HANDBOOK OF
INTERCULTURAL
TRAINING
2ND EDITION

For Rae in thanks for the past 35 years.
D .L

For Ebha, Monika, and Priyanka
R. S. B.

HANDBOOK OF
INTERCULTURAL
TRAINING
2ND EDITION

LINCOLN CHRISTIAN COLLEGE AND SEMINARY

DAN LANDIS & RABI S. BHAGAT
EDITORS

SAGE Publications
International Educational and Professional Publisher
Thousand Oaks   London   New Delhi

For information address:

 SAGE Publications, Inc.
2455 Teller Road
Thousand Oaks, California 91320
E-mail: order@sagepub.com

SAGE Publications Ltd.
6 Bonhill Street
London EC2A 4PU
United Kingdom

SAGE Publications India Pvt. Ltd.
M-32 Market
Greater Kailash I
New Delhi 110 048 India

Printed in the United States of America

Library of Congress Cataloging-in-Publication Data

Main entry under title:

Handbook of intercultural training / editors, Dan Landis and Rabi S.
  Bhagat. — 2nd ed.
    p.cm.
    Includes bibliographical references and indexes.
    ISBN 0-8039-5833-1. — ISBN 0-8039-5834-X (pbk.)
    1. Intercultural communication.   2. Culture conflict.
3. Adjustment (Psychology)   4. Multicultural education.   I. Landis,
Dan.   II. Bhagat, Rabi S.
GN496.H36   1996
303.48′2—dc20

This book is printed on acid-free paper.

96 97 98 99 10 9 8 7 6 5 4 3 2 1

Production Editor: Diana E. Axelsen   Typesetter: Christina M. Hill

Contents

PART II:
Contextual Dimensions of Intercultural Training

PART III:
Area Studies: Intercultural Training for Critical Parts of the World

Foreword

DURING the past week in Shanghai, I had the privilege of conducting in-depth discussions with 15 Chinese managers and employees of a U.S. company. They are struggling with many difficulties as they attempt to build their new organization. On my return, I had the privilege of reading the manuscript for this book. The connections between the field and the classroom, between effective performance and disciplined inquiry, have never been clearer.

As I work with organizations in China, I find that many fundamental questions, both theoretical and intensely practical, are raised. The authors of this book deal directly with a surprising number of these questions. I know that many individuals and organizations involved in intercultural relations confront these same issues. Professors, students, trainers and consultants, and those responsibile for training trainers and consultants will therefore be intrigued and encouraged by this new edition of the handbook.

The authors survey and summarize the most relevant theories and results of research from a variety of disciplines. From their own work and experience, they offer new models, promising hypotheses, and practical guidelines. In other words, they look not only at what we collectively have learned but also at how we can discover more and how we actually do our work. Some of them even touch on why we do this work.

What are the connections between the content of these chapters and the challenging tasks and responsibilities of intercultural trainers? What are the fundamental questions this handbook helps us resolve? Let's return to Shanghai, the commercial capital of the People's Republic of China.

The managers and the employees have worked for this new company for only a few months. Already, they have many concerns. Some of these cannot be addressed through training. A different structure for the organization is needed, for example, and some appropriate policies, procedures, and systems must be put into place.

Other concerns can be very effectively addressed by intercultural training programs—provided they are carefully designed, professionally conducted, and accurately evaluated. Let's look at these concerns and some possible training responses.

The five senior Chinese managers report to North American executives, one in Hong Kong and the other in New York. The Chinese managers have little understanding of their bosses. The executives have little understanding of China, their organization in Shanghai, and their subordinates who are trying to build that organization. What kind of training would enhance clarity, cooperation, and performance? For the U.S. executives, perhaps a program on intercultural management; for their Chinese subordinates, a program on working for a foreign boss; and for all of them together, a workshop on intercultural communication and organizational development. How can these training events be designed to ensure they will be effective? When should they be done? How should the needs assessment be conducted? What methods are most appropriate, and how should they be sequenced? Would any relevant models and theories inform and guide the design efforts? These questions are carefully considered in several of the chapters that follow.

Looking more closely at the five Chinese managers, we find one grew up in Hong Kong, one in Taiwan, one in Australia, and two in Shanghai. Three are men; two are women. They range in age from 28 to 48. There is some real diversity here. In fact, the managers are often working at cross-purposes with one another. Morale is suffering. Perhaps we should recommend several sessions on multicultural team building. This raises more questions, both theoretical and practical, on program design.

The Shanghai operation desperately needs a chief financial officer. Both candidates are Canadian. They will increase the diversity of the team. How do we select the one who can best adapt to the challenges of living in Shanghai, earn the respect of Chinese colleagues, and work most effectively day-to-day with them? What specific knowledge, skills, and attitudes are necessary for success in another culture? How can we define success—and measure it? Critical questions. See the pertinent chapters.

A chief engineer must also be selected. Soon. This person will probably come from one of the company's operations in Germany. Still more diversity in the Shanghai office and more need for carefully designed sessions to consolidate the team.

In addition, of course, both the Canadian and the German team members, as well as their spouses and families, will need specially designed predeparture programs. Or, even better, a program for both of them together, an objective of which will be preliminary multicultural team building. As we prepare them for 3 years in China, what intercultural competencies should we concentrate on developing? What transition and acculturation skills should we strengthen? How can we equip each member of the families to establish strong support groups and to learn continually from one another and from their ongoing cultural contact? For the employees, how can we increase not only their cultural adaptation but also their professional performance? Useful insights and guidelines are provided by a number of authors in this handbook.

Once the foreign expatriates are in place and the organization begins to grow, more men and women from Shanghai and elsewhere in China must be hired. How can these new Chinese employees be integrated into what is still, in many respects, a North American organization? Don't they need a corporate and intercultural orientation program? Some interesting design, delivery, and evaluation challenges here.

A group of top-level executives from New York is planning to visit Shanghai. A different kind of intercultural program, a China briefing, would be illuminating and useful for them. Three members of the group, including the president of the company, will go on to Beijing to begin negotiations for a promising joint venture. This venture may be very important to the future of the company. All three would benefit significantly from participating in an intercultural negotiation simulation during which they would try to resolve difficult issues with seasoned (and carefully prepared) Chinese enterprise managers, government officials, and a secretary of the Communist Party.

While in Beijing, the executives will call on the U.S. Embassy for assistance. They will ask embassy personnel for advice on how to approach the industrial ministry, which will have jurisdiction over their joint venture, and how to resolve differences and difficulties with their JV partner once the venture is up and running. How culturally astute will the embassy personnel be? What level of language proficiency and intercultural competence will they have achieved? Will each of them have had the benefit of intercultural training designed specifically for them and their responsibilities?

The success of the Shanghai organization depends, more than most people realize, on the purchasing manager, a local Chinese person who must locate and purchase the highest quality materials not only from within China but also from Japan and Malaysia. Success also depends on the marketing manager. This person is responsible for selling the Shanghai products in Korea, Japan, Singapore, North America, Europe, and Scandinavia. What particular cultural insights and interaction skills do the purchasing and marketing managers need? How would we design programs uniquely suited to each of them and their departments? What expertise would be required on the program staff? What special methods, materials, and content do *they* really need?

The Shanghai operation will require the transfer of much technology, some of it highly sophisticated. Large numbers of Chinese employees must develop new management and technical skills. Trainers will be brought into Shanghai from New York, Los Angeles, Munich, and Taipei. How can they package years of experience and complex information, pass it along to the Chinese, and do so in a way that the Chinese can fully comprehend it, *accept* it, and consistently apply it? What are Chinese patterns of thinking and learning? The transfer will more likely take place if the trainers are given an opportunity to participate in an intensive program on international technology transfer through training.

As a part of the technology transfer process, significant numbers of Chinese will be sent to the United States and Germany. How will they be selected, prepared, oriented on-site, supervised, and integrated into the local organization? (Let's bear in mind that very few of them speak English. Even fewer speak German.)

Someone else is coming to the United States, but under different circumstances and with very different needs. The daughter of the oldest Chinese manager has been accepted at a university in Bloomington, Indiana. She will be entirely on her own. How can we provide meaningful preparation, orientation, and ongoing support and intercultural training for her? And what about the faculty who will be teaching her? How can we design and conduct programs on teaching a multicultural class and on supervising international students as teaching assistants that will be engaging and convincing for professors from a wide variety of disciplines?

Three years from now, when the daughter and another foreign student (from New Zealand) are considering marriage, she may come

to the foreign student advisor for guidance. What are the distinctive objectives, designs, and methods for programs on cross-cultural counseling?

Consider how many of the people above, having lived in a foreign culture, will probably return home: the Western expatriates in Hong Kong and China, the overseas Chinese managers on assignment in Shanghai, the U.S. Embassy personnel, the Chinese employees in the U.S. and Germany, and, perhaps, the Chinese manager's daughter. Each of these stands to benefit, both personally and professionally, from a reentry program. The same program? Let's hope not. The participants differ so much from one another in their personal and professional needs that different designs should be created for each. Read the chapter on reentry.

Let's suppose the company has the good sense to invest in all of this intercultural training. It will have to provide special training programs for some of its in-house trainers. What competencies should be developed? What specific knowledge, training skills, personal qualities, and ethical standards are necessary to become an intercultural trainer who is both effective and responsible? Some external trainers may be hired. What qualifications should the company look for as it evaluates vendors of intercultural training services? These questions are of real concern to many of the authors here.

Having made this investment, the company will want to know how the training has affected the individual participants and the whole organization (including, perhaps, their customers). As trainers, we too, of course, must know the consequences of our efforts. Accurate evaluation keeps us honest (and usually humble) and enables us to improve every component of our programs. How can we measure and demonstrate the impact of intercultural training? We must all learn more in this area, as some of the authors emphasize.

Who in the world could provide this range of intercultural training programs? Imagine the company invited all the authors of this handbook to meet in the conference facilities at the Portman Shangrila in Shanghai Centre, one of the best hotels in China. Their assignment: design, conduct, evaluate, *and integrate* all of these training programs in the most thoroughly professional, highly effective manner possible. Just think what this combination of commitment, experience, and expertise could create and accomplish!

The chances of such an extraordinary team ever assembling, of course, are few. No organization will ever enjoy the benefit of these authors' combined capability. At least not directly. But what about indirectly? If all of us who do intercultural training and prepare trainers not only read these chapters but also carefully think through the theories, models, research findings, and principles for practice, and if we frequently draw on and apply them, then the many individuals and organizations with whom we work will benefit. We ourselves will benefit. And the promising profession we have chosen will continue to develop. The depth and extent of the development will be evident, no doubt, in the next edition of this handbook.

GEORGE W. RENWICK
Renwick and Associates

Preface to the Second Edition

MUCH has changed in the 13 years since we wrote the Preface to the first edition. We are certainly older, one of us now is a grandparent three times over, and his then-teenage daughter is herself a mother of a teenager. Charles Osgood, who had just fallen seriously ill, has since passed away; this has left an unfillable void in our field. Jerry Frank, the editor of the first edition, has also died; it has left us with one less fine friend. And, the original publisher has been sold amid a scandal that still reverberates in publishing circles.

The Society for Intercultural Education, Training, and Research has added the term *International* to its name, an addition that reflects its increasingly cross-national character. Baby SIETAR societies have sprung up in Europe, Japan, and elsewhere. Local chapters abound in places like Chicago and New York. The number of consulting (or "relocation") firms seems to increase every year, paced by a growth in firms providing "diversity" advice. The *International Journal of Intercultural Relations,* the professional journal of the field, is entering its third decade and can count approximately 600 papers published under the IJIR imprint. Clearly, major changes have taken place in the field.

But, many things have not changed. This is still a contentious field, one that has yet to attain academic respectability. As a field of study, it remains buried within other, often less than hospitable, academic feifdoms—psychology, communications, education, management, and so on. As a field of application, there remains no agreed-on qualifications for people practicing "intercultural training." To parody the Red Queen, "A trainer is what I chose to say it is, no more and no less!" SIETAR periodically revisits the issue of qualification but just as periodically shys away from the issue, though as we write, a new commission has been formed to study the problem and recommend solutions. Perhaps when the third edition appears, some progress will have been made.

Perhaps one problem that impedes progress is still the lack of theory—a theory that would tell us why certain training programs work, for whom, and when. To be sure, attempts have been made to develop mid-level theories, but none have attained the popularity necessary to be widely accepted. So, much of the field remains intuitive, with a smattering of theory here and there. The chapters in this edition verify that description. Many of the authors labored intensively to bring order out of atheoretical writings and findings. The results of those labors are impressive.

This edition also reflects the changing world. The fall of the Soviet Union, the opening up of China, and the looming peace in the Middle East, as well as the increasingly international character of business, results in consideration of the unique intercultural training aspect of those regions. At the same time, some problems remain. Racism and the lack of diversity in the workforce remain issues in the United States, with the current attacks on affirmative action reaching a fever pitch in the run to the 1996 elections. The ethics of trainers are as much an issue today as they were in 1980, as is the lack of a defensible definition of intercultural competence. All of these issues are reflected in the chapters of this new edition.

We owe great thanks to our editor, Marquita Flemming, who showed inordinate patience as we cajoled authors to meet ever-lengthening deadlines. Her faith in this project allowed it to be completed. Landis also thanks the staff of the Defense Equal Opportunity Management Institute, who provided a sabbatical home while this book was being created and who were very understanding when he would stay home to complete a chapter or two. He is also very grateful to Chittibabu Govindarajulu and Manimekalai Chittibabu, who kept the *International Journal of Intercultural Relations* afloat so that a sabbatical could be realized and this book completed. Bhagat thanks Allison Faulk, Kristin Prien, Ramesh Balakrishnan, and Joy Ward in Memphis for assisting with the preparation of this handbook. He also takes this opportunity to express his appreciation to his wife, Ebha; and his children, Monika and Priyanka, for allowing him to spend many hours editing the various drafts of the chapters of this book.

From the Preface to the First Edition

THIS handbook deals with a problem that is central to today's complex world: How can people best live and work with others who come from very different cultural background?

This book was formally born at the 1980 meetings of the Society for Intercultural Education, Training, and Research (SIETAR) held in Mt. Pocono, Pennsylvania. But its origin dates farther back than a few cold, beer-filled nights in the mountains near Scranton. We, the editors, have been involved in cross-cultural research, education, and training for some years now, although we scarcely qualify as "grand old men" of the field. We have both been impressed with the desire of people to subject themselves to the rigors of working in strange cultures. We have had extensive interaction with people who prepare others for cross-cultural experiences, frequently called "trainers." We have also been impressed with the intuitive feelings of many trainers and just as equally impressed by the naivete of others who are also called "trainers." At times, we have been blessed with that exhilaration that comes from a successful training session or have been beset by the depression when it fails. At times, we look over the work of others and stand in awe; at other times, we are ashamed and furious. But most of all, like many behavioral and social scientists who have a background in extensive empirical analysis, we have been more impressed by the lack of communication and theoretical rigor in this important applied field. As Lewin noted years ago, nothing is so practical as a good theory. Well, the lack of a good theory—despite much that passes as one—may be the reason that training is still an art whose replicability is more a matter of chance than design. Thus, this book was conceived.

For the serious trainer and cross-cultural scientist, much here will be interesting, intriguing, and even useful. For the practitioner who is not interested in developing his or her activities on a more rational, careful basis, these volumes will disappoint and perhaps even anger. We can do little for such individuals. For them, handbook volumes remain on someone else's shelf. It is our hope that even if this proves to be the case, perhaps once in a while they will be borrowed and scanned. That will be one measure of the success of this enterprise, which has involved over three dozen scholars and trainers.

AUTHORS' NOTE: This is an abbreviated version of the Preface to the first edition.

The other measure is the anger quotient. We expect to be controversial because this is a contentious field, as anyone who has attended a planning meeting for a cross-cultural training program can attest. We have asked our contributors to take chances with their ideas. We want these chapters to stand as good contributions 20 and 30 years from now, much as S. S. Stevens's *Handbook of Experimental Psychology* (New York, John Wiley, 1951) is still treasured by the best graduate students.

A Model of Intercultural Behavior and Training

DAN LANDIS

RABI S. BHAGAT

THE aims of this chapter are threefold. The first is to present a model of intercultural behavior that includes most, if not all, of the critical variables identified in the literature. The model is thus multivariate in nature and would require latent variable techniques (Loehlin, 1992) for full analysis. The second aim is to examine the relationship between the model and existing cross-cultural training techniques. The third aim is to lay out the organization of this volume as a guide for the reader.

Model Development

In the first edition of this handbook, Brislin, Landis, and Brandt (1983) presented a model of intercultural behavior. That model was based on an explicitly psychological perspective; that is, those authors considered intercultural behavior to be the result of forces (both internal and external) acting on an individual. Social and historical contexts have an impact as they affect internal memory or dispositional states. The model was presented in the hope that it would stimulate programmatic and multivariable research designed to explicate the various antecedents. Sadly, that has not been the case. Such research has proved to be either too difficult or too costly or was not seen as important by funding agencies. For whatever reason, the fulfillment of the 1983 hope has been elusive.

Yet, if the intervening decade has taught us anything, it is that the need to understand intercultural behavior is even more important. The 1980s saw an explosion in the internationalization of business. The fall of the Soviet empire, increasing relations with the People's Republic of China, as well as the passage of the North American Free Trade Act (NAFTA) are but three events driving business and individuals across national and cultural boundaries. Less salutary are the events in Somalia, the former Yugoslavia, and Kuwait, all of which still required intercultural behavior. We could go on and on, but the point is clear: National boundaries are becoming more and more porous, with people and capital becoming interchangeable on either side of the border.

Model building is not just the occupation of academics frantically scrambling for tenure and promotion. There are pragmatic outcomes of value. A reasonably good model alerts us to the complex of variables that act as antecedents to intercultural behavior, be it successful or unsuccessful. As several chapter authors note, fewer than 50% of American overseas managers are successful in completing their assignments. The attendant costs for these failures are estimated at between $250,000 and $1,000,000. A reasonably good model suggests the relationship, be it positive or negative, between the variables that act to moderate those costs.

A reasonably accurate model also suggests variables most amenable to modification by either training or selection. It may also suggest areas where training might be self-defeating as one training module inhibits the effect of another. Because much of the research in the intervening period has focused on single module effects, however, the potential of an overarching model has been lost or ignored.

Despite all of these positives and the history of missed opportunities, we go once more into the lists. We take it as axiomatic that the description and prediction of intercultural behavior require a serious and sustained effort at theory building.

In developing a model that can guide training and research programs, we start with the idea that the desired behavior has many antecedents. Consistent with the earlier framework of Brislin et al. (1983), we continue to view intercultural behavior as an action that can produce significant change in the judgments of the actor's social or skill competence. Such changes might become positively or negatively reinforced by the process of interacting with people from different cultural backgrounds.

In Figure 1.1, we present a framework that depicts contextual influences on intercultural behavior. Variables of cultural variation are most distal in terms of their influences on intercultural behavior. We make here the distinction between subjective and objective culture, though it is not shown in the figure. As Osgood noted, "objective" culture consists of the physi-

cal constructions that a people make of their world, the shards that archaeologists puzzle over (Osgood, May, & Miron, 1975). More interesting to us are the social constructions that the same people make of their relations with one another—the "subjective" culture (Triandis, 1972). The first we see as being quite distal; the later are quite intimate psychological variables—or at least more proximate. Included in the former are the dimensions of culture variation, such as individualism-collectivism, power distance, and so on (Hofstede, 1980; Kim, Triandis, Kagitçibaci, Choi, & Yoon, 1994), which are linked to ecological characteristics (Berry, 1994). These dimensions are more or less perceived or accepted by the actor.

These variables, combined with certain others, we label as *social-psychological* related. Here lie all the normative views that occur when contemplating behavior with persons judged to be different. Constructions of the ingroup and the out-group, norms and roles appropriate from people in those groups, power and influence from individuals in the groups, and so on constitute this set of variables.

The most proximate set of variables are those that are characteristic of the individual. The image of the self, abilities and aptitudes, personality traits, cognitive and perceptual sets, and other relatively enduring characteristics of the individual make up the set of variables that are *intrapsychological*. Although these variables are relatively proximate to the occurrence of intercultural behavior, on the one hand, they may be relatively impervious to change. On the other hand, the research on modification of these traits in an intercultural context is still wanting.

The distal-proximal view of intercultural behavior is useful in that it alerts people to the major groupings of variables that have an influence on the actions of interest. It is not, however, a model in the sense of suggesting the potency and direction of influences. Such a representation is presented in Figure 1.2.

The model is explicitly individualistic in focus, one that looks at modifiable events impinging on the actor with the actor having effects on the hosts and they on him or her. At the very distal level, we note a number of variables that the individual brings to the situation. Past experiences, both directly and indirectly encountered, lead to a more or less enhanced sensitiv-

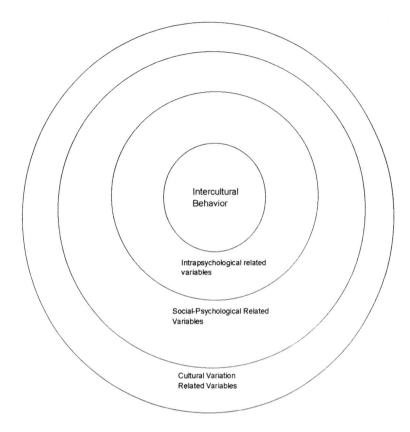

Figure 1.1. Contextual Influences on Intercultural Behavior

ity to behavioral cues (intercultural sensitivity). The level of sensitivity affects the awareness of differences in roles, norms, and values (Schwartz, 1994a), which in turn are influenced by perceived differences in the appropriateness of resource exchanges (Foa & Foa, 1974). All of these distal variables affect the level of social categorization that researchers make between in-groups and out-groups. How inclusive the groups are, how distinct the people in each group are, how permeable the boundaries between groups are, and how much affectivity is a consequence of transiting the boundaries are all functions of those most distal variables enumerated above.

M. Bennett (1986) offered a dynamic view of intercultural sensitivity, suggesting it is a process, not a state, that moves from ethnocentric to ethnorelative stages. Our model does not deny the dynamic nature, but rather treats it as a state for each intercultural act. So, by extend-

ing the model in Figure 1.1 through time, one can see that any given state is a product of many successive acts, which have allowed the individual to traverse the stages from denial, defense, minimization, acceptance, and adaptation to integration (M. Bennett, 1986).

Schwartz (1994a, 1994b) proposed a system of value structures that appear to be universal. These values fall into 10 "value types," almost of all which appear in a very large and heterogeneous sample of cultures. Like the Foa and Foa (1974) theory of resource exchange, value types appearing next to one another (e.g., security and power) are less in conflict than those more distal (e.g., security and stimulation). Although all cultures sampled appear to contain the major value types, they do differ in terms of the relative importance of each. Struch and Schwartz (1989) found that the perceived dissimilarity of value types affected the level of perceived intergroup conflict on aggression.

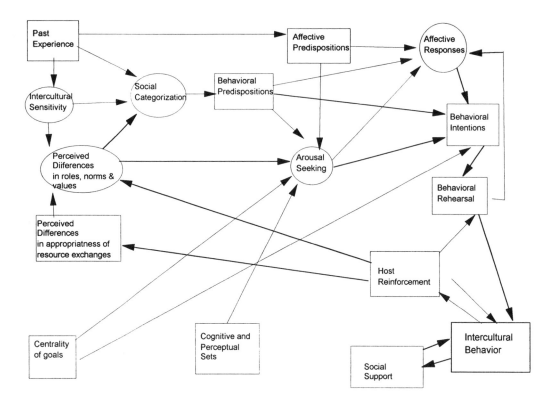

Figure 1.2. Antecedents of Intercultural Behavior

We would predict that, all things being equal, the amount of disparity between the individual's core value types and those perceived of the host culture will be a significant antecedent of intercultural behavior. Another distal variable arises, not from the past experience of the person, but from the extent to which personal goals are consonant with the reasons for engaging in intercultural behavior.

What we call *centrality of goals* has its theoretical origin in two lines of research. The first is a long line of studies indicating that the cognitive dissonance effect only occurs when the behavior is viewed as a central part of the actor's view of him- or herself (Bem, 1967; Festinger, 1957). The second comes from contact theory, wherein a condition on the reduction of prejudice is a function of the acceptance of superordinate goals (Allport, 1954; Stephan, 1987). Although the acceptance of superordinate goals might occur without a change in

the self-image, it is unlikely in the emotionally labile atmosphere of the intercultural encounter.

Goals, as discussed in the previous paragraph, are distinct from values in that they refer to the particular set of tasks at hand. Hence, they will show considerable variation between individuals and organizations. At the same time, goals may be in conflict with values and lead to intrapersonal tension with a negative impact on ability to successfully complete an intercultural assignment.

Social categorization (Bond & Hewstone, 1988; Brewer, in press; Taifel & Turner, 1986) is both descriptive (e.g., who is in and who is out) and antecedent to other variables. It leads to a set of behavioral predispositions—a set of probabilities for certain kinds of actions below threshold level but correlated with two subsequent effects: arousal seeking and behavior intentions. More about them later.

Past experiences also lead, we believe, to a set of affective predispositions. Like behavioral predispositions, these are a set of probabilities to react emotionally when in an intercultural situation. Fear, trait anxiety (Spielberger, 1966), and exhilaration are three of the possible emotions. We consider them to be analogous to the fractional anticipatory goal responses that Osgood used in devising a theory of meaning based on Hull's model of learning (Osgood, Suci, & Tannenbaum, 1957).

The last set of predisposing variables are cognitive-perceptual in nature. Much of the research on personality variables in intercultural behaviors (e.g., Kealey & Ruben, 1983) has focused on these constructs without labeling them as such. In the first edition of this handbook, Brislin et al. (1983) outlined a line of research that went back at least to the work of Gardner (e.g., Gardner, Holzman, Klein, Linton, & Spence, 1959) and others at the Menninger Clinic during the 1950s. Within the realm of intercultural behavioral research, the focus on these sets has led to a search for relationships between such variables as flexibility, cognitive complexity, field independence-field dependence, and leveling and sharpening on the one hand, and success in intercultural interactions on the other hand.

We suggest that the three dispositional components (affective, cognitive, and behavioral) are jointly predictive of a characteristic we call *arousal seeking*. This we define as the desire to seek nonhomeostatic states. It is an increasing of the inclusiveness of social categories, an individuation of persons in the out-group, and an increase of the level of anxiety. When this increase in arousal is also accompanied by a consonance of the behavior with a saliency of goals, then little or no stress results; when not, stress is likely and may even be severe (Barna, 1983). In the Brislin, Landis, and Brandt model, the term *behavioral seeking* was used for this constellation of variables. We now believe, however, that behavior is but one aspect of this characteristics; there are cognitive and affective antecedents as well.

The contemplation of seeking higher levels of arousal engenders an affective and behavioral response. The affective response is likely to be complex but will mainly be on a dimension of fear/exhilaration. The responses identified as uncertainty reduction (Gudykunst,

1985) and intercultural anxiety (Stephan & Stephan, 1985) also fit into this category. Which set of responses occurs will be conditioned by the level and type of affective predispositions that exist. The behavioral response is the forming of an intention. Here, we follow the model of interpersonal behavior described by Triandis (1977), with a few significant additions. Triandis's formulation was that behavioral intentions are captured by the following relation:

$$BeInt = w_1A + w_2S + w_3PcVc$$

where:

A = Affective response to the individuals who are the targets of the behavior

S = Social appropriateness of the behavior (e.g., roles and norms)

PcVc = Perceived consequences of the behavior

and:

w_1–w_3 are individual difference regression weights.

In the context of intercultural behavior, the behavior might be "engaging in criticism of a person from another culture." The BeInt would represent the cognitive act of intending to do the action. The A component would involve the emotional response (usually marked by responses on the Evaluative factor of the semantic differential [Osgood et al., 1957]). Consideration should be given here, though Triandis did not, to the affect toward the target, aside from the behavior. So, some behaviors would be done, even though they might be repugnant, if the target is either liked or disliked. A reasonable formulation would make the A component the product of the affect toward the behavior times the affect toward the target. Thus, if the target is extremely disliked, that component will go to zero and the behavior will not occur. Similarly, if the behavior itself is extremely repugnant, the behavior will not occur even if the person is well liked. The S component includes the actor's assessment of the appropriateness of the behavior, given the cultural background of the actor. We would add that when the target is from a different culture and when the setting is the target's culture, then the S component must include an assessment of the appropriateness of the behavior in that culture. Indeed, a logical extension would be to consider the S component as the disparity between the two cultures. Finally, The $PcVc$ component is a product of the likely consequences of the behavior and the value of each of those consequences. Again, one should consider the disparity between the $PcVc$'s of the actor's culture and the host culture as perceived by the actor. In many cases, particularly when the actor is new to the host culture, the disparity can be considered to be null—even if, in reality, it is large. As the sojourner becomes more familiar with the host culture, the disparity will grow and then decrease as the actor's subjective culture begins to change and the consequences reorder themselves and take on new values. Finally, the w weights are empirically determined and may be unique to the person, culture, and behavior.

In our model, behavioral intentions are affected by behavioral predispositions. So, the intention to do a behavior is a function of the past experiences (either objective or subjective) of the individual (analogous to the assessment of PcVc), the affective response to both the behavior and the target, as well as the extent to which the behavior is consonant with the self-image (centrality of goals) and the level of desired arousal seeking.

After the intention is formed, one needs to consider its relation to behavior. The Triandis model posits the following relationship:

$$\text{ProbBeh} = F*(w_1H + w_2BehInt)$$

where:

ProbBeh = Probability that the behavior will occur

H = past occurrence of the behavior

w_1 and w_2 are individual difference regression coefficients

F = facilitating conditions

We would add a further relation: that the behavior will be rehearsed except when the behavior is well practiced. In the latter case, little or no rehearsal is necessary. So, the Triandis equation applies equally well to both observable and nonobservable behaviors. Hence, the final emitting of the behavior is a product of the level of rehearsal and the intentions to commit the action. Psychology has generally been leery of theory involving behaviors that are not observable. With the rise of cognitive psychology, however, such concerns have lost most of their force as consciousness found its way back into respectable theory construction. Surely, as the behavior is rehearsed, affective responses will be released. The response may be anxiety (as the actor anticipates a negative response from the target) or satisfaction (as the actor anticipates an acceptance by the target). This feedback loop continues (and it may be quite fast) until the actor is convinced that the behavior will have the desired results. At the point, the behavior will or will not occur.

Finally, because we are dealing with intercultural behavior, we need to consider two additional sets of variables. Rarely are managers sent overseas by themselves. If they are not accompanied by family members, there is often a social support network consisting of countrymates. Social support is conceptualized as emotional concern, instrumental aid, and information that individuals entering into an intercultural behavior are likely to receive from significant others who are interested in governing the outcome of the intercultural behavior. In addition to the country- or organization-mates, the targets will provide some sort of cues as the acceptability of the behavior. The cues provided by hosts may lead the person to re-rehearse the behavior and to modify the action accordingly (Adelman, 1988; Fontaine, 1986).

As a coda to the above discussion, we maintain that the same considerations apply whether the target is intercultural or intracultural. So, when dealing with prejudice within a culture, the prediction and modification of behavior is, in principle, no different from that involving dealing on an equal basis with a foreign manager. The difference will come in the level of certain variables (e.g., affective responses), as well as the strength of the relationships between variables.

Applications to Training

As the various chapters of this handbook show, training in an increasingly shrinking, highly interdependent world is no longer a luxury, but a necessity that most organizations have to confront in a meaningful fashion. The areas in which our model have formal application are as follows:

1. *Designing of rigorous training programs.* The major motivation for developing the 1983 edition of the *Handbook of Intercultural Training* (Landis & Brislin, 1983) was to provide rigorous background for designing effective intercultural training programs. Although much has been accomplished in the past 13 years, we still need to develop guidelines for designing program design. The model articulated in this chapter, as well as the other chapters in this handbook, should be helpful in this area.

2. *Implementing of training programs.* A majority of the training programs started in organizations are not appropriately conceptualized in terms of the various essential theoretical issues. It is our hope that our model will provide appropriate guidelines for designing training programs that involve changes in trainees' cognitions and in affective reactions. We get the impression that a large majority of training programs are conducted because they are well advertised, not because they are well designed. Effective implementation of cross-cultural training programs can only take place in the context of a rigorously articulated theoretical framework.

3. *Training in a culturally diverse world.* As the workforce in various countries becomes increasingly culturally diverse, the need to train individuals to become effective in dealing with such new complexities increases. The model in this chapter, as well as the other chapters of the handbook, provides guidelines for conceptually training in a culture-general and in a culture-specific sense.

4. *Evaluating of training programs.* Unlike training conducted in a given cultural setting, training conducted in cross-cultural settings should be evaluated in the context of a meaningful framework. One important way of looking at this problem is to ask whether views of all relevant parties are to be presented. If an American corporation has a branch in Japan and trains Americans to live in that country, the points of view of a number of populations might be considered: (a) the top management of the corporation, (b) immediate supervisors of the trainees, (c) the trainees themselves, (d) friends of the trainees, both at work and at nonwork settings, and (e) the Japanese counterparts of the trainees. The various chapters of this handbook provide important guidelines for evaluation of training programs by considering those points of view pertinent to the type of training being conducted. Psychometric issues from an evaluation research point of view are not the only ones to consider in evaluating the effectiveness of cross-cultural training programs.

5. *Understanding the reasons for success and failure of cross-cultural training programs.* We are confident that the model in this chapter and the various other chapters should provide us with important insights as to why some training programs succeed when they ought to fail and why some training programs fail when they ought to succeed. Many contextual factors need to be fully understood in evaluating the causes of success and failure of cross-cultural training programs. By understanding contextual factors, we can get a better grasp of the intensity of the individual's learning experiences.

Having described the antecedents of the intercultural act and given a general rationale for the importance of a reasonable theoretical model, it is necessary to examine the impact of training on the structure. J. Bennett (1986) provides a helpful schema (in some respects, similar to that proffered by Kohls, 1987, and Bhawuk, 1990) based on the viewpoint of the trainer. She notes that individuals who have had an orientation approach typically focus on cognitive/behavioral goals, use culture-specific content, and structure the training around an intellectual approach. Trainers with a training background are usually more interested in achieving affective/behavioral goals for specific cultures in an experiential framework. Finally, trainers from a pedagogical background include all three goals—cognitive, behavioral, and affectual—in their objectives, add *why* as well as *how* in both culture-specific and culture-general foci, and use both intellectual and experiential approaches. Thus, the background of the trainer will often determine the type of training offered. Within each broad training category, several subtypes can be identified. These subtypes can be grouped into four categories according to where they fall on two orthogonal dimensions: culture-specific versus culture-general goals and affective versus cognitive goals (J. Bennett, 1986). So, for example, Bennett's Quadrant A (culture-specific and affective goals) includes such approaches as area simulations, bicultural workshops, and culture-specific events. In the opposite quadrant (cognitive and culture-general) are such approaches as intercultural communication courses, "learning how to learn" methodology, and culture-general curriculum.

Culture assimilators (see Chapter 10, this volume) are seen as fitting in the quadrant defined by culture-specific and cognitive goals. This assignment is an oversimplification because, on the one hand, several studies have shown behavioral effects (e.g., Landis, Brislin, & Hulgus, 1985; Weldon, Carston, Rissman, Slobodin, & Triandis, 1975) and, on the other hand, the development of the culture-general assimilator (Brislin, Cushner, Cherrie, & Yong, 1986) has suggested that this technique may fit into more than one sector. But, more to the point, the model in Figure 1.2 suggests that, depending on content to some extent, these various techniques will impact at different points in the causal structure.

The developmental strategies of M. Bennett (1986) are focused on moving a person from an ethnocentric to an ethnorelativistic level of intercultural sensitivity. So, at the ethnocentric end, simple cultural awareness activities would seem to be most effective. As a person moves through each stage, more and more intense and experiential activities may be useful. Bennett suggests that, at the end (integration), activities focused on developing a system of ethics to guide behavior are necessary. Our model suggests that these activities will affect the extent to which social categories are seen as impenetrable or porous. We would predict that, at the point when a system of ethics has been developed to guide intercultural interactions, the boundaries between "us" and "them" will be perceived as very thin and that the host nationals will be categorized as individuals, rather than only as members of a group.

Assimilators (see Chapter 10, this volume), whether culture general or specific, would seem to have their major impact on modifying the individual's perception of the host national's role, norm, and value structure. They may also increase or decrease the tendency to seek new experiences (arousal seeking). Landis, Brislin, and Hulgus (1985) demonstrated that such training may well increase intercultural anxiety as prior attributions are shown to be inappropriate and new ones have yet to be formed. Building on the Landis, Brislin, and Hulgus findings, Merta, Stringham, and Ponterotto (1988) developed a program for training counselors in cross-cultural sensitivity. Alternatively, the assimilator experience may increase curiosity, particularly if the foreign assignment is viewed as central to the individual's personal goals. The latter variable thus becomes an important moderator. Kraemer's cultural self-awareness model (1973, 1974), which focuses on learning about one's own culture, may also be useful in making the contrast between the home and host cultures' roles, norms, and values.

A potentially useful training technique for changing values is that of value self-confrontation (Grube, Mayton, & Ball-Rokeach, 1994). This technique, which has yet to be applied in the cross-cultural training setting, is based on the idea of creating a state of dissatisfaction in the individual through feedback and interpretations of his or her own and significant others' values. Because the dissatisfaction is a negative affective state, some individuals will change their values to become more consistent with their views of themselves. Grube et al. (1994) report that, of 27 studies using value self-confrontation, 96% found significant value change, 73% showed attitude change, and a smaller number found behavioral change. This approach, which is well grounded theoretically in belief system theory (Ball-Rokeach, Rokeach, & Grube, 1984) would seem to hold promise as a cross-cultural training technique.

Experiential training, if it realistically portrays the target culture, may provide some change in perceived role, norms, and values of the host milieu. Contact of this type, however, is more than likely to increase anxiety and be an inhibitor of culture learning. Such training is best used later in the sequence, perhaps to increase the level of arousal seeking or even to provide a safe way to rehearse appropriate behaviors.

Intellectual or lecture-type training may also be useful at this stage, particularly when the sojourn is likely to be short and extremely task focused. The thrust is simply to provide enough information to complete the task, no more nor less. Alternatively, if the purpose of the sojourn is not only short but also recreational in nature, this may be the method of choice. It is certainly the basis for innumerable guidebooks.

The model suggests that affectional dispositions play a significant part in the process. The method of choice here may be some sort of anxiety counterconditioning or stress reduction techniques. By and large, these have not been used in intercultural training, and they are not referred to in the chapters in this handbook. That does not mean, however, that they do not have a place in the armamentarium of the cross-cultural trainer. In the first edition, Barna (1983) made a persuasive case that the cross-cultural encounter is an inherently stressful event, a conclusion echoed by Stephan and Stephan (1992), Walton, (1990), and Kealey (1989). A related treatment was used by Furuto and Furuto (1983) where groups met to participate in "spiritual, cultural, and social experiences" (p. 153). These groups were contrasted with a "cognitive" treatment and found to have superior, positive attitude changes.

At the level of behavioral rehearsal, some form of behavioral modeling may be useful (David, 1972; Eachus, 1965; Higgenbotham, 1979). These techniques often require the person to perform some act that is then recorded and presented to the learner. The self-confrontational aspect of the situation permits behavioral experimentation without the pressure of an actual situation. Our model suggests that this technique may work best when it is accompanied by the development of new behavioral intentions and reinforced by host nationals.

Figure 1.2 also suggests that the primary reinforcer of intercultural behavior is the counterpart national. Yet, training of this person has been largely ignored in the literature. We would argue that this person's behavior should be viewed as an intercultural act, subject to the same moderators as those of the sojourner. In other words, he or she is performing intercultural behavior in his or her own country, the function of which is to give reinforcement to the sojourner. The effectiveness of that behavior will be a function of the same variables outlined in Figure 1.2. A reasonable extension is to develop training programs for host nationals before the sojourner arrives. As an example, within the academic community, such training is provided sporadically, if at all. Rarely are university faculty, staff, and students provided with guidelines for interacting with the foreign student, yet the horror stories abound whenever foreign student advisors congregate.

Organization of This Volume

The similarity between international and intracultural interactions is reflected in the content of this volume. Several contributions (e.g., Dansby & Landis [Chapter 11]; Landis, Dansby, & Tallarigo [Chapter 14]; Shachar & Amir [Chapter 22]) deal with relationships between dominant and subordinate groups within the same culture.

We have organized this second edition along the same lines as the first edition; namely, one set of chapters deals with theoretical and methodological issues inherent in understanding intercultural relations and training. Many of these chapters are updates of ones appearing in the first edition. The two new contributions are Ward on acculturation (Chapter 7) and Paige on trainer competencies (Chapter 8). Both of these topics have become important for different reasons in the years since the first edition. The fall of the Soviet state and the opening up of borders around the world have led to renewed interest in the process of *acculturation,* which is the process of coming to know and accept the roles, norms, and values of a culture different from one's own. Ward deals with a more enduring process than that normally placed under the rubric of intercultural training. Also, in the intervening years, the profession of intercultural training has exploded beyond a cottage industry. This increase in demand has resulted in people entering the profession with little or no training. Paige considers what skills are necessary for trainers and how those skills might be obtained.

A second set of chapters considers, roughly, the contexts in which training takes place, as well as specific techniques. All of these chapters are new to this edition. The focus is somewhat on training within the United States (e.g., Dansby & Landis [Chapter 11]; Ferdman [Chapter 16]). This intracountry focus is of special interest to people concerned with relations between majority and minority groups.

A third set of chapters deals with issues specific to particular parts of the world and, in one case, with a specific population. We selected

areas that are problematic in this last decade of the 20th century: Eastern Europe and Russia, China, Central and South America, and Israel. Two special populations are also considered here: the returning sojourner (an issue generally ignored in American institutions) and, in a unique contribution, those of differing sexual orientation.

SUMMARY

In the first edition of this handbook (Landis & Brislin, 1983), Brislin et al. (1983, pp. 7-8) summarized what was known about the positive effects of cross-cultural training. The intervening years have not changed those conclusions, and they bear repeating here (with updated references):

Changes in people's thinking (cognitions)

1. A greater understanding of host nationals from the host nationals' own point of view (Albert & Adamapoulos, 1980).
2. A decrease in the use of negative stereotypes in thinking about hosts (Albert & Adamopoulos 1980; Landis, Brislin, Tzeng, & Thomas, 1985; Lefley, 1985).
3. A development of complex, rather than oversimplified, thinking about another culture, as well as an increase in knowledge about other cultures (Landis, Day, McGrew, Miller, & Thomas, 1976; Malpass & Salancik, 1977; Stohl, 1985).
4. In longer programs (approximately 10 weeks), an increase in the general attitude called *world-mindedness,* as well as greater knowledge about one's own culture (Carlson & Widaman, 1988; Sharma & Jung, 1985; Steinkalk & Taft, 1979; Stohl, 1985).

Changes in people's affective reactions (feelings)

5. Greater enjoyment and anxiety reduction among people who interact with hosts (Kamal & Marayuma, 1990; Landis, Brislin, & Hulgus, 1985; Lowe, Askling,

& Bates, 1984; Merta, Stringham, & Ponterotto, 1988; Randolf, Landis, & Tzeng, 1977; Rohrlich & Martin, 1991; Stephan & Stephan, 1992).
6. An increase in the feeling, from a given person's perspective, that he or she has a good working relation with hosts (Fiedler, Mitchell, & Triandis, 1971) and is enjoying overseas duty (Gudykunst, Hammer, & Wiseman, 1977).

Changes in people's behavior

7. Better interpersonal relationships in work groups composed of people from different cultural backgrounds (Fiedler et al., 1971; Waters, 1990).
8. Better adjustment to the everyday stresses of life in another culture and better job performance (Cushner, 1989; Fiedler et al., 1971 with reference to the study by O'Brien, Fiedler, & Hewlett, 1971). Better job performance was found among people who had already lived in another culture. Training seemed to help them integrate their diverse and perhaps confused experiences.
9. Greater ease while interacting with hosts, as perceived by the hosts themselves (Landis, Brislin, & Hulgus, 1985; Randolf et al., 1977; Weldon et al., 1975).
10. Assistance in setting and achieving people's own goals related to better interpersonal relations with hosts (Katz, 1977).

Although the above findings have proved to be robust, the lack of articulation with theory has prevented a full understanding of why this is so, as well as the ability to discover the effects of contextual moderators. In other words, we know that training appears to produce positive effects, but we are at a loss to understand why. We have yet to understand why certain training works in one setting and fails in another. The model presented in this chapter is a reaffirmation of the faith that good theory development will eventually provide the answers to these questions.

References

Adelman, M. (1988). Cross-cultural adjustment: A theoretical perspective on social support. *International Journal of Intercultural Relations, 12,* 183-204.

Albert, R., & Adamopoulos, J. (1980). An attributional approach to culture learning: The culture assimilator. In M. Hamnett & R. Brislin (Eds.), *Research in culture learning: Language and conceptual studies.* Honolulu: University Press of Hawaii.

Allport, G. W. (1954). *The psychology of prejudice.* Reading, MA: Addison-Wesley.

Ball-Rokeach, S., Rokeach, M., & Grube, J. (1984). *The great American values test: Influencing behavior and belief through television.* New York: Free Press.

Barna, L. (1983). The stress factor in intercultural relations. In D. Landis & R. Brislin (Eds.), *Handbook of intercultural training: Vol. 2. Issues in training methodology* (pp. 19-49). Elmsford, NY: Pergamon.

Bem, D. J. (1967). Self-perception: An alternative interpretation of cognitive dissonance phenomenon. *Psychological Review, 74,* 183-200.

Bennett, J. M. (1986). Modes of cross-cultural training: Conceptualizing cross-cultural training as education. *International Journal of Intercultural Relations, 10,* 117-134.

Bennett, M. J. (1986). A developmental approach to training for intercultural sensitivity. *International Journal of Intercultural Relations, 10,* 179-200.

Berry, J. (1994). Ecology of individualism and collectivism. In U. Kim, H. Triandis, C. Kagitçibasi, S-C Choi, & G. Yoon (Eds.), *Individualism and collectivism* (pp. 77-84). Thousand Oaks, CA: Sage.

Bhawuk, D. (1990). Cross-cultural orientation programs. In R. Brislin (Ed.), *Applied cross-cultural psychology* (pp. 325-346). Newbury Park, CA: Sage.

Bond, M., & Hewstone, M. (1988). Social identity theory and the perception of intergroup relations in Hong Kong. *International Journal of Intercultural Relations, 12,* 153-170.

Brewer, M. (in press). When contact is not enough: Social identity and intergroup cooperation. *International Journal of Intercultural Relations.*

Brislin, R., Cushner, K., Cherrie, C., & Yong, M. (1986). *Intercultural interactions: A practical guide.* Newbury Park, CA: Sage.

Brislin, R. W., Landis, D., & Brandt, M. (1983). Conceptualizations of intercultural behavior and training. In D. Landis & R. Brislin (Eds.), *Handbook of intercultural training: Vol. 1. Issues in theory and design* (pp. 1-34). Elmsford, NY: Pergamon.

Carlson, J., & Widaman, K. (1988). The effect of study abroad during college on attitudes toward other cultures. *International Journal of Intercultural Relations, 12,* 1-17.

Cushner, K. (1989). Assessing the impact of a culture-general assimilator. *International Journal of Intercultural Relations, 13,* 125-146.

David, K. (1972). Intercultural adjustment and applications of reinforcement theory to problems of "culture." *Trends, 4,* 1-64.

Eachus, H. (1965, September). *Self-confrontation for complex skill training: Review and analysis* (AD 624062). Wright-Patterson AFB: Air Force Systems Command.

Festinger, L. (1957). *A theory of cognitive dissonance.* Evanston, IL: Row, Peterson.

Fiedler, F., Mitchell, T., & Triandis, H. (1971). The culture assimilator: An approach to cross-cultural training. *Journal of Applied Psychology, 55,* 95-102.

Foa, U., & Foa, E. (1974). *Social structure of the mind.* Springfield, IL: Charles C Thomas.

Fontaine, G. (1986). Roles of social support systems in overseas relocation: Implications for intercultural training. *International Journal of Intercultural Relations, 10,* 361-378.

Furuto, S., & Furuto, D. (1983). The effects of affective and cognitive treatment on attitude change toward ethnic minority groups. *Interna-*

tional Journal of Intercultural Relations, 7, 149-165.

Gardner, R., Holzman, P., Klein, G., Linton, H., & Spence, D. (1959). Cognitive control: A study of individual consistencies in cognitive behavior [Special issue]. *Psychological Issues, 1*(4).

Grube, J., Mayton, D., & Ball-Rokeach, S. (1994). Inducing change in values, attitudes, and behaviors: Belief system theory and the method of value self-confrontation. *Journal of Social Issues, 50*(4), 153-173.

Gudykunst, W. (1985). A model of uncertainty reduction in intercultural encounters. *Language and Social Psychology, 2,* 79-98.

Gudykunst, W., Hammer, M., & Wiseman, R. (1977). An analysis of an integrated approach to cross-cultural training. *International Journal of Intercultural Relations, 1*(2), 99-110.

Higgenbotham, H. (1979). Comments on cognitive behavior modification. In R. Brislin, Orientation programs for cross-cultural preparation. In A. Marsella, R. Tharpe, & T. Ciborowski (Eds.), *Current perspectives in cross-cultural psychology.* San Diego: Academic Press.

Hofstede, G. (1980). *Culture's consequences: International differences in work-related values.* Beverly Hills, CA: Sage.

Kamal, A., & Maruyama, G. (1990). Cross-cultural contact and attitudes of Qatari students in the United States. *International Journal of Intercultural Relations, 14,* 123-134.

Katz, J. (1977). The effects of a systematic training program on the attitudes and behaviors of white people. *International Journal of Intercultural Relations, 1*(1), 77-89.

Kealey, D. (1989). A study of cross-cultural effectiveness: Theoretical issues, practical applications. *International Journal of Intercultural Relations, 13,* 387-428.

Kealey, D., & Ruben, B. (1983). Cross-cultural personnel selection: Criteria, issues, and methods. In D. Landis & R. Brislin (Eds.), *Handbook of intercultural training: Vol. 1. Issues in theory and design* (pp. 155-175). Elmsford, NY: Pergamon.

Kim, U., Triandis, H. C., Kagitçibasi, C., Choi, S-C, & Yoon, G. (1994). *Individualism and collectivism: Theory, methods, and applications.* Thousand Oaks, CA: Sage.

Kohls, R. (1987). Four traditional approaches to developing cross-cultural preparedness in adults: Education, training, orientation, and briefing. *International Journal of Intercultural Relations, 11,* 89-106.

Kraemer, A. (1973). *Development of a cultural self-awareness approach to instruction in intercultural communication* (Report 73-17). Arlington, VA: HumRRO.

Kraemer, A. (1974). *Workshop in intercultural communication* (Report). Arlington, VA: HumRRO.

Landis, D., & Brislin, R. (Eds.). (1983). *Handbook of intercultural training* (3 vols.). Elmsford, NY: Pergamon.

Landis, D., Brislin, R., & Hulgus, J. (1985). Attributional training versus contact in acculturative training: A laboratory study. *Journal of Applied Social Psychology, 15,* 466-482.

Landis, D., Brislin, R., Tzeng, O., & Thomas, J. (1985). Some effects of acculturative training: A field study. *International Journal of Group Tensions, 15,* 69-91.

Landis, D., Day, H., McGrew, P., Miller, A., & Thomas, J. (1976). Can a black culture assimilator increase racial understanding? *Journal of Social Issues, 32,* 169-183.

Lefley, H. (1985). Impact of cross-cultural training on black and white mental health professionals. *International Journal of Intercultural Relations, 9,* 305-318.

Loehlin, J. (1992). *Latent variable models* (2nd ed.). Hillsdale, NJ: Lawrence Erlbaum.

Lowe, G., Askling, L., & Bates, A. (1984). The impact of intercultural contact on host families. *International Journal of Intercultural Relations, 8,* 45-60.

Malpass, R., & Salancik, G. (1977). Linear and branching formats in culture assimilator training. *International Journal of Intercultural Relations, 1,* 76-87.

Merta, R., Stringham, E., & Ponterotto, J. (1988). Simulating culture shock in counselor trainees: An experiential exercise for cross-cultural training. *Journal of Counseling and Development, 66,* 242-245.

O'Brien, G., Fiedler, F., & Hewlett, T. (1971). The effects of programmed culture training upon the performance of volunteer medical teams in Central America. *Human Relations, 24,* 209-231.

Osgood, C. E., May, W., & Miron, M. (1975). *Cross-cultural universals of affective word meaning.* Urbana: University of Illinois Press.

Osgood, C. E., Suci, G., & Tannenbaum, P. (1957). *The measurement of meaning.* Urbana: University of Illinois Press.

Randolf, G., Landis, D., & Tzeng, O. (1977). The effects of time and practice on culture assimilator training. *International Journal of Intercultural Relations, 1*(4), 105-119.

Rohrlich, B., & Martin, J. (1991). Host country and reentry adjustment of student sojourners. *International Journal of Intercultural Relations, 15,* 163-182.

Schwartz, S. H. (1994a). Are there universal aspects in the structure and contents of human values? *Journal of Social Issues, 50*(4), 19-46.

Schwartz, S. H. (1994b). Beyond individualism/ collectivism: New cultural dimensions of values. In U. Kim, H. C. Triandis, C. Kagitçibasi, S-C Choi, & G. Yoon (Eds.), *Individualism and collectivism: Theory, method, and applications* (pp. 85-122). Thousand Oaks, CA: Sage.

Sharma, M., & Jung, L. (1985). How cross-cultural social participation affects the international attitudes of U.S. students. *International Journal of Intercultural Relations, 9,* 377-387.

Spielberger, C. (1966). *Anxiety and behavior.* San Diego: Academic Press.

Steinkalk, E., & Taft, R. (1979). The effect of a planned intercultural experience on the attitudes and behaviors of the participants. *International Journal of Intercultural Relations, 3,* 187-197.

Stephan, C., & Stephan, W. (1992). Reducing intercultural anxiety through contact. *International Journal of Intercultural Relations, 16,* 89-106.

Stephan, W. G. (1987). The contact hypothesis in intergroup relations. *Review of Personality and Social Psychology, 9,* 13-40.

Stephan, W. G., & Stephan, C. (1985). Intergroup anxiety. *Journal of Social Issues, 41,* 157-176.

Stohl, C. (1985). The A.M.I.G.O. Project: A multicultural intergroup opportunity. *International Journal of Intercultural Relations, 9,* 151-175.

Struch, N., & Schwartz, S. (1989). Intergroup aggression: Its predictors and distinctness from intergroup bias. *Journal of Personality and Social Psychology, 56,* 364-373.

Taifel, H., & Turner, J. (1986). The social identity theory in intergroup behavior. In S. Worchel & W. G. Austin (Eds.), *Psychology of intergroup relations* (2nd ed., pp. 7-24). Chicago: Nelson-Hall.

Triandis, H. C. (1972). *The analysis of subjective culture.* New York: Wiley-Interscience.

Triandis, H. C. (1977). *Interpersonal behavior.* Monterey, CA: Brooks/Cole.

Walton, S. (1990). Stress management training for overseas effectiveness. *International Journal of Intercultural Relations, 14,* 507-527.

Waters, H. (1990). Preparing the African-American student for corporate success: A focus on cooperative education. *International Journal of Intercultural Relations, 14,* 365-376.

Weldon, D., Carston, D., Rissman, A., Slobodin, L., & Triandis, H. (1975). A laboratory test of effects of culture assimilator training. *Journal of Personality and Social Psychology, 21,* 300-310.

PART I

Theory and Method
in Intercultural Training

2

The Role of Culture Theory
in the Study of Culture and Intercultural Training

DHARM P. S. BHAWUK

HARRY C. TRIANDIS

THIS chapter presents the role of culture theory in the study of culture and intercultural training. The chapter is divided into three sections. First, a model of building intercultural expertise through training is presented. This model examines the role of theory in the study of learning—in particular, the role of culture theory in intercultural learning. It is based on current thinking about the way people develop expertise (Anderson, 1990). The model suggests that theory-based training is more effective than other kinds of intercultural training.

In the second section, individualism and collectivism, a theory that dominated research in cross-cultural psychology in the 1980s (Kagitçibasi, 1994) and that can be the basis of intercultural training, is discussed. Individualism and collectivism has important implications for intercultural training, and we think it is important for both trainers and trainees to be familiar with this theory.

Finally, in the third section, the methodology used to study cultures is discussed. The role of emic (culture specific) and etic (culture general) in the study of cultures is analyzed, and then a discussion of the study of subjective culture is presented. Also discussed is the effectiveness of specific methods of studying cultures (e.g., experiments; ability, personality, and attitude tests; observations of behavior; translations; interviews and surveys; content analyses; the use of the Human Relations Area Files). Examples from the study of individualism and collectivism are presented to emphasize the role of culture theory in the study of culture.

Development of Intercultural Expertise Through Training

Theories serve both predictive and explanatory functions. The literature on development of expertise suggests that experts and novices differ in their ability to use a theory: Experts use theory to organize knowledge, as well as to retrieve information to solve problems. Novices do not use theory. This difference has led us to propose a role for culture theory in intercultural training.

The Role of Theory in the
Development of Expertise

The *identical-elements theory* was proposed by Thorndike and Woodworth (1901). According to this theory, transfer from training to work environments would occur as long as the two situations had identical elements. Critics of the identical-elements theory have argued that the analysis of transfer need not be limited to situations with identical elements. Ellis (1965) argued that Thorndike and Woodworth did not intend for the identical-element view to be specific to the stimulus and response components. Their elements consisted of such items as general principles and attitudes, as well as more specific components. We share this view of identical-elements theory and believe that knowledge acquisition and application take place through the assimilation of principles and theories.

The *transfer-through-theory principle* suggests that training should focus on general principles. This was demonstrated in a classic study by Hendrickson and Schroeder (1941), which showed the value of theory for learning to perform a task. They allowed two groups of people to practice shooting at an underwater target until each was able to hit the target consistently. Then the depth of the target was changed, and only one of the groups was taught the principle of refraction of light and how it affected shooting a target underwater. In the next session of target shooting, the group that was trained with the theory on refraction of light performed significantly better than the other group. This experiment demonstrated the value of theory for learning. In the same vein, we propose that culture theories are useful in the development of intercultural expertise.

Anderson (1990) described how people develop expertise. According to him, skill learning occurs in three steps. The first step is the *cognitive stage,* in which a description of the procedure is learned. In this stage, knowledge is "declarative," and people have to make an effort to recall and apply what they have learned. The second step is the *associative stage,* in which people convert their declarative knowledge of a domain into a more efficient procedural representation. Thus, in this stage, people learn the steps of performing a task and, while performing it, follow each step in the proper sequence. This process is referred to as *proceduralization.* The third step, in which the skill becomes more and more rapid and automatic, develops through practice and is called the *autonomous stage.* People know the task so well that they can perform it very quickly without following each step. People in this stage are sophisticated users of knowledge in a particular domain and use broad principles to categorize and solve a number of problems.

In studies that focused on the development of expertise in geometry, Anderson (1982) found that, as subjects develop expertise, dramatic changes occur in the degree to which they rely on procedural versus declarative knowledge. Greeno (1974) found that students remembered the steps they took to solve a problem after they solved the problem a few times. Elements of a problem are repeated in many other problems of the same type. These common elements constitute learning labeled *tactical learning* (Anderson, 1990). People recognize these common elements as they becomet proficient, develop a tactic around them, and approach the solution of a certain kind of problem in a certain way. This process helps them solve problems more rapidly. According to Anderson, tactical learning involves proceduralization.

Larkin (1981) compared the solutions given by novices and experts to physics problems. He found that, unlike novices, experts solve problems by using theories (e.g., Newton's second law of motion). Anderson (1990) called the use of principles and theories in problem solving *strategic learning.* This is similar to Hendrickson and Schroeder's (1941) experiment in which students who learned the principle of refraction of light were able to effectively shoot an underwater target. Building on the notion that theories have a role in the development of expertise, we propose a model of intercultural expertise development, discussed below.

A Model of Intercultural Expertise Development

We propose to define a *lay person* as one who has no knowledge of another culture, an ideal type for all practical purposes, considering that even the Sherpas in the remote Nepalese mountains or the pygmies in Africa have been exposed to people from other cultures. Some evidence suggests that people who have spent 2 or more years in another culture develop cross-cultural sensitivity through their intercultural interactions, even in the absence of any formal training (Bhawuk & Brislin, 1992). We posit that people with extended intercultural experience or those who have gone through a formal intercultural training program (e.g., a culture-specific orientation program) that discusses differences between two cultures will develop some degree of intercultural expertise; we call them *novices*. In other words, novices are people with some intercultural skills or expertise, usually for a culture other than their own. These people are still in the first stage of learning (the cognitive or declarative stage).

We propose that *experts* are novices who have acquired the knowledge of culture theories so that they can organize cognitions about cultural differences more meaningfully around a theory (e.g., the way experts use Newton's second law of motion to classify physics problems). These people are at the second stage of learning (the associative or proceduralization stage). We posit that people can arrive at this stage by going through a theory-based intercultural training program.

Advanced experts are experts who not only have the knowledge of the theory but also have had the amount of practice needed to perform tasks automatically. These people are at the third stage of learning (the autonomous stage). A behavioral modeling training, following a theory-based training, would enable experts to become advanced experts. Thus, the model of intercultural expertise development posits that intercultural training using culture theory will make a person an expert, whereas training that does not use theory will only result in novices; and to be an advanced expert, one would need to go through behavioral training or to avail the

opportunity to practice different behaviors so that they become habitual (see Figure 2.1). Also shown in the figure are the linkages between stages of learning and stages of intercultural expertise development. In the next section, we discuss the theory of individualism and collectivism, a theory that has potential for the improvement of intercultural training.

Individualism and Collectivism

The constructs of individualism and collectivism have been used in most of the social sciences since the 1600s (Triandis, 1995). They drew the attention of researchers, however, especially social psychologists and organizational scientists, following the seminal work of Hofstede (1980). Using the work value responses of 117,000 IBM employees in 66 countries, Hofstede found four value-based factors useful in analyzing culture: power distance, uncertainty avoidance, individualism, and masculinity. His level of analysis was the countries, rather than the individuals who provided the data, and so, strictly speaking, the constructs he proposed are sociological, rather than psychological (Hofstede, 1994). In his studies, English-speaking countries were found to be high on individualism, whereas Asian and Latin American countries were found to be low on individualism.

Hofstede (1980) defined *individualism* as the emotional independence of individuals from "groups, organizations, and/or other collectives" (p. 221). He contrasted individualists with collectivist societies in which people are born into extended families or kinship systems that protect them in exchange for giving their loyalty to the collectives. A person's identity is derived from the social system, rather than from individual attributes. Hofstede (1994) suggested that, at the cultural level, individualism and collectivism may well be a bipolar construct but that, at the individual level, it may be a multidimensional construct. Since the 1980s, Triandis and colleagues have conducted a series of studies to understand these constructs both at the psychological and the cultural levels.

Hui and Triandis (1986) carried out a systematic study to define the constructs of individualism and collectivism. They asked a sample of psychologists and anthropologists from all over the world to respond to a questionnaire in the

20

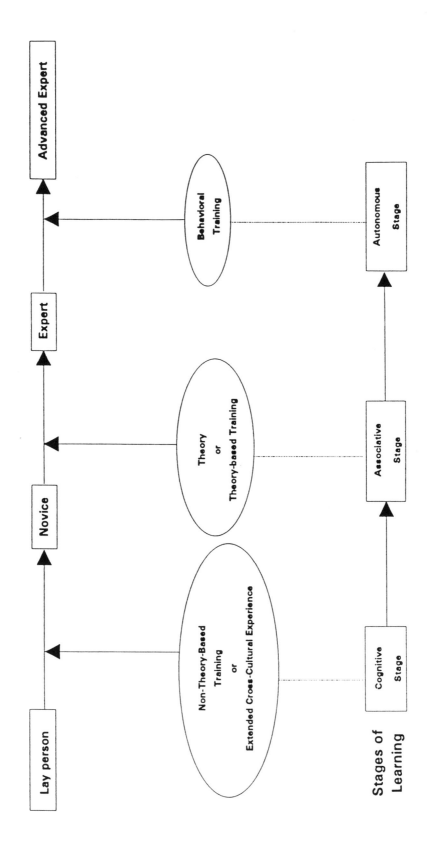

Figure 2.1. A Model of Intercultural Expertise Development

way an individualist or a collectivist would respond. They found collectivism to be a cluster of a wide variety of beliefs and behaviors that could be categorized into the following seven categories: (a) the feeling of concern about how their decisions would affect others in their collectivity; (b) the sharing of material resources; (c) the sharing of such nonmaterial resources as time, affection, and fun, or the sacrificing of some interesting activities for a member of the collective; (d) the willingness of people to accept the opinions and views of others, or in other words, the willingness to conform; (e) the feeling of concern about saving face or about gaining the approval of the collective; (f) believing in the correspondence of one's own outcomes, both positive and negative, with the outcomes of others; and (g) the feeling of involvement in others' lives.

Collectivism also requires the subordination of individual goals to the goals of a collective. Underlying the seven characteristics is the term *concern.* Concern does not refer to affection and worry only; it is rather "a sense of oneness with other people, a perception of complex ties and relationships, and a tendency to keep other people in mind" (Hui & Triandis, 1986, p. 231). According to these researchers, *collectivism* is a syndrome of feelings, emotions, beliefs, ideology, and actions related to interpersonal concern. Hui and Triandis argued that collectivism is not equivalent to altruism. Collectivism recognizes the group, and not the individual, as the basic unit of survival.

The researchers participating in the study had a high level of consensus in recognizing collectivism as an etic or universal concept. Hence, this concept can be meaningful in understanding and explaining the similarities and differences between cultures.

Comparing Americans and Chinese, Hsu (1981) concluded that individualists are independent-minded, inner-directed, and resentful of conformity, whereas collectivists believe in interdependence and are inclined to conform. According to Hsu, in China, conformity tends to govern all interpersonal relations and has social and cultural approval.

Triandis, Bontempo, et al. (1986) found that, at the cultural level, each construct of individualism and collectivism consists of two factors: (a) "separation from in-groups" and "self-reliance with hedonism" (individualism) and (b) "family integrity" and "interdependence with

sociability" (collectivism). They suggested that individualism and collectivism are not the two opposite poles of a bipolar construct, but rather are two independent constructs. This is a refinement of the early conceptualization of individualism and collectivism as bipolar opposites proposed by earlier researchers (Hofstede, 1980; Wagner & Moch, 1986).

Triandis, Leung, Villareal, and Clark (1985) emphasized the distinction between the cultural and psychological levels of individualism and collectivism. At the cultural level, as in Hofstede's analysis (each culture is treated as an observation or a subject), they recommended using the terms *individualism* and *collectivism.* They suggested using the terms *allocentrism* and *idiocentrism* at the psychological level, corresponding to collectivism and individualism, respectively. Allocentrism and idiocentrism refer to the individual differences existing in all cultures (both allocentrics and idiocentrics can be found in all cultures). Allocentric individuals subordinate their personal goals to the interests of their collectivity and may derive satisfaction in doing so; idiocentric individuals set their personal goals above the interest of any collectivity (Triandis et al., 1985). Allocentrics in individualist cultures join communes and other collectives; idiocentrics in collectivist cultures try to escape the dominance of their in-groups.

Triandis, McCusker, and Hui (1990) proposed a further refinement of the theory by defining the antecedents and consequents of individualism and collectivism. Affluence, social mobility, and small family size appear to be the antecedents for self-reliance and independence, good skills when entering new groups; loneliness seems to be the consequent of individualism. They found that the content of the self includes more group-linked elements in collectivist than in individualist cultures; members of collectivist cultures perceive their in-groups as more homogeneous than their out-groups, and the opposite pattern is found among members of individualistic cultures. As predicted, the researchers found that people in collectivist cultures perceive more intimate and subordinate social behaviors as likely toward their in-group members and more dissociative and superordinate behaviors toward members of their out-groups than do members of individualistic cultures. Collectivists were found to emphasize values that promote the welfare of their in-group; individualists were found to emphasize values that promote individual goals.

Individualism and collectivism are also useful in predicting everyday behavior. Wheeler, Reis, and Bond (1989) examined the effects of these constructs on everyday social interaction by using the Rochester Interaction Record (RIR). Consistent with their predictions, they found that Hong Kong students had longer but fewer interactions (half as many) with fewer people, had a higher percentage of group and task interactions, and indicated greater self- and other-disclosure than U.S. norms.

Triandis (1995) proposed, after reviewing both theoretical and empirical studies, that individualism and collectivism have four universal defining attributes: (a) independent versus interdependent self, (b) goals independent from in-groups versus goals compatible with in-groups, (c) emphasis on attitude versus norms, and (d) emphasis on rationality versus relatedness. According to him, individualists (a) have an independent self, (b) choose goals that suit them individually, (c) behave consistently with their personal attitudes, beliefs, and values, and (d) base their relationship on a careful computation of the costs and benefits of their interpersonal relationships. Contrary to these characteristics, collectivists (a) have an interdependent self, (b) have goals compatible with those of their in-groups, (c) exhibit norm-driven behavior (e.g., they conform to social pressure and are dutiful), and (d) give priority to relationships even when that is not cost-effective.

Triandis (1995) proposed that individualism and collectivism are of two types—vertical and horizontal—depending on whether people view their selves as "same as" or "different from" others. In vertical collectivism and individualism, people view their selves to be different from those of others; India and China provide examples of vertical collectivism, and the United States and France provide examples of vertical individualism. In horizontal collectivism and individualism, people view their selves as the same as those of others; the Israeli kibbutz and Eskimo cultures provide examples of horizontal collectivism, and Sweden and Australia provide examples of horizontal individualism.

Vertical and horizontal individualism and collectivism fit well conceptually with other culture theories. For example, Fiske (1990, 1992) proposed that communal sharing, market pricing, equality matching, and authority ranking are the four basic forms of social behavior found in every culture. These four basic behaviors correspond to collectivism, individualism, horizontal, and vertical dimensions proposed by Triandis (1995); vertical individualism corresponds to market pricing and authority ranking, vertical collectivism corresponds to communal sharing and authority ranking, horizontal individualism corresponds to equality matching and market pricing, and horizontal collectivism corresponds to equality matching and communal sharing. A discussion of the relationship of vertical and horizontal individualism and collectivism with other contemporary culture theories, and the measurement of these constructs, can be found elsewhere (Singelis, Triandis, Bhawuk, & Gelfand, 1995; Triandis, 1995; Triandis & Bhawuk, in press).

The value of individualism and collectivism in intercultural training can be estimated by its effectiveness in predicting both daily social behaviors across cultures (Wheeler et al., 1989) and in explaining such phenomena as cultural distance, concept of self, and perception of in-group versus out-group (Triandis et al., 1990). Furthermore, Triandis, Brislin, and Hui (1988) proposed a way of using this theory in briefing people from either type of culture when they visit the other type of culture. The first author found this concept extremely useful in orienting developmental workers and volunteers from Western industrialized countries working in Nepal in that the orientation could go beyond superficial do's and don'ts and provide a meaningful framework for participants to categorize their intercultural experiences. In short, individualism and collectivism provide a parsimonious conceptualization to explain and predict intercultural interaction and can be effectively used in orientation programs that are both short and long in duration. If individualism and collectivism are important aspects of culture, how can they be studied? In the next section, we address this question and discuss the methodology for studying culture.

Methodology for Studying Culture

Culture is a very complex entity, and a good account of how to study it can be found in the *Handbook of Method in Cultural Anthropology*

(Naroll & Cohen, 1970) and in the *Handbook of Cross-Cultural Psychology* (Vol. 2; Triandis & Berry, 1980). We start by discussing the constructs of *emic* and *etic* and their importance in studying cultures and in making cross-cultural comparisons. We then present the subjective culture approach to cross-cultural research (Triandis, 1972). Finally, we critically evaluate the effectiveness of different research methods in studying cultures. In each case, we use examples from the study of individualism and collectivism and thus link the earlier two sections of this chapter with this section.

The Role of Emics and Etics in the Study of Culture

Emics and etics are perhaps the two most crucial constructs in the study of culture because they emphasize two perspectives. Emics focus on "the native's point of view"; etics focus on the cross-cultural scientist's point of view. As noted earlier, collectivism and individualism are etics, but they take different forms in different cultures and thus provide emics. For example, in Indonesia, a point of view (see Triandis et al., 1993) found among women is that leaving one's in-group is "dangerous." That is a local manifestation of an etic because probably in all cultures people feel uneasy about leaving their in-group. But in individualistic cultures, many people feel good about the freedom from the influence of the in-group and see little danger in leaving an in-group. In collectivist cultures, the sense that danger is associated with being away from the in-group is stronger; in Indonesia, women see this danger as extreme, whereas males do not. Thus, in this case, it is an Indonesian female emic.

Emics and etics have their origin in linguistics—emic from phon*emic* and etic from phon*etic*—and represent the culture-specific and culture-general elements of cultures (Pike, 1967). These words also represent two distinct approaches to studying culture. The *emic approach* is predominantly followed by anthropologists who believe that each culture has unique ideas, behaviors, and concepts and that its uniqueness must be the focus of their study. The *etic approach* is mainly followed by cross-cultural scientists (both anthropologists and psychologists) who believe that cultures have

both specific and universal dimensions and are interested in observing these universals. It is now generally accepted that similarities between cultures must be established before their differences can be studied, because if a framework of universal constructs is not observed, it is impossible to distinguish a cultural difference from a misperception of the method (Campbell, 1968). In other words, "differences must be embedded into a framework of similarities" (Triandis, 1994, p. 85).

Emics are essential for understanding a culture, but their uniqueness makes them inappropriate for cross-cultural comparisons. Etics are theoretical concepts that allow generalizations about relationships among variables across cultures. For example, even animals other than humans have pecking orders, and thus social hierarchy is an etic. But it takes emic forms, such as touching the feet in Nepal and India, bowing in Japan, and using a title in the United States. If researchers were interested in the relationship of social distance (also an etic) and giving status, they would need to operationalize both variables emically in each culture. Yet, the relationship may well be etic: When social distance is minimal, people give less status than when social distance is moderate, and as social distance increases, people give more status up to a point when the social distance is high, at which point they would like to give little status, and what they do depends on a computation of the advantages and disadvantages of giving status. The general shape of the relationship between status and social distance may be universal, but the specific shape will vary with culture (e.g., Triandis et al., 1990).

Studying cultural similarities and differences has two approaches. First, one could start with a construct generated in one's own culture and use it in another culture. In doing this, one is imposing the construct developed in one's culture, and therefore this approach is referred to as *pseudoetic* or *imposed etic*. This approach allows the researcher to find out how the original construct changes in the second culture, and thus a derived emic of that culture can be identified. The two emics can then be compared if, and only if, there is a common ground or a derived etic between the two emics (Berry, 1969).

The second approach is recommended by Triandis (1972, 1994) and requires that one start with a theoretical construct (e.g., social distance). The theoretical construct should be discussed with researchers in all of the cultures, and the construct should be operationalized simultaneously. The etic (culture-general) and emic (culture-specific) aspects of the constructs should be identified. Items should be developed to measure both the etic and emic aspects of the construct in all cultures by using focus groups, and the items should be locally standardized by using Thurstone's procedure (see Edwards, 1957, chap. 5). This procedure provides locally standardized and equivalent measures of the theoretical constructs. It is usually easy to interpret the findings of a study that uses such a procedure.

A related methodological issue in the study of cultures is the level of analysis. Hofstede (1980) presented data that make the case that correlations obtained from individual-level data may not always replicate correlations obtained when cultures or nations are used as the units of observation. He used the terms *individual correlations* and *ecological correlations* to distinguish these two sets of analyses. He also noted a distinction between studies that attempt to establish the generality of some law (the more of variable *X,* the more of variable *Y*), as opposed to studies that attempt to show cultural differences. We get a two-by-two table of types of studies by crossing etic emphasis versus emic emphasis with individual- versus ecological-level of analysis. The etic-individual studies might include attempts to show the universality of a phenomenon (Lonner, 1980). The emic-individual studies might include studies of subjective culture, such as the ones that established the meaning of the word *philotimo* (Vassiliou & Vassiliou, 1973). The etic-ecological are the hologeistic (whole-world) studies described by Naroll, Michik, and Naroll (1980). The emic-ecological are attempts to show that certain cultures are high and other cultures low on some variable, and Hofstede's studies are in this category.

The level of analysis influences how one samples cultures. For example, for etic-individual or etic-ecological research, one needs to select the broadest possible sample of cultures. This should be done in such a way that the cultures are sufficiently geographically distant to make cultural diffusion unimportant as a variable shaping cultures. This distance is necessary to avoid the so-called Galton's problem—the spurious increase in correlations when cultures next to each other are included in

the sample. For emic-ecological studies, however, one would want to keep time, place, context of measurement, instrument, sampling of individuals, and other variables as similar as possible because the broader the sample, the greater the chance that the specific emic elements will "wash out." Also, in exploring a limited problem, such as the rather distinctive suicide rates in various countries, one gets more information by comparing similar countries (e.g., the Scandinavian countries—Norway has very low rates, and Sweden has very high rates) than by comparing very different countries (e.g., France and Japan—rate differences may be due to a large number of factors).

It is relevant to note here Leung and Bond's (1989) discussion of pancultural, cross-cultural or ecological, and intracultural analyses. They discussed a number of problems with each of these approaches and also proposed a method that extracts etic dimensions at the individual level and eliminates response sets, a problem that has been identified in cross-cultural studies for some time (Hui & Triandis, 1989; Triandis, 1972).

The Leung and Bond (1989) procedure can be understood best if we consider a study conducted in 10 cultures. Suppose that, in each culture, data are collected from 100 people who fill out an instrument with 20 items. The *pancultural analysis* refers to analyzing 1,000 observations (100 respondents times 10 cultures) for each variable or item on the instrument. The *ecological analysis* refers to analyzing 10 observations (1 each for the cultures, which is the average of the 100 respondents) for each variable or item on the instrument. This is similar to Hofstede's ecological analysis discussed earlier. The *intracultural analysis* refers to analyzing 10 sets (1 for each culture) of 100 observations for each variable or item of the instrument.

Leung and Bond (1989) proposed a factor analysis of the variables following a twofold standardization of the scores. First, standardization is done within subject and then across items. (This procedure is similar to that used by Osgood, May, and Miron, 1975, to analyze the affective meaning of words across cultures.) A strong etic is found when the factor analysis extracts factors in agreement with the factors extracted from the pancultural or ecological factor analyses. The differences between their procedure and the pancultural analysis is that, in the former method, the data are standardized, whereas in the later method, the raw data are used. Factors extracted by the Leung-Bond procedure but not found in the pancultural or ecological analyses are weak etics, according to these researchers. Factors found in the intracultural analyses but not found in the Leung-Bond procedure are emic factors; those extracted from pancultural and ecological analyses but not found in the Leung-Bond analysis are cultural factors. Thus, it is possible to identify both the etics (strong and weak) and emics of the constructs under study by following the Leung-Bond procedure. We now turn to the discussion of the subjective culture approach to studying cultures.

Subjective Culture Studies

Triandis (1972) defined *subjective culture* as "a cultural group's characteristic way of perceiving the man-made part of its environment" (p. 3) and provided a theoretical framework for the study of subjective culture. He referred to roles, tasks, norms, ideals, cognitive structures, values, and affect (evaluations) as elements of subjective culture, and to cognitive learning, categorization, conditioning, and instrumental learning as basic psychological processes through which proximal antecedents, such as occupations, social situations, language, and religion, act on these elements. The proximal antecedents themselves are shaped by the physical environment or resources and historical events. Economic activities, social organization, and political organization are also important determinants of subjective culture. A detailed description of the study of subjective culture is beyond the scope of this chapter; the interested reader should refer to Triandis (1972, 1994).

Triandis (1972) recommended that cross-cultural studies be undertaken by teams of researchers representing the various cultures being studied. The research strategy should be determined jointly. Then, each investigator should check the cultural appropriateness of the methods in his or her culture, and adjustments in procedure should be made to make all materials culturally appropriate. Typically, one will have a theory in which several etic constructs are interrelated; the model described above provides one such broad framework that includes the concepts and the probable relationships between them.

For example, Davidson, Jaccard, Triandis, Morales, and Díaz-Guerrero (1976) examined the relationship between behavioral intentions and norms as proposed by Triandis (1972). They examined the relationship between the intention to have one more child and the norm of whether or not the women felt a moral obligation to have one more child. This norm was highly predictive of the behavioral intentions in the case of less-educated Mexican women. The educated Mexican and American samples, however, responded on the basis of their attitudes, not this norm. In both the American and Mexican operationalizations of the norms, pretest interviews determined the best way to word the questions that measured the norm. The questions were not identical or parallel word for word, but the theoretical constructs were the same. This research showed that both American and Mexican women saw that their behavioral intentions to have one more child were related to their norms and attitudes. But the Mexican women with a lower education gave more importance to norms than to attitudes; the Mexican women with more education gave most attention to their attitudes (e.g., Would I like a family with an extra child?).

In subjective cultural studies, therefore, the attempt is to get the advantages of both emic and etic approaches. One obtains data from many persons on many emically constructed instruments. The broad variables reflected in the instruments, or extracted from statistical analyses, however, are etic. Thus, one can do both relatively accurate descriptions of a culture and approximate cultural comparisons. But the amount of work that is needed increases considerably and makes the approach a daunting venture. We now turn to the evaluation of various research methods for studying cultures.

Multimethod Approaches

In cross-cultural studies, it is most desirable to use more than one method to test a hypothesis. The reason is that each culture is likely to have its own way of reacting to each method (each method has a unique meaning in each culture). Therefore, the use of many methods that converge strengthens our conviction that we have really established an important point about cultural similarities and differences. Ideally, we should do systematic observations and experiments and also analyze the subjective culture of the peoples we are studying.

Experiments

It is useful to distinguish *presentation experiments,* as when a person is shown different kinds of stimuli and is asked to respond, from *manipulation experiments,* as when a person is placed in a social situation different from the social situation of a control group. In presentation experiments, the key question is, Are the stimuli presented equivalent in meaning across cultural groups? In manipulation experiments, the key question is, Are the manipulations equivalent in meaning?

It is quite obvious that equivalence in manipulation cannot be established unless one gets similarities in responses to the manipulation. This task requires very complex operations in which the researcher, during pretests, keeps changing the manipulation until many results are similar. The objective differences in the manipulation can then be reported; they constitute the "cultural differences."

An example illustrates the importance of selecting the correct experimental task for the particular population. Irwin, Schafer, and Feiden (1974) asked Mano farmers in Liberia and West Africa and U.S. undergraduates to do a rice-sorting and a card-sorting task. The researchers found that whereas the U.S. sample performed more card sorts than the Mano sample, the Mano subjects performed more rice sorts than the U.S. subjects. In other words, a drop in performance level was associated with an unfamiliar task. People arrive at laboratories with a battery of existing skills that have been developed over 20 or more years of experience. Such skills are likely to make cross-cultural experiments very difficult to do because it is very difficult for the researcher to control or manipulate them.

Brown and Sechrest (1980) examined a number of threats to the validity of experimental findings. They showed various ways to control for threats to validity (e.g., by manipulating at least one variable in each culture, by running several groups, by doing manipulation checks, by replicating the experiment several times).

Nevertheless, experiments are extremely difficult to do in cross-cultural settings.

When interpreting the results of experiments, it is necessary to keep in mind that the manipulations may not be equally appropriate and may not have the same meaning in various cultures; thus, they may result in artifactual, rather than valid, findings. Furthermore, the replicability of experiments is often low (Amir & Sharon, 1987), and it is often difficult to interpret the findings because of insufficient context. Experiments may also be culturally objectionable or even unethical, particularly when they require deception. Nevertheless, in some examples, experiments have provided useful information (Bochner, 1980; Ciborowski, 1980). In such cases, the interpretation of the results has relied very heavily on ethnographic information and on manipulations that gave the same results in both cultures.

Experimental design has been used by many researchers to examine many types of behavior as predicted by the theory of individualism and collectivism—for example, social loafing (Earley, 1989) and group loyalty (James & Cropanzano, in press).

An important precursor to conducting an experiment is to use a *scenario study,* in which the manipulations are presented to subjects from the relevant cultures. The situations the subjects will find themselves in during the experiment should be described in exhaustive detail. The same stimuli (if possible) that will be presented in the actual experiment should be presented in the scenarios. Cultural differences in the way people from the various cultures respond should be examined for possible differences in the meaning of the manipulation that are over and above the differences expected in the experiment. In general, the results of the scenario study and the experiment should be the same. If serious discrepancies are found, they must make sense theoretically.

Ability, Personality, and Attitude Tests

The use of tests in cross-cultural research is quite problematic because a test usually measures one or, at most, a few variables out of context. If the results show cultural similarities, the problems of interpretation of the results are much reduced, but a frequent finding is that researchers report cultural differences.

One must realize that two cultural groups differ in perhaps 10,000 ways—race, social class, material goods, socialization, familiarity with the stimuli presented, the responses, and so forth. How can an inference be made from a score on an IQ test that "race" results in different "intelligence"? To start with, what is the meaning of "intelligence" in various cultures? In many African cultures, to be intelligent means to know what the elders want you to do and to do it. In many cultures, to be wise (slow, and not make mistakes) and intelligent are the same. Many cultures of conquered peoples (e.g., Africans brought to North America as slaves, Mexican American descendants of residents of the Southwest in 1848, American Indians) have an "oppositional cultural framework" (Gibson & Ogbu, 1991), wherein if the majority says "good," they are likely to say "bad." Thus, for example, American Indians often see a person who behaves "intelligently," according to the white definition of intelligence, as "crazy." Among African Americans, sometimes, to be a "good student" means to try to be white and can lead to ostracism or worse.

Reasons for differences in scores are often attributed to the most visible attributes, such as race, when in fact they may be due to any of the other 9,999 attributes that are confounded with race! Many challenges to the validity of the statement—that some cultural differences are due to race—can be identified. Differences on tests may be due to differences in the motivation of the participants (Why should I respond *quickly?*), experimenter bias, differences in familiarity with the materials, differential comprehension of instructions, interactions of anxiety with cultural group (test anxiety is higher among some groups than among others), differential reliability, and differential validity (see Triandis, 1994, chap. 3).

One important factor that can lead to differences on tests is differences in response sets. Some cultural groups assume they must only answer those questions they are absolutely sure to know the answers to; other groups assume that guessing is acceptable. In the case of attitude tests, in different cultures there are yes-sayers and nay-sayers in different mixes (Triandis & Triandis, 1962). In some cultures, if you say "agree," it sounds as if you are hiding something. You need to say "I strongly agree." In other cultures, to say "I strongly agree" sounds arrogant. In short, cultural differences are found in the meaning of the scale positions on attitude scales, and ignoring such differences can result in major misinterpretations of the results. Hui and Triandis (1989), in a study of effects of culture and response formats, found that Hispanics exhibit a stronger tendency for extreme checking (about half the time, on the average) than non-Hispanics but only when 5-point scales are used. Use of a 10-point scale was found to reduce the extreme responses of the Hispanics to the level of non-Hispanics, and the extreme responses of the non-Hispanics were not affected by the scales. Thus, differences in response set can have a highly significant difference in the attitude scores; it simply reflects this response style.

One way to get around such cultural differences is to standardize the responses of each individual. For example, if a person has given 50 answers, remove the mean of these answers from each score and divide by the standard deviation of the 50 scores. This calculation must be done carefully, however, because standardization can eliminate "true" cultural differences.

Indeed, serious problems are associated with a testing approach to cross-cultural studies. But testing should not be dismissed entirely. There are ways to adapt tests to the cross-cultural enterprise. If the researcher starts with a careful analysis of what is learned in each culture and constructs the test with items that are over-learned in both cultures, there is hope that a comparison can be made. Additional requirements are that the administration of the tests should be done by members of the same ethnic group as the persons tested, in the vernacular of those persons, and with "comprehension checks" to establish that respondents understood the instructions and the format of the questions. After the data have been collected, it is necessary to conduct several checks and to discard items that make the inter-item correlation patterns of the two cultural groups nonidentical; that is, each item must be correlated with the total score, and the correlations across cultures must be similar.

Individualism and collectivism have implications for understanding attributions of ability versus effort. Evidence suggests that collectivists (e.g., Japanese) usually explain their success by pointing to help they receive from others (Kashima & Triandis, 1986), and failure by pointing to their own lack of effort (Holloway,

Kashiwagi, Hess, & Azuma, 1986). In contrast, Americans are more likely to attribute success to their ability, and failure to task difficulty. This difference became evident in an intercultural group recently. Triandis requires students in his cross-cultural psychology course to form an intercultural group and to write papers by reflecting on their own experience with theoretical concepts learned in the class. One group recently reported that, in the group meeting after the midterm examination, a Chinese student attributed her poor performance to her lack of effort and an American student attributed it to confusing questions and poor grading. The group had a Eureka! experience when a third member pointed out how the attributions made by the two group members were a straight textbook case of how collectivists and individualists make attributions! Later, the American student admitted that he had not worked hard enough. Thus, it seems possible to integrate a number of concepts of research in ability tests with the theory of individualism and collectivism. Other issues, such as the academic success of children of migrant Asians, can also be examined better in the light of individualism and collectivism, and researchers are beginning to realize this.

Observations of Behavior

Observations of behavior (Longabaugh, 1980) are usually organized by taking note of who interacts with whom, how frequently, and in what setting. Special attention is sometimes given to frequency of eye contact, distance between persons, position of the head and orientation of the body, loudness of the interaction, or facial expressions used. From such raw materials, observers sometimes infer broader categories of meaning, such as offers help, suggests responsibility, reprimands, seeks dominance, acts sociably, seeks attention, offers support, touches, seeks help, assaults sociably, and is aggressive (Whiting & Whiting, 1975).

Another approach examines and clarifies the environment in which the interaction takes place (Barker & Schoggen, 1973). The frequency of interaction in various settings is obtained. Some settings may exist in one culture but not in another; to address this problem, one can sample particular settings (e.g., schools), take a time sample of behaviors in them, and examine how frequently particular behaviors take place.

One needs to examine the methodology to determine whether the observer was able to become unobtrusive and what is likely to have been the reactivity of the subjects. Did the researcher provide information on the reliability of the recording? Did the code system for recording the observations have clear definitions of time boundaries, behavioral boundaries, and ways of making inferences? How were coder errors corrected? How were the data reduced, analyzed, and interpreted?

Wheeler et al. (1989) provided an example of the use of observations (in this case, self-observations) and culture theory (individualism and collectivism) in studies of daily social behaviors across cultures (Hong Kong and United States) discussed earlier. Triandis (1990) observed frequencies of people seen in such public places as streets, squares, restaurants, and movies alone or together in two cities, one in an individualist culture (Urbana, Illinois, USA) and another in a collectivist culture (Kozane, Greece). He found that the Greeks ride together more often than alone, relative to Americans (alone/together ratio was .8 to 2.7, mean = 1.49, for Greece; and 3.05 to 8.67, mean = 3.94, for United States). The pedestrian data were strikingly similar. Triandis used this observation to support the theoretical argument that collectivists spend more leisure time with others than do individualists.

In summary, errors can occur because the reactions of the subjects to the observer, to the code system, and to the definitions of boundaries for behavior were culture-bound. The use of multiple observers, code systems that have been pretested in many cultures, and extensive observer training are likely to reduce these problems, and by using this method one can study many aspects of individualism and collectivism.

Translations

The translation of pragmatic material, such as information that makes references to objects, is likely to be quite satisfactory, but the translation of poetry or philosophical discourse is likely to be unsatisfactory (Triandis, 1964). Therefore, translations should be used with caution, and a researcher undertaking a serious work on translations should consult other sources (Brislin, 1976, 1980).

An important idea in translating questions for questionnaires, instructions for experimental settings, and similar kinds of materials is decentering (Werner & Campbell, 1970). To get a text "decentered," one starts with the text in one language—say, *A*—and has it translated into language *B,* and then uses a different set of interpreters to translate *B* back to *A* and thus obtain a version that is a bit different, which we can call *A'*. Now the original text *A* and the back-translated text *A'* can be compared. Discrepancies may suggest a revision in the original *A*. A new original text is constructed and again translated, so we have *A''*, which goes into *B'*. This is again translated back into *A*, this time, giving us *A'''*. We can now compare *A''* with *A'''*, and the two texts might be similar or even identical. Then we can stop the process. But if the texts are not similar, we continue iterating (going back and forth between *A* and *B* and changing) the texts until we reach two versions of the text that are almost identical.

Back translation appears to be an excellent way to obtain equivalence, but it is important to be cautious. There are many problems, including the fact that many words are derived from the same roots but develop different meanings in different languages. For example, the word *sympathetic* in English suggests an action of understanding another person. But in many languages of the Latin group, such as French (*sympatique*), Italian (*simpatico*), it is a quality of a person who is "nice," "pleasant," or "agreeable." The original meaning (in Greek) was someone who feels the same way as another. The English meaning is rather close to the original, whereas the modern Greek, French, Italian, and Spanish have deviated from it. The problem in translation is the strong tendency to translate *simpatico* into *sympathetic* because they "look" alike. Because the connotations are very different, the translation is poor, though it "looks good" superficially.

Cross-cultural researchers should not be satisfied with a simple "double translation" and should strive for decentering. Additional studies, such as administering the two versions to bilinguals and examining their responses to the two versions (see Marin, Triandis, Betancourt, & Kashima, 1983; Triandis & Davis, 1965), can be useful but must also be used with caution because bilinguals give more socially desirable responses when using the language of a reference group.

Interviews and Surveys

Problems of sampling should be examined by cross-cultural researchers. If the society is homogeneous, a few well-selected informants can provide the needed information, but as the complexity and heterogeneity of the society increase, more careful sampling is needed. In industrialized societies, area sampling is often used, requiring that the whole country be broken down into numerous segments and that individuals be selected randomly from each segment. This is difficult to do in many developing countries because of inadequate maps or lists of addresses.

Who should be the interviewer is another issue. Answers obtained from respondents may differ, depending on who sponsors and who conducts the study, as well as the dress and mannerisms of the interviewer. If several interviewers are used, it is useful to interview the interviewers at the end of the study to find out what has not gone according to plan.

What questions should be asked is also an issue. The concern here is whether one should take an emic or an etic approach—that is, ask different culture-specific questions or ask the same questions in all cultures. If the same questions are to be used, researchers should avoid emic concepts (e.g., "a date" has little meaning in a culture where chaperons are used). It is often useful to use random probes—that is, select some respondents at random and ask them why they answered the way they did. One should also examine what ideas the respondents have about the interviewer, the questions, and whether the questions appear to them as biased or threatening. Some of these issues are discussed in detail by Pareek and Rao (1980).

Special attention should be given to norms. In some cultures, people are very courteous and try to give answers that will please the interviewer; in others, they are reticent; and in still others, they play various games (e.g., "fool the interviewer," whereby respondents tell the biggest lies they can get away with). To avoid such problems, the interviewer must develop rapport. Questions that create rapport, show concern, and capitalize on the needs of the respondent should be asked first. Emphasizing norms is a defining attribute of collectivism; hence, it is necessary for a researcher to pay special attention to norms when conducting research in a collectivist culture.

Interviewers should be familiar with the culture and know the social structure of the villages in which they interview. In many cultures, women interviewers must be used to interview women. In interviewing in villages, it may be desirable to obtain the endorsement of a powerful person from the village—the chief, local doctor, priest, or medicine man. When there are competing or conflicting authorities, it may be necessary to employ different interviewers who obtain permission from different authorities. In short, one must adjust procedures to make them acceptable to the culture.

Content Analyses

Existing cultural products, such as written materials (e.g., children's stories, newspaper stories), myths, speeches, movies, formal and informal communications, or even artistic products such as pots with various themes painted on them, can be analyzed systematically to measure attitudes, motives, opinions, values, and other attributes (Brislin, 1980). Basically, responses are classified according to the judgments of one or more analysts, according to predetermined rules, with care taken to ensure that different analysts classify the responses in similar categories. In conducting a content analysis, it is useful to develop procedures for sampling the materials to be analyzed, to define categories and subsequently code the materials into them, and to establish the reliability of the coding procedure and the validity of the results (Brislin, 1980, p. 401).

One should select materials that are popular (seen by many people—e.g., successful films produced in the various cultures); materials used to develop and instill norms (e.g., school primers in the various cultures); and materials that are diverse (e.g., both films and primers). Random selection is highly desirable in sampling but is often impossible. Rules are developed to transform the specific materials into a frequency in a category. The key to coding is to make the rules explicit so that different analysts can classify the materials in the same way. Special problems and difficulties in doing this are discussed by Brislin (1980, pp. 403ff). To ad-

dress the reliability issues, quite dissimilar people, preferably from different cultures, should classify the materials and should be trained to get high interrater reliability. To address the validity issues, a number of questions might be asked: Can the data be used to predict other events? What variables predict the data? Do these various links form a coherent theory?

Content analysis can provide useful information about cultural change, especially the effect of modernity on collectivism. A systematic study of films, stories, cartoons, and so forth can give researchers insight in the dynamics of cultural change. For example, a theme currently found in India(n) films is the disintegration of the extended family; when the nuclear family becomes the norm in that country, this theme will receive less attention in films. Also, by comparing themes of successful films from an individualistic versus a collectivist culture (e.g., in the United States vs. in Japan), one could demonstrate differences in emphases placed by these cultures (e.g., one may value fantasy, whereas the other may stress family). This method seems to be underused despite its potential.

Human Relations Area Files

The Human Relations Area Files are based on the ethnographic works (Goodenough, 1980) of anthropologists. They include reports on the social system, politics, religion, aesthetics, technology, and other aspects of the culture. The files have organized the material from the ethnographies of about 900 cultures (Barry, 1980) by classifying the information according to a two-digit code with almost 100 categories, such as language, food quest, clothing, machines, property, labor, fine arts, family, state, law, and socialization. Each of these is further broken down. For instance, socialization includes techniques of training in weaning, food consumption, cleanliness, sex, aggression, independence, and transmission of cultural norms, skills, and beliefs. Each paragraph in the files is coded and filed under the categories it contains, so one paragraph dealing with several topics is filed under several headings and thereby allows a researcher to find it in many ways.

A researcher who looks under the heading "transmission of cultural norms" will find all the paragraphs that deal with this topic from all the ethnographies in which the topic was mentioned. Thus, very quickly, the researcher can identify features of variation in this activity. Researchers examining relationships among variables across cultures code the location of each culture on each variable and compute the relationships by using chi-square or rank-order correlations.

Critics have attacked this method, arguing that ethnographies may be inadequate bases for research because informants may not know what is important from a scientific point of view and because there is no guarantee the anthropologist will see what is important. In addition, the anthropologist cannot write about everything experienced in the culture. What is selected is supposed to be what is worth recording, but in fact it may not be a crucial element in a particular society. Furthermore, when coders read ethnographies and rate cultures on a dimension, they may make mistakes in coding. Other problems are the paucity of data on certain topics (ethnographers simply did not report on those topics), the possibility that one will compute so many correlations that some will be statistically significant by chance, and the problem that most cultures are changing and it is unclear whether a 1920 culture is the same as the one in 1960. Naroll (1962) suggested several checks on the quality of the data reported in ethnographies; the interested reader should refer to it.

It seems possible to study cultural differences by using the files if one follows Berry's (1994) ecological approach in studies of individualism and collectivism. He proposed that if one knows "societal size" (mean size of local community, settlement pattern, political stratification, and occupational specialization) and "social conformity" (social stratification, differences in emphasis on socialization from compliance to assertion, and obligation to conform to social norm), the two aspects of the "ecocultural" dimension, then one can predict whether people in that society will be allocentric (collectivistic) or idiocentric (individualistic). These two factors of the ecocultural dimension are rooted in anthropological literature; theoretically, allocentrism will vary as a function of social conformity, whereas idiocentrism will vary as a function of societal size (Berry, 1994). Berry's theorizing provides a unique opportunity to use the files to examine the predictions that people in gathering, hunting, and industrial societies are individualists, whereas those in agricultural and irrigation societies are collectivists.

Conclusion

In the first part of the chapter, we discussed the role of culture theory in intercultural training by proposing a model. Intercultural training has hitherto focused on identifying important cultural differences between two cultures, developing critical incidents focusing on these differences, and training people with these scenarios. We presented a model that proposes a role for culture theory in intercultural training. It is proposed that people who get theory-based intercultural training would become "experts," whereas those who go through traditional atheoretical orientation programs would be no more than "novices." Those people who have gone through both theory-based training and a behavioral modeling type of training that provides an opportunity to practice the behaviors and thus to perform a task automatically would become "advanced experts."

In the second part of the chapter, we discussed the theory of individualism and collectivism and described its relationship to other theories. This theory has implications for intercultural training because training material based on this theory can be used to prepare people from a large geographical area (say, North America) to live in another part of the world (say, Asia).

In the third part of the chapter, we discussed the methodology for studying cultures. It is clear there is no royal road to studying cultures. The methods used depend on the research problem, the knowledge of the investigators, the cultural acceptability of various techniques, the sophistication of the respondents, and many other variables. In general, emic approaches, such as ethnographic field techniques, systematic observations, and content analyses, should be used to start with, when the researcher knows relatively little about the culture and when the interest is in getting a holistic picture that consists of many interrelated elements. In this strategy, data collection tends to be maximally appropriate; however, estimates of neither accuracy nor replicability of the data are usually obtained. Although the data have depth and are usually collected ethically, one cannot really depend on the findings.

Testing, experimentation, questionnaires, and so forth are useful when the researcher has limited goals, knows a great deal about the culture, and has some well-developed theory to test (Malpass, 1977). They tend to be obtrusive, however, and are often culturally inappropriate. Also, although one can often establish internal validity, it is difficult to establish external validity without doing an enormous amount of work. Surveys are often based on a limited theory and have limited goals. They can accomplish what they try to do (e.g., predict an election) but often do not increase greatly researchers' understanding of cultures.

Approaches that combine the emic and etic approaches are used in most of the social sciences. Unstructured interviewing, questionnaires based on these interviews, and validation with some other method are the essential elements of studies of subjective culture. Such approaches can be used when the researcher knows a good deal about the culture and has relatively broad goals. The amount of work required is great, but so is the payoff in terms of understanding cultural similarities and differences.

References

Amir, Y., & Sharon, I. (1987). Are social psychology's laws cross-culturally valid? *Journal of Cross-Cultural Psychology, 18,* 383-470.

Anderson, J. R. (1982). Acquisition of cognitive skill. *Psychological Review, 89,* 369-406.

Anderson, J. R. (1990). *Cognitive psychology and its implications* (3rd ed.). New York: Freeman.

Barker, R. G., & Schoggen, P. (1973). *Qualities of community life.* San Francisco: Jossey-Bass.

Barry, H. (1980). Description and uses of the Human Relations Area Files. In H. C. Triandis & J. W. Berry (Eds.), *Handbook of cross-cultural psychology* (Vol. 2, pp. 445-478). Boston: Allyn & Bacon.

Berry, J. W. (1969). On cross-cultural comparability. *International Journal of Psychology, 4,* 119-128.

Berry, J. W. (1994). Ecology of individualism and collectivism. In U. Kim, H. C. Triandis, C. Kagitçibasi, S-C Choi, & G. Yoon (Eds.), *Individualism and collectivism: Theory, method, and applications* (pp. 77-84). Thousand Oaks, CA: Sage.

Bhawuk, D. P. S., & Brislin, R. W. (1992). The measurement of intercultural sensitivity using the concepts of individualism and collectivism. *International Journal of Intercultural Relations, 16,* 413-436.

Bochner, S. (1980). Unobtrusive methods in cross-cultural experimentation. In H. C. Triandis & J. W. Berry (Eds.), *Handbook of cross-cultural psychology* (Vol. 2, pp. 319-388). Boston: Allyn & Bacon.

Brislin, R. W. (1976). *Translation: Applications and research.* New York: Gardner.

Brislin, R. W. (1980). Translation and content analysis of oral and written materials. In H. C. Triandis & J. W. Berry (Eds.), *Handbook of cross-cultural psychology* (Vol. 2, pp. 389-444). Boston: Allyn & Bacon.

Brown, E. D., & Sechrest, L. (1980). Experiments in cross-cultural research. In H. C. Triandis & J. W. Berry (Eds.), *Handbook of cross-cultural psychology* (Vol. 2, pp. 297-318). Boston: Allyn & Bacon.

Campbell, D. T. (1968). A cooperative multinational opinion sample exchange. *Journal of Social Issues, 24,* 245-258.

Ciborowski, T. (1980). The role of context, skill, and transfer in cross-cultural experimentation. In H. C. Triandis & J. W. Berry (Eds.), *Handbook of cross-cultural psychology* (Vol. 2, pp. 279-296). Boston: Allyn & Bacon.

Davidson, A. R., Jaccard, J. J., Triandis, H. C., Morales, M. L., & Díaz-Guerrero, R. (1976). Cross-cultural model testing: Toward a solution of the etic-emic dilemma. *International Journal of Psychology, 11,* 1-13.

Earley, P. C. (1989). Social loafing and collectivism: A comparison of the United States and the People's Republic of China. *Administrative Science Quarterly, 34,* 565-581.

Edwards, A. L. (1957). *Techniques of attitude scale construction.* New York: Appleton-Century-Crofts.

Ellis, H. C. (1965). *The transfer of learning.* New York: Macmillan.

Fiske, A. P. (1990). *Structures of social life: The four elementary forms of human relations.* New York: Free Press.

Fiske, A. P. (1992). The four elementary forms of sociality: Framework for a unified theory of social relations. *Psychological Review, 99,* 689-723.

Gibson, M., & Ogbu, J. U. (Eds.). (1991). *Minority status and schooling: A comparative study of immigrant and involuntary minorities.* New York: Garland.

Goodenough, W. H. (1980). Ethnographic field techniques. In H. C. Triandis & J. W. Berry (Eds.), *Handbook of cross-cultural psychology* (Vol. 2, pp. 29-56). Boston: Allyn & Bacon.

Greeno, J. G. (1974). Hobbits and orcs: Acquisition of a sequential concept. *Cognitive Psychology, 6,* 270-292.

Hendrickson, G., & Schroeder, W. (1941). Transfer of training in learning to hit a submerged target. *Journal of Educational Psychology, 32,* 206-213.

Hofstede, G. (1980). *Culture's consequence.* Beverly Hills, CA: Sage.

Hofstede, G. (1994). Foreword. In U. Kim, H. C. Triandis, C. Kagitçibasi, S-C Choi, & G. Yoon (Eds.), *Individualism and collectivism: Theory, method, and applications* (pp. ix-xiii). Thousand Oaks, CA: Sage.

Holloway, S. D., Kashiwagi, K., Hess, R. D., & Azuma, H. (1986). Causal attributions by Japanese and American mothers and children about performance in mathematics. *International Journal of Psychology, 21,* 269-286.

Hsu, F. L. K. (1981). *American and Chinese: Passage to differences.* Honolulu: University of Hawaii Press.

Hui, C. H., & Triandis, H. C. (1986). Individualism-collectivism: A study of cross-cultural researchers. *Journal of Cross-Cultural Psychology, 17,* 225-248.

Hui, C. H., & Triandis, H. C. (1989). Effects of culture and response format on extreme response style. *Journal of Cross-Cultural Psychology, 20,* 296-309.

Irwin, M. H., Schafer, G. N., & Feiden, C. P. (1974). Emic and unfamiliar category sorting of Mano farmers and U.S. undergraduates. *Journal of Cross-Cultural Psychology, 5,* 407-423.

James, K., & Cropanzano, R. (in press). Dispositional group loyalty and individual action for the benefit of an in-group: Experimental and correlational evidence. *Organizational Behavior and Human Decision Process.*

Kagitçibasi, C. (1994). A critical appraisal of individualism and collectivism: Toward a new formulation. In U. Kim, H. C. Triandis,

C. Kagitçibasi, S-C Choi, & G. Yoon (Eds.), *Individualism and collectivism: Theory, method, and applications* (pp. 56-65). Thousand Oaks, CA: Sage.

Kashima, Y., & Triandis, H. C. (1986). The self-serving bias in attributions as a coping strategy: A cross-cultural study. *Journal of Cross-Cultural Psychology, 17,* 83-98.

Larkin, J. (1981). Enriching formal knowledge: A model for learning to solve textbook physics problems. In J. R. Anderson (Ed.), *Cognitive skills and their acquisition* (pp. 311-334). Hillsdale, NJ: Lawrence Erlbaum.

Leung, K., & Bond, M. H. (1989). On the empirical identification of dimensions for cross-cultural comparison. *Journal of Cross-Cultural Psychology, 20,* 133-151.

Longabaugh, R. (1980). The systematic observation of behavior in naturalistic settings. In H. C. Triandis & J. W. Berry (Eds.), *Handbook of cross-cultural psychology* (Vol. 2, pp. 57-126). Boston: Allyn & Bacon.

Lonner, W. (1980). The search for psychological universals. In H. C. Triandis & W. W. Lambert (Eds.), *Handbook of cross-cultural psychology: Vol. 1. Perspectives* (pp. 143-204). Boston: Allyn & Bacon.

Malpass, R. S. (1977). Theory and method in cross-cultural psychology. *American Psychologist, 32,* 1069-1079.

Marin, G., Triandis, H. C., Betancourt, H., & Kashima, Y. (1983). Ethnic affirmation versus social desirability: Explaining discrepancies in bilinguals' responses to a questionnaire. *Journal of Cross-Cultural Psychology, 14,* 173-186.

Naroll, R. (1962). *Data quality control: A new research technique.* New York: Macmillan.

Naroll, R., & Cohen, R. (Eds.). (1970). *A handbook of method in cultural anthropology.* New York: Columbia University Press.

Naroll, R., Michik, G. L., & Naroll, F. (1980). Holocultural research methods. In H. C. Triandis & J. W. Berry (Eds.), *Handbook of cross-cultural psychology* (Vol. 2, pp. 479-522). Boston: Allyn & Bacon.

Osgood, C. E., May, W. H., & Miron, M. S. (1975). *Cross-cultural universals of affective meaning.* Urbana: University of Illinois Press.

Pareek, U., & Rao, T. V. (1980). Cross-cultural surveys and interviewing. In H. C. Triandis & J. W. Berry (Eds.), *Handbook of cross-cultural psychology* (Vol. 2, pp. 127-180). Boston: Allyn & Bacon.

Pike, K. L. (1967). *Language in relation to a unified theory of the structure of human behavior.* The Hague, The Netherlands: Mouton.

Singelis, T. M., Triandis, H. C., Bhawuk, D. P. S., & Gelfand, M. (1995). Horizontal and vertical dimensions of individualism and collectivism: A theoretical and measurement refinement. *Cross-Cultural Research, 29,* 240-275.

Thorndike, E. L., & Woodworth, R. S. (1901). The influence of improvement in one mental function upon the efficiency of other functions. *Psychological Review, 9,* 374-382.

Triandis, H. C. (1964). Cultural influences upon cognitive processes. In L. Berkowitz (Ed.), *Advances in experimental social psychology* (Vol. 1, pp. 1-48). San Diego: Academic Press.

Triandis, H. C. (1972). *The analysis of subjective culture.* New York: John Wiley.

Triandis, H. C. (1980). Values, attitudes, and interpersonal behavior. In H. E. Howe & M. M. Page (Eds.), *Nebraska Symposium on Motivation, 1979* (pp. 195-260). Lincoln: University of Nebraska Press.

Triandis, H. C. (1990). Cross-cultural studies of individualism and collectivism. In J. Berman (Ed.), *Nebraska Symposium on Motivation, 1989* (pp. 41-133). Lincoln: University of Nebraska Press.

Triandis, H. C. (1994). *Culture and social behavior.* New York: McGraw-Hill.

Triandis, H. C. (1995). *Individualism and collectivism.* Boulder, CO: Westview.

Triandis, H. C., & Berry, J. W. (Eds.). (1980). *Handbook of cross-cultural psychology* (Vol. 2). Boston: Allyn & Bacon.

Triandis, H. C., & Bhawuk, D. P. S. (in press). Culture theory and the meaning of relatedness. In P. C. Earley & M. Erez (Eds.), *New perspectives on international industrial/organizational psychology.* San Francisco: Jossey-Bass.

Triandis, H. C., Bontempo, R., Betancourt, H., Bond, M., Leung, K., Brenes, A., Georgas, J., Hui, C. H., Marin, G., Setiadi, B., Sinha, J. B. P., Verma, J., Spangenberg, J., Touzard, H., & de Montomollin, G. (1986). The measurement of etic aspects of individualism and collectivism across cultures. *Australian Journal of Psychology, 38,* 257-267.

Triandis, H. C., Brislin, R. W., & Hui, C. H. (1988). Cross-cultural training across the individualism-collectivism divide. *International Journal of Intercultural Relations, 12,* 269-289.

Triandis, H. C., & Davis, E. E. (1965). *Some methodological problems concerning research on negotiations between monolinguals* (Technical Report No. 28). Urbana: University of Illinois.

Triandis, H. C., Leung, K., Villareal, M., & Clark, F. L. (1985). Allocentric vs. idiocentric tendencies: Convergent and discriminant validation. *Journal of Research in Personality, 19,* 395-415.

Triandis, H. C., McCusker, C., Betancourt, H., Iwao, S., Leung, K., Salazar, J. M., Setiadi, B., Sinha, J. B. P., Touzard, H., & Zaleski, Z. (1993). An etic-emic analysis of individualism and collectivism. *Journal of Cross-Cultural Psychology, 24,* 366-383.

Triandis, H. C., McCusker, C., & Hui, C. H. (1990). Multimethod probes of individualism and collectivism. *Journal of Personality and Social Psychology, 59,* 1006-1020.

Triandis, H. C., & Triandis, L. M. (1962). A cross-cultural study of social distance. *Psychological Monographs, 76*(21), [Whole No. 540].

Vassiliou, V., & Vassiliou, G. (1973). The implicative meaning of the Greek concept of philotimo. *Journal of Cross-Cultural Psychology, 4,* 326-341.

Wagner, J. A., & Moch, M. K. (1986). Individualism-collectivism: Concept and measure. *Group & Organization Studies, 11,* 280-304.

Werner, O., & Campbell, D. T. (1970). Translation, working through interpreters, and the problem of decentering. In R. Naroll & R. Cohen (Eds.), *A handbook of method in cultural anthropology* (pp. 398-422). New York: Columbia University Press.

Wheeler, L., Reis, H. T., & Bond, M. H. (1989). Collectivism-Individualism in everyday social life: The middle kingdom and the melting pot. *Journal of Personality and Social Psychology, 57,* 79-86.

Whiting, B., & Whiting, J. (1975). *Children of six cultures: A psycho-cultural analysis.* Cambridge, MA: Harvard University Press.

┌─────────┐
│ **3** │
└─────────┘

Ethics in Intercultural Training

R. MICHAEL PAIGE

JUDITH N. MARTIN

This chapter focuses on the ethics of intercultural training. Significant developments have occurred in the field of intercultural communication since the original version of this chapter appeared in the first *Handbook of Intercultural Training* (Landis & Brislin, 1983). The theoretical and empirical literatures have expanded substantially, and more is known today about intercultural phenomena than in 1983. Intercultural training, the applied domain of the field, has also grown considerably, and so has the training literature. Most notably, domestic multicultural or diversity training has assumed a prominent place in our work. We are now seeing a convergence of domestic and international training whereby both are informed in process and content by intercultural communication perspectives. The issue of ethics itself has continued to receive attention, to a limited degree in the literature and to a greater degree by professional associations that have deliberated such issues as codes of ethics for intercultural practitioners, guidelines for ethical practice, and credentialing.

In our reexamination of ethics, we thought these important developments needed to be considered. Consequently, we give more explicit attention, particularly in our use of examples, to domestic diversity training. We also bring our reviews of the literature up to date to take into account the theoretical advances in the field. Finally, the perspectives we offer on ethics in intercultural training have been informed by an ongoing dialogue with our colleagues about these issues. In that regard, we conducted a survey in 1994 of nine experienced trainers regarding ethics in intercultural training. The results of that survey are incorporated into our discussion.

Our concern with ethics is based on the belief that intercultural training is an inherently transformative form of education, for learners and trainers alike. Such work demands of its practitioners the highest form of professionalism, which we define as a lifelong commitment to their own professional development, a deep concern for the welfare of their clients, and ethical behavior in all aspects of their work. What that ethical behavior consists of is the theme of this chapter.

We address the following key questions in this chapter: What are the ethical dilemmas facing intercultural trainers? What does ethical conduct mean for interculturalists? What can the professional associations do to promote ethical practices? We define *intercultural training* as educative processes intended to promote culture learning, by which we mean the acquisition of behavioral, cognitive, and affective competencies associated with effective interaction across cultures. Such interactions can occur within and across societies—that is, in both domestic and international settings.

We begin the chapter with a discussion of ethics in conceptual and philosophical terms to lay the foundation for our analysis of ethics in intercultural training. Second, we examine intercultural training as a field and present a historical overview of its development so that this discussion can be placed in context. Third, we analyze the major ethical issues for trainers and illustrate them with examples and with the results of our survey of experienced trainers. Fourth, we present a detailed set of recommendations regarding ethical conduct for trainers. We conclude the chapter with a discussion of professionalization of intercultural training wherein we make recommendations in favor of a licensure program for trainers.

Our intention is to continue a dialogue with those already deeply concerned with ethics and to initiate one with those newer to the field. It is particularly important to us that the future generation of intercultural trainers be given greater guidance and assistance so that their professional behavior, and ours, will ultimately strengthen our work. The collectivity that will determine these matters in the years ahead is the international community of intercultural trainers. In 1983, we stated, "Our operating assumption is that a commonly agreed-upon set of professional ethics does not currently exist" (Paige & Martin, 1983, p. 37). Today, we believe that an ethics of intercultural training is emerging that represents the consensus of trainers worldwide. Although specific issues in certain countries remain unresolved (e.g., the matter of certifying intercultural trainers), there is

substantial agreement on the principles we discuss below.

Ethics

Ethics may be thought of as principles of conduct that help govern the behavior of individuals and groups. As Goulet (1973, pp. 331-332) explains, ethical theories represent a community's perspective on what is good and bad in human conduct and lead to norms (prescriptive and concrete rules) that regulate action. Ethics represent what ought to be and help set standards for human behavior. Ethical behavior, then, is whatever is defined as good and appropriate by the collectivity. Ethics may be referred to as *universalistic* when the behavioral standard is accepted by virtually all societies (e.g., human rights), *particularistic* or *culture specific* when they are adhered to by a given cultural community but not by others (e.g., ancestor worship), and *situational* when a shared universal or cultural standard does not automatically apply but is more a function of the specific circumstances (e.g., telling "white lies"). Debate over ethics can occur on all of these levels. An *ethical issue* can be defined as any aspect of human endeavor that demands a set of standards as a framework for human behavior.

Specifically, we are concerned here with the development of a universal ethics of intercultural training. This presents a conundrum for interculturalists because, as Wendt (1982) points out in his insightful essay on human rights, their respect for different cultures inclines them away from applying ethical standards universally. Thus, we acknowledge that establishing ethical principles at this level is a difficult task. As Howell (1981) emphasizes, although some ethical principles are universal (valid in all cultures), others are products of a given culture and thus are particularistic (Barnlund, 1980; Herskovits, 1973; Kleinjans, 1975). Are we to infer that, extrapolated to training, a universal ethics of training is impossible to establish, that ethics can only be discussed in particularistic or situational terms? Not according to scholars who have attempted to identify some universally accepted guidelines for ethical intercultural behavior. For example, Kale (1994) outlines a universal code of ethics in intercultural communication founded on the human spirit and peace as the fundamental human value. Similarly, Hatch (1983) proposes the "humanistic principle" on which to base a universal criterion for judging particular cultural values. Barnlund suggests that the universal training ethic should be to further dialogue between groups.

A most useful perspective is provided by Howell (1981), who offers the principle of social utility as a universal standard to guide trainer behavior: "No action is ethical if it harms persons affected, and the action that benefits affected persons accumulates ethical quality" (p. 8). Howell's principle suggests that intercultural trainers must always be concerned with the welfare of the learners. This dictum presents a frame of reference we refer to as the *ethics of culture teaching and learning*. In addition, trainers must think of the welfare of those with whom their learners will eventually come into contact. This second frame of reference we refer to as the *ethics of culture contact*. Let's now examine these two frameworks in more detail.

Ethics of Culture
Teaching and Learning

Howell (1981) makes two key points about intercultural training with respect to culture learning: (a) Learners should be provided with sufficient information about the host culture so that they can make an informed decision about entering into it or not, and (b) training should promote the acquisition of enough personal flexibility regarding one's own and the target culture's ethics so as to enable the sojourner to be empathic with the new culture and to deal effectively with cultural differences. As a starting point for an ethics of intercultural training, we agree with Howell's standards. They presuppose, however, that the learners have a choice about entering a host culture and, having made that choice, will readily adapt to or become assimilated into it. But what of individuals who did not elect to live in a culture other than their own (e.g., refugees, colonized peoples, those in minority or subordinated culture groups)? Their involvement in another culture is dictated, not by choice or volition, but by circumstances generally beyond their control.

Some important theoretical advances in the past 10 years allow us to modify Howell's two key points and to take the above issue into con-

sideration. The first is the shift in focus from an assimilation model of intercultural communication (which Howell's work reflected) to a more pluralistic notion. Early models assumed that culture learning was a matter of the individual learner adapting to the new culture and that the sojourn was voluntary. The audience this model most often had in mind was the international sojourner, such as student, diplomat, or businessperson. When the analysis was expanded to take into consideration other populations whose intercultural experiences were neither voluntary nor necessarily positive, the theoretical predictions regarding cultural adaptation shifted. Recent years have seen the reality of ethnic identity resurgence in many countries, including the United States. Ethnic group revitalization is challenging single culture group dominance, albeit not without considerable controversy and tension (see Schlesinger, 1992). It is now clearer that the condition under which persons find themselves in another culture has a strong relationship to the nature of their adaptation to it, one pattern perhaps being outright resistance to assimilation.

Intercultural trainers need to be aware of these circumstances so that training can take into account how individuals feel about their presence in another culture. If they feel oppressed by the dominant culture but under great pressure to conform to it, for example, their training needs will be very different from those who voluntarily seek a cross-cultural experience. Theory thus informs practice, and intercultural training has become more differentiated because of research inquiries into these issues.

The second theoretical advance is the long overdue recognition that power and power differentials inherent in the social and political context play a critical part in intercultural interaction (Gallois, Franklyn-Stokes, Giles, & Coupland, 1988; Nakayama & Martin, 1993). Although some scholars recognized and wrote about the importance of power (Brislin, 1981, 1991; Folb, 1982; Lum, 1982), with the exception of Singer (1987), it was missing from most theoretical models. New insights into training have followed these theoretical reflections. For example, more attention is being placed on the power differentials between trainers and learners themselves, on what the trainer represents—symbolically and otherwise—to the learner. These insights are particularly important for diversity training, wherein the issues of power inequities abound.

What does the above discussion mean for an ethics of training? Stringer (1993) suggests that intercultural trainers, most notably diversity trainers, will inevitably encounter program participants who have experienced and are immersed in the emotions of oppression, as well as others from the dominant culture who fear they will be attacked, confronted, and blamed for that oppression. Drawing on Bennett (1986), Stringer and Taylor (1991) present a "support and challenge" intercultural communication model as the ethical foundation for training—that is, a nonjudgmental, nondefensive, and nonthreatening training atmosphere (support) within which attitudes and behaviors that hurt other people and impede intercultural effectiveness can be addressed and changed (challenge). Those authors say that training based on the intercultural communication perspective can explain how these negative attitudes and behaviors occur and can be changed. Learners who have experienced discrimination and the "isms" in their lives will have had their concerns dealt with and will come away from the program feeling better understood and having promoted positive social change. Others will have had issues brought to their attention and can begin to alter their own patterns of behavior and the institutionalized mechanisms that have maintained discriminatory practices. All will have practiced the intercultural communication ethic of support for, rather than resistance to, diversity.

We agree with these ideas and believe they apply to both domestic diversity and international programs. As an initial attempt to formulate an ethics of culture teaching and learning, we state the following principles:

1. *Intercultural trainers should always be mindful of the welfare of the learners. In particular, learners should be given opportunities to acquire the knowledge, skills, and values that will help them function effectively in their cross-cultural circumstances.*
2. *To promote the welfare of the learners and culture learning, intercultural training should be conducted in a supportive,*

nonthreatening environment. The ethos of the training environment should be one of acceptance of, adaptation to, and integration of diversity into one's own life.
3. *Intercultural trainers should understand and be prepared to respond to the significantly different ways in which learners perceive intercultural relations.*
4. *Intercultural training should address the issues of oppression, discrimination, and the "isms" from an intercultural communication perspective and as they pertain to the settings within which the participants are living/working or are intending to live/work.*

Ethics of Culture Contact

Intercultural trainers prepare individuals to function effectively in cross-cultural situations. In many instances, when those individuals enter another culture, they will intentionally or unintentionally be agents of change. This change can come about in many ways, one simply being the introduction of new ideas into another culture through the normal course of interpersonal interactions. The more dramatic form of change agentry occurs when the intended outcome of culture contact is transformation of the culture or society—for example, religious conversion efforts, modernization-oriented development programs, and the introduction of new technologies.

Trainers should be cognizant of the purposes learners have for acquiring intercultural competence and the degree to which that competence will be applied to promoting change in the target culture. What are the ethical issues for trainers and for those being trained who envision themselves as change agents in the future? Kagan (1972) discusses this matter in his intriguing paper on ethics and concepts of cultural therapy. Although he does not address intercultural trainers directly, his purpose is to provide guidelines for those functioning as "cultural therapists" or change agents, and his writing has important ethical implications for trainers preparing such people.

Kagan first proposes that cultural intervention is justified when (a) a culture's practices are injurious to its members (e.g., racism, female circumcision), (b) the culture does not allow individuals or groups to self-actualize (e.g., excessive state control over life choices), (c) a culture contains maladaptive practices (e.g., obsessive work norms, extreme xenophobia), and (d) a society can authentically be helped without destroying the fabric of its culture (e.g., the introduction of new and culturally appropriate technologies). The author then presents an approach to cultural therapy in which change agents promote individual awareness of one's culture and alternatives to it, help make unconscious patterns of behavior and belief conscious, change reinforcement contingencies that maintain maladaptive behaviors, and help move cultures to the point where individuals and groups are allowed to be responsible for their own choices. We believe these are important ideas for intercultural trainers and that they should be communicated to learners in training programs. Nieto (1992), speaking of an education that promotes social reconstruction, emphasizes that educators must go beyond the previously established training goals, such as culture learning and respect for cultural variability, to the more change-oriented goals of *affirmation* of subordinated groups, *solidarity* with those groups, and *critique* of oppressive social structures. She suggests educators see themselves and their learners as potential social change agents.

The works of these authors suggest the following ethical principles for training practice.

1. *Trainers should help learners understand the dynamics of cultural intervention and change agentry.*
2. *Trainers should promote learner awareness of culture-bound and unconscious patterns of belief and behavior.*
3. *Trainers should promote changes in the existing patterns of learner behavior if they will be maladaptive in the new culture.*
4. *Trainers should provide opportunities for learners to gain skills in identifying and helping others change their maladaptive behaviors.*
5. *Trainers should provide opportunities for learners to become responsible for their*

own choices and to help others become responsible for theirs.

These authors present some important perspectives that help us move toward an ethics of intercultural training.

Historical Overview of Intercultural Training

Although individuals have been helping others prepare for intercultural interactions for centuries, intercultural training as a field of professional activity in the United States is still relatively new. The field (and its practitioners) emerged in response to fundamentally important post-World War II adjustments in the international order and has been growing steadily ever since. As with any professional field, intercultural training exhibits many of the growing pains of a developing field, some directly related to ethical issues. The literature on the sociology of professions identifies the characteristics of a profession: It possesses a distinctive body of knowledge shared by its members. It has a sanctioned and specified program of academic study and related experience leading to the acquisition of knowledge and skills. It has strict procedures by which its members are certified and equally strict membership rules. It has a set of professional ethics that governs professional behavior and that sets standards against which the activities of members are judged. To the degree that a field of human endeavor acquires these professional qualities, its practitioners receive the right to govern themselves, the respect of the public at large, high status and esteem, and the ability to practice the craft without excessive external intervention. The field becomes self-sustaining and self-perpetuating (Elliot, 1972; Etzioni, 1969; Jackson, 1970).

Given these criteria, one could argue that the field of intercultural training has not yet achieved the status of a profession. A brief overview of the historical development of the field, however, provides a context in which to examine ethical issues involved in intercultural training. On the basis of the above discussion, guidance about ethical issues should come from

(a) the conceptual base of knowledge (the ethical issues inherent in intercultural interaction and training) and (2) professional associations (the ethical standards identified and promoted by the organizations that regulate this professional field). Keep these items in mind as we examine the historical development of intercultural training.

Post-World War II:
The Birth of Intercultural Training

Many trace the birth of intercultural training (and intercultural communication) in the United States to the establishment of the Foreign Service Institute in 1946 (Leeds-Hurwitz, 1990). The field emerged in the social-political context of the postwar era, when the United States was a leader in rebuilding and reestablishing international bonds. Diplomats, technical assistance workers, and corporate personnel discovered that they were often unprepared for the challenges of living and working overseas.

As Leeds-Hurwitz (1990) recounts, the U.S. government responded to this need by establishing the Foreign Service Institute (FSI) and by staffing it with several notable anthropologists and linguists, such as Edward T. Hall, George Trager, and Ray L. Birdwhistell. These scholars offered a new type of training program that went beyond the existing emphasis on language training. They were interested in studying the "out of awareness" aspects of communication (proxemics, paralinguistics, kinesics), as well as linguistics, and their training reflected this more holistic approach. They focused on helping the trainees become aware of and adapt to cultural variations in the verbal and nonverbal aspects of interaction. The content of training was cognitive knowledge, and this early work of the FSI formed the foundation for the later university model. In sum, the focus of the FSI's training was on practical predeparture guidelines for assisting government and business personnel to communicate more effectively in their work overseas.

The 1960s and the
University Training Model

The field of intercultural training continued to flourish through the 1950s and 1960s into the era of the civil rights movement, the U.S. Peace Corps, and the Vietnam War. It is interesting to note that although there was much need for intercultural training in the United States (e.g., race relations), those calling themselves intercultural trainers continued to work primarily on international rather than domestic programs. The most influential organization regarding the development of the intercultural training field was the U.S. Peace Corps. During the 1960s, Peace Corps trainers conducted programs for thousands of trainees and experimented with a variety of intercultural training models. Much of the later research on training effectiveness and the predictors of success in intercultural relations was inspired by these experiences with the Peace Corps.

The dominant training model during the 1960s was the so-called *university model,* which emphasized a cognitive-centered, lecture-dominated, information-transfer pedagogy. As Hoopes (1979) recounts, "They [trainers] sat trainees down in classrooms and presented information to them about the target country and culture" (pp. 3-4). Peace Corps staff members in the field quickly learned, however, that this approach to culture learning left the future volunteers dramatically lacking in the skills required for living and working effectively in a new cultural setting. To Hoopes (1979), it was becoming increasingly clearer that,

Skills in communication and cross cultural adjustment turned out to be as much or more important than country specific information. Perhaps even more significant was the dawning recognition that becoming effective overseas involved a heavy measure of self-understanding and awareness. (p. 4)

Although the perceived failure of the university model to adequately prepare trainees led the Peace Corps to search for an alternative approach, these early years did produce a cadre of trainers who became concerned with the ethics as well as the practice of training. The fundamental ethical issue for trainers was how best to determine the effects of their programs in order to improve them. The most sensitive and ethical trainers were motivated by their concern for the physical and psychological well-being of the trainees in their new assignments; those trainers kept abreast of the training literature, subjected their programs to extensive evaluation, and carefully introduced new elements into their training design. They did not adopt new techniques uncritically, and they strove to acquire the skills required to use a variety of training approaches. The foundations of an ethics of intercultural training began to emerge that included a deep commitment to ongoing professional development, a sensitivity to the trainees' needs and concerns, a willingness to challenge traditional learning theories and approaches, and building a knowledge base through research and evaluation. When it seemed the university model was not working, some trainers, according to Althen (1975), adopted another approach—the human relations sensitivity model.

The 1970s and the Human Relations Sensitivity Model

Intercultural training in the 1970s gained in respectability and credibility as conceptual foundations of knowledge were being formalized in graduate programs and professional associations. In 1974, the Society for Intercultural Education, Training, and Research (SIETAR) was formed expressly for the purpose of legitimating and promoting the fledgling field of intercultural training. Related organizations (e.g., the American Society for Training and Development [ASTD], the National Association for Foreign Student Affairs [NAFSA], the Speech Communication Association [SCA], the International Communication Association [ICA]) all formed divisions devoted to the study of intercultural relations.

Intercultural training in the United States was occurring in a social-political context of racial tension and political unrest after the Vietnam War. It is significant that while intercultural communication scholars were studying the effects of racism and prejudice (Rich, 1974; Smith & Asante, 1973) and some U.S. trainers were designing and implementing interracial training (Katz, 1978; Chapter 11, this volume, details the extensive race relations training developed by the U.S. military), many more continued to concentrate on international training and ignored the intercultural conflict at home.

Much of the training (whether domestic or international) was based on the human relations sensitivity training model (Hoopes, 1979). Sensitivity training was distinctly different from

the university model in that the focus was almost entirely on experiential, participative learning. Experiential learning activities were designed to promote personal growth, rather than the acquisition of information, and the training pedagogy emphasized confrontation with the trainees' own and others' value and belief systems, attitudes, and prejudices. This approach to intercultural training fell into disfavor rather quickly for several reasons. First, it was excessively confrontational and stressful. Second, it required processing and debriefing skills that many trainers did not possess. Finally, it created such resistance and frustration among the trainees that learning was inhibited (Hoopes, 1979).

In retrospect, we can see that the embracing of the human relations sensitivity model was in direct reaction to the failure of the passive, cognitive, university training model. The new approach, however, lacked a sound conceptual framework, which was necessary for the trainees to acquire an understanding of intercultural issues. Instead, trainees were thrown into confrontational situations with little or no conceptual guidance.

The experiences of this period in training history highlighted a second area of ethical concern: the intensive nature of the intercultural training experience itself. Specifically, trainers were pondering to what degree training could or should attempt to replicate the emotional challenges and other demands of the intercultural experience. The human relations approach built confrontation and stress right into the training program on the assumption that those trainees who could cope best with this kind of training would be the most effective in intercultural interactions. Although excessive confrontation proved to be counterproductive and the extreme form of sensitivity training was soon abandoned, trainers realized that intercultural effectiveness required considerable "emotional muscle." The question therefore remained on how best to help trainees acquire a realistic and affective understanding of the ways they would be tested in future intercultural contexts.

The 1980s and the Integrated/ Alternative Learning Model

In the 1980s, intercultural communication as a field continued to grow and was described as a semiprofession (Paige & Martin, 1983). The knowledge base was expanding (Brislin, Cushner, Cherrie, & Yong, 1986; Landis & Brislin, 1983; Martin, 1986; Paige, 1986), more graduate programs were established, and professional development opportunities increased. Advanced programs in intercultural theory and application were being offered by, among others, the East-West Center in Honolulu, Hawaii; the Intercultural Communication Institute in Portland, Oregon; and SIETAR, with its summer workshops and master workshops at its annual congress.

The topic of ethics appeared more frequently in the conceptual writings in intercultural communication (Barnlund, 1980). By the late 1980s, most undergraduate intercultural communication texts included at least a brief discussion of the relationship among ethics, culture, and communication. The lively debate within professional organizations about standards and ethics took on a global dimension as SIETAR expanded to become SIETAR International, with worldwide affiliates such as SIETAR Europa, SIETAR Japan, and SIETAR Canada. For example, in the early 1980s, SIETAR attempted to develop a certification procedure that would provide a professional "accreditation" for intercultural trainers, similar to those established for social workers and therapists. A committee was established to deliberate the matter, and widespread debate about it occurred within the SIETAR membership, but ultimately no consensus could be reached concerning the standards and procedures for certification. By the mid-1980s, the issue was dropped.

The 1980s witnessed the phenomenon of the globalization of the economy. To an unprecedented degree, businesses were "going international" to expand their markets, enhance their competitiveness, and increase their productivity and profitability. These international involvements required sending employees and their families abroad, individuals who would have the capacity to live and work effectively overseas. Those selected for overseas assignments needed to be prepared, and for many corporations intercultural training was the answer. Throughout the 1980s, international business training grew as an area of application and continues to be a major focus of intercultural training.

Another phenomenon emerged during the 1980s that had important implications for the field: the increasing diversity of the U.S. workforce (more women, persons of color, immigrants, and refugees). Diversity training emerged to help businesses turn diversity into an asset and combat the racism, sexism, and intergroup conflict being experienced in the workplace. In fact, diversity training was an offshoot of human relations training, but it was substantially different in approach. Throughout the decade, intercultural trainers increased their involvement in the issues of domestic diversity. Intercultural training approaches to personal and organizational change—approaches that rejected extreme confrontation as a pedagogy—were applied to diversity training. The conceptual models of intercultural communication were employed to help learners understand the cultural, behavioral, perceptual, and communicative aspects—the tangible manifestations—of racism, sexism, discrimination, misunderstanding, and miscommunication. An important synergy occurred as intercultural trainers and human relations trainers began working together, sharing insights and expertise about this highly challenging area of training.

Throughout this period, the knowledge base continued to grow and approaches to training became more sophisticated (Brislin et al., 1986: Gudykunst & Hammer, 1983; Landis & Brislin, 1983; Martin, 1986; Paige, 1986). The dominant model of the 1980s was the integrated or alternative learning model, which uses experiential as well as cognitive learning approaches. Most trainers stressed the integration of theory and practice, the combining of informational, conceptual, and experiential learning, and the acquisition of skills the trainees could apply outside the training situation. Training should be designed to help trainees become interculturally competent—linguistically, behaviorally, attitudinally, and psychologically equipped to live and work effectively within a second cultural environment.

Current State of the
Field of Intercultural Training

Currently, the issues of domestic intercultural relations have taken center stage and are demanding the attention of intercultural trainers.

The dismantling of the Berlin Wall, the break-down of the Soviet empire (see Chapters 19 and 20, this volume) and subsequent social disruptions, and the severe ethnic conflict in Eastern Europe and East Africa all point to the continued importance of understanding intergroup relations and the need for professional training to facilitate intercultural interaction.

The current training model continues to be an integrated and comprehensive one. Interest continues in wedding theory with practice and in linking the training applications in the domestic and international contexts (Bennett & Bennett, 1994; Brislin & Yoshida, 1994a, 1994b; Gochenour, 1993; Pusch, 1994). Interest is also increasing in looking at the political, historical, and social contexts of training. Much of the research in the 1980s was contextual and not very useful for trainers. In addition, interest is growing in examining the impact of power differentials in intercultural relations, as well as in training settings themselves.

Status of Professional/
Ethical Issues in the Field

As noted in the beginning of this section, we should be able to look to the conceptual literature and professional associations for guidelines on professional ethics in the field of intercultural training. We must conclude, however, that serious shortcomings remain: The literature on ethics is limited, and professional associations have not fully realized their role in addressing ethical issues.

With few exceptions (Althen, 1994; Hammer, 1992; Paige, 1993c), very little discussion of ethics has taken place in the intercultural training literature in recent years (Blanchard, 1993). Some contributions to our thinking have been made by the intercultural communication theory and research literatures. But a review of the intercultural communication textbooks reveals only a cursory treatment of ethics that focuses almost exclusively on two issues: (a) the universality (or lack) of ethical systems and (b) the ethical issues of intercultural relations (Borden, 1991; Gudykunst, 1991; Lustig & Koester, 1993; Samovar & Porter, 1991). From the research literature come important guidelines regarding the use of human subjects in research, the ethical obligations of the researcher to the subjects, and the responsibilities of the researcher to the host culture (Brislin, Lonner, & Thorndike, 1973; Hoopes, Pedersen, & Renwick, 1978; Hursh-Cesar & Roy, 1976; Triandis, 1983; Warwick, 1980). These ethical guidelines for researchers, however, have limited transferability to trainers and have also come under recent criticism for ignoring the sociopolitical issues of privilege and power in researcher-subject relations (Clifford, 1992; Gonzalez, Houston, & Chen, 1994; Rosaldo, 1989; Stanfield & Dennis, 1993).

Finally, we turn to the experienced intercultural trainers as a source of professional ethics. Here, we discover a mixed picture. Many qualified trainers are highly principled, sensitive to ethical issues of their work, and adhering to strict standards in designing, implementing, and evaluating their programs. They are acutely aware of the ethical issues inherent in transformative education and the obligations they have to learners, organizations, and themselves. They have discussed codes of professional conduct for many years. Unfortunately, these discussions have not been systematically entered into the intercultural training literature, with the exception of the growing body of knowledge on program evaluation (Black & Mendenhall, 1990; Blake & Heslin, 1983; Brislin, 1993; Hammer & Martin, 1992; Renwick, 1979). SIETAR International and NAFSA: Association of International Educators have made important contributions to the field by bringing newcomers together with intercultural training experts in professional development workshops, but the opportunities for dialogue between these groups remain limited. As the field currently exists, many newcomers are learning their trade without the guidance of a formalized set of professional ethics.

By way of summarizing the historical development of the field as a context for discussing contemporary ethical issues, we reiterate the points made in our earlier writing that intercultural training is subject to abuse as a function of its relative newness, its conceptual eclecticism, and most important, the lack of stated professional standards. Trainers are functioning in a marketplace environment where individual consultants and consulting firms are in competition with each other, where few mechanisms govern the work of practitioners. Such an environment, in our view, contributes to abuses, such as exaggerated claims about the services and expertise being offered, the accepting of contracts beyond the scope of the trainer's skills, and programs poorly designed and implemented.

Ethical Issues in Intercultural Training

In this section, we discuss ethical issues in intercultural training. First, we report the findings of our survey of experienced trainers. Then, we expand on our discussion of the culture contact and culture teaching/learning issues. With respect to the latter, we focus on the ethical issues related to (a) the transformative potential of intercultural education, (b) the dynamics of teaching and learning (learning environment and pedagogy), and (c) the psychological risks inherent in intercultural education.

Perspectives of Experienced
Intercultural Trainers

We begin our discussion of ethical issues with a summary of the results of a survey we conducted in 1994 of a small but select group of highly experienced intercultural trainers ($N = 9$). The respondents ranged in age from 31 to 60, had spent an average of 8 years as trainers, and were involved in the areas of business ($n = 4$), the public sector ($n = 2$), education ($n = 2$), and the nonprofit sector ($n = 1$). The majority were working in the area of domestic training ($n = 5$); several others listed international or both as their focus of training. In terms of educational background, two were college graduates, four had M.A. degrees, and three had Ph.D.'s.

In the survey, we put the following two open-ended questions to our respondents:

1. What general ethical issues are you most concerned about in your professional work as a trainer?
2. What do you think is the single most important ethical issue facing the field of intercultural training today?

In response to the first question about general ethical issues, the answers clustered around the following themes: *client issues* (e.g., clients taking advantage of our expertise; clients wanting a kind of training we don't think is appropriate for the circumstances); *trainer issues* (e.g., ill-prepared trainers; trainers who don't know themselves—their biases, strengths, weaknesses; trainers who are experiencing burnout; trainers who have their own personal agenda); and *training issues* (e.g., trainers who don't know how to do intercultural communication or diversity training but are in it because these are "hot" training areas; trainers who do not know how to establish a positive learning environment). Diversity training received the most comments in response to the first question; the respondents expressed great concern about the challenges of diversity training, the potential for burnout, the involvement of nontrainers or inexperienced trainers and the potential for negative results, and the need for very skilled diversity trainers.

When asked about the most important ethical issue facing intercultural trainers (second question), the respondents gave us 11 items dealing with *lack of trainer skills and credentialing* ($n = 5$), *diversity training and trainer problems* ($n = 4$), and *inappropriate trainer motives* ($n = 2$). Regarding trainer skills, the concern was with trainers who do not have the necessary preparation and skills to do their work (diversity training was singled out for particular attention). One respondent recommended the credentialing of trainers, one commented on the need for mechanisms of accountability, and another talked about the necessity to live the intercultural life, not just talk about it. Diversity training comments focused on the ethical issues regarding institutions that announce they value diversity but are unwilling to change; value conflicts between trainers and the groups they are working with; overgeneralizing learners as racist in diversity programs; and the need, not always realized, to be more inclusive regarding diversity (in particular, with respect to sexual orientation). The comments on motives took trainers to task who are simply in the field to make money and will take on any kind of program but are not really committed to the client or to the field.

Reflecting on the survey results, which are quite consistent with the more anecdotal evidence we have from conversations with colleagues in recent years, we are struck by two things: (a) the continuing problem of unskilled trainers and (b) the expressed concerns regarding diversity training. In this section, we return to these issues. We first place them in the conceptual framework of ethics already presented (the culture contact and culture learning context).

We have identified two major varieties of ethical issues: those associated with culture teaching and learning and those related to culture contact. Intercultural trainers must pay attention to both of these areas. They must recognize that (a) although the training itself may be entirely adequate, those being trained might use their skills for unethical purposes and (b) the ultimate purposes of training may be highly ethical, but the training is of dubious quality. We pursue the culture contact questions first because these are raised at the very onset of a trainer-client relationship.

Culture Contact Issue

As a starting point, we believe that trainers should examine the reasons why their clients are seeking to acquire intercultural competencies. If, in the trainer's opinion, the long-term purposes are not ethically sound, the trainer must consider whether or not to conduct the program. We suggest that the ethical response is for trainers to refuse a contract if they are unconvinced of the ethical merit of the client's purposes or are concerned that the applications of skills gained in training would violate the principles established by Hatch (1983), Howell (1981), and Kale (1994). Some might argue that the immediate objective of providing individuals with intercultural abilities is a sufficient rationale for providing their training services. We disagree. We believe such a position ignores the culture contact issue. Specifically, we strongly argue against training for persons or organizations whose primary motive is to exploit or deceive (e.g., those who would engage in unethical business practices or who would practice deception in attempts to gain religious converts). Further, we urge trainers to convey the ethical dimension of intercultural relationships so that those who are acquiring new skills will use them in an ethical manner. This is an imperative for those who will be working in change agent roles. As trainers, we are confronted with this issue directly when our services are first sought, and it should be addressed in the earliest stage of contract negotiation with a potential client.

In response to the culture contact issue, we suggest the following principle for an ethics of training:

Intercultural trainers should determine the client's purposes in seeking training and enter into a contract only if they are convinced that the skills and knowledge acquired from training will be applied in a positive and beneficial manner.

Culture Teaching and Learning Issue

Once a trainer is satisfied that the client's purposes are ethical, it is necessary to confront the questions related to such topics as training as a process and trainer-learner relationships. In this regard, we address three major areas. The first area pertains to our view of *intercultural training as transformative education.* Given the potential of training to effect change in persons and organizations, what are the ethical obligations of trainers engaged in such education? The second area is that of the *intercultural training environment and pedagogy* (the learning climate, methodologies, technologies, and approaches used by trainers). We are particularly concerned with the fit between pedagogy and learner needs, learning styles, and so forth. The third area is what we refer to as the *psychological risks inherent in intercultural training* for learners and trainers. Intercultural experiences are psychologically stressful (Adler, 1975, 1976; Brislin et al., 1986; Paige, 1993b). What does this mean for an ethics of training?

Intercultural Training as Transformative Education

We strongly maintain the position, first stated in 1983, that intercultural training is inherently transformative in intent and potential, both of persons and of organizations or groups. With respect first to persons, we advanced the concept of the person-transformation imperative, the notion that *training designed to promote certain personal qualities and skills is oriented toward effecting personal transformations among learners.* Training for these qualities (e.g., tolerance of ambiguity, nonjudgmentalism, ethnorelativism regarding cultural differences, cognitive and behavioral flexibility) requires learners to assume new modes of thinking, valuing, and behaving. Such training is change oriented. Moreover, in its emphasis on changes in areas of personal life not normally addressed by traditional education, it is very demanding.

We examine this last point in greater detail. It is our theoretical contention that human beings are usually ethnocentric. One's self-identity or sense of personhood is anchored in those culturally influenced belief systems, worldviews, behavioral repertoires, value orientations, and cognitive classification systems acquired through socialization and upbringing. These come to represent reality and truth (Berger & Luckmann, 1967), as well as highly valued ways of thinking and behaving. They define one as a person and as a member of a cultural community. They provide the lens through which people view all reality and the rest of the world. Geertz (1963) points out that learned orientations toward one's kinfolk, religion, ethnic group, and community become deeply rooted "primordial attachments" and serve as powerful motivating forces in an individual's life. We agree with M. Bennett (1993), therefore, that it is not the normal condition of human beings to be ethnorelative—that is, culturally relativistic, appreciative of contradictory belief and behavior systems, or nonjudgmental when confronted with alternative cultures.

If we accept the foregoing theoretical statements as correct, we can see that intercultural training may be potentially threatening to the learner because it challenges existing and preferred beliefs, values, and patterns of behavior. It is directed at promoting personal change, cognitive restructuring, or what Kuhn (1962), Mestenhauser (1981), and M. Bennett (1993) refer to as a *paradigm shift*. We agree with Adler (1976) and Mestenhauser that substantive culture learning cannot occur without the acquisition of a new worldview. Let's not forget Adler's (1976) useful observation that multiculturalism—the ability to operate effectively in a multiplicity of cultural settings and to integrate those diverse cultural perspectives into one's personality—can pose acute personal dilemmas. The loss of personal identity, confusion of self-concept, loss of adequate peer group support, and other negative consequences can result from the acquisition of a multicultural frame of reference. J. Bennett

(1993), in a particularly insightful analysis, distinguishes between encapsulated (dysfunctional) and constructive (functional) forms of cultural marginality. Some learners, at a certain stage of intercultural development, find themselves overwhelmed by their marginality. As new learners begin to encounter the issues associated with personal change, they may become anxious and resistant to learning.

Trainers should be aware of the dynamics of personal change. They should know how to assist learners struggling with their own transformations. They need to be especially sensitive to learners who, being more rigidly attached to their existing cultural orientations, will likely be openly resistant to change.

Trainers working with organizations seeking to restructure themselves—for example, to create workplace environments more attentive to the needs of women and minorities—must similarly be aware of the dynamics of organizational change. Predictably, as the culture of the organization shifts, some members will feel threatened. They may see their power eroding. They may be uneasy about the direction of the organization and uncertain about the outcomes. They may feel anxious about the process. Consequently, the trainer should anticipate resistance and be prepared to address it.

In light of this discussion, we suggest the following principle for an ethics of training:

Trainers must be knowledgeable about the transformative potential inherent in intercultural training and must be prepared to assist individuals and organizations experiencing stress and anxiety over personal and organizational change. Moreover, trainers must have command over approaches that can address individual and organizational resistance to change.

Intercultural Training Environment and Pedagogy

One central challenge to the field has been to identify training environments and pedagogies that best promote intercultural learning. This is a major issue because learners bring to the training program different learning styles, learning needs, levels of intercultural experience and competence, and degrees of openness to such learning. Most experienced trainers would agree that no single training method is sufficient to meet the diverse needs of learners. And most would concur that the learning environment must be supportive of learners. But what do these general principles mean in practice? When we look more closely at training, we find that the problems of environment and pedagogy are quite complex.

By *learning environment,* we mean the social-psychological climate within which learning occurs (e.g., supportive, hostile, challenging, engaging, structured). Concerning the person-environment relationship, psychologists and social psychologists have produced a rich literature that suggests (a) environments acquire distinct personalities (in part, as a function of the selected pedagogies) and impose themselves on the learner and (2) the degree of congruity-incongruity between the learner's needs/learning styles and that environment will influence learning outcomes (Lewin, 1936; Moos, 1979; Murray, 1979). Intercultural trainers as a rule have not paid sufficient attention to this literature and its implications for training. Irrespective of the degree of cultural heterogeneity that exists among trainees, they are generally placed into the same learning environments and exposed to the same learning methodologies. Many learners, for example, find relatively unstructured learning environments to be uncomfortable learning settings because they are too ambiguous. Trainers need to be (a) sensitive to these issues, (b) skilled in constructing learning environments that support a variety of learners, and (c) capable of explaining the environment to the learners.

Pedagogy refers the instructional methods employed in training (the way content is delivered). Three considerations are important here. First, trainers must determine the type of learning environment that will most effectively facilitate intercultural learning for their participants. Our guiding principle has been that a supportive learning environment is the most appropriate environment for intercultural learning because it encourages an atmosphere of trust. Such an atmosphere lessens resistance and encourages learners to take more risks in exploring difficult issues. Second, a central issue in pedagogy has been to ascertain which types of learning activities promote different facets of intercultural learning. It is imperative for the trainer to have a sound understanding of the impact of alternative learning activities on (a) af-

fective, behavioral, and cognitive outcomes; (b) movement of learners toward intercultural competence and sensitivity; and (c) participants with different kinds of learning styles. Third, the trainer must know a great deal about the learners to establish a sound learning environment and to incorporate appropriate learning activities. The cultural orientation of the learner—for example, whether the person is from an individualist versus a collectivist culture—has received a great deal of attention in the intercultural training literature (Bhawuk & Brislin, 1992; Hofstede, 1980; Triandis, Brislin, & Hui, 1988). Triandis et al. (1988) suggest that the individualism-collectivism distinction is a crucial one for trainers because "allocentric" (collectivist) persons have very different learning needs and styles than "idiocentric" (individualistic) persons. Collectivist cultures are generally high-context cultures (Hall, 1977), in which meaning is embedded in the situation; allocentric learners extract meaning intuitively from the situation by being sensitive to nonverbal cues and the circumstances surrounding the situation. Only minimal information need be made explicit. By way of contrast, in low-context cultures, explicit, unambiguous information is required to be transmitted, and learning is more linear, cognitive, and direct. Low-context culture learners, to function effectively in high-context cultures, must acquire skills in intuiting meaning from context and circumstances, rather than in analyzing information received from extensive verbal communication.

Let's apply these environment and pedagogy considerations to experiential learning, the instructional method that has received the most attention in intercultural training. This approach requires learners to be active participants in the learning process, and it is intended to engage them cognitively, behaviorally, and emotionally (Gochenour, 1993; Paige, 1993b). Some have argued, however, that experiential learning is culture-bound with respect to learning styles. Kondo (1993) studied how Japanese learners responded to BAFA BAFA, an experiential culture learning simulation that requires role playing followed by an immediate debriefing. The participants thought the activity did not leave sufficient time for reflection, the preferred learning style of many persons in Japanese culture. Because it requires behavioral and emotional involvement, experiential learning can be quite threatening, especially for learners more comfortable with abstract and conceptual forms of learning. Used too early in a training program, experiential activities can create a stressful learning environment. But if a supportive environment has already been established, learners may be much more willing to participate in such activities.

Furthermore, the notion of integrating learning styles into experiential learning (Fry & Kolb, 1979; Kolb, 1984) has made an important contribution to the field of intercultural training. As described by Kolb (1976), the four basic learning modes—experiencing, reflecting, conceptualizing, and experimenting—can be combined to facilitate intercultural learning. Learners can be prepared to use these learning skills by means of the structured learning exercise. This activity takes learners through the four styles and has the advantages of (a) meeting the learning style needs of all learners at some point, (b) expanding their capacity to learn in different ways, (c) maintaining their interest and involvement in training, and (d) providing them with a model that can help them systematically structure their own culture learning. The environment created by this pedagogy is one of attention to learner diversity and expansion of learning skills. Bennett and Paige (1994) also suggest that the intercultural learning environment should balance support with challenge in terms of program content, as well as process. A highly challenging process such as experiential learning (e.g., simulations) should not occur simultaneously with similarly challenging content (e.g., a discussion of racism or oppression), at least not until a supportive learning environment has been established and the learners are ready for that level of challenge.

With respect to learning environments and pedagogy, then, we suggest the following principle for an ethics of training:

Trainers must strive to create a learning environment that is supportive of learners and use a pedagogy that responds to diverse needs and learning styles. Trainers should also be prepared to assist learners who are not responding well to certain learning approaches and be prepared to offer alternatives. Finally, trainers must know their audiences and the contexts (social, cultural, historical, political, eco-

nomic) within which training is occurring so as to create appropriate environments.

Psychological Risks Inherent in Intercultural Training

Few life transitions are as fraught with uncertainty and risk as the movement from one's own culture to a new and unfamiliar cultural setting. Intercultural training deals with personal and organizational transition and thus, in our view, is an inherently challenging form of education that can pose many types of risks for the learners. Furthermore, most trainers think a pedagogy that will prepare learners to handle the challenges of intercultural communication and interaction must, by necessity, identify those challenges and provide learners with the opportunity to respond to them. Pusch (1994), for example, points out, "The trainer must decide how the participants can be encouraged to take greater risks, moving from the less difficult intellectual and emotional demands . . . to exploring their own attitudes and behaviors in greater depth" (p. 121).

What are these risk factors associated with training? Originally, we commented on the risks of self-disclosure and failure. These two risk factors have been discussed in greater detail by Paige (1993b), who has also expanded the analysis to include the risks of embarrassment, threat to one's cultural identity, cultural marginality and cultural alienation, and self-awareness. According to Paige, these occur because intercultural training,

first . . . requires learners to reflect upon matters with which they have had little firsthand experience. . . . Second, . . . includes highly personalized behavioral and affective learning. . . . Third, "learning how to learn," a process-oriented pedagogy (Hughes-Weiner, 1986), replaces learning facts. . . . Fourth . . . involves epistemological explorations regarding alternative ways of knowing and validating what we know, i.e., the meaning of truth and reality. (p. 3)

In light of this discussion, we suggest the following principle for an ethics of training:

The ethical trainer will understand the risks associated with training and will be able to (a) properly sequence such events into the overall program and (b) properly debrief the participants following such events (help trainees interpret what has occurred to them in cognitive, affective, and behavioral terms).

Intercultural trainers encounter ethical issues in terms of the process, as well as the purposes, of training. Although it may seem obvious that trainers should not conduct programs for those who one knows would use their skills unethically, it is our view that trainers are at a disadvantage because it is not always clear how trainees will later apply their competencies. Critical questioning at the early stages may or may not reveal potential future abuses. Accordingly, trainers should endeavor to address ethical issues in intercultural communication and relations during the training program so that trainees become aware of the obligations facing them.

The discussion of problems in intercultural training programs has centered on three major issues we believe to be important. These could be further refined, and others could be identified. By focusing on the transformative, environmental, and risk elements inherent in intercultural training, we have attempted to present a framework with which trainers can assess their own activities and professional behavior.

We now illustrate some of the issues mentioned by our respondents and suggested by our conceptual model.

Illustrations of Ethical Issues

Here we focus on two specific examples or illustrations of ethical issues in intercultural training. The first—religious proselytizing—represents the ethical problems associated with the purposes to which training is put. The second—the diversity training case—illustrates the ethical problems that can arise within the training context. These are not inherently unethical activities, but they are areas that raise serious questions regarding ethical practice.

Dubious Culture Contact:
Deceptive Religious Proselytizing

Should an intercultural trainer train missionaries and others if their known purpose is to proselytize in other countries/cultures and gain converts to their religion? This question has come up many times over the years, and we addressed it in the first version of this chapter (Paige & Martin, 1983). For the trainer negotiating a contract with a client, the ethical principle concerns the manner in which the religious organization represents its goals and intentions. Most religious organizations and denominations provide services to others in the spirit of compassion, hospitality, and authentic interest; indeed, the sharing of religious belief may not be a central objective. Many religions also have clear goals relating to mission and conversion, but these are presented openly and honestly. If the trainer has reason to believe, however, that deceptive practices are being used to gain converts, our position is that the trainer should refuse to provide services to that group or terminate an existing relationship.

Here are two cases that involve deceptive practice. The most egregious case is the cult, which uses all manner of deception and psychological manipulation to recruit and retain new members. No credible intercultural trainer would get involved in conducting training for a cult. The second case pertains to religious groups that actively proselytize international students, aggressively seeking converts. Some years ago, our colleagues in an international student office at a U.S. university surveyed the literature from Christian religious groups ministering to international students. They found that a wide range of services was being offered, including free English classes, holiday homestays with church families, and programs for international students' wives and children. These services were not at issue by themselves. But several of these groups were definitely misrepresenting their intentions; that is, they were deliberately misleading international students into thinking their services were unrelated to religious purposes. In those cases, the literature aimed at religious group members was filled with advice about how to proselytize—for example, by first offering hospitality and friendship. The subject of one document was how to convert Islamic students to Christianity.

In our view, such deceptive practices do a distinct disservice to the legitimate religious organizations that have long been active in assisting international students. It is acceptable to discuss religious beliefs if there is informed consent, by which we mean the participants know the purpose of the discussion in advance and are there voluntarily. It is another thing altogether to misrepresent the purpose of a gathering, for the purpose of attracting an audience, and then turn it into something else.

With respect to religious proselytizing, our ethical principle is as follows:

> If a group seeks to acquire intercultural skills for the purpose of more effectively deceiving and manipulating persons from other cultures, the ethical response would be to reject the contract.

Challenging Culture Teaching and
Learning: The Diversity Training Case

Few areas of intercultural training have been more controversial and problematical than diversity training. Its content is extremely challenging (e.g., racism and discrimination, inequalities in interpersonal and intergroup relations), and its goals, derived from perceived deficiencies in society, often include social reconstruction, personal and organizational transformation, and the advancement of specific groups. The content and goals are threatening to some, and resistance to such training is often serious. Consequently, it must be designed and implemented with great skill. Moreover, many societies or organizations have no clear social consensus on what the outcomes of diversity training should be; as a case in point, witness the debate over multicultural education in the United States (Banks & Banks, 1993; Nieto, 1992). And as the respondents in our survey suggested, there is serious concern about the quality in diversity training and the lack of preparedness of some trainers working in this area.

One of the most serious ethical debates regarding diversity training pertains to our aforementioned culture learning issue of learning environment and pedagogy. What kind of environment should be created to promote learning about this difficult content area? What types of instructional methods are most appropriate? When the diversity training is directed at majority or dominant culture group members, how should it be designed? What ethical issues are involved in diversity work? The learning environment/pedagogy debate has focused on the value of an openly confrontational approach (e.g., learners are directly challenged

to acknowledge their racism or sexism), the approach that characterized human relations training in the 1970s, versus an intercultural communication approach that emphasizes a balance between support and challenge in content and process. Although the more confrontational training model had fallen into disfavor by the end of the 1970s, it appears to have resurfaced as one form of diversity training, particularly when that training is directed at majority culture learners.

Starosta (1990) reports on the case of a psychodrama, intended to serve as an example of prejudice training, that was presented at a professional association conference. At the session, "the trainer then adopted a persona who, for much of an hour, verbally confronted audience members with intensely prejudicial statements of a racist, ageist, sexist, and ethnocentric nature" (p. 2). After a perfunctory debriefing of approximately 35 minutes, the trainer left even though he had said "he would refuse to perform his psychodrama for a corporate client unless he was guaranteed a complete three days to perform the exercise and to debrief it, because he recognized it to be a very intense experience, which required careful debriefing" (p. 2). Afterward, many audience members (most of whom were themselves trainers or intercultural scholars) were very uneasy; some, by their own admission, felt "emotionally distraught" (p. 3). To the author, it was unethical of the trainer to manipulate the audience's feelings and emotions without a substantive debriefing. Furthermore, this was not the most effective way to reduce prejudice and discrimination; in fact, this type of training could exacerbate prejudice. Starosta offers this important observation:

> A trainer voluntarily assumes certain responsibilities when he or she accepts an assignment to modify the attitudes and behaviors of a client. The trainer explicitly enters into a bond to make the trainee a more flexible or healthier person following training than before. She or he promises to safeguard the mental well-being of the trainee and to guide the trainee safely through any anxieties that are aroused as a by-product of the training technique that is chosen. . . . The expertise and the professionalism of the trainer are often the only safety net to protect a client from lasting emotional damage. (p. 1)

We agree with the author's observations and would add that, in our view, an intercultural approach to diversity training has significant advantages over an aggressively confrontational model of training. First, the concepts of intercultural communication provide a framework for understanding: how and why racism, sexism, and other forms of prejudice and discrimination occur; the cultural origins of these patterns; and the ways in which these are manifested in daily communication and interaction, as well as in their more institutionalized forms. Second, the support and challenge model of intercultural communication is far more likely to retain learners, rather than lose them. We are convinced that confrontation drives learners into M. Bennett's (1993) defense stage; support and challenge encourage them to move past defense into acceptance, adaptation, and integration. Third, excessive confrontation can be harmful to the learners, as evidenced by the response of even experienced trainers to the psychodrama discussed above.

With respect to diversity training, but not limited to it, we present the following ethical principle for the trainer's code of conduct:

> *Trainers working on highly emotional issues such as prejudice and discrimination should at all times be mindful of the challenges these issues pose for their clients. Trainers should create learning environments and use training methods that will encourage such learning, rather than interfere with it, or worse, leave learners emotionally damaged.*

The Ethical Intercultural Trainer

We discuss in this section how individual trainers can respond to the ethical issues that have been identified. The discussion is organized around three major themes: knowledge, pedagogical skills, and professional development. Regarding conceptual foundations, a model of critical variables in intercultural training is presented that includes an examination of training content areas. To contribute to the pedagogical area, a specific model for sequencing intercultural training activities is proposed. Professional development opportunities are then identified.

Table 3.1 Critical Variables in Intercultural Training Programs

Goals and Objectives
Types of Training Activities
Learner Characteristics
Trainer Characteristics
Risk Elements of the Training Activity
Behavioral Requirements of the Training Activity
Social-Psychological Learning Environments
Training Content and Training Activities

The First Requirement of the Ethical Trainer: Acquisition of Knowledge

If trainers are to be aware of the ethical issues associated with their work, they must have a strong conceptual grasp of the dynamics of training and intercultural learning. Table 3.1 presents those variables we believe are operative in intercultural training programs. The list is selective, of course, and is based on our practical experience and understanding of the relevant literature. The variables are presented here to familiarize the reader with factors that trainers should be aware of if they are to be effective in their work. They are "critical variables" in that they affect the processes and outcomes of training. For more details regarding the knowledge base, readers are referred to Chapter 8 (this volume), on trainer competencies.

Goals and Objectives. Goals and objectives represent a critical variable to consider in intercultural training. The purpose of training is often formulated as broad goals, all too frequently presented in vague and ambiguous terms (e.g., "the purpose of this program is to promote cultural awareness and appreciation"). If the goal statements end here, and they often do, numerous and conflicting interpretations of training are likely to emerge. Trainers and trainees will be confused about the purposes of training. In essence, the ethical trainer needs to be very clear and concrete about the purposes of training.

One way to do this is to articulate the specific objectives of the program. We suggest that trainers differentiate objectives into three culture learning domains: *cognitive, affective,* and *behavioral* (Triandis, 1977). For example, let's examine a predeparture orientation program for

U.S. students preparing to study in a Third World nation. One objective of training would be to transmit factual knowledge about the target nation and culture(s) and thus increase the trainees' cognitive knowledge. Another objective would be to acquaint the trainees with the types of emotional reactions they may experience in confronting a new and different cultural environment. Sessions devoted to this outcome would be focused on the affective domain. Trainers would also design learning activities to promote the acquisition of new behaviors appropriate to the target culture and essential to cross-cultural adjustment and effectiveness. The specification of objectives into these domains will help trainers in making more appropriate decisions regarding training methodologies. Trainees will be cognizant of the goals of training and, more important, will begin to conceptualize cross-cultural learning as a multifaceted phenomenon. What actually is expected of them in the training milieu, as well as in the target culture, will be unambiguously identified. The interrelationship of the affective, behavioral, and cognitive domains of cultural adjustment and second-culture functioning can be examined.

Types of Training Activities. Intercultural trainers can use a broad array of training approaches to accomplish program goals. Certain types of activities are thought to promote learning in a specific domain better than others. In addition, some learners are more responsive to some types of learning activities than to others. The experienced trainer will select activities according to his or her level of skill, the characteristics of trainees, and the objectives of the learning activities. We have identified some of the most common training activities; they include lectures, discussions, critical incidents/case studies, role plays and simulations, and small-group problem solving. These and other training activities are the subject of an extensive literature to which the reader can refer (Brislin & Yoshida, 1994a; Gochenour, 1993; Landis & Brislin, 1983; Paige, 1993a).

Learner Characteristics. The literature suggests that observable learning outcomes are, in part, a function of the characteristics of the learners. Background characteristics (e.g., prior cross-cultural experience), learning style, level of cultural self-awareness, the learner's sense of ethnic or cultural identity, learner familiarity with certain types of activities, and learners' familiarity with each other all affect the training program. Trainers must know the individual participants in terms of these characteristics and how these qualities, at the group level, will influence the training environment. For example, highly heterogeneous groups could require more time and different approaches to training than more homogenous ones. For training design purposes, then, it is vital for trainers to take the characteristics of the learners into consideration. For the purpose of evaluating intercultural training, the early identification of these characteristics as baseline data is essential.

Trainer Characteristics. In intercultural training, the success of an activity often depends on the trainer's skill level and familiarity with the task. Trainers must be familiar with the activities they are using, in terms of such things as the risk elements associated with the task, its behavioral requirements, and the type of learning style for which it is best suited. Unfortunately, few training manuals describe training activities in these terms.

Risk Elements of the Training Activity. We have suggested that culture learning poses various risks that, if ignored, can inhibit rather than promote learning. Activities that focus on affective and behavioral learning are inherently more risky for the learner because they touch on self-concept, self-awareness, emotions, and new behavior. Initially, learners are likely to respond to such tasks with caution and may find themselves evaluating the target culture in a negative manner. The trainer must be aware of possible reactions to stressful activities, such as learner withdrawal, avoidance, or even hostility. Consequently, the trainer must establish an environment conducive to culture learning and should structure training activities so as to minimize these potentially counterproductive responses.

Behavioral Requirements of the Training Activity. Each learning activity can be characterized according to the behavioral requirements it imposes on learners. Our discussion of sequencing incorporates these behavioral considerations into the model. Basically, we suggest that trainers begin with activities that pose fewer risks (e.g., of self-disclosure, embarrassment, or failure), are more familiar to learners, and initially require less active involvement. Trainers unfamiliar with the requirements of a given activity will risk using it at an inappropriate time.

Social-Psychological Learning Environments. Extensive research conducted during the past 20 years clearly indicates that (a) learning environments acquire their own social-psychological qualities, (b) those qualities influence all forms of learning, (c) teachers strongly influence the type of environment that emerges, and (d) social climates can be adjusted. Although scant research has been done on the social climate of intercultural training programs (Hammer, 1982, is an exception), an extrapolation of evidence from the classroom learning environment literature suggests that intercultural learning would be advanced in environments characterized by (a) supportive leaders, (b) a high degree of structure, (c) affiliation among the participants and between participants and teachers, (d) a task orientation, (e) activities that challenge the learners, (f) learner involvement, (g) a comfortable physical environment, and (h) a pace of learning congruent with the learners' needs. At the outset, trainers should have in mind the type of learning environment they want to establish. The overall training design, the selection and sequencing of learning activities, and the ground rules for classroom communication and interaction should all be directed toward the creation and maintenance of that idealized learning environment. Minimally, trainers must understand how these can influence the environment and how the learning atmosphere, in turn, can promote or inhibit intercultural learning.

Training Content and Training Activities. Table 3.2 presents the content foundations of intercultural training and intercultural competence. They can be incorporated into learning activities appropriate to the cognitive, affective, and behavioral domains. For example, a training session devoted to target culture information would represent primarily cognitive learning. In contrast, a training session designed to give participants opportunities to practice target culture communication styles would be focused on behavioral learning. It is important for the trainer to have the content of training firmly established so that the appropriate learning activities can be selected. In other words, the trainer will relate the content areas to the training design and the training methods. The juxtaposition of the critical variables associated with training (Table 3.1) with the content areas (Table 3.2) can allow the trainer to design the program carefully.

The Second Requirement of the Ethical Trainer: Developing Pedagogical Skills

Ethical trainers will constantly reflect on and refine their training pedagogy. As an example, we have suggested that trainers make every effort to familiarize themselves with a set of critical variables and that they design training programs with these in mind. Two more areas need to be considered: sequencing and facilitation skills.

Sequencing Skills. One questions frequently asked is, How should different types of training activities be sequenced to produce the most effective learning? We think this is a central issue related to pedagogy and here we attempt to provide a partial answer. But a caveat is in order: No absolute intercultural training formula will cover all training circumstances. Design decisions will emerge as a function of the skill level of the training staff, the characteristics of the learners, the pedagogical preferences of the trainers, and the goals and objectives of the program. The cultural, political, social, and economic contexts of the program are also very important considerations.

Table 3.3 presents our model for sequencing intercultural training activities. It lists six frequently used types of approaches; these are presented in a sequencing order according to (a) the behavioral requirements of the activity, (b) the learning domains(s) of the activity, and (c) the degree of risk associated with the activity. The first type of learning activity, for example, is the lecture. It does not require active participation or the performance of unfamiliar behaviors. Its focus would be on the cognitive learning domain through the acquisition of information. The risk of personal disclosure or failure would be correspondingly low. By way

TABLE 3.2 Content Foundations of Intercultural Training

Intercultural Communication Phenomena

      Culture and Communication
      Language and Communication
      Nonverbal Behavior and Communication
      Role of Values, Beliefs, and Norms in Communication
      Cognitive Differentiation: Categories, Classification Systems
      Learning Styles
      Communication Styles
      Culture Learning, Adjustment, "Shock"

Characteristics of the Intercultural Communication and Interaction Process

      Alternative Responses to Cultural Differences
      Stages of Development Toward Intercultural Communication Competence/Sensitivity
      Describing, Interpreting, and Evaluating Intercultural Events and Persons

Intercultural Relations and Cultural Differences

      Intercultural Relations Continuum: From Similarity to Difference
      Cultural Differences That Make a Difference: Values, Attitudes, Beliefs, Behaviors
      Cultural Differences Associated With Race, Ethnicity, Gender, Nationality, Socioeconomic Status,
          Religion, Sexual Orientation, Etc.

Factors That Inhibit and Promote Intercultural Communication

      Personal Characteristics: Degree of Flexibility, Openness, Emotional Resilience, Etc.
      Situational Variables: Degree of Status Equality, Shared Goals, Cooperation, Supportive Environment,
          Role and Work Assignment Clarity, Etc.
      Cultural Variables: Language Differences and Language Ability of Interactants, Cultural Differences
          and Target Culture Skills of the Interactants

Area Studies/Target Culture Knowledge

      History
      Political and Economic Systems
      Religions
      Ethnic Diversity
      Etc.

of contrast, simulation games (the sixth type) require learners to become actively involved in the performance of new behaviors in unfamiliar roles. Simulations are designed to promote learning primarily in the affective and behavioral domains. The risks are much greater. Simulations and lectures represent two significantly different types of learning activities that address different learning objectives, require different levels of learner activity, and present quite different levels of risk to the learner.

Our suggestion is that trainers begin with the cognitively oriented, low-risk, and more familiar types of learning activities and then move progressively toward the high-risk and more affectively oriented activities. By starting with more familiar and less personally threatening activities, the trainer can build a solid level of

trust among the learners (and between the learners and trainers) and establish an environment conducive to more intensive learning. Given that some learning activities will confront the learner with new and disturbing information and will challenge existing assumptions, it is important to prepare the training community for such learning. It is our view that unless the learners establish relationships among themselves and with the trainers, they are likely to be resistant, especially with respect to affective and behavioral learning.

In summary, the sequencing model presented here is designed to structure activities in a manner that allows learners time to become acquainted with each other and with their trainers and that allows trainers time to establish trust and a positive learning environment.

TABLE 3.3 Sequencing Intercultural Training Activities

Sequencing Order of Learning Activities	Behavioral Requirements of Learning Activities	Familiarity and Risk Levels Associated With Learning Activities	Culture Learning Emphasis
1. Lectures	Passive	Low risk of failure, self-disclosure, embarrassment, etc; familiar activity for most learners	Cognitive
2. Discussions	Active	Low risk; familiar activity for most learners	Cognitive
3. Group problem solving	Active	Medium risk; familiar activity for some learners	Cognitive
4. Critical incidents, case studies	Passive (reflection) and active (discussion)	Medium risk; unfamiliar activity for many learners	Cognitive; Affective
5. Role plays	Active	High risk; unfamiliar activity for many learners	Affective; Behavioral
6. Simulations	Active	High risk; unfamiliar activity for most learners	Affective; Behavioral

Facilitation Skills. The effective facilitation of intercultural learning is a complex skill; some may view it, in the manner of fine teaching, as an art. One serious challenge facing trainers is that regardless of how careful they are in sequencing learning activities, the psychological demands and stresses are such that they will encounter resistance to learning. This may be expressed as withdrawal, frustration, aggression, or hostility. Perhaps the most important facilitation skill is the ability to debrief, which means being able to place learning into a conceptual perspective. The specific objectives of debriefing are (a) to minimize rationalization of culturally inappropriate behavior, (b) to reduce negative emotional responses, (c) to reduce current and future resistance to learning, and (d) to assist the learner in understanding what has occurred. Debriefing should be anticipated for learning events designed to challenge existing cognitive orientations, to promote awareness and acceptance of new value systems, or to promote affective learning. In extreme cases, the trainer should be prepared to terminate an activity if the emotional response becomes too difficult for the group to handle.

The Third Requirement
of the Ethical Trainer: Commitment
to Professional Development

Intercultural training is an ever-changing field. Research and evaluation studies provide new insights into the nature and consequences of training. Books and articles appear regularly and present new theories, conceptualizations, and methodologies. New clienteles and problems emerge that confront trainers with new challenges. As a result of these changes, intercultural training expertise is a time-bound phenomenon that should not be taken for granted. Rather, trainers should make every effort to upgrade their skills constantly. We suggest that trainers continuously pursue their own professional development by

actively participating in international and domestic professional associations such as SIETAR International, the American Society for Training and Development, and so forth;

conducting relevant research and disseminating the results via professional news-

letters, journals, and presentations at professional meetings;
contributing to the theoretical literature on
intercultural training;
keeping abreast of the recent literature;
attending professional training workshops;
acquiring advanced academic training; and
contributing to the professional development
of others through mentoring, conference
workshops and presentations, and training
of trainers sessions.

The more experienced trainers should assist
those who are newer to the field by offering
internship and apprenticeship opportunities and
by advising prospective trainers on academic
programs, workshops, and so forth. Less experienced trainers should seek out these opportunities. The workshops and training programs
sponsored by SIETAR International (Washington, DC) and the Intercultural Communication
Institute's Summer Institute for Intercultural
Communication (Portland, OR) are examples of
the professional development programs available to trainers.

Professionalization of
Intercultural Training

We conclude this chapter with recommendations regarding the professionalization of the
intercultural training field, a matter we consider
central to the development of an ethics of training. Professional associations—in particular,
SIETAR International—have played a significant role in this endeavor. We believe, however,
the time has come for the field to codify its ethics in the manner of most other professional societies. A published code, authored and author-
ized by the field's most experienced and
distinguished members, will provide ethical
standards and guidelines for education, research, and training. NAFSA: Association of
International Educators has gone farther than
SIETAR International by formulating standards
of professional behavior for its practitioners
(e.g., international student advisors), by adopting a program of institutional self-study, and by
establishing a consulting program to assist institutions in their efforts to internationalize
their programs. Although SIETAR International has worked on a code of ethics for a number of years, it has not yet been promulgated.

This work should be completed as soon as possible.

Perhaps the most significant item on the professionalization agenda is licensure for intercultural trainers. In 1983, we recommended
that this be examined by our professional association and opined, "Ultimately, the need for
licensure may depend on the degree to which
trainers adhere to a professional set of ethics. If
serious abuses continue, this question will become more critical" (Paige & Martin, 1983,
p. 57). All evidence suggests that the problem
of incompetent trainers (trainers who lack the
necessary knowledge, skills, experience, and an
understanding of the ethical issues to be working in this field) continues to exist. Although
licensure, of and by itself, will not eliminate the
problem, it would be a major advance for the
profession. The development and implementation of a licensure program would require the
professionals to address issues more systematically and completely than they have to date.

On the basis of our assessment of the profession, we now recommend in favor of a licensure
program. It would have a number of advantages. First, it would formalize the knowledge
base needed by intercultural trainers. This
would be done in the context of specifying and
accrediting the graduate-level academic programs needed for entry into the profession. Second, a licensure program would articulate the
types of cross-cultural experiences deemed
mandatory for trainers. Opportunities to acquire these could be built into the academic programs in the form of internships and mentor relationships with experienced trainers. Third, it
would require a code of ethics. Fourth, it would
establish far greater accountability for individual trainers and training organizations by providing clients with standards for hiring and
evaluating them. Fifth, it would symbolize the
profession's commitment to governing itself
and to maintaining its standards, hallmarks of
any profession and essential factors in creating
an atmosphere of trust between trainers and clients. Sixth, it would establish sanctions to be
employed in cases of unethical practice.

We are aware of the enormous amount of
work that will be required to accomplish this
task. Undoubtedly, it will stir up a great deal of
controversy. Will licensure requirements lend
themselves to standardization across countries,
or will they have to be country-specific? Will a
licensure examination be required, and if so,

what form will it take? What will be the agreements and disagreements over the body of knowledge? These are just a few issues that will arise. In the final analysis, however, we believe the effort will be worthwhile because it will enhance the status of the field as a profession, a significant element of which will be the codification of an ethics of intercultural training.

Professional associations can promote ethics in other ways. We recommend the following:

1. *Professional associations should continue to actively assist in the training of future trainers.* This can be done in a variety of ways, including sessions at annual meetings devoted to professional development, the sponsoring of workshops and programs, the offering of internships, and the identification of learning opportunities available to prospective trainers.
2. *Professional associations should identify the formal academic programs most suit-* *able for prospective intercultural trainers.* Whether a licensure program is established or not, the need is for appropriate academic programs, and newcomers to the field need assistance in making decisions regarding academic options. Professional associations can be helpful in providing such advice.
3. *Professional associations should encourage the publication of relevant training and research findings.* We are pleased with the advances in the literature that have occurred in the past decade. They have been substantial, especially in the area of theory and application (the Training Section of the *International Journal of Intercultural Relations* has made a useful contribution in this area). We have also noted some inadequacies, particularly in the area of research regarding intercultural training. We would like to see more funding made available for research.

SUMMARY

The complexities and demands of culture learning require exceptional competencies of the intercultural trainer. These include a high degree of self-awareness and a recognition of one's skill limitations, sensitivity to the needs of the learners, the ability to respond to problems that culture learners encounter, an awareness of the ethical issues involved in cross-cultural training, conceptual/theoretical understanding, program design and implementation skills, and research and evaluation skills. These skills and knowledge can be learned, but we caution prospective trainers against expecting to acquire them in a short period of time. We have conceptualized the ethical issues, underscored the need for the ongoing professional development of trainers, and argued for a new commitment to professionalization in the form of a licensure program for intercultural trainers. In conclusion, if we wish our field to become an authentic profession, then we must be exemplary in our pursuit of excellence. And excellence means that we are guided in all aspects of our work by an understanding of and a commitment to the ethics of our profession.

References

Adler, P. S. (1975). The transitional experience: An alternative view of culture shock. *Journal of Humanistic Psychology, 15*(4), 13-23.

Adler, P. S. (1976). Beyond cultural identity: Reflections upon cultural and multicultural man. In L. A. Samovar & R. E. Porter (Eds.), *Intercultural communication: A reader* (pp. 362-380). Belmont, CA: Wadsworth.

Althen, G. L. (1975). Human relations training and foreign students. In D. S. Hoopes (Ed.), *Readings in intercultural communication* (Vol. 1, pp. 73-86). Pittsburgh, PA: Intercultural Communications Network.

Althen, G. L. (1994). *Learning across cultures.* Washington, DC: National Association for Foreign Student Affairs: Association of International Educators.

Banks, J. A., & Banks, C. A. (Eds.). (1993). *Multicultural education: Issues and perspectives* (2nd ed.). Boston: Allyn & Bacon.

Barnlund, D. (1980). The cross-cultural arena: An ethical void. In L. A. Samovar & R. E. Porter (Eds.), *Intercultural communication: A reader* (3rd ed., pp. 378-383). Belmont, CA: Wadsworth.

Bennett, J. M. (1986). Modes of cross-cultural training: Conceptualizing cross-cultural training as education. *International Journal of Intercultural Relations, 10*(2), 117-134.

Bennett, J. M. (1993). Cultural marginality: Identity issues in intercultural training. In R. M. Paige (Ed.), *Education for the intercultural experience* (pp. 109-135). Yarmouth, ME: Intercultural Press.

Bennett, J. M., & Bennett, M. J. (1994). Multiculturalism and international education: Domestic and international differences. In G. Althen (Ed.), *Learning across cultures* (pp. 145-173). Washington, DC: National Association for Foreign Student Affairs: Association of International Educators.

Bennett, J. M., & Paige, R. M. (1994). *Training in international and multicultural programs*. Portland, OR: Institute for Intercultural Communication.

Bennett, M. J. (1993). Toward ethnorelativism: A developmental model of intercultural sensitivity. In R. M. Paige (Ed.), *Education for the intercultural experience* (pp. 21-71). Yarmouth, ME: Intercultural Press.

Berger. P. L., & Luckmann, T. (1967). *The social construction of reality.* Garden City, NY: Doubleday.

Bhawuk, D. P. S., & Brislin, R. (1992). The measurement of intercultural sensitivity using the concepts of individualism and collectivism. *International Journal of Intercultural Relations, 16*(4), 413-436.

Black, J. S., & Mendenhall, M. (1990). Cross-cultural training effectiveness: A review and a theoretical framework. *Academy of Management Review, 15,* 113-136.

Blake, B. F., & Heslin, R. (1983). Evaluating cross-cultural training. In D. Landis and R. W. Brislin (Eds.), *Handbook of intercultural training* (pp. 203-223). Elmsford, NY: Pergamon.

Blanchard, K. (1993). Cultural adjustment, power, and personal ethics. In T. Gochenour (Ed.), *Beyond experience: The experiential approach to cross-cultural education* (pp. 107-112). Yarmouth, ME: Intercultural Press.

Borden, G. A. (1991). *Cultural orientation: An approach to understanding ICE.* Englewood Cliffs, NJ: Prentice-Hall.

Brislin, R. W. (1981). *Cross-cultural encounters.* Elmsford, NY: Pergamon.

Brislin, R. W. (1991). *The art of getting things done: A practical guide to the use of power.* New York: Praeger.

Brislin, R. W. (1993). *Understanding culture's influence on behavior* (Chap. 6, pp. 169-206). Orlando, FL: Harcourt Brace Jovanovich.

Brislin, R. W., Cushner, K., Cherrie, C., & Yong, M. (1986). *Intercultural interactions: A practical guide.* Newbury Park, CA: Sage.

Brislin, R. W., Lonner, W. J., & Thorndike, R. M. (1973). *Cross-cultural research methods.* New York: John Wiley.

Brislin, R. W., & Yoshida, T. (Eds.). (1994a). *Improving intercultural interactions: Modules for cross-cultural training programs.* Thousand Oaks, CA: Sage.

Brislin, R. W., & Yoshida, T. (1994b). *Intercultural communication training: An introduction.* Thousand Oaks, CA: Sage.

Clifford, J. (1992). Traveling cultures. In L. Grossberg, C. Nelson, & P. Treichler (Eds.), *Cultural studies* (pp. 96-116). New York: Routledge.

Elliot, P. (1972). *The sociology of professions.* Cambridge, UK: Cambridge University Press.

Etzioni, A. (1969). *The semi-professions and their organizations.* New York: Teachers, Nurses, Social Workers Free Press.

Folb, E. (1982). Who's got the room at the top? Issues of dominance and nondominance in intracultural communication. In L. A. Samovar & R. E. Porter (Eds.), *Intercultural communication: A reader* (3rd ed., pp. 132-141). Belmont, CA: Wadsworth.

Fry, R., & Kolb, D. A. (1979). Experiential learning theory and learning experience in liberal arts education. In *New directions for experiential learning: Enriching the liberal through experiential learning* (No. 6, pp. 79-91). San Francisco: Jossey-Bass.

Gallois, C., Franklyn-Stokes, A., Giles, H., & Coupland, N. (1988). Communication accommodation in intercultural encounters. In Y. Y. Kim & W. B. Gudykunst (Eds.), *Theories in intercultural communication* (pp. 157-185). Newbury Park, CA: Sage.

Geertz. D. (1963). The integrative revolution: Primordial sentiments and civil politics in the new states. In C. Geertz (Ed.), *Old societies and new states: The quest for modernity in Asia and Africa* (pp. 105-157). New York: Free Press.

Gochenour, T. (Ed.). (1993). *Beyond experience: The experiential approach to cross-cultural education.* Yarmouth, ME: Intercultural Press.

Gonzalez, A., Houston, M., & Chen, V. (Eds.). (1994). *Our voices: Essays in culture, ethnicity, and communication.* Los Angeles: Roxbury.

Goulet, D. (1973). *The cruel choice.* New York: Atheneum.

Gudykunst, W. B. (1991). *Bridging differences: Effective intergroup communication.* Newbury Park, CA: Sage.

Gudykunst, W. B., & Hammer, M. R. (1983). Basic training design: Approaches to intercultural training. In D. Landis & R. W. Brislin (Eds.), *Handbook of intercultural training* (Vol. 1, pp. 118-154). Elmsford, NY: Pergamon.

Hall, E. T. (1977). *Beyond culture.* New York: Anchor.

Hammer, M. R. (1982). *The effects of an intercultural communication workshop on American participants' intercultural communication competence.* Unpublished doctoral dissertation, University of Minnesota.

Hammer, M. R. (1992). The research connection: Ethics and the incompetent interculturalist. *SIETAR Communique, XXII*(3), 1, 3.

Hammer, M. R., & Martin, J. N. (1992). The effects of cross-cultural training on American managers in a Japanese-American joint venture. *Journal of Applied Communication Research, 20,* pp. 161-182.

Hatch, E. (1983). *Culture and morality: The relativity of values in anthropology.* New York: Columbia University Press.

Herskovits, M. (1973). *Cultural relativism: Perspectives in cultural pluralism.* New York: Vintage.

Hofstede, G. (1980). *Culture's consequences: International differences in work-related values.* Beverly Hills, CA: Sage.

Hoopes, D. S. (1979). Notes on the evolution of cross-cultural training. In D. Hoopes & P. Venturas (Eds.), *Intercultural sourcebook* (pp. 3-5). LaGrange Park, IL: Intercultural Communications Network.

Hoopes, D. S., Pedersen, P. B., & Renwick, G. W. (Eds.). (1978). *Overview of intercultural education, training, and research* (Vol. 2). Washington, DC: Society for Intercultural Education, Training, and Research.

Howell, W. S. (1981, November). *Ethics of intercultural communication.* Paper presented to the Speech Communication Association, Anaheim, CA.

Hursh-Cesar, G., & Roy, P. (Eds.). (1976). *Third World survey: Survey research in developing nations.* New York: Macmillan.

Jackson, J. A. (1970). *Professions and professionalization.* New York: Herder & Herder.

Kagan, S. (1972). *Ethics and concepts of cultural therapy* (ERIC Document Reproduction No. ED 069 379). Washington, DC: Office of Economic Opportunity.

Kale, D. W. (1994). Peace as an ethic for intercultural communication. In L. A. Samovar & R. E. Porter (Eds.), *Intercultural communication: A reader* (3rd ed., pp. 435-441). Belmont, CA: Wadsworth.

Katz, J. (1978). *White awareness: Handbook for anti-racism training.* Norman: University of Oklahoma Press.

Kleinjans, E. (1975). A question of ethics. *International Educational and Cultural Exchange, 10*(4), 20-25.

Kolb, D. A. (1976). *Learning Style Inventory: Technical manual.* Boston: McBer.

Kolb, D. A. (1984). *Experiential learning.* Englewood Cliffs, NJ: Prentice-Hall.

Kondo, Y. (1993). *Validating the intercultural communication training methods on Japanese: Intercultural communication workshop.* Unpublished doctoral dissertation, University of Minnesota.

Kuhn, T. S. (1962). *The structure of scientific revolutions.* Chicago: University of Chicago Press.

Landis, D., & Brislin, R. W. (1983). *Handbook of intercultural training* (Vols. 1-3). Elmsford, NY: Pergamon.

Leeds-Hurwitz, W. (1990). Notes in the history of intercultural communication: The Foreign Service Institute and the mandate for intercultural training. *Quarterly Journal of Speech, 76,* 262-281.

Lewin, K. (1936). *Principles of topical psychology.* New York: McGraw-Hill.

Lum, J. (1982). Marginality and multiculturalism: Another look at bilingual-bicultural education. In L. A. Samovar & R. E. Porter (Eds.), *Intercultural communication: A reader* (3rd ed., pp. 384-388). Belmont, CA: Wadsworth.

Lustig, M. W., & Koester, J. (1993). *Intercultural competence: Interpersonal communication across cultures.* New York: HarperCollins.

Martin, J. N. (Guest Editor). (1986). Special issue: Theories and methods in cross-cultural orientation. *International Journal of Intercultural Relations, 10*(2).

Mestenhauser, J. (1981). Selected learning concepts and theories. In G. Althen (Ed.), *Learning across cultures* (pp. 116-127). Washington, DC: National Association for Foreign Student Affairs: Association of International Educators.

Moos, R. H. (1979). *Evaluating educational environments.* San Francisco: Jossey-Bass.

Murray, H. A. (1979). *Explorations in personality.* New York: Oxford University Press.

Nakayama, T. K., & Martin, J. N. (1993, November). *The white problem, or toward a postcolonial intercultural communication.* Paper presented at the Annual Meeting of the Speech Communication Association, New Orleans.

Nieto. S. (1992). *Affirming diversity: The sociopolitical context of multicultural education.* White Plains, NY: Longman.

Paige, R. M. (Ed.). (1986). *Cross-cultural orientation: New conceptualizations and applications.* Lanham, MD: University Press of America.

Paige, R. M. (Ed). (1993a). *Education for the intercultural experience.* Yarmouth, ME: Intercultural Press.

Paige, R. M. (1993b). On the nature of intercultural experiences and intercultural education. In R. M. Paige (Ed.), *Education for the intercultural experience* (pp. 1-19). Yarmouth, ME: Intercultural Press.

Paige, R. M. (1993c). Trainer competencies for international and intercultural programs. In R. M. Paige (Ed.), *Education for the intercultural experience* (pp. 169-199). Yarmouth, ME: Intercultural Press.

Paige. R. M., & Martin, J. N. (1983). Ethical issues and ethics in cross-cultural training. In D. Landis & R. W. Brislin (Eds.), *Handbook of intercultural training* (Vol. 1, pp. 36-60). Elmsford, NY: Pergamon.

Pusch, M. (1994). Cross-cultural training. In G. Althen (Ed.), *Learning across cultures* (pp. 109-144). Washington, DC: National Association for Foreign Student Affairs: Association of International Educators.

Renwick, G. W. (1979). *Evaluation handbook.* Yarmouth, ME: Intercultural Press.

Rich, A. L. (1974). *Interracial communication.* New York: Harper & Row.

Rosaldo, R. (1989). *Culture and truth: The remaking of social analysis.* Boston: Beacon.

Samovar, L. A., & Porter, R. E. (1991). *Communication between cultures.* Belmont, CA: Wadsworth.

Schlesinger, A. M., Jr. (1992). *The disuniting of America.* New York: Norton.

Singer, M. (1987). *Intercultural communication: A perceptual approach.* Englewood Cliffs, NJ: Prentice-Hall.

Smith, A. L., & Asante, M. K. (1973). *Transracial communication.* Englewood Cliffs, NJ: Prentice-Hall.

Stanfield, J. H., II, & Dennis, R. M. (Eds.). (1993). *Race and ethnicity in research methods.* Newbury Park, CA: Sage.

Starosta, W. (1990). Thinking through intercultural training assumptions in the aftermath. *International Journal of Intercultural Relations, 14*(1), 1-6.

Stringer, D. M. (1993). *Domestic vs. international training differences and similarities.* Seattle: Executive Diversity Services.

Stringer, D. M., & Taylor, L. (1991). Guidelines for implementing diversity training. *Training & Culture Newsletter, 3*(5), 1, 10-11.

Triandis, H. C. (1977). Theoretical framework for evaluation of cross-cultural training effectiveness. *International Journal of Intercultural Relations, 1*(4), 19-45.

Triandis, H. C. (1983). The essentials of studying culture. In D. Landis & R. W. Brislin. *Handbook of intercultural training* (Vol. 1, pp. 82-117). Elmsford, NY: Pergamon.

Triandis, H. C., Brislin, R., & Hui, C. H. (1988). Cross-cultural training across the individualism-collectivism divide. *International Journal of Intercultural Relations, 12,* 269-289.

Warwick, D. P. (1980). The politics and ethics of cross-cultural research. In H. C. Triandis (Ed.), *Handbook of cross-cultural psychology* (Vol. 1, pp. 319-372). Boston: Allyn & Bacon.

Wendt, J. R. (1982). Uncle Sam and the bad news bear: Human rights as intercultural communication. In M. Burgoon (Ed.), *Communication yearbook 5* (pp. 571-589). New Brunswick, NJ: Transaction Books.

4

Designing Intercultural Training

WILLIAM B. GUDYKUNST

RUTH M. GUZLEY

MITCHELL R. HAMMER

THE effective design of intercultural training (ICT) programs is critical to their success. A well-designed training program not only keeps the trainees actively involved but also contributes to meeting the goals of the program (Black & Mendenhall, 1990). An abundance of material has been written on ICT design (see Gudykunst & Hammer, 1983, for early citations), but even today very few authors who address ICT design issues do it in a systematic fashion. By training design, we mean the selection and sequencing of training techniques to accomplish the specific goals of a training program. Our purpose in writing this chapter is to present ICT design in a systematic fashion so that trainers can increase the effectiveness of their programs.

We begin by examining problems that affect the design of ICT programs. Next, we look at the goals and objectives of ICT. Following this, we present a typology of training techniques

based on two critical issues in ICT: didactic versus experiential learning, and culture-general versus culture-specific content. After isolating the major training techniques available for use in ICT, we illustrate how these techniques can be combined into two specific training designs (one theory-based and one not theory-based). We conclude by examining additional issues that must be taken into consideration when designing ICT (needs assessments, selecting theories to guide training, timing of training, selection and sequencing of training techniques, and evaluation of training).

Problems Affecting the Design of Intercultural Training

Black and Gregersen (1991) argue that training design is critical to the success of ICT. They surveyed U.S. expatriate managers located in

Japan, Korea, Taiwan, and Hong Kong regarding the effect of a variety of antecedents on work, interaction, and general adjustment in their host cultures. Black and Gregersen found that only 25% of the respondents had received predeparture training and that the training received was brief (a few hours).[1] This training "was not significantly related to either work or general adjustment" (p. 510). Contrary to expectations, a negative relationship was found between the training and interaction adjustment; this finding "may suggest that the combination of low quantity and insufficient quality of training may have resulted in inaccurate expectations" (p. 510).

A variety of problems and potential problems are associated with the design of ICT. One of the most obvious is related to the increasing demand for ICT by U.S. organizations in response to a growing diversity in the U.S. population and workforce, as well as to the growth of the global market. The Western propensity for quick-fix solutions has led to the increasing demand for relatively short-term ICT, which by some reports ranges anywhere from a 4-hour, half-day session to 3 weeks (Caudron, 1991; Forsberg, 1993), depending on the complexity of the training (e.g., minimal awareness to intense language training). Unrealistic expectations of what can be accomplished in short-term training are exemplified by such statements as, "Cultural differences become moot with training" (Forsberg, 1993, p. 80).

Although some empirical evidence suggests that short-term experiential culture sensitivity training is effective in increasing cultural awareness and potentially changing attitudes (Hammer & Martin, 1992; Pruegger & Rogers, 1994) and although diversity consultants' testimonials attest to its success in improving client relations (Forsberg, 1993), these results should be viewed with caution. Sue (1991) points out that "cultural diversity training, when applied to organizations, is a complex and long-term process. . . . Our biases, prejudices, and stereotypes run deep and die hard!" (p. 104). Salyer (1993) argues that cultural sensitivity is a matter of progression that takes place over time.

A second problem affecting the design of ICT is that most of the training conducted is not theoretically grounded (Landis & Brislin, 1983). Although empirical evidence exists that cross-cultural training is effective in skill development (see Black & Mendenhall, 1990),

explanations for the effectiveness are not available (Hammer & Martin, 1992). The variety of contexts toward which ICT is directed (e.g., expatriate adjustment to host culture, skills for dealing with foreign clients, intercultural skills for operating in a diverse workforce), points to the importance of such models or theoretical frameworks. We believe that training should be based on explicit models or theories designed to explain the interaction toward which training is directed. To illustrate, if training is directed toward helping trainees adapt to new cultural environments, it should be based on a model or theory of cultural adjustment. Similarly, if training is designed to help people communicate effectively in a multicultural workplace, it should be based on a theory of intergroup effectiveness.

A third potential problem influencing ICT design is related to the variety of labels associated with it—for example, intercultural training, diversity training, cultural diversity training, cultural diversity awareness training, multicultural training, cross-cultural training, and multicultural education. Although there is some overlap in the content associated with training conducted under each of these labels, there may also be some distinctions among them. Forsberg (1993), for example, argues that diversity training is aimed at improvement of relationships internal to the organization and that cultural training is aimed at improvement of relationships external to the organization. Such differences in labels may lead to confusion for training participants unless the logic behind the label used is defined, along with the associated training objectives.

The differences in terminology may be the result of philosophical differences in what type of training is necessary to manage a diverse workforce. Digital Equipment Corporation's philosophy of "valuing differences," for example, focuses on individual growth and development, as well as on changing the attitudes and perspectives of individual employees to facilitate better interactions in a diverse workforce (Waler & Hanson, 1992). Core groups, which are voluntary and led by trained employees, are an integral part of Digital's commitment to ICT. They consist of "groups of seven to nine employees [including top management] who commit to coming together on a monthly basis to examine their stereotypes, test the differences in their assumptions, and build significant relationships with people they regard as different" (Walker & Hanson, 1992, p. 121). In sharp contrast, Pepsi-Cola International recognizes cultural differences in its global workforce but has chosen to neutralize such differences in favor of creating a corporate culture and performance vocabulary that "transcends international boundaries" (Fulkerson & Schuler, 1992, p. 272). Pepsi's Executive Leadership Program (which includes executives from around the world), for instance, "is seen as culturally neutral. Although cultural differences are discussed, the focus is on how best to demonstrate the practice regardless of the country of application" (p. 260).

Although some elements of ICT are general in nature (e.g., how stereotypes develop) and serve as a foundation, other aspects of the training need to be designed to fit an organization's culture, purpose, and stage of commitment to managing a diverse workforce, as well as to individual needs (Sue, 1991). "One-size-fits-all" cultural diversity programs are not likely to have components that address complexities unique to the demands of the specific trainees.

Pepsi's culturally neutral approach is reported to be successful, yet it does point to the possibility of a fourth problem in training design: cultural bias. Fulkerson and Schuler (1992) contend that,

> the essence of leadership . . . is the same around the world. Leadership is the same in that people need to be motivated and aligned with the strategic business vision. . . . [T]he exact application of the skills taught in these programs may be different, but the outcome (improved business performance) is the same. (p. 269)

Such beliefs reflect an ethnocentric view of leadership. Hofstede (1991) argues that "management techniques and training packages have almost exclusively been developed in individualist countries, and they are based on cultural assumptions which may not hold in collectivist cultures" (p. 66).

A fifth problem associated with the design of ICT is the reluctance of organizational management and/or program designers and trainers to confront prejudices that need to be examined before behavioral and attitudinal change can take place. As a result, training content is diluted and may reinforce the very prejudices it

was intended to address. One such example is offered by Barlow and Barlow (1993) from their work on steering committees formed to select both instructors and cultural diversity awareness training programs for law enforcement.

The project was begun with a high degree of enthusiasm and commitment to having a significant impact on officers' knowledge, appreciation, and behavior toward diverse cultures. However, after the first series of training programs, committee members fell into the trap of supporting programs based upon popularity rather than substantive merit. Relying almost exclusively on the participants' program evaluations, the committee reinvited instructors who received high marks and terminated the services of those with lower scores. Some consideration was given to the strong possibility that the "best" programs may be those that the officers don't like, because they confront prejudices and challenge perceptions and attitudes. Yet, ultimately, invitations were extended to instructors with high ratings, despite the uneasy recognition that high ratings may be given to instructors who make participants feel comfortable with their prejudices and the way they are currently doing their jobs. (p. 78)

Corvin and Wiggins (1989) would agree and contend that a strong antiracism component is a necessary part of any multicultural training program.

As uncomfortable as it may be to confront bias and prejudice in ICT sessions, it is necessary in order to break down rigid stereotypes. As the United States becomes more multicultural, the tensions are likely to continue to increase in the workplace, as well as in society in general. Those tensions cannot be covered up with awareness training that remains on the surface of cultural differences. Sue (1991) notes that "if we are to truly become a multicultural society, we cannot continue to avoid this battleground" (p. 104). It is important to note, however, that developing training that sensitizes people to their biases is not enough. Results of management training at Xerox Corporation suggests that training must also "provide them with the necessary tools and information they [need] to deal with these biases" (Sessa, 1992, p. 46).

A sixth problem that affects the design of ICT is the political climate and corporate culture of the organization in which training is conducted.[2] The political climate and corporate culture affect whether or not training is conducted, who is trained, who requests the training, who conducts the training, the type of training conducted, and the resources committed to training. The decision of whether or not to conduct training is partially a function of political considerations in an organization. To illustrate, do the people who think training is needed have the power in the organization to convince the decision makers to conduct training? Hall and Gudykunst (1989) found that the more ethnocentric the corporate culture of an organization, the less likely the organization is to offer training to its employees.

Political considerations and the corporate culture also influence the resources that are committed to training once a decision to conduct training is made. Hall and Gudykunst (1989) observed that the more ethnocentric the corporate culture of an organization, the fewer resources they commit to selection and training of overseas personnel. The resources committed to training, in turn, influence who conducts training, the length of the training conducted, and who is trained (e.g., employees only, employees and family).

Political considerations in the organization and the corporate culture in the organization also affect what training is conducted. Trainers may be pressured to focus on specific goals or to conduct training in a particular way. To illustrate, trainers may be pressured to train trainees how to socialize host nationals in the corporate culture when the trainers think they should focus on helping trainees understand how to adjust to local practices in the host culture. Hall and Gudykunst (1989) found that the more ethnocentric the corporate culture of an organization, the more likely it is to use its own personnel in managerial positions in overseas operations (as opposed to hiring host nationals; for more on this point, see Chapter 3, this volume).

Last, but certainly not least, it is important to recognize that ICT alone is not enough to improve intercultural relations; the organizational culture must reinforce the training. Rowe argues that,

all the ways that the organization treats people—their performance-review system, their career-development system—none of it's going to fit [without awareness of diversity] because all of that needs to be designed to meet the [diverse] needs of people that are there. Forward-thinking companies are beginning to see, for example, that instead of having a separate diversity program, you make diversity a part of *all* the [different types of] training. (quoted in Laabs, 1993, p. 26)

Sue (1991) points to the complex nature of the multicultural workforce today and states that the associated challenges cannot be met by cultural diversity training alone, but rather must be accompanied by intervention in recruitment, retention, and promotion.

United States companies, our schools, and mental health services are often seeking either quick profits or easy solutions. There are no "quick fixes," "magic wands," or simple solutions. Success is directly proportional to the investment of time, energy, and financial resources devoted to the development of a truly multicultural organization. It begins at the top levels of government, business, and industry. (p. 100)

Hence, ICT that does not have the continual commitment and support of all levels of organizational management is not likely to succeed (Jackson & Associates, 1992).

Our focus in this chapter is on ICT, not on other issues of organizational support (e.g., recruitment, retention). It is important to keep these issues in mind, however, because they do affect training outcomes. We address issues of designing training that cut across the various forms of ICT (e.g., adjustment training, effective communication in multicultural workplaces), but the example training designs proffered emphasize intercultural adjustment. We begin our discussion of design issues in ICT by looking at goals and objectives of training.

Goals and Objectives of Intercultural Training

There appears to be general agreement that the goals of training are different from the goals of education. Nadler (1970), for example, sees training as "those activities which are designed to improve human performance on the job the employee is presently doing or is being hired to do" (p. 40). Education, in contrast, is not linked to specific jobs, but rather is aimed at improving individuals' overall competence. Not all ICT is job oriented, but virtually all ICT conducted is aimed at improving trainees' performance in specific intercultural situations.

As indicated earlier, the broad objectives of ICT can vary greatly. To illustrate, ICT can be directed at helping trainees adjust to living in new cultural environments, interact effectively with members of other groups in culturally diverse environments, or counsel members of other cultural groups. The specific goals of ICT need to be derived from the broad objectives of the training, the theory or approach used to guide the training, and the specific trainees.

Although goals have to be specific to particular training programs, most ICT involves some form of change in three areas: cognition, affect, and behavior. Cognitively, ICT generally is aimed at helping trainees understand how their culture, stereotypes, and attitudes influence their interactions with members of other cultures. Cognitive ICT goals, therefore, focus on knowledge and/or awareness. Affectively, ICT generally is aimed at helping trainees effectively manage their emotional reactions (e.g., anxiety) when interacting with members of other cultures. Behaviorally, ICT generally is designed to help trainees develop the skills they need to interact effectively with members of other cultures. The specific skills depend on the broader objectives of the training (e.g., cultural adjustment, effective communication).

The first step in designing ICT is to isolate the specific goals for the training. The goals must be derived from several sources. First, the broad objectives of the training must be kept in mind. To illustrate, although there will be some overlap in the goals of ICT across training programs, the specific goals of ICT will differ if the broad objectives are to help trainees adjust to new cultures or effectively communicate in multicultural workplaces. Second, the needs of the trainees must be taken into consideration in determining the specific training goals. This goal source is based on a needs assessment that trainers conduct with trainees (see discussion of needs assessment in the last section of this chapter). Trainees who are going abroad for 3 years with their families, for example, have needs different from those of trainees going abroad for 6 months without their families.

Third, the model or theory guiding the training will influence the specific goals used to design training (see the two examples in the section below). Theories and models used to guide training affect what can be accomplished in training programs and, therefore, must be selected before specific goals are derived.

Once the objectives and goals of ICT have been determined, trainers must design the training to be conducted. This task involves deciding on the specific training techniques that will be used to meet the objectives and the order in which the techniques will be used. In the following section, we overview the major training techniques used in ICT.

Training Techniques

As pointed out earlier, one major problem in the literature on ICT design and techniques is the lack of articulated theory underlying the various designs and techniques in use. In this section, we present a typology for classifying training techniques. The typology originally was presented by Gudykunst and Hammer (1983). Many examples used in the earlier version are omitted here, and new examples are presented. The examples we present may appear to emphasize intercultural adjustment training, but most, if not all, can be used in programs designed to improve the effectiveness of communication in culturally diverse environments, to increase the cultural sensitivity of counselors, and so forth.

Training techniques used in ICT can be classified on the basis of two central issues in ICT: the approaches used in training (didactic vs. experiential approaches to training) and the content of the training (culture-general vs. culture-specific approaches to training). The didactic approach to ICT is based on the assumption that a cognitive understanding of a culture, its people, and customs is necessary to effectively interact with people of that culture (Harrison & Hopkins, 1967). This approach generally involves a lecture/discussion format in which similarities and differences between cultures are presented and discussed. The experiential approach to ICT, in contrast, is based on the assumption that people learn best from their experiences. To illustrate, if trainees are going to a new culture, they might engage in a structured activity (e.g., a simulation, role play) designed to confront them with situations they will face in the new culture. Trainees react cognitively, emotionally, and behaviorally to the situations. After the experience, the trainees discuss the experiences with the trainer and draw conclusions from their experiences.

Culture-specific training usually refers to "information about a given culture and guidelines for interaction with members of that culture" (Brislin & Pedersen, 1976, p. 6), or more generally, training that is "*specific* to a particular culture" (Triandis, 1977, p. 21). Although there is general agreement on what constitutes culture-specific training, there is no agreement on what culture-general training is. Brislin and Pedersen, for example, see culture-general training as referring to "such topics as cultural awareness and sensitivity training that allow one to learn about himself [or herself] as preparation for interaction in *any* culture" (p. 6). Downs (1969) takes a slightly different position, arguing that culture-general training is aimed at increasing trainees' understanding and/or appreciation of culture's influence on behavior.

By combining these two issues, we can classify the training techniques used in ICT into one of four types: didactic culture general, didactic culture specific, experiential culture general, and experiential culture specific. We briefly overview these techniques in the remainder of this section (for additional techniques, see Gudykunst & Hammer, 1983).

Didactic Culture General

Didactic culture-general approaches to ICT are designed to present culture-general information to trainees. These techniques include, but are not limited to, lecture/discussion techniques, videotapes, and culture-general assimilators.

Lecture/Discussion Techniques

The major didactic culture-general technique used in ICT is lecture/discussion. To illustrate, how trainees' attitudes (e.g., ethnocentrism) influence their communication with members of other cultures can be addressed by lecture/discussion techniques. Characteristics of culture and how it influences trainees' behavior also can be presented through lectures and discussion (e.g., see Brislin's, 1993, 12 characteristics of culture).

Once characteristics of culture are presented, major differences between cultures can be illustrated through lecture/discussion techniques. To illustrate, Triandis, Brislin, and Hui (1988) isolate characteristics of individualistic and collectivistic cultures and ways that individualists and collectivists can adapt their behavior to effectively communicate with each other. For individualists to communicate more effectively with collectivists, Triandis et al. suggest that individualists recognize that collectivists pay attention to group memberships and use group memberships to predict collectivists behavior; recognize that when collectivists' group memberships change, their behavior changes; recognize that collectivists are comfortable in vertical, unequal relationships; recognize that collectivists see competition as threatening; recognize that collectivists emphasize harmony and cooperation in the ingroup; recognize that collectivists emphasize face (public self-image) and help them preserve their face in interactions; recognize that collectivists do not separate criticism from the person being criticized and avoid confrontation whenever possible; cultivate long-term relationships; be more formal than usual in initial interactions; and follow collectivists' guide in disclosing personal information.

For collectivists to interact effectively with individualists, Triandis et al. (1988) suggest that collectivists recognize that individualists' behavior cannot be predicted accurately from group memberships; recognize that individualists will be proud of their accomplishments and say negative things about others; recognize that individualists are emotionally detached from their in-groups; recognize that individualists prefer horizontal, equal relationships; recognize that individualists do not see competition as threatening; recognize that individualists are not persuaded by arguments emphasizing harmony and cooperation; recognize that individualists do not form long-term relationships and that initial friendliness does not indicate an intimate relationship; recognize that individualists maintain relationships when they receive more rewards than costs; recognize that individualists do not respect others on the basis of position, age, or gender as much as collectivists; and recognize that out-groups are not viewed as highly different from ingroups.

Videotapes

Two videotape series used widely in ICT are Copeland and Griggs's *Going International* (1983) and *Valuing Diversity* (1987). These videos are not theoretically based, but if the trainer selects carefully, they can be used to illustrate intercultural communication processes.

The *Going International* series contains seven videotapes. The purpose of the series is to help trainees develop cross-cultural adaptation skills and prepare them for a successful, enjoyable intercultural experience abroad. The three most useful videos for ICT are "Bridging the Cultural Gap," "Beyond Culture Shock," and "Welcome Home Stranger." The series fits topics on intercultural value orientations and intercultural adjustment. Each tape is approximately 30 minutes long and contains intercultural critical incidents, interviews with experts, and practical suggestions.

The *Valuing Diversity* series consists of 3½ hours of videotapes. The purpose of the series is to sharpen trainees' understanding of the human dynamics that cause problems among people who are different. The videos most useful in ICT include "Managing Differences," "Diversity at Work," and "Communicating Across Cultures." Each of these videos is approximately 30 minutes long.

Culture-General Assimilators

Culture-general assimilators involve the use of critical incidents from many different cultures that allow trainees to learn principles that cut across specific cultures.

Critical incidents consist of short stories that involve the interaction of people from different cultures. Incidents have characters with names, a plot line, and an ending that involves some sort of problem and/or misunderstanding. In analyzing reasons for the problems and misunderstandings, trainees begin to learn about culturally influenced knowledge that can have major impacts on

people's intercultural interactions. (Brislin & Yoshida, 1994b, p. 121)

Brislin, Cushner, Cherrie, and Yong (1986) present 100 incidents from a variety of cultures. The critical incidents revolve around the themes of anxiety, disconfirmed expectancies, belonging, ambiguity, confrontation with one's prejudices, work, time and space, language, roles, importance of group versus individual, rituals and superstitions, hierarchies, values, categorization, differentiation, ingroup/outgroup distinction, learning styles, and attribution. Trainees may read and analyze the incidents on their own or work in groups to discuss their individual/group interpretations and attributions. This form of the assimilator is more fully described in Chapter 10.

Didactic Culture Specific

Didactic culture-specific techniques are designed to present culture-specific information to trainees. These techniques include, but are not limited to, area orientation briefings, language training, culture-specific assimilators, and culture-specific reading.

Area Orientation Briefings

Kohls (1979) presents a conceptual model for area studies based on his work in Korea. The model includes three parts: (a) factual information about the specific country, (b) information about the attitudes of the country's people, and (c) a discussion of the problems trainees who go to the country will face. The factual information that should be presented includes history, family and social structure, religion, philosophy, education, fine arts, economics and industry, politics and government, medicine, science, and sports. Kohls argues that the factual information is the least important to be presented because intelligent trainees can gather this information on their own.

Information about the attitudes of a country's people involves presenting personality profiles of the people, as well as information on the attitudes, values, and behavior of the people in the target culture. Kohls (1979) argues that this type of information is important for trainees' effectiveness in the target culture and that this information often cannot be found in books (this is true for most cultures, but many books on some cultures, such as Japan, provide this type of information).

Information on problems that foreigners face in the target culture also must be presented. To illustrate, Kohls (1979) isolates 12 problems North Americans will face in Korea:

Foreigners are "un-persons"
General staring and rudeness in public
Passive resistance as a communication strategy
Extreme poverty and beggars
Koreans' reactions to the influence of the
    United States in their country
Theft, bribery, and dishonesty
Cleanliness and sanitation
Health problems
Strange smells
Adjusting to the food
Learning to share
Lack of privacy

Although area orientation briefings generally are used for adjustment training, they can be used for other forms of training as well. To illustrate, if the broad objective is to increase effectiveness of communication in intercultural workplaces, culture/ethnic group briefings can be given for the various groups working in the organization.

Language Training

Boyer (1990) points out that people "should become familiar with other languages and cultures so that [they] will be better able to live, with confidence, in an increasingly interdependent world" (p. B4). Living in another culture without learning some of the host language is counterproductive to successful intercultural adjustment.

Triandis (1983) points out that the importance of speaking another language depends, at least in part, on where the persons are:

In some cultures foreigners are expected to know the local language. A Frenchman [or woman] who arrives in the United States without knowing a word of English, or an American who visits France with only a bit of French, is bound to find the locals rather unsympathetic. For example, I have found a discrepancy between my friends' and my own experience in Paris. Their accounts stress discourtesy of the French, while I have found the French to be quite courteous. I suspect the difference is that I speak better French than the majority of visitors and am therefore treated more courteously. In contrast, in other cultures the visitor is not expected to know the local language. In Greece, for example, one is not expected to know the language although a few words of Greek create delight, and increase by order of magnitude (a factor of ten) the normal hospitable tendencies of that population. (p. 84)

Some attempt at using the local language is necessary to indicate an interest in the people and/or culture.

Most language training tends to be didactic, and therefore it is discussed here. Many language books and teachers, however, incorporate experiential techniques (e.g., role plays) into language teaching.

Culture-Specific Assimilators

Culture-specific assimilators use programmed learning to teach members of one culture specific information about another culture. Brislin and Pedersen (1976) describe culture-specific assimilators as,

a series of episodes that previous visitors to a given country have labeled as problem situations. Each episode describes an interaction between a visitor . . . and a host national. After reading about the interactions, trainees examine four different interpretations. If trainees make the right choice that explains the interaction, they are reinforced. If they make a mistake, they are told why their choice is wrong and asked to restudy the episode and make another choice. Trainees proceed at their own rate, and no trainee can proceed beyond any one incident until he or she has discovered the correct interpretation of that interaction between people. (p. 90)

The difference between it being used in a culture-general assimilator and a culture-specific assimilator lies in the explanation provided for the behavior. In the culture-general assimilator, the explanation is based on a broad principle of cultural differences (e.g., individualism-collectivism). In the culture-specific cultural assimilator, the explanation would be based on specific characteristics of the culture.

Culture-specific assimilators have been developed for many cultures and ethnic groups in the United States (see Albert, 1983; Chapter 10, this volume). Triandis (1984) provides a theoretical framework for the efficient construction of culture-specific assimilators.

Culture-Specific Reading

Three potentially useful sources for trainers who want to include culture-specific reading in their ICT are the *Interact* series of books published by the Intercultural Press, Brigham Young University's *Culturegram* series, Alison Lanier's *Updates* series[3] (all three are available from Intercultural Press, P.O. Box, 700, Yarmouth, ME 04096), and the *Human Relations Area Files.*

The *Interact* series includes culture-specific volumes on Australia, Japan, Mexico, Thailand, and the Arab world. The authors discuss how nationals from these countries express and structure their worldviews in comparison with middle-class people in the United States.

The *Culturegram* series contains cultural minibriefings on the values, customs, and lifestyles of nationals in 90 countries. Each pamphlet is approximately four pages long.

The *Updates* series provides practical information concerning everyday living and working (e.g., topics include history, language, doing business, social customs, operating a household, health and medical care, leisure and entertainment) in a new cultural environment (e.g., Belgium, Britain, Hong Kong, France, Indonesia, Kuwait, West Germany). The volumes in the series are designed especially to meet the needs of families relocating abroad. The series contains 15 volumes of intercultural information, and each volume (approximately 110 pages in length) is updated periodically.

The *Human Relations Area Files* is perhaps the largest ethnographic computer database and consists of detailed descriptive information on 300-plus cultural groups. A descriptive list of major categories and themes (e.g., labor and leisure, age stratification, gestures, in-group antagonism) can be found in Murdock's (1971) *The Outline of Cultural Materials,* and specific cultural group descriptions can be found in Murdock's (1972) *The Outline of World Cultures.*

Experiential Culture General

Experiential culture-general techniques are designed to help trainees experience how their culture, stereotypes, and attitudes influence their behavior. Training techniques in this category include, but are not limited to, intercultural communication workshops, culture-general assimilators, and self-assessments.

Intercultural Communication Workshops

Intercultural communication workshops (ICWs) are designed to encourage participants to learn through their interaction with members of other cultures in a small group setting. ICWs are designed to help participants understand how culture influences their thoughts and behaviors. More specifically, Althen (1975) argues that,

> from an intercultural communication workshop a participant can learn about the subject of culture generally, about the cultures representant in the group, and about the problems of communication which exist when members of differing cultures come together. Perhaps most important, he [or she] can learn about himself [or herself], since the encounter with contrasting value and behavior systems will normally illuminate his [or her] own with marked effect. (p. 80)

ICWs, therefore, provide an opportunity for participants to meet many objectives of ICT.

ICWs involve a small group of people from different cultures (e.g., about 10) meeting over an extended period of time to interact with each other. Facilitators guide participants' interaction but do not formally teach the group. The idea is for participants to learn from the experiences they have in the ICW. This is accomplished, in part, by the facilitators helping the participants analyze the interactions they have and draw conclusions from these interactions.

Facilitators in ICWs may use a variety of specific training techniques to help the participants improve their intercultural understanding. These techniques might include, but are not limited to, (a) discussing cultural differences among the members of the group, (b) discussing the communication taking place among the members of the group, (c) using role plays to help participants understand how conflict or decision making takes place in other cultures, and (d) discussing critical incidents or having participants engage in a field experience and then discussing the different reactions to the experience. Although other techniques are used, the primary emphasis in ICWs is the analysis of the interaction taking place among the participants.

Culture-General Simulations

Culture-general simulations are experiential exercises designed to simulate general interaction between members of different cultures. One of earliest simulations in this category is the contrast-American simulation (Stewart, 1966; Stewart, Danielian, & Foster, 1969). Stewart (1966) identified American values in five categories: (a) form of activity, (b) form of social relations with others, (c) modality of motivation, (d) perception of the world, and (e) perception of self. Once the American values were isolated, Stewart isolated contrast-American values (values that are the opposite of American values). Based on the value differences, a series of role plays was developed wherein an American interacted with a contrast-American. A contrast-American actor responds to American trainees on the basis of the contrast-American values. Stewart et al. (1969) argue that this approach "engages the trainee behaviorally and emotionally while simultaneously exposing him [or her] to cultural values and assumptions different from his [or her] own" (p. 45).

One of the most widely used culture-general simulations is BAFA BAFA (Shirts, 1973). BAFA BAFA simulates two hypothetical cultures: alphas and betas. Alpha culture is a masculine, collectivistic culture; beta culture is a feminine, individualistic culture (Shirts does not use these terms to describe the cultures; see Hofstede, 1980, for descriptions of individualism-collectivism and masculinity-femininity; note that alpha culture is a patriarchy, but it can be run as a matriarchy). Trainees are divided into the two cultures, and they are taught the rules of their culture. Once they understand the rules of their culture, observers go to the other culture to gather information. After the observers report their observations, visitors are exchanged. After everyone has visited the other culture, the experiences are debriefed by the trainers. Discussion of BAFA BAFA brings out all aspects of entering a new cultural environment. Running BAFA BAFA and debriefing requires a minimum of 3 hours.

Many other culture-general simulations require less time (e.g., the Albatross—Gochenour, 1977a; the Owl or "X-ians"—Gochenour, 1977b; Alpha-Omega—Hoppe, Michalis, & Reinking, 1995; Ecotonos—Nipporica Associates, 1993; Barnga—Thiagarajan & Steinwachs, 1990). Trainers may use one of these simulations or more than one. To illustrate, Alpha-Omega is similar to BAFA BAFA, but it involves much less time and does not involve entering a new culture (rather, interactions between alphans and omegans take place on "neutral" territory). Alpha-Omega, however, can be debriefed just like BAFA BAFA. It is possible, therefore, to run Alpha-Omega early in a training program to develop cultural awareness and then to run BAFA BAFA later to give trainees a chance to apply the knowledge they learned in the program.

Batchelder and Warner's (1977) experiential manual includes three major sections: ideas, exercises, and assessment. The idea section includes articles on values of experiential education, cross-cultural learning, and cross-cultural resources. The exercises section includes language orientation exercises, ESL classroom exercises, global sensitivity exercises, the Owl simulation, the Albatross simulation, and many others. The final section on assessment includes articles on assessing experiential learning overseas and sample experiential formats.

Weeks, Pedersen, and Brislin's (1975) manual offers 59 experiential exercises that address clarification of values, identification of roles, recognition of feelings and attitudes, and community interaction, among other topics. Exercises such as "Value Statements," "Cultural Value Checklist," and "The Parable" can be used in sessions on identity and cultural values. Exercises such as "Letters to the Editor," "A Newspaper Incident," "We and You," and the "Multicultural Person" can be used in sessions on intergroup attribution process, stereotypes, and prejudice. Because the manual was developed in 1975, some of the exercises need to be modified for nonsexist language usage and gender equity issues.

Hoopes and Ventura's (1979) sourcebook includes sections on role playing, simulations, the contrast-American technique, the culture assimilator, self-awareness inventories, workbook approaches, critical incidents, case studies, other group exercises, and area-specific training. This volume differs from the other two in that the focus is on how to design the training methodologies, rather than on presenting specific exercises.

Self-Assessments

Another way that trainees can experientially learn in ICT is through completing self-assessment instruments designed to determine their attitudes and/or perceptions of their communication competence. Gudykunst (1994) presents approximately 20 self-assessment questionnaires that readers can complete to assess their attitudes, motivations, and perceptions of their competence. He includes, for example, measures of uncertainty and anxiety experienced when communicating with strangers, as well as measures of approach/avoidance tendencies, prejudice, ethnocentrism, and uncertainty orientation. Trainees can complete the self-assessment questionnaires and then discuss how their attitudes and motivations influence their ability to communicate effectively with people from other cultures or ethnic groups. Many other self-assessments (e.g., assessments of individualism-collectivism, cross-cultural awareness, nonverbal communication knowledge) are presented by the contributors in Brislin and Yoshida's (1994a) modules for ICT.

Experiential Culture Specific

Experiential culture-specific techniques are designed to help trainees experience interaction with members of other cultures and learn from these experiences. Techniques in this category include, but are not limited to, bicultural ICWs, culture-specific simulations, and culture-specific role plays.

Bicultural Communication Workshops

Although the ICW originally was designed as a culture-general training technique, it can be used as an experiential culture-specific training technique by limiting participants to members of two cultures (e.g., members of the host and visitor cultures; members of specific minority groups working in an organization and members of the majority group working in an organization).

If bicultural ICWs are conducted, the facilitators should include members of both cultures represented. Each facilitator should be thoroughly familiar with the other culture and be able to effectively communicate with members of other cultures. If the participants are bilingual, it also is advisable to hold some sessions in one language and some sessions in the second language to help the participants understand how language influences their intercultural communication.

Culture-Specific Simulations

Few culture-specific simulations are available. One simulation that is available is the Markhall simulation (available from Training Resources Group, 1021 Prince Street, Alexandria, VA 22314). This simulation is designed to help trainees understand the influence of culture on management styles, work life, and worker interaction in Japan and the United States. The United States "Ace Card Company" is characterized as having leader-centered decision making, one-way communication, short-term employment, specialized tasks, segmented work situations, and individual accountability. The Japan "Creative Card Company" is characterized by participative decision making, two-way communication, long-term employment, nonspecialized tasks, integrated work situations, and collective accountability.

The simulation does not involve interaction between members of the two cultures but does illustrate cultural differences. Trainees learn about cultural differences when they participate as members of the culture and when the simulation is debriefed.

Culture-Specific Role Plays

Culture-specific role plays are designed to help trainees learn how to interact in specific situations with members of a specific culture. To illustrate, a culture-specific role play might be designed to help trainees in the United States negotiate a contract with a Japanese.

Culture-specific role plays often involve interaction between members of the two specific cultures (e.g., Americans role-playing Americans and Japanese role-playing Japanese). They can, however, also involve members of the same culture (e.g., Americans role-playing both the American and Japanese roles). Each method has advantages. To illustrate, when both cultures are represented, trainees gain experience interacting with members of the other culture. This experience is easily transferred to "real" interactions with members of other cultures. When trainees role-play members of the other culture, however, they also gain insight into how to modify their behavior when interacting with members of the other culture.

Illustrations of Training Designs

ICT designs involve putting training techniques together in a systematic way designed to meet the goals of training. Space does not permit a wide variety of training designs to be presented here. We therefore concentrate on two examples of ICT designs that focus on intercultural adjustment. The first design is derived from Brislin and Yoshida (1994b). This design is based on the authors' knowledge and experiences, not on an explicit theory of cultural adjustment. The second design illustrates how training design can be derived from an explicit theory of cultural adjustment.

Brislin and Yoshida's Approach

Brislin and Yoshida (1994b) argue that ICT needs to address awareness and knowledge about culture and its influence on behavior, the emotional challenges individuals face when communicating with members of other cultures, and the skills trainees need for effective intercultural communication in another culture. They argue that most clients of ICT assume it can take place in a very short period of time (e.g., a few hours). The authors, however, contend that 3 days is the minimum time necessary to conduct a reasonable ICT program.

Brislin and Yoshida (1994b) isolate three goals for ICT designed to help trainees adjust to living in a new cultural environment:

1. awareness, knowledge, and information about culture, cultural differences, and the specific culture in which trainees will be living;
2. attitudes related to intercultural communication, such as people's feeling about others who are culturally different (e.g., tolerance, prejudice, or active enthusiasm about developing close relationships); and the emotional confrontation people experience when dealing with cultural differences in everyday communication; and
3. skills, or new behaviors that will increase the chances of effective communication when living and/or working with people from other cultural backgrounds. (p. 24)

Brislin and Yoshida examine these three issues in some detail and then suggest a training design based on these three goals.

Brislin and Yoshida's (1994b) training design is divided into four phases: awareness, knowledge, emotional challenges, and behavioral skills. Space does not permit an elaborate discussion of each phase, but we briefly overview their suggestions for each phase (there are no clear boundaries among the four phases).

Brislin and Yoshida (1994b) suggest introducing an awareness of culture by beginning with a discussion of the characteristics of culture (Brislin, 1993, isolates 12 characteristics). To illustrate, "culture consists of concepts, values, and assumptions about life that guide behavior and that are widely shared by people" (p. 118) and "culture becomes clearest when people interact with others from very different backgrounds" (p. 119). Major differences in cultures (e.g., individualism-collectivism) also are introduced during this phase. While presenting the various characteristics of culture, the trainer can draw on the trainees' experiences and use their experiences to help them understand how culture influences their behavior.

Once trainees are aware of how culture influences their behavior, knowledge useful in intercultural interaction and adjustment can be presented. Brislin and Yoshida (1994b) argue that critical incidents are an effective way to provide this knowledge. During this phase, the critical incidents used would be culture general, rather than culture specific (see Brislin et al., 1986, for 100 critical incidents).

Emotional challenges often arise when trainees are confronted with cultural differences (Brislin & Yoshida, 1994b). The authors suggest critical incidents and role playing as ways to help trainees address the emotional challenges they face. When using critical incidents, the discussion should focus on emotional reactions of the people involved in the incidents. Brislin and Yoshida point out that "people become especially upset, and experience great stress, if they have no idea why problems occurred" (p. 126). The focus of the discussion, therefore, needs to be on helping trainees understand why people have different emotional reactions.

Scripted role playing also can help trainees address the emotional challenges they will face in another culture. Use of the term *scripted* implies that the role play is well planned. Trainees are given approximately 20 minutes to plan the role play prior to enacting it. The topic of the role plays may be the same as the critical incidents used or different, depending on the trainers' goals.

Awareness, knowledge, and an ability to face emotional challenges are not sufficient for success in intercultural encounters. According to Brislin and Yoshida (1994b), practice in engaging in the behaviors needed to increase trainees' success also must occur. They point out that trainers must give trainees "exact reasons" for adapting new behaviors. The authors also suggest that the first behavior presented be "non-threatening and easy to carry out" (p. 130; e.g., designing a business card they might use in the new culture). Obviously, learning appropriate behaviors is culture specific, not culture general. Brislin and Yoshida suggest providing training with very specific behaviors the train-

ees can enact in the new culture. To illustrate, they suggest that, when training individuals to go to Japan, trainees be taught how to apologize in a Japanese way because apologies are important in the Japanese culture. Specific techniques for apologizing, therefore, are taught.

Brislin and Yoshida (1994b) argue that a final session must summarize the training and allow trainees time to answer questions. They suggest that the trainer provide trainees with notes that are used to summarize what they have learned. Brislin and Yoshida (1994b) suggest that if more time than 3 days is available, "(a) trainees be introduced to various behaviors that they will be asked to perform in other cultures, and that (b) these behaviors be performed in social contexts similar to those that will be experienced in the host culture" (p. 134).

Brislin and Yoshida's (1994b) approach is not based on a theory of cultural adjustment. It does, however, incorporate a theory of cultural differences (e.g., individualism-collectivism) in its examination of culture. The program outlined emphasizes didactic culture-general and didactic culture-specific techniques but does incorporate experiential culture-specific techniques in the role plays. Experiential culture-general techniques do not appear to be incorporated into this training design.

Theory-Based Training Design

We use anxiety/uncertainty management theory (AUM; Gudykunst, 1988, 1993, 1995; Gudykunst & Hammer, 1988; Gudykunst & Sudweeks, 1992) to illustrate a theory-based training program. AUM theory is based on the assumption that managing uncertainty and anxiety is necessary for effective intergroup communication and intercultural adjustment (see Gao & Gudykunst, 1990; Hammer, Wiseman, Rasmussen, & Bruschke, 1992, for empirical tests of the assumption). When AUM theory is applied to intercultural adjustment, the argument is that the basic cause of intercultural adjustment is sojourners' abilities to manage their uncertainty and anxiety. Other concepts often associated with intercultural adjustment (e.g., interaction with host nations) affect the amount of uncertainty and anxiety that sojourners experience. Space does not permit a summary of the theory or a complete outline of a training program. We therefore overview a training program based on AUM theory and introduce components of the theory to provide the rationale for training sessions included.

The major goals of an adjustment training program based on AUM theory would be (a) to help trainees understand how their ability to manage their uncertainty and anxiety influences their ability to adapt to new cultures, (b) to help trainees successfully manage their uncertainty in new cultural environments, and (c) to help trainees successfully manage their anxiety in new cultural environments. The theory suggests that the first goal must be addressed prior to addressing the second and third. If trainees do not understand that their uncertainty and anxiety are directly related to their ability to adapt to new cultural environments, they will not be open to sessions focusing on managing uncertainty and anxiety. Although the goals focus on uncertainty and anxiety, we do not mean to imply that the ICT focuses exclusively on uncertainty and anxiety. Other factors (e.g., interaction with host nations, being mindful) must be incorporated to meet the second and third goals.

We would begin the training program with an introductory session. In this session, we would explain the purposes of the training program. Assuming that this is the only ICT program the trainees will attend (ideally, trainees would participate in language instruction outside the training program), we would design the program to meet both trainees' long-term adjustment needs and their immediate survival needs on entering the culture. If trainees mentioned specific needs during the needs assessment (see below), we would indicate that these needs also would be met in the programs. We also would conduct an introductory exercise to allow the trainees to get to know each other. We would begin the actual training immediately after the introductory session.

For trainees to understand how their uncertainty and anxiety influence their ability to adapt to new cultural environment, they must see this through their own experience. In other words, the first goal cannot be met by using didactic training techniques; it requires experiential learning. We therefore would begin with a culture-general simulation such as BAFA BAFA.

After running the simulation, we would debrief it, focusing on how uncertainty and anxiety influence trainees' ability to adjust to the new culture. To illustrate, after soliciting alphans' views of betans, betans' views of alphans, and trainees' feelings on entering the new culture, we would examine the views of the members of the other culture and ask trainees what they have in common. Inevitably, the views expressed are ethnocentric interpretations or judgments of the members of other cultures, not descriptions of behavior. We would discuss how these interpretations and judgments influenced the trainees' ability to predict the behavior of members of other cultures. Once it was clear that ethnocentric interpretations and judgments are not useful in accurately predicting host nationals' behavior, we would help trainees understand how they can describe host nationals' behavior and, on the basis of these descriptions, make an educated guess as to what it might mean in their culture. Making an educated guess involves understanding cultural differences.

Cultural differences cannot be discussed in detail here, but the basic ideas can be presented, and cultural variability can be discussed in a later session. We would then point out that we cannot describe others' behavior and make an educated guess if we communicate on automatic pilot or mindlessly (see Langer, 1989). Rather, we must be mindful of our communication. We would indicate that we will return to mindfulness in the next session and turn to the list of feelings. The feelings listed will be similar to those involved when individuals experience culture shock, as well as the anxiety present anytime trainees communicate with members of other cultures. In concluding this session, we would indicate that we will discuss how to manage the feelings in a later session.

In the next session, we would emphasize the importance of being mindful if we are going to make accurate predictions (manage uncertainty) and manage our anxiety (Axiom 47 of AUM theory; Gudykunst, 1995). This could be accomplished in many ways. Because the preceding session was exclusively experiential, we would probably use didactic techniques in this session (to mix training techniques). This use might involve a short lecture on being mindful and the use of critical incidents to help the trainees understand the importance of creating new categories (or looking for individuating information about individuals from other culture), being open to new information, and being aware of alternative perspectives (the three characteristics of mindfulness; Langer, 1989).

The third session would be devoted to managing anxiety. Managing anxiety is addressed prior to managing uncertainty because accurate predictions cannot be made when anxiety is high (an assumption of AUM theory; Gudykunst, 1995). This session could be organized in many ways (e.g., many factors influence the amount of anxiety individuals experience in AUM theory). One critical issue that must be addressed, however, is helping trainees learn specific techniques for managing their anxiety (e.g., breaking from the situation, meditation, yoga). It is important for trainees to recognize that any technique that works in the trainees' home culture will work in new cultural environments (see Gudykunst & Sudweeks, 1992). This task can easily be accomplished through role-playing exercises. Other influences on managing anxiety (e.g., rigid attitudes toward host nationals; negative expectations, including negative stereotypes; ability to tolerate ambiguity) could be illustrated through the use of critical incidents.

The fourth session would focus on managing uncertainty. The goal of this session would be to help trainees learn how to make accurate predictions about host nationals' behavior. To accomplish this, cultural similarities and differences must be addressed. We do not think it generally is useful for trainees to be taught specific interpretations for specific behaviors in the host culture (the exception, of course, is if specific taboos would get trainees into trouble if they violate them). Trainees will never remember all of the interpretations they are taught, and more important, there is never a one-to-one correspondence between specific behaviors and specific interpretations of those behaviors. If trainees find that interpretations they are taught are not accurate in some situations, they may reject other things they learned in a training program.

Because specific interpretation are not being taught, trainees need a framework within which they can interpret the behavior of members of the host culture. We therefore would introduce major dimensions of cultural variability (e.g., individualism-collectivism, uncertainty avoidance; Hofstede, 1991) that trainees can use to initially interpret host nationals' behavior (before they have much culture-specific knowledge). Cultural variability is incorporated into the most recent version of AUM theory (Gudykunst, 1995). To illustrate, person-based information is emphasized in reducing uncertainty in individualistic cultures, whereas group-based information is emphasized in collectivistic cultures (Axiom 57 of AUM theory; Gudykunst, 1995). Triandis et al.'s (1988) suggestions for individualists to interact with collectivists and for collectivists to interact with individualists could be used here. In addition to cultural differences, other influences on managing uncertainty need to be addressed (again, there are many from which to choose). The importance of positive expectations (Axiom 24), for example, could be introduced through the use of critical incidents. Similarly, the quantity and quality of contact with host nationals (Axiom 34), as well as the intimacy of relationships with host nationals (Axiom 35), could be addressed through critical incidents or discussion of relationships and uncertainty in the home culture.

The fifth session would focus on giving trainees an opportunity to apply what they have learned in interactions with host nationals. Ideally, host nationals would be available for this session. If no host nationals are available, the objective can be accomplished by culture-specific role playing. AUM theory suggests several important issues to be addressed in this session. To illustrate, gathering the appropriate type of information is critical to making accurate predictions (Axiom 38). Role plays can be set up wherein trainees have the opportunity to gather information about host nationals, and the role plays would then be debriefed in terms of the utility of the information gathered in making accurate predictions. Similarly, AUM theory suggests that the ability to be mindful when negative expectations are activated is critical to effective communication (Axiom 46). Role plays could be designed wherein trainees' negative expectations are activated to provide them an opportunity to practice being mindful.

The sixth session of the training program would be devoted to presenting survival skills that trainees will need when they arrive in the new culture. What is addressed in this session depends on the concerns the trainees expressed during the needs assessment. It is advisable, however, to make sure some basics are covered. These basics might include such activities as using local transportation systems (e.g., taxis, buses, trains) in the host culture. Using public telephones, ordering food in restaurants, and finding a place to live are other survival needs with which most trainees will be concerned.

The final session should be a wrap-up session. In this session, trainees would be asked to summarize what they have learned in the sessions (this is based on the experiential learning assumption that adults remember the conclusions they draw for themselves better than the conclusions they are told by others). Also during this session, trainees might be asked to develop a plan for continuing their learning about the new culture after they arrive in the culture. Trainees also should be given the opportunity to ask any questions that have not been addressed in the program. Finally, the program should be evaluated (see below).

Like Brislin and Yoshida's (1994b) suggested program, this program can be accomplished in 3 days. If more time is available, each session could be expanded to cover the factors that influence uncertainty and anxiety more thoroughly and to give trainees more practice interacting with host nationals (e.g., using situation-specific role plays). In addition, if trainees are not receiving language training, survival language skills could be incorporated. If less time is available, the sessions suggested here can be shortened and combined. We believe that, minimally, the first four sessions must be completed in some form for the program to be effective.

Additional Considerations in Designing Intercultural Training

Several additional considerations must be weighed in designing ICT. In this section, we focus on needs assessment, selecting a theory to guide training, timing of training, selecting and sequencing training techniques, and evaluating training.

Needs Assessment

Trainers should conduct needs assessments of the trainees participating in ICT programs.[4]

One purpose of the needs assessment is to understand the trainees' needs vis-à-vis the training program to ensure that these needs are met. Do the trainees have special needs, such as enrolling their children in school when they arrive in the new culture? If these needs are not addressed in the training program, the trainees may dismiss the other things they learn in the program.

A second purpose of the needs assessment is to understand how trainees perceive the issues the training program is designed to address. Do the trainees have any specific problems in intercultural communication, for example, if the goal is effective communication? Alternatively, do the trainees anticipate having to address any specific problems in the new culture if the training involves intercultural adjustment? Again, if these needs are not addressed in the training programs, the trainees may reject other things they learn in the program.

A third reason for the needs assessment is to obtain insight into who the trainees are. To illustrate, are the trainees highly ethnocentric? If so, the trainer can anticipate how they might react to particular training sessions. Are the trainees opposed to experiential learning? If so, the trainer can avoid these techniques or anticipate initial negative reactions when the technique is introduced. Understanding the trainees allows the trainer to anticipate problems, and the training program can be designed in a way that will maximize trainees' learning.

Selecting a Theory to Guide Training

Many trainers do not see theories as having practical value, and they do not base their training on explicit theories. Rather, their training usually is based on their intuitive feelings for what is needed or their compilation of training techniques with which they are familiar. We believe that Kurt Lewin was correct when he said, "There is nothing so practical as a good theory." The question is, What constitutes a good theory? The criteria for evaluating theories often involve logical consistency, parsimony, and explanatory ability. These criteria alone can lead to theories that are highly abstract being evaluated positively. Highly abstract theories, however, are difficult to apply or use in designing training. The more concrete theories are, the easier they are to apply (but the less parsimonious they are).

The theory selected to guide the training program must be consistent with the training objectives, be applicable to the trainees and the members of the culture with which the trainees will be interacting, and make sense to the trainer (see Gudykunst, 1983; Kim & Gudykunst, 1988a, 1988b; and Wiseman, 1995, for theories available). A training program for effective communication in multicultural workplaces cannot be based on a theory of cultural adjustment. Rather, it must be based on a theory that focuses on effective intergroup communication. The theory used also must be applicable to the trainees and to the members of other cultures. Using an ethnocentric theory of effective communication (e.g., one limited to European Americans), for example, will not help trainees communicate more effectively with members of other cultures. Finally, the theory must make sense to the trainers. If the theory does not make sense to the trainers, they cannot consistently apply it in the training program and help the trainees use the theory to meet the goals of the training (this does not mean the theory needs to be presented to trainees, but they must understand its basic assumptions and how to apply them in their interactions).

Timing of Training

If the ICT is designed to help trainees adapt to living in a foreign culture, the timing of the training is critical. The ICT must address broad issues of trainees' intercultural adjustment, as well as the survival problems trainees will face on arriving in the host culture. When trainees are receptive to these two types of training in both predeparture and postarrival training depends on the timing of the training.

Issues of intercultural adjustment involve learning how to adapt to the new culture, how to communicate effectively with host nationals, and how to establish relationships with host nationals, to name only a few. These issues are critical to trainees' success in the host culture, but trainees perceive training designed to meet these goals as unrelated to meeting their needs when they are close to departing for the new culture and immediately after arriving in the new culture. Immediately prior to departure and immediately after arrival, trainees are concerned most with meeting their survival needs. Survival needs related to entering the new culture include, but are not limited to, making sure trainees' passports are in order, knowing how to get to the hotel after arriving, knowing how to find a place to live, knowing how to enroll children in school, and knowing how to shop for food.

To maximize trainees' receptiveness to ICT designed to address intercultural adjustment and survival needs, ideally specific types of training should be conducted at specific times. To illustrate, ICT designed to meet trainees' survival needs should be conducted close to departure (e.g., between 0 and 3 months prior to departure) and on arrival in the new culture (e.g., between arrival and 3 months postarrival). ICT designed to help trainees adjust to living a new culture should be conducted several months before departure (e.g., 3 to 6 months) and several months after arrival (e.g., 3 to 6 months). Several months prior to departure, trainees will not be highly concerned with meeting their survival needs, and they therefore will be open to training designed to help them adjust to the new culture. Similarly, when they arrive in the new culture, trainees will not recognize the importance of communicating effectively and establishing relationships with host nationals until their survival needs are met in the host culture.

Although it is ideal to spread out the different types of training, this often is not feasible (e.g., because a company decides to do training just before departure or the personnel are not selected 6 months in advance). If training cannot be spread out as suggested and if it is being conducted just prior to departure, trainees should be assured that their immediate survival needs will be addressed. When the are addressed, however, depends on the training design being used.

Selecting and Sequencing Training Techniques

Selecting and sequencing the training techniques are critical to the success of ICT programs. In selecting training techniques, trainers should be concerned with the efficacy of the technique on meeting the training objective; some techniques are more appropriate than others to meet certain objectives. To illustrate, it is difficult for trainees to learn how to manage their affective reactions to interacting with members of other cultures by using didactic techniques.

Ideally, training programs should combine a variety of training techniques. One obvious reason is that different objectives require different training techniques. But another reason is that adult learning theory suggests different people learn best through different techniques. To illustrate, some people learn best through didactic techniques, whereas others learn best through experiential techniques. By using a variety of techniques, trainers ensure that they will use the, at some point during the training, techniques individual trainees prefer.

Training techniques should be varied throughout training programs. If several sessions in a row involve strictly experiential learning, some trainees (e.g., those opposed to experiential learning) may be turned off and withdraw. By intermixing the various techniques, trainers can maximize trainees' involvement.

Evaluating Training

All ICT should be evaluated. If training is not evaluated, one cannot know whether it is effective. Evaluation of training can help trainers assess the effectiveness of the overall program, individual sessions, and the sequencing of the sessions. Evaluation also helps trainers develop persuasive arguments for their effectiveness.

Space does not permit a discussion here of the techniques required to successfully evaluate ICT. Discussions of ICT program evaluations are available in Brislin and Yoshida (1994b), as well as in Chapter 9, this volume.

SUMMARY

In this chapter, we overviewed the major issues in designing ICT. In concluding, we want to emphasize that ICT programs should be designed on the basis of good theories or models developed based on research. There is no excuse for conducting ICT based on the trainers' intuition. Intercultural trainers must be thoroughly familiar with the major theories and research in the areas in which they are conducting training, and they must use the theories and research to design their training.

Notes

1. Tung (1981) and Dunbar and Ehrlich (1986) report similar percentages of people being trained.

2. We want to thank Rabi Bhagat for suggesting that this issue be addressed.

3. As we were completing the chapter, we heard a rumor that these updates are being discontinued.

4. We are not suggesting that training be based on a needs assessment. Rather, training should be theoretically based, but a needs assessment is necessary to understanding trainees' perceptions of their needs. If these needs are not addressed in some way, trainees may reject the other material presented.

References

Albert, R. (1983). The intercultural sensitizer or culture assimilator. In D. Landis & R. W. Brislin (Eds.), *Handbook of intercultural training* (Vol. 2, pp. 186-217). Elmsford, NY: Pergamon.

Althen, G. (1975). Human relations training for foreign students. In D. Hoopes (Ed.), *Readings in intercultural communication* (Vol. 1). Pittsburgh: Intercultural Communication Network.

Barlow, D. E., & Barlow, M. H. (1993). Cultural diversity training in criminal justice: A progressive or conservative reform? *Social Justice, 20,* 69-84.

Batchelder, D., & Warner, E. (Eds.). (1977). *Beyond experience: The experiential approach to cross-cultural education.* Brattleboro, VT: Experiment in International Living.

Black, J. S., & Gregersen, H. B. (1991). Antecedents to cross-cultural adjustment for expatriates in

Pacific Rim assignments. *Human Relations, 44,* 497-515.

Black, J. S., & Mendenhall, M. (1990). Cross-cultural training effectiveness: A review and a theoretical framework for future research. *Academy of Management Review, 15,* 113-136.

Boyer, E. (1990, June 20). Letter to the editor. *Chronicle of Higher Education,* p. B4.

Brislin, R. W. (1993). *Understanding culture's influence on behavior.* Orlando, FL: Harcourt Brace Jovanovich.

Brislin, R. W., Cushner, K., Cherrie, C., & Yong, M. (1986). *Intercultural interactions: A practical guide.* Beverly Hills, CA: Sage.

Brislin, R. W., & Pedersen, P. (1976). *Cross-cultural orientation programs.* New York: Gardner.

Brislin, R. W., & Yoshida, T. (Eds.). (1994a). *Improving intercultural interactions: Modules for cross-cultural training programs.* Thousand Oaks, CA: Sage.

Brislin, R. W., & Yoshida, T. (1994b). *Intercultural communication training: An introduction.* Thousand Oaks, CA: Sage.

Caudron, S. (1991). Training ensures success overseas. *Personnel Journal, 70,* 27-30.

Copeland, L., & Griggs, L. (Producers). (1983). *Going international* [videotape]. (Available from Copeland Griggs Productions, 302 23rd Avenue, San Francisco, CA 94121)

Copeland, L., & Griggs, L. (Producers). (1987). *Valuing diversity* [videotape]. (Available from Copeland Griggs Productions, 302 23rd Avenue, San Francisco, CA 94121)

Corvin, S., & Wiggins, F. (1989). An antiracism training model for white professionals. *Journal of Multicultural Counseling and Development, 17,* 105-114.

Downs, J. (1969). Fables, fancies, and failures in cross-cultural training [Special issue]. *Trends, 7*(3).

Dunbar, E., & Ehrlich, M. (1986). *International human resource practices: Selecting, training, and managing the international staff.* New York: Columbia University Teachers College.

Forsberg, M. (1993, May). Cultural training improves relations with Asian clients. *Personnel Journal, 72,* 79-85.

Fulkerson, J. R., & Schuler, R. S. (1992). Managing worldwide diversity at Pepsi-Cola International. In S. E. Jackson & Associates, *Diversity in the workplace: Human resources initiatives* (pp. 248-276). New York: Guilford.

Gao, G., & Gudykunst, W. B. (1990). Uncertainty, anxiety, and adaptation. *International Journal of Intercultural Relations, 14,* 301-317.

Gochenour, T. (1977a). The albatross. In D. Batchelder & E. Warner (Eds.), *Beyond experience* (pp. 125-129). Brattleboro, VT: Experiment in International Living.

Gochenour, T. (1977b). The owl. In D. Batchelder & E. Warner (Eds.), *Beyond experience* (pp. 131-136). Brattleboro, VT: Experiment in International Living.

Gudykunst, W. B. (Ed.). (1983). *Intercultural communication theory.* Beverly Hills, CA: Sage.

Gudykunst, W. B. (1988). Uncertainty and anxiety. In Y. Y. Kim & W. B. Gudykunst (Eds.), *Theories in intercultural communication* (pp. 123-156). Newbury Park, CA: Sage.

Gudykunst, W. B. (1993). Toward a theory of interpersonal and intergroup communication: An anxiety/uncertainty management (AUM) perspective. In R. Wiseman & J. Koester (Eds.), *Intercultural communication competence* (pp. 33-71). Newbury Park, CA: Sage.

Gudykunst, W. B. (1994). *Bridging differences: Effective intergroup communication* (2nd ed.). Thousand Oaks, CA: Sage.

Gudykunst, W. B. (1995). Anxiety/uncertainty management (AUM) theory: Current status. In R. Wiseman (Ed.), *Intercultural communication theory* (pp. 1-58). Thousand Oaks, CA: Sage.

Gudykunst, W. B., & Hammer, M. R. (1983). Basic training design. In D. Landis & R. Brislin (Eds.), *Handbook of intercultural training* (Vol. 1, pp. 118-154). Elmsford, NY: Pergamon.

Gudykunst, W. B., & Hammer, M. R. (1988). Strangers and hosts. In Y. Y. Kim & W. B. Gudykunst (Eds.), *Cross-cultural adaptation* (pp. 106-139). Newbury Park, CA: Sage.

Gudykunst, W. B., & Sudweeks, S. (1992). Applying a theory of intercultural adaptation. In W. B. Gudykunst & Y. Y. Kim (Eds.), *Reading on communicating with strangers* (pp. 358-368). New York: McGraw-Hill.

Hall, P. H., & Gudykunst, W. B. (1989). The relationship of perceived ethnocentrism in corporate cultures to the selection, training, and success of international employees. *International Journal of Intercultural Relations, 13,* 183-201.

Hammer, M. R., & Martin, J. N. (1992). The effects of cross-cultural training on American managers in a Japanese-American joint venture. *Journal of Applied Communication Research, 20,* 161-182.

Hammer, M. R., Wiseman, R., Rasmussen, J., & Bruschke, J. (1992, November). *A comprehensive test of uncertainty/anxiety reduction theory: The intercultural adaptation context.* Paper presented at the Speech Communication Association Convention, Chicago.

Harrison, R., & Hopkins, R. (1967). The design of cross-cultural training. *Journal of Applied Behavioral Science, 3,* 431-460.

Hofstede, G. (1980). *Culture's consequences.* Beverly Hills, CA: Sage.

Hofstede, G. (1991). *Cultures and organizations: Software of the mind.* New York: McGraw-Hill.

Hoopes, D., & Ventura, P. (Eds.). (1979). *Intercultural sourcebook: Cross-cultural training methodologies.* Washington, DC: Society for Intercultural Education, Training, and Research.

Hoppe, A., Michalis, D., & Reinking, T. (1995). Alpha-omega negotiation. In S. Sudweeks & R. Guzley, *Instructors' resource manual for building bridges* (pp. 77-83). Boston: Houghton Mifflin.

Jackson, S. E., & Associates (1992). *Diversity in the workplace: Human resources initiatives.* New York: Guilford.

Kim, Y. Y., & Gudykunst, W. B. (Eds.). (1988a). *Cross-cultural adaptation.* Newbury Park, CA: Sage.

Kim, Y. Y., & Gudykunst, W. B. (Eds.). (1988b). *Theories in intercultural communication.* Newbury Park, CA: Sage.

Kohls, R. (1979). Conceptual model for area studies. In D. Hoopes & P. Ventura (Eds.), *Intercultural sourcebook.* Washington, DC: Society for Intercultural Education, Training, and Research.

Laabs, J. J. (1993, September). Diversity training is a business strategy. *Personnel Journal, 72,* 25-28.

Landis, D., & Brislin, R. W. (Eds.). (1983). *Handbook of intercultural training* (Vol. 2). Elmsford, NY: Pergamon.

Langer, E. (1989). *Mindfulness.* Reading, MA: Addison-Wesley.

Murdock, G. (1971). *The outline of cultural materials* (4th ed.). New Haven, CT: Human Relations Area Files.

Murdock, G. (1972). *The outline of world cultures* (4th ed.). New Haven, CT: Human Relations Area Files.

Nadler, L. (1970). *Developing human resources.* Houston: Gulf.

Nipporica Associates. (1993). *Ecotonos.* Yarmouth, ME: Intercultural Press.

Pruegger, V. J., & Rogers, T. B. (1994). Cross-cultural sensitivity training: Methods and assessment. *International Journal of Intercultural Relations, 18,* 369-387.

Salyer, M. (1993). Educators and cultural diversity: A six-stage model of cultural versatility. *Education, 113,* 503-508.

Sessa, V. I. (1992). Managing diversity at the Xerox Corporation: Balanced workforce goals and caucus groups. In S. E. Jackson & Associates, *Diversity in the workplace: Human resources initiatives* (pp. 37-64). New York: Guilford.

Shirts, G. (1973). *BAFA BAFA: A cross-cultural simulation.* Delmar, CA: Simile II.

Stewart, E. (1966). The simulation of cultural differences. *Journal of Communication, 16,* 291-304.

Stewart, E., Danielian, J., & Foster, R. *Simulating intercultural communication through role playing* (Technical Report 69-3). Washington, DC: Human Resource Research Organization.

Sue, D. W. (1991). A model for cultural diversity training. *Journal of Counseling and Development, 70,* 99-105.

Thiagarajan, S., & Steinwachs, B. (1990). *Barnga.* Yarmouth, ME: Intercultural Press.

Triandis, H. C. (1977). Theoretical framework for evaluation of cross-cultural training effectiveness. *International Journal of Intercultural Relations, 1,* 19-46.

Triandis, H. C. (1983). Essentials of studying culture. In D. Landis & R. Brislin (Eds.), *Handbook of intercultural training* (Vol. 1, pp. 82-117). Elmsford, NY: Pergamon.

Triandis, H. C. (1984). A theoretical framework for the more efficient construction of cultural assimilators. *International Journal of Intercultural Relations, 8,* 301-330.

Triandis, H. C., Brislin, R. W., & Hui, H. (1988). Cross-cultural training across the individualism-collectivism divide. *International Journal of Intercultural Relations, 12,* 269-289.

Tung, R. I. (1981). Selection and training of personnel for overseas assignment. *Columbia Journal of World Business, 16,* 68-71.

Waler, B. A., & Hanson, W. C. (1992). Valuing differences at Digital Equipment Corporation. In S. E. Jackson & Associates, *Diversity in the workplace: Human resources initiatives* (pp. 119-137). New York: Guilford.

Weeks, W., Pedersen, P., & Brislin, R. (1975). *A manual of structured experiences for cross-cultural learning.* Washington, DC: Society for Intercultural Education, Training, and Research.

Wiseman, R. (Ed.). (1995). *Intercultural communication theory.* Thousand Oaks, CA: Sage.

5

The Challenge of
International Personnel Selection

DANIEL J. KEALEY

IN the 1960s, the founding of the Peace Corps in the United States sparked an interest in developing methods that would help in identifying those volunteers who would succeed on their assignment and in screening out those individuals who would likely fail on the overseas assignment. The Peace Corps initiative spawned a substantial amount of research on international selection. In 1983, Kealey and Ruben reviewed the literature on international selection and concluded that the evidence supported a general set of criteria to be associated with success in another culture.

But knowing the criteria for success in another culture does not necessarily mean being able to accurately assess people on those criteria. Ever larger numbers of individuals are working in foreign countries in business, the military, government service, and the development field. The purposes for sending people overseas vary greatly, depending on the sponsoring organization. Not surprisingly, how cross-cultural success is defined and measured can also vary substantially, depending on the type of international sojourn in question.

Table 5.1 provides a taxonomy of selection situations by type of sojourner, role to be performed in the new environment, and skills required for effectiveness on the assignment. As can be inferred from the table, although the roles of international personnel do differ enormously, the skills required for being effective in any of those roles are similar in nature. For example, skills in understanding local culture, respecting local people, and tolerating cultural differences are important for success for all 12 types of sojourners. Other skills, such as learning the local language and collaborating with host nationals, will differ in importance, depending on the type of sojourn in question. Accordingly, one challenge in international personnel assessment is learning how to assess the environmental context and specific job demands in order to identify and prioritize the

TABLE 5.1 A Taxonomy of International Personnel Selection Situations

Types of Sojourners: People who move to another culture on a temporary basis

	Development Workers		Business Personnel		Government Officers		Foreign Students		Military Personnel		Other	
Purpose of Sojourn	*Voluntary*	*Government*	*Joint Venture*	*Subsidiary*	*Diplomats*	*Multilateral*	*Academic*	*Applied*	*Defense*	*Peace Keepers*	*Media*	*Missionaries*
Transfer skills and knowledge	✓	✓										
Establish business for profit			✓	✓								
Represent interests of one's country or organization					✓	✓						
Obtain degree or professional experience							✓	✓				
Keep the peace/Monitor									✓	✓		
Gather news/Assess information											✓	
Convert/Care for local people												✓
Skills Required for Effectiveness												
Understand local culture	✓	✓	✓	✓	✓	✓	✓	✓	✓	✓	✓	✓
Respect local people	✓	✓	✓	✓	✓	✓	✓	✓	✓	✓	✓	✓
Tolerate differences	✓	✓	✓	✓	✓	✓	✓	✓	✓	✓	✓	✓
Adapt one's own method	✓		✓	✓			✓				✓	
Collaborate with colleagues	✓											
Learn local language	✓					✓	✓	✓				✓
Socialize with local people	✓											

skills required for success. More on this subject later.

Given the increasing numbers and variety of personnel living and working outside their own cultures, concerns are being expressed about the effectiveness of these people on their assignments and their capacity to adjust to different living and working conditions. Problems associated with the sending of expatriates are well documented and include the following:

- Only about 20% of international development workers perform highly effectively overseas (Kealey, 1990).
- Although many technical cooperation personnel do achieve operational goals, they seldom succeed in preparing local staff to take over, with the result that "many aid projects have a negative impact on institutional development" (Forss, Carlesen, Froyland, Sitari, & Vilby, 1988, p. 28).
- A board of inquiry into the death of a Somali civilian in the custody of Canadian peacekeeping troops pointed out that "the Somali way of doing things" proved difficult for the Canadians to understand and accept (Canada, Department of National Defense, 1993). The need for intercultural skills on the part of UN peacekeepers is now evident because they are the fastest-growing expatriate category—in 1994, numbering about 70,000, from 70 providing countries and serving in 17 host countries ("Shamed Are the Peacekeepers," 1994).
- Failure rates, as measured by early returns, are about 15% to 40% for American busi-

ness personnel, and of those who stay, less than 50% perform adequately (Baker & Ivancevich, 1971; Copeland & Griggs, 1985).
- Although most international workers are considered technically competent, they lack the cross-cultural skills needed for effective performance (Gertsen, 1990).
- Poor adaptation of the spouse and family is often cited as a main reason for early return (Kealey, 1990; Stephens & Black, 1991).
- It is estimated that U.S. firms alone lose $2 billion per year in direct costs because of premature returns. Early return rates are highest for assignments in developing countries (Nauman, 1992).

Part of the problem lies in the fact that most organizations continue to base their selection decisions primarily on technical competence and experience and ignore the nontechnical skills and knowledge required for success in another culture. But this may be changing as the pressures of globalization force companies and organizations to recruit managers who can operate effectively in different cultures.

The purpose of this chapter is threefold. Part 1 essentially updates the state of knowledge with respect to selection criteria and the challenge of defining and measuring cross-cultural success. Part 2 focuses on some critical issues of theory and practice. Part 3 looks at the future challenge of establishing an effective methodology for international personnel selection.

PART 1:
CURRENT STATE OF KNOWLEDGE

The Search for
Predictors of Overseas Success

There appear to be individuals marked by a strikingly effective capacity for cross-cultural communication, regardless of circumstances; and there are other individuals who are marked by an equally striking incapacity for cross-cultural communication, regardless

of circumstances. . . . [T]he development of methods to identify such "universal communicators" would seem to open up some urgent and challenging perspectives for cross-cultural social research. (Gardner, 1962, p. 248)

In 1983, Kealey and Ruben reviewed the literature on identifying reliable criteria associated with overseas success. The largest number of published empirical studies of overseas adjustment and selection dealt with Peace Corps volunteers (PCVs), but significant research on personnel in international business, technical cooperation, and the military was also found. Additionally, they found an abundance of related research studying different groups participating in intercultural exchanges. Kealey and Ruben concluded that, contrary to popular opinion, there was a substantial consensus on the nontechnical criteria required for success in another culture. There was empirical support for the importance of at least six criteria across all groups studied: *empathy, respect, interest in local culture, flexibility, tolerance,* and *technical skill.* In addition, four other criteria—*initiative, open-mindedness, sociability,* and *positive self-image*—were identified as relevant for three of the four groups. Accordingly, the case was made that the research supported the existence of a "cross-cultural" or an "overseas type" (see Kealey & Ruben, 1983, for detailed discussion).

Three main characteristics appear to best describe the overall findings in the literature since 1983. First, the research continues to replicate previous findings and thus confirms the validity of a set of general traits and skills needed to be successful in another culture. Personal characteristics, such as motivation, communication, flexibility, empathy, respect, tolerance for ambiguity, and self-confidence, continue to be empirically validated for their importance in enhancing cross-cultural success (see Gersten, 1990; Hannigan, 1990; Searle & Ward, 1990; Van den Broucke, De Soete, & Bohrer, 1989; Ward & Kennedy, 1992). Second, the literature also looks at a broader range of criteria to determine their potential relevance to cross-cultural success. For example, several articles published in the *International Journal of Intercultural Relations* (*IJIR*) examine variables such as work role clarity (Black & Gregersen, 1990), cultural identity and cultural knowledge (Ward & Searle, 1991), attributional complexity (Stephan & Stephan, 1992), life changes and proneness to depression (Searle & Ward, 1990), and collectivism/individualism (Bhawuk & Brislin, 1992). These studies go beyond the more traditional exploration of personality-related variables to look at factors associated with success that are perhaps more amenable to modification through cross-cultural training programs or better project planning. Certainly,

such factors as work role clarity and cultural knowledge (both of which were found to be associated with higher levels of personal and professional satisfaction overseas) can be more easily addressed and controlled for than modifying or assessing characteristics, such as an individual's flexibility or capacity for relationship building. Third, the research focuses substantially on foreign students and international business personnel.

Focus on Foreign Students and International Business Personnel

With respect to the study of sojourner groups, of nine *IJIR* studies dealing specifically with predictors of cross-cultural success, seven dealt with the adaptation of foreign students. For example, Searle and Ward (1990; Ward & Searle, 1991) have been active establishing a research program aimed at constructing and testing predictive models of psychological and sociocultural adjustment. Their research, focused on a study of foreign students studying in New Zealand, has begun to identify both personal and situational factors associated with successful adaptation. Hannigan (1990) reviewed the literature on international students (and PCVs) and identified three broad categories of criteria associated with cross-cultural success/failure: skills, attitudes, and personality characteristics. Other studies on foreign students (Bhawuk & Brislin, 1992; Stephan & Stephan, 1992; Van den Broucke et al., 1989) have looked at a combination of traditional variables of study, such as ethnocentrism and extroversion, with new ones, such as neuroticism, conscientiousness, and creativity. Although conducting studies of foreign students is easy, given their accessibility, evidence (see Tanaka, Takai, Kohyama, & Fujihara, 1994) suggests that international foreign student exchange is increasing at a rapid rate and may well be driving the interest in researching predictors of foreign student success. Until recently, research on foreign students has generally tended to explore their adaptation patterns and coping strategies.

The argument can be made, however, that the field of international business and management is fast becoming the real driving force in research on cross-cultural selection. Although much of this research is anecdotal in nature, tending to survey the opinions of international managers on selection criteria and related issues (see Brandt, 1991; Fuchsberg, 1992; Geber, 1992; Howard, 1992; Tung, 1981, 1988), some empirical investigations are aimed at building predictive models of intercultural effectiveness. The work of Black (1988), Black and Gregersen (1990, 1991), and Black, Mendenhall, and Oddou (1991) is most noteworthy in this regard. Globalization is leading more and more companies to become international in order to remain competitive. International joint venturing is becoming commonplace. But, as noted earlier, the substantial failure rates of international business personnel is sounding an alarm bell for corporate management. The failure rate for companies undertaking international joint ventures is estimated at 50% to 80% (Blake, 1992; Nauman, 1992). No doubt in response to these difficulties, a substantial literature on global managers is evolving that overwhelmingly concludes, "The intercultural abilities of managers on overseas assignments are increasingly important to bottom-line performance of multinational businesses. . . . Cross-cultural difficulties can result in increased organizational costs and even premature return home" (Stening & Hammer, 1992, p. 79). The intercultural abilities being identified reveal no surprises: Characteristics such as flexibility, tolerance, diplomacy, adaptability, and language continue to be validated for their relevance in enhancing overseas success. What is troublesome in the business world, however, is the conclusion that interculturally competent personnel remain in short supply.

Research on International Development Workers

Although research on identifying criteria associated with successful performance on an international development posting has dwindled since the 1960s and 1970s, Kealey (1988, 1989, 1990, 1994a) has continued to focus much of his research on this sojourner group. Results of a major international study, begun in 1992, on overseas screening and selection have recently been published by the Canadian International Development Agency (see Kealey, 1994b). Fifteen countries, the World Bank, and the United Nations Development Program participated in this study aimed at identifying current trends, problems, and solutions for making technical assistance advisers more effective on their development assignments. Results confirmed that the need to identify selection criteria and methods for overseas personnel assessment was a major priority for most international development agencies. In identifying the criteria these development agencies employ in screening candidates for international assignments, complete consensus was found on the importance of 12 criteria for development success: tolerance, respect, interest in local culture, flexibility, communication skills, patience, listening ability, empathy, cross-cultural sensitivity, commitment, realistic expectations, and technical competence (see Kealey, 1994b, for more details).

Profile of the Model Cross-Cultural Collaborator

With a view to summarizing the current state of knowledge on identifying what it takes to be successful working in another culture, the profile of skills listed in Table 5.2 can be said to represent the core nontechnical requirements for the screening and selection of international personnel. All of the identified skills have been researched empirically to determine their relevance to explaining and predicting success in another culture. Three major categories of personal or nontechnical skills are required for effective collaboration across cultures: *adaptation skills, cross-cultural skills,* and *partnership skills.*

In terms of theoretical underpinnings, the three categories of skills relate directly to the three major challenges to be encountered when undertaking an international assignment. First, it is essential to be able to deal calmly and competently with the emotional upheaval inevitably experienced by oneself and one's family in making the transition to a new country. Although the severity of transition stress is usually much less for experienced internationalists and single people, compared with "first timers" and families, a significant degree of frustration is experienced by all, and adaptation skills are therefore needed to become personally well adjusted in the new culture. If one fails to become personally adjusted, it is virtually impossible to be professionally effective. Second, the overseas challenge involves the need to understand

TABLE 5.2 A Profile of the Model Cross-Cultural Collaborator

Adaptation Skills	*Cross-Cultural Skills*	*Partnership Skills*
• Positive attitudes	• Realism	• Openness to others
• Flexibility	• Tolerance	• Professional commitment
• Stress tolerance	• Involvement in culture	• Perseverance
• Patience	• Political astuteness	• Initiative
• Marital/Family stability	• Cultural sensitivity	• Relationship building
• Emotional maturity		• Self-confidence
• Inner security		• Problem-solving

ADAPTATION SKILLS:

This set of skills is related to one's ability to cope personally, maritally, and as a family with the overall living and working conditions overseas. Adaptation skills enable people to develop a sense of well-being, of comfort, and of feeling "at home" in the host culture. Overseas assignments are frequently difficult and full of the unexpected (both personally and professionally). Being able to react appropriately is an advantage in the adjustment process.

Positive Attitudes: One of the best predictors of professional effectiveness overseas is positive attitudes on the part of the expatriate. Feelings of being positive, excited, strong, and determined about undertaking the collaborative venture are indicators of potential to succeed. Ambivalence and concern about undertaking the assignment are negative indicators.

Flexibility: This is the ability to modify ideas and behavior, to compromise, and to be receptive to new ways of doing things. It is important to avoid being rigid and judgmental; these attitudes will lead to rejection on the part of host colleagues.

Stress Tolerance: Making a transition to a new culture, a new home, and a new job is a stressful undertaking for most people. Being able to cope with and overcome transition stress is important both on a personal and a family basis.

Patience: This is the ability to be calm and steadfast despite opposition, difficulties, or adversity. Establishing effective working relationships takes time and often involves substantial frustration. Learning to be patient is critical for success.

Marital/Family Stability: An overseas assignment affects the whole family. A dissatisfied or poorly adjusted family is detrimental to the advisor's professional output and is sometimes destructive to the family relationship. The bond and communication between husband and wife must be strong, and the couple should demonstrate a sense of partnership with respect to the posting. Adolescent children should demonstrate willingness and, ideally, excitement about the undertaking.

Emotional Maturity: This means one is emotionally and interpersonally well balanced. Psychopathological tendencies, such as drug addiction, psychotic reactions, and schizoid behavior, are absent.

Inner Security: This is the ability to be comfortable with and accepting of oneself. One is not excessively concerned about advancement and economic gain in one's personal and professional life. The need to be acknowledged or rewarded is minimal. Ability to deal with the new environment without excessive worry about one's personal and professional security is evident.

CROSS-CULTURAL SKILLS:

These are the particular skills needed to enable one to participate in the local culture and to find culturally appropriate ways of living and working within the host culture. These skills have been acknowledged as important by many international organizations, as well as by expatriate personnel and national colleagues.

Realism: It is important to be as realistic as possible about the way of life overseas and the living and working conditions that one will confront. Awareness of the constraints that will challenge one's professional capacity and how to overcome these obstacles is an important skill.

Tolerance: It is important to be accepting of the way of life overseas and the living and working conditions that one confronts. Such acceptance demands a capacity to live with the unknown and to work in situations of ambiguity. This is difficult for people who need control. Being content to live with differences and avoiding judging the host culture against the values of one's home culture are important components of tolerance.

TABLE 5.2 (Continued)

Involvement in Culture:	Being intrigued about different cultures and wanting to learn about them is associated with effective collaboration across cultures. On a cross-cultural posting, this interest usually leads to a sincere desire to get to know the country, its people, and its traditions. Having local people as friends and learning some of the local language help prepare the ground for effective working relationships. Research confirms that showing an interest in and making an effort to speak the local language particularly serve to promote goodwill and acceptance.
Political Astuteness:	The ability to assess relations between people within and between institutions, as well as the ability to develop strategies for organizational change and individual learning that will not threaten local officials but rather will gain their support, is essential for many international workers. One must be able to accurately perceive others, especially in social situations and across cultures.
Cultural Sensitivity:	This is the important ability to recognize differences and similarities between cultures and to understand how social and cultural realities affect the professional attitudes and practices of individuals and organizations.

PARTNERSHIP SKILLS:

This set of skills focuses primarily on the professional demands of the assignment and the need to establish effective working relationships with national colleagues and partners. In the past, expatriate personnel worked within an apprenticeship model where they were the experts and the nationals were the apprentices. These relationships were often characterized by substantial distance, minimal understanding, and limited trust between the foreign expert and the national colleague. Establishing an effective partnership relationship requires closeness, understanding, and trust between the parties. The challenge is to learn to work as colleagues so that both learn from each other and support each other in ways conducive to effective skills acquisition. This takes considerable energy, conviction, and skills on the part of both parties. What follows is a description of the core skills needed for partnership building. They are a mix of personal skills and qualities, as well as interpersonal and relational abilities.

Openness to Others:	This is the ability to question oneself and to become genuinely open to the behavior and ideas of others. It entails an effort to understand the attitudes, perceptions, and values of others in a cultural context and a willingness to consider views that conflict with one's own. A component of this skill is respect and empathy for other people. Showing *respect* is to respond to others in a way that helps them feel valued and that demonstrates concern about their needs and feelings. *Empathy* is the capacity to put oneself in another person's shoes, important for both partners because there will be many cases of differing priorities and interests between them.
Professional Commitment:	International assignments are both demanding and stressful. To succeed requires a substantial belief in the overseas mission, strong commitment to one's profession, and a determination to contribute to the development process.
Perseverance:	This means persisting in an undertaking despite counterinfluences, opposition, or discouragement. It is tenacity. When confronted with obstacles, one looks for ways to overcome the barriers.
Initiative:	This is the capacity to originate action, to get things started, and to keep them going. An effective international advisor does not need to be told what to do or react passively to the directions or desires of others.
Relationship Building:	This is the ability to build and maintain effective professional and personal relationships with people. It requires a belief in the importance of people, an ability to listen, and an overall capacity to be trusting, friendly, cooperative, and socially outgoing. This skill is critical for effective collaboration across cultures. It is an ability to lead people, to bring them together in a way that all feel part of something they believe in and are committed to working toward goals together.
Self-Confidence:	This is the ability to affirm oneself in the presence of others. It is faith in oneself and one's abilities to act with minimal supervision or direction. One realistically trusts and acts on one's own talents.
Problem-Solving:	This is the ability to analyze a situation, identify the key issues, and recommend and implement actions to resolve crises or to achieve project goals.

the new environment: the culture, the people, day-to-day customs and practices. This requires possession of a set of cross-cultural skills that enable an individual to become an effective communicator in the host country. Third, the overseas challenge involves learning how to perform in a new setting where the "rules of the game" are unknown and where the professional roles and responsibilities are more complicated and demanding than in one's own culture (see Kealey & Protheroe, 1995). Whether in international business, or providing development

assistance, or being a missionary, the demand overseas is for a professional collaboration with colleagues that, on the one hand, is vastly more difficult (because of the differences in culture and professional standards and practices) and that, on the other hand, is even more critical for success than what might be required in one's own culture. Accordingly, the set of partnership skills that make up the final component of the model of cross-cultural collaborator is essential for establishing effective collaboration with one's colleagues in the host country.

SUMMARY

1. The state of knowledge with respect to the question What does it take to be successful in another culture? was already substantial in 1983 (see Kealey & Ruben, 1983). Now, it is even more extensive. Studies have replicated previous findings, thus continuing to confirm the evidence for an "overseas type." Other studies have expanded knowledge by identifying new criteria associated with overseas success.

2. The profile of the effective cross-cultural collaborator was presented as a summary or résumé of the core criteria needed to live and work effectively in another culture. This profile goes beyond the identification of personality characteristics (not easily amenable to change) to identify a broader range of cross-cultural skills and knowledge (more amenable to change through training and education programs).

3. Despite the increasing consensus on identifying the skills needed for achieving success cross-culturally, this knowledge can only serve to guide the overseas screening and selection process. That is to say, the general profile of skills and knowledge must be weighted or prioritized according to the particular demands of the position, the country, the host institution, the duration of the assignment, and so forth. Accordingly, there is no substitute for excellence in undertaking job analysis, institutional analysis, and culture analysis; these situational variables

profoundly influence the cross-cultural selection task.

4. Although research investigations are increasing sample sizes, as well as the variables of study, there is still a lack of longitudinal studies that better enable researchers to draw conclusions about the predictive power of the variables being studied. Most studies continue to rely on a concurrent design methodology. Finally, although the research continues to be generally atheoretical, models attempting to link predictors and criterion are being developed. This effort is discussed at more length in the next part of this chapter.

Defining and Measuring Cross-Cultural Success

Establishing a method to predict overseas success of a particular population requires a profound examination of the cross-cultural situation involved and of the criteria used for determining success and failure of the experiences. (Van den Broucke et al., 1989, p. 79)

Defining and measuring cross-cultural success remain a critical part of the recipe for effective cross-cultural personnel selection. In 1983, Kealey and Ruben referred to Tucker's (1974) review of the literature on screening and selection that identified the "criterion problem" as a major impediment to the development of a predictive knowledge base on selection. The point was simply that success overseas had never been adequately described or measured. The review of literature by Benson (1978) and the research by Ruben and Kealey (1979) and Hawes and Kealey (1981) began to address this problem and resulted in the need to conceive of adaptation in other than unidimensional terms. In their field study of Canadian advisers posted to six countries, Hawes and Kealey derived an empirically based definition and description of the concept of overseas effectiveness. *Overseas effectiveness* is the capacity to live and work effectively on an international assignment. To be effective overseas is to be personally and family adjusted, professionally competent, and interculturally active. *Personal and family adjustment* means being happy and satisfied with life and conditions in the host country; *professional competence* is the capacity to demonstrate technical skill in a culturally appropriate manner; and *intercultural interaction* refers to being socially involved with nationals and demonstrating interest in and knowledge of the host culture.

This view of overseas effectiveness as constituting three main components—personal/ family adjustment, professional competence, and intercultural interaction—has been generally confirmed by many studies of cross-cultural adaptation and effectiveness undertaken in the 1980s and 1990s. For example, the research by Black and colleagues (see Black, 1988; Black & Gregersen, 1991) conducting studies of international business has determined that adjustment abroad consists of three conceptually distinct factors: general living adjustment, work adjustment, and interaction adjustment. Other researchers limit their study of cross-cultural adjustment to two components. For example, Searle and Ward (1990) and Ward and Searle (1991) distinguish between *psychological adjustment* (feelings of well-being) and *sociocultural adjustment* (the ability to interact or "fit in" the local culture). Given that their research is based primarily on studies of foreign students, the need to include the component of professional competence may not be seen as relevant for this population. Exploratory research undertaken by Hammer, Gudykunst, and Wiseman in 1978 spawned substantial follow-up research and debate on the culture-specific versus culture-general nature of intercultural effectiveness.

Gudykunst and Hammer (1984) argue very strongly that their three dimensions of intercul-

tural effectiveness identified in 1978 apply to all intercultural transitions. The ability to deal with psychological stress, the ability to communicate effectively, and the ability to establish interpersonal relationships remain "consistent with previous research and current conceptualizations of intercultural effectiveness" (Gudykunst & Hammer, 1984, p. 8).

What is perhaps most encouraging about recent research on intercultural effectiveness is not just the replication of previous findings but also the development of new theoretical models to explain intercultural adjustment and effectiveness. Accordingly, Church's conclusion in 1982 that "there has been a minimal attempt to apply theoretical concepts in the socio-psychological literature to the dynamics of sojourner adjustment" (Church, 1982, p. 363) is no longer valid for the intercultural field. The work of Grove and Torbiorn (1985), Anderson (1994), Searle and Ward (1990), and Bhawuk and Brislin (1992) is illustrative in this regard. For example, the research by Grove and Torbiorn presents a model that explains adjustment as a function of three psychological constructs: applicability of behavior, clarity of mental frame, and level of mere adequacy. Although this work deals primarily with only one aspect of overseas success—personal adjustment—it does attempt to develop a more profound understanding of this process and highlights the role of cross-cultural training in reducing the distress in international transistors. Along similar lines, but much more comprehensive in identifying the multiplicity of factors influencing cross-cultural adaptation, is Anderson's (1994) model based on socio-psychological adjustment theory. She argues strongly that cross-cultural adaptations "represent in essence a common process of environmental adaptation" (p. 293).

Gudykunst and Hammer (1988) have developed a communication-based theory to explain intercultural adaptation. They postulate that the combined reduction of uncertainty and anxiety are "necessary and sufficient conditions for intercultural adaptation" (p. 302) and that success in this regard is a function of eight variables: (a) knowledge of the host culture, (b) shared networks, (c) intergroup attitudes, (d) favorable contact, (e) stereotypes, (f) cultural identity, (g) cultural similarity, and (h) second-language competence. Although their theory remains to be fully tested, data from a study in

1990 (Gao & Gudykunst, 1990) did offer partial support for their hypotheses. Parker and McEvoy (1993) also present an intriguing model of expatriate adjustment based on Black's (1988) three-component model of intercultural adjustment. They go much beyond this previous research to build a model based on "three major categories of factors influencing the degree of intercultural adjustment: individual, organizational, and contextual" (p. 357). To test their model, they also present data from 169 adults working in 12 countries and conclude that adjustment overseas is influenced by controllable factors, such as expatriate selection and management practices, but also by uncontrollable factors, such as the degree of culture novelty. Finally, Gertsen (1990) also reviewed literature on intercultural competence to derive "a more precise formulation of the concept" (p. 341). She concludes there are three main interdependent dimensions of intercultural competence: an affective dimension (appropriate personality and attitudes), a cognitive dimension (knowledge of culture), and a behavioral communicative dimension (e.g., ability to listen, display respect).

Cross-Cultural Success:
Culture General or Culture Specific?

The recent research models of intercultural adjustment, some of which are discussed above, assume that this process is generalizable across people and across situations. Nevertheless, substantial debate remains on this issue in the intercultural field. It is not easy to generalize findings from one study or situation to the next when the type of personnel, country of assignment, nature of the sojourn, length of stay, and so on vary so greatly from one circumstance to the next. Benson (1978) concluded that the quest for a general definition of overseas adjustment was futile because "there are as many kinds of overseas adaptation as there are cross-cultural situations" (p. 32). Perhaps it is most reasonable to conclude both culture-specific and culture-general aspects are applicable to any definition of cross-cultural success. Indeed, it will always remain a challenge for any organization that sends people overseas to define clearly and concretely their expectations in terms of success on the assignment.

With this in mind, Kealey (1994a) undertook an extensive study of the adaptation and effectiveness of Canadian technical advisers posted to Egypt. One chief aim of the research was to define and describe concretely the overseas behavior of successful Canadian advisers in Egypt. Highly effective technical advisers were identified through performance ratings obtained from Canadian supervisors and colleagues, as well as from Egyptian supervisors and colleagues. This group was then interviewed and observed on the job to determine precisely what characteristics and what behavior overseas made them different from advisers who were rated poorly in terms of performance. Results established five major outcomes demonstrated by successful advisers in Egypt that can be said to constitute a description of the expected type of cross-cultural success for personnel posted to Egypt by the Canadian International Development Agency.

The argument can be made that these behavioral outcomes (see Table 5.3) are likely valid for all long-term technical advisers working on an international development posting. But they would not be fully applicable to short-term advisers, nor would they all apply to other sojourner groups, such as foreign students and international business personnel.

SUMMARY

1. The "criterion problem" identified by Tucker in 1974 was being addressed by interculturalists in 1983. Research during the past several years has continued to develop the knowledge base in this regard.
2. The intercultural field no longer suffers from a so-called criterion problem. The components of overseas effectiveness identified by Hawes and Kealey (1981) and Hammer et al. (1978) continue to be confirmed in research investigations. Most researchers agree on three major components required for intercultural effectiveness: personal and family adjustment,

TABLE 5.3 Indicators of Cross-Cultural Success: What Successful Advisors Do in Egypt

1. Personal Satisfaction

Successful advisors express enjoyment and satisfaction in living and working in Egypt (although they may initially experience difficulty or stress in adjusting to Egypt). The indicators of successful personal adjustment include the following:

- Engaging in enjoyable activities in Egypt
- Expressing satisfaction with overall living and working conditions in Egypt
- Avoiding any stereotyping of Egyptians
- No idealizing of Canada and judging Egypt against Canadian standards
- Expressing satisfaction as a family unit (for those posted with spouse and children)

2. Professional Satisfaction

Despite acknowledging frustrations with a different managerial and professional style in Egypt, successful advisors tend to express overall positive regard for their Egyptian counterparts and are challenged by both the technical and cultural realities they confront. They also report that they do not feel constrained by either personal or professional conditions within Egypt. Other indicators of professional satisfaction include the following:

- Believing that one's technical expertise is useful to Egypt
- Understanding Egyptian technical conditions and Egyptian ways of operating in the specific technical area

3. Trust and Confidence

Ultimately, the advisors who are rated most effective in Egypt succeed in winning the confidence, trust, and respect of their Egyptian colleagues. One advisor recalled vividly the day his Egyptian counterpart, on his own initiative, came into his office to discuss ideas for improving project success. For the advisor, this was an indicator that he had finally been accepted by the Egyptians, and their level of comfort with him enabled them to initiate contact. Other indicators of having succeeded in winning the trust and respect of Egyptians include the following:

- Regular interaction with Egyptians socially on and off the job
- Expressing interest in and using some Arabic on and off the job
- Demonstrating factual knowledge about Egypt and the role of Islam
- Mutual personal self-disclosure and exchanging of greetings as friends in the Egyptian way

4. Transfer of Skills and Knowledge

Successful advisors express substantial commitment and try their best to teach and train Egyptian colleagues in their field of expertise. Success in this regard is often demonstrated by:

- The advisors reporting that they actually receive more from contact with Egyptian colleagues than being able to give to them
- Developing a strategy or plan on how they will try to transfer skills and knowledge and fighting the tendency "to take over" and become operational
- Never giving up on trying to help their Egyptian colleagues develop new skills and techniques

5. Sustainable Institutional Development

The advisors identified in this study as the most successful expressed a strong awareness of the need for development to encompass an institutional focus and be sustainable. The successful advisors expressed greater awareness of the more macrolevel factors affecting the potential success of their work. At times, they became discouraged about any Canadian projects having a sustainable impact, but their commitment to contributing to Egypt's development remained strong. Advisors concerned about sustainable development also tended to demonstrate the following:

- Substantial tolerance and openness toward Egyptian culture and conditions
- Strong desire to collaborate and connect with a broad spectrum of personnel in the host institution
- Readiness to get involved in activities beyond their specific job responsibilities
- Interest in learning about the experience of other aid projects in Egypt

professional competence, and intercultural interaction. Different authors may use different terms in reporting findings, but the consensus on these three components of intercultural effectiveness in the research community is now well established.

3. Despite the consensus on a three-component construct of intercultural effectiveness, the need to specify indicators for measuring individual success in achieving all components leads inevitably to generating more specific definitions of success that may only apply to certain cultures and/or certain types of sojourns. Kealey's (1994a) research on development advisers in Egypt illustrated this point. Accordingly, adopting the view that the concept of cross-cultural success is both culture specific and culture general is realistic, practical, and not at all contradictory.

4. The research on intercultural adjustment and effectiveness is also becoming more sophisticated (more probing) and is leading to the development of theoretical models that can be tested for their ability to predict and enhance the intercultural effectiveness of individuals and organizations. The work of Grove and Torbiorn (1985), Gudykunst and Hammer (1988), and Parker and McEvoy (1993) is illustrative in this regard. Through efforts such as these, knowledge of the dynamics of the process for achieving intercultural success is deepening.

5. By way of counterbalancing a generally positive review of knowledge of the components of intercultural effectiveness, two characteristics of intercultural research limit the overall success in establishing sound intercultural theory and practice. First, many researchers still tend to confuse or "mix up" a study of the criterion that predicts intercultural effectiveness with the study of the criterion itself: defining and measuring intercultural effectiveness. Perhaps the best example of this problem in the literature is the tendency to identify communication skills as both the predictor and measure of intercultural effectiveness. Second, and perhaps, in part, because of this problem of confusing predictor and criterion, there remains a dearth of solid empirical research that defines and describes concretely and comprehensively the outcome behavior demonstrated by successful intercultural personnel. Research studies still focus too much on general dynamics of adjustment and ignore the challenge of identifying and specifying successful behavior in another culture.

6. Overall, one can conclude that the knowledge of what constitutes effective performance in another culture is substantial, generalizable to many different groups and situations, and useful for guiding the recruitment and selection process. The growth of intercultural knowledge and expertise has been very encouraging since 1983, when the first edition of this handbook was published.

PART 2:
ISSUES IN THEORY AND PRACTICE

Concepts and theory remain underdeveloped in the sojourner adjustment literature. . . . Most of the concepts used constitute not so much theories, allowing generation and tests of predictive hypotheses, but rather post hoc descriptions of adjustment data already obtained." (Church, 1982, p. 562)

In Part 1, an attempt was made to review the status of knowledge on two issues: (a) What does it take to be effective in another culture? and (b) how can cross-cultural success be defined and measured? The case was made that the knowledge base on these two critical issues is now very substantial. Interculturalists now know a lot about the type of person who is successful in another culture and what this person actually does while on assignment in another culture. Despite success in building this useful knowledge base on cross-cultural selection, the research foundations remain atheoretical and limited in their empirical rigor. The fact that much of the research on cross-cultural selection is not theory driven should come as no surprise. Research in this field has generally been initiated by organizations involved in sending people overseas. Their agendas are usually very practical and of some urgency. They simply want to know how to select people who will adjust and be effective overseas because the costs of failure are substantial. Not only is the financial loss significant (estimates to maintain one family overseas for 1 year range from $150,000 to $250,000 U.S.), but also, for many, the damage to one's reputation as an effective international organization is even more bothersome.

Even though research on cross-cultural personnel selection has been driven primarily by practitioners, the need to explain, predict, and better control cross-cultural outcomes is leading gradually to the development and testing of theoretical models of intercultural adjustment and effectiveness. Some of this emerging research was reviewed briefly in Part 1. The aim of Part 2 is to focus specifically on three critical theoretical issues that confront the field of international personnel selection: (a) the role of personal versus situational factors in explaining cross-cultural success, (b) the development of a comprehensive model that links selection criteria (the predictors, or independent variables) with cross-cultural success (the criterion, or dependent variable) and that specifies the conditions that moderate the relationship, and (c) the validity of peer ratings versus self-ratings in assessing an individual's potential for personal and professional success in another culture.

The Role of Personal Versus Situational Variables in Explaining and Predicting Cross-Cultural Success

As Kealey and Ruben discussed in 1983, some researchers (Benson, 1978; David, 1972; Dinges, 1983; Guthrie, 1975; Stening, 1979) argue against the relevance of personality variables in predicting overseas success. They cite evidence to demonstrate that personality tests, psychological interview ratings, and the like have been, at best, inconsistent in their capacity to predict outcomes in another culture. They proceed in different ways to make the case that

overseas outcomes are more a function of the situation than of the individual. This position is perhaps best expressed by Stening (1979):

> In summary, though one traditionally held view is that personality is central to almost all problems of intercultural adjustment (e.g., Group for the Advancement of Psychiatry, 1958; Klineberg, 1964), current opinion is that personality is not very useful in predicting intercultural adjustment (e.g., David, 1972; Guthrie, 1975). The degree of adjustment achieved by the sojourner is likely to depend as much on such factors as the precise nature of his role and the particular environment in which he is placed as upon his personality. (p. 289)

Interestingly, Furnham and Bochner (1986), in their book on culture shock, argue that the "person versus situation" debate in social and personality psychology can be traced back to the inability of psychologists and psychiatrists to predict success in screening people for the Peace Corps in the United States. They refer to Mischel's (1973, 1984) admitting his own failure to predict success for PCVs in Africa as leading him to his reconceptualization of personality and behavior away from viewing behavior as trait determined to seeing it more as situation specific. But Guthrie and Zektick (1967) led the way in rejecting personality testing for overseas postings, arguing that, in unfamiliar cultural settings, situational variables are more critical than personality traits in influencing performance in the field. This idea led Guthrie and others (Furnham & Bochner, 1986) to emphasize training and social support as more important than selection for ensuring an effective adaptation to a foreign culture.

This issue of the role of personal versus situational factors is critical for international personnel selection. If the "situationist" position is accepted as valid, there is no need to worry about how to screen and select people for overseas positions. My opinion is that the situationist position is untenable and that any readiness to dismiss the need to look carefully at personality and attitudes for ensuring successful outcomes in another culture is unjustified and dangerous. Cross-cultural outcomes are a function of both personal and situational factors. Support for the fundamental role of personality and attitudes derives from the following:

- As presented in Part 1, the knowledge base on the personal criteria associated with overseas success is substantial and generalizable across groups and situations (see "Profile of the Model Cross-Cultural Collaborator" in Part 1).

- Those who dismiss personality fail to distinguish between the characteristics themselves and the measurement of these characteristics. Traditionally, personality test results based on self-report questionnaires have shown little predictive power, but behavior-based assessment methodologies and peer ratings are demonstrating some success in predicting overseas outcomes (see Kealey, 1989; Ruben & Kealey, 1979).

- Those who argue that behavior is situation specific and that creating the right environment and social supports will ensure successful intercultural outcomes forget or ignore the fact that situations are as much a function of persons as the person's behavior is a function of the situation (Bowers, 1973). This interactionist position was strongly supported by my longitudinal study of the performance of Canadian technical advisers posted to 20 developing countries (see Kealey, 1988, for details). Essentially, different people interpret the same situation differently. For example, when I recently interviewed three Canadian advisers in Egypt, I received three very different assessments of what it was like living and working in Egypt even though the work roles and living and working conditions of the three advisers were basically similar. How individuals perceive and react to other people and situations varies enormously. Indeed, any individual's assessment of another person or situation likely tells you as much or more about the individual than it does about the situation.

From the foregoing, it follows that the important challenge in selection is to predict how an individual will likely interpret, react to, and cope with the new environment overseas. Although the case can be made (see Arvey, Bhagat, & Salas, 1991) that there is an urgent need to research the influence of situational factors, such as political realities, economic conditions, and institutional constraints on individual success and failure, maintaining an interest in studying the relevance of personality and attitudes to predicting outcomes in a new culture remains important. This is not to say that the social skills training approach emphasized by Furham and Bochner (1986) is irrelevant to enhancing success overseas. It is to say, however, that unless an individual first possesses certain personal traits and interpersonal attitudes, no amount of training will ever enable that person to achieve a high level of cross-cultural success.

Models of Intercultural Adjustment and Effectiveness

In terms of theoretical challenges for the field of international personnel selection, the current need is to develop comprehensive models that attempt to demonstrate how personal and situational variables combine or interact to produce cross-cultural success. Such models must also include identifying the conditions or factors that moderate any established cause-effect relationships between predictors and the criterion of cross-cultural success. Development and testing of such comprehensive models are important for the field of cross-cultural personnel selection for several reasons. First, such models will provide a framework and direction for research that will lead to more consistent and more powerful findings. Second, on a more practical level, these models will help those involved in the recruitment, selection, and training of overseas personnel be aware of both the personal and situational requisites for overseas success. This awareness will be useful in enabling recruitment specialists to focus more on matching the strengths of the person with the demands of the job and the environment. Third, comprehensive models for explaining intercultural adjustment and effectiveness have the potential to inform the broader field of intercultural education and training aimed at enhancing overall cross-cultural understanding between groups and individuals, domestically and internationally.

What can be said about the status of such comprehensive models? Do such models exist?

Have they been tested? Have the research findings been replicated? Most of the models discussed previously either focus on only one aspect of cross-cultural success (e.g., Grove & Torbiorn's [1985] model focuses on the dynamics of personal adjustment) or tend to ignore the personal/attitudinal variables (e.g., Gudykunst & Hammers' [1988] theory of intercultural adaptation). The model of acculturative stress developed by Berry and Kim (1988), though only focused on the adjustment component of cross-cultural success, is comprehensive, especially in identifying the myriad of variables that moderate the relationship between acculturation and mental health. But more comprehensive models are being developed. Examples are those of Landis and Bhagat (Chapter 1, this volume), Parker and McEvoy (1993), Kealey (1988), and Nauman (1992). For some, postulating such models is futile, given the enormous number and variety of factors that influence adjustment and performance in another culture. With the advent of more sophisticated techniques for dealing with multivariate data, however, being able to identify cause-effect patterns between the predictors of overseas performance and the criterion is no longer a pipe dream.

Kealey's (1988) comprehensive model to explain and predict cross-cultural adjustment and effectiveness overseas was tested with Canadian advisers in a 3-year longitudinal study. An extensive array of variables (some 21 predictor variables, 14 outcome measures, and 3 situational variables) was investigated, and results provided some empirical support for a model of the dynamics of effective transfer (see Kealey, 1988, for details). The model established by Parker and McEvoy (1993) includes coverage of individual, organizational, and contextual factors, as well as a comprehensive description of adjustment and performance. They have begun to test parts of their model and have confirmed that "intercultural adjustment is affected by some controllable factors such as expatriate selection and management practices, but also by some uncontrollable factors such as culture novelty" (p. 355). Landis and Bhagat's model adopts a much more psychological perspective than that of Parker and McEvoy (1993), Black (1988), Black et al. (1991), and

Gudykunst and Hammer (1988) but remains to be tested.

The Issue of Self-Perception Versus Other Perception

The point has been made in this chapter that some researchers have mistakenly dismissed the relevance of personality characteristics for predicting outcomes in another culture. The fact that personality test results have never proved to be good predictors of actual performance in the field does not mean the characteristics being measured by such tests are irrelevant to overseas outcomes. In fact, research confirms overwhelmingly that certain personality-related variables are critical for success in any culture (see the profile in Part 1). The problem is one of measurement, and the conclusion justified to date is that traditional self-report psychological inventories are not very useful in predicting failure or success on an international assignment.

One major problem with self-report inventories derives from the fact that the way people see themselves and assess their own competencies is often very different from the way they are seen and assessed by others (see Ichheiser, 1949; Miller, 1982; Norman, 1969). Data from Kealey's (1988) 20-country study of Canadian technical advisers support this finding. In Kealey's study, participants who rated themselves on 15 predictor variables were also rated by their peers and supervisors on the same 15 characteristics. Results showed little or no correlation between the two sets of ratings. With respect to assessing performance in the field, ratings were gathered from the field research team (who interviewed and observed behavior on the job), the advisers themselves, and adviser colleagues and counterparts. A substantial correlation was found between colleague and researcher ratings ($r = .39$, $p = .001$); minimal between colleagues and self (the adviser) ($r = .13$, $p = .05$); and insignificant between researchers and self ($r = .08$, $p = .17$). These results clearly challenge the practice of relying on self-report methods for the screening and selection of international personnel. This issue is addressed at more length in Part 3 of this chapter.

SUMMARY

1. Although situational factors play a substantial role in influencing overseas cross-cultural success, the role of personal/attitudinal factors is also crucial. This importance has been established and confirmed through an increasingly wide array of research. Accordingly, the challenge is to better understand how personal and situational factors interact to influence overseas outcomes. The development of comprehensive models of intercultural adjustment is a step toward enhancing the knowledge base in this regard.

2. Development and testing of comprehensive models for explaining and predicting intercultural adjustment and effectiveness are necessary for the intercultural field to establish itself as a unique and rigorous field of study. The need is to demonstrate a greater quality and depth in developing theory and in applying findings. Such models are now appearing in the literature. Testing for their relevance and power to explain and predict cross-cultural outcomes is still in the beginning stages.

3. The issue of self-perception and other perception is important in international selection because it deals directly with the problem of establishing reliable and valid measures of both predictor variables and criterion outcomes. Self-report mechanisms are unreliable; peer and colleague assessments, especially those based on behavioral assessment techniques, offer the greatest promise.

PART 3:
TOWARD AN EFFECTIVE SELECTION METHODOLOGY

When Americans are sent abroad . . . they should first be carefully selected for their suitability. Then . . . they should be . . . thoroughly informed about the culture. . . . Unless we are willing to select and train personnel, we simply waste our time and money overseas. (Hall, 1990, p. xiii)

Although many people involved in recruiting and selecting international personnel readily agree that cross-cultural skills and knowledge are important for achieving international success, very little is done to either specify these criteria or assess people on such skills. Personnel managers often report that they have a limited pool of candidates to choose from and that they see little point to extensive screening and selection procedures. Others assume that the high-performing manager at home will also be the top performer in another culture. Still others who express a genuine belief in the importance of cross-cultural skills do not feel competent to identify or assess candidates on these skills. It is perhaps not surprising, then, that the two most common criteria used for selecting international

managers have not changed during the last 30 years. *Technical expertise and previous overseas experience* were identified as the key criteria in the 1960s and 1970s (see Ivancevich, 1969; Miller, 1972); and recently, Black and Mendenhall (1990), Gertsen (1990), and Laabs (1991) confirmed that this same practice holds true today.

But this practice may be gradually changing. The research reported previously on the substantial early return rates and less than adequate performance of overseas personnel (see discussion in Part 1) is leading companies and other international organizations to look more carefully at their screening and selection procedures. Within the Organization for Economic Cooperation and Development (OECD), members of the Development Assistance Committee (DAC) have concluded that "donors should select experts not only for professional competence but also for their ability to exchange and transfer experience" (OECD, 1991, p. 11). Recently, the Canadian International Development Agency launched a major project on overseas screening and selection aimed at developing new tools and procedures for screening international development personnel.

Although some people would still argue that interculturalists lack adequate knowledge about what it takes to be effective in another culture or that it is just too complicated to predict outcome overseas because of the enormity of factors that influence performance, a major goal of this chapter has been to argue another position. Part 1 reviewed literature that led to the conclusion that knowledge about what it takes to be effective in another culture, as well as about what constitutes cross-cultural success, is indeed substantial. More than 30 years of empirical research have resulted in identifying a core set of personal and interpersonal skills that are important for collaborating effectively across cultures (see profile in Part 1). Accordingly, the challenge in the field of cross-cultural personnel selection is assessment, not criteria. That is to say, although researchers know much about the criteria associated with cross-cultural success, their knowledge and skill on how to validly and reliably assess people on these criteria remain weak.

Why Is International Personnel Selection So Difficult?

For many reasons, the task of selecting people for international assignments is difficult, much more challenging than selection for domestic assignments. Difficulties include those discussed below.

Reliability and
Validity of Assessment Tools

As discussed previously, a substantial effort has been made to determine the usefulness of established psychological inventories for predicting intercultural adjustment and effectiveness. Results of this research (see Kealey, 1988, 1994b, for literature review) have demonstrated that such tools have little predictive power. Although many of the traits measured by these tests have been associated with intercultural success, the tests themselves are unreliable for the international assessment situation. Among the reasons, the following are important:

- People tend to respond inconsistently to test items. They become frustrated and angry responding to items that appear to have no relevance to living overseas.
- Socially desirable responding is extraordinarily high on these tests when used for overseas screening. Generally, candidates try to make themselves look good and therefore hide their "true selves." As a result, these tests tend to reveal greater homogeneity of response and thus severely limit predictive power.
- These tests are all self-report. At best, they will only reveal how an individual tends to perceive him- or herself. The problem is simply that how one sees oneself is often very different from how one is seen by others. Recent research indicates that peer-assessed behavioral traits offer the best promise for more effective screening.
- Many psychological inventories are clinical instruments designed for diagnosing psychopathology. Applying them in an overseas selection process without any adaptation/modification has proved, not surprisingly, to be difficult.
- Outcome on an overseas assignment is influenced by a myriad of personal and situational factors. Psychological tests do not adequately deal with the impact that new environments have on people.

There are other reasons why psychological inventories have proved to be of little use in predicting outcome overseas. For one, the best predictor of behavior is behavior. What people say and what people do are often inconsistent. As Kealey and Ruben (1979) point out:

> It is not uncommon for an individual to be exceptionally well versed on the theories of cross-cultural effectiveness, possess the best of motives, and be sincerely concerned about enacting the role accordingly, yet still be unable to demonstrate those understandings in their own behavior. (p. 19)

Accordingly, the most promising avenue for more effective international screening/selection tools lies in the development of relevant and reliable behavioral assessment techniques (see Kealey & Ruben, 1983; Koester & Olebe, 1988).

Lack of Job, Institution, and Culture Analysis

For any individual to achieve cross-cultural success, a set of minimal conditions likely exists for ensuring that this takes place. Although one can never fully predict or control how individuals will interpret and react to the situation overseas, this lack does not mean that interculturists should ignore trying to clarify the situation overseas. Situational factors can be identified and categorized. Cole and Bruner (1971) and David (1972) identified the following 10 situations that can influence intercultural adjustment:

Urban versus rural setting
Job conditions
Living conditions
Host country friends
Contact with other sojourners
Health problems
Legal status
Lack of interests
Language difficulties
Opposite-sex contacts

The study of the demands of these situations is vital in order to take better account of them in the selection process. Techniques for undertaking institutional analysis, sociocultural analysis, and job analysis have been developed with some rigor during the past several years. What is needed now is to undertake this type of situational analysis as one of the first activities in planning international assignments. Although rarely done, this analysis is critical for specifying and prioritizing selection criteria.

Kealey and Ruben (1983) discuss the case of individuals assigned for a short time to work in cultures very like their own, dealing almost exclusively with individuals from their own company, living in a compound, and interacting socially with members of the expatriate community.

A profile and weighting system for the selection of persons for such positions would be quite different from one for individuals who are going to very different cultures, for three to five years, to work primarily with nationals, and to live in the local community. (p. 171)

For short-term personnel, technical skills would be weighted more heavily than behavioral-social-communicative skills, and capacity for professional task performance would be considered more important than transfer of skills and intercultural interaction.

Lack of Integrated Process

Unfortunately, overseas personnel assessment often operates in a vacuum on its own, inadequately linked to the initial overseas job scoping and project planning phase, as well as to the preparation and training activities that take place after selection is completed. Personnel assessment will be much better if specific data on field conditions and job expectations are fed into this process. Also, cross-cultural training will be more effective if it addresses the real needs of departing personnel; these needs or gaps in knowledge and skill will be identified as part of the personnel assessment process per se. Together, these phases are essential components of a process aimed at enhancing success on an international posting.

The Need to Assess Spouse and Family

Another difficulty confronted by international recruitment and selection experts is the critical importance of spouses and children to the success of the international assignment (see Black & Stephens, 1989; Kealey, 1990; Tung, 1981). Despite the fact that this is readily acknowledged by many in the international arena, spouses are not generally interviewed or screened as part of the selection process. Gertsen's (1990) Danish business study found that only 6% of the 80 multinationals surveyed interviewed spouses, because they thought it was interfering with the employee's private life. More recent research (Kealey, 1994b; Stephens & Black, 1991) indicates that the problems of spouses overseas are escalating and increasingly interfering with the potential success of international sojourners. Estimates range from 30% to 60% of accompanying spouses experience serious difficulties in adapting to their foreign posts.

Lack of Follow-Up
Monitoring and Research

Often, companies and other international organizations have very little idea about the effectiveness of their selection procedures. The reason simply derives from the fact that few of them have any systematic follow-up monitoring of the performance of overseas personnel. It is most often still assumed that "no news is good news." If the person and his or her family stay on for the duration of the assignment, the assignment is considered a success. But, as mentioned earlier, some pessimistic research findings on international business personnel should lead organizations to look more carefully at defining their overseas performance expectations and at developing a system for monitoring performance and measuring success. Undertaking activities along these lines will only serve to verify the usefulness and effectiveness of any selection procedure being used for screening international personnel.

Predicting Adjustment Versus
Predicting Effectiveness

Another major difficulty in assessing personnel for international positions derives from the multifaceted nature of cross-cultural success. Increasing evidence suggests the criteria that predict personal adjustment overseas differ from the criteria associated with professional effectiveness (see Kealey, 1989). Literature in the intercultural field aimed at identifying factors associated with success and failure on an international assignment continue to focus on measuring self-reported levels of personal adjustment and job satisfaction. But Kealey's 1990 research that attempted to measure a variety of overseas outcomes determined that certain interpersonal skills (flexibility, respect, attentiveness, cooperation, control, and sensitivity) associated with success at transferring skills and knowledge to local colleagues were also associated with greater difficulty in adjusting to a foreign culture. Kealey offered different explanations for these findings, but the implications of such findings for cross-cultural personnel selection are important. The argument is made that management should be concerned about an individual's capacity to perform in the overseas situation. Assessing this

type of performance potential is more difficult than assessing the capacity to adjust. In fact, if personal adjustment capacity is the primary focus of concern, overseas personnel assessment can be simplified. For example, substantial empirical evidence indicates that previous overseas experience is associated with greater ease and quickness in adapting to living and working conditions. But as Kealey's data (1988) again point out, previous overseas experience is not at all associated with greater levels of professional effectiveness or greater intercultural interaction overseas.

The Reality of the Individual

A final difficulty in conducting effective cross-cultural personnel assessment derives from the reality of the individual. The ideal candidate never exists. Although the profile of the model cross-cultural collaborator is derived from the study of international sojourners, no individual possesses all of the identified characteristics. The profile of skills and knowledge is, in effect, an abstraction. It comprises all those characteristics that have been found, during years of study, to have some empirical validity. But in the real world, any individual always presents his or her own unique pattern of strengths and weaknesses. As this profile of personality, attitudes, and behavior is identified during assessment, the challenge is to determine which individual pattern best fits the demands of the job and the overall conditions that will influence performance.

This challenge, to match the strengths of the individual with the demands of the situation, is indeed a difficult and demanding task, and it becomes even more difficult when one confronts another reality in overseas personnel assessment. Individual strengths themselves imply weaknesses and vice versa. For example, if one is strong on initiative, self-confidence, and relationship building, one is often weak on patience, sensitivity, and tolerance. But all six of these skills are generally considered important for cross-cultural success. This dilemma is always present in cross-cultural personnel selection. How can it be resolved? The answer lies in understanding the demands of the job and the environment overseas. For example, for most project manager or team leader positions, priority should be given to initiative, self-confidence, and relationship building, and every effort should be made to assist the selected team leader in improving his or her deficiencies in other skills, such as patience, sensitivity, and

tolerance. Strategies in this regard are discussed at more length elsewhere (see Kealey, 1994b).

SUMMARY

1. Seven situations make the task of doing effective cross-cultural personnel selection very difficult: (a) lack of reliable tools, (b) poor analysis of the host environment, (c) an unintegrated selection process, (d) ignoring the role of spouse and family, (e) no monitoring of field performance, (f) the multidimensional nature of intercultural effectiveness, and (g) the limitations of all individuals.

2. Research to assess the reliability and validity of assessment procedures remains of vital importance for this field. Unfortunately, this type of research is time-consuming and costly. Organizations should seek ways to collaborate on this type of research (see Kealey, 1994a, for discussion of a potential international collaboration on this issue).

3. Perhaps the most ignored constraint to establishing an effective cross-cultural personnel assessment procedure (and perhaps also the easiest constraint to address) is the lack of adequate job, culture, and institutional analysis. Effective methodologies have been developed for undertaking these activities; they need to be adapted and applied by those involved in planning international projects and in scoping the work needed to be completed by personnel posted to another culture.

4. The most pressing action to undertake toward the goal of enhancing the usefulness of any procedures for cross-cultural personnel selection is to develop an integrated planning, recruitment, selection, and preparation process. Part 3 of this chapter offers guidelines for addressing this issue.

A Model for an Integrated International Selection Process

As discussed previously, effective selection tools in themselves cannot guarantee that inter-

national personnel will adapt and perform effectively on the overseas assignment. For this reason, the development of the profile of skills and knowledge for each international position and the linking of selection and training are important activities to undertake. Table 5.4 outlines the main components of an integrated screening and selection system for enhancing the overall intercultural effectiveness of international personnel.

Goal 1:
Establishing the Profile
of Skills and Knowledge

Establishing the profile of skills and knowledge for each international position is the sine qua non of effective cross-cultural personnel selection. Unfortunately, this task is traditionally focused on identifying the technical knowledge and skills requirements. Little emphasis is paid to identifying the nontechnical requirements. Many international positions will identify cross-cultural adaptability and flexibility as a desirable individual capacity. This is too much, too general, and very limited in terms of the nontechnical skills that need to be identified.

The profile of skills and knowledge outlined in Part 1 can serve to guide international managers in this task of establishing the nontechnical skills and knowledge requirements. But the need is to undertake rigorous analysis of job requirements, cultural constraints, and the host organization environment in order to prioritize the selection criteria that make up the general profile of the model cross-cultural collaborator. Some criteria in the profile will undoubtedly be considered of minor importance; other, new criteria (not listed in the profile) may well be identified as a result of analyzing job requirements and environmental conditions. As mentioned previously, the challenge in selection is always that of trying to match the skills of the individ-

TABLE 5.4 International Selection: A Three-Phase Model

Goal	Establishing the Profile of Skills and Knowledge	Planning and Implementing the Selection Procedures	Training and Monitoring the Overseas Performance
Tasks	1. Job analysis	1. Prescreening program (self-assessment)	1. Design training based on needs analysis
	2. Sociocultural analysis	2. Identify selection committee	2. Establish training contract with the individual
	3. Institutional analysis	3. Administer selection instrument	3. Conduct training
	4. Counterpart screening	4. Conduct selection interviews	4. Monitor performance overseas
Outputs	1. Project objectives identified	1. Personnel selected with best potential to succeed	1. Trained personnel equipped with the knowledge and skills needed to succeed overseas
	2. Scope of work, including job requirements and constraints	2. Training needs of international personnel identified	
	3. Selection criteria for international personnel established		

ual with the needs and constraints of the job, culture, and host institution.

Goal 2:
Planning and Implementing
the Selection Procedures

Prescreening or preselection programs offer considerable value in enhancing any cross-cultural personnel assessment process. A prescreening program is intended to provide prospective international candidates an opportunity to learn about the job, the country of posting, and the personal and professional challenges of living and working in another culture. These programs are usually designed to take place over 1 or 2 days. The major objective of such programs is to enable participants to make an informed decision whether or not they are ready to pursue their interest in an international assignment. Too often, people present themselves as candidates for international assignments without having adequately thought through their motivations, expectations, and implications for all family members of an international posting.

With respect to implementing the screening and selection procedures per se, most organizations involved in international recruitment establish some type of selection board or committee responsible for making the final selection decision. Of course, many considerations must be taken into account when making international selection decisions. But the need to screen carefully for personal skills and knowledge is of vital importance for enhancing the potential success of international endeavors.

What, then, is the best approach for screening overseas candidates? The principle of converging evidence is always the most practical and proven guideline in establishing any screening and selection procedure. This means simply that the more differing and multiple the sources of information one has on a particular candidate, the more reliable the resulting selection decision. In this regard, "assessment center" methodologies perhaps offer the most potential for effective international screening because they elicit a variety of responses, both verbal and behavioral, to the different situations presented to all candidates. Assessment center techniques include role plays, behavioral observation, case studies, paper-and-pencil tests, and a variety of group-based selection activities. Such methodologies have been used most extensively for career planning and personnel development within business corporations. Their application to international selection is less common because of the time needed and budget required to undertake such procedures.

But even if an assessment center process cannot be employed by a designated international selection committee, a combination of structured and open-ended interviews, paper-and-pencil tests, and reference checks and behavioral assessment is highly recommended. In selecting from among these approaches, evidence argues strongly for the inclusion of behavioral or performance-based measures of an individual's capabilities, in addition to the more traditional self-report and verbal methods exemplified by the questionnaire and interview.

Finally, the selection interview should still be considered the preeminent international selection procedure. New research is providing valuable insights and knowledge on how to conduct more effective job interviewing. This new knowledge should be applied and adapted for the international selection situation.

Goal 3:
Training and Monitoring
the Overseas Performance

The last phase of an integrated cross-cultural selection process deals with linking the results of assessment process with predeparture training and, ultimately, with monitoring the overseas performance of selected personnel.

The effectiveness of any overseas screening and selection process (in terms of ensuring intercultural success) is increased to the degree that it is linked with the training and preparation provided to selected international personnel. As mentioned previously, the ideal candidate for an international assignment will never be found and probably does not exist. But results of the overseas assessment procedure should result in identifying the strengths and weaknesses of the selected candidate. This resulting profile serves, then, to identify the "gaps" in the knowledge and skills required for effective performance on the international assignment. These identified gaps in the required knowledge and skills of the selected candidate should enable the training specialists to customize their predeparture and in-country training to meet the specific needs of selected personnel. In this way, the overseas screening and assessment serve as a needs analysis for designing an effective cross-cultural training and preparation process.

With respect to the monitoring of overseas performance, the first challenge is to define cross-cultural success for the assignment in question, next to establish indicators of cross-cultural success, and finally to determine a methodology and procedures for collecting outcome performance measures on selected international personnel. In this regard, although self-report assessments may be acceptable as reasonable measures of personal adjustment and professional satisfaction, they are not sufficient for measuring actual professional effectiveness on the assignment. The measurement of professional performance in another culture must go beyond self-report and call on the input of peers, national colleagues, and supervisors, both national and domestic.

References

Anderson, L. (1994). A new look at an old construct: Cross-cultural adaptation. *International Journal of Intercultural Relations, 18*(3), 293-328.

Arvey, R. D., Bhagat, R. S., & Salas, E. (1991). Cross-cultural and cross-national issues in personnel and human resources management: Where do we go from here? *Research in Personnel and Human Resources Management, 9,* 367-407.

Baker, J., & Ivancevich, J. (1971). The assignment of American executives abroad: Systematic, hap-

hazard, or chaotic? *California Management Review, 13,* 39-44.

Benson, P. G. (1978). Measuring cross-cultural adjustment: The problem of criteria. *International Journal of Intercultural Relations, 2,* 21-37.

Berry, J., & Kim, U. (1988). Acculturation and mental health. In P. S. Dasen, J. Berry, & N. Sartorious (Eds.), *Health and cross-cultural psychology* (pp. 207-238). Newbury Park, CA: Sage.

Bhawuk, D., & Brislin, R. (1992). The measurement of intercultural sensitivity using the concepts of individualism and collectivism. *International Journal of Intercultural Relations, 16*(4), 413-437.

Black, J. (1988). Work role transitions. A study of American expatriate managers in Japan. *Journal of International Business Studies, 19,* 277-294.

Black, J., & Gregersen, H. (1990). Expectations, satisfaction, and intention to leave of American managers in Japan. *International Journal of Intercultural Relations, 14*(4), 485-307.

Black, J., & Gregersen, H. (1991). Antecedents to cross-cultural adjustment for expatriates in Pacific Rim assignments. *Human Relations, 44*(5), 201-222.

Black, J., & Mendenhall, M. (1991). The U-curve adjustment hypothesis revisited: A review and theoretical framework. *Journal of International Business Studies, 22*(2), 225-247.

Black, J., Mendenhall, M., & Oddou, G. (1991). Toward a comprehensive model of international adjustment. An integration of multiple theoretical perspectives. *Academy of Management Review, 16,* 291-317.

Black, J., & Stephens, G. (1989). The influence of the spouse on expatriate adjustment and intent to stay in assignments. *Journal of Management, 15,* 529-544.

Blake, R. W. (1992). *The international success of small and medium-sized companies: Assessing the role of culture and cultural adaptability.* St. Johns, Newfoundland: Memorial University.

Bowers, K. S. (1973). Situationism in psychology: An analysis and critique. *Psychological Review, 80,* 307-336.

Brandt, E. (1991, March). Global HR. *Personal Journal,* pp. 38-45.

Canada, Department of National Defense (DND). (1993). *Board of inquiry: Canadian airborne regiment battle group.* Ottawa, Canada: Author.

Church, A. (1982). Sojourner adjustment. *Psychological Bulletin, 91*(3), 540-571.

Cole, M., & Bruner, S (1971). Cultural differences and inferences about psychological processes. *American Psychologist, 26,* 867-876.

Copeland, L., & Griggs, L. (1985). *Going international.* New York: Random House.

David, K. (1972). Intercultural adjustment and applications for reinforcement theory to problems of culture shock. *Trends. 4*(3), 1-64.

Dinges, N. (1983). Intercultural competence. In D. Landis & R. Brislin (Eds.), *Handbook of intercultural training: Vol. 1. Issues in theory*

and design (pp. 176-203). Elmsford, NY: Pergamon.

Forss, K., Carlesen, J., Froyland, E., Sitari, T., & Vilby, K. (1988). *Evaluation of the effectiveness of technical assistance personnel* (Study commissioned by the Danish Internaional Development Agency, the Royal Norwegian Ministry of Development Cooperation, and the Swedish International Development Agency). Stockholm, Sweden: SIDA.

Fuchsberg, G. (1992, January 10). As costs of overseas assignments climb, firms select expatriates more carefully. *Wall Street Journal,* pp. 7-8.

Furnham, A., & Bochner, S. (1986). *Culture shock: Psychological reactions to unfamiliar environments.* New York: Metheun.

Gao, G., & Gudykunst, W. (1990). Uncertainty, anxiety, and adaptation. *International Journal of Intercultural Relations, 14*(3), 301-319.

Gardner, G. (1962). Cross-cultural communication. *Journal of Social Psychology, 58,* 241-256.

Geber, B. (1992, July). The care and breeding of global managers. *Training,* pp. 32-37.

Gertsen, M. (1990). Intercultural competence and expatriates. *Journal of Human Resource Management, 4,* 341-361.

Grove, C., & Torbiorn, I. (1985). A new conceptualization of intercultural adjustment and the goals of training. *International Journal of Intercultural Relations, 9*(2), 205-238.

Gudykunst, W., & Hammer, M. (1984). Dimensions of intercultural effectiveness: Culture specific or culture general. *International Journal of Intercultural Relations, 8*(1), 1-11.

Gudykunst, W., & Hammer, M. (1988). Strangers and hosts: An extension of uncertainty reduction theory to intercultural adaptation. In Y. Y. Kim & W. Gudykunst (Eds.), *Cross-cultural adaptation* (pp. 106-140). Newbury Park, CA: Sage.

Guthrie, G. (1975). A behavioral analysis of culture learning. In R. Brislin, S. Bochner, & W. Lonner (Eds.), *Cross-cultural perspectives on learning* (pp. 212-232). New York: Halstead.

Guthrie, G., & Zektick, I. (1967). Predicting performance in the Peace Corps. *Journal of Social Psychology, 71,* 11-21.

Hall, E. (1990). *The silent language.* New York: Anchor.

Hammer, M., Gudykunst, W., & Wiseman, R. (1978). Dimensions of intercultural effectiveness: An exploratory study. *International Journal of Intercultural Relations, 2,* 382-392.

Hannigan, T. P. (1990). Traits, attitudes, and skills that are related to intercultural effectivenss and their implications for cross-cultural training: A review of the literature. *International Journal of Intercultural Relations, 14*(1), 89-112.

Hawes, F., & Kealey, D. J. (1981). An empirical study of Canadian technical assistance: Adaptation and effectiveness on overseas assignment. *International Journal of Intercultural Relations, 5,* 239-258.

Howard, C. (1992, June). Profile of the 21st-century expatriate manager. *HR Magazine,* pp. 93-100.

Ichheiser, G. (1949). *Misunderstandings in human relations: A study of false social perception* (Supplement to the September issue of *American Journal of Sociology*). Chicago: University of Chicago Press.

Ivancevich, J. (1969). Perceived need satisfaction of domestic versus overseas managers. *Journal of Applied Psychology, 53,* 274-278.

Kealey, D. J. (1988). *Explaining and predicting cross-cultural adjustment and effectiveness: A study of Canadian technical advisers overseas.* Unpublished doctoral dissertation, Queens University, Department of Psychology, Kingston, Ontario, Canada.

Kealey, D. J. (1989). A study of cross-cultural effectiveness: Theoretical issues, practical applications. *International Journal of Intercultural Relations, 13,* 387-428.

Kealey, D. J. (1990). *Cross-cultural effectiveness.* Hull, Canada: CIDA.

Kealey, D. J. (1994a). *Interpersonal and cultural dimensions of Canadian development assistance in Egypt.* Hull, Canada: CIDA.

Kealey, D. J. (1994b). *Overseas screening and selection: A survey of current practice and future trends.* Hull, Canada: CIDA.

Kealey, D. J., & Protheroe, D. P. (1995). *Cross-cultural collaborations: Making North-South cooperation more effective.* Hull, Canada: CIDA.

Kealey, D. J., & Ruben, B. D. (1983). Cross-cultural personnel selection: Criteria, issues, and methods. In D. Landis & R. Brislin (Eds.), *Handbook of intercultural training* (Vol. 1, pp. 155-175). Elmsford, NY: Pergamon.

Koester, J., & Olebe, M. (1988). The behavioral assessment of intercultural communicative effectiveness. *International Journal of Intercultural Relations, 12,* 233-246.

Laabs, J. (1991, August). The global talent search. *Personnel Journal,* pp. 38-44.

Miller, D. (1982). *The individual and society: Unpublished works of G. H. Mead.* Chicago: University of Chicago Press.

Miller, E. (1972). The overseas assignment: How managers determine who is to be selected. *Michigan Business Review, 24*(3), 12-19.

Mischel, W. (1973). Toward a cognitive social learning reconceptualization of personality. *Psychological Review, 80,* 252-283.

Mischel, W. (1984). Convergences and challenges in search for consistency. *American Psychologist, 39,* 351-364.

Nauman, E. (1992). A conceptual model of expatriate turnover. *Journal of International Business Studies, 23*(3), 499-532.

Norman, W. (1969). To see ourselves as others see us: Relations between self-perceptions and peer perceptions. *Multivariate Behavioral Research, 4,* 417-443.

Organization for Economic Cooperation and Development (OECD). (1991). *New directions for technical cooperation.* Paris, France: Development Assistance Committee (DAC).

Parker, B., & McEvoy, G. (1993). Initial examination of a model of intercultural adjustment. *International Journal of Intercultural Relations, 17*(3), 355-381.

Ruben, B., & Kealey, D. (1979). Behavioral assessment of communication competency and the prediction of cross-cultural adaptation. *International Journal of Intercultural Relations, 3,* 15-47.

Searle, W., & Ward, C. (1990). The prediction of psychological and sociocultural adjustment during cross-cultural transitions. *International Journal of Intercultural Relations, 14*(4), 449-465.

Shamed are the peacekeepers. (1994, May 2). *Globe and Mail,* p. A17.

Stening, B. (1979). Problems in cross-cultural contact: A literature review. *International Journal of Intercultural Relations, 3,* 269-315.

Stening, B., & Hammer, M. (1992). Cultural baggage and the adaptation of expatriate American and Japanese managers. *Management International Review, 32*(1), 77-89.

Stephan, C., & Stephan, W. (1992). Reducing intercultural anxiety through intercultural contact. *International Journal of Intercultural Relations, 16*(1), 89-107.

Stephens, G., & Black, J. (1991). The impact of spouses' career orientation on managers during international transitions. *Journal Management Studies, 28*(4), 417-429.

Tanaka, T., Takai, J., Kohyama, T., & Fujihara, T. (1994). Adjustment patterns of international students in Japan. *International Journal of Intercultural Relations, 18*(1), 55-76.

Tucker, M. (1974). *Screening and selection for overseas assignment: Assessments and recommendations to the U.S. Navy.* Denver, CO: Center for Research and Education.

Tung, R. (1981). Selection and training of personnel for overseas assignments. *Colombia Journal of World Business, 16*(1), 68-78.

Tung, R. (1988). *The new expatriate.* Cambridge, MA: Ballinger.

Van den Broucke, S., de Soete, G., & Bohrer, A. (1989). Free-response self-description as a predictor of success and failure in adolescent exchange students. *International Journal of Intercultural Relations, 13*(1), 73-93.

Ward, C., & Kennedy, A. (1992). Locus of control, mood disturbance, and social difficulty during cross-cultural transitions. *International Journal of Intercultural Relations, 16*(2), 175-194.

Ward, C., & Searle, W. (1991). The impact of value discrepancies and cultural identity on psychological and sociocultural adjustment of sojourners. *International Journal of Intercultural Relations, 15*(2), 209-227.

6

Intercultural Competence
A Research Perspective

NORMAN G. DINGES

KATHLEEN D. BALDWIN

The ambitious, sometimes grandiose models of intercultural competence that have been proposed in the past (see Dinges, 1983, for a review) unfortunately have not been matched by an equally ambitious empirical research program, although significant progress has been made in the last decade. Anecdotal, impressionistic reports of interculturally effective persons and small sample cross-sectional studies constituted a large share of the earlier literature (Dinges, 1983). More recent research has included an increase in attempts to conduct controlled studies informed by theoretical models. Although the results of quantitative empirical research are not to be taken as the sole standard of evidence, the control of significant variables (e.g., subject variables, task variables, context variables) has increased the credibility of research conclusions. Excellent reviews of intercultural competence research prior to 1972 (David, 1972) and between 1972 and 1977

(Benson, 1978) have been supplemented by more recent theoretical/methodological reviews (Collier, 1989; Hannigan, 1990). This chapter is designed to extend the review of this literature to the current status of intercultural competence research.

Framework for the Review

The empirical studies of intercultural competence conducted since 1983 are summarized in Table 6.1. Identified are the author(s), purpose and design, methods and subjects, and results for each investigation.

This review deals specifically with studies that focused on effective intercultural performance, rather than on the majority of studies that have dealt with more global aspects of

(text continues on page 113)

TABLE 6.1 Summary of Studies

Author	Purpose and Design	Method and Subjects	Results
Nishida (1985)	• Explored the relationship between language and communication skills and patterns of success and failure in the cross-cultural adjustment of Japanese university students using seven interpersonal communication skills selected by Ruben and Kealey (1979) as important to cross-cultural adjustment. • Quasi-experimental/(pretest-posttest)	• 17 Japanese university students in an English class (8 female, 9 male). Subjects had visited the U.S. in 1982 and had taken an English course at an American university. • Cross-sectional • Questionnaire and ratings on listening, speaking, and writing structure.	• Only ambiguity tolerance was correlated with culture shock; speaking and listening skills were closely correlated with interactional effectiveness.
Hammer (1987)	• Replicated and tested the degree of fit via confirmatory factor analysis of Hammer, Gudykunst, and Wiseman's (1978) three-factor model and Abe and Wiseman's (1983) five-factor model of perceived cultural effectiveness. • Quasi-experimental	• 210 North American sojourners at a U.S. university who (a) lived in a foreign culture 3 months or longer, (b) reported satisfaction with stay in the foreign culture, and (c) thought they functioned well in the other culture. • Cross-sectional • Questionnaire	• Three-factor model is a good fit to data: ability to establish interpersonal relationships, ability to effectively communicate, and ability to manage intercultural stress.
Martin (1987)	• Investigated effects of a sojourn on perceived intercultural competence. • Quasi-experimental	• 175 student sojourners enrolled in intercultural communication courses in the United States, having just returned from studies in foreign countries. • Cross-sectional • Questionnaire	• Sojourners with the most intercultural experience (3 to 12 months) rated their ability significantly higher than those with no experience on awareness of self and culture and ability to facilitate communication.
Gudykunst, Nishida, & Chua (1987)	• Examined whether social penetration theory (four stages of relationship development: orientation, exploratory affective exchange, affective exchange, stable exchange) can be extended to intercultural relationships. • Quasi-experimental • 3 (relationship type) × 3 (dyadic composition)	• 39 Japanese students who had lived in the United States from 1 month to 3 years and 37 North Americans with whom the Japanese students had developed relationships. • Cross-sectional • Questionnaire	• Social penetration theory is generalizable to intercultural relationships and is related to perceived intercultural effectiveness and communication satisfaction.

(continued)

TABLE 6.1 (Continued)

Author	Purpose and Design	Method and Subjects	Results
Weissman & Furnham (1987)	• Investigated the relationship between sojourners' fulfilled and unfulfilled expectations in relationship to adjustment.	• 59 Americans from middle-class families who had enrolled their children in the American School in London; a majority of the parents were 45 years of age or younger. • Questionnaire • Longitudinal	• Few differences were found between expectations and experiences. • Mental health and sex differences were related to expectations. • Mental health was related to confidence; poor mental health was related to threats to one's security.
Koester & Olebe (1988)	• Adaptation and creation of the Behavioral Assessment Scale for Intercultural Communication (BASIC) effectiveness.	• 263 college students • Development of questionnaire	• The BASIC demonstrates reliability and validity and correlated highly with another measure of communication effectiveness.
Dinges & Lieberman (1989)	• Satisfied communication competence of persons within specific situations and measured influence of persons culturally similar or dissimilar to themselves. • Quasi-experimental • (2) culture of judge × (2) culture of subject participants × (3) situation × (2) other within situation.	• 64 undergraduate students in Hawaii, 18 to 24 years of age; 32 Japanese Americans and 32 Caucasians • Subjects judged videotaped experimental situations.	• Situational factors are more influential factors involved in measuring intercultural communication competence than are actual traits possessed by individuals. • Many Significant Person × Situation × Other in Situation interactions.
Kealey (1989)	• Purpose is both theoretical and applied. Focused on explaining and predicting cross-cultural adjustment and effectiveness by testing theories on overseas outcome, explored relationship between interpersonal skills and capacity to accurately perceive and understand people from other cultures, clarified relationship between predictors of acculturative stress and effectiveness overseas, looked at background and situational factors in a sojourner outcome, and developed an instrument for assessing people on the skills critical to overseas success. • Quasi-experimental	• 277 Canadian technical assistance advisors sent overseas. • Longitudinal ($N = 89$) and concurrent ($N = 188$) • Questionnaire and interviews	• Reassertion of the importance of personality traits as predictors of overseas behavior, along with situational variables supporting an interactionist position. • Development of a theoretical model to explain the relationship between acculturative stress and effectiveness.

Author	Purpose and Design	Method and Subjects	Results
Olebe & Koester (1989)	• Tested construct operationalization equivalence, item equivalence, and scalar equivalence of the Behavioral Assessment Scale for Intercultural Communication (BASIC) for cross-cultural equivalency.	• Original data used to develop the BASIC were used (263 college students—U.S. and international students.) • BASIC Questionnaire	• Results favor the BASIC's conceptual, construct operationalization, and item equivalence.
Wiseman, Hammer, & Nishida (1989)	• Examination of the relationship between intercultural communication competence and knowledge of the host culture and cross-cultural attitude. • Quasi-experimental	• 887 subjects; 206 students in a university near Tokyo; 681 students in three major universities in the United States. Average age was 21. • Cross sectional	• Strongest predictors (in order of strength) of communication competence were one's ethnocentrism; one's perceived social distance from the other culture. • Higher degrees of ethnocentrism were associated with less culture-general understanding; greater degrees of perceived knowledge of a specific culture were related to greater culture-general understanding. • Positive regard for members of another culture was minimally related to understanding the other culture, knowledge of other cultures in general, and impressions of the other culture.
Martin & Hammer (1989)	• Investigated what behaviors are associated with impressions of communication competence for self and other in both intracultural and intercultural communication contests. • Quasi-experimental	• 602 Caucasian undergraduate students enrolled in speech communication courses. • Mean age 20.6 years. • Questionnaire	• The communicative function (empathy, flexibility, display of respect) was related to impressions of communication competency. • Behaviors identified for both intracultural and intercultural context include speaking more slowly, speaking more clearly, making sure one understands, and talking about cultural topics in an intercultural situation.

(continued)

TABLE 6.1 (Continued)

Author	Purpose and Design	Method and Subjects	Results
Dean & Popp (1990)	• Investigated agreement between American managers in Saudi Arabia and French managers in the United States on subjective evaluation of the importance of 16 personal abilities for Intercultural Communication Effectiveness (ICE). • Quasi-experimental	• 92 subjects: 61 American managers in Saudi Arabia; 31 French managers in the United States. • Managers had lived in the host culture for at least 6 months. • Questionnaire	• American and French managers differed significantly in their rating of importance for ability to communicate interpersonally and ability to adjust to different cultures. • No difference between evaluation of ability to deal with different societal systems, ability to establish interpersonal relationship, or ability to understand others. • Results suggest culture-general and cultural-specific abilities for intercultural communication competence.
Searle & Ward (1990)	• Empirically differentiated psychological and sociocultural forms of adjustment during the process of cross-cultural transitions. • Quasi-experimental	• 105 Malaysian and Singaporean university students living in New Zealand. • Mean age 21.23 years. • Questionnaire	• Although psychological and sociocultural forms of adjustment are related, they are predicted by different variables. • Social difficulty, life changes, extraversion, and satisfaction with host contact predicted psychological adjustment. • Expected difficulty, cultural distance, and depression were the most powerful predictors of sociocultural adjustment.
Sudweeks, Gudykunst, Ting-Toomey, & Nishida (1990)	• Examined relational themes and patterns of discourse that focus on partners' interpretations of their interaction in intercultural relationships. • Quasi-experimental	• 9 female Japanese and 9 female North Americans with whom the Japanese had formed intimate relationships. • Mean age 25.7 years. • Interview/self-report	• Four themes of communication in intercultural relationship development were identified: communication competence, similarity, involvement, and turning points (episodes associated with changes in relationships).

Author	Purpose and Design	Method and Subjects	Results
Black & Gregersen (1991)	• Explored the impact of job, personal, and general factors on three facets of cross-cultural adjustment from data collected from American expatriate managers in Pacific Rim assignments. • Quasi-experimental	• 220 upper-level executives registered with the American Chamber of Commerce in Japan, Korea, Taiwan, and Hong Kong; average duration of employment 13.7 years; mean age 43.9 years. • Questionnaire survey	• Both self-provided and company-provided predeparture training were related to interaction adjustment; however, the latter was not related to work or general adjustment. • Four of the nine in-country variables were related to work adjustment, and all three job variables were related to work adjustment during international and domestic relocations. • Interaction with home nationals was related to work adjustment; interaction with host was significantly related to interaction adjustment.
Cui & Van Den Berg (1991)	• Confirmatory factor analysis to test construct validity of intercultural effectiveness as a theoretical construct.	• 257 American businesspeople in Beijing and Shanghai in 1988. • 20-item self-report questionnaire	• The three factors (communication competence, cultural empathy, communication behavior) are good indicators of intercultural effectiveness.
Redmond & Bunyi (1991)	• Explored to what extent six dimensions of intercultural communication competence (communication effectiveness, adaptation, social integration, language competence, knowledge of host culture, social decentering) contribute to the amount of stress reported by international students. • Quasi-experimental	• 631 international students; 203 female, 428 males; average age 28 years. • Survey questionnaire	• Adaptation and social decentering were the best predictors of the amount of stress reported. • Reported communication effectiveness, adaptation, and social integration were the best predictors of the reported effectiveness in handling stress.
Cui & Awa (1992)	• Examined the factorial structures of the five dimensions of intercultural effectiveness (language and interpersonal skills, social interaction, cultural empathy, personality traits, managerial ability) in reference to cross-cultural adjustment and job performance. • Quasi-experimental	• 74 business people who had been working in China; average age 42 years. • Survey questionnaire	• The factorial structures of intercultural effectiveness differ in reference to cross-cultural adjustment and job performance. • Cross-cultural adjustment emphasized personality traits; overseas job performance required interpersonal skill. • Marital status, presence of sojourner's family, and occupation of sojourners were found to influence adjustment and job performance.

(continued)

TABLE 6.1 (Continued)

Author	Purpose and Design	Method and Subjects	Results
Ward & Kennedy (1992)	• Investigated the impact of locus of control on the psychological adjustment process. • Quasi-experimental/exploratory	• 84 New Zealanders resident in Singapore. • Mean age 37.8 years. • Questionnaire	• Psychological distress, as assessed by a measurement of general mood disturbance, was predicted by external locus of control, personal relationship dissatisfaction, sociocultural adjustment problems, and high incidence of host national contact. • Depression was dependent on external locus of control and a high incidence of life changes.
Parker & McEvoy (1993)	• Tested Black's (1988) three-facet model of expatriate adjustment. • Quasi-experimental	• 169 adults working abroad in 12 countries; 74 in Western Europe, 60 in Asia, 35 in North and South America. • Mean age 36 years. • Questionnaire	• Intercultural adjustment is affected by controllable factors, such as those related to organizational and management practices, but also by some uncontrollable factors, such as the degree of culture novelty.
Ward & Kennedy (1993)	• Examination of psychological and socio-cultural adjustment during cross-cultural transitions in two groups of sojourners, Malaysian and Singaporean students in New Zealand (Study 1) and Malaysian students in Singapore (Study 2). • Quasi-experimental	• Study 1: 145 Malaysian and Singaporean university students living in New Zealand 2 to 8 months; 69 female and 76 male; mean age 21.93 years. • Study 2: 156 Malaysian university students living in Singapore 1 to 9 years; 46 female and 110 male; mean age 20.91. • Questionnaire	• Locus of control, life changes, social difficulty, and social support variables predicted psychological adjustment during cross-cultural transitions. • Length of residence in the host culture, cultural distance, interaction with host nationals and co-nationals, extroversion, acculturation strategies, and mood disturbance predicted sociocultural adaptation. • Culture-specific results also emerge.
Ward & Kennedy (1993)	• Examination of differences between psychological and sociocultural adjustment during cross-cultural transitions. • Development of predictive models of psychological and sociocultural adjustment. • Quasi-experimental	• 178 New Zealand American Field Service (AFS) students residing in 23 countries; mean age 17.35 years; average length of residence in host country 10.88 weeks. • Questionnaire	• Homesickness, external locus of control, life changes, and social difficulty accounted for 55% of the variance in psychological adjustment. • Cultural distance, language ability, satisfaction with host national contact, cultural separation, and mood disturbance explained 52% of the variance in sociocultural adjustment. • Students residing abroad experienced greater sociocultural difficulties than those residing in New Zealand.

intercultural adjustment (e.g., Mahmoudi, 1992). Studies are included, however, that use such terminology as *effectiveness, adjustment,* and *adaptation* interchangeably if they measure variables similar to those included among the factors considered to comprise intercultural competence. We first examine the goals and designs of these studies and then describe the research methods used and the results obtained. The overall research effort is constructively criticized from the standpoint of recent theoretical and methodological advances.

Goals and Design

By far, the most frequent goal of intercultural competence research has been the identification of variables that could be used as predictors of effective intercultural performance, followed by empirical attempts to understand the correlates of differentially effective adaptations (e.g., Cui & Van Den Berg, 1991). Although the number of studies focusing specifically on variables related to intercultural competence have increased (e.g., Dinges & Lieberman, 1989; Wiseman, Hammer, & Nishida, 1989), operationalizing competence criteria remains underdeveloped. Additionally, fewer researchers have examined intercultural competence criteria from the reciprocal cultural perspectives of the persons involved (Hecht, Sedano, & Ribeau, 1993; Nishida, 1985). A positive trend in recent research has been a significant attempt to study intercultural competence as a behavioral phenomenon related to general theories of human competence in an intercultural context (e.g., Hammer, 1987).

The situational dimension of intercultural competence has received increasing attention as an important design variable. Complex empirical results describing the interaction of person by situation outcomes is a significant gain in understanding the extent to which situational and environmental variables account for intercultural effectiveness variance (e.g., Cui & Awa, 1992; Dinges & Liebermann, 1989). More typically, study designs have been a variation on the theme of quasi-experimental research, as well as the use of confirmatory factor analysis to identify the underlying structure of intercultural competence (e.g., Cui & Van Den Berg, 1991).

The majority of studies (especially the pre-1983 era) have used relatively simple designs, relying on opportunistic observations or a single set of measurements collected at one point in time. The more recent empirical research continues to be predominantly cross-sectional in nature; however, a growing number of studies have attempted to employ longitudinal designs (Kealey, 1989; Weissman & Furnham, 1987). With the exception of some earlier Peace Corps studies, the subject samples have been relatively small, and comparative sampling frames have not been aggressively pursued. Some studies have made significant advances with regard to sampling size (Martin & Hammer, 1989), but these are the exception rather than the rule. On the more optimistic side, the last several years have seen a gradual evolution of research design and measurement refinements. Multivariate approaches combining grounded measures of intercultural competence obtained at different points in the sojourn are starting to appear (e.g., Kealey, 1989) and are likely to produce greater understanding.

Methods

The research methods employed to study intercultural competence have departed little, if at all, from the standard approach to social science research. Despite their notoriously poor correlation with the behavioral indices of intercultural competence, personality inventories and standardized trait measures continue to be used, albeit possessing more psychometrically sound and sophisticated properties than earlier measures. Self-report data obtained from structured and semistructured interviews and surveys have continued to receive extensive use. Specialized instruments for the measurement of intercultural communication competence have been developed (e.g. Koester & Olebe, 1988), but adaptations of existing self-report measures have been predominant. Almost all of the measurement methods have relied on retrospective self-report or reports by significant others, although behavioral measures have begun to appear in more recent investigations (e.g. Dinges & Liebermann, 1989).

Results

Empirical studies since 1983 have made significant progress in addressing the restricted range and complexity of variables that characterized previous research. Although the operationalization of such variables continues to be problematic, the review of studies below demonstrates the progress that has been made.

Intercultural Competence

Wiseman et al. (1989) examined the relationship between intercultural communication competence and knowledge of the host culture and cross-cultural attitudes. Their conceptualization of intercultural communication competence included culture-specific understanding of other, culture-general understanding, and positive regard for other. Using Gudykunst, Wiseman, and Hammer's (1977) three-factor model of cross-cultural attitude as the predictor variables, (including cognitive, stereotypes of the other culture; affective, ethnocentrism; and conative, behavioral intentions), Wiseman et al. found ethnocentrism to be the strongest predictor of the culture-specific understanding dimension of communication competence; perceived social distance followed as the next strongest predictor. Higher levels of ethnocentrism were related to less culture-general understanding; greater degrees of perceived knowledge of specific culture were associated with greater culture-general understanding. Additionally, the culture-general dimension was positively correlated with perceived social distance. Increased positive regard was modestly related to less ethnocentrism, greater knowledge of the other culture, and greater perceived social distance.

Dean and Popp (1990) explored similar variables by examining the agreement between American managers in Saudi Arabia and French managers in the United States on culture-general and culture-specific interpretations of five personal abilities perceived as being important for intercultural communication competence. American and French managers differed significantly on ability to communicate interpersonally (Factor I), an indication that this ability is culture specific. Ability to adjust to different cultures (Factor II) was also found to be culture specific. Factor III, ability to deal with different societal systems; Factor IV, ability to establish interpersonal relationships; and Factor V, ability to understand others were culture general, an indication of no significant differences in ratings between French and American managers on these factors.

Adding to the legacy of intercultural sojourner research, Martin (1987) investigated the relationship between previous intercultural experience and perceived intercultural competence. Three groups of student sojourners with different amounts of past intercultural experience (none, less than 3 months, and 3 to 12 months) were assessed on four intercultural competence dimensions: (a) awareness of self and culture, (b) awareness of implications of cultural differences, (c) interpersonal flexibility, and (d) ability to facilitate communication. Sojourners with the most intercultural experience rated their ability significantly higher than those with no experience on the first and fourth dimension. Awareness of self and culture accounted for 59% of the explained variance, whereas awareness of the implications of cultural differences accounted for 22% of the variance.

In a study on a larger scale, Martin and Hammer (1989) attempted to identify behaviors associated with impressions of communication competence for self and other in intracultural and intercultural interaction contexts. They asked 602 subjects to describe communication competence for themselves and for another person in four conversational contexts: (a) with another American, (b) with a foreign student, (c) with a Japanese student, and (d) with a German student. Each subject was asked to describe (a) what he or she would you do to create a favorable impression and be seen as a competent communicator and (b) what he or she would expect the other person to do to create a favorable impression and be viewed by the respondent as a competent communicator. Everyday communicators identified three specific categories that were similar across both intracultural and intercultural contexts: nonverbal behaviors, verbal (topic/content) behaviors, and conversational management behaviors. One communicative function dimension associated with impressions of communication competence was also identified. The behaviors most frequently identified as important to communication competence for self were similar to those identified for other: show of interest, friendliness, politeness, and make the other person comfortable and be myself/act natural. Behaviors identified as important to communication competence for others included do the same as I do, show interest, friendliness, honesty, and politeness. Nonverbal behaviors associated with communication competence included direct eye contact, listening carefully, smiling, paying attention, and using gestures. The nonverbal behaviors identified for other included direct eye contact, listening carefully, smiling, and nodding head and paying attention. Frequent topics associated with communication competence for self included seeking common ground, seeking topics of shared interest, sharing information about self, talking about own country, and comparing countries and cultures. Topics listed for other included sharing information about own country, seeking topics of mutual interest, sharing information about self, expressing feelings, and expressing themselves.

Dinges and Lieberman (1989) focused examination on assessing intercultural competence in terms of situational variables that affected responses to stressful intercultural employment situations. The influence of situational factors on judgments of observers was measured by assessing the communication competence of persons culturally similar or dissimilar to themselves. Three aspects of the employment setting depicted Japanese American and Caucasian American participants responding to varying levels of stress in each situation (e.g., job interview, promotion seeking, job termination). Each situation was evaluated by 16 judges, 4 of each gender and culture combination, and was designed to vary the magnitude of stressfulness for each participant. Results indicated that the type of situation and the other participants within the situation were more powerful determining factors in the judges' assessments of intercultural communication competence than were individual competence traits assessed alone.

Dimensions of Intercultural Effectiveness

Several studies have attempted to identify and validate the dimensions related to intercultural effectiveness. Cui and Van Den Berg (1991) tested the factorial validity of intercultural effectiveness as a theoretical construct involving cognitive, affective, and behavioral components. LISREL VI procedure was used to test the fit of the factorial structure model of intercultural effectiveness on data obtained from 70 business expatriates from other countries who were living in China. Results of confirmatory factor analysis indicated that all of the factor loadings were significant; they ranged from 0.34 to 0.75, with communication competence as the single best scale for factor loadings, followed by personality traits, cultural empathy, and communication behavior. The three factors of communication competence, cultural empathy, and communication behavior were considered good indicators of intercultural effectiveness. Although important in terms of the statistical sophistication of the techniques used to analyze the data, one potential drawback of this study is the small sample size, which may have contributed to unstable factor coefficients.

Cui and Awa (1992) examined intercultural effectiveness based on the five underlying dimensions of interpersonal skills, social interaction, cultural empathy, personality traits, and managerial ability. These underlying factors were studied in relation to cross-cultural adjustment and job performance (two unique yet correlated aspects of cross-cultural adaptation). In terms of cross-cultural adjustment, all factors combined accounted for 59.7% of the variance. Factor I, personality traits (including patience, flexibility, empathy, and tolerance), accounted for 24.4% of the variance. Factor II, interpersonal skills (including the abilities to establish and maintain relationships, to initiate conversation with strangers, and to speak the language), accounted for 11.7% of the total variance. Factor III, social interaction (including an understanding of the political and economic systems, demonstrating respect, and appropriate social behavior), explained 8.7% of the variance. Factor IV, managerial ability (including motivation, success in the home country, and creativity), explained 8.0% of the variance. Factor V, cultural empathy (including previous overseas experience, awareness of cultural differences, empathy for working style, and nonjudgmental behavior), accounted for 6.9% of the total variance. Factor analysis for effective job performance revealed four factors that accounted for 51% of the variance. Factor I, interpersonal skills (including ability to speak the host language, establish relationships, maintain relationships, initiate conversation with a stranger, and knowledge of the culture), accounted for 24.9% of the variance. Factor II, cultural empathy (including empathy for working style and culture, tolerance for ambiguity and uncertainty, awareness of cultural differences, and being nonjudgmental), accounted for 11.5% of the variance. Factor III, managerial ability (including motivation, creativity, understanding economics, and problem-solving ability), explained 7.9% of the variance. Factor IV, personality traits (including patience and flexibility), explained 7.3% of the variance.

Focus on the behavioral dimensions of intercultural effectiveness has led researchers to develop and explore practical tools and assessment methods for the measurement of intercultural effectiveness. Additionally, studies have focused on testing previously identified behavioral skills considered to be important in facilitating intercultural effectiveness. For example, Hammer (1987) employed confirmatory factor analysis to test the degree of fit of the three-factor model originally developed by Hammer, Gudykunst, and Wiseman (1978) and the five-factor model developed by Abe and Wiseman (1983) in determining the degree to which each model provided a reasonable fit to data obtained from 210 North American sojourners. The Hammer et al. model involved three general behavioral skill domains that North American sojourners perceived as important in facilitating their intercultural effectiveness: (a) ability to manage psychological stress, (b) ability to effectively communicate, and (c) ability to establish interpersonal relationships. In Abe and Wiseman's study, the five behavioral abilities were identified as (a) ability to communicate interpersonally, (b) ability to adjust to different cultures, (c) ability to adjust to different societal systems, (d) ability to establish interpersonal relationships, and (e) ability to understand others. The three-factor model developed by Hammer et al. provided the best fit to the data and thus supported the hypothesized importance of abilities relating to stress management, effective communication, and establishment of interpersonal relationships in promoting intercultural effectiveness; it is thus the more parsimonious model of the dimensions of intercultural effectiveness.

Koester and Olebe (1988) used a behavioral approach to the measurement of intercultural communication effectiveness as the theoretical and methodological foundation for their creation of the Behavioral Assessment Scale for Intercultural Communication (BASIC) effectiveness. The BASIC is derived from original work by Ruben (1976), which departed from typical personality approaches of conceptualizing intercultural communication competence while recognizing the role of situational variables and their influence on behaviors during interactions. The revised BASIC consisted of eight items and was based on the original nine Ruben scales. Items on the BASIC are (a) display of respect, (b) interaction posture, (c) orientation to knowledge, (d) empathy, (e) task-related roles, (f) relational roles, (g) interaction management, and (h) tolerance for ambiguity. The BASIC appears to effectively measure intercultural communication effectiveness, supported by results indicating that all eight items load on one underlying dimension while also overcoming some of the limitations of the original Ruben scales.

Olebe and Koester (1989) attempted to establish construct validity for the revised BASIC by determining (a) whether the internal structure of the instrument was invariant regardless of the respondents' cultures, (b) whether the items have the same meaning and are operationalized similarly regardless of participants' cultures, and (c) whether the items of the BASIC relate similarity to other measures of communication effectiveness regardless of culture. Results indicated a similar internal structure of BASIC despite the participants' cultures. Factor analysis of the U.S. subjects' responses revealed a one-factor solution that accounted for 48.4% of the total variance. Additionally, a second factor analysis of non-U.S. responses revealed another one-factor solution accounting for 47.5% of the total variance. No significant differences were found between U.S. and non-U.S. subjects on the BASIC items; this finding indicated that the items possessed similar meaning and were operationalized similarly regardless of subjects' culture. Multiple regression for each subject group revealed that the eight BASIC items accounted for 41% of the variability in intercultural effectiveness for the U.S. group (multiple $R = .64$, multiple $R^2 = .41$). The three most important predictors of intercultural effectiveness (all significant $p < .02$ or greater) were task roles, empathy, and respect. Remarkably, the eight items also accounted for 41% of the total variability in intercultural effectiveness for the non-U.S. group, whereas only interaction management was a significant predictor $(p < .03)$.

Several studies have explored the influences of both individual variables (e.g., perceptions, language, and communication skills; relationships and levels of intimacy) and situational variables on intercultural effectiveness and cross-cultural adjustment. Nishida (1985) examined the relationship between language, communication skills, and patterns of success and failure in the cross-cultural adjustment of Japanese university students. Seven communication skills identified previously by Ruben and Kealey (1979) as important to cross-cultural adjustment were examined: (a) empathy, (b) respect, (c) role behavior flexibility, (d) orientation to knowledge, (e) interaction posture, (f) interaction management, and (g) tolerance for ambiguity. Additionally, language, communication skills, and performance were considered to be major influences on intercultural communication. Comparisons between pre- and posttest measures on the dimensions of culture shock, psychological adjustment, and interactional effectiveness at the end of the subject's stay in the U.S. revealed that only tolerance for ambiguity predicted success or failure in Japanese student adjustment. The remaining six communication skills were not good predictors of shorter term Japanese student adjustment to new cultures and environments.

Gudykunst, Nishida, and Chua (1987) extended Altman and Taylor's (1973) theory of social penetration involving four stages of relationship development (orientation, exploratory affective exchange, affective exchange, and stable exchange) to explore the effect of different levels of intimacy on intercultural communications in Japanese-North American interpersonal relationships. A 3 (relationship type—high intimacy, mixed intimacy, or low intimacy) × 3 (dyadic composition—determined by combinations of the gender of the partners) design was used to examine social penetration on perceived personalization, synchronization, and difficulty. For high-intimacy pairs, partners sensed more personalized and synchronized communication but less difficulty in communication than low-intimacy dyads. Relationship type accounted for 62% of the variance in personalized communication, 20% of synchronized communication, and 15% of difficulty in communication. Additionally, mixed pairs had significantly less agreement than low-intimacy dyads on the amount of personalized communication and less agreement than low-intimacy dyads. Pairs with higher intimacy had lower dispersion scores than the lower intimacy pairs. Greater concordance was

also found among higher intimacy pairs than the lower intimacy dyads; no pattern appeared for the mixed pairs.

In a related study, Sudweeks, Gudykunst, Ting-Toomey, and Nishida (1990) examined intercultural effectiveness in terms of themes that emerge in intercultural relationships. Of particular interest were themes related to developing and sustaining such relationships. Japanese and North American partners in low-, moderate-, and high-intimacy, same-sex dyads were interviewed, and four main themes with subthemes related to relationship development were identified: (a) communication competence (subthemes: language/cultural knowledge, empathy, and accommodation); (b) similarity (subthemes: cultural, background/lifestyle, and attitude similarity); (c) involvement (subthemes: intimacy level of communication and shared networks); and (d) turning points or episodes associated with changes in the relationship (subthemes: relational tests, responsiveness, and understanding). The results suggested that communication competence was necessary for intercultural relationships to survive and contributed greatly to higher levels of intimacy. Lack of cultural similarity had less impact on communication in relationships defined as intimate, whereas in low-intimacy dyads, the negative effect was greater. Communication competence was found to be relevant and interconnected with each of the other themes and thus indicated that some basic language and cultural knowledge must exist to recognize similarities and differences between cultural views.

Intercultural Adjustment

Several studies have focused on factors relevant to the prediction of overseas adjustment outcomes for different types of sojourners. Kealey (1989) used a longitudinal and concurrent design to study the overall adjustment and effectiveness of Canadian technical advisors living in developing countries. The longitudinal group completed both predeparture and follow-up measures 3 to 12 months after arriving in the foreign country; the concurrent group was administered both predictor and outcome measures at one time. Although favoring an interactionist position with respect to personal traits and situational variables, the author nonetheless asserted that personal traits are more relevant in explaining and predicting overseas adjustment outcomes. Knowledge of the local culture and participation were found to be associated with effectiveness in working with nationals and the transferring of skills and knowledge to peers. In addition, the results suggest that previous overseas experience moderated adjustment stress for over 50% of the sample.

A contrasting study by Parker and McEvoy (1993) investigated a model of intercultural adjustment based on individual, organizational, and contextual factors that were predicted to influence the degree of intercultural adjustment. A unique feature of this model is that personality characteristics are not identified as a major separate predictor category, but rather are included within the individual factors, such as prior international and work experience, demographic characteristics, motivation, free time spent with host country expatriates, and perception and relational skills. Compensation and benefits, promotional opportunities, length of assignment, work assignment, and organization size fall under the organizational category; the contextual category includes such factors as urban or rural location, family and spacial adaptation, and culture novelty. This model was tested by using data from 169 participants living and working in foreign countries. Results indicated that adjustment was mainly affected by such organizational variables as compensation levels and perceived opportunities for promotion and returning home. General living adjustment was primarily affected by individual variables such as previous international experience, length of time spent with hosts, and degree of cultural novelty.

Black and Gregersen (1991) similarly attempted to explore cross-cultural adjustment by examining relationships among individual, organizational, job, and nonwork antecedents and three facets of cross-cultural adjustment: (a) anticipatory (previous international experience and organization), (b) in-country (individual and job), and (c) nonwork (association with home and host nationals, cultural novelty, and spacial interaction and general adjustment). Previous international work experience was not related to any of the three factors of adjustment. Self-initiated, predeparture training was related to interaction adjustment, but company training was not related to work or general adjustment. Interaction with home nationals was signifi-

cantly related to work adjustment, and interaction with host nationals was related to interaction adjustment. Spacial interaction adjustment was related to expatriate interaction adjustment, and spacial general adjustment was also related to expatriate general adjustment.

Intercultural stress as an important dimension of intercultural adjustment has received continuing research attention. For example, Redmond and Bunyi (1991) examined the relationship between intercultural communication competence and stress derived from data gathered from 644 international students attending a university in the United States. *Intercultural communication competence* was defined as consisting of communication effectiveness, adaptation, social integration, language competence, knowledge of the host culture, and social decentering. Two facets of intercultural communication competence—adaptation and social decentering—accounted for 16% of the variance in amount of stress reported. Regression analysis revealed that communication effectiveness, adaptation, and social integration accounted for 46% of the variance in reported effectiveness in handling stress. Communication effectiveness, adaptation, and social integration appear to be related to the amount of stress reported. In a related study, Weissman and Furnham (1987) examined the relationship between predeparture expectations of expatriates and experiences 6 months after arriving in England. Those who were poorly adjusted were more concerned with change and the possibility of having negative experiences. The authors suggest an element of a self-fulfilling prophecy in that low expectations lead to poor experiences with little differences in expectations and experience, whereas high expectations are unattainable and result in disappointment.

Several studies on cross-cultural adjustment have focused on differentiating psychological and sociocultural forms of adjustment. Searle and Ward (1990) attempted empirically to differentiate psychological and sociocultural types of adjustment during cross-cultural transitions for Malaysian and Singaporean students living in New Zealand. Depression (psychological well-being) and social difficulty (sociocultural competence) were examined in relationship to expected difficulty, cultural distance, quantity and quality of extraversion, life changes, and individual variables including age, gender, length of residence, and previous cross-cultural training and experiences. Social difficulty, satisfaction with host contacts, extraversion, and life changes accounted for 34% of the variance in psychological adjustment. Cultural distance, expected difficulty, and depression accounted for 36% of the variance in sociocultural adjustment. No significant differences were found on psychological or sociocultural adjustment or length of residence in New Zealand.

Ward and Kennedy (1992) attempted to construct predictive models of psychological and sociocultural adjustment during cross-cultural transitions by examining the relationship between locus of control and subject gender, extraversion, life changes, cultural distance, acculturation, quality and quantity of contact with host nations and co-nations, and personal relationship satisfaction of 84 New Zealand adults residing in Singapore. Locus of control, personal relationship satisfaction, social difficulty, and host national contact accounted for 32% of the variance in psychological adjustment. Length of residence in Singapore, cultural distance, cultural identity, and mood disturbance accounted for 42% of the variance in sociocultural adaptation. Psychological well-being was predicted by an internal locus of control.

Focusing on non-American cultural groups has contributed to the understanding of potential similarities and differences with regard to intercultural communication competence. Ward and Kennedy (1993) investigated the cross-cultural transitions and adjustment of two separate samples of sojourners. The psychological and sociocultural adjustment of Malaysian and Singaporean students in New Zealand were compared with the adjustment of Malaysian students in Singapore. Each group was assessed in the following areas: cross-cultural experience, cultural knowledge, personality, life changes, cultural distance, acculturation, attitudes toward host country, and quality and quantity of interpersonal relations. With the first population, psychological adjustment was predicted by a low incidence of life changes, an internal locus of control, satisfying co-national relations, and social adaptation. Extroversion, cultural distance, cultural separation, quantity of interaction with hosts, and mood disturbance were predictive of sociocultural adjustment. For the Malaysian students in Singapore, an internal locus of control, a low incidence of life

changes, sociocultural adaptation, and increased interaction with hosts were the most significant predictors of psychological adjustment. Cultural identity, cultural distance, length of residence in the host culture, quantity of interaction with hosts, and psychological adjustment were revealed as the most powerful predictors of sociocultural adjustment. No significant differences were found in psychological adjustment between the two groups, but the Malaysian and Singaporean students experienced greater difficulty with sociocultural adjustment; this finding suggests that problems may be greater for those making small cross-cultural transitions.

Ward and Kennedy (1993) further explored cross-cultural adjustment by exploring differences between sociocultural and psychological adjustment, as well as by developing a predictive model. They assessed the following areas for 178 New Zealand American Field Service students living in 23 countries: personality (extraversion and locus of control); life changes; homesickness, cultural distance, acculturation; attitudes toward host country; language ability; amount of contact with host and other nationals; relationship satisfaction with other nationals, host nationals, and host family; and outcome measures of sociocultural and psychological adjustment. Stepwise regressions revealed that homesickness, external locus of control, life changes, and social difficulty accounted for 55% of the variance in psychological adjustment. Cultural distance, language ability, satisfaction with host national contact, cultural separation, and mood disturbance accounted for 52% of the variance in sociocultural adaptation. Students who were resident abroad experienced greater sociocultural difficulties than students residing in New Zealand.

Critique

Concerns previously addressed by Dinges (1983) are still relevant with regard to the more recent empirical research on intercultural competence. A continuing concern is the limitation of sample size and variety. With the exception of some earlier Peace Corps studies and some military research, the samples have typically been small and restricted to populations considered captive in that their participation was part of their organizational obligations. The

Wiseman et al. (1989), Martin and Hammer (1989), and Redmond and Bunyi (1991) studies are a welcome exception.

Most intercultural competence research still has the tendency to "study down"—or at best, across—in that the subjects are relatively powerless, nonaffluent, and of lower status than those who conducted the research. Research using student sojourners and university populations are undeniably all too common but will probably continue to be relied on in light of the increasing costs of obtaining alternative representative samples. Intercultural competence research using other populations, such as international research organization staff, diplomatic personnel, multinational corporation executives, and quasi-diplomatic military personnel, remains the exception. Studying "up" in terms of a sampling emphasis on affluent, powerful, and well-connected sojourners could prove enlightening with regard to intercultural context factors. The few studies reviewed above that did study up are a welcome sign for future research prospects (e.g. Black & Gregersen, 1991; Dean & Popp, 1990; Kealey, 1989).

The frequently identified intercultural goals of tolerance and understanding undoubtedly reflect the social values of many intercultural specialists, but perceived personal power (most typically measured in the proxy variable of locus of control) may have far more weight in predicting both intercultural effectiveness and adjustment. This variable deserves far more specific definition and operationalization in future intercultural competence research, especially in relation to the goals of high-ranking, high-status, high-resource sojourners.

Greater variation in the sampling of performance settings could also contribute to clarification of generic competencies that are important to effective functioning in a great variety of intercultural situations, as opposed to those that are highly specific to situational demands. Without broader sampling of both populations and performance contexts, generic and specific intercultural competence distinctions will very likely remain vague. Parker and McEvoy (1993) made an important contribution in attempting to incorporate organizational and contextual variables with the more typical individual variables used in studying adjustment as an important component of intercultural competence.

The trend to employ behaviorally oriented measures is a positive sign for future research

on intercultural competence. The positive findings of recent research that has employed behavioral measures indicate that their use to predict desirable intercultural performance may improve research outcomes. The failure of earlier and a few more current studies of intercultural competence to predict overseas performance was probably due to the misuse of personality measures intended for study of the structure and dynamics of personality, and not for the prediction of future performance, especially insofar as that performance would occur in situations about which very little was known. The abilities and communicative-behavior variables that are becoming more typical in intercultural competence research are a step in the right direction but need considerable refinement and much clearer operationalization. These concepts and their associated variables are more clearly related to intercultural task considerations but should not be taken as synonymous with competence. Behaviorally oriented measures should also consider putting more emphasis on subjective competence variables as described by Bowerman (1978), as well as the link between overt and covert behaviors in producing action chains that lead to intercultural competence.

The previous decade has seen a welcome decline in the number of studies focused solely on the search for the elusive general "traits" presumed to be the critical underlying predispositions for intercultural competence. This past approach has resulted in composite-trait stereotypes that have contributed little more to the understanding of intercultural competence and has probably been a major nonproductive diversion from more important research. A recent review and critique (Ross & Nisbett, 1991) of the empirical and conceptual limitations of trait concepts is recommended to intercultural competence researchers. Considering the development of newer, more psychometrically sophisticated and comprehensive personality measures, it might now be beneficial to replicate some of the past studies by using an interactionist model of intercultural competence to determine whether any more variance is now accounted for by person-based trait measures.

Consideration of the temporal dimension is an important, understudied aspect of intercultural competence. Probably of greatest research importance is the individual variation in coping patterns over time, rather than the monumental stage and phase models that all sojourners are presumed to experience. Such models may be important in understanding the broader dynamics of human adjustment in stressful environments, but they contribute little to identifying effective intercultural performance. A focus on criteria research in which multidimensional standards of exemplary performance are identified at different points in time and across tasks is clearly indicated. Attempts to predict future performance from prior measures must be particularly sensitive to the variation in adaptive demands and changes in the task environment over time. Stress and coping paradigms, especially those incorporating social cognition, are highly recommended in this regard. Additionally, stress and coping paradigms that examine the positive and negative consequences of stressful events at different levels of analysis (physiological, cognitive, affective, behavioral, social, cultural), as well as developmental and ecological factors, would seem to match the complexity of the intercultural competence phenomena (e.g., Aldwin & Stokols, 1988).

Much more attention will have to be given to task-environment variables that enable or constrain effective intercultural behaviors. With few exceptions, it continues to be difficult, if not impossible, to know the diversity and difficulty of tasks faced by subjects in intercultural competence research. Biological survival tasks are obviously important but have not been adequately appreciated for their role in overall intercultural effectiveness. Indeed, there appears to be a "biophobic" character to much intercultural competence research, which until recently has been typical of the standard social science model of cultural adaptation (e.g.,

Barkow, Cosmides, & Tooby, 1992). Moreover, the extensive realm of psychosocial tasks involved in intercultural competence that were conspicuous by their absence in past research is only now receiving the attention it deserves.

Person X situation research strategies that systematically examine the contributions of person variables, task variables, and the interaction between them have typically found the interaction sources of variance to be more useful in explaining performance and are recommended as the basis of future research designs (e.g., Dinges & Lieberman, 1989). Some earlier studies (e.g., Selltiz et al., 1963) were more sensitive to these issues and were much more assiduous in including setting variables in the assessment of the intercultural interaction potential, and cultural variations in which adaptive demands differed (e.g., Jones & Popper, 1972). Although very little has been done to develop taxonomies of overseas settings in which the behavioral elicitation potential of different intercultural situations is identified, the trend to recognize contextual factors in recent research is encouraging. Most contemporary intercultural competence researchers would very likely identify themselves as "interactionists." This predominance means that the task and environment dimensions of intercultural competence will receive more attention in the future.

Perhaps the most serious limitation of intercultural competence research continues to be its insularity from the social sciences and the lack of interdisciplinary perspective in design, measurement, and interpretation of results. This deficiency is not surprising in light of the serious obstacles that continue to compromise most interdisciplinary collaboration in cross-cultural research (e.g., Dinges, 1977).

SUMMARY

The expanding empirical literature on intercultural competence continues to show significant methodological gaps but encouraging, if still somewhat modest, relationships between predictor and criterion variables. The increasing sophistication of design, sampling, measurement, and interpretation, however, is a positive trend that may be hampered only by the limitations of the conceptual frameworks

by which the research has been guided. Behaviorally oriented measures based on the task environment in which intercultural competence is to be assessed are strongly recommended for future studies, as are more phenomenologically oriented approaches that provide representational validity of the subjects' actual experience in intercultural situations (Collier, 1989).

The insularity of present theory and research from the social sciences in general and the lack of an interdisciplinary perspective in particular will have to be overcome if significant progress is to be made in theory and research. The professional socialization and educational training of many intercultural researchers leads to avoidance of biological dimensions and social power variables, to mention but a few areas of neglect. Many alternative models of human stress, coping, and adaptation have proved effective in understanding and improving human competence, and there is reason to hope that these could be profitably employed in intercultural competence research.

References

Abe, H., & Wiseman, R. L. (1983). A cross-cultural confirmation of the dimensions of intercultural effectiveness. *International Journal of Intercultural Relations, 7,* 53-67.

Aldwin, C., & Stokols, D. (1988). The effects of environmental change on individuals and groups: Some neglected issues in stress research. *Journal of Environmental Psychology, 8,* 57-75.

Altman, I., & Taylor, D. (1973). *Social penetration: The development of interpersonal relationships.* New York: Holt, Rinehart & Winston.

Barkow, J., Cosmides, L., & Tooby, J. (1992). *The adapted mind: Evolutionary psychology and the generation of culture.* New York: Oxford University Press.

Benson, P. (1978). Measuring cross-cultural adjustment: The problem of criteria. *International Journal of Intercultural Relations, 2,* 21-37.

Black, J. S., & Gregersen, H. B. (1991). Antecedents to cross-cultural adjustment for expatriates in Pacific Rim assignments. *Human Relations, 44,* 497-515.

Bowerman, W. (1978). Subjective competence: The structure, process, and function of self-referent causal attributions [Special issue]. *Journal for the Theory of Social Behavior, 14.*

Collier, M. J. (1989). Cultural and intercultural communication competence: Current approaches and directions for future research. *International Journal of Intercultural Relations, 13,* 287-302.

Cui, G., & Awa, J. E. (1992). Measuring intercultural effectiveness: An integrating approach. *International Journal of Intercultural Relations, 16,* 311-328.

Cui, G., & Van Den Berg, S. (1991). Testing the construct validity of intercultural effectiveness. *International Journal of Intercultural Relations, 15,* 227-241.

David, K. (1972). Intercultural adjustment and applications of reinforcement theory to problems of "culture shock." *Trends, 4,* 1-64.

Dean, O., & Popp, G. E. (1990). Intercultural communication effectiveness as perceived by American managers in Saudi Arabia and French managers in the U.S. *International Journal of Intercultural Relations, 14,* 405-424.

Dinges, N. (1977). Interdisciplinary collaboration in cross-cultural social science research. In R. Brislin & M. Hamnett (Eds.), *Topics in culture learning* (Vol. 5, pp. 136-143). Honolulu: University of Hawaii Press.

Dinges, N. (1983). Intercultural competence. In D. Landis & R. Brislin (Eds.), *Handbook of intercultural relations: Vol. 1. Theory and practice* (pp. 176-202). Elmsford, NY: Pergamon.

Dinges, N. G., & Lieberman, D. A. (1989). Intercultural communication competence: Coping with stressful work situations. *International Journal of Intercultural Relations, 13,* 371-385.

Gudykunst, W. B., Nishida, T., & Chua, E. (1987). Perceptions of social penetration in Japanese-North American dyads. *International Journal of Intercultural Relations, 11,* 171-189.

Gudykunst, W. B., Wiseman, R., & Hammer, M. (1977). An analysis of an integrated approach to cross-cultural training. *International Journal of Intercultural Relations, 1,* 99-110.

Hammer, M. (1987). Behavioral dimensions of intercultural effectiveness: A replication and extension. *International Journal of Intercultural Relations, 11,* 65-88.

Hammer, M., Gudykunst, W., & Wiseman, R. (1978). Dimensions of intercultural effectiveness: An exploratory study. *International Journal of Intercultural Relations, 2,* 382-393.

Hannigan, T. P. (1990). Traits, attitudes, and skills that are related to intercultural effectiveness and their implications for cross-cultural training: A review of the literature. *International Journal of Intercultural Relations, 14,* 89-111.

Hecht, M. L., Sedano, M. V., & Ribeau, S. R. (1993). Understanding culture, communication, and research: Applications to Chicanos and Mexican Americans. *International Journal of Intercultural Relations, 17,* 157-165.

Jones, R., & Popper, R. (1972). Characteristics of Peace Corps host countries and the behavior of volunteers. *Journal of Cross-Cultural Psychology, 18,* 68-87.

Kealey, D. J. (1989). A study of cross-cultural effectiveness: Theoretical issues, practical applications. *International Journal of Intercultural Relations, 13,* 387-428.

Koester, J., & Olebe, M. (1988). The Behavioral Assessment Scale for Intercultural Communication Effectiveness. *International Journal of Intercultural Relations, 12,* 233-246.

Mahmoudi, K. M. (1992). Refugee cross-cultural adjustment: Tibetans in India. *International Journal of Intercultural Relations, 16,* 17-32.

Martin, J. N. (1987). The relationship between student sojourner perceptions of intercultural competencies and previous sojourn experience. *International Journal of Intercultural Relations, 11,* 337-355.

Martin, J. N., & Hammer, M. R. (1989). Behavioral categories of intercultural communication competence: Everyday communicators' perceptions. *International Journal of Intercultural Relations, 13,* 303-332.

Nishida, H. (1985). Japanese intercultural communication competence and cross-cultural adjustment. *International Journal of Intercultural Relations, 9,* 247-269.

Olebe, M., & Koester, J. (1989). Exploring the cross-cultural equivalence of the Behavior Assessment Scale for Intercultural Communication. *International Journal of Intercultural Relations, 13,* 333-347.

Parker, B., & McEvoy, G. M. (1993). Initial examination of a model of intercultural adjustment. *International Journal of Intercultural Relations, 17,* 355-379.

Redmond, M. V., & Bunyi, J. M. (1991). The relationship of intercultural communication competence with stress and the handling of stress as reported by international students. *International Journal of Intercultural Relations, 17,* 235-254.

Ross, L., & Nisbett, R. E. (1991). The person and the situation: The perspective of social psychology. New York: McGraw-Hill.

Ruben, B. D. (1976). Assessing communication competency for intercultural adaptation. *Group and Organization Studies, 1,* 334-354.

Ruben, B., & Kealey, D. (1979). Behavioral assessment of communication competency and the prediction of cross-cultural adaptation. *International Journal of Intercultural Relations, 3,* 15-48.

Searle, W., & Ward, C. (1990). The prediction of psychological and sociocultural adjustment during cross-cultural transitions. *International Journal of Intercultural Relations, 14,* 449-464.

Selltiz, C., Christ, J. R., Havel, J., & Cook, S. W. (1963). *Attitudes and social relations of foreign students in the United States.* Minneapolis: University of Minnesota Press.

Sudweeks, S., Gudykunst, W. B., Ting-Toomey, S., & Nishida, T. (1990). Developmental themes in Japanese-North American interpersonal relationships. *International Journal of Intercultural Relations, 14,* 207-233.

Ward, C., & Kennedy, A. (1992). Locus of control, mood disturbance, and social difficulty during cross-cultural transitions. *International Journal of Intercultural Relations, 16,* 175-194.

Ward, C., & Kennedy, A. (1993). Where's the "culture" in cross-cultural transition? *Journal of Cross-Cultural Psychology, 24,* 221-249.

Weissman, D., & Furnham, A. (1987). The expectations and experiences of a sojourning temporary resident abroad: A preliminary study. *Human Relations, 40,* 313-326.

Wiseman, R. L., Hammer, M. R., & Nishida, H. (1989). Predictors of intercultural communication competence. *International Journal of Intercultural Relations, 13,* 349-370.

7

Acculturation

COLLEEN WARD

The term acculturation *has been used during the 20th century in reference to what may be considered one of the more elusive, albeit ubiquitous constructs in the behavioral sciences.*

—Olmeda, 1979, p. 1061

ACCULTURATION refers to changes that occur as a result of continuous firsthand contact between individuals of differing cultural origins (Redfield, Linton, & Herskovits, 1936). Originally of primary interest to anthropologists and sociologists, acculturation was first used in reference to group-level phenomena; more recently, however, it has been studied by psychologists as an individual-level variable (Graves, 1967). Acculturation may occur in a wide range of sociocultural contexts and among a variety of groups. It is most often discussed in connection with those individuals who make cross-cultural relocations, such as sojourners, immigrants, and refugees. The acculturative experience, however, is not limited to those who engage in geographical movement; it is also relevant to sedentary communities, such as indigenous (native) peoples and ethnic groups in plural societies (Berry & Kim, 1988).

Acculturation may be viewed as a state or a process. As a *state,* the amount or extent of acculturation is typically defined and measured in relationship to culture-specific cognitive, behavioral, and affective markers. Often, the core markers or identifying features of acculturation are considered in conjunction with related indices, such as level of education, socioeconomic status, media usage, and patterns of friendship. In contrast, acculturation as a *process* is viewed in a broader context and explores dimensions of change over time. This perspective encompasses a range of conceptual frameworks and includes the identification of antecedents and consequences of culture contact and change.

This chapter considers both state and process facets of acculturation. It commences with the introduction of the theoretical frameworks for the study of acculturation—its definition, measurement, and outcomes. A conceptual model of acculturation is then presented. The process of acculturation is considered with special reference to changes over time, and selected predictors of successful adaptation during cross-cultural transition are reviewed. Particular emphasis is placed on acculturative strategies and their psychological and social consequences. Finally, the relevance of these issues is discussed for intercultural trainers.

The Process of Acculturation

Theoretical Frameworks
and Conceptual Muddles

No doubt, contemporary research on acculturation has matured beyond the oft-cited anecdotal accounts of cross-cultural transition and popular armchair theorizing about the stages and characteristics of successful adaptation. Gone are the days of naive reliance on Oberg's (1960) notion of "culture shock," indiscriminately used as both a description and explanation of acculturative distress. But although (a) extensive research on culture contact and change has emerged in the last two decades, (b) diverse groups such as immigrants, native peoples, refugees, and sojourners have been studied, and (c) more sophisticated approaches have been adopted, theory and research on acculturation continue to be plagued by fundamental conceptual and methodological problems. Few attempts have been made to integrate the massive and expanding literature that is punctuated by sustained debates as to the most appropriate theoretical frameworks for the investigation of acculturation and by the lack of agreement about the definition of key constructs.

Early theory and research on acculturation were very much influenced by medicine and psychiatry and assumed a clinical perspective on issues relating to culture contact and change. Certainly, Oberg's (1960) writings centered on anxiety during cross-cultural transitions, but even earlier workers, such as Pedersen (1949), discussed pathological transition phenomena, such as refugee neurosis. Psychoanalytical approaches to acculturation, though fairly limited, have also been imbued with a clinical flavor. Garza-Guerrero (1974), for example, referred to cross-cultural transition in terms of loss and mourning, emphasizing the anxious, depressive, and hostile components of the experience; Arredondo-Dowd (1981) more recently described the despair, homesickness, and disorganization accompanying the experience of immigration. What is clear from many of the early commentaries on acculturation is the emphasis on the symptoms of culture shock and the pathological nature of the transition process.

More recent approaches have framed culture contact and change in quite different terms and have placed varying degrees of emphases on af-
fective, behavioral, and cognitive components of acculturation. Theoretical frameworks have been borrowed from areas of mainstream psychology and applied specifically to work on acculturation. Major influences have been drawn from (a) the stress and coping literature, (b) research on social learning and skills acquisition, and to a lesser extent, (c) developments in the field of social cognition and intergroup perceptions.

In the first instance, acculturation has been viewed as entailing a series of stress-provoking life changes that tax adjustive resources and demand coping responses. This view of the acculturative experience has been shaped by early research on the impact of life changes on physical and mental health (Holmes & Rahe, 1967) and later theorizing on mediating factors in stress and coping reactions (Lazarus & Folkman, 1984). More specifically, it has been argued that any life change, whether positive or negative, is intrinsically stressful, in that it produces disequilibrium and requires adaptive reactions. Both retrospective and prospective studies in health psychology have substantiated the link between life stresses, physical illness, and psychiatric symptomatology (Johnson & Sarason, 1979), and related research has supported the contention that life changes increase overall susceptibility to illness (Holmes & Masuda, 1974). Nevertheless, stress and coping responses are believed to be mediated by a variety of factors, including both personal and situational influences. Frequency and duration of life changes, as well as personal resources (e.g., perceptions of self-efficacy) and deficits (e.g., limited cognitive capacity), and situational factors (e.g., timing of life changes) affect stress reactions (Lazarus, 1976).

Cross-cultural psychologists have recognized the relevance of the life events literature to the acculturation experience, noting the vast array of changes confronted by immigrants, sojourners, refugees, and native peoples (Furnham & Bochner, 1986; Spradley & Phillips, 1972). Adopting a stress and coping framework, researchers have examined the influence of life changes (Lin, Tazuma, & Masuda, 1979), personality (Ward & Kennedy, 1992), individuals' cognitive appraisal of the change (Chataway & Berry, 1989), and social support (Adelman, 1988) on outcomes of acculturation, particularly physical and mental health. Although this has been a very popular approach to the study of acculturation and one that has been implicitly relied on by a number of investigators, the most impressive example of research in this area has been Berry's work on acculturation and acculturative stress (e.g., Berry, Kim, Minde, & Mok, 1987; Berry, Kim, Power, Young, & Bujaki, 1989).

In contrast to stress and coping perspectives, social learning approaches emphasize the role of learning in the acquisition of culturally appropriate skills. This approach has been derived from social and experimental psychology and has adapted Argyle's (1969) work on social skills and interpersonal behaviors to the specific domain of acculturation. Along these lines, Argyle has identified that practice, feedback, demonstration, and guidance as the most important components of the learning process and has emphasized the significance of experience and the effectiveness of training, modeling, and social interaction in the facilitation of social skills acquisition (Trower, Bryant, & Argyle, 1978). In the main, Argyle has drawn parallels between the learning of motor and social skills and has acknowledged the importance of motivation and reinforcement in the learning process.

Cross-cultural researchers have extended this line of inquiry to the acculturation domain and have considered factors that promote learning of new social skills and that facilitate adaptation to an unfamiliar cultural milieu. On the most obvious count, general knowledge about a new culture (Pruitt, 1978) has been considered in relation to cross-cultural adaptation. Length of residence in host culture (Zaidi, 1975), amount of contact with host nationals, previous experience abroad (Klineberg & Hull, 1979), and cross-cultural training (Brislin, Landis, & Brandt, 1983) are also relevant to the learning process and have been examined in conjunction with acculturation. In addition, similarities and differences between culture of origin and culture of contact, known as *cultural distance,* have been assessed in relation to outcomes of cross-cultural transitions (Furnham & Bochner, 1982). Although Argyle acknowledged the significance of perceptual, performance, and cognitive skills in social interactions, most research on acculturation has highlighted the behavioral dimension of adaptation. While this theoretical framework has been adopted by many researchers in the acculturation field, the most notable advocates of the social learning approach have been Furnham and Bochner (1986) in their book *Culture Shock.*

On the whole, social cognition approaches to acculturation have not been as well developed, although the adoption of favorable attitudes toward members of the new culture and the changes in values as part of the acculturation process have been investigated. Much of the cognitive perspective on acculturation is akin to the skill acquisition approach but applied to the cognitive domain. For example, Taft (1977) has referred to cognitive aspects of enculturation, such as beliefs, values, attitudes, and schema, and has discussed the changes in these domains as part of the acculturation experience. Along similar lines, the length of acculturative period (Szapocznik, Scopetta, Kurtines, & Aranalde, 1978) and generational differences (Feather & Wasejluk, 1973) have been assessed as predictors of value convergence during cross-cultural transitions. Cognitive elements such as expectations (Weissman & Furnham, 1987), attitudes (Chang, 1973; Heath, 1970), identity, perceptions and stereotypes (Sewell & Davidsen, 1961; Triandis & Vassiliou, 1967; Wong-Rieger, 1984), and attributions (Brislin, 1981) have also been studied in conjunction with acculturation; however, these are not always examined as ends in themselves, but are often viewed as mediators of broader patterns of adaptation.

Outcomes of Acculturation

What defines adaptive responses to culture contact and change? What are the characteristics of a successful cross-cultural transition? Mental or physical health? Psychological satisfaction? Competent work performance? Good grades? Satisfying relationships with members of the host or dominant culture? Positive attitudes toward the transition? Identification with host nationals? Diverse indices of acculturation and cross-cultural adjustment have been examined in the immigrant, sojourner, and refugee literature. Church's (1982) review of sojourner adaptation, for example, presented only a thin slice of the acculturative pie but detailed the investigation of acculturative outcomes, including broader worldview, reduction in ethnocentrism, and greater self-awareness and self-esteem. Empirical studies have also relied on attitudes toward host culture (Ibrahim, 1970), psychological distress (Masuda, Lin, & Tazuma, 1982), perceptual maturity (Yoshikawa, 1988), mood states (Stone Feinstein & Ward, 1990), health evaluations (Babiker, Cox, & Miller, 1980), feelings of acceptance and satisfaction (Brislin, 1981), the nature and extent of interaction with hosts (Sewell & Davidsen, 1961), the acquisition of culturally appropriate behaviors and skills (Bochner, Lin, & McLeod, 1979, 1980), academic competence (Perkins, Perkins, Guglielmino, & Reiff, 1977), and job performance (Harris, 1972) as assessments of sojourner and immigrant adaptation.

Recent approaches to defining and investigating adaptation and adjustment have been guided by both psychometric and conceptual criteria. On the first count, a number of investigators have undertaken factor analytical studies to capture identifying features of adjustment. Some of the best-known research along these lines was conducted by Hammer, Gudykunst, and Wiseman (1978), who requested individuals who had lived abroad to identify specific abilities that are important in facilitating effective functioning in a new cultural milieu. Factor analysis of 24 cited abilities revealed the emergence of three intercultural effectiveness domains: (a) ability to manage psychological (intercultural) stress, (b) ability to communicate effectively, and (c) ability to establish interpersonal relationships. Although the concept of intercultural effectiveness has proved popular, attempts to replicate the original findings have not been completely consistent (Abe & Wiseman, 1983; Gudykunst & Hammer, 1984; Hammer, 1987). Of course, the usefulness of factor analysis as a conceptual tool is often restricted by limitations of item pools. It is also influenced by the theoretical preferences of relevant researchers and the conceptual terms they generate as factor labels. As would be expected, then, factor analytical approaches to intercultural effectiveness and intercultural competence have shared some similarities but have also been marked by salient differences (cf. Cui & Awa, 1992; Kealey, 1989; Martin, 1987; Tanaka, Takai, Kohyama, & Fujihara, 1994).

Substantial variation has also occurred in theoretically based reviews of acculturation and adjustment, although a number of authors have distinguished affective, behavioral, and cognitive dimensions of adaptation. Black

and Mendenhall (1990) and Mendenhall and Oddou (1985), for example, identified self-maintenance of psychological well-being, interpersonal interactions with host nationals, and appropriate cognitive dispositions such as values and attitudes as the defining features of successful adaptation to a new cultural milieu. Despite the apparent comprehensiveness of this approach, Searle and Ward (1990) have argued that adaptive outcomes of the acculturative enterprise are more meaningfully divided into psychological (emotional/affective) and sociocultural (behavioral) domains. In short, individuals who are exposed to acculturative demands are motivated to maintain psychological well-being or satisfaction and to acquire culturally appropriate knowledge and skills. The distinction of a uniquely cognitive domain of adaptive outcomes, including variables such as identity, attitudes, and values, remains more contentious. First, a serious debate is still ongoing as to what constitutes an appropriate or adaptive cognitive response to the acculturative experience. Second, many cognitive components of acculturative outcomes may be conceptually subsumed under or blended with psychological (e.g., self-perceptions) and sociocultural (e.g., perceived problems) adjustment domains. Consequently, on the whole, cognitive factors may be better understood as mediators of the affective and behavioral outcomes.

Ward and colleagues, then, have advanced a bipartite framework for the study of acculturation and adaptation and have integrated stress and coping and social learning approaches to culture contact and change. In the first instance, the acculturative outcome is defined in terms of physical and psychological well-being; in the second instance, it is defined in terms of behavioral competence. In my studies of culture contact and change and in those of various colleagues and past students, we have argued that psychological and sociocultural adjustment are interrelated but that they are largely predicted by different types of variables and show different patterns of variation over time. (This is further detailed in the model presented below.)

The mainstream psychological literature earlier recognized the complementarity of the stress and coping and social skills perspectives on human behavior. Trower et al. (1978), for example, previously linked the social skills domain to psychology of adjustment by noting that certain forms of adaptation difficulties can be caused or exacerbated by lack of social competence. They also commented that the causal relationship between the two domains may occur in either direction, with social inadequacy leading to isolation and psychological disturbance, as well as psychological distress affecting behavior, including an array of social interactions. The connection between affective and behavioral components of adjustment has also been acknowledged by those who have primarily concerned themselves with stress and coping. Along these lines, Folkman, Schaeffer, and Lazarus (1979) emphasized that the management of stressful circumstances includes instrumental control of the situation and maintenance of personal integrity and morale.

Although Ward and colleagues have been the most vocal proponents of the psychological and sociocultural distinction, this perspective on acculturative outcomes has been implicitly adopted by a number of researchers in their investigations of cross-cultural transition and adjustment. For example, in their work on intercultural effectiveness, Hammer et al. (1978) confined their study to adapted sojourners who both reported satisfaction with their sojourn and believed they effectively functioned in their new cultural milieux. Similarly, earlier work by Kealey (1989) distinguished psychological adjustment (stress, psychological and psychosomatic symptoms, and general satisfaction) from culture-specific knowledge and skills.

A Model of the
Acculturation Process

The model presented on the next page has been developing and continues to expand in the evolution of research on cross-cultural transition and adjustment (see Figure 7.1). Integrating clinical and social psychological perspectives on culture contact and change, it distinguishes psychological and sociocultural adjustment and incorporates selected predictors of adjustive outcomes of acculturation. In doing so, it also offers an organizing framework for the synthesis of the acculturation literature. The model is largely guided by the general work of Lazarus and Folkman (1984), draws heavily on models proposed by Berry (1994),

and is additionally shaped by some of my own earlier research on stress, coping, and change (Ward, 1988).

The model considers culture contact as a major life event that is characterized by stress, disorientation, and learning deficits and demands cognitive appraisal of the situation and behavioral, cognitive, and affective responses for stress management and the acquisition of culture-specific skills. These factors, as well as their psychological and sociocultural outcomes, are likely to be influenced by both societal-level and individual-level variables. On the macrolevel, characteristics of both the society of settlement and the society of origin are important. Discriminating features of these societies may include sociopolitical and demographic factors such as ethnic composition and salient attitudes toward ethnic and cultural outgroups. Although these macrofactors undoubtedly affect individual acculturation and are included in this model, they have not, in the main, been investigated to the same extent as individual-level factors that encompass both characteristics of the acculturating individual and situational aspects of the acculturative experience. On the first count, factors such as personality, language ability, and social support may be important; in the second instance, features such as type of acculturative group (e.g., sojourners, immigrants) and amount of contact with host nationals may be more relevant.

The State of Acculturation

As previously mentioned, acculturation may be viewed as a process or as a state. The model introduced on the next page frames acculturation as an ongoing process whereby emotions, cognitions, and behaviors of persons from one culture are modified as a result of firsthand contact with persons from different cultures (Moyerman & Forman, 1992). The model also considers the antecedents, mediators, and adaptational consequences of the dynamic acculturative process. In contrast, researchers may conceptualize acculturation as a state and concern themselves with its definition and measurement. From this perspective, emphasis is placed on the defining cognitive, affective, and behavioral features of the acculturated individual.

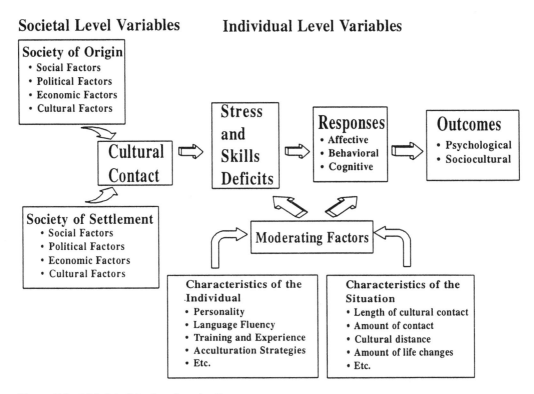

Figure 7.1. A Model of the Acculturation Process

Sayegh and Lasry (1993) have provided a comprehensive and cohesive discussion of the various models and measurements of the acculturative state. On the most basic level, they distinguish bipolar, unidimensional models and multidimensional models of acculturation. The unidimensional perspective has been the forerunner of acculturation theory (Park, 1929; Stonequist, 1935), as evidenced in sociological treatises that originally described acculturation as relinquishing the values, norms, and behaviors of heritage culture and substituting those of the dominant, assimilative culture. Social psychologists have also tended to rely on this more simplistic conceptualization, which casts home and host cultures as competing and mutually exclusive domains.

This approach is exemplified in the construction and scoring of many acculturation indices. For example, the Acculturation Rating Scale for Mexican Americans (ARSMA), developed by Cuellar, Harris, and Jasso (1980), was designed to assess the level of acculturation through the use of Likert-scale responses to items pertain-ing to language, ethnic pride and identity, ethnic interaction, cultural heritage, and generational proximity, with the scoring classification ranging from Mexican to Anglo orientation and the midpoint assumed to reflect a bicultural perspective. The same approach was taken in the construction of the Suinn-Lew Asian Self-Identity Acculturation Scale (Suinn, Ahuna, & Khoo, 1992; Suinn, Richard-Figueroa, Lew, & Vigil, 1987), which taps language, identity, friendship choice, behaviors, family history, and attitudes, and Lai and Linden's (1993) acculturation scale for Asian Americans, which similarly assesses low and high levels of acculturation, with intermediate scores indicative of biculturalism.

Although proponents of the unidimensional models view acculturation as "acceptance of new cultural traits and loss of native cultural traits" (Orozo, Thompson, Kapes, & Montgomery, 1993, p. 150), a number of researchers have recognized that the measurement and experience of acculturation may vary across different domains. Acculturation, for example, may be assessed behaviorally or attitudinally, as in Padilla's (1980) study that distinguished behavioral facets of acculturation in terms of language preference and attitudinal aspects in relation to ethnic loyalty. In later research, Keefe and Padilla (1987) reported that ethnic loyalty remained fairly stable over generations of acculturating Mexican Americans despite significant differences in cultural awareness and language usage. Substantial evidence suggests that acculturation is manifest earlier in convergence of behaviors, rather than in attitudes (Rosenthal, Bell, Demetriou, & Efklides, 1989; Triandis, Kashima, Shimada, & Villareal, 1986).

Several researchers have criticized the unidimensional, bipolar conceptualization of acculturation (e.g., Mendoza, 1984; Szapocznik & Kurtines, 1980), challenged the supposition that movement toward a new culture is at the expense of loss of heritage culture, and offered revised and expanded measurements of acculturation. Along these lines, Szapocznik, Kurtines, and Fernandez (1980) assessed two dimensions of acculturation—monoculturalism versus biculturalism, and low- versus high-cultural involvement. In contrast, Moghaddam's (1988) mobility model of cultural integration measures assimilation versus cultural heritage maintenance and normative versus nonnormative behaviors. In some instances, the bidimensional view of acculturation reflects the independent assessment of the individual's relationship to both culture of origin and culture of contact (e.g., Zak, 1973, 1976). Montgomery (1992), for example, constructed an acculturation index that independently assessed participation in and enjoyment of both Mexican and Anglo activities, such as media and language usage and ethnic identity; however, his scoring technique for the acculturation rating scale still relied on a bipolar conceptualization of acculturation—that is, movement from a Mexican to an Anglo orientation. The same is true for Wong-Rieger and Quintana's (1987) Multicultural Acculturation Scale.

Although Hutnik (1986) and Lasry and Sayegh (1992) have also advocated the independent assessment of heritage and contact culture identification, perhaps the best-known acculturation model of this type has been advanced by John Berry (1984, 1994). Berry has proposed two dimensions of acculturation based on (a) maintenance of cultural identity and (b) maintenance of relationships with other groups. Variations along these two continua result in a fourfold classification of acculturation modes. More specifically, individuals who maintain a strong identity with their heritage culture but are also motivated to maintain group ties with other cultures are believed to adopt an integration strategy. Those who maintain a strong identity with heritage culture but are unmotivated to sustain intergroup relations are seen to adopt a separatist strategy. In contrast, those who maintain a weak identity with culture of origin but are strongly motivated to relate to the contact culture are viewed as assimilated. The final category, marginalized, is exemplified by a weak cultural identity and poor relations with the cultural outgroups.

Berry et al. (1989) have presented an in-depth description of the construction and validation of culture-specific measurements of acculturation attitudes for French Canadians and Portuguese, Hungarian, and Korean immigrants in Canada. Each acculturation index, which has retained validity and reliability over samples, is composed of four subscales that represent independent measures of separation, integration, marginalization, and assimilation. Each subscale includes a range of statements accompanied by Likert response options. In more recent research, Ward and Kennedy (1994a) and Dona and Berry (1994) have used Berry's conceptual model of acculturation to construct two factor scales that, in combination with a median split technique, can be used to identify the four acculturation domains.

Psychological and Sociocultural Adjustment During Acculturation

This section considers factors that affect acculturative outcomes. More specifically, discussion commences with an overview of individual-level variables that influence psychological and sociocultural adaptation. Both characteristics of the acculturating person (e.g., expectations, previous experience) and the acculturation situation (e.g., amount and length of contact, cultural distance) are described. Subsequently, a brief discussion of societal-level variables affecting the acculturation process is presented.

The Influence of
Individual-Level Variables

Stages of Acculturation
and Adjustment Over Time

Early writings on acculturation, particularly the popular literature on culture shock, were often anecdotal and frequently limited to descriptive accounts of the stages of cross-cultural transition. Oberg (1960) detailed four stages of culture shock, with reactions commencing with the euphoric honeymoon stage and progressing through crisis, recovery, and finally adjustment. Adler (1975) referred to stages of contact, disintegration, reintegration, and independence during cross-cultural sojourns; Garza-Guerrero (1974) cited phases of cultural encounter, reorganization, and new identity. Beyond these descriptive accounts, Lysgaard (1955) proposed a U-curve of adjustment during cross-cultural relocation based on his empirical study of Scandinavian Fulbright grantees in the United States. He reported that students who had resided in the United States from 6 to 18 months were significantly less adjusted than those who had been there either less than 6 months or more than 18 months. The U-curve hypothesis was further extended by Gullahorn and Gullahorn (1963), who maintained that the adjustment curve is repeated on reentry to the home environment.

Although popular and intuitively appealing, evidence for the U-curve has been "weak, inconclusive and overgeneralized" (Church, 1982, p. 542). A major problem has been that primarily cross-sectional research has been used to evaluate the U-curve proposition, which would be more adequately assessed by longitudinal studies (e.g., Davis, 1971; Klineberg & Hull, 1979; Selby & Woods, 1966; Sewell & Davidsen, 1961). A second difficulty arises in connection with the selection of various adjustment indices that have transversed cognitive, affective, and behavioral variables. Although originally discussed with reference to psychological well-being and satisfaction, the U-curve proposition has also been investigated in relationship to attitudes (e.g., Selltiz, Christ, Havel, & Cook, 1963), academic adaptation, sociocultural adjustment (Zaidi, 1975), and knowledge of the host culture (Torbiorn, 1982).

A number of researchers have been critical of the U-curve proposition, with some being particularly skeptical about the initial phase of psychological euphoria documented by Lysgaard (1955) and recounted by Oberg (1960) in his description of the honeymoon stage of cross-cultural relocation. Contrary to prediction, empirical research with Peace Corps volunteers has demonstrated that high levels of anxiety are experienced by nearly all volunteers during their first few weeks on assignments (Guthrie & Zektick, 1967; Thomson & English, 1964), and our qualitative and quantitative studies with foreign students have suggested that the entry period is characterized primarily by psychological malaise. The distinction of psychological and sociocultural adaptation, however, demands more precise hypothesizing about the nature of adjustment over time. In line with the social skills literature, it may be argued that the pattern of sociocultural adaptation resembles a learning curve, improving over time and eventually leveling off as new culture-specific skills are acquired. The stress and coping literature, in contrast, suggests that psychological adjustment problems would be greatest at the initial point of culture contact and change, but after that point, it may follow a less predictable pattern over time.

To examine these propositions, my colleagues and I conducted a series of longitudinal investigations of sojourner adjustment. Our first study followed a group of Malaysian and Singaporean students who were initially interviewed and tested within a month of arrival to New Zealand and then again after 6- and 12-month periods (Ward & Kennedy, in press). As predicted, sociocultural difficulties peaked during the initial stages of transition, dropped sharply over the first 6 months, and continued to fall slightly during the second 6-month period. In contrast, psychological adjustment followed a U-curve, but in the opposite direction of that described by Lysgaard (1955). Students' level of depression was significantly greater at 1 month and at 1 year of residence than at the intermediate 6-month period. In addition, qualitative data indicated that the emotions experienced on arrival were even more negative, with 68% of the students retrospectively describing their sojourn in exclusively negative terms at that time, compared with only 5% describing it in those terms after a 1-month period.

Similar findings emerged in a study of Japanese students who were tested within 24 hours of arrival to New Zealand and then again at

4-, 6-, and 12-month periods (Ward, Okura, Kennedy, & Kojima, 1995). The greatest sociocultural problems occurred at entry; they steadily decreased at 4 and at 6 months and rose slightly, but not significantly, at the 1-year period after students returned from a holiday break in Japan. The level of depression was also highest during the entry period, with a significant drop and only minor variations over the subsequent three time periods.

Finally, a study of the psychological and sociocultural adaptation of New Zealand overseas volunteers included both predeparture measures and subsequent field testings at 2- and 12-month periods. Consistent with studies of student sojourners, the results indicated that sociocultural adaptation problems declined over time on the foreign assignments. In contrast, no significant differences were found in psychological adjustment at the 2- and 12-month field testings; however, depression was significantly more pronounced during field assignments than before departure from New Zealand (Ward & Kennedy, 1994b).

In the main, then, longitudinal research suggests that sociocultural adjustment follows a learning curve, with adaptation problems decreasing steadily, and that psychological adjustment difficulties peak in the early stages of transition (also see Westermeyer, Neider, & Callies, 1990) and is more variable over time. More longitudinal studies are needed, however, particularly with immigrants and refugees.

Training and Previous Experience

Culture-specific knowledge, acquired both before and during a cross-cultural transition, is associated with enhanced sociocultural adaptation (Hull, 1978; Klineberg & Hull, 1979; Pruitt, 1978; Ward & Searle, 1991). Along these lines, it has been frequently argued that the sources of relevant knowledge may come via previous cross-cultural experience and/or training. On the first count, Parker and McEvoy (1993) found that greater international experience was linked to improved adaptation and the ability to meet the challenges of a new cultural environment. On the whole, however, more substantial research has been undertaken on the effects of training on cross-cultural adjustment.

Training has been found to have positive effects in a number of areas, including affective, behavioral, and cognitive domains (Black & Mendenhall, 1990; Chemers, 1969; Chemers, Lekhyananda, Fiedler, & Stolurow, 1966; Earley, 1987; Hammer & Martin, 1990; Landis, Brislin, & Hulgus, 1985; Landis, Brislin, Swanner, Tseng, & Thomas, 1985; Lefley, 1986; Mitchell, Dossett, Fiedler, & Triandis, 1972; O'Brien, Fiedler, & Hewlett, 1970; Worchel & Mitchell, 1972). The powerful effects of cross-cultural training were more comprehensively documented by Deshpande and Viswesvaran (1992), who undertook a meta-analysis to examine the impact of training on the following variables: (a) self-development (e.g., psychological well-being, increased self-confidence), (b) interpersonal skills with host nationals, (c) cognitive skills (better understanding of host social systems and values), (d) adjustability (the development of expected behaviors in a new culture), and (e) work performance. They reported that, in all cases, a positive relationship was found between training and outcome. Programs exerted a direct effect on self-development and perceptions; in the case of performance, relations, and adjustability, however, these outcomes were also strongly moderated by additional factors.

Intercultural Communication and Language Fluency

Adequate communication has been regarded by many as the key component of intercultural effectiveness (Gudykunst & Hammer, 1988; McGuire & McDermott, 1988); in fact, it has often been used as a measure of intercultural competence. As expected, language fluency bears a straightforward relationship to sociocultural adjustment; it is associated with increased interaction with members of the host culture (Gullahorn & Gullahorn, 1966; Sewell & Davidsen, 1961) and a decrease in sociocultural adjustment problems (Sano, 1990; Ward & Kennedy, 1993b). Its relationship to psychological adjustment, however, is not always as straightforward.

Certainly, a number of studies have linked language fluency to psychological well-being, adjustment, and general satisfaction (e.g., Gullahorn & Gullahorn, 1966; Sewell & Davidsen, 1961). Ying and Liese (1991) found higher levels of depression in U.S.-based Taiwanese students who had poor English ability. Similarly, lack of language fluency has been associated with increased psychological and psychosomatic symptoms in Indian immigrants to the United States (Krishnan & Berry, 1992) and in Greek Cypriot immigrants to the United Kingdom (Mavreas & Bebbington, 1990). In some instances, however, researchers have failed to document a relationship between language fluency and psychological adjustment (e.g., Ward & Kennedy, 1993b); in other cases, an inverse relationship between language ability and psychological satisfaction or well-being has been observed. For example, Takai (1989) reported that increased linguistic fluency in Japanese was associated with decreased satisfaction in foreign students. He suggested that this finding was related to the higher expectations they had for friendship, coupled with rejection by the Japanese in their relatively homogeneous society.

Expectations

Expectations have long been regarded as a crucial factor in determining adaptation to a new cultural environment; indeed, many intercultural training techniques are based on the assumptions that it is necessary to prepare sojourners and immigrants for life in a new country by teaching them what to expect abroad (Kim, 1988; Landis & Brislin, 1983). Although a number of theorists have emphasized the significance of expectations in the adaptation process, few investigators have empirically examined them. Nevertheless, two hypotheses regarding expectations have been advanced. First, it has been suggested that realistic expectations facilitate adjustment. A second, more refined hypothesis considers accuracy and the evaluative component of expectations and includes both the direction and extent of expectation-experience mismatches.

Some research has documented the what-you-expect-is-what-you-get phenomenon. For example, Searle and Ward (1990) found that expectations about sociocultural difficulties were related to actual sociocultural adaptation problems. Likewise, Hawes and Kealey (1980) reported an association between expectations of a rewarding sojourn and a competent performance on overseas assignment with self-rated satisfaction in Canadian technical assistants on international development projects; however, these studies were limited by retrospective ratings of expectations.

In a rare longitudinal study, Weissman and Furnham (1987) reported that expectations were remarkably similar to experiences of Americans who had relocated to the United Kingdom; however, they were unable to substantiate a relationship between expectation-experience discrepancies and psychological adjustment. In contrast, Black and Gregersen (1990), who also considered the direction of expectation-experience mismatch, found that overmet general expectations about life in Japan were associated with increased general satisfaction and decreased likelihood of premature departure in American managers. Similar findings were reported by Rogers and Ward (1993), who monitored sojourner reentry. In this instance, they found that when reentry was more difficult than expected, greater discrepancies between expectations and experiences were associated with elevated levels of depression.

The precise influence of expectations on psychological and sociocultural adjustment has yet to be determined; however, it seems reasonable to conclude that although expectations about sociocultural difficulties are fairly accurate, overly optimistic expectations about cross-cultural transitions are likely to result in psychological adaptation problems.

Modes of Acculturation

Many studies have considered the relationship between acculturation status and various measures of stress and well-being. For the most part, these studies have relied on the unidimensional, bipolar conceptualization of acculturation and have related a "more-or-less acculturated" index to other measures, such as psychosomatic distress or symptom checklists. Although Moyerman and Forman (1992) found relationships between acculturation and addiction, affective, impulse control, and anxiety disorders in their meta-analytic study, this line of research has been rather controversial. Studies have shown that acculturation is related both to more (Singh, 1989) and to less stress (Padilla, Wagatsuma, & Lindholm, 1985); similarly, it has been related to both more (Kaplan & Marks, 1990) and less depression

(Ghaffarian, 1987; Torres-Rivera, 1985). In fact, Rogler, Cortes, and Malgady's (1991) review of Hispanic research reported that 12 studies supported a positive relationship between acculturation and mental health, 13 supported a negative relationship, 3 suggested a curvilinear relationship, and 2 produced both positive and negative effects. To explain these inconsistencies, some researchers have argued that intermediate or bicultural modes of acculturation are most adaptive (Buriel, Calzada, & Vasquez, 1982), whereas others have maintained that the effects of acculturation are moderated by such factors as age (Kaplan & Marks, 1990), gender (Mavreas & Bebbington, 1990), and religion (Neffe & Hoppe, 1993). It is likely that these factors, in addition to limitations of acculturation measurements, have contributed to the inconsistent findings.

A smaller number of researchers have relied primarily on Berry's (1974, 1984, 1994) model to consider the relationship between acculturation and acculturative stress. Studies with native peoples and immigrants have documented a positive relationship between integration, assimilation, and adjustment. In contrast, separation and marginalization are related to psychological maladjustment and psychosomatic problems (Berry & Annis, 1974; Berry et al., 1987; Berry, Wintrob, Sindell, & Mawhinney, 1982). Similar trends have also been borne out in research by Schmitz (1992), who reported that integration was associated with reduced levels of both neuroticism and psychoticism; that separation was associated with higher levels of neuroticism, psychoticism, and anxiety; and that assimilation was linked to higher levels of neuroticism, in his study of East German migrants to West Germany. He argued further that assimilation is linked to impairment of the immune system, that segregation is related to cardiovascular problems, and that separation is associated with drug and alcohol addiction.

Extending research on acculturation and adaptation, Ward and Kennedy (1994a) attempted to combine Berry's theorizing on the two dimensions and four modes of acculturation with their own research on psychological and sociocultural adjustment of sojourners. Using the Acculturation Index in their study of New Zealanders on overseas assignments, the authors found that those who strongly identified with culture of origin displayed fewer symptoms of depression. This finding appears to be conceptually consistent with Berry and

Blondell's (1982) contention that links to one's ethnic community are crucial for mental health, to Muhlin's (1979) findings that demonstrated a strong inverse relationship between density of an ethnic group and mental illness, and to Mena, Padilla, and Meldonado's (1987) research that documented a negative correlation between stress level and ethnic loyalty. Ward and Kennedy's study further found that host national identification, by contrast, did not directly affect psychological adjustment of sojourners but that host and co-national identification did produce an interaction effect. More specifically, psychological adjustment was adversely affected by host national identification only when co-national identification was weak (that is, assimilation produced significantly more psychological adjustment problems than did integration). No other significant differences were found in psychological adjustment across the four acculturation modes.

In contrast, host and co-national identification produced a divergent pattern of influence on sociocultural adaptation. Strong host national identification was associated with lowered sociocultural adaptation problems. This is consistent with Ward and Kennedy's (1993a, 1993b, 1993c) earlier findings that identification with host culture predicted decrements in sojourners' and immigrants' social difficulties. Co-national identification, however, did not produce a main effect on sociocultural adaptation, but the interaction between the two factors indicated that the greatest number of adaptation problems was experienced by the separated, followed by the marginalized, who had, in turn, more difficulties than the integrated and assimilated.

In conclusion, studies that have relied on unidimensional conceptualizations of acculturation and examined its relationship to psychological adaptation have produced varied results. This variation is likely to be influenced both by the measurement itself and by Person × Situation interactions. In contrast, research that has used Berry's quadrimodal categorization of acculturation has demonstrated the positive association between integration and both psychological and sociocultural adjustment.

Personality

There has been much anecdotal evidence and armchair theorizing about adaptive personality

Acculturation   135

qualities and the acculturative experience. Authoritarianism, rigidity, and ethnocentrism, for example, have been assumed to impede psychological adjustment (Locke & Feinsod, 1982), whereas extraversion and sensitivity, the embodiment of the "universal communicator" (Gardner, 1962), are thought to facilitate adaptation. Despite extensive theorizing, however, relatively few studies have empirically documented the influence of personality traits on either psychological well-being or intercultural competence. Two possible exceptions to this pattern are bodies of research on locus of control and extraversion.

Locus of control has received noticeable attention in the cross-cultural transition literature. In the main, studies have linked external locus of control and psychological and emotional disturbances (Dyal, 1984; Kuo & Tsai, 1986). Kuo, Gray, and Lin (1976) found that external locus of control was a more powerful predictor of psychiatric symptoms in Chinese immigrants to the United States than demographic, socioeconomic, or life change variables. Dyal, Rybensky, and Somers (1988), who investigated locus of control in Indo- and Euro-Canadian women, reported an association between external responses, depression, and psychosomatic complaints, and Hung (1974) demonstrated a link between external locus of control and anxiety in Taiwanese students in the United States. Despite the speculation that external locus of control may be adaptive under certain circumstances, particularly in Asian contexts (e.g., Anath, 1978; Partridge, 1987), no direct evidence indicates that it functions positively in either Asian societies or with Asian sojourners. In fact, our own research has demonstrated a consistently positive effect of internal locus of control on psychological well-being irrespective of sojourners' origins or destinations (Kennedy, 1994; Ward & Kennedy, 1992, 1993b, 1993c). These findings are congruent with more general theory and research on personality and mental health, including theorizing on self-efficacy (Bandura, 1977) and learned helplessness (Seligman, 1975).

Extraversion has proved a more slippery personality variable in the prediction of psychological adjustment despite its popularity with theorists. Research has generated positive, negative, and insignificant relationships between extraversion and sojourner adjustment (Armes & Ward, 1989; Padilla et al., 1985; Van den Broucke, de Soete, & Bohrer, 1989). Our

own research has produced inconclusive findings. In a study of Malaysian and Singaporean students in New Zealand, research indicated that extraversion was predictive of enhanced psychological well-being (Searle & Ward, 1990). In native English-speaking expatriates in Singapore, however, extraversion was associated with increased feelings of boredom, frustration, depression, and poor health (Armes & Ward, 1989). Considering these conflicting trends, we have since advanced the cultural fit proposition, arguing in favor of the personality-situation interaction and suggesting that, in many cases, it is not the personality domain per se that predicts cross-cultural adjustment, but rather the "cultural fit" between the acculturating individual and host culture norms. Along these lines, we recently surveyed a sample of Americans in Singapore and compared their extraversion scores on the Eysenck Personality Questionnaire to normative Singaporean data. Analysis indicated that those Americans whose scores were less discrepant with Singaporean norms experienced less psychological distress; this finding gives tentative support to the cultural fit proposition (Ward & Chang, 1995).

Other personality factors associated with psychological adjustment have been coping with humor (Kennedy, 1994), personal flexibility (Gullahorn & Gullahorn, 1962; Ruben & Kealey, 1979), and tolerance of ambiguity (Cort & King, 1979). Despite the relatively poor showing of personality in the prediction of cross-cultural adaptation, many believe it is premature to dismiss its influence on the adjustment process. Along these lines, it has been argued that greater attention should be paid to the Person × Situation interaction and the notion of cultural fit (Church, 1982; Ward & Kennedy, 1992).

Life Changes

Research on life changes and acculturation has supported the general link between life events, physical illness, and psychological distress (Monroe, 1982). Greater incidences of life changes have been associated with increased health problems (Masuda, Lin, & Tazuma, 1980, 1982), depression, and global mood disturbances (Ward & Kennedy, 1992, 1993b, 1993c) in refugee and sojourner samples. In a related endeavor, Spradley and Phillips (1972) have attempted to quantify the amount of readjustment required during cross-cultural transition in their Cultural Readjustment Rating Questionnaire. Although rarely cited in the acculturation literature, the questionnaire parallels Holmes and Rahe's (1967) Social Readjustment Rating Questionnaire, has proven useful in the study of both American and Chinese sojourners, and holds potential for further research on cross-cultural transition and adjustment.

Social Support

Social support has been viewed as a major resource in the stress and coping process and as a significant mediator of psychological adjustment (Adelman, 1988; Fontaine, 1986). Despite the variety of operationalizations of the social support construct, strong empirical evidence indicates that social support facilitates psychological well-being during acculturation.

A number of researchers have defined social support in terms of relationship satisfaction. For example, Stone Feinstein and Ward (1990) reported that loneliness and quality of spousal relationship were the most significant predictors of psychological well-being of U.S. women in Singapore. Spousal support does seem particularly important during cross-cultural transitions; Ward and Kennedy (1992) noted that marital relationship satisfaction was also one of the most significant predictors of psychological adjustment of New Zealand sojourners in Singapore. Similarly, Naidoo (1985) found that immigrant Asian women in Canada experienced substantially less stress when they had supportive husbands.

It is a common finding that social support and relationship satisfaction are linked to broader patterns of psychological well-being. Hammer (1987), for example, demonstrated that the presence or absence of social support relates to the probability of physical and mental illness during cross-cultural sojourns. Dyal et al. (1988) noted a relationship between social support and a general reduction of depressive symptoms in the process of acculturation; in fact, some researchers have argued that most variables associated with depression are actually related to the quality of personal relationships during the acculturation experience (e.g., Golding & Burnam, 1990). A wide range of studies has documented the detrimental effects of the absence of social support. Leon (cited in Brein & David, 1971), for example, reported that lack of social interaction was associated with increased anxiety, insomnia, and excessive alcohol consumption in U.S. housewives in Colombia. Lasry (1988) found that poor social relations in Jewish immigrants to Canada were related to an increase in psychiatric symptoms. Ward and Searle (1991) observed that loneliness was the major predictor of psychological distress in foreign students in New Zealand. Despite the agreement that social support is necessary for psychological well-being, the actual source of social support during cross-cultural transition remains a more controversial issue.

Some studies have suggested that co-national relations are the most salient and powerful source of social support for both sojourners and immigrants. Ward and Kennedy (1993c), for example, found that satisfaction with co-national relations was a strong predictor of psychological adjustment in Malaysian and Singaporean students in New Zealand. Berry et al. (1987) found that Korean immigrants with close Korean friends experienced less acculturative stress during their relocation to Canada. Sykes and Eden's (1987) study also found that fellow nationals were the most significant source of emotional support. These findings are consistent with Bochner, McLeod, and Lin's (1977) functional model of friendships, which specifies the function of co-national networks in terms of social support and cultural maintenance.

Certainly, expatriate enclaves provide support opportunities, but quality of relationships with other groups, particularly members of the dominant culture, may also affect adjustment. Furnham and Alibhai (1985) produced evidence that suggests both host and co-national support affects sojourner well-being. In our own research, satisfaction with relationships with host nationals and the quality of interactions with hosts have also been significantly related to psychological adjustment of sojourners (Searle & Ward, 1990; Stone Feinstein & Ward, 1990).

Empirical evidence, then, points to beneficial effects of both host and co-national support systems. But interactions with members of one's own cultural group and members of other groups can have wider reaching consequences.

Kang (1972), for example, argued that co-national social networks may facilitate psychological adjustment of sojourners but may actually impede sociocultural adaptation. This contention warrants further scrutiny.

Relations With Host Nationals or Members of the Dominant Culture

Many authors have considered positive and extensive social interactions with host nationals a necessary precondition for effective sojourner adjustment (e.g., Brein & David, 1971; Davis, 1971; Klineberg & Hull, 1979). Unfortunately, the relationship between contact and adjustment is not always straightforward. Indeed, in his 1982 review, Church stated that "the number, variety and depth of social encounters with host nationals may be the most important yet complex variables related to sojourner adjustment" (p. 551). This is likely to hold true for immigrants and refugees, as well as for native peoples whose relationships with members of the majority culture are thought to be a salient influence on psychological and sociocultural adaptation.

Some studies have confirmed a relationship between amount of social contact with host nationals and general adjustment or satisfaction in immigrants and sojourners (Berry et al., 1987; Gullahorn & Gullahorn, 1966; Lysgaard, 1955; Selltiz et al., 1963; Sewell & Davidsen, 1961). In fact, Torbiorn (1982) found that sojourners who spent more time with host nationals were happier than those who spent the majority of their time with co-nationals, and Richardson (1974) reported that dissatisfied immigrants, compared with satisfied ones, had more compatriot and fewer host national friends. Other studies, however, have found that more extensive contact between sojourners and locals is related to increased psychological distress (Ward & Kennedy, 1992, 1993c). Again, this finding suggests interactive influences—in this case, between sojourner and host characteristics.

Although there is some controversy about the relationship between host national contact, attitudes, and psychological well-being, the common agreement seems to be that contact with members of the majority culture offers valuable opportunities to learn culture-specific skills. Sojourners who have more extensive in-teractions with host nationals and those who are more satisfied with these relationships experience less sociocultural adaptation problems (Church, 1982; Searle & Ward, 1990; Ward & Kennedy, 1993b, 1993b). This finding is consistent with the social skills approach to cross-cultural transition and adaptation and has been discussed previously by Bochner (1982).

Cultural Distance

Babiker et al. (1980) first introduced the concept of cultural distance to account for the distress experienced by sojourners during the process of acculturation. They initially argued that the degree of psychological adjustment problems was a function of the dissimilarities between culture of origin and culture of entry. To examine this proposition, they constructed a Cultural Distance Index, an individual difference measure of the perceived discrepancies between social and physical aspects of home and host culture environment.

Babiker et al.'s hypothesis about the link between cultural distance and psychological well-being was borne out in their original research, which demonstrated that cultural distance was related to symptoms of anxiety and medical consultations in foreign students in Scotland. In more recent research, the link between cultural distance and psychological disturbance has been further substantiated in other studies of sojourners (Ward & Searle, 1991). These findings are not surprising and may be interpreted within the stress and coping framework in conjunction with the underlying assumption that those who experience greater cultural distance likewise experience greater incidences of life changes during cross-cultural transition.

The concept of cultural distance, however, can also be situated within social learning approaches to acculturation. Along these lines, the acquisition of new culture-specific skills is likely to be more difficult as cultural distance increases. Following this line of argument, Furnham and Bochner (1982) investigated the relationship between cultural distance and sociocultural adaptation in foreign students in the United Kingdom and substantiated a relationship between social difficulty and cultural distance. In our own research, a robust relationship has been consistently observed between cultural distance and sociocultural adjustment problems (Searle & Ward, 1990; Ward & Kennedy, 1992, 1993b, 1993c).

Type of Acculturating Group

Although there has been much discussion about the distinctions among sojourners, immigrants, refugees, and native peoples, few systematic studies of psychological or sociocultural adaptation in these groups have been conducted. A major exception is research by Berry et al. (1987), which assessed the level of acculturative stress—more specifically, psychological and psychosomatic symptoms—across the various groups. Results indicated that native peoples and refugees experienced the greatest level of acculturative stress; immigrants and ethnic groups the lowest level; and sojourners an intermediate level of stress. Wong-Rieger and Quintana (1987), however, while documenting the lowered levels of life satisfaction in refugee populations, found that Hispanic immigrants to the United States reported lower life satisfaction than Hispanic sojourners.

Related research has drawn comparisons between sojourners and home-based nationals, showing that sojourners have more psychological and sociocultural adaptation problems, compared with local residents (Chataway & Berry, 1989; Furnham & Bochner, 1982; Furnham & Tresize, 1981; Zheng & Berry, 1991). Sojourners have also been shown to experience greater sociocultural, but not psychological, problems, when compared with compatriots who remain at home (Ward & Kennedy, 1993b; Zheng & Berry, 1991). Again, more systematic research on psychological and sociocultural adjustment is required across acculturating groups.

The Influence of Societal-Level Variables

Cultural Origins, Destinations, and Level of Modernization

Culture of origin and culture of settlement can affect psychological and sociocultural adjustment in a number of ways. In some instances, influences may be linked to overall cultural similarities and dissimilarities. This was considered in a previous section as an individual difference measure of perceived cultural distance; it may also be examined on the macrolevel in relation to national or cultural origins and destinations, as well as level of modernization. For example, our research has demonstrated that greater sociocultural adaptation problems were experienced by Malaysian students in New Zealand (culturally and ethnically dissimilar and geographically distant), compared with Malaysian students in Singapore (culturally and ethnically similar and geographically proximal). No significant differences were found, however, in psychological adjustment between these groups of Malaysian sojourners (Ward & Kennedy, 1993a). Along similar lines, Sinha, Mishra, and Berry (1992) found that the nomadic Bihors, compared with the sedentary and more modernized Oraon tribe in India, experienced more acculturative stress, including physical and psychological symptoms, during their contact with the larger society.

In other instances, cultural variations in psychological or sociocultural adjustment do not appear to be simply attributable to cultural distance. For example, Hinkle (1974) reported that Hungarian immigrants to the United States experienced more psychological and physical illness than did Chinese; likewise, Cochrane and Stopes-Roe (1977) found that Indian immigrants were better adjusted than Pakistani immigrants in the United Kingdom. It is unclear whether these differences relate to sociopolitical, economic, or psychological factors. Both dispositional and situational variables may contribute to adjustment, including the possibility that some ethnic or cultural groups may be more broadly adaptable than others. Unfortunately, these group-level differences have not been systematically evaluated.

Social, political, and economic characteristics of the society of settlement may also affect psychological well-being and sociocultural adaptation. Torbiorn (1982), for example, found that expatriates are generally more content in industrialized, economically developed countries. Along similar lines, Korn-Ferry International (1981) reported that American expatriates were less satisfied with assignments outside Europe. These findings, however, are limited to a specific type of sojourner, such as those found in the employment of multinational companies. In contrast to this trend, some research indicates that morale and satisfaction of

Peace Corps volunteers are higher in rural locales where patterns of indigenous culture are more commonly observed (Guskin, 1966). Again, it is likely that an interaction between characteristics of the acculturating group and features of the culture of settlement affects the adjustment process. Certainly, further research should be undertaken in this area.

Cultural Pluralism, Prejudice, and Discrimination

The probable effects of race prejudice on acculturation strategies and psychological and social adjustment of immigrants and refugees have been widely discussed (e.g., Abbott, 1989; Berry et al., 1989; Moghaddam, Ditto, & Taylor, 1990) in the acculturation literature. A number of researchers have speculated that attitudes held by members of the dominant culture strongly influence patterns of immigrant, sojourner, and refugee adaptation (e.g., Tanaka et al., 1994; Ward & Searle, 1991). Unfortunately, few investigations have empirically examined host culture attitudes toward acculturating groups of immigrants and sojourners.

A small number of studies, however, have considered the effects of *perceived* discrimination or prejudice. Along these lines, Aycan and Berry (1994) found that perceived discrimination by Turkish immigrants in Canada was related to sociocultural adaptation problems. Similarly, in our recent unpublished study of American sojourners in Singapore, both psychological and sociocultural adjustment increased in relation to Americans' perceptions of negative Singaporean attitudes toward resident expatriates (Ward & Chang, 1995).

SUMMARY

This chapter has presented an overview of theory and research on acculturation. Distinguishing state and process views of acculturation, a theoretical framework has been offered for synthesizing the massive and expanding research on culture contact and change. The framework combines the stress and coping literature and social skills theory in the construction of predictive models of psychological and sociocultural adjustment. It also incorporates both individual- and societal-level variables as moderating influences on acculturative outcomes.

The proposed model not only facilitates the development of acculturation theory and research but also addresses a number of general concerns raised by intercultural trainers. On the most fundamental level, for example, Martin (1986) has lamented that there has been very little conceptual clarity as to what constitutes cross-cultural orientation and which outcomes should be considered. In response to this, the acculturation model offers the basic distinction of psychological and sociocultural adjustment and suggests that these adjustment outcomes should be integrated with training objectives. On a second count, Martin has recognized that variables that are not intrinsically "cultural" influence individuals' behavior during the process of cross-cultural transition and adaptation, and she has called on researchers to identify these personal and situational factors. Again, this model presents a combination of personal and situational, cultural and "noncultural," and individual- and societal-level variables and describes their roles and interactions in the prediction of acculturative adjustment. On a third count, Martin has acknowledged that both culture-general and culture-specific aspects of training are relevant to cross-cultural orientation programs. This chapter has reiterated Martin's contention that both culture-general and culture-specific factors play a role in the adjustment process and has identified both cross-cultural similarities and differences in factors that predict successful adaptation to new cultural milieux.

In addition to addressing general conceptual issues, the model and accompanying review have provided specific empirical information for both cross-cultural researchers and intercultural trainers. A wide range of moderating influences on psychological and sociocultural adjustment have been identified, described, and critically evaluated. These have included both individual-level variables, such as personality, expectations, and acculturation modes, as well as situational factors, such as length and amount of intercultural contact, and cultural distance. In the end, I hope this chapter has offered conceptual clarification and theoretical synthesis of the vast and expanding field of acculturation research and has provided useful empirical information and practical knowledge for researchers and trainers.

References

Abbott, M. (Ed.). (1989). *Refugee resettlement and well-being*. Auckland: Mental Health Foundation of New Zealand.

Abe, H., & Wiseman, R. (1983). A cross-cultural confirmation of the dimensions of intercultural effectiveness. *International Journal of Intercultural Relations, 7*, 53-67.

Adelman, M. B. (1988). Cross-cultural adjustment: A theoretical perspective on social support. *International Journal of Intercultural Relations, 12*, 183-205.

Adler, P. S. (1975). The transitional experience: An alternative view of culture shock. *Journal of Humanistic Psychology, 15*, 13-23.

Anath, J. (1978). Psychopathology in Indian females. *Social Science and Medicine, 12*, 177-178.

Argyle, M. (1969). *Social interaction*. New York: Methuen.

Armes, K., & Ward, C. (1989). Cross-cultural transitions and sojourner adjustment in Singapore. *Journal of Social Psychology, 12*, 273-275.

Arrendondo-Dowd, P. M. (1981). Personal loss and grief as a result of immigration. *Personnel and Guidance Journal, 2*, 376-378.

Aycan, Z., & Berry, J. W. (1994, July). *The influences of economic adjustment of immigrants on their psychological well-being and adaptation*. Paper presented at the XII International Congress of the International Association for Cross-Cultural Psychology, Pamplona, Spain.

Babiker, I. E., Cox, J. L., & Miller, P. M. (1980). The measurement of cultural distance and its relationship to medical consultations, symptomatology, and examination of performance of overseas students at Edinburgh University. *Social Psychiatry, 15*, 109-116.

Bandura, A. (1977). Self-efficacy: Toward a unifying theory of behavior change. *Psychological Review, 84*, 191-215.

Berry, J. W. (1974). Psychological aspects of cultural pluralism. *Topics in Culture Learning, 2*, 17-22.

Berry, J. W. (1984). Cultural relations in plural societies. In N. Miller & M. Brewer (Eds.), *Groups in contact* (pp. 11-27). San Diego: Academic Press.

Berry, J. W. (1994). Acculturation and psychological adaptation. In A.-M. Bouvy, F. J. R. van de Vijver, P. Boski, & P. Schmitz (Eds.), *Journeys into cross-cultural psychology* (pp. 129-141). Lisse: Swets & Zeitlinger.

Berry, J. W., & Annis, R. C. (1974). Acculturative stress. *Journal of Cross-Cultural Psychology, 5*, 382-406.

Berry, J. W., & Blondell, T. (1982). Psychological adaptation of Vietnamese refugees in Canada. *Canadian Journal of Community Mental Health, 1*, 81-88.

Berry, J. W., & Kim, U. (1988). Acculturation and mental health. In P. Dasen, J. W. Berry, & N. Sartorius (Eds.), *Health and cross-cultural psychology* (pp. 207-236). Newbury Park, CA: Sage.

Berry, J. W., Kim, U., Minde, T., & Mok, D. (1987). Comparative studies of acculturative stress. *International Migration Review, 21*, 490-511.

Berry, J. W., Kim, U., Power, S., Young, M., & Bujaki, M. (1989). Acculturation attitudes in plural societies. *Applied Psychology, 38*, 185-206.

Berry, J. W., Wintrob, R., Sindell, P. S., & Mawhinney, T. A. (1982). Psychological adaptation to culture change among the James Bay Cree. *Naturaliste Canadien, 109*, 965-975.

Black, J. S., & Gregersen, H. B. (1990). Expectations, satisfaction, and intention to leave of American expatriate managers in Japan. *International Journal of Intercultural Relations, 14*, 485-506.

Black, J. S., & Mendenhall, M. (1990). Cross-cultural training effectiveness: A review and a theoretical framework for future research. *Academy of Management Review, 15*, 113-136.

Bochner, S. (1982). The social psychology of cross-cultural relations. In S. Bochner (Ed.), *Cultures in contact: Studies in cross-cultural interaction* (pp. 5-44). Elmsford, NY: Pergamon.

Bochner, S., Lin, A., & McLeod, B. M. (1979). Cross-cultural contact and the development of an international perspective. *Journal of Social Psychology, 107*, 29-41.

Bochner, S., Lin, A., & McLeod, B. M. (1980). Anticipated role conflict of returning overseas students. *Journal of Social Psychology, 110,* 265-272.

Bochner, S., McLeod, B. M., & Lin, A. (1977). Friendship patterns of overseas students: A functional model. *International Journal of Psychology, 12,* 277-297.

Brein, M., & David, K. H. (1971). Intercultural communication and adjustment of the sojourner. *Psychological Bulletin, 76,* 215-230.

Brislin, R. (1981). *Cross-cultural encounters.* Elmsford, NY: Pergamon.

Brislin, R. W., Landis, D., & Brandt, M. E. (1983). Conceptualizations of intercultural behavior and training. In D. Landis & R. W. Brislin (Eds.), *Handbook of intercultural training* (pp. 1-35). Elmsford, NY: Pergamon.

Buriel, R., Calzada, S., & Vasquez, R. (1982). Relationship of traditional Mexican American culture to adjustment and delinquency among three generations of Mexican-American male adolescents. *Hispanic Journal of Behavioral Sciences, 1,* 41-55.

Chang, H.-B. (1973). Attitudes of Chinese students in the United States. *Sociology and Social Research, 58,* 66-77.

Chataway, C. J., & Berry, J. W. (1989). Acculturation experiences, appraisal, coping, and adaptation: A comparison of Hong Kong Chinese, French, and English students in Canada. *Canadian Journal of Behavioral Science, 21,* 295-301.

Chemers, M. M. (1969). Cross-cultural training as a means of improving situational favorableness. *Human Relations, 22,* 531-546.

Chemers, M. M., Lekhyananda, D., Fiedler, F. E., & Stolurow, L. (1966). Some effects of cultural training on leadership in heterocultural task groups. *International Journal of Psychology, 1,* 301-314.

Church, A. T. (1982). Sojourner adjustment. *Psychological Bulletin, 91,* 540-572.

Cochrane, R., & Stopes-Roe, M. (1977). Psychological and social adjustment of immigrants to Britain: A community survey. *Social Psychiatry, 12,* 195-207.

Cort, D. A., & King, M. (1979). Some correlates of culture shock among American tourists in Africa. *International Journal of Intercultural Relations, 3,* 211-225.

Cuellar, I., Harris, L. C., & Jasso, R. (1980). An acculturation scale for Mexican American normal and clinical populations. *Hispanic Journal of Behavioral Sciences, 2,* 199-217.

Cui, G., & Awa, N. E. (1992). Measuring intercultural effectiveness: An integrative approach. *International Journal of Intercultural Relations, 16,* 311-328.

Davis, F. J. (1971). The two-way mirror and the U-curve: America as seen by Turkish students returned home. *Sociology and Social Research, 56,* 29-43.

Deshpande, S. P., & Viswesvaran, C. (1992). Is cross-cultural training of expatriate managers effective? A meta-analysis. *International Journal of Intercultural Relations, 16,* 295-310.

Dona, G., & Berry, J. W. (1994). Acculturation attitudes and acculturative stress of Central American refugees. *International Journal of Psychology, 29,* 57-70.

Dyal, J. A. (1984). Cross-cultural research with the locus of control construct. In H. M. Lefcourt (Ed.), *Research with the locus of control construct* (Vol. 3, pp. 209-306). San Diego: Academic Press.

Dyal, J. A., Rybensky, L., & Somers, M. (1988). Marital and acculturative strain among Indo-Canadian and Euro-Canadian women. In J. W. Berry & R. Annis (Eds.), *Ethnic psychology: Research and practice with immigrants, refugees native peoples, ethnic groups, and sojourners* (pp. 80-95). Lisse: Swets & Zeitlinger.

Earley, P. C. (1987). Intercultural training for managers: A comparison of documentary and interpersonal methods. *Academy of Management Journal, 30,* 685-698.

Feather, N., & Wasejluk, G. (1973). Subjective assimilation among Ukrainian migrants: Value similarity and parent-child differences. *Australian and New Zealand Journal of Sociology, 9,* 16-31.

Folkman, S., Schaeffer, C., & Lazarus, R. S. (1979). Cognitive processes as mediators of stress and coping. In V. Hamilton & D. M. Warburton (Eds.), *Human stress and cognition* (pp. 265-298). New York: John Wiley.

Fontaine, G. (1986). Roles of social support in overseas relocation: Implications for intercultural training. *International Journal of Intercultural Relations, 10,* 361-378.

Furnham, A., & Alibhai, N. (1985). The friendship networks of foreign students: A replication and extension of the functional model. *International Journal of Psychology, 20,* 709-722.

Furnham, A., & Bochner, S. (1982). Social difficulty in a foreign culture: An empirical analysis of culture shock. In S. Bochner (Ed.), *Cultures in* contact: *Studies in cross-cultural interactions* (pp. 161-198). Elmsford, NY: Pergamon.

Furnham, A., & Tresize, L. (1981). The mental health of foreign students. *Social Science and Medicine, 17,* 365-370.

Furnham, S., & Bochner, S. (1986). *Culture shock: Psychological reactions to unfamiliar environments.* New York: Methuen.

Gardner, G. H. (1962). Cross-cultural communication. *Journal of Social Psychology, 58,* 241-256.

Garza-Guerrero, A. (1974). Culture shock: Its mourning and the vicissitudes of identity. *Journal of the American Psychoanalytic Association, 22,* 408-429.

Ghaffarian, S. (1987). The acculturation of Iranians in the United States. *Journal of Social Psychology, 127,* 565-571.

Golding, J. M., & Burnam, M. A. (1990). Immigration, stress, and depressive symptoms in a Mexican-American community. *Journal of Nervous and Mental Disease, 178,* 161-171.

Graves, T. D. (1967). Psychological acculturation in a tri-ethnic community. *Southwestern Journal of Anthropology, 23,* 337-350.

Gudykunst, W. B., & Hammer, M. R. (1984). Dimensions of intercultural effectiveness: Culture specific or culture general? *International Journal of Intercultural Relations, 8,* 1-10.

Gudykunst, W. B., & Hammer, M. R. (1988). Strangers and hosts: An uncertainty reduction based theory of intercultural adaptation. In Y. Y. Kim & W. B. Gudykunst (Eds.), *Cross-cultural adaptation: Current approaches* (pp. 106-139). Newbury Park, CA: Sage.

Gullahorn, J. E., & Gullahorn, J. T. (1966). American students abroad: Professional vs. personal development. *Annals, 368,* 43-59.

Gullahorn, J. T., & Gullahorn, J. E. (1962). Visiting Fulbright professors as agents of cross-cultural communication. *Sociology and Social Research, 46,* 282-293.

Gullahorn, J. T., & Gullahorn, J. E. (1963). An extension of the U-curve hypothesis. *Journal of Social Issues, 19,* 33-47.

Guskin, A. E. (1966). Tradition and change in a Thai university. In R. B. Textor (Ed.), *Cultural frontiers of the Peace Corps* (pp. 87-106). Cambridge: MIT Press.

Guthrie, G. M., & Zektick, I. N. (1967). Predicting performance in the Peace Corps. *Journal of Social Psychology, 71,* 11-21.

Hammer, M. R. (1987). Behavioral dimensions of intercultural effectiveness: A replication and extension. *International Journal of Intercultural Relations, 11,* 65-88.

Hammer, M. R., Gudykunst, W. B., & Wiseman, R. L. (1978). Dimensions of intercultural effectiveness: An exploratory study. *International Journal of Intercultural Relations, 2,* 382-393.

Hammer, M. R., & Martin, J. M. (1990, November). *The effect of cross-cultural training on information exchange, uncertainty reduction, and anxiety reduction of American managers in a Japanese/American joint venture.* Paper presented to the International and Intercultural Division of the Speech Communication Association Annual Convention, Chicago.

Harris, J. G. (1972). Prediction of success on a distant Pacific Island: Peace Corps style. *Journal of Clinical and Consulting Psychology, 38,* 181-190.

Hawes, F., & Kealey, D. (1980). *Canadians in development.* Ottawa: Canadian International Development Agency.

Heath, G. L. (1970). Foreign student attitudes at International House, Berkeley. *International Educational and Cultural Exchange, 5,* 66-70.

Hinkle, L. (1974). The effect of exposure to culture change, social change, and changes in interpersonal relationships on health. In B. S. Dohrenwend & B. P. Dohrenwend (Eds.), *Stressful life events: Their nature and effects* (pp. 9-44). New York: John Wiley.

Holmes, T. H., & Masuda, M. (1974). Life change and illness susceptibility. In B. S. Dohrenwend & B. P. Dohrenwend (Eds.), *Stressful life events: Their nature and effects* (pp. 45-72). New York: John Wiley.

Holmes, T. H., & Rahe, R. H. (1967). The Social Readjustment Rating Scale. *Journal of Psychosomatic Research, 11,* 213-218.

Hull, W. F. (1978). *Foreign students in the United States of America: Coping behavior within the educational environment.* New York: Praeger.

Hung, Y. Y. (1974). Socio-cultural environment and locus of control. *Psychologica Taiwanica, 16,* 187-198.

Hutnik, N. (1986). Patterns of ethnic minority identification and modes of social adaptation. *Ethnic and Racial Studies, 9,* 150-167.

Ibrahim, S. E. M. (1970). Interaction, perception, and attitudes of Arab students toward Americans. *Sociology and Social Research, 55,* 29-46.

Johnson, J. H., & Sarason, I. G. (1979). Recent developments in research on life stress. In

V. Hamilton & D. M. Warburton (Eds.), *Human stress and cognition* (pp. 205-233). New York: John Wiley.

Kang, T. S. (1972). A foreign student group as an ethnic community. *International Review of Modern Sociology, 2,* 72-82.

Kaplan, M. S., & Marks, G. (1990). Adverse effects of acculturation: Psychological distress among Mexican American young adults. *Social Science and Medicine, 31,* 1313-1319.

Kealey, D. (1989). A study of cross-cultural effectiveness: Theoretical issues and practical applications. *International Journal of Intercultural Relations, 13,* 387-428.

Keefe, S. M., & Padilla, A. M. (1987). *Chicano ethnicity.* Albuquerque: University of New Mexico Press.

Kennedy, A. (1994). *Personality and psychological adjustment during cross-cultural transitions: A study of the cultural fit proposition.* Unpublished master's thesis, University of Canterbury, New Zealand.

Kim, Y. Y. (1988). *Communication and cross-cultural adaptation.* Philadelphia: Multilingual Matters.

Klineberg, O., & Hull, W. F. (1979). *At a foreign university: An international study of adaptation and coping.* New York: Praeger.

Korn-Ferry International. (1981). *The repatriation of the American international executive.* New York: Author.

Krishnan, A., & Berry, J. W. (1992). Acculturative stress and acculturation attitudes among Indian immigrants to the United States. *Psychology and Developing Societies, 4,* 187-212.

Kuo, W. H., Gray, R., & Lin, N. (1976). Locus of control and symptoms of distress among Chinese-Americans. *International Journal of Social Psychiatry, 22,* 176-187.

Kuo, W. H., & Tsai, V.-M. (1986). Social networking, hardiness, and immigrants' mental health. *Journal of Health and Social Behavior, 27,* 133-149.

Lai, J., & Linden, W. (1993). The smile of Asia: Acculturation effects on symptom reporting. *Canadian Journal of Behavioral Science, 25,* 303-313.

Landis, D., & Brislin, R. W. (Eds.). (1983). *Handbook of intercultural training.* Elmsford, NY: Pergamon.

Landis, D., Brislin, R. W., & Hulgus, J. F. (1985). Attributional training versus contact in acculturative learning: A laboratory study. *Journal of Applied Social Psychology, 15,* 466-482.

Landis, D., Brislin, R. W., Swanner, G., Tseng, O., & Thomas, J. (1985). Some effects of acculturative training: A field evaluation. *International Journal of Group Tensions, 15,* 68-91.

Lasry, J. C. (1988). Immigrants' mental health and social relations in Montreal. In J. W. Berry & R. C. Annis (Eds.), *Ethnic psychology: Research and practice with immigrants, refugees, native peoples, ethnic groups, and sojourners* (pp. 125-134). Lisse: Swets & Zeitlinger.

Lasry, J. C., & Sayegh, L. (1992). Developing an acculturation scale: A bidimensional model. In N. Grizenko, L. Sayegh, & P. Migneault (Eds.), *Transcultural issues in child psychiatry* (pp. 67-86). Montreal: Editions Douglas.

Lazarus, R. S. (1976). *Patterns of adjustment.* New York: McGraw-Hill.

Lazarus, R. S., & Folkman, S. (1984). *Stress, coping, and appraisal.* New York: Springer.

Lefley, H. (1986). Evaluating the effects of cross-cultural training: Some research results. In H. Lefley & P. Pedersen (Eds.), *Cross-cultural training for mental health professionals* (pp. 265-307). Springfield, IL: Charles C Thomas.

Lin, K., Tazuma, L., & Masuda, M. (1979). Adaptational problems of Vietnamese refugees: I. Health and mental status. *Archives of General Psychiatry, 36,* 955-961.

Locke, S. A., & Feinsod, F. (1982). Psychological preparation for young adults traveling abroad. *Adolescence, 17,* 815-819.

Lysgaard, S. (1955). Adjustment in a foreign society: Norwegian Fulbright grantees visiting the United States. *International Social Science Bulletin, 7,* 45-51.

Martin, J. (1986). Training issues in cross-cultural orientation. *International Journal of Intercultural Relations, 10,* 103-116.

Martin, J. (1987). The relationship between student sojourner perceptions of intercultural competencies and previous sojourn experience. *International Journal of Intercultural Relations, 11,* 337-355.

Masuda, M., Lin, K., & Tazuma, L. (1980). Adaptational problems of Vietnamese refugees: II. Life changes and perceptions of life events. - *Archives of General Psychiatry, 37,* 447-450.

Masuda, M., Lin, K., & Tazuma, L. (1982). Life changes among Vietnamese refugees. In R. C. Nann (Ed.), *Uprooting and surviving* (pp. 25-33). Boston: Reidel.

Mavreas, V., & Bebbington, P. (1990). Acculturation and psychiatric disorder: A study of Greek

Cypriot immigrants. *Psychological Medicine, 20,* 941-951.

McGuire, M., & McDermott, S. (1988). Communication in assimilation, deviance, and alienation states. In Y. Y. Kim & W. B. Gudykunst (Eds.), *Cross-cultural adaptation: Current approaches* (pp. 90-105). Newbury Park, CA: Sage.

Mena, F. J., Padilla, A. M., & Maldonado, M. (1987). Acculturative stress and specific coping strategies among immigrant and later generation college students. *Hispanic Journal of Behavioral Sciences, 9,* 207-225.

Mendenhall, M., & Oddou, G. (1985). The dimensions of expatriate acculturation. *Academy of Management Review, 10,* 39-47.

Mendoza, R. H. (1984). Acculturation and sociocultural variability. In J. L. Martinez, Jr. & R. H. Mendoza (Eds.), *Chicano psychology* (pp. 61-75). San Diego: Academic Press.

Mitchell, T. R., Dossett, D., Fiedler, F., & Triandis, H. (1972). Cultural training: Validation evidence for the cultural assimilator. *International Journal of Psychology, 7,* 97-104.

Moghaddam, F. M. (1988). Individualistic and collectivistic integration strategies among immigrants: Toward a mobility model of cultural integration. In J. W. Berry & R. C. Annis (Eds.), *Ethnic psychology: Research and practice with immigrants, refugees, native peoples, ethnic groups, and sojourners* (pp. 69-79). Lisse: Swets & Zeitlinger.

Moghaddam, F. M., Ditto, B., & Taylor, D. (1990). Attitudes and attributions related to symptomatology in Indian immigrant women. *Journal of Cross-Cultural Psychology, 21,* 335-350.

Monroe, S. M. (1982). Life events and disorder: Event-symptom associations and the course of disorder. *Journal of Abnormal Psychology 91,* 14-24.

Montgomery, G. T. (1992). Comfort with acculturation status among students from South Texas. *Hispanic Journal of Behavioral Sciences, 14,* 201-223.

Moyerman, D. R., & Forman, B. D. (1992). Acculturation and adjustment: A meta-analytic study. *Hispanic Journal of Behavioral Sciences, 14,* 163-200.

Muhlin, G. L. (1979). Mental hospitalization of the foreign-born and the role of cultural isolation. *International Journal of Psychiatry, 25,* 258-266.

Naidoo, J. (1985). A cultural perspective on the adjustment of South Asian women in Canada. In I. R. Lagunes & Y. H. Poortinga (Eds.), *From a different perspective: Studies of behavior across cultures* (pp. 76-92). Lisse: Swets & Zeitlinger.

Neffe, J. A., & Hoppe, S. K. (1993). Race/ethnicity, acculturation, and psychological distress: Fatalism and religiosity as cultural resources. *Journal of Community Psychology, 21,* 3-20.

Oberg, K. (1960). Cultural shock: Adjustment to new cultural environments. *Practical Anthropology, 7,* 177-182.

O'Brien, G. E., Fiedler, F., & Hewlett, T. (1970). The effects of programmed culture training upon the performance of volunteer medical teams in Central America. *Human Relations, 24,* 209-231.

Olmeda, E. L. (1979). Acculturation: A psychometric perspective. *American Psychologist, 34,* 1061-1070.

Orozo, S., Thompson, B., Kapes, J., & Montgomery, G. T. (1993). Measuring the acculturation of Mexican Americans: A covariance structure analysis. *Measurement and Evaluation in Counseling and Development, 25,* 149-155.

Padilla, A. M. (1980). The role of cultural awareness and ethnic loyalty in acculturation. In A. M. Padilla (Ed.), *Acculturation: Theory models and some new findings* (pp. 47-84). Boulder, CO: Westview.

Padilla, A. M., Wagatsuma, Y., & Lindholm, K. J. (1985). Acculturation and personality as predictors of stress in Japanese and Japanese-Americans. *Journal of Social Psychology, 125,* 295-305.

Park, R. E. (1929). Human migration and the marginal man. *American Journal of Sociology, 33,* 881-893.

Parker, B., & McEvoy, G. M. (1993). Initial examination of a model of intercultural adjustment. *International Journal of Intercultural Relations, 17,* 355-380.

Partridge, K. (1987). How to become Japanese: A guide for North Americans. *Kyoto Journal, 4,* 12-15.

Pedersen, S. (1949). Psychopathological reactions to extreme social displacements. *Psychoanalytic Review, 26,* 344-354.

Perkins, C. S., Perkins, M. L., Guglielmino, L. M., & Reiff, R. F. (1977). A comparison of adjustment problems of three international student groups.

Journal of College Student Personnel, 18, 382-388.

Pruitt, F. J. (1978). The adaptation of African students to American society. *International Journal of Intercultural Relations, 21,* 90-118.

Redfield, R., Linton, R., & Herskovits, M. J. (1936). Memorandum for the study of acculturation. *American Anthropologist, 38,* 149-152.

Richardson, A. (1974). *British immigrants and Australia: A psycho-social inquiry.* Canberra: Australian National University Press.

Rogers, J., & Ward, C. (1993). Expectation-experience discrepancies and psychological adjustment during cross-cultural reentry. *International Journal of Intercultural Relations, 17,* 185-196.

Rogler, L., Cortes, D., & Malgady, R. (1991). Acculturation and mental health status among Hispanics: Convergence and new directions for research. *American Psychologist, 46,* 585-597.

Rosenthal, D., Bell, R., Demetriou, A., & Efklides, A. (1989). From collectivism to individualism? The acculturation of Greek immigrants in Australia. *International Journal of Psychology, 24,* 57-71.

Ruben, B. D., & Kealey, D. J. (1979). Behavioral assessment of communication competency and the prediction of cross-cultural adaptation. *International Journal of Intercultural Relations, 3,* 15-47.

Sano, H. (1990). Research on social difficulties in cross-cultural adjustment: Social situational analysis. *Japanese Journal of Behavioral Therapy, 16,* 37-44.

Sayegh, L., & Lasry, J. C. (1993). Immigrants' adaptation to Canada: Assimilation, acculturation, and orthogonal cultural identification. *Canadian Psychology, 34,* 98-109.

Schmitz, P. G. (1992). Immigrant mental and physical health. *Psychology and Developing Societies, 4,* 117-131.

Searle, W., & Ward, C. (1990). The prediction of psychological and socio-cultural adjustment during cross-cultural transitions. *International Journal of Intercultural Relations, 14,* 449-464.

Selby, H. A., & Woods, C. M. (1966). Foreign students at a high pressure university. *Sociology of Education, 39,* 138-154.

Seligman, M. E. P. (1975). *Helplessness: On depression, development, and death.* San Francisco: Freeman.

Selltiz, C., Christ, J. R., Havel, J., & Cook, S. W. (1963). *Attitudes and social relations of foreign students in the United States.* Minneapolis: University of Minnesota Press.

Sewell, W. H., & Davidsen, O. M. (1961). *Scandinavian students on an American campus.* Minneapolis: University of Minnesota Press.

Singh, A. (1989). Impact of acculturation on psychological stress: A study of the Oraon tribe. In D. M. Keats, D. Munro, & L. Mann (Eds.), *Heterogeneity in cross-cultural psychology* (pp. 210-215). Lisse: Swets & Zeitlinger.

Sinha, D., Mishra, C., & Berry, J. W. (1992). Acculturative stress in nomadic and sedentary tribes of Bihar, India. In S. Iwawaki, Y. Kashima, & K. Leung (Eds.), *Innovations in cross-cultural psychology* (pp. 396-407). Lisse: Swets & Zeitlinger.

Spradley, J. P., & Phillips, M. (1972). Culture and stress: A quantitative analysis. *American Anthropologist, 74,* 518-529.

Stone Feinstein, E., & Ward, C. (1990). Loneliness and psychological adjustment of sojourners: New perspectives on culture shock. In D. M. Keats, D. Munro, & L. Mann (Eds.), *Heterogeneity in cross-cultural psychology* (pp. 537-547). Lisse: Swets & Zeitlinger.

Stonequist, E. V. (1935). The problem of the marginal man. *American Journal of Sociology, 41,* 1-12.

Suinn, R. M., Ahuna, C., & Khoo, G. (1992). The Suinn-Lew Asian Self-Identity Acculturation Scale: Concurrent and factorial validation. *Educational and Psychological Measurement, 52,* 1041-1046.

Suinn, R. M., Richard-Figueroa, K., Lew, S., & Vigil, P. (1987). The Suinn-Lew Asian Self-Identity Acculturation Scale: An initial report. *Educational and Psychological Measurement, 47,* 401-402.

Sykes, I. J., & Eden, D. (1987). Transitional stress, social support, and psychological strain. *Journal of Occupational Behavior, 6,* 293-298.

Szapocznik, J., & Kurtines, W. M. (1980). Acculturation, biculturalism, and adjustment among Cuban Americans. In A. M. Padilla (Ed.), *Psychological dimensions of the acculturation process: Theory, models, and some new findings* (pp. 139-160). Boulder, CO: Westview.

Szapocznik, J., Kurtines, W. M., & Fernandez, T. (1980). Bicultural involvement and adjustment in Hispanic-American youths. *Interna-*

tional Journal of Intercultural Relations, 4, 353-365.

Szapocznik, J., Scopetta, M. A., Kurtines, W. M., & Aranalde, M. A. (1978). Theory and measurement of acculturation. Inter-American Journal of Psychology, 12, 113-130.

Taft, R. (1977). Coping with unfamiliar cultures. In N. Warren (Ed.), Studies in cross-cultural psychology (pp. 121-151). San Diego: Academic Press.

Takai, J. (1989). The adjustment of international students at a third culture-like academic community in Japan: A longitudinal study. Human Communication Studies, 17, 113-120.

Tanaka, T., Takai, J., Kohyama, T., & Fujihara, T. (1994). Adjustment patterns of international students in Japan. International Journal of Intercultural Relations, 18, 55-75.

Thomson, C. P., & English, J. T. (1964). Premature return of Peace Corps volunteers. Public Health Reports, 79, 1065-1073.

Torbiorn, I. (1982). Living abroad: Personal adjustment and personnel policy in the overseas setting. Chichester, UK: Wiley.

Torres-Rivera, M. A. (1985). Manifestations of depression in Puerto Rican migrants to the United States and Puerto Rican residents of Puerto Rico. In I. R. Lagunes & Y. H. Poortinga (Eds.), From a different perspective: Studies of behavior across cultures (pp. 63-75). Lisse: Swets & Zeitlinger.

Triandis, H. C., Kashima, Y., Shimada, E., & Villareal, M. (1986). Acculturation indices as a means of confirming cultural differences. International Journal of Psychology, 21, 43-70.

Triandis, H. C., & Vassiliou, V. (1967). Frequency of contact and stereotyping. Journal of Personality and Social Psychology, 7, 316-328.

Trower, P., Bryant, B., & Argyle, M. (1978). Social skills and mental health. New York: Methuen.

Van den Broucke, S., de Soete, G., & Bohrer, A. (1989). Free response self-description as a predictor of success and failure in adolescent exchange students. International Journal of Intercultural Relations, 13, 73-91.

Ward, C. (1988). Stress, coping, and adjustment in victims of sexual assault: The role of psychological defense mechanisms. Counseling Psychology Quarterly, 1, 165-178.

Ward, C., & Chang, W. C. (1995). "Cultural fit": A new perspective on personality and sojourner adjustment. Manuscript submitted for publication.

Ward, C., & Kennedy, A. (1992). Locus of control, mood disturbance, and social difficulty during cross-cultural transitions. International Journal of Intercultural Relations, 16, 175-194.

Ward, C., & Kennedy, A. (1993a). Acculturation and cross-cultural adaptation of British residents in Hong Kong. Journal of Social Psychology, 133, 395-397.

Ward, C., & Kennedy, A. (1993b). Psychological and socio-cultural adjustment during cross-cultural transitions: A comparison of secondary students at home and abroad. International Journal of Psychology, 28, 129-147.

Ward, C., & Kennedy, A. (1993c). Where's the culture in cross-cultural transition? Comparative studies of sojourner adjustment. Journal of Cross-cultural Psychology, 24, 221-249.

Ward, C., & Kennedy, A. (1994a). Acculturation strategies, psychological adjustment, and socio-cultural competence during cross-cultural transitions. International Journal of Intercultural Relations, 18, 329-343.

Ward, C., & Kennedy, A. (1994b, July). Before and after cross-cultural transition: A study of New Zealand volunteers on field assignments. Paper presented at the XII International Congress of the International Association for Cross-Cultural Psychology, Pamplona, Spain.

Ward, C., & Kennedy, A. (in press). Crossing cultures: The relationship between psychological and sociocultural dimensions of cross-cultural adjustment. In J. Pandey, D. Sinha, & P. S. Bhawuk (Eds.), Asian contributions to cross-cultural psychology. New Delhi, India: Sage.

Ward, C., Okura, Y., Kennedy, A., & Kojima, T. (1995, August). The U-curve on trial: A longitudinal study of psychological and sociocultural adjustment during cross-cultural transition. Paper presented at the International Union of Psychological Science Asian-Pacific Regional Conference of Psychology, Guangzhou, China.

Ward, C., & Searle, W. (1991). The impact of value discrepancies and cultural identity on psychological and socio-cultural adjustment of sojourners. International Journal of Intercultural Relations, 15, 209-225.

Weissman, D., & Furnham, A. (1987). The expectations and experiences of a sojourning temporary resident abroad: A preliminary study. Human Relations, 40, 313-326.

Westermeyer, J., Neider, J., & Callies, A. (1990). Psychosocial adjustment of Hmong refugees during their first decade in the United States. *Journal of Nervous and Mental Disease, 177,* 132-139.

Wong-Rieger, D. (1984). Testing a model of emotional and coping responses to problems in adaptation: Foreign students at a Canadian university. *International Journal of Intercultural Relations, 8,* 153-184.

Wong-Rieger, D., & Quintana, D. (1987). Comparative acculturation of Southeast Asian and Hispanic immigrants and sojourners. *International Journal of Intercultural Relations, 8,* 153-184.

Worchel, S., & Mitchell, T. R. (1972). An evaluation of the effectiveness of the cultural assimilator in Thailand and Greece. *Journal of Applied Psychology, 56,* 472-479.

Ying, Y.-W., & Liese, L. H. (1991). Emotional well-being of Taiwan students in the U.S.: An examination of pre- to post-arrival differential. *International Journal of Intercultural Relations, 15,* 345-366.

Yoshikawa, M. J. (1988). Cross-cultural adaptation and perceptual development. In Y. Y. Kim & W. B. Gudykunst (Eds.), *Cross-cultural adaptation: Current approaches* (pp. 140-148). Newbury Park, CA: Sage.

Zaidi, S. M. H. (1975). Adjustment problems of foreign Muslim students in Pakistan. In R. W. Brislin, S. Bochner, & W. J. Lonner (Eds.), *Cross-cultural perspectives on learning* (pp. 117-130). New York: John Wiley.

Zak, I. (1973). Dimensions of Jewish-American identity. *Psychological Reports, 33,* 891-900.

Zak, I. (1976). Structure of ethnic identity of Arab-Israeli students. *Psychological Reports, 38,* 239-246.

Zheng, X., & Berry, J. W. (1991). Psychological adaptation of Chinese sojourners in Canada. *International Journal of Psychology, 26,* 451-470.

8

Intercultural Trainer Competencies

R. MICHAEL PAIGE

Intercultural sensitivity is not natural. It is not part of our primate past, nor has it characterized most of human history. Cross-cultural contact usually has been accompanied by bloodshed, oppression, or genocide. . . . Education and training in intercultural communication is an approach to changing our "natural" behavior. With the concepts and skills developed in this field, we ask learners to transcend traditional ethnocentrism and to explore new relationships across cultural boundaries. This attempt at change must be approached with the greatest possible care.

—M. Bennett, 1993, p. 21

[I]ntercultural education is inherently transformative. It is preparing learners for a major transition in their lives and it is, in fact, a part of that transition. As such, it poses serious risks for the learner. Competent intercultural educators will recognize these risks, systematically assess learning activities in light of them, and sequence those activities accordingly.

—Paige, 1993a, p. 18

THIS chapter is about competence in intercultural training, a matter that has generated much discussion in recent years (Black & Mendenhall, 1990; Hammer, 1989; Paige, 1986, 1993b). Of great concern among professional trainers are individuals entering and practicing in this field who do not possess the requisite knowledge, education, experience, and training skills to be doing the work they are doing. The purpose of this chapter is to specify what constitutes competence for intercultural trainers. What knowledge do they need? What kind of intercultural experience do they need to have had? What types of skills are required of them? Which personal qualities will help them be more effective in their work?

In this chapter, the term *intercultural trainer* is applied to those individuals whose work involves them as educators and trainers in the cultural lives of persons, groups, and organizations either in a domestic setting (diversity training) or in the international arena (international training). Their work consists of the following kinds of activities:

> Training designed to prepare individuals to live and work effectively in cultures other than their own through the acquisition of relevant knowledge, skills, and attitudes
>
> Training designed to promote an organization's capacity to function effectively in cultural settings other than its own
>
> Training directed toward assisting individuals, groups, and organizations in managing cultural diversity
>
> Training directed toward social and cultural change intended to reduce racism, sexism, homophobia, and other forms of discrimination or inequity that may pertain in a given society
>
> Training directed toward social and cultural change intended to reduce intergroup conflict and to promote more harmonious intergroup relations

Fundamentally, intercultural trainers are concerned with human relations. Their goal is to promote more effective intercultural interactions between persons and groups by making learners aware of the impact of culture on their lives. Their approach is to educate from an intercultural communication perspective, and in so doing, they enable learners to effect their own intercultural development. In one sense, they may be thought of as cultural interventionists because they deal with the issues of cultural awareness, transition, and transformation. Although it is still most common to refer to these professionals as *trainers* (the convention I follow in this chapter), I adhere to the position taken by J. Bennett (1986) that intercultural trainers should more properly be thought of as educators, given the breadth of content, the complexities of the issues, and the range of learning objectives and instructional methods that characterize this field.

The intercultural trainer's role is complex. First, *trainers are consultants* who advise their clients on a wide range of issues. As an extensive literature suggests, many skills are required of consultants working in international and intercultural contexts (see Casino, 1983, for an excellent treatment of this subject). Second, *trainers are curriculum specialists* who

must be able to design programs often quite unlike traditional forms of education in terms of process and content. They must possess a great deal of knowledge and expertise to do this effectively. Third, *trainers are educators* who are responsible for creating appropriate learning environments and facilitating the learning process. Fourth, *trainers are often "change agents"* who are actively involved in facilitating individual as well as organizational transformations. Fifth, *trainers are assessment specialists* who can evaluate programs and their impact.

Clearly, to be a competent practitioner in this profession requires considerable knowledge, experience, and skill. As Paige and Martin (Chapter 3, this volume) point out, intercultural training is inherently transformative (change oriented) and thus is exceptionally demanding of both trainers and learners. It is education in the most profound sense of the term (the facilitation of learning in the cognitive, affective, and behavioral domains). It can be very stressful.

Intercultural training is now a global phenomenon, and my analysis of trainer competencies is intended to have validity for intercultural trainers wherever they may practice. It is important to note, however, that intercultural training has been strongly influenced by North American social and behavioral science perspectives, as well as by instructional approaches. Experiential education, for example, is more popular in North America than in some other parts of the world and is generally viewed by trainers in the West as a significant and necessary component of training methodology. Intercultural trainers elsewhere, as a function of their own academic training and the different cultural contexts in which they practice, may disagree on the validity of experiential education, or certain manifestations of it, for their audiences. They may question some of the principles I am enunciating and may bring others to the attention of the intercultural field. I welcome that dialogue and expect that, through a continuing discourse, the conceptual sense of what constitutes trainer competencies will achieve an even greater universality.

This chapter is organized into two parts, one conceptual and the other applied. In Part 1, trainer competencies are conceptualized in terms of knowledge, skills, and personal qualities. Each of these categories is discussed in detail. In Part 2, trainer competencies are examined in a more practical manner. The consequences of inadequate trainer knowledge and skills are conceptualized and then illustrated by two case studies.

PART 1:
FOUNDATIONS OF TRAINER COMPETENCE

The basic foundations of trainer competence are education and experience. Education is necessary for the acquisition of the theoretical body of knowledge that guides the trainer in all aspects of the craft, from the development of a philosophy of training to the actual design, implementation, and evaluation of programs. Experience translates knowledge into actual training skills. In this regard, relevant experiences are of two types: substantive life experience in culturally diverse settings and experience with training itself. Education and experience are lifelong pursuits for the professional trainer who recognizes that one can never know all there is to know or fully master all of the skills related to intercultural training. New knowledge is continuously being generated, and new social issues arise that require trainers to review and refine their approaches. Competent trainers, thus, are also *reflective trainers,* persons who reflect on each training program, relate it to the literature and their own past training experiences, and learn from it. Each training program, in its own way, is a test of their theoretical knowledge and skills. Each provides an opportunity for reflective trainers to refine their theories, improve their training design, and develop their training skills.

My conceptual model for trainer competencies is organized into four categories: knowledge, skills, personal qualities, and ethics. This model is based on my earlier writings on this topic (Paige, 1986, 1993b) but differs from them in certain respects. Some ideas are expanded; others are synthesized.

Trainer Competencies: Knowledge

The first category of trainer competencies is *knowledge,* what intercultural trainers need to know. Knowledge is the foundation of training expertise. The nine areas that together constitute the core of knowledge for intercultural trainers are the following:

Intercultural phenomena
Intercultural learning
Intercultural training: Design issues
Intercultural training: Learner issues
Intercultural training: Trainer issues
Intercultural training: Content
Intercultural training: Pedagogy
International training issues
Diversity training issues

Intercultural Phenomena

Trainers need a thorough conceptual foundation in intercultural communication and relations. According to Paige (1993a, 1993b), they must understand the psychological and social dynamics of the intercultural experience and have a command of key concepts, such as intercultural effectiveness, competence, development, adjustment, learning, culture shock, cultural differences, and reentry adjustment. Many authors (Brislin, Cushner, Cherrie, & Yong, 1986; Brislin & Yoshida, 1994; Paige, 1993a; Weaver, 1993) have emphasized the importance of stress in intercultural encounters, its causes and consequences, and strategies for coping with it (see Chapter 7, this volume).

It is essential that trainers are theoretically familiar with the causes and consequences of culture contact, misunderstandings, and conflict, as well as with the factors that promote effective intercultural interactions. This knowledge enables them to assess where the learners are, what they are or will be experiencing in their lives, what types of developmental stages they are going through, what their learning needs are, what training should address, and how it should address it. They must also know themselves: who they are, culturally speaking, what their training strengths and weaknesses are, and what their so-called hot buttons are (issues that trigger powerful emotional responses in them). In the final analysis, an ignorant trainer will most likely be an incompetent one. Lacking the necessary knowledge foundation, such a trainer can do more harm than good.

Intercultural Learning

The competent trainer will understand the dynamics of intercultural learning, the stages of development associated with it, and the ways to help facilitate it among the learners. Understanding the stages of intercultural development is crucial because it provides the trainer with an important tool for assessing learner needs, interpreting learner performance in the program, and responding with appropriate learning activities in the training design. A number of developmental models have been constructed, but the model presented by Milton Bennett (1986a, 1986b, 1993) is the most conceptually sophisticated one and the most important for intercultural trainers. He discusses intercultural sensitivity in terms of how learners respond to cultural difference and identifies six major stages of development: the *ethnocentric stages* of denial, defense, and minimization and the *ethnorelative stages* of acceptance, adaptation, and integration.

Intercultural trainers, especially those working in the multicultural field in the United States, should also be familiar with conceptual models of ethnic identity development (Salett & Koslow, 1994). Among the best known and most important are those by Banks (1988), Cross (1978), Helms (1990), and Parham (1989). The learners' levels of intercultural sensitivity and sense of ethnic identity will strongly influence their response to training, their degree of openness to intercultural learning. Competent trainers will understand how these developmental factors can be taken into account in the training design to effectively facilitate learning.

Learning styles also influence the ways participants will respond to various intercultural learning activities in the training setting. The most commonly used instrument to assess learning styles, one that many trainers have found to be quite valuable, is Kolb's (1976) Learning Style Inventory (LSI) and its deriva-

tive, the Learning Type Measure (Excel, 1993). An effective intercultural training pedagogy will use learning activities that address all of Kolb's basic four learning styles: concrete experience, reflective observation, abstract conceptual, and active experimentation. The systematic use of these four learning styles can also promote culture learning (Kolb, 1984).

Intercultural Training: Design Issues

An understanding of intercultural training design is a core area of knowledge. Competent trainers know how complex intercultural training is and what elements must be considered in putting together a sound program. Overall training design consists of organizational and learner needs assessments, goal and objective setting, staff selection and preparation, identification of content and training methods, and the implementation of the program and formative and summative evaluations. It also includes being able to determine the logistical needs of the program, how much and what type of learning can be realized within different periods of time, what training can and cannot accomplish, and how training relates to actual performance. Skilled trainers have criteria for selecting among alternative training approaches and know what content items are appropriate for learners. The competent trainer will address these issues methodically in developing the program design.

Intercultural Training: Learner Issues

The competent trainer will understand the challenges associated with learning in an intercultural setting, the stages of development leading toward intercultural competence, the role of training and trainers in the learning process, and the nature and sources of learner resistance to training. Intercultural learning is quite profound; it includes learning about oneself as a cultural being, learning about one's own culture, and learning about a target culture. It involves deep, significant, and at times, painful reflection. It can threaten the learners' sense of cultural identity and worldview; they may, for example, think their values will be compromised by the intercultural experience. They may resist changing or adapting to another culture on the ground that this will violate their own integrity. As the learners proceed through their learning experiences, trainers must be adept at *debriefing* those experiences—that is, helping the learners conceptualize what is happening to them.

Trainers must also be aware of the dynamics of the trainer-learner relationship. At times, the learners will be very dependent on the trainer (e.g., for information and guidance). McCaffery (1993) suggests that the aim of trainers should be "to move people toward developing/ enhancing the skills they need to become independently effective cross-cultural sojourners" (p. 226). He adds this means knowing how to avoid the dependency syndrome and how to assist learners in learning how to learn (managing their intercultural transitions, gaining fluency in everyday life and communication skills, and developing their knowledge). At other times, learners will be resistant for various reasons (e.g., fatigue, training overload, perceived threats to their cultural sense of self). Competent trainers must know how to manage learner resistance, or else they risk serious disruptions to the program and the learning process.

Intercultural Training: Trainer Issues

Intercultural training can be as challenging for trainers as it is for learners. Trainers often deal with issues that threaten the learners; as learners' anxiety increases, so does their level of resistance to training. Trainers must be prepared to handle learner resistance and frustration because these are often directed at the trainers.

It is also essential that intercultural trainers know themselves: their strengths and weaknesses as trainers, their own cultural identity, their hot buttons, and their own biases and prejudices. As professionals, they must know these things and be able to handle them. For example, skilled trainers will not facilitate learning activities they are unfamiliar with or have a bias against. They will work out ways to handle their own negative feelings when a hot button is pushed (e.g., let a co-trainer know in advance what those are and have the co-trainer respond when the situation arises).

Intercultural Training: Content

Intercultural trainers must have a mastery of content. First, they must understand it themselves. Second, they must know what content is appropriate for different types of programs and for programs of different lengths. Intercultural communication concepts and theories are central and will represent the core of the program (the foundation for further learning). Trainers must also be familiar with the distinction between culture-general and culture-specific training, know how to balance these in the training design, and know when to incorporate each into the learning process.

Intercultural Training: Pedagogy

Intercultural training pedagogy differs from mainstream education in many respects (Paige, 1993a; Paige & Martin, Chapter 3, this volume). Not only must trainers know about the different training methodologies, but they also must know how to sequence them appropriately. They must understand how different approaches relate to different learning styles, to learners from various cultural backgrounds, and to the goals and objectives of training. The risks for the learner are higher in intercultural programs, and trainers must know how and when certain activities, as a function of their content and the process being employed, will be particularly high risk. Trainers must be skilled in debriefing as well.

International Training Issues

Many intercultural trainers prepare sojourners (e.g., businesspersons, students, diplomats) to live, work, and study in other countries. Those trainers must be familiar with the culture-specific and culture-general content requirements of international training. Culture-specific content will include detailed information regarding the job assignment, the culture variables (value orientations, communication styles, patterns of behavior) to which they must adjust and adapt, and so forth. Given that the learners will be making a transition in their lives, they must also be introduced to culture-general content regarding the intercultural experience. Trainers preparing individuals who will be working in so-called Third World countries, especially those working on development assistance projects, must have considerable knowledge of social change and development, change agentry, and the thorny dominant-subordinate relationship issues that occur between the "helpers" and those being helped.

Diversity Training Issues

Diversity training, as Paige and Martin (Chapter 3, this volume) point out, is extremely challenging and very demanding of the trainer (for one organization's approach, see Chapter 11). It focuses on serious social problems, such as race and gender relations, that are as yet unresolved. Its purpose is to promote positive intergroup relations, improve the social environment of the workplace and other settings, and eliminate racism and other forms of discrimination. These are some of the most difficult goals to accomplish and require trainers who have a great deal of knowledge about the historical, cultural, political, and economic realities of the learners. They must also be knowledgeable about the issues of power (dominance and subordination), oppression, socioeconomic inequalities, and marginality as experienced and perceived by their clients.

Diversity training, because of the nature of its content, is almost always controversial, politicized, and stressful. The issues addressed provoke strong emotional responses. All of these factors must be understood if the intercultural training design is to be appropriate and the program itself successful.

Trainer Competencies: Skills

In addition to a substantial mastery of the knowledge areas identified above, intercultural trainers need skills to turn that knowledge into effective design, implementation, and evaluation of training. The six categories of skills that intercultural trainers must acquire and master are the following:

Organizational and learner needs assessments
Training design: Goals and objectives
Training design: Content
Training design: Pedagogy
Program implementation
Program evaluation

Organizational and Learner Needs Assessment

Before an intercultural training program can be designed, the competent trainer will conduct a thorough needs assessment of the client's organization and those who will participate in the program. The client's goals may vary from comparatively short-term training designed to develop specific intercultural skills to much longer programs intended to significantly change the entire organization. It is critical for the trainer to determine the client's expectations with respect to the organization and its members.

Among the questions to be asked during the organizational analysis phase, the most central are the following:

What are the organization's expected outcomes of training?
To what degree, if any, is the organization seeking to change itself?
Why is the organization seeking training at this point in time?
What is the organization's history regarding the issues it is seeking to address in training?
What is the organization's current situation regarding those issues?
What is the nature of the organization's commitment to training, and where is the impetus coming from (e.g., top management, employees)?

The second set of questions pertains to the needs of the learners. Some of the major questions include:

What are the demographics of those who will be involved in training?
With respect to gender, race, ethnicity, nationality, and other characteristics, how

homogeneous or heterogeneous is the group?

How do the prospective learners feel about training (e.g., supportive, apprehensive)?

What knowledge, skills, and attitudes do the learners have regarding the issues to be addressed?

Are the training issues likely to be stressful ones for them?

What are their learning styles?

A needs analysis enables the trainer to gather the information needed to put together an appropriate training team, come to an agreement with the client on the time frame required for the program, design the program, and implement it. It is an essential component of intercultural training.

Training Design: Goals and Objectives

Training design begins with the needs assessment, during which information is generated that helps the trainer develop the goals and objectives of the program. *Goals* are broader and more general statements regarding the purposes of training. *Objectives* are more specific statements about organizational and learner outcomes. Learner outcomes, for example, can be categorized into the cognitive, behavioral, and affective (values, attitudes) domains of learning. These have to be established in the context of how much time should be devoted to training. Here is where trainer expertise is essential. The competent trainer will be able to set realistic goals and objectives, distinguish between the more immediate and longer term outcomes, set a time frame necessary for accomplishing the program's goals and objectives, and communicate all of this to the client.

Training Design: Content

It takes considerable skill to design an intercultural training program. One key element of training design is selecting the appropriate content. Trainers must select program content based on the needs of the learners and the goals and objectives of the program. Intercultural programs of any kind must include core intercultural communication concepts. Trainers must be familiar with the distinction between

culture-general and culture-specific content because most programs will include a combination of these.

Training Design: Pedagogy

Trainers must be able to select from a wide array of instructional methods those appropriate to the content of training and the intended learning outcomes (cognitive, behavioral, affective). They must be able to select and sequence learning activities in the context of the participants' learning styles and needs, the goals and objectives of training, the levels of intercultural sensitivity and competence represented in the group, the risks that different activities pose for learners, and the overall goals and objectives of training.

Program Implementation

In the actual process of conducting a training program, trainers must be able to function in a variety of roles, such as teachers, program administrators, and advisors. Intercultural training pedagogy also involves the ability of trainers to debrief learning activities (help learners make conceptual sense of what they are experiencing through a process of reflection). This task is particularly important for the more challenging, experienced-based learning exercises.

Program Evaluation

Intercultural trainers should be able to evaluate a program both while it is being implemented (formative assessment) and after it is completed (summative). The most immediate concern, of course, is how well the training program itself is progressing. Here, the trainer needs to be observant and have good intuition, qualities that can be developed over time.

The long-term question is whether the training program achieved its goals. This cannot be answered entirely at the conclusion of training because the participants have not yet had a chance to put into practice what they learned. At that point in time, neither they nor the organization can know whether the longer term goals and objectives have been attained. Evaluation models structured more longitudinally (at different points in time) will yield more information (for information on evaluation of training programs, see Chapter 9, this volume).

The competent trainer will understand evaluation principles and be able to construct and implement an evaluation scheme for the client.

Trainer Competencies: Personal Qualities

One question intercultural trainers are asked most frequently is, What personal qualities are associated with intercultural competence? Intercultural theory and research have identified specific behaviors, values, and attitudes related to intercultural competence (Lustig & Koester, 1993; Martin, 1989; Storti, 1989). Those most frequently and consistently mentioned in the literature are the following:

Tolerance of ambiguity
Cognitive and behavioral flexibility
Cultural identity
Patience
Enthusiasm and commitment
Interpersonal skills
Openness to new experiences and people
Empathy
Respect
Sense of humor

My premise here is that the interculturally competent person is far more likely to be a competent intercultural trainer. If trainers do not possess the knowledge, skills, and qualities they are trying to instill in others, they cannot be effective as trainers. These personal qualities, in my view, are just as important for conducting effective training programs as they are for effective intercultural communication and relations. Moreover, trainers who lack these qualities will not have credibility with the learners, many of whom will view their trainers as role models. The learners will see a contradiction between what they are being taught and what they are seeing in the trainer's own performance.

Let's then examine these qualities as they pertain to intercultural trainers and effective training programs.

Tolerance of Ambiguity

Every training situation—the program, training staff, and group of learners—is unique and inherently ambiguous. Trainers cannot anticipate exactly how well the group will come together, what problems individual learners will experience, what new learner needs might arise, which logistical problems might occur, and so forth. Trainers who cannot tolerate ambiguity are as likely to fail in training as they would be in a new cultural setting. Examples of trainer intolerance of ambiguity are rigid and unyielding adherence to the training plan, stress and anger over unexpected changes in any aspect of training, and negativity toward individual learners who are "not on track." None of these promote a supportive learning environment.

Cognitive and Behavioral Flexibility

Intercultural competence requires the ability to adapt to new ways of thinking and behaving. By extension, intercultural training competence requires the capacity to rethink and restructure programs in response to the complex dynamics of training (e.g., variations in pace of learner development, nature of acceptance and resistance to training as the program unfolds, differences in learning styles). Learners, as a function of their own life experiences, can bring new insights into training. This provides flexible trainers with the opportunity to reconceptualize, expand their own knowledge, and integrate these insights into training. The competent intercultural trainer will be able to respond cognitively and behaviorally to the dynamics of training.

Cultural Identity

Competent intercultural trainers must have a clear sense of their own cultural identity, according to Hammer (1989). *Cultural identity* refers to the sense persons have of their own values, attitudes, beliefs, style of communication, and patterns of behavior. Put another way, it means what cultural community they identify themselves with. As Adler (1976) pointed out many years ago, persons immersed in cross-cultural situations face many challenges—for example, confusion regarding cultural identity. As they become more competent in a second culture and language, they expand themselves culturally in their adaptation to the new culture's ways, some of which will contrast substantially with their own, others of which they will accept quite readily. As this process continues, they will seriously ponder what their core values and beliefs are. They may start to feel marginal in both cultures, a phenomenon very insightfully analyzed by J. Bennett (1993). This uncertainty about core cultural identity is normal but unsettling.

Learners in intercultural training programs also ponder these kind of questions and turn to trainers for answers. On the one hand, trainers who have not resolved these identity issues in their own lives cannot respond effectively to these questions. On the other hand, those who have integrated different cultural frames of reference into their lives and are comfortable with a multicultural sense of self can serve as excellent role models and resource persons. They can answer these questions on the basis of their own life experiences. In addition, they can conceptualize how culture influences human beings. Most important, they will provide opportunities for learners to examine themselves as cultural beings. In these ways, competent intercultural trainers can assist others in dealing with the identity issues associated with culture learning.

Patience

Patience is truly a virtue in intercultural training, just as in intercultural encounters. In their discussion of intercultural adjustment, Grove and Torbiorn (1993) introduce three psychological constructs: *applicability of behavior, clarity of mental frame of reference,* and *level of mere adequacy.* These refer, respectively, to the perceptions individuals hold regarding (a) how congruent their behaviors are with others in the culture, (b) how accurate their perspectives are of the culture and how it functions, and (c) how well they think they are doing in that culture as judged against their internal standards of personal competence (pp. 74-77). Grove and Torbiorn theorize that new cultural environments quickly challenge people to question their behavior. With the realization that they do not understand the behaviors of others or which behaviors are appropriate for

them in the new culture, they also question their mental framework. All of this contradicts how well they expected to perform, one response to which is to blame themselves for not learning more quickly and performing at the level of their own standards. Grove and Torbiorn suggest that people should be more patient with themselves and, in fact, temporarily lower their level of adequacy standard.

Patience is extremely important for trainers as well. It is critical for the quality and effectiveness of their relationship with the learners. For example, a trainer who has expectations that the learners will be able to acquire intercultural information and develop intercultural skills far more quickly than they in actuality can, will become frustrated with them. This frustration and impatience can discourage learners. Moreover, the inevitable logistical problems and delays will test the patience of the best trainer. The competent trainer will be able to adjust to these things; that often means exercising patience.

Enthusiasm and Commitment

Through their own enthusiasm and commitment to intercultural experiences, competent trainers inspire learners to undertake their own journeys. Such trainers balance the many challenging and stressful aspects of intercultural encounters with the knowledge that significant learning and personal growth, even positive organizational transformation, will be the longer term outcomes. They model this enthusiasm in their own behavior, values, attitudes, and life experiences. They fully understand the demanding nature of intercultural experiences, yet appreciate these as opportunities for personal and professional development. Their gift as trainers, as is the case for all fine teachers, is to be able to motivate a learner by means of their own enthusiasm and commitment to their subject.

Interpersonal Skills

Intercultural trainers work with a wide variety of individuals from their own society and from other countries and cultures. To be effective in their work, they must have very strong interpersonal skills. They must be adept at working in heterogeneous environments, sensitive to the needs and concerns of others, and able to communicate and interact effectively.

Openness to New Experiences and People

Openness is a personal quality that leads many into intercultural and international fields in the first place, and it is an essential quality of competent trainers. I equate openness with M. Bennett's (1993) ethnorelative states of acceptance, adaptation, and integration—all of which assume that the culture learner is a willing and interested seeker of new intercultural experiences.

Openness can be expressed by trainers in many ways—for example, showing a sincere interest in the backgrounds and experiences of the learners, being willing to learn along with the program participants regarding matters they are less familiar with, and demonstrating through their own life experiences their interest in other cultures.

Empathy

Competent trainers are empathic persons who can put themselves in the place of others. As M. Bennett (1979) and Howell (1982) point out, this means acquiring the ability to sense how the others, as a function of their own cultural orientations and background, are perceiving and feeling about training. The empathic trainer will know what the learners are experiencing and attempt to respond as effectively as possible. Empathy is also a quality the trainer hopes to transmit to the learners as an attribute that will promote their intercultural competence.

Respect

I use the term *respect* to connote attitudes and ways of being that attach significance and importance to others and to the field in which they work. Competent trainers respect their learners and their craft. Respect is demonstrated by how well people treat others, and as such it is a core quality for promoting positive intercultural interactions. Respect also means honoring the field one works in by striving to

improve one's professional knowledge and skills. This means, as Paige (1993b) points out, that trainers have an honest respect for what the field demands and what practitioners still need to learn and do.

Sense of Humor

A sense of humor is a particularly useful attribute that can help trainers and learners alike cope with the pressures of training and the stresses of intercultural learning. Learners who can laugh at themselves and see the humor in their situations will have an easier time adjusting to new cultural circumstances. Trainers can use well-timed humor to break the tension of training and maintain a supportive learning environment.

The above-mentioned personal qualities are ones I suggest a person should look for in an intercultural trainer. Undoubtedly, other personal attributes could be included, and some on this list could be seriously questioned as a function of the cultural setting where the training is being conducted and the cultural backgrounds of the trainers and learners. As I point out elsewhere (Paige, 1993b, p. 194), "No ideal typology can do complete justice to the variation in style and approach that exists among competent trainers." But assuming the qualities mentioned are important for intercultural trainers, it is useful to recognize that these attributes are demonstrated in the real world by patterns of behavior. Those patterns can be adjusted, with practice and time and experience, to better fit the demand of intercultural training and culture learning.

Trainer Competencies: Ethical Behavior

Competent trainers are, by my definition, ethical trainers. They know what the field's guiding ethical principles are and possess the necessary skills to apply them in virtually every aspect of their work. They are aware of the pressures that intercultural experiences and intercultural training can place on the individual. Accordingly, they attempt to create training environments that are both sufficiently supportive and challenging to effectively prepare learners for the intercultural experiences ahead or equip them to function more effectively in the intercultural world in which they live and work. The ethical trainer's primary concern is for the welfare of the learner.

Ethical trainers thus constantly strive to be the best trainers they can be. They are committed to their own professional development through such means as keeping up with relevant theoretical and research literatures, strengthening their training skills, communicating with their professional colleagues, and participating in professional association activities. They are also committed to the professionalization of the field as a whole; they share their professional expertise with others through mentoring, presenting at workshops and conferences, writing books and articles, conducting research, and the like.

The hallmark of competent and ethical trainers is that they hold very high standards for themselves and others in the profession. Their commitment to the professional development

of themselves and others is one of the most tangible and important demonstrations of this.

To lend greater specificity to this brief discussion, I present a set of behaviors that I believe characterize the ethical trainer:

Is a lifelong learner
Is committed to own professional development
Is committed to professional development of others
Is aware of and helps manage risks that training poses for learners
Shares knowledge and skills with others
Is openly self-reflective and critical
Markets skills and programs accurately
Is sensitive to needs of learners
Uses content and processes congruent with skills
Establishes supportive learning environments

PART 2:
CONSEQUENCES OF
INADEQUATE TRAINER KNOWLEDGE AND SKILLS

The consequences of inadequate trainer knowledge and skills can be extremely serious. Learners, organizations, and trainers themselves can all suffer if the trainer is not suitably prepared to do the job. Intercultural training is difficult enough for highly skilled trainers; it is absolutely no place for the amateur.

Tables 8.1 and 8.2 identify the consequences, respectively, of an insufficient knowledge base and inadequate training skills. The less the trainer knows, as indicated in Table 8.1, the more likely it is that the training program will be seriously flawed. Individual and organizational learning objectives will be inadequately and inappropriately conceptualized, program content will be incongruent with the desired goals and objectives, the sequencing of learning activities will be haphazard, and as often as not, the program will pose risks for the learners and generate resistance to training the trainer had not anticipated.

Many skills are required of the intercultural trainer; the consequences, as shown in Table 8.2, are considerable if the trainer lacks them. A

fundamental problem can occur at the very onset of the trainer-client relationship if the trainer is unskilled in conducting suitable learner and organizational needs assessments. Those assessments are critical for everything that follows, from design to implementation to evaluation. The classical problems include promising more than the trainer and the program can deliver within the given period of time; using canned programs that ignore the unique circumstances of the client's organization and the persons within it; introducing issues that are highly emotional within the organization, but not knowing how to handle them; sticking rigidly to the initial training design when the circumstances call for revision of the design; and emphasizing learner satisfaction with the program itself as the criterion of training program success instead of other, far more important learner and organizational outcomes.

To illustrate these issues in a more practical way, a set of case studies is presented in the following section. These are intended to show

TABLE 8.1 Consequences Arising From Lack of Trainer Knowledge

1. Inability to conceptualize culture learning outcomes

   a. Tendency to emphasize cognitive learning
   b. Tendency to de-emphasize behavioral learning
   c. Tendency to ignore affective learning
   d. Failure to balance learning objectives in training design

2. Inability to conceptualize necessary and appropriate content

   a. Tendency to emphasize culture "facts"
   b. Tendency to emphasize culture-specific information
   c. Tendency to de-emphasize culture-general phenomena
   d. Tendency to de-emphasize culture learning issues

3. Tendency to select learning activities inappropriate to learner needs and desired learning outcomes

4. Tendency to sequence learning activities inappropriately and without any guiding criteria

   a. Tendency to introduce high-risk content and process learning activities too early in the program

5. Tendency to underestimate risks that learning activities pose for learners

6. Tendency to inappropriately emphasize *culture knowing,* rather than *culture learning*

7. Tendency to use learning activities unfamiliar to the trainer

more exactly how and why intercultural training programs can falter.

Case Studies of Intercultural Training

Two case studies are presented, one pertaining to an international training program and the other to a diversity program. The purpose of these cases is to illustrate in a practical way the serious problems that can arise when a trainer is not properly equipped for the task. Neither case study is a report of an actual situation. Rather, each is a composite of actual similar situations. A commentary is provided at the conclusion of each case. The emphasis of the commentary is a critique of the trainer, whose performance is evaluated by using the conceptual model of the competent trainer. Other aspects of the case are also analyzed so that the situation can be seen in its larger perspective. I suggest that, before proceeding to the commentaries, readers conduct their own critique and arrive at their own conclusions.

Case Study 1:
International Training

Martin, an MBA student, was hired by a friend at a small U.S. computer software company to "conduct a 2-day culture briefing" for 10 employees. They would shortly be embarking with their families on a 3-year overseas assignment in Thailand in the company's first joint international venture, and this briefing would be their only cultural preparation. It seemed like an easy enough assignment to Martin. After all, he had been a Peace Corps volunteer for 2 years in Thailand, working on a small-business development project; he thought he was very familiar with the language and culture. This job had come his way because his friend knew of his Peace Corps experience. Although Martin had no prior intercultural training experience and limited business experience of his own, the money was good and he gladly accepted the assignment. This would be a good opportunity to gain some experience in international training, an area he was thinking of going into after the MBA.

TABLE 8.2 Consequences Arising From Lack of Intercultural Training Skills

1. Inability to conduct relevant organizational needs analysis

   a. Tendency to place too much reliance on information from a limited number of sources
   b. Tendency to focus too heavily on individual learner outcomes, rather than on organizational objectives for and consequences of intercultural training
   c. Inability to conceptualize organizational development, change, and transformation dynamics
   d. Tendency to ignore the organizational climate or culture

2. Inability to conduct learner needs assessment

   a. Tendency to ignore learning style diversity, intercultural sensitivity, emotions/feelings regarding the training issues and program, patterns of interpersonal intergroup relations, history of interpersonal and intergroup conflict, learner perceptions of own needs, and stress factors being experienced by learners

3. Inability to design an appropriate intercultural training program

   a. Tendency to promise too much within too limited a period of time—that is, to overstate the individual and organizational objectives that can be achieved
   b. Inability to provide a philosophical, theoretical, or research-based frame of reference for training design decisions
   c. Tendency to articulate individual and organizational learning objectives

4. Inability to properly implement the program

   a. Inability to establish a supportive learning environment
   b. Tendency to give insufficient time to particular learning activities
   c. Tendency to inadequately debrief learning activities
   d. Inability to handle learner resistance and emotions
   e. Tendency to stick too rigidly to the training plan regardless of the circumstances

5. Inability to evaluate and assess the program

   a. Tendency to rely too heavily on immediate end-of-program evaluations and ignore formative and longer term assessments of individual learner and organizational development
   b. Tendency to overemphasize learner satisfaction as the criterion of success and to ignore other measures, most notably affective and behavioral learning

Martin designed his program to focus on Thai culture specifics: values, customs, what to do and what not to do. He delivered his information in a lecture format, left some time for questions, and gave lots of examples based on his own personal experience. He thought things were going well until midway through the second day, when at lunch several participants began anxiously bringing up issues he had not considered. One commented, "This is all very nice, but my main problem is my wife and 14-year-old daughter. They don't really want to go, and I don't know what to do about it. We're worried about schooling, what my wife will do there, things like that. Nobody in the company has talked to us about these issues." Another observed, "Martin, we don't have much time left, and I really want to know how all of this is going to apply to my working relationships with my Thai business partners. I don't even know yet exactly what my assignment is going to be and with whom I'm going to be working." A third added, "Some of my friends who have been overseas talk a lot about culture shock, and you haven't said much about it at all. Are we going to get to that?" Martin was stumped.

Commentary on Case Study 1

Martin made a number of serious errors with this consultancy. Not being an intercultural trainer, he did not have a sound understanding of what should go into a program preparing people for overseas assignment. Neither did the company. But a competent trainer would have determined this during the negotiation of the consulting contract, would have advised the company on what was needed, and would clearly have indicated that a 2-day program was totally inadequate. After all, these employees and their families would be living in Thailand for 3 years.

Specifically, Martin failed to determine in advance what the employees thought their own needs were, what kind of preparation (if any) they had already had, and what their prior international or intercultural experience was. In a serious oversight, Martin failed to take the employees' families into consideration at all. They were not invited to the program. He did not know whether they were being assisted and prepared in any way, and he had no idea of what their concerns might be or of the employees' concerns regarding their families. He also neglected to find out about the nature of the work assignments and thus could not speak credibly about the central concern of the employees: the nature of their work life with their Thai counterparts.

As a consequence of his failure to conduct an appropriate needs assessment, both the content and the instructional methodology of his training design were faulty. The content was focused too heavily on Thai culture specifics, though not enough on the cultural dynamics of the Thai workplace. Martin was not prepared to discuss the particular work settings into which the learners would be entering. Moreover, he neglected an entire array of issues that should have been addressed, such as culture shock and adjustment, coping strategies, intercultural communication and interaction in the workplace, and intercultural competence and sensitivity. He neglected family issues altogether and thus failed to address the concerns employees had on how the impending move would affect their families.

Regarding teaching methods, Martin failed to incorporate alternative and relevant learning activities, such as case studies and critical incidents, and the use of resource persons (e.g., Thai businesspersons, returnees who had worked in Thailand). Moreover, he focused too much on his own experiences and failed to relate them to the situation the participants would be entering.

In the final analysis, Martin would have been much more valuable to the firm and its employees if he had conducted a sound needs assessment, conceptualized and suggested to the company an appropriate intercultural training program for the employees and their families, and implemented the program by using the appropriate training methodologies. In conclusion, Martin was not equipped for the task and should not have accepted the assignment.

This case study points out some serious errors an organization can make. Here, the firm did not understand intercultural training, as evidenced by the short period of time given to it and the fact that family members were not involved. It also erred by ignoring the intercultural training background of the consultant. This firm both assumed Martin knew a great deal about Thailand and, because of his country expertise, that he would be a good choice as a trainer. Whether or not Martin understood Thai culture well, he did not know intercultural training. Unfortunately, a great deal was at stake in this situation. The success of the joint venture and the well-being of the employees and their families could be seriously jeopardized by the inadequate attention given to high-quality intercultural preparation.

Case Study 2:
Diversity Training in the United States

Maria was a psychologist and student counselor at a large U.S. public university, where she worked predominately with students of color. Recently, her institution had embarked on a diversity program to recruit more "minority students" and to improve their retention rate. Although she applauded the effort, she had seen many such students struggle over the years with what she perceived to be the insensitivity and racism of the predominately white faculty. Thus, when it was announced that the diversity program mandated the faculty to undergo five sessions of training to "teach and relate more effectively with the students from diverse backgrounds," Maria immediately asked to be one of the trainers. Her supervisor agreed, knowing how committed she was to eliminating racism and prejudice on campus. He also thought she was the right choice because she had conducted a number of antiracism programs for students. Although he knew that Maria was quite outspoken about these issues and even angry at times, he agreed with her that "it was time for the faculty to get the message." They shared the view that "if this institution wants to support diversity and not just pay lip service to it, its own professors had better get their house in order."

Maria argued persuasively that the antiracism component should be central to the diversity effort and that discussion with the faculty on this issue should come at the beginning of the program. She assumed that the faculty would want to avoid the racism issue. She thought the best approach to counteract this assumed opposition would be to confront them directly and powerfully with examples from her students' own personal experiences. She had had enough of abstract, academic discussions of racism. By personalizing the discussion and by speaking about it with conviction "from the heart," she thought, the faculty would have to accept that they indeed were part of the problem and would have to change. This would a golden opportunity to tell the faculty about things that had deeply troubled her for a long time.

The program began with Maria's 2-hour presentation to 50 faculty members on the topic of racism on campus. Barely 30 minutes into her presentation, one participate angrily asked her, "Are you accusing us of being racist? Is this what diversity is all about—being forced to come and listen to this garbage?" Another responded, "Yes, that's exactly what she's saying. We've got a lot to learn, and you should listen to what she has to say." In no time, audience members were arguing with each other, and about 10 of them got up and left. Maria, distraught and angry, said to the audience, "If you don't want to hear this, I suggest you go," at which point a few more left the room. She then continued with the session.

The next day, a group of five faculty from the previous night's session complained to the university chancellor about the diversity program. At that meeting, they stated that the tone of the diversity program was one of hostility toward faculty and that it was assumed the faculty were racist. Maria's supervisor, on hearing of the complaint, called her in to explain what the furor was all about. She explained, "Some of the faculty are just hard-core racists who want to kill the whole program. Those who stayed were with me."

Commentary on Case Study 2

This was a training disaster in numerous respects. The institution itself had initially erred in making the training program mandatory, a move guaranteed to create suspicion among some faculty. But the content of teaching and relating more effectively with students of color was not particularly threatening. In fact, some faculty looked forward to the training sessions. By starting with the antiracism component and in the way she did, Maria compounded the problem significantly. Her evening session set a confrontational and negative tone for the entire five-session program. In so doing, it turned some against the whole diversity initiative.

Maria made a second critical error by failing to establish a supportive learning environment. Rather, she created a hostile atmosphere by using the training session as a forum for dealing with her own personal agenda regarding racism and her negative feelings about faculty. Worse, she began the program in a manner that seemed accusatory to certain audience members. The unfortunate result was that the session polarized faculty and generated serious opposition to the program. The stage was thus set for future conflict that could jeopardize the entire diversity effort.

Clearly, the university should have begun the program on a much more positive and visionary note. A major initiative such as this could have started with a full faculty convocation during which the overall principles of the diversity effort and the reasons for mandatory participation would be discussed. Such an approach would have made it clear that this initiative had the full support of the university administration. Knowing this, the faculty might have felt less threatened and thus been more willing to participate in the training sessions.

The most significant problem here was the training design. Contrary to the diversity training principles set out by J. Bennett (1986) and Stringer and Taylor (1991), the process (confronting faculty) and the content (racism) were far too challenging for the first session. Rather than establishing a supportive learning environment, Maria's approach (accusing faculty of racism) created a tense and negative learning atmosphere. The content sequencing was also seriously flawed. Given the explanation that these sessions were to be about effective teaching and relationships with students of color, this is what the first session should have emphasized. The overall program design, including the racism component, could have been explained.

In the final analysis, Maria could have played a much more constructive role in the program if she had had an intercultural perspective on training (understood the content and process issues of diversity training in intercultural terms). She then would have attempted to establish a positive learning atmosphere, to support and not just confront learners, to conceptualize racism in cultural and not just personal or institutional terms, and to educate learners about how culture affects human relations, communication, and perception of others. She would have placed racism in a larger context, pointing out how the institutional culture was and was not the more inclusive climate the university was striving to create. Maria could certainly have drawn on her own experiences and those of her students to provide concrete examples, but her confrontational approach negated the value of those examples. Maria basically lacked the necessary intercultural training skills and knowledge to successfully conduct this session.

This case study also reveals a common mistake of employers, which is to hire someone to do training on the basis of international experience, race, ethnicity, gender, or some other quality not necessarily related to intercultural training expertise. Having had an international living experience or experienced racism, for example, does help establish an individual's credibility with the learners. It does not automatically mean that the person will be an effective trainer.

SUMMARY

Intercultural training has become increasingly sophisticated during the past three decades. Those seeking to work in this field have an extensive body of knowledge to learn, many skills to acquire, and a set of personal qualities to develop. This obviously cannot be done overnight. It takes years of relevant academic study, immersion in cross-cultural settings, and experience in intercultural programs to become an authentically competent trainer.

In closing, I would say to those currently working in the field that they should always strive to serve as standard-bearers for excellence in intercultural training and to demonstrate this in every aspect of their work. For prospective interculturalists, my best advice is, first, to understand the very challenging nature of the field you are entering and second, if it genuinely feels right for you, to make a firm commitment to it. The best guarantee that you will become a competent intercultural trainer is to have made that commitment from the heart and done everything possible to prepare yourself for working in this profession.

References

Adler, P. S. (1976). Beyond cultural identity: Reflections upon cultural and multicultural man. In L. A. Samovar & R. E. Porter (Eds.), *Intercultural communication: A reader* (pp.362-380). Belmont, CA: Wadsworth.

Banks, J. (1988). Stages of ethnicity: Implications for curriculum reform. In J. Banks, *Multiethnic education: Theory and practice* (pp. 193-202). Boston: Allyn & Bacon.

Bennett, J. M. (1986). Modes of cross-cultural training: Conceptualizing cross-cultural training as education. *International Journal of Intercultural Relations, 10*(2), 117-134.

Bennett, J. M. (1993). Cultural marginality: Identity issues in intercultural training. In R. M. Paige (Ed.), *Education for the intercultural experience* (pp. 109-135). Yarmouth, ME: Intercultural Press.

Bennett, M. J. (1979). Overcoming the Golden Rule: Sympathy and empathy. In D. Nimmo (Ed.), *Communication yearbook 3* (pp. 407-422). Washington, DC: Intercultural Communication Association.

Bennett, M. J. (1986a). A developmental approach to training for intercultural sensitivity. *International Journal of Intercultural Relations, 10*(2), 179-196.

Bennett, M. J. (1986b). Toward ethnorelativism: A developmental model of intercultural sensitivity. In R. M. Paige (Ed.), *Cross-cultural orientation: New conceptualizations and applications* (pp. 21-69). Lanham, MD: University Press of America.

Bennett, M. J. (1993). Toward ethnorelativism: A developmental model of intercultural sensitivity. In R. M. Paige (Ed.), *Education for the intercultural experience* (pp. 21-71). Yarmouth, ME: Intercultural Press.

Black, J. S., & Mendenhall, M. (1990). Cross-cultural training effectiveness: A review and a theoretical framework. *Academy of Management Review, 15,* 113-136.

Brislin, R. W., Cushner, K., Cherrie, C., & Yong, M. (1986). *Intercultural interactions: A practical guide.* Beverly Hills, CA: Sage.

Brislin, R. W., & Yoshida, T. (Eds.). (1994). *Intercultural communication training.* Thousand Oaks, CA: Sage.

Cross, W. E. (1978). The Thomas and Cross models of psychological nigrescence: A review. *Journal of Black Psychology, 5*(1), 13-31.

Excel, Inc. (1993). *Learning Type Measure.* Barrington, IL: Author.

Grove, C., & Torbiorn, I. (1993). A new conceptualization of intercultural adjustment and the goals of training. In R. M. Paige (Ed.), *Education for the intercultural experience* (pp. 73-108). Yarmouth, ME: Intercultural Press.

Hammer, M. R. (1989). Intercultural communication competence. In M. K. Asante & W. R. Hammer (Eds.), *The handbook of international and intercultural communication* (pp. 247-260). Newbury Park, CA: Sage.

Helms, J. E. (1990). *Black and white racial identity: Theory, research, and practice.* Westport, CT: Greenwood.

Howell, W. S. (1982). *The empathic communicator.* Belmont, CA: Wadsworth.

Kolb, D. A. (1976). *Learning Style Inventory: Technical manual.* Boston: McBer.

Kolb, D. A. (1984). *Experiential learning.* Englewood Cliffs, NJ: Prentice-Hall.

Lustig, M. W., & Koester, J. (1993). *Intercultural competence: Interpersonal communication across cultures.* New York: HarperCollins.

Martin, J. N. (Guest Editor). (1989). Intercultural communication competence [Special issue]. *International Journal of Intercultural Relations, 13*(3).

McCaffery, J. A. (1993). Independent effectiveness and unintended outcomes of cross-cultural orientation and training. In R. M. Paige (Ed.), *Education for the intercultural experience* (pp. 219-240). Yarmouth, ME: Intercultural Press.

Paige, R. M. (1986). Trainer competencies: The missing conceptual link in orientation. *International Journal of Intercultural Relations, 10*(2), 135-158.

Paige, R. M. (1993a). On the nature of intercultural experiences and intercultural education. In R. M. Paige (Ed.), *Education for the intercultural experience* (pp. 1-19). Yarmouth, ME: Intercultural Press.

Paige, R. M. (1993b). Trainer competencies in international and intercultural programs. In R. M. Paige (Ed.), *Education for the intercultural experience* (pp. 169-199). Yarmouth, ME: Intercultural Press.

Parham, T. A. (1989). Cycles of psychological nigrescence. *Counseling Psychologist, 17*(2), 187-226.

Salett, E. P., & Koslow, D. R. (Eds.). (1994). *Race, ethnicity, and self: Identity in multicultural perspective.* Washington, DC: National Multicultural Institute.

Storti, C. (1989). *The art of crossing cultures.* Yarmouth, ME: Intercultural Press.

Stringer, D., & Taylor, L. (1991). Guidelines for implementing diversity training. *Training & Culture Newsletter, 3*(5), 1, 10-11.

Weaver, G. R. (1993). Understanding and coping with cross-cultural adjustment stress. In R. M. Paige (Ed.), *Education for the intercultural experience* (pp. 137-167). Yarmouth, ME: Intercultural Press.

9

Measuring Impacts
of Cross-Cultural Training

BRIAN F. BLAKE

RICHARD HESLIN

SHANNON C. CURTIS

EMPIRICAL evaluations of cross-cultural training (CCT) programs must be considered except as an intrinsic part of the more general topic of cross-cultural training (Martin, 1986). In an attempt to bring order to what could be an amorphous and unstructured field, a variety of emphases have been selected that range across the goals, the content, and/or the techniques used in the training (Bennett, 1986).

In this chapter, we attempt to make two contributions to these studies. First, we describe the *conceptual schema,* a theoretical model of the CCT evaluation process, incorporating components of the framework originally proposed in the first edition of this handbook (Blake & Heslin, 1983). Second, we describe a *design schema,* a perspective for use in choosing among alternative research procedures.

Conceptual Schema

Evaluating the effectiveness of CCT programs is complex. To simplify it, we break down the process into components by using a flowchart of the phases of a training activity and by highlighting the important aspects of this evaluation process. The framework emphasizes knowledge about the effects of CCT on individual participants, rather than on the sponsoring organization or host culture. It highlights the variety of alternative approaches possible by identifying potential stumbling blocks the investigator may face.

The underlying theme of the schema is that successful evaluations represent a wedding of the scientific method with an awareness of the organizational context in which the evaluation is conducted. An emphasis on scientific method brings the focus to the data's validity and reliability and the importance of precise delineations of all relevant ideas. Emphasizing the organizational context alerts us to the fact that the evaluation must be conducted so that it helps policy decisions and increases the effectiveness of the organization.

As diagramed in Figure 9.1, components along the upper level of the model pertain to the training program itself and its outcomes. The lower level refers to the broader context within which the evaluation study is done. Both levels converge in the conclusions reached about the program's value. The researcher should feed back his or her conclusions to all people in the organization who have a stake in the selection and training process. We now turn to each component of CCT.

Selection

Wide variation occurs in how much organizations take care in selecting people for cross-cultural assignment and training. At one extreme is the use of programs with little prior screening of participants; they assign all who are eligible because of particular rotation systems within an organization. At the other extreme is the use of a range of criteria for screening people, such as indices of (a) intellectual ability (e.g., intelligence test, level of education); (b) specialized training (e.g., college major, professional identity, job experience); (c) motivation (e.g., requiring that only volunteers be taken); (d) linguistic ability (e.g., training in the language of the host country; cf. Tanaka, Takai, Kohyama, & Fujihara, 1994); and (e) personal characteristics (e.g., flexibility, tolerance; cf. Redmond & Bunyi, 1993).

Devising suitable selection procedures can be a problem. Identifying selection criteria related to successful performance in a foreign culture is more difficult than had originally been thought. For example, personality traits and social behavior typically have not been highly predictive of the intercultural adjustment of sojourners (Brein & David, 1971). So, how should one select people for overseas assignment? Despite the difficulty of the task, evidence suggests what things do, and do not, relate to cross-cultural effectiveness. For example, an extensive study by Kealey (1989) indicates that the successful sojourner is highly motivated and interested in and committed to being involved in the local culture. Assuming, then, that motivation is important, it is sad to discover that Americans seem to have an arrogant attitude. They believe they have little to learn from competitors, whereas Japanese and Europeans believe they have much to learn from their competitors (Kupfer, 1988).

Not only is it important to select people who are motivated, but also demographic variables, such as gender, have been found to relate to how a person handles being in a foreign country (Furnham & Bochner, 1986). Specifically, women from the United States, Germany, and Poland living in England were twice as likely to commit suicide as English women. No difference was found in suicide rate between men from the United States, Germany, and Poland compared with men from England. The selection problem can be compounded by the criteria the organization uses, such as the person's technical capabilities or prior performance, rather than the ability to adapt to a foreign environment.

Whether the criteria are appropriate or not, the organization selects those who will participate in a given CCT. As a result, the conclusions drawn about the effectiveness of a training program must consider any potential confounds resulting from subject selection (see Cook & Campbell, 1979).

Training

CCT techniques have been classified in various ways (e.g., Bennett, 1986). Gudykunst, Hammer, and Wiseman (1977), for example, have categorized approaches to CCT training as (a) intellectual, (b) area simulation, (c) self-awareness, (d) cultural awareness, (e) behavioral, and (f) interactional. Mendenhall and his colleagues (Black & Mendenhall, 1990; Mendenhall & Oddou, 1985, 1986) have proposed another schema. Their proposed model of CCT divides the skills required into those that deal with three major aspects of life: (a) *self* (e.g., developing self-confidence, avoiding depression and anxiety); (b) *other* (skills that foster relationships with host nationals); and (c) *perception* (appropriate views and attitudes toward the other culture). These taxonomies are useful in many ways, but for this chapter in training

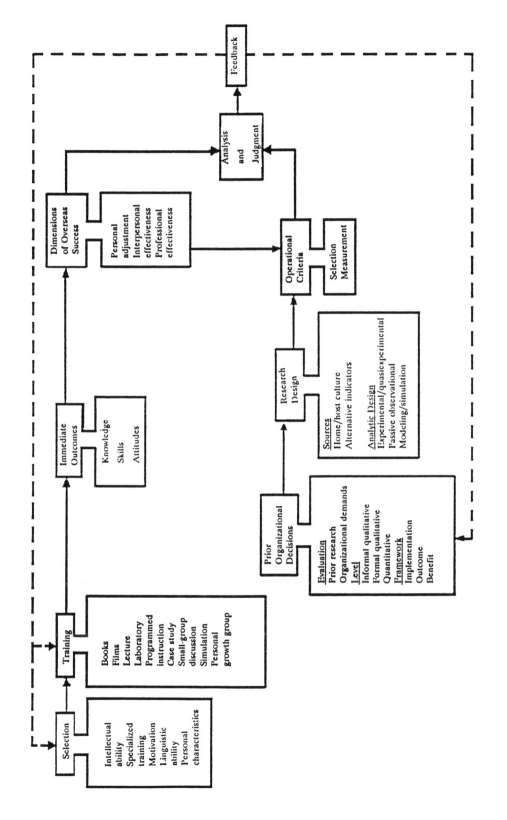

Figure 9.1. A Schematic Representation of Cross-Cultural Training and Evaluation

evaluation, we focus on techniques, rather than on desired changes in the trainee. Our categories are (a) intellectual or area study, (b) laboratory, (c) case study, (d) group discussion, (e) simulation, (f) role playing, and (g) personal growth emphasis. We now look briefly at these different training techniques (our discussion assumes equally competent trainers for all of the techniques—an assumption that, of course, needs to be addressed with each application; Paige, 1986).

Books, films, and lectures have usually been considered *intellectual* approaches to CCT. This approach, called the *intellectual model* (Bennett, 1986) or *area studies training programs* (Bird, Heinbuch, Dunbar, & McNulty, 1993), reflects a belief that understanding a country and its people will give a person the tools to work and get along with members of the host country. By diligent study, one can know their history, values, beliefs, practices, their "shoulds" and "should nots," and their prejudices, taboos, and general expectations of what responsible behavior, good citizenship, and the good life are.

Each of the different emphases within the area studies approach has its advantages and disadvantages. *Books* can deal with a wide variety of topics—for example, the history of the host country, its cuisine, politics, and agriculture. Books are portable and can be read by the trainee at his or her own pace and in a variety of locations, including either the home or the host culture. Booklets give thumbnail sketches of a host country (e.g., the "Culturegrams" published by Brigham Young University) or general instruction for traveling abroad (e.g., *Handbook for U.S. Students Abroad,* published by Youth for Understanding, a student exchange program). A book provides more than simply knowledge of the host culture; it may even generate not only sympathy and understanding but also anxiety and even hostility toward it. So, the expectation "To know them is to love them" that underlies much of the intellectual or area studies approach could have some unintended negative consequences. Of course, the kind of potential participant that becomes anxious or hostile toward another culture on learning about it is the kind one wishes to discourage from participating anyway.

Film can provide an especially vivid experience. Seeing the people and their dwellings makes the nature of the host country much clearer to the trainee. *Lectures* have the advantage that the message is being given by a live source. The lecturer can repeat points that might be poorly comprehended and can skip sections that are too elementary for a particular audience.

The use of *laboratories,* in which trainees can practice exercises, helps strengthen materials learned from books, films, and lectures. A recent example of the laboratory approach being used in training involved Japanese managers practicing the components of creative thinking (increased divergent thinking and reduced tendency toward premature convergence). In this study, the technique resulted in a significant impact of the training and was comparable to that found with U.S. groups (Basadur, Wakabayashi, & Takai, 1992). Language learning is one skill taught in a laboratory setting. When we teach language, we usually have a limited goal for the trainee—that he or she can function at least minimally in the host country environment. However, it has been pointed out (a) by Segalowitz (1980) that language learning fosters cognitive flexibility and creativity, (b) by Lambert (1992) that it is one way to improve intelligence, and (c) by Triandis (in press) that it fosters a feeling of being in control (especially in that language's country), teaches the person how to learn other languages, and gives the person a sense of efficacy and confidence.

We classify such techniques as the culture assimilator (Albert, 1983; Fiedler, Mitchell, & Triandis, 1971) as *programmed instruction.* Programmed instruction has the advantage of providing ongoing testing and feedback to the trainee. The trainee knows immediately whether he or she is understanding the important distinctions.

Many business schools have used *case study* techniques extensively. Such a technique presents a trainee with a complex and realistic situation and is usually more involving than the intellectual and laboratory techniques. A series of case studies can present the participants with a variety of real-life scenarios that involve dealing with members of the host country or working within constraints resulting from host country beliefs and practices. The trainee's awareness of the complexity and variety of factors that must be considered grows with familiarity with the host culture.

In *group discussion,* participants play a more active, involving role as they discuss the ideas and problems being considered. They are free to question the reasoning and decisions of co-members. They may or may not be required to arrive at group consensus on their decisions.

Simulations put the person in a situation that is highly arousing and that usually involves resolving some difficulty facing the person or group. A well-constructed simulation can sensitize a participant to an important concept, such as a conflict between two valued actions. Simulation techniques vary in nature. Furthermore, many simulations extend over time so that decisions a person or group makes at Time 1 may have positive or negative ramifications at Times 2, 3, 4, and so on.

Role playing as a training technique brings the trainee into a situation that can have high similarity to what he or she will experience in the host culture. Goldman (1992) used this technique with Japanese managers focusing on differences between Japanese and U.S. cultures in negotiation style. Established orientation programs, such as the Intercultural Communication Program, use role playing with persons of different cultures in the training process (Brislin & Pedersen, 1976). In that kind of situation, the trainee is with someone who can identify from moment to moment all the verbal and nonverbal behaviors that are "foreign" to a host country national. Furthermore, the trainee faces his or her fears and prejudices as he or she role-plays with "one of them."

The last technique we discuss is the use of *personal growth* groups and procedures. It focuses on the trainee's self-understanding. The trainer hopes that if the trainee understands his or her motivation, fears, and defenses, he or she can respond to situations in appropriate ways. The personal growth group epitomizes the National Training Laboratory T-group model, which relies on sensitivity and encounter groups.

These groups can vary in structure. For example, Brislin (1993) described a structured form of experiential training that uses a replica of a South Pacific village for training Peace Corps volunteers. The volunteers spend weeks in the primitive village, learning language and customs and relating to people from South Pacific cultures. This realistic experience results in some trainees dropping from the program. They would have otherwise gone to the host country and then probably asked to be relieved of duty; the process would have incurred cost to

the program and embarrassment to themselves. The Pacific village setting confronts them with the full experience of loss of control and difficulty with functioning that one can experience in those conditions.

CCT Effectiveness

The effectiveness of some techniques has been investigated. For example, the culture assimilator yielded positive effects in various studies in the laboratory and field (see Fiedler et al., 1971). Good results have also been obtained by using techniques tailored to a particular cross-cultural need. The study mentioned earlier in which Japanese managers focused on differences between the Japanese and U.S. cultures in negotiation style showed that role playing is useful for exploring the differences between cultures in business negotiation style (Goldman, 1992).

The relative effects of the various alternative approaches we have been considering have received some attention. O'Brien and Plooij (1977), for example, found that critical-incident training (programmed instruction) has a stronger effect on retention and generalization of cultural knowledge than essay training (book) or no training at all. Furthermore, a few studies have evaluated the effectiveness of combinations of training techniques. For example, Landis, Brislin, and Hulgus (1985) explored the joint effectiveness of role playing (simulation) and culture assimilator training (programmed instruction). They found significant differences between trained and untrained individuals in knowledge of the African American culture and observed better behavioral performance among persons receiving assimilator training followed by role playing than among individuals receiving the reverse sequence of training experiences. Gudykunst et al. (1977) concluded that a 6-hour lecture training was less effective for navy personnel than a 3-day seminar in which simulation (role play), programmed instruction, lecture, and interaction techniques were integrated.

On a continuum of training experiences ranging from *vicarious* to *immediate,* one could place actually meeting and talking with members of a host country fairly close to the *immediate* end. Although talking with a bilingual member of the host country should have some positive benefits, the problem of underrepresenting the differences between the two cultures is also real. For example, Stephan and Stephan (1992) reported that actual contact with Moroccans was found to reduce anxiety in a group of white American college students on an educational ship. Similarly, McDaniel, McDaniel, and McDaniel (1988) found training that emphasized multicultural *experiences* transferred best and training that emphasized multicultural *attitudes* transferred most poorly to application by schoolteachers.

The relative effectiveness of techniques may well lie in the direction of something other than a "which is better" mentality. An approach to training that considers (a) resources available, (b) time constraints, (c) the motivation of the potential trainees, and (d) the fit between a technique and the needs that are relevant for a given overseas assignment has a high likelihood of succeeding. Furthermore, combinations of techniques may optimize the learning from each and thus give the participants opportunity to rehearse skills and apply information received from books, lectures, films, and programmed instruction. Such an effort has yielded good results (Harrison, 1992).

In Harrison's (1992) study, civilian employees in a U.S. military agency were exposed to (a) information about Japan through a culture assimilator format or (b) training that used modeling and rehearsal as intrinsic aspects or (c) both. Participants in the condition that exposed them to both techniques showed a significantly higher level of learning than those in either condition by itself. All three conditions were better than the control condition. Nevertheless, the results were supportive of the effectiveness of the combined-conditions approach.

The external validity of a given study of training effectiveness must be carefully considered. The present schema suggests that the relative effectiveness of the various training techniques is contingent on the other classes of factors portrayed in Figure 9.1. These other factors should be controlled, measured, and/or clearly described before a conclusion can be reached about a technique's effectiveness.

Immediate Outcomes

A training episode can affect a trainee in several ways that can be classified in terms of knowledge, skills, and attitudes. We have looked at studies and techniques that dealt with some of them. All three of these categories are relevant to the goals of most CCT programs. The given expatriate assignment, however, will decide the particular skills, knowledge, and attitudes that are relevant. The immediate measurement of training impact is often seen as unimportant and is contrasted in a negative light to the real situation in the other country. But, in the final analysis, whatever measures the evaluator can get will be used in evaluating a program. Most often, the measures the evaluator can get are of immediate outcomes—tests and demonstrations at the training site.

In the measurement of training outcome, both immediate and overseas, the needs and goals of the organization must be considered. These are discussed in more detail below, but for the measurement of immediate outcomes, the assessed learning reflects the organization's view of what is important and necessary for the assignment. That limitation is merely a reflection of the obvious fact that any particular training program will have its own set of emphases that reflect the organizational goals and the particular task.

Dimensions of Overseas Success

Dimensions of overseas success are the three overlapping domains implicitly or explicitly assumed in most programs' goals: (a) personal adjustment, (b) interpersonal effectiveness, and (c) professional effectiveness. The organization uses these three domains as yardsticks in evaluating the immediate outcome and structure of its operational criteria (see Figure 9.1). Not included under "Dimensions of Overseas Success" are cost/time minimizations or similar standards of evaluation that do not pertain to adaptation to a host country. Such criteria as cost/time minimization are part of "Operational Criteria" of Figure 9.1.

Unfortunately, something of a theoretical and empirical vacuum exists about the definition of cultural adaptation. After reviewing 245 studies, Hawes and Kealy (1979) concluded that intercultural adjustment or "overseas effectiveness" has not been thoroughly defined, described, or measured. Nevertheless, the consensus is that adaptation is a multidimensional phenomenon. For example, Hammer, Gudykunst, and Wiseman (1978) examined 24 abilities thought to be important for intercultural effectiveness. A factor analysis of these data yielded three dimensions of intercultural effectiveness: (a) ability to deal with psychological stress, (b) capacity to relate effectively, and (c) skill in establishing interpersonal relationships.

The model proposed here, distinguishing among three major areas—personal adjustment, interpersonal effectiveness, and professional effectiveness—is based on the assumption that recurring aspects of human functioning devolve into three core dimensions: (a) feelings, (b) relations with others, and (c) handling of problem-solving, task-focused demands (see Heslin & Blake, 1973). Use of this three-dimensional approach is substantively supported by the conclusion of Hawes and Kealy (1979) that overseas effectiveness consists of three components: (a) personal/family adjustment and satisfaction, (b) intercultural interaction, and (c) professional effectiveness. Although labeled differently, the components are conceptually similar. The present taxonomy also converges with the distinction among conative, affective, and cognitive realms drawn in the assessment of sojourner satisfaction of Hammer et al. (1978).

Prior Organizational Decisions

Moving to the bottom of Figure 9.1, with its focus on the concerns of the organization, we are reminded that CCT evaluation is more than a simple extension of basic scientific methods. The missions or policies of the organization influence evaluation activity. Organizational and political forces affect what questions are asked, when, and by whom. Because of the variety of goals and the people interested in the performance overseas, the evaluator's role is often ambiguous and subject to conflicting expectations.

The most basic decision the sponsoring organization makes is whether to conduct an evaluation at all. This decision may reflect pressures from forces external to the organization (e.g., governmental mandate, client request) or from internal organizational policy that may require an evaluation. Before the evaluation, the organization decides what the focus of the evaluation should be. The evaluator may or may not be a party to that decision. The decisions of

whether and how to evaluate may also be based on previous empirical research or on a pilot study. One use of a pilot study is to conduct an evaluability analysis before conducting a full-scale evaluation study. The evaluability analysis identifies aspects of a program that can be measured to meet the study's objectives (Rutman, 1980).

A third decision pertains to how rigorous the evaluation should be. Will conclusions be based predominantly on anecdotal data, unsystematic observations, or other informal qualitative procedures? Will the organization insist on more systematically obtained, though still inherently qualitative, data such as that used in ethnographic (Goodenough, 1980) or content analytical (Brislin, 1980) studies? Will highly quantitative, systematic data be needed and useful? Although the quantitative level is valued as a basis for decision making, do not overlook qualitative analysis ("depth" in program evaluation).

The evaluation framework is a major decision that shapes what gets measured. For example, a study can document how well a CCT program is being *done* (e.g., participation rates, use of materials). Unfortunately, most published CCT evaluations use an *outcome* framework; they concentrate on the degree to which trainees have been affected by the CCT. Few published studies are *benefit* analyses, simultaneously quantifying positive/negative impacts of the CCT and costs in time, money, and so on.

More complex benefit and outcome analyses are not necessarily more valuable than simpler accomplishment studies. A thorough accomplishment study can be highly informative (Scheirer, 1981), whereas cost-benefit assessments sometimes demand questionable assumptions (Thompson, 1980).

Research Design

An important aspect of the evaluation procedure is the source of the data. A sojourner may be quite successful from the viewpoint of the sponsoring organization but unsuccessful in the eyes of people in the host country. A balanced evaluation should consider both home and host culture data sources by using both home and host nationals as evaluators.

Within each cultural group, use alternative data sources:

Self-reports
Judgments of significant others (especially spouses, coworkers, and supervisors)
Archival/objective measures
Evaluator observations
Measures of the sojourner's overt behavior

Although they are difficult to obtain, the increased use of behavioral measures would improve CCT evaluations. Peace Corps studies often relied on supervisors' ratings to assess performance, but with mixed results. Even so, most published CCT evaluation studies have relied wholly or partly on trainee self-reports and interviews. This reliance on self-reports is not entirely inappropriate, though, because self-report data have been found to relate to successful adaptation to host cultures (Mischel, 1965).

The ongoing trend is toward the broadening of CCT evaluation research by using multiple measures obtained from different kinds of people. This is precisely the orientation our model postulates to be most desirable: a combination of home and host culture sources, with multiple sources within each culture.

Clearly, all the alternative types of data are not equally appropriate for a given CCT evaluation. Judgments of spouses may not be as useful a source for indexing the work performance dimension as for interpersonal effectiveness or personal adjustment. Overt behavior may be more appropriate for work performance and interpersonal effectiveness dimensions than for personal adjustment. Similarly, information coming from host country sources may be better for evaluations of interpersonal effectiveness on work performance than for evaluation of personal adjustment.

An evaluation study may spring from various analytical paradigms. First, it may use an experimental or quasi-experimental design (Brown & Sechrest, 1980; Cook & Campbell, 1979) to conduct a causal analysis of CCT impacts, or second, it may use a passive observational (survey) design to identify correlates of CCT training. Third, modeling or mathematically simulating likely consequences of CCT experiences in individuals is possible. Current published studies within an outcome or benefit framework emphasize an experimental/quasi-experimental paradigm, whereas implementa-

tion and selection studies often employ passive observation. Modeling/simulation is currently a rarity but could well be considered, given the potential power and flexibility of these techniques. The three frameworks can overlap at times. For example, path analysis of cross-sectional data to yield conclusions of a causal nature combine facets of all three frameworks.

Operational Criteria

Operational criteria are the observable indicators used, the actual yardsticks on which the CCT program is measured. The choice of operational criteria obviously reflects the missions, resource base, and other aspects of the sponsoring organization. Therefore, many criteria (e.g., time to CCT completion, appropriate number and nature of trainees, cost per trainee completion) flow from the system maintenance needs of the organization. Beyond these pragmatic concerns, however, it is essential that operational criteria directly reflect the dimensions of success assumed in the CCT objectives (see Figure 9.1). Criteria must be *selected* to ensure their *content validity,* which means that in combination they must include all of the various components of success assumed in the CCT objectives. Further, they must be *measured* to ensure their *construct validity* so that observed variation between trainees on an operational criterion can safely be assumed to represent variability on the particular theoretical dimension underlying that criterion. Given the previously mentioned problem in theoretically defining successful intercultural adjustment, given the frequent vagueness of CCT objectives, and given the need for content and construct validation to flow from clearly specified theoretical constructs, validation of criteria can be very difficult.

One approach to construct validation is to use multiple criterion measures of a previously specified success dimension. The use of multiple measures allows a test of convergence among alternative measures of the same theoretical construct and an indexing of constructs too complex to measure by a single method (Berry, 1980). Conversely, suitably selected measures can test a criterion's discriminant validity—that is, its independence of factors from which it should be separate, such as acquiescence bias. Although this approach has long been accepted for the measurement of social and psychological variables, it is especially relevant when cross-cultural variation may be present.

Analysis and Judgment

Analysis of information generated in the evaluation study and judgments about the value of the CCT are combined in our model; this indicates our contention that study results are often combined with other considerations in reaching a conclusion about a program's value.

Feedback

Our model assumes that effective CCT evaluations must result in the dissemination of results to appropriate parties to enlighten subsequent organizational decisions about CCT programming, trainee selection, and evaluation efforts. Although rarely emphasized in previously published studies of CCT evaluation, feedback of results to trainees and to sponsoring organizations must be considered an intrinsic part of evaluation. Indeed, the tendency of evaluators to consider the publication of a technical report on their project as having dispatched their responsibility for dissemination must be considered close to irresponsible and shortsighted in a world where money goes to efforts that bear consumable fruit.

Conclusion on the Conceptual Schema

Our model does not pretend to encapsulate all past CCT evaluations or to highlight all important factors in conducting an evaluation. We hope, however, that the model can provide a point of departure for what is sorely needed within the CCT realm: effective evaluation of training.

Design Schema

Let's flirt with heresy here and suggest that, unless we are careful, our empirical evaluations of CCT programs will be all talk and no result. Let's risk being drawn and quartered by traditionalists for observing that we often strive to

meet standards of good research that were developed for basic theoretical investigations but that do not apply *in toto* to CCT evaluation.

Evaluations of training programs, as we have just seen, are principally of three types. At this point, let's refer to these simply as Types A, B and C.

Type A. In a Type A study, the evaluators intend to generalize the specific empirical results to a delimited number of real-life contexts. Illustratively, a study is undertaken to assess the value of participation in CCT Program X to inexperienced corporate managers preparing for assignment to the Middle East. The sample of persons who qualify for participation in Program X is drawn and measured on a variety of criteria (dimensions representing desired standards of cultural adaptation). This study has two principal criteria: (a) peer ratings of one's effectiveness on the job and (b) self-reported satisfaction with one's personal relationships with members of the host culture. A comparison of those who had completed Program X with those who had not done so reveals that trainees displayed 10% higher ratings of job effectiveness and 15% greater satisfaction. Generalizing to the population of qualified corporate managers, the study authors conclude that Program X provides a trainee with a 10% improvement in job effectiveness and a 15% improvement in satisfaction after that person enters the host culture.

Type B. The focus here is to test theoretical propositions that should pertain to a wide variety of people and cultures. For example, a study hypothesized that sojourners who are better informed about a host culture before traveling there will adapt more thoroughly and quickly to that culture, everything else being equal. Accordingly, a sample of sojourners to the Middle East is queried about their prior knowledge of the culture to which they are about to be exposed—for example, typical social roles and unique cultural nuances. Then, they are assessed on variables reflecting their subsequent degree of cultural adaptation. Correlations between the various independent (knowledge) variables and the variety of criteria measures (adaptation) reveal a pattern: The better informed the person, the more extensive his or her adaptation. The study recommends that because prior knowledge facilitates adaptation, a CCT program for sojourners should make provision for such knowledge.

Type C. In the Type C approach, the researcher wants to demonstrate that a CCT program based on a certain theoretical premise is effective in a range of contexts. Let's use a hypothetical example. The theoretical assumption is that increased knowledge of the target culture prior to contact will contribute to one's adaptation to that culture. A training program is developed to inculcate that specialized knowledge of given aspects of the target culture. The program is then provided to trainees in a variety of environments that could potentially undermine its impact on trainees. The trainees are subsequently compared with equivalent persons without training on two major criteria: (a) peer ratings of effectiveness on the job and (b) self-reported satisfaction with one's personal relationships with members of the host culture. The study evaluators conclude that Program X is effective with inexperienced sojourners, but not with seasoned ones, and is successful with trainees whose own cultures are quite disparate from the target culture, but not with persons from cultures fairly similar to the host's.

Most published examples of CCT programs are either Type A or Type C; usually, they are not of Type B. Much of our thinking about "good research" procedures, though, springs from Type B. Classic works by Cook and Campbell (1979), Campbell and Stanley (1966), and others on experimental and quasi-experimental designs have had a great impact on the methodology used in contemporary social science. These standards of what constitutes good research procedures are widely accepted.

The problem is that these techniques, which were developed to assess the validity of theoretical constructs, often have been applied uncritically to research with different objectives and done in different contexts. Unfortunately, useful evaluations of CCT programs must meet standards somewhat different from those appropriate for basic theoretical research.

In this chapter, let's contrast Types A, B, and C and suggest appropriate standards for these three disparate approaches. Although we incorporate concepts from the seminal works of Campbell and others, we also draw shamelessly and extensively from the insights of Calder, Phillips, and Tybout (1981). In overview, we

first compare the objectives of three types and then discuss procedures—sample, operational definitions, research setting or context—appropriate for each. Then, we consider an issue equally pertinent to all three types: the threats to the validity of a study's conclusions and how to ward off these threats.

The principal point is that the CCT evaluator must appreciate which type of research is included and then design the study accordingly. Techniques suitable for one type are not appropriate for another.

Research Objectives

Type A. Calder et al. (1981) refer to this approach as *effects application.* It attempts to describe events in a delimited range of real-world situations (in that world represented by the subject sample). The ultimate objective of this research form is to obtain concrete numerical findings (effects) that can be applied directly to the real-world situation of interest. "It is the effects themselves that are generalized rather than [their] being linked by inference to theoretical constructs and the hypothesized theoretical network then used to deduce patterns of outcomes" (Calder et al., 1981, p. 198).

To generalize the effects, it is necessary to have measured them in a research setting that corresponds to the real-world situation. It is practically impossible to obtain complete correspondence between the research setting and its real-world counterpart because of the myriad subtle distinctions that exist between the two environments. What is necessary is a degree of correspondence sufficient to permit the generalization of numerical results from the research setting to the environment sampled in the research setting.

Type B. In contrast, the Type B research approach can be labeled *theory application* in the Calder et al. (1981) framework. The principal goal of such research is to construct scientific theories that provide a general understanding of the real world. Type B research is restricted to the assessment of scientific theories. In contrast, the theoretical framework involved in Type A research can be scientific, but it also can be simply intuitive or derived from common sense.

Theory application demands procedures that test the theoretical propositions by creating situations that have the potential to disprove the theory. The specific research context (e.g., a university laboratory, the particular host cultures used to test the hypothesis) and the precise numerical effects are not of interest in their own right. Their value resides in their implication for the theory's adequacy. Further, the scientific theories are assumedly valid in any real-world situation to which they apply, not just to the particular situations represented in the research setting.

Type C. Referred to as *intervention falsification* by Calder and colleagues (1981), Type C research involves the testing of a CCT program (intervention) based on theoretical insights. The success of the training program not only relies on the validity of the assumptions about the operation of the core theoretical variables but also rests on the actions of theoretically irrelevant variables that can make or break the program's effectiveness. It is possible that the theoretical underpinnings of the program may be quite valid but that the program's execution may be shoddy. The program then would be ineffective even though it is based on a viable theory. Hence, research procedures to test the theory must be separate from those employed to test the CCT program.

Unlike effects application, no attempt is made to generalize any specific numerical outcome found in testing the intervention theory. Only the degree of success (or lack thereof) of the CCT is generalized beyond the research setting. Also, unlike theory falsification, no attempt is made to conclude that specific processes underlying the intervention are widely applicable; that is, the demonstrated effectiveness of the CCT program is not seen to imply the validity of the theoretical propositions on which the program is based.

A Caveat

We should not be tempted to think that effects application and intervention falsification are hard-nosed and realistic, whereas a theory falsification approach is fuzzy or simply speculative. Wrong! If anything, the converse is true.

Effects and intervention falsification ultimately involve reasoning by induction; that is,

we assume that because a CCT program had particular impacts in the research setting, it will have similar impacts on the real-world environment to which the research setting corresponds. Induction per se, then, cannot claim to demonstrate a logical necessity why the CCT program must have a specific impact. Critics can point out, legitimately, that because an event occurred in the past, it does not necessarily mean it will occur again in exactly the same fashion. This Achilles heel of inductive methods is rendered even more suspect when one realizes that the research has only relatively few observations on which to base the study's conclusions.

In contrast, theory falsification is more closely aligned with the use of deductive logic. Once a theory's propositions have been subjected to rigorous testing and have survived, we can deduce from the theoretical premises a conclusion that should be true in given real-life situations. We do not assume, as discussed earlier, that CCT programs based on the theory's propositions will necessarily be effective in any specific real-life situations.

Research Procedures

In a Type A effects application study, procedures are required that ensure the research setting accurately represents the real-world environment of interest. These procedures have been termed *correspondence procedures.* *Theory falsification procedures,* however, are needed in Type B to guarantee that the theoretical postulates are rigorously tested. *Intervention falsification procedures* of Type C assess the CCT program under conditions that can potentially cause it to fail in the real world. Let's now look at these points in more detail.

Respondent Sample

When *effects application* is the goal, correspondence procedures demand that research respondents match the individuals composing the real-world setting of interest. In our illustrative Type A case, inexperienced corporate managers preparing for assignment to the Middle East comprise the population of interest. Ideally, a match could be achieved by the researcher's drawing a probability sample of persons from this population. But, because strict statistical sampling of the population is rarely possible, other steps must be taken to generate representative data. One possibility is to replicate the study with different subgroups drawn from the target population. For example, we might conduct the study first with managers from one corporation, then replicate it with managers from a second corporation, again with persons from a third corporation, and so on. Another, though less satisfactory, possibility is to select for the investigation "modal cases," persons whose profile is the most prevalent in that population.

Because in many studies a statistically representative sample cannot be obtained, it often boils down to the researcher's admittedly subjective judgment that, indeed, the sample is adequately representative of the target population.

It is a different story for *theory falsification,* however. The only thing required is that participants be chosen so as to provide a rigorously unbiased test of the theory. In our Type B example, we need a sample of sojourners who vary with respect to prior knowledge of the Middle Eastern culture in question and in their degree of adaptation to that culture.

Optimally, though, we would want a sample that also is homogenous on variables irrelevant to the hypothesis (e.g., the language spoken in one's own culture). This homogeneity can eliminate "noise" in the data that is due to inconsequential differences among respondents. In our case, homogeneity would permit us to avoid the noise due to variation among the respondents in expressive styles associated with their native languages. Homogeneity, then, decreases the chance of making a Type II error.

A representative sample of the real-world population is not needed because the goal is not to perform a statistical generalization of the precise numerical results. The theory's validity is generalized beyond the research setting.

Next, in the *intervention falsification* realm, we need a sample that includes the full range of applicable individual differences; that is, some individual characteristics—be they demographic, such as young versus old, or experiential, such as seasoned versus neophyte trainees—may potentially determine the degree of success of a program. The sample must include representatives of all of those groups. Further, enough instances of each category must be included to permit a test of whether the CCT is effective with people in each of the groups. So, for example, the sample of young neophytes

must be large enough to allow an adequately powerful test of the impact of the CCT on that particular respondent group.

Operational Definitions

By *operational definitions,* we mean the concrete measures used to gauge the independent and dependent variables. For example, we could operationally define adaptation to the host culture by the number of days absent from work due to illness, by ratings on an attitude scale reflecting the degree of stress experienced daily, by reported judgments of supervisors about the quality of one's job performance, or by a variety of other indices.

In *effects application,* as we noted earlier, our prime objective is to make the research situation correspond to the real-world context to which we want to generalize. We can maximize the similarity between the operational definitions and their real-world analogues by using naturally occurring events and behaviors as the operational definitions. In the example above, the number of days absent or the supervisor judgments would be more appropriate than the more obtrusive use of an attitude scale of perceived stress. In our daily lives, most of us are not asked to fill out such scales.

In *theory falsification,* the operational definition does not have to be natural. Instead, the operational definition must be clearly interpretable in terms of the underlying construct; that is, a trainee's score on the operational definition must represent clearly the theoretical dimension, and not systematically reflect other variables. In our example, the number of days absent may be a relatively poor operational definition for cultural adaptation because absences can be due to many factors beyond the adequacy of one's adaptation—for example, previously occurring health conditions, environmental issues prevalent in the host culture. A self-report measure of perceived stress would be better for theory falsification—if the theoretical definition of *successful adaptation* presumes a feeling of comfort and tranquility.

For *intervention falsification,* the operational definitions must be identical to the way the intervention is to be conducted in the real world. The CCT program must be implemented in the same way it will be performed in the real world—the same trainers, same materials, same recruitment procedures, and so on. The criterion measures also must be those found in the real-world environment. Unlike theory falsification, the training program and impact measures should not be "cleaned up" to enhance the interpretability of the study's results in terms of the applicable theory.

Study Context

We should choose a setting for *effects application* statistically representative of the environmental variation present in the real world in which the CCT program will take place. The real-world situations are often heterogeneous on a number of background factors (e.g., characteristics of the physical facility in which the training will be offered, season of the year at which the training takes place). Variability in these background variables should be present in the research setting.

Ideally, a statistically random sample of these background factors would be used to capture this variation. Typically, though, it is impossible to represent systematically all variation in the real-world situation within a single study. In practice, it frequently boils down to the investigator's judgment that all the important background factors have been duly represented.

However the background factors enter into the research, representativeness is routinely best achieved by a nonlaboratory setting—because the trainee responses can be less sensitive to "guinea pig" effects, to experimenter bias (Blake & Heslin, 1971), and other such artifacts.

For *theory falsification,* we should choose a setting that is "clean" of extraneous influences on subjects and that allows the use of precise operational definitions. Most often—but not always—a controlled laboratory environment is the most expeditious way to keep the study free from variation in factors not of theoretical interest. These controlled settings permit standardization of CCT program features and of the impact measures. Further, it is typically easier to obtain a homogeneous sample of trainees for the test because the investigator can have greater control over who participates in a given training session. Similarly, in this setting, the researcher can use operational definitions constructed to be clear of undesired factors, without concern about their being naturally occurring.

A research context encompassing the environmental heterogeneity that can influence the success of the training program is a necessity for *intervention falsification.* The CCT must be shown to perform successfully in the face of this real-life variability. The test itself can be either in a controlled laboratory environment or in an uncontrolled natural setting. Either way, the setting need not be representative of any specific real-world situation (as would be true for effects application); it must only expose the CCT program to conditions that could cause the program to fail.

Validity Threats

The four forms of validity pertain to the legitimacy or accuracy with which a study can answer the following questions:

1. *Statistical conclusion validity.* Is participation in the CCT related to one's scores on the criteria of evaluation?
2. *Internal validity.* Given that a relationship exists, is it because of the CCT participation itself?
3. *Construct validity.* How do I describe this effect in theoretically relevant terms?
4. *External validity.* Given a plausible relationship between CCT and the dimensions of impact, how generalizable is this effect to other people, times, and settings?

Statistical Conclusion Validity

Statistical conclusion validity refers to the sources of error variance and to the appropriate use of statistical tests in determining (a) the existence of an association between CCT participation and scores on the immediate outcomes and the dimensions of overseas effectiveness and (b) the precise magnitude of that relationship. Five threats are particularly relevant to this form of validity.

1. *Low statistical power.* The statistical analysis permitted by a given design may be so insensitive as to fail to detect a relationship contained in the data or to underestimate the strength of the relationship. Prime culprits are the use of a small sample, particular statistical tests known to be fairly insensitive, and an overly restrictive alpha level.

2. *Fishing and multiple comparisons.* When numerous tests of differences between treatment and control conditions and/or between time periods are made, the probability that some of the comparisons will yield apparent differences by chance alone is increased. Failure to use appropriate multivariate or other statistical tests to adjust for this threat can result in spurious conclusions.

3. *Measure reliability.* Measures of operational criteria can yield scores containing substantial proportions of random error. The threat of low-measure reliability can result in failure to detect CCT impacts that could otherwise be found by using measures with suitable reliability.

4. *Training implementation reliability.* The way the treatment is implemented may vary from trainer to trainer and from one trainee group to another from one time to another. In theory falsification, this lack of standardization can inflate error variance and decrease the chance of detecting CCT impacts. The unreliability, though, is a realistic aspect of effects application and so is not a bias per se. In intervention falsification, the time period, trainee group, and so on should be a part of the design, and so the degree of unreliability would be estimated by the statistical analysis. It would not be a bias.

5. *Random irrelevancies in the research setting.* Frequently, features of the training setting (e.g., physical layout, sponsoring agency) affect the data gathered by increasing the error variance. In theory falsification, these factors can reduce the sensitivity of the design and so mask the real CCT impact. By the same reasoning as above for training implementation, this threat pertains more to theory falsification than to the other two types.

Designs that cannot rule out the above threats to statistical conclusion validity may provide misleading conclusions.

Internal validity

Internal validity is the degree to which the design legitimately permits one to conclude that a specific CCT program did or did not cause an effect on the criterion. Threats to internal validity raise the specter that the particular impact observed in the study might not, in fact, have been caused by the CCT program per se. A study's conclusions can be said to be internally valid only if no other causal factors are present that can act as plausible alternative explanations for the observed effects.

Outstanding threats to the internal validity of CCT evaluations include the following.

1. *History.* An effect could be due to an event that occurred between Time 1 and Time 2 and that is unrelated to the CCT program itself. Impacts of abrupt changes in governmental or corporate policy, natural disasters, and other such events might be mistakenly thought to be the result of CCT unless the research design controls for such contingencies.

2. *Maturation.* An observed effect could be due to a person growing wiser, more experienced, or in other ways changing between Time 1 and Time 2 for reasons other than the CCT experience.

3. *Testing.* A change from Time 1 to Time 2 may be traceable to an individual's having taken the "test" more than once, such as obtaining a higher score on the criterion because of recall of the questions or familiarity with the measurement environment.

4. *Instrumentation.* An effect might be due, not simply to the CCT, but to a change in the measuring instrument from Time 1 to Time 2 or to a difference in instruments between training and control conditions. For example, interviewers in a hypothetical study might use a subtly different approach at Time 2 than at Time 1 because of their better grasp of the procedure.

5. *Selection.* An apparent effect of CCT program observed by comparing criterion scores of those receiving CCT with those who do not can be spurious when the kinds of people admitted to training are different from those included in the control condition (e.g., intelligence, past experiences with the culture).

6. *Mortality.* This threat occurs when particular kinds of people drop out of a condition while other kinds remain. This loss renders the sample of people systematically different at Time 2 from Time 1, and the people in that condition at Time 2 possibly different from the kinds of individuals in other conditions that did not encounter such a loss. Conclusions will be invalid if these differences become entangled with the effects of CCT per se.

7. *Ambiguity about the direction of causality.* Surveys and other designs in which all criterion measures are collected at the same time are especially prone to this threat. Consider, for

example, a study comparing job productivity, appreciation of a culture, or other criterion scores of those who had previously participated in a CCT program with the scores of those who had not. Did the CCT experience produce better criterion scores, or did those who were already superior on the evaluation dimensions tend to volunteer (or be assigned by supervisors) for training?

8. *Diffusion or imitation of treatment.* Imagine a situation in which individuals in the training and control conditions can communicate with each other, or imagine other situations in which the information in the CCT is conveyed to those in the control condition. Under these circumstances, the conclusions based on criterion differences between conditions would be questionable because there may not be truly separate conditions to be compared.

The eight threats to internal validity apply equally to all three types of research.

Construct Validity

Internal validity has little to do with the theoretical definition of the CCT program or the dimension of impact. Rather, it refers to the relationship between the operational definition of the CCT (the specific instance included in the study) and the precise criterion scores analyzed irrespective of their theoretical representation. *Construct* validity, however, pertains to the fit between operational and theoretical definitions, to the ability to infer from the concrete measures used in the study the relevant theoretical definitions—for example, "Has a program designed to enhance cross-cultural tolerance really changed tolerance or just knowledge, and is the measure of tolerance more a measure of intelligence than tolerance?" Threats to construct validity arise when an operationally defined CCT impact dimension can be construed in terms of more than one theoretical definition; this can render it difficult to explain or even describe the obtained results meaningfully. Four such threats are especially appropriate to CCT evaluations:

1. *Inadequate explication of constructs.* Confusion about which are the "important" facets of the CCT program or about the reason for the observed impacts of the CCT may reflect the fact that the theoretical framework underlying the CCT program was specified in a vague or superficial manner.

2. *Mono-operation bias.* Many CCT evaluations are designed to have only one presentation of the CCT program or only one measure to represent each possible dimension of impact. Because a single instance may underrepresent important facets of a complex phenomenon, as well as contain irrelevancies, construct validity will be lower in such single-instance designs than when several instances are used simultaneously to operationalize a given theoretical construct. Multiple presentations of the CCT program and multiple indices of each impact dimension are invaluable for construct validity.

3. *Mono-method bias.* Even if one has avoided a mono-operation bias threat, irrelevancies may still be integral to the design. Suppose all administrations of the CCT are presented in the same way (e.g., by the same trainer, in the same physical environment, all impact measures are collected by using self-report attitudes questionnaires). In such a case, the influence of the method of administration of the measures upon the criterion scores cannot be dissociated from the influence of the CCT itself.

4. *Subject effects and researcher effects.* Artifactual findings may result when the study stimulates individuals' fears of being evaluated (Blake & Heslin, 1971; Rosenberg, 1969), when individuals' responses are influenced by researcher characteristics or cues (Blake & Heslin, 1971), or by other aspects of the evaluation setting.

As should be obvious at this point, construct validity is the *sine qua non* for theory falsification and is still quite important for intervention falsification. It is least applicable to effects application.

External Validity

External validity pertains to the generalization of a study's conclusions beyond the sample of people, time, and settings included in the evaluation study. External validity flows from the degree of correspondence among the sample of people/time/settings in a study, the populations they actually represent, and the populations to which generalization is desired. External validity is at the heart of effects application, in that the objective is to generalize the specific empirical observations to given real-world contexts. The more external validity, the better it is for theory falsification; this form of validity, though, is not essential to theory falsification. The objective with the latter is to see whether the hypothesis is supported in the given research context. If so, then the theory itself is extrapolated beyond the research setting as evidence mounts. For intervention falsification, external validity is not a necessity within a given study. The goal here is to assess the success of the training program in designated settings. These settings can represent worst-case scenarios and other atypical contingencies.

Let's review five threats:

1. *Interaction of multiple treatments.* When individuals participate in more than one training experience, it is difficult to generalize evaluation results to situations in which the entire set of training experiences is not present. Hence, the validity of an evaluation of a given CCT is endangered when individuals may have participated in more than one formal training program and the other programs are not included in the analyses, or when individuals are engaged in informal learning (e.g., through direct contacts) outside the program and that informal learning will probably not occur with the program in the future.

2. *Interaction of testing and CCT.* The measurement of criterion scores at Time 1 can sometimes sensitize individuals to particular facets of the CCT program and thereby alter the impact of those facets. The calculated impacts, however, should not be generalizable to more "typical" situations in which criterion scores are not measured prior to CCT participation.

3. *Interaction of selection and CCT.* A major threat to external validity can occur when the trainees participating at the time of evaluation are substantially different from those participating at other times (e.g., because of changes in trainee selection procedures). To the extent that obtaining results depends on characteristics of the participants (e.g., intelligence, gender, experience), the results are not generalizable to other people with different characteristics.

4. *Interaction of setting and CCT.* This threat pertains to the dependence of the CCT impacts on the setting in which the CCT takes place. This threat may be particularly applicable to CCT programs evaluated in settings (e.g.,

universities, retreats) substantially different from the settings in which the training is typically conducted.

5. *Interaction of history and CCT.* It is possible that the observed impacts of the CCT program have been altered by events irrelevant to the program itself (e.g., exposure to media coverage of important events occurring in the culture of interest). Clearly, the observed impacts would be modified at a future time in which those events are not occurring.

On the one hand, in comparing alternative research designs, one should gravitate toward those designs judged to be freer from threats to the most important types of validity. In evaluating the conclusions drawn in a study that used a particular design, on the other hand, one should consider all types of validity. In this way, one can differentiate conclusions that are legitimate from those that are not.

Concluding Points

Whichever type of study and whichever forms of validity are of concern to us, two issues merit attention. First, a rule of thumb invariably adopted by researchers engaged in theoretical development is to be highly cautious. Suppose an investigator concluded that evidence was not found for a causal impact of a certain CCT and that, in reality, the program actually did have an impact. This erroneous conclusion would be far less troublesome than would be the case if an investigator erroneously concluded that there was an impact when there truly was not. This conservative vent has led researchers to fear a Type I error more than a Type II error.

Perhaps this basic research rule of thumb may not inevitably be suitable for all CCT evaluations. The political and financial climate of organizations conducting CCT programs, as well as the hidden agendas and formal objectives of program evaluations, are often different from those of basic research. Failing to identify impacts that are actually there may be more disastrous than concluding that an impact exists when it actually does not. Too often, program managers, organizational sponsors, and others interpret the conservative conclusion that no clear impact was observed as meaning that the CCT program was found to have had no impact of any sort. Under such circumstances, uncritical adoption of the basic research rule of thumb may be dysfunctional.

Second, and above all, no ideal design is applicable to all CCT evaluations. Even the classical experimental design is suspect in regard to external validity, whereas several quasi-experimental designs are quite powerful and permit high levels of internal and external validity without sacrifice of construct and statistical conclusion validity (see Cook & Campbell, 1979). But many of them can be cumbersome, expensive, and in other ways unsuitable for practical use.

The investigators must select a design to meet the requirements of the specific CCT evaluation in question. They must first determine which of the three types they are working with. Then they must review the various forms of validity and prioritize the more important ones in light of the project objectives and the organizational culture in which it is embedded. Finally, they must select a design and, as appropriate, add as many modifications as necessary to safeguard it from the principal threats. We hope the design schema will be helpful in these activities.

References

Albert, R. D. (1983). The intercultural sensitizer or cultural assimilator: A cognitive approach. In D. Landis & R. W. Brislin (Eds.), *Handbook of intercultural training: Vol. 2. Issues in training methodology* (pp. 186-217). Elmsford, NY: Pergamon.

Basadur, M., Wakabayashi, M., & Takai, J. (1992). Training effects on the divergent thinking attitudes of Japanese managers. *International Journal of Intercultural Relations, 16,* 329-346.

Bennett, J. M. (1986). Modes of cross-cultural training: Conceptualizing cross-cultural training as education. *International Journal of Intercultural Relations, 10,* 117-134.

Berry, J. W. (1980). Introduction to methodology. In H. C. Triandis & J. W. Berry (Eds.), *Handbook of cross-cultural psychology: Vol. 2. Methodology* (pp. 1-28). Boston: Allyn & Bacon.

Bird, A., Heinbuch, S., Dunbar, R., & McNulty, M. (1993). A conceptual model of the effects of area studies training programs and a preliminary investigation of the model's hypothesized relationships. *International Journal of Intercultural Relations, 17,* 415-436.

Black, J. S., & Mendenhall, M. (1990). Cross-cultural training effectiveness: A review and theoretical framework for future research. *Academy of Management Review, 15,* 113-136.

Blake, B. F., & Heslin, R. (1971). Evaluation apprehension and subject bias in experiments. *Journal of Experimental Research in Personality, 5,* 57-63.

Blake, B. F., & Heslin, R. (1983). Evaluating cross-cultural training. In D. Landis & R. W. Brislin (Eds.), *Handbook of intercultural training: Vol. 1. Issues in theory and design* (pp. 203-223). Elmsford, NY: Pergamon.

Brein, M., & David, K. (1971). Intercultural communications and the adjustment of the sojourner. *Psychological Bulletin, 76,* 215-230.

Brislin, R. (1980). Translation and content analyses of oral and written materials. In H. C. Triandis & J. W. Berry (Eds.), *Handbook of cross-cultural psychology: Vol. 2. Methodology* (pp. 389-444). Boston: Allyn & Bacon.

Brislin, R. (1993). *Understanding culture's influence on behavior.* Fort Worth, TX: Harcourt Brace Jovanovich.

Brislin, R., & Pedersen, P. (1976). *Cross-cultural orientation programs.* New York: Halsted.

Brown, L., & Sechrest, L. (1980). Experiments in cross-cultural research. In H. C. Triandis & J. W. Berry (Eds.), *Handbook of cross-cultural psychology: Vol. 2. Methodology* (pp. 297-318). Boston: Allyn & Bacon.

Calder, B. J., Phillips, L. W., & Tybout, A. M. (1981). Designing research for application. *Journal of Consumer Research, 8*(2), 197-207.

Campbell, D., & Stanley, J. (1966). *Experimental and quasi-experimental designs for research.* Chicago: Rand McNally.

Cook, T., & Campbell, D. T. (1979). *Quasi-experimentation: Design and analysis for field settings.* Chicago: Rand McNally.

Fiedler, F., Mitchell, T., & Triandis, H. (1971). The cultural assimilator: An approach to cross-cultural training. *Journal of Applied Psychology, 55,* 95-102.

Furnham, A., & Bochner, S. (1986). *Culture shock: Psychological reaction to unfamiliar environments.* New York: Methuen.

Goldman, A. (1992). Intercultural training of Japanese for U.S.-Japanese interorganizational communication. *International Journal of Intercultural Relations, 16,* 175-216.

Goodenough, W. (1980). Ethnographic field techniques. In H. C. Triandis & J. W. Berry (Eds.), *Handbook of cross-cultural psychology: Vol. 2. Methodology* (pp. 9-56). Boston: Allyn & Bacon.

Gudykunst, W., Hammer, M., & Wiseman, R. (1977). An analysis of an integrated approach to cross-cultural training. *International Journal of Intercultural Relations, 1,* 99-110.

Hammer, M., Gudykunst, W., & Wiseman, R. (1978). Dimensions of intercultural effectiveness: An exploratory study. *International Journal of Intercultural Relations, 2,* 382-393.

Harrison, J. K. (1992). Individual and combined effects of behavior modeling and the culture assimilator in cross-cultural management training. *Journal of Applied Psychology, 77,* 952-962.

Hawes, F., & Kealy, D. J. (1979). *Canadians in development: An empirical study of adaptation and effectiveness on overseas assignment.* Ottawa: Canadian International Development Agency.

Heslin, R., & Blake, B. (1973). The involvement inventory. In J. W. Pfeiffer & J. E. Jones (Eds.), *The 1973 annual handbook for group facilitators* (pp. 87-94). Iowa City, IA: University Associates Press.

Kealey, D. J. (1989). A study of cross-cultural effectiveness: Theoretical issues, practical applications. *International Journal of Intercultural Relations, 13,* 378-428.

Kupfer, A. (1988, March 14). How to be a global manager. *Fortune,* pp. 52-54, 58.

Lambert, W. F. (1992). Challenging established views on social issues: The power and limitations of research. *American Psychologist, 47,* 533-542.

Landis, D., Brislin, R. W., & Hulgus, J. F. (1985). Attributional training versus contact in acculturative learning: A laboratory study. *Journal of Applied Social Psychology, 15*(5), 466-482.

Martin, L. (Ed.). (1986). Theories and methods in cross-cultural orientation [Special issue]. *International Journal of Intercultural Relations, 10,* 103-254.

McDaniel, C. O., Jr., McDaniel, N. C., & McDaniel, A. K. (1988). Transferability of multicultural evaluation from training to practice. *International Journal of Intercultural Relations, 12,* 19-33.

Mendenhall, M., & Oddou, G. (1985). The dimensions of expatriate acculturation. *Academy of Management Review, 10,* 39-47.

Mendenhall, M., & Oddou, G. (1986). Acculturation profiles of expatriate managers: Implications for cross-cultural training programs. *Columbia Journal of World Business, 21,* 73-79.

Mischel, W. (1965). Predicting the success of Peace Corps volunteers in Nigeria. *Journal of Personality and Social Psychology, 1,* 510-517.

O'Brien, G. E., & Plooij, D. (1977). Comparison of programmed and prose culture training upon attitudes and knowledge. *Journal of Applied Psychology, 62,* 499-505.

Paige, R. M. (1986). Trainer competencies: The missing conceptual link in orientation. *International Journal of Intercultural Relations, 10,* 135-158.

Redmond, M., & Bunyi, J. M. (1993). The relationship of intercultural communication competence with stress and the handling of stress as reported by international students. *International Journal of Intercultural Relations, 17*(2), 235-254.

Rosenberg, M. (1969). The conditions and consequences of evaluation research. In R. Rosenthal & R. Rosnow (Eds.), *Artifacts in behavioral research* (pp. 280-349). San Diego: Academic Press.

Rutman, L. (1980). *Planning useful evaluations: Evaluability assessment.* Beverly Hills, CA: Sage.

Scheirer, M. A. (1981). *Program implementation: The organizational context.* Beverly Hills, CA: Sage.

Segalowitz, N. S. (1980). Issues in the cross-cultural study of bilingual development. In H. C. Triandis & A. Heron (Eds.), *Handbook of cross-cultural psychology: Vol. 4. Developmental* (pp. 55-92). Boston: Allyn & Bacon.

Stephan, C. W., & Stephan, W. G. (1992). Reducing intercultural anxiety through intercultural contact. *International Journal of Intercultural Contact, 16,* 89-106.

Tanaka, T., Takai, J., Kohyama, T., & Fujihara, T. (1994). Adjustment patterns of international students in Japan. *International Journal of Intercultural Relations, 18,* 55-76.

Thompson, M. (1980). *Benefit-cost analysis for program evaluation.* Beverly Hills, CA: Sage.

Triandis, H. C. (in press). Intercultural training. In D. Landis & R. W. Brislin (Eds.), *Handbook of cross-cultural training.*

PART II

Contextual Dimensions of Intercultural Training

10

The Intercultural Sensitizer

KENNETH CUSHNER

DAN LANDIS

THE overall goals of intercultural training aim to affect the cognitive, affective, and behavioral domains of trainees and subsequently people's overall adjustment and effectiveness in cross-cultural settings. Analysis of the many training designs that have emerged over the years (Bhawuk, 1994; Brislin, Cushner, Cherrie, & Yong, 1986; Brislin & Pedersen, 1976) suggests that, overall, intercultural training has attempted to (a) help people communicate more effectively, (b) help people deal with the inevitable stresses that accompany an intercultural encounter, (c) enable people to develop and maintain interpersonal relationships with those whose backgrounds are different from their own, and (d) enable people to accomplish the various tasks they originally set out to do in a new context or setting.

Of all the training approaches that have been developed, the *intercultural sensitizer (ICS),* also known as the *culture assimilator,* has been exposed to the most intense scrutiny and analy-sis and has repeatedly demonstrated positive impact on people's cognitive, affective, and behavioral processes. The intent of this chapter is to (a) present an overview of the purposes and design of the ICS, (b) differentiate between culture-specific and culture-general sensitizers, (c) review available research on the instrument, (d) explore the variety of uses of this approach to training, and (e) suggest guidelines for construction and use of future sensitizers.

History and General Description

The ICS or culture assimilator is a cross-cultural training strategy that employs the critical incident approach (Flannagan, 1954) to present culture clashes between individuals from different cultural backgrounds. Through the use of short vignettes, or *critical incidents,* trainees read scripted accounts of situations in which individuals from different cultures interact with the intent of pursuing some common goal. Toward the end of the incident, a clash of cultures is evident and the various parties are unable to satisfactorily accomplish their task. More often than not, an unintended misinterpretation of events is at the base of the problem or a misunderstanding of the subjective meaning is given to a particular behavior. The reader is presented with a number of alternatives to explain the problem and is asked to select the one that best explains the problem *from the other's point of view.*

Development of the ICS can be traced to the University of Illinois in 1962, where researchers (led by Larry Stolurow, working with Osgood, Fiedler, and Triandis) proposed the creation of a computer program that could be used to provide cross-cultural training to students (Albert, 1983).[1] It was here the term *culture assimilator* was proposed, the first assimilator being developed to address communication and interaction between Arab and American students. Construction of such instruments has not altered much over the years. In the first case, Arab students were asked to relate a variety of culture clashes they encountered with their American peers and to explain the problem as best they could from their perspective. American students were then asked to review the incidents and to explain them as best they could from their perspective. Episodes, or short scenarios, were constructed, followed by four or five alternative explanations or attributions, one of them being the one provided by the Arab respondents and the remaining foils coming from those most often presented by the Americans. Such has been the general format for the development of most ICSs.

A typical training program would have trainees read a number of such critical incidents, perhaps as many as 20 or more. Such an approach to training encourages individuals to develop a more sophisticated understanding of the distinction between objective and subjective culture. Osgood and Triandis (Osgood, 1977; Triandis, 1972) suggested that culture operates at two levels—an objective level, as well as a subjective level. *Objective elements of culture,* on the one hand, are the visible, tangible elements of culture and include such things as the artifacts people make, the food they eat, and the clothing they wear—things that are relatively easy to pick up, analyze, visualize, and touch. *Subjective elements of culture,* on the other hand, are the invisible, intangible elements of a group of people and include such things as values, attitudes, and norms of behavior—things that are generally kept in the mind and that are much more difficult to pick up, analyze, and visualize. It is thought that the greatest problems in intercultural understanding and communication occur at the level of people's subjective cultural differences and that effective intercultural education and training should focus on this dimension of culture.

Subjective elements of culture are most evident when people make judgments or attributions about others on the basis of the behavior they observe. People are constantly making judgments about others, and they do so rather quickly. People judge others to be well intentioned, ill-mannered, well educated, hardworking, and so forth generally within the first few minutes of an encounter. Behavior itself, however, is not data. Behavior occurs within a given context to satisfy one's needs. To accurately understand what a person's intentions are, one must understand the context in which it occurs. Culture provides one such context. Without an adequate cultural context, another's behavior is akin to noise and can be rather meaningless. Knowledge of culture enables one to interpret the motivations of others in the same way they would for themselves. People are thus more accurate in their judgments of others. Misunderstanding the reasons or motivations for people's behavior, or making misattributions, is a common problem in an intercultural context. The goal, then, is for people to make *isomorphic attributions,* or similar judgments about the causes of another's behavior. Making isomorphic attributions thus helps improve intercultural understanding and relations and is the major goal of training with the ICS.

The assumption behind culture assimilator training is that, as the trainees receive feedback on their responses, they begin to understand the subjective culture of the target group and subsequently to select more appropriate responses.

Perhaps an example will be helpful. Most Euro-Westerners may view the idea of arranged marriages as antiquated and with disdain. With insight into the reasoning and practice of such behavior *from an insider's point of view,* outsiders can begin to more fully understand the motivations of such behavior and are thus less likely to make inaccurate or negative judgments about people whose culture dictates such practice. From a Euro-Western perspective, one may question how anyone else could possibly take a role in selecting one's marriage partner. From another perspective, it may be seen that one's parents understand both their children and the demands placed on adults far greater than most young people themselves are capable of doing. Parents, then, are best suited to select a mate who would be compatible with their child, as well as with an extended family collective. Young people who marry as a result of such practice learn to love one another and thus grow into love, rather than fall in love and then marry. Understanding another culture's perspective, and subsequently the reasons behind one's actions, makes people more accurate in their interpretations of observed behavior. Thus, the attributions a person makes of others become similar to the judgments the person would make about him- or herself.

An example of a critical incident follows:

On the Flathead Indian Reservation, tribal chiefs are engaged with ranchers in negotiating water rights. The ranchers are disturbed because the water table is being lowered. They believe it is in everybody's interest to scientifically manage the supply of water. They also believe that much of the problem is because of excessive water use on the reservation. Although the Indian team consists of tribal elders with whom the ranchers have long relations, the Indians, though quite friendly, do not seem very concerned about the problem and do not act as though the negotiations are serious. The Indians brought along a lawyer from the firm that handles legal affairs for the tribe. As the conference proceeds, the tribal lawyers take a progressively larger role in expressing the position of the Indians. The ranchers become more frustrated and threaten to take matters into their own hands.

The critical incident is just that, an event. It is not the same as the scenario part of a sensitizer item. Much work is still necessary to make the entire item appear reasonable and the conclusions logical.

Forms of Intercultural Sensitizers

Over the years, two forms of ICSs have been developed. *Culture-specific assimilators* are designed to prepare people for experiences in highly specified settings. *Culture-general assimilators* are designed to prepare people for experiences that are common in a variety of cross-cultural encounters.

Culture-Specific Assimilators

Prior to the mid-1980s, ICSs or culture assimilators were developed for highly specific purposes; that is, they were designed to prepare individuals from one cultural group for interactions with another specific cultural group. And, they were developed in hard-copy format. A variety of culture-specific assimilators have been developed for a variety of uses, including the preparation of French bankers to live and work in Thailand, for American adolescents about to embark on volunteer programs in Honduras, and for white and black servicemen living and working together in the United States military (see Albert, 1983, for a comprehensive listing of culture-specific assimilators).

Culture-specific assimilators have demonstrated considerable effectiveness at helping individuals achieve the goals of their intercultural experience when the target or host culture is well known. One major difficulty with the use of culture-specific assimilators, oddly enough, seems to be its strength; that is, the high degree of specificity generally results in a lack of widespread usefulness or availability. Developed for quite particular audiences and often for highly specific purposes (e.g., adolescent volunteer medical workers to Honduras on an Amigos de las Americas Program), these assimilators are generally not readily available to or easily obtained by the general public. One truly needs to have a wide-ranging network of colleagues in the field of cross-cultural training to gain access to the culture-specific assimilators that have been developed.[2]

Culture-General Assimilators

Stimulated by large-scale programs such as the Peace Corps, as well as by organizations that support foreign students, a rich and diverse body of research has developed that focuses on the experiences of people who spend much time in cultures other than their own. In reviewing this literature, Brislin (1981) was struck by the similarities in people's experiences despite the wide range of roles they had and the large number of countries in which they lived. Despite such diverse roles as businessperson, diplomat, Peace Corps worker, teacher in an urban setting, social worker, foreign student, and technical assistance adviser, people go through similar experiences adjusting to life abroad and/or to extensive interaction with people from other cultures. Examples of these experiences are a sense of uprootedness, feelings that one has been centered out for special attention, difficulties in developing relationships, and realizations that one's previous knowledge may be inadequate.

Brislin (1981) organized his treatment of the commonalities in cross-cultural experiences according to nine broad categories: (a) the historical myths people bring with them to another culture, (b) people's attitudes, traits, and skills, (c) people's thought and attribution processes, (d) the groups people join, (e) the range of situations in which people have to interact, (f) people's management of cross-cultural conflict, (g) the tasks people want to accomplish, (h) the organizations people are a part of, and, given an understanding of the above, (i) the processes of short- and long-term adjustment.

Prompted by this analysis and by work done in 1983 by Brislin and Landis at the East-West Center, the first culture-general assimilator was developed (Brislin et al., 1986; Cushner & Brislin, 1996). Such an assimilator was designed to prepare individuals for the kinds of experiences they are certain to have regardless of the particular background of the individuals and regardless of their roles in the new settings. These common experiences became the basis for the development of a culture-general assimilator. Such an approach to training is of special interest because people are increasingly coming into contact with others from a variety of backgrounds. Culture-general training—that is, preparation for the kinds of experiences one is certain to encounter—rather than training for

highly culture-specific interactions is often preferred.

The culture-general assimilator (Brislin et al., 1986) presents 100 critical incidents that were developed to sensitize individuals to 18 culture-general themes (see Table 10.1) thought to be common across most intercultural interactions. The range of such experiences forms the basis for the incidents, as well as for the 18 essays that expand on the general themes brought out in the incidents.

The 18 themes are further grouped according to three main categories: (a) people's experiences that engage the emotions, (b) knowledge areas that people learn as a result of being socialized within any given culture, and (c) the bases of cultural differences and how people learn to process information. A brief description of the 18 culture-general themes developed in the culture-general assimilator is presented in Table 10.1.

Research Implications of the Intercultural Sensitizer

The ICS has been the most thoroughly researched of all cross-cultural training strategies. Time and time again and across a variety of audiences, the ICS has proved to have positive impact on people's cognitive, affective, and behavioral domains. This section reviews relevant studies of culture assimilators in three categories: (a) a brief review of studies done on culture-specific assimilators through the mid-1980s, (b) research carried out on the culture-general assimilator in the decade following its development, and (c) more recent analysis of culture assimilators.

Early Studies on
Culture-Specific Assimilators

A number of studies have been conducted with a variety of culture-specific assimilators, and they are reviewed in detail elsewhere (e.g., Albert, 1983). For example, Fiedler, Mitchell, and Triandis (1971) found that Americans who received culture assimilator training prior to going to Honduras were better adjusted and performed their work better than untrained Americans. Worchel and Mitchell (1970) reported that persons trained with a Thai assimilator gave

TABLE 10.1 Eighteen Themes of the Culture-General Assimilator

People's Experiences That Engage the Emotions:

1. *Anxiety.* As people encounter many unfamiliar demands, they are likely to become anxious about whether or not their behavior is appropriate.

2. *Disconfirmed expectations.* People may become upset or uncomfortable, not because of the specific circumstances they encounter, but because the situation differed from what they expected.

3. *Belonging.* People have the need to fill a niche, to feel that they belong, and to feel at home, but they often cannot because they have the status of "outsider."

4. *Ambiguity.* When living and working across cultures, the messages one receives are often unclear; yet, decisions must be made and appropriate action must be taken. People who are effective at working across cultures are known to have a high tolerance for ambiguity.

5. *Confrontation with one's prejudices.* People may discover that previously held beliefs about a certain group of people may not be accurate or useful when interacting with another culture.

Knowledge Areas That People Learn as a Result of Being Socialized Within Any Given Culture:

6. *Communication and language use.* Communication differences are probably the most obvious problem that must be overcome when crossing cultural boundaries. Cross-cultural communication, attitudes toward language use, the difficulties of learning another language, and its relation to education are addressed in this area.

7. *Roles.* People perform a generally accepted set of behaviors in relation to the roles they adopt. Tremendous differences exist with respect to the occupants of these roles and how these roles are enacted in different social groups.

8. *Individualism versus collectivism.* All people act at times in their individual interest, and at other times according to their group allegiances. The relative emphasis on group versus individual orientation varies from culture to culture and may have a significant impact on people's decision-making processes, their choice of peers and associates, and the degree to which they perform effectively on their own.

9. *Rituals versus superstition.* All cultures have rituals that help people meet their needs as they cope with life's everyday demands. People in all cultures also engage in behaviors that "outsiders" may label superstitious. One's rituals may be seen by others as based on superstitions.

10. *Social hierarchies—class and status.* People often make distinctions based on various markers of high and low status. These distinctions differ from culture to culture.

11. *Values.* People's experiences in such broad areas as religion, economics, politics, aesthetics, and interpersonal relationships become internalized. Understanding these internalized views and the range of possible differences is important to cross-cultural understanding.

12. *Work.* Differences in the amount of time people spend on task versus socializing, who has the onus of control, and the way decisions are made may differ significantly across cultures.

13. *Time and spatial orientation.* Culture determines people's orientation toward time and the degree to which one feels bound by the clock. In addition, people's use of space may also be quite different.

Bases of Cultural Differences and How People Learn to Process Information

14. *Categorization.* Because people cannot attend to all the information they perceive, they group similar bits of information into categories and then respond according to that category. Different cultures may put the identical piece of information into different categories. This variation causes confusion when people who use different sets of categories must interact.

15. *Differentiation.* People make finer distinctions between elements in categories that are of great importance to them.

16. *In-group—out-group distinctions.* People the world over classify people into in-groups—those with whom they are comfortable and can discuss their concerns—and out-groups—those who are generally kept at a distance. People entering other cultures or new groups must recognize that they will often be considered out-group members and that they will never participate in some behaviors associated with in-group membership.

17. *Learning styles.* The style in which people learn best may differ from culture to culture.

18. *Attribution.* People observe the behavior of others and reflect on their own behavior. Judgments about the causes of behavior are called *attributions.* Effective intercultural interaction is facilitated when people can make *isomorphic* (shared or agreed-on) attributions about the behavior of others.

more favorable self-reports concerning contacts with members of the Thai culture and their work in Thailand than did untrained persons. Fiedler et al. found that persons using a Greek assimilator saw themselves as significantly better adjusted and as having better interpersonal relations and higher productivity than untrained individuals. In yet other studies, whites trained with an assimilator designed to improve white-black interactions made attributions that were more similar to those made by members of the target culture (Weldon, Carston, Rissman, Slobodin, & Triandis, 1975). Trained participants refused to engage in racial stereotyping more often than untrained individuals. In addition, trained individuals perceived the attitudes of blacks and whites involved in conflict episodes as more positive than untrained individuals. An unintended finding was that black confederates preferred untrained to trained individuals as people with whom to interact. Landis, in a comment graciously included in Weldon et al.'s article, suggested that the assimilator training acted to increase the anxiety that past behaviors were no longer appropriate and that the time between training and testing was not enough for new responses patterns to become solidified. Hence, the trained persons would seem unsure of themselves, in contrast with untrained individuals.

Landis, Brislin, and Hulgus (1985) used a Solomon four-group design to investigate the effect of the culture assimilator and contact in acculturative training of whites and blacks. Five groups were defined: assimilator/contact, contact/assimilator, assimilator only, contact only, and control. Dependent variables included the TICS (25 items), anxiety (state, self-evaluation), task evaluation, and a behavioral task. Subjects were evaluated blind by black raters on the basis of videotapes made during the behavioral task.

Results indicated that the assimilator/contact group was superior to the other groups for both the primary (competence) and secondary (affect) ratings. The assimilator-only group was not different from the control group. All groups made significantly greater isomorphic (TICS) attributions than the control subjects. All groups were also more anxious on the posttest than pretest, with the control and assimilator-only groups being the major contributors of this effect. The order was as predicted, although the differences were not significant. Trainee perception was affected by training. The assimilator and control groups rated their coworkers significantly more competent than did the other groups; this finding may, in turn, explain the anxiety effect.

Hart, Day, Landis, and McGrew (1978) completed a field evaluation of Landis et al.'s army assimilator (1975; and reviewed in Albert, 1983). The first chapter of the Hart et al. report was a reprise of the article by Landis, Day, McGrew, Thomas, and Miller (1976). Chapters 2 and 3, however, went beyond and attempted to assess the external validity. Because the results appear to indicate ineffectiveness of the assimilator technique, the report bears closer scrutiny.

In the first evaluation, it was reasoned that commanders' performances on the assimilator should be correlated with their subordinates' views of them in regard to racial issues and policies in the unit. The study did not actually measure commanders' performances on the assimilator (which would require a measure of acquisition), however, but only knowledge. Knowledge was achieved by presenting the assimilator in a test format (without rationales). Fifty commanders were in the first set of subjects, with their subordinates constituting the second sample. The enlisted sample thus constituted approximately 700 respondents (in a ratio of 6 whites, 5 blacks, and 3 Hispanics from each company). Response rate among the enlisted men was approximately 83%.

The enlisted men rated their commanders on three variables: the Racial Policies Scale (five questions, alpha = .74 to .94); and two single-item responses dealing with the racial climate and the handling of racial problems. The five Racial Policies items were averaged to form a single datum; the single-item scales were treated separately—hence, three bits of data from each enlisted respondent.

When commanders' scores on the test version of the assimilator and subordinates' scores were correlated, two significant correlations out of nine were found, well within the number that could be expected by chance. Indeed, no significant correlation occurred for the black enlisted men's group; this finding suggests that a commander's untrained level of knowledge had little impact on how he was perceived by his subordinates.

A second evaluation was done to address issues of causation by using a controlled experimental design. In this study, the assimilator was part of a 1-day seminar in which 40 assimilator items were divided into two 20-item sets. Between the sets, the seminar participants discussed the items and reflected on the information in the items.

The subjects were senior command NCO's (E7-E9) of units. The 80 subjects were divided into two groups: experimental and control. They then participated in the seminar (experimental) or did nothing (control). Two months later, the 80 participants received a questionnaire tapping into their perceptions of their effectiveness with regard to racial issues. A second group of the three immediate subordinates received another questionnaire designed to evaluate the race relations performance of the seminar participants. Finally, the immediate supervisors also received a survey. By and large, all of the surveys were identical except, of course, the participants evaluated themselves, whereas all the others evaluated the participant.

Unfortunately, the sample attrition was quite high and thus rendered any conclusions highly suspect and tentative. For example, of the 40 command personnel assigned to the experimental group, only 22 actually appeared. Of the 240 subordinates who were sent surveys, the return rate was 16%; 29% of the supervisors and only 40% of the participants completed the survey.

Because of the sample attrition, data analyses were difficult. Attempts were made to control for selection bias, although the efforts were not very convincing. In any case, the analysis provided no evidence of assimilator impact—the relevant F tests were all nonsignificant.

The problems in the last study are many and do not need to be restated. They do point, however, to the need for carefully controlled studies of the assimilator-impact studies that have, with few exceptions (Landis, Brislin, & Hulgus, 1985; Weldon et al., 1975) yet to be done.

Assessing the Culture-General Assimilator

Recent studies of the culture-general assimilator have shown it to be of considerable use in preparing individuals for interactions in culturally diverse settings. A number of studies have analyzed the impact of the culture-general assimilator in college classrooms, for the orientation of adolescent exchange participants, and in the preparation of teachers and teacher education students for the kinds of cross-cultural interactions they are certain to encounter in the increasingly diverse classrooms in the United States (Bhatkal, 1990; Broaddus, 1986; Cushner, 1989; Ilola, 1991; Pacino, 1988; Ramirez, 1992; Yarbro, 1988). Some of these are highlighted below.

The first empirical study comparing a culture-general assimilator-trained group with a control group was carried out by Broaddus (1986). Designed to test the usefulness of the materials in university undergraduate courses, Broaddus's study introduced the culture-general assimilator to half of a large lecture course in social psychology. The other half became a wait control group that received the culture-general assimilator at a later time. Assignment to the two groups was on a random basis. At the point when half the class had been exposed to the materials (the trained group) and half had not, Broaddus administered various dependent variable measures. Using a criterion introduced by Malpass and Salancik (1977), Broaddus showed that trained students answered 15 of the more difficult items (which they had not seen before) more accurately than the controls.

This finding suggests that trained people are better able to analyze new cross-cultural problematic encounters to which they had not been previously exposed, after they had analyzed many other critical incidents and relevant essays during training. Trained students also scored significantly higher than controls on a newly developed scale—the Inventory of Cross-Cultural Sensitivity (ICCS), a set of statements in five subscales (cultural integration, behavioral response, intellectual interaction, attitude toward others, and empathy), designed to measure various aspects of people's attitudes toward and behaviors concerning intercultural interaction (Cushner, 1986). Trained students scored higher on the factors concerned with attitude toward others and empathy, as measured by such items as the following: It is important to consider people's feelings before making a decisions, There is usually more than one good way to get things done, I may defend the viewpoint of others, I think people are basically alike, and Certain prejudices I have hinder the way I interact with people (negatively scored). These items were mixed in with many others that did not discriminate trained from-untrained students, and so it is unlikely that students were simply responding to the above items to flatter themselves or to present themselves in a desirable light. Rather, such results can be interpreted to suggest that because many critical incidents examine the nature of cultural relativity, sensitivity to the viewpoint of others, and understanding of the attributions made by others, this result reflects internalization of the ideas presented during training.

Cushner (1989) used a modified version of the culture-general assimilator in the preparation of adolescent exchange students from 14 countries about to live in New Zealand for 1 year. As the basis of their orientation and training to life in an overseas setting, the trained group spent 6 hours analyzing 19 cultural-general critical incidents rewritten to speak directly to the experiences of adolescents (Cushner & Grove, 1990). The control group participated in the more traditional, yet quite comprehensive, AFS orientation to life in New Zealand.

In pretest assessment, subjects were asked to complete 10 critical incidents taken from the culture-general assimilator. Subjects were also asked to describe a cross-cultural encounter they had experienced and to explain it to the best of their ability. No significant differences were evident in subject responses between the control and treatment groups.

Data and interviews were collected on subjects over a period of 6 months after training. In the first evaluation conducted immediately after training, subjects were asked to complete a series of 10 of the more difficult and previously unseen critical incidents (difficulty as determined by the validation sample of experienced sojourners conducted during the development of the culture-general assimilator). Treatment group responses were significantly higher than the control group ($p < .05$). Subjects were asked once again to relate a cross-cultural encounter they had experienced and to explain the encounter to the best of their ability. Results of this study indicated that, compared with the control group, trained individuals were more knowledgeable about concepts relevant to cross-cultural interaction and better able to apply those concepts to personal cross-cultural misunderstandings.

All subjects completed the Culture Shock Adjustment Inventory (CSAI; Juffer, 1982) and the Means-Ends Problem-Solving Test (MEPS;

Spivak, Platt, & Shure, 1976) approximately 6 months into their experience. Trained subjects were better adjusted ($p < .05$) to their new context as evidenced on one of four scales of the CSAI (Perceived Control of the Environment). In addition, trained subjects were more proficient in handling hypothetical interpersonal problem-solving situations in a cross-cultural setting ($p < .05$).

An additional observation centered around the number of transfers required by students throughout the year. Although not significant, seven from the control group required changes in host families, whereas only three of the trained group required such changes. This outcome would certainly be welcome by anyone working in adolescent exchange programs, considering the significant upheavals, embarrassment, and stresses such unanticipated family changes bring about.

Yarbro (1988) administered a version of the culture-general assimilator to 50 school teachers enrolled in teacher education courses. The assimilator was administered over two class periods in a discussion format; that is, the programmed instruction format was discarded in favor of a guided discussion and group agreement on appropriate responses. A control group received a similar pretest and posttest. Dependent variables were the subscales of the ICCS, a measure of cultural incident productivity, responses to a set of culture assimilator items presented in test format, and the Marlowe-Crowne Social Desirability Scale.

Results indicated significant ($p < .05$) differences between the experimental and control groups on the culture assimilator test items and on the production of critical incidents. The ICCS and Marlowe-Crowne results were not significant. The author, in attempting to explain the results, pointed to the small sample size, the potentially insensitive ICCS, and the delay in administering the ICCS (approximately 1 week following training).

These studies have demonstrated that trainees are more knowledgeable about concepts relevant to cross-cultural interaction; are better able to generate, analyze, and apply such concepts to personal cross-cultural incidents; and are more sophisticated in their thinking and analysis of cross-cultural issues present in diverse classroom settings. On the basis of these investigations, it has been concluded that the culture-general assimilator is capable of bringing about marked improvement in individuals' knowledge about factors related to cross-cultural interaction and adjustment. In addition, trained individuals seem better able to achieve their goals in an intercultural setting, in part, by assisting individuals to confront unfamiliar situations with more confidence and a more complex frame of reference. As such, it makes a good tool for preparing people to live and work in highly diverse settings.

Recent Analysis of
Culture-Specific Assimilators

A number of studies have extended the application and further enhanced understanding of the impact of the ICS. A few of these are detailed below.

Harrison (1992) compared the effects of assimilator and behavioral modeling, although he seems unaware of the Landis, Brislin, and Hulgus (1985) study. The assimilator and behavioral modeling experiences focused on the following aspects of Japanese culture: "greater harmony and avoidance of conflict displayed by Japanese employees compared with Americans, and the stronger collective orientation of Japanese employees compared with the stronger individualism of Americans" (Harrison, 1992, p. 955). Sixty assimilator items were developed from several sources. The items were rated in terms of their reflection of the two a priori dimensions. Thirty-four items tapped one of the two dimensions, 20 involved conflict avoidance, and 14 involved collective orientation; the remainder dealt with broader cultural issues and themes.

Behavioral modeling involved the development of two modules, each focusing on one of the two a priori factors. Four elements were involved: (a) learning points or principles, (b) a film of a model using the principles, (c) a role play in which participants rehearse the procedures, and (d) social reinforcement from the trainer and other group members.

The experimental design involved six conditions: (a) behavioral modeling, (b) culture assimilator training, (c) both behavioral modeling and assimilator, (d) an assimilator-comparison

using an assimilator without rationales, (e) a behavioral modeling comparison using only video presentation (no role play), and (f) a no treatment group.

Dependent measures included a 13-item Likert scale of reactions, assessing reactions to the design, opinion, or information. Other measures included a measure of learning, an multiple-choice test of eight items covering customs, and the two a priori dimensions. Finally, for those conditions involving the behavioral modeling, a role-play assessment was developed. Unlike the Landis, Brislin, and Hulgus (1985) study, however, role play was not combined with the assimilator group, so no assessment of the interaction was possible.

Results indicated that the combination produced higher levels of learning and behavior than either of the single conditions; however, the overall F for the behavior was not significant. Effect sizes for the learning condition were sizable, particularly when compared with the no training condition. Results were more equivocal, though in the correct direction for the behavioral measures.

Limitations included the relatively small sample size (65, with about 10 per group), the lack of strong motivation in the groups (e.g., they were not actually being prepared to go to Japan), and a failure to control for time in training (e.g., the combined group was in training the longest).

Pollard (1989) developed a gender-based assimilator and administered it to high school students from Latin America and West Germany ($n = 53$). Three questions were addressed (a) to test the influence of similarity of gender stereotypes between U.S. host parents and exchange students on functioning, (b) to test the effect of a gender orientation on functioning in the United States, and (c) to determine which gender-related issues were problematic.

For Question 1, all parents and students ($n = 53$) completed an instrument called the Pan-Cultural Check List (Williams & Best, 1981) for measuring sex role stereotypes. Adjustment during placement was measured by the use of Hopkins' Observer's Ratings (Hopkins, 1982) and completed by a Youth for Understanding representative. The ratings scale covers four areas (adjustment to host country, family, academic work in school, and adjustment to school environment). Results indicated no relationship between the agreement of host and student on student functioning (correlations ranged from .29 downward to −.08).

For Question 2, 18 students (one third of students in the DE, NJ, PA region) were randomly selected (8 from Latin America and 10 from West Germany). A culture assimilator that focused on gender issues was constructed and administered at the beginning of the year. The orientations took place in small groups and involved group discussion of the items, answers, and rationales. At the end of the year, each student was rated by using the Hopkins scale. The results were weakly supportive of the hypothesis (the direction was as predicted, but most of the differences were nonsignificant). In general, the results were more positive for the German students than for the Latin American students.

With regard to problematic issues, a structured interview was used with 8 students. Students were less concerned with the stereotype than with the behavioral manifestation of the stereotype. For example, the Latin American students seemed puzzled by the host mother working outside the home and thus being unable to fulfill the role of the mother as an "at-home companion."

In general, the benefits of training with the ICS seem to include (a) greater understanding of hosts, as judged by the hosts themselves; (b) a decrease in the use of negative stereotypes on the part of trainees; (c) the development of complex thinking and isomorphic attributions about the target culture, which replaces the oversimplified, facile thinking to which hosts react negatively; (d) greater enjoyment among trainees who interact with members of the target culture, a feeling reciprocated by hosts; (e) better adjustment to the everyday stresses of life in other cultures; and, (f) better job performance in cases in which performance is influenced by specific cultural practices that can be covered in the training materials.

Uses of the
Intercultural Sensitizer

Trainers have used the ICS in a number of ways. People can read and react to the incidents on their own because the materials form a self-contained learning package that is easy to use. As is common in many training situations, trainees typically do not have significant cross-cultural experiences from which to draw when they are presented with new information. Training can be facilitated by having trainees read a number of incidents prior to any formal training session. The incidents, then, provide a foundation from which further learning can take place.

The materials can also be used in training programs involving many people whose considerable interaction is desirable. In such an arrangement, the incidents can be used as the basis for group discussions or can become scripts for role-playing sessions.

The 18-theme framework presented in the culture-general assimilator (Brislin et al., 1986) has also been used as a foundation for the development of culture assimilators specific to a given organization or purpose. In such a process, members of a given organization become familiar with the 18 themes and prepare a number of critical incidents that speak to a specific group or particular context. An added outcome of such activity is that the developers themselves become quite knowledgeable and skilled with many of the concepts of training. For instance, the culture-general assimilator has become the framework for the preparation of interpreters for the deaf, who work between the culture of the hearing and the culture of the hearing impaired. It has also been used as a foundation for a high school curriculum designed to prepare Israeli Arabs and Jews for cross-cultural contact (see Chapter 22, this volume); as orientation for students from 17 island nations who needed to learn about formal schooling prior to their study at Guam Community College; and for the preparation of teachers as they learn to work across culture, gender, and exceptionality (Cushner, McClelland, & Safford, 1996).

Thinking on Why the
Intercultural Sensitizer Is Effective

Information on the process by which training works or how and why training has its effects has also been the target of research. Landis, Brislin, and Hulgus (1985) argued that cross-cultural experiences cause anxiety because people come to realize that information previously learned in their own culture is not always useful in the host culture. People discover that if they use their previous knowledge, they will sometimes be wrong: They will make mistakes. Nobody likes to be confronted with the fact that he or she is wrong. This realization causes anxiety, which is communicated to hosts and thus compounds the adjustment problem. The information presented in culture assimilators can assist people in expanding their knowledge so that they make fewer mistakes in the host culture. One basic piece of knowledge trainees learn is that hosts have a point of view that often differs from that of sojourners. When trainees learn the host viewpoint, they are more likely to make isomorphic attributions and thus reduce the probability of total misunderstanding and miscommunication.

The sensitizer may encourage what Brislin, Landis, and Brandt (1983) called *behavioral training rehearsal* in their model of intercultural behavior (see also Chapter 1, this volume); that is, the trainee cognitively practices the correct behaviors in the absence of an actual other person. In other words, the trainee develops a script that is to be triggered in the appropriate situation. The motive for the development of this script is the intercultural anxiety generated from the knowledge that previous attributions and behaviors are likely to be inappropriate. Because the script always comes to a favorable conclusion, anxiety is reduced. If the interaction takes place before the script is finalized, however, anxiety will be at some enhanced level and the behavior will be uncertain and tentative. Hence, we would suggest that time and practice are essential elements of a successful intercultural training session using sensitizers. An interesting experiment would be to instruct a subgroup of trained subjects to cognitively practice the behaviors being depicted in the scenario while another subgroup is given a filler, but still cognitively engaging, task for the same period of time. The prediction would be that the practiced and training group would show less intercultural anxiety (see below) when interacting with a member of the target group.

This point of view is elaborated by the work of Walter and Cookie Stephan. In a number of publications (Stephan & Stephan, 1985, 1989,

1992), they have postulated that intercultural anxiety arises from a fear of four types of situations and their consequences: (a) negative psychological consequences, (b) negative behavioral consequences, (c) negative evaluations by out-group members, and (d) negative evaluations by in-group members. It is suggested that any type of intercultural interaction, even that provided by the ICS, produces some level of intercultural anxiety. That being the case, it would be useful to develop sensitizer items that focus on the four types of intercultural anxiety proposed by the Stephans. A reduction in the anxiety during training should be a powerful enhancement to the effectiveness of the training.

A more fundamental source of intercultural anxiety is proposed by Gudykunst and his colleagues (Ge & Gudykunst, 1990; Gudykunst, 1983, 1985a, 1985b; Gudykunst & Nishida, 1984; Gudykunst, Sodetani, & Sonoda, 1987; Gudykunst, Yang, & Nishida, 1985; as well as Chapter 4, this volume). Several axioms are proposed for uncertainty theory—for example, "Increases in uncertainty produce decreases in liking, and the converse is true." Again, one function of the ICS would be to reduce uncertainty and thus increase liking. This proposition, however, to our knowledge, has not been directly tested by using ICS materials.

Trainees also begin to develop a framework that enables them to anticipate the kinds of problems or conflicts that may emerge, as well as a related vocabulary that allows them to talk about specific concepts that may be at play. They are thus better able to pose specific questions when confronted with ambiguous situations and thus begin to understand and address potential problems before they become too debilitating.

As intriguing as many of these suggestions are, they remain just that, provocative ideas. We have ample evidence that changes are produced in trainees (although the extent of those changes is still problematic), but we can only guess as to underlying causation. We have rarely tested the ICS against other methods to explore the potential positive and negative interactions, yet we know that any technique is unlikely to be used in isolation. Clearly, more theoretical formulation is yet to be done; we hope this chapter encourages that effort.

Construction
of Critical Incidents

Triandis (1984) developed a theoretical framework for developing items for ICSs based on agreed-on dimensions of cultural variation. A number of dimensions are suggested as factors along which culture assimilator items could be constructed, including (a) perceptual differentiations made, (b) information processing strategies, (c) cognitive structures, and (d) behavior.

What Perceptual
Differentiations Are Made?

Triandis (1984) suggested that three such areas become the focus of culture assimilator items. In-group/out-group distinctions become critical in the comparison between some cultures, as in the example incident. In some countries (e.g., Latino), a system of enlarging the ingroup is used (*compadrazgo*—including ritual relatives in the familistic system). In high-familism cultures, voluntary organizations do not function well because the emphasis is on the family as the primary social and financial support for the individual. In low-familism cultures, the important relationship is the spouse (e.g., the in-group is defined as a dyad, not a collective).

Sex differentiation is perhaps the most obvious way cultures differ. Role differentiation is greater in Mediterranean cultures (Greek, Italian, Latino). Some jobs are performed only by women; some jobs only men can do. Women's jobs tend to be centered in the home, with women often feeling threatened when men enter the kitchen. *Machismo* is the Latin version of this and leads to men being "in the street or other public places" and to a double standard of morality, with men free to have mistresses. Women, however, are saddled with *Marianismo*, which is characterized by submission, self-sacrifice, and stoicism. Industrialized cultures will often have large segments of the population lagging behind the cultural variation, and the fault line may be over the issue of appropriate sex role behavior. The repudiation of President Clinton may be partly because of the failure of his wife to play the role of *Marianismo*.

Finally, age differentiation is another area of focus. Respect for the aged, for instance, is based solely on age, not on accomplishments.

Information Processing Strategies

Triandis focuses on two major issues: ideologism-pragmatism and associative-abstractive. Ideologues use a broad structure within which all experience is fitted; the pragmatist starts with experience and forms a generalization. With regard to interpersonal interactions, the ideologue insists on setting general principles first; the pragmatist works on specific details, letting the general principles take care of themselves.

Associative-abstractive refers to differences in communication styles in which, in some cultures, communication is by association, whereas in others, communication proceeds by abstracting ideas seen as essential to the dialogue. The associative uses poetic language; the abstractive is scientific.

Another related dimension is field independence-dependence of Witkin and Berry (1975) and others. Triandis makes the association that associative cultures are field dependent, whereas abstractive cultures are field independent. Men tend to be field independent; women tend to be field dependent (more people oriented). Triandis does suggest an inconsistency, however, when he notes that merchants who deal with the public are more field sensitive and that most merchants are men.

Cognitive Structures

Triandis identifies ten areas of concern under this heading:

1. *Values.* Considers Kluckhohn and Strodbeck's (1961) five basic value orientations of (a) beliefs about innate human nature; (b) preferences for subjugation, harmony, or mastery over nature; (c) focus on past, present, or future time; (d) emphasis on doing, versus being, versus being-in-becoming; and (e) emphasis on individualism versus collectivism.
2. *Human nature as good, bad, or neither.*

3. *Human nature as changeable.* In societies that believe that human nature is not fixed, expenditures for education and so forth are likely to be large.

4. *Mastery, harmony, or subjugation to nature.* Masters prefer solutions that control nature (e.g., building dams); subjugation is more passive and rejects control mechanisms as detrimental to nature and, at best, ineffective (e.g., environmentalists).

5. *Past-present-future orientation.* Time is more important in associative cultures (e.g., Latino), presumably because interpersonal relationships are much more important and because such interactions (particularly with people in the in-group) do not follow a prescribed time sequence.

6. *Doing—being—being-in-becoming.* North Americans, for instance, prefer doing, whereas Latino cultures value the striving for higher levels of life—related to the using of poetic language full of allusion and metaphor.

7. *Power distance* (Hofstede, 1980). In high-power countries, rank has its privileges; in low-power countries, there are few rank differentiations. Because, presumably, there is conflict about rank in the United States, the United States is a middle-power distant country, whereas Scandinavia and Austria are low and Latin America and the Philippines are high. In Austria, everybody has status (e.g., Mr. Plumber, Ms. Stockbroker). Triandis also points to the use of Vous/Tu (Is/Du; Ousted/Tu). In high-power distant countries, the low-status person uses Vous, the high use Tu. In low-power distant countries, either will use both, depending on the degree of intimacy.

8. *Uncertainty avoidance versus tolerance for ambiguity.* Again, in Hofstede's data, the highest scores for this dimension were obtained by Greece, Japan, and most Hispanic countries. Low scores were found in Hong Kong, Singapore, and Scandinavia. It might be that countries with a history of instability (e.g., revolutions) would move toward a "tight" control to reduce anxiety.

9. *Individualism versus collectivism.* Reflects a preference for independence from groups.

10. *Masculinity versus femininity.* In high-masculine countries, the emphasis is on personal advancement and earnings, whereas in high-feminine countries, the emphasis is on service and on having a nice physical environment. Japan, Austria, Venezuela, Italy, and Switzerland are high on the masculine dimension; Sweden, Norway, the Netherlands, and Denmark reflect more feminine characteristics.

Behavior

Triandis looks at three issues here:

1. *Association-dissociation.* The degree to which people are helpful and supportive. These, it would seem, are correlated with associative cultures, as well as with the dimension that human behavior is either good or bad.

2. *Superordination versus subordination.* Correlates with the value dimension of power distance.

3. *Intimacy versus formality.* The degree to which touching and the expression of emotions are encouraged. Related to this is the degree to which people have personal contact.

The general approach to preparing critical incidents is as follows:

1. Identify relevant themes/issues for your purposes. You may select from the 18-theme cultural-general framework or the dimensions suggested by Triandis or identify specific themes/issues of relevance to your needs. The emphasis, however, is to use the incident to inform others about a cultural issue or theme underlying the incident—not merely to relate the story.

2. Generate episodes by identifying incidents through personal experience, by interviewing others, by reading the research and/or ethnographic literature, or through observation and analysis.

3. Construct episodes or stories, being certain to include only relevant information;

verifying content; refining generalizations, abstractions, and specifics; and speaking to your intended audience. The resulting incident should be clear, concise, straightforward, interesting, and believable while maintaining the original conflict situation.

4. Elicit attributions by identifying different interpretations (attributions) of the incident through interviews, ethnographic data, and open-ended questions completed by experienced and inexperienced individuals.

5. Select attributions to use.

6. Complete critical incidents with feedback and explanations; relevant cultural knowledge can be transmitted in the explanation.

7. Modify the set to be sure the entire item hangs together in a logical fashion. Although the incident may have started out in someone's experience, you are permitted to take liberties to engage the learner, to make the answer non-obvious, and to make each alternative reasonable from some point of view.

A complete ICS item is included in the Appendix to this chapter.

Use of Technology in the Presentation of Cultural Information

ICSs are, for the most part, presented by using print technology as books, handouts, or monographs. The technique was originally developed, however, with a view to making the learning computer aided. Unfortunately, computers of the early 1960s were too unwieldy to make their use practical. With the advent of the PC in the late 1970s and succeeding advances in processor capability, storage capability, and overall size, the technology is no longer forbidding. Indeed, with the use of CD-ROM technology now available even on notebook-size computers, the possibility of interactive ICSs in a multimedia format becomes a real possibility.

In 1993, working from a contract with the Community Relations Service of the Department of Justice, Landis developed a computerized version of the ICS that could be run on any IBM-compatible PC with a minimum amount of storage space. This version of the ICS allows any number of items from any number of assimilators to be used and mixed together in any order. A statistics file is also created that permits a tracking of the learner's progress. Version 2.0[3] includes items from the Landis et al. (1976) army assimilator; the Landis, Fross, et al. (1985) assimilator for non-Southerners coming to Southern universities and colleges; a set of items from the 1983 summer workshop at the East-West Center; and a set of items created for community mediators.

As the availability of sophisticated computers increases around the world, one can expect to see versions incorporating motion, color, and sound, as well as true interactive capabilities. A caution, however: The key to the effectiveness of an ICS is the content. If the content is not believable, the options not feasible, or the rationales not logical, the impact will be degraded and the credibility of the entire set compromised.

SUMMARY

The development and use of the ICS or culture assimilator approach to cross-cultural training was described. The literature on both culture-specific as well as culture-general assimilators was reviewed. Finally, approaches to the development of assimilators were reviewed.

Clearly, despite the popularity of the ICS technique, its theoretical and empirical foundations still need elaboration. Perhaps the next decade will see more research designed to provide that elaboration.

APPENDIX

SAMPLE ICS ITEM*

Next-Door Neighbors

Chris and Margaret are two English teachers currently working in Barcelona, Spain. They live in a small but comfortable apartment in a building near the center of the city and are pleased to find that their neighbors (on the same floor) often stop to exchange pleasantries on the stairs. Chris and Margaret believe they should get to know them better and on several occasions invite them to their apartment for a drink or a meal. Although they are thanked for their offer, none of the neighbors ever come. Also, although the neighbors seem to be very social—often having large gatherings of their relatives over during the weekends—Chris and Margaret are never invited to these functions. As a consequence, they begin to feel uneasy in any interactions with the neighbors, believing they are not really liked or wanted in the building.

How would you explain to Chris and Margaret the neighbors' apparent unwillingness to have any extensive personal interaction with them?

The reader is then presented with a number of alternative explanations and is asked to select the one that seems most appropriate. Sample alternative explanations include:

1. They are accustomed to restricting home-based social activities to those involving family only.
2. They are probably wary of any intimate contact with foreigners.
3. They probably believe that they would not know how to talk to or entertain foreigners and so are reluctant to invite them over.
4. Chris and Margaret have probably unwittingly offended them in some way.

Following the incident and alternative explanations, the reader is provided with feedback on his or her choices as follows:

Rationales

1. *You chose 1.* This is the best response. In Mediterranean and many other cultures, there is a strong identification with the family and less concern for others outside it (familialism). Social bonds and activities are thus generally restricted to the extended family group, especially when the activities are home based. People are defined much more by their role within the family, and a complex support network exists that becomes both self-supporting and exclusive. Relationships with people such as neighbors or work colleagues are thus de-emphasized, and although friendships may develop, these friends are generally not invited to participate in family activities. Thus, although the neighbors do not dislike or seek to avoid contact with Chris and Margaret, they would feel very uneasy about inviting them into their homes or entering Chris and Margaret's home, considering they hardly knew them.
2. *You chose 2.* Although this may appear to be the case, it does not explain why the neighbors are reluctant to socialize. There is a more specific and helpful explanation. Please choose again.
3. *You chose 3.* The story has little evidence for this. The neighbors appear willing to chat with Chris and Margaret

on an informal basis but apparently do not wish to get more intimately involved. There is a more adequate explanation. Please choose again.

4. *You chose 4.* This seems unlikely, and if it were the case, the neighbors would probably shun or ignore Chris and

Margaret when they ran into them. Please choose again.

*This sample item is adapted from Brislin, Cushner, Cherrie, & Yong, 1986. Copyright © Sage Publications, Inc. 1986.

Notes

1. A little-known fact is that the original studies were supported by the Advanced Projects Research Agency of the Department of Defense, presumably as a way of creating a technology for training troops serving in foreign countries. The fact that the assimilator technology was never really used in the DoD may reflect a lack of belief that such training was really critical to mission effectiveness in the early years of the Vietnam War.

2. The most recent culture-specific assimilator is one for Venezuela developed by Tolbert and McLean (1995).

3. The ICS is available from D. K. Research Group, P.O. Box 1074, Oxford, MS 38655.

References

Albert, R. (1983). The intercultural sensitizer or culture assimilator: A cognitive approach. In D. Landis & R. Brislin (Eds.), *Handbook of intercultural training: Vol. 2. Issues in training methodology* (pp. 186-217). Elmsford, NY: Pergamon.

Bhatkal, R. (1990). *Intercultural sensitivity training for preservice teachers using a culture-general assimilator with a peer interactive approach and media analysis.* Unpublished doctoral dissertation, University of Nebraska, Lincoln.

Bhawuk, D. P. S. (1990). Cross-cultural orientation programs. In R. Brislin (Ed.), *Applied cross-cultural psychology* (pp. 325-346). Newbury Park, CA: Sage.

Brislin, R. (1981). *Cross-cultural encounters: Face-to-face interaction.* Elmsford, NY: Pergamon.

Brislin, R., Cushner, K., Cherrie, C., & Yong, M. (1986). *Intercultural interactions: A practical guide.* Beverly Hills, CA: Sage.

Brislin, R., Landis, D., & Brandt, M. (1983). Conceptualizations of intercultural behavior and training. In D. Landis & R. Brislin (Eds.), *Handbook of intercultural training: Vol. 1. Issues in theory and design* (pp. 1-34). Elmsford, NY: Pergamon.

Brislin, R., & Pedersen, P. (1976). *Cross-cultural orientation programs.* New York: John Wiley.

Broaddus, D. (1986). *Use of the culture-general assimilator in intercultural training.* Unpublished doctoral dissertation, Indiana State University, Terre Haute.

Cushner, K. (1986). *Inventory of cross-Cultural Sensitivity.* Assessment instrument developed by the author.

Cushner. K. (1989). Assessing the impact of a culture-general assimilator. *International Journal of Intercultural Relations, 13,* 125-146.

Cushner, K., & Brislin, R. (1996). *Intercultural interactions: A practical guide* (2nd ed.). Thousand Oaks, CA: Sage.

Cushner, K., & Grove, C. (1990). *They are talking about me! And other stories about exchange students.* New York: AFS Intercultural Programs.

Cushner, K., McClelland, A., & Safford, P. (1996). *Human diversity in education: An integrative approach* (2nd ed.). New York: McGraw-Hill.

Fiedler, F., Mitchell, T., & Triandis, H. (1971). The culture assimilator: An approach to cross-cultural training. *Journal of Applied Psychology, 55,* 95-102.

Flannagan, J. (1954). The critical incident technique. *Psychological Bulletin, 51,* 327-358.

Ge, G., & Gudykunst, W. B. (1990). Uncertainty, anxiety, and adaptation. *International Journal of Intercultural Relations, 14,* 301-318.

Gudykunst, W. (1983). Uncertainty reduction and predictability of behavior in low- and high-context cultures: An exploratory study. *Communication Quarterly, 31,* 49-55.

Gudykunst, W. (1985a). The influence of cultural similarity, type of relationship, and self-monitoring on uncertainty reduction processes. *Communication Monographs, 52,* 203-217.

Gudykunst, W. (1985b). A model of uncertainty reduction in intercultural encounters. *Language and Social Psychology, 2,* 79-98.

Gudykunst, W., & Nishida, T. (1984). Individual and cultural influences on uncertainty reduction. *Communication Monographs, 51,* 23-36.

Gudykunst, W., Sodetani, L., & Sonoda, T. (1987). Uncertainty reduction in Japanese-American/ Caucasian relationships. *Western Journal of Speech Communication, 51,* 256-278.

Gudykunst, W., Yang, S., & Nishida, T. (1985). A cross-cultural test of uncertainty reduction theory: Comparisons of acquaintances, friends, and dating relationships in Japan, Korea, and the United States. *Human Communication Research, 3,* 407-455.

Harrison, J. K. (1992). Individual and combined effects of behavior modeling and the culture assimilator in cross-cultural management training. *Journal of Applied Psychology, 77,* 952-962.

Hart, R. J., Day, H. R., Landis, D., & McGrew, P. (1978, September). *Culture assimilator for training army personnel in racial understanding* (ARI Technical Paper 314). Monterey, CA: ARI Field Unit.

Hofstede, G. (1980). *Cultures' consequences: International differences in work-related values.* Beverly Hills, CA: Sage.

Hopkins, R. S. (1982). *Defining and predicting overseas effectiveness for adolescent exchange students.* (Available from Youth for Understanding, 3501 Newark Street, NW, Washington, DC 20016)

Ilola, L. (1991, April). *The use of structured social interaction with the culture-general assimilator to increase cognitive problem solving about intercultural interactions in an ethnically diverse population.* Paper presented at the Annual Meeting of the American Educational Research Association, Chicago.

Juffer, K. A. (1982). *Technical description of CSAI, I.* Unpublished manuscript, Western Illinois University, Macomb.

Kluckhohn, F., & Strodbeck, F. (1961). *Variations in value orientations.* New York: Harper & Row.

Landis, D., Brislin, R., & Hulgus, J. (1985). Attributional training versus contact in acculturative learning: A laboratory study. *Journal of Applied Social Psychology, 15,* 466-482.

Landis, D., Day, H. R., McGrew, P. L., Thomas, J. A., & Miller, A. B. (1976). Can a black "culture assimilator" increase racial understanding? *Journal of Social Issues, 32,* 169-183.

Landis, D., Fross, J., Holman, J. E., Swanner, G., Bishop, L., Gideon, B., Reisenwitz, T., & Williams, E. (1985). *Through the magnolia curtain: A survival guide to Southern universities and colleges.* University: University of Mississippi, Center for Applied Research and Evaluation.

Malpass, R., & Salancik, G. (1977). Linear and branching formats in culture assimilator training. *International Journal of Intercultural Relations, 1,* 76-87.

Osgood, C. (1977). Objective indicators of subjective culture. In L. Adler (Ed.), *Issues in cross-cultural research* (Annals of the New York Academy of Sciences, Vol. 285. New York: New York Academy of Sciences.

Pacino, M. (1988). *Intercultural communication and its use in education as a training tool for school personnel (administrators, counselors, and teachers).* Unpublished doctoral dissertation, Ball State University, Muncie, IN.

Pollard, W. R. (1989). Gender stereotypes and gender roles in cross-cultural education: The cultural assimilator. *International Journal of Intercultural Relations, 13,* 57-72.

Ramirez, H. (1992). *The effects of cross-cultural training on the attributions and attitudes of preservice teachers (LEP instructors).* Unpublished doctoral dissertation, University of Illinois, Urbana-Champaign.

Spivak, G., Platt, J. J., & Shure, M. (1976). *The problem-solving approach to adjustment.* San Francisco: Jossey-Bass.

Stephan, C., & Stephan, W. (1992). Reducing intercultural anxiety though intercultural contact. *International Journal of Intercultural Relations, 16,* 89-106.

Stephan, W., & Stephan, C. (1985). Intergroup anxiety. *Journal of Social Issues, 41,* 157-176.

Stephan, W., & Stephan, C. (1989). Antecedents of intergroup anxiety in Asian-Americans and Hispanic-Americans. *International Journal of Intercultural Relations, 13,* 203-216.

Tolbert, A. S., & McLean, G. N. (1995). Venezuelan culture assimilator for training United States professionals conducting business in Venezuela. *International Journal of Intercultural Relations, 19,* 111-125.

Triandis, H. C. (1972). *The analysis of subjective culture.* New York: Wiley-Interscience.

Triandis, H. C. (1984). A theoretical framework for the more efficient construction of culture assimilators. *International Journal of Intercultural Relations, 8,* 301-330.

Weldon, D., Carston, D., Rissman, A., Slobodin, L., & Triandis, H. (1975). A laboratory test of effects of culture assimilator training. *Journal of Personality and Social Psychology, 32,* 300-310.

Williams, J. E., & Best, D. (1981). *Measuring sex stereotypes.* Beverly Hills, CA: Sage.

Witkin, H. A., & Berry, J. W. (1975). Psychological differentiation in cross-cultural perspective. *Journal of Cross-Cultural Psychology, 6,* 4-87.

Worchel, G., & Mitchell, T. (1970). *An evaluation of the effectiveness of the Thai and Greek culture assimilators.* Seattle: University of Washington, Organizational Research Group.

Yarbro, C. L. M. (1988). *An assessment of the ability of the culture-general assimilator to create sensitivity to multiculturalism in an educational setting.* Unpublished doctoral dissertation, University of Houston, College of Education.

Intercultural Training in the Military

MICKEY R. DANSBY

DAN LANDIS

OUR nation was founded on the principle that the individual has infinite dignity and worth. The Department of Defense, which exists to keep the Nation secure and at peace, must always be guided by this principle." Thus begins the Department of Defense Human Goals, a brief charter outlining the broad philosophy for equal opportunity (EO) and diversity within the Department of Defense (DoD). This document, signed by the secretary of defense, deputy secretary of defense, service secretaries, and military chiefs of the services, lists a number of objectives, including "To make military and civilian service in the Department of Defense a model of equal opportunity for all" and "To create an environment that values diversity and fosters mutual respect and cooperation among all persons." The DoD strives to implement these lofty goals through two primary means: policy directives and training.

Military training in matters of intercultural diversity and EO is multi-tiered, starting with basic instruction at the various service entry points (e.g., basic recruit training, service academies, ROTC) and continuing through the senior career levels. Although each service develops its own directives and program of training, the core for this training comes from one source: the Defense Equal Opportunity Management Institute (DEOMI) at Patrick Air Force Base, Florida. Since 1971, this institute has been responsible for training the EO advisors who manage and conduct training programs for the services. In essence, DEOMI "trains the trainers" for DoD (and the U.S. Coast Guard, which falls under the Department of Transportation) in matters of intercultural relations, EO, and diversity. Because of its central role, discussion of DEOMI's work plays a crucial role in developing the theme of this chapter.

AUTHORS' NOTE: The opinions expressed in this chapter are those of the authors and do not necessarily reflect positions of the Department of Defense or any of its agencies.

Our goal in this chapter is to give the reader a perspective on the background, philosophy, and status of intercultural training in the military. We begin with historical background to set the context for the rest of the chapter.

Historical Background

In the previous edition of this book, Day (1983) provided an in-depth review of the development of DEOMI and the services' race relations training programs. Rather than repeat that material, we summarize key elements and update Day's work to give the reader an appreciation of current practice in the DoD. We begin with a thumbnail history of intercultural training in the military.

Integration of the Armed Forces

The foundation of intercultural relations in the military is based largely on the integration of blacks into the services following World War II. Although minority contributions to U.S. defense prior to World War II are well documented (e.g., see Binkin, Eitelberg, Schexnider, & Smith, 1982; MacGregor, 1981; Nalty, 1986; Young, 1982), their participation in World War II and decisions in the postwar period are watershed events in understanding intercultural relations in the military.

Substantial numbers of black servicemembers served during World War II. More than 900,000 served in the Army (almost 9% of the Army during their peak period), about 167,000 in the Navy (around 4%), and more than 17,000 in the Marine Corps (2.5%) (Binkin et al., 1982). With limited exceptions, these individuals served in segregated units (Lovejoy, 1977; MacGregor, 1981). Their notable contributions to the war effort, though sometimes clouded by controversy (Hope, 1979; MacGregor, 1981; Nalty, 1986), could not be overlooked. Because many black servicemembers returning to their homes suffered discrimination at the hands of a society they had fought to defend, President Truman was moved to action (MacGregor, 1981; Nalty, 1986). Eventually, Truman's concerns resulted in the landmark Executive Order 9981.

Issued on July 26, 1948, Executive Order 9981 called for "equality of treatment for all persons in the armed services without regard to race, color, religion or national origin." It also established the President's Committee on Equality of Treatment and Opportunity in the Armed Services (often known as the Fahy committee) to serve as a vehicle for implementing the policy by advising the president and the service secretaries on how to "effectuate the policy" (MacGregor, 1981). Despite its broad powers, the committee faced an arduous task in carrying out its charter because of the opposition of many high-ranking military and civilian officials in the military establishment.[1]

It took the impetus of another war (in Korea) and research supporting integration based on the effectiveness of integrated units during this war to move the desegregation effort from policy to reality. (Both the Army's internal study and a contract study called Project CLEAR supported integration; furthermore, with larger numbers of black soldiers involved in the Korean conflict, efficiency demanded integration as a pragmatic necessity [MacGregor, 1981].) Finally, by October 1954, the secretary of defense was able to announce the abolishment of the last racially segregated (active duty) unit in the armed forces (MacGregor, 1981).

President Truman's July 1948 executive order racially integrating the forces had a profound effect on the American military services. Another event leading to a permanent change in the face of America's armed forces occurred in the same year. In June, Congress passed the Women's Armed Services Act of 1948 (P.L. 625; Holm, 1992). When President Truman signed this law, he ensured a permanent place for women in the armed forces. Although P.L. 625 placed severe limits on women's service (e.g., their strength could never exceed 2% of the force, women were restricted from serving as general officers; interestingly, during the life of the law, the 2% ceiling was never reached), it made it possible for women, many of whom had served during World War II, to continue in the services during peacetime. In 1967, P.L. 90-130 removed the limits on women's representation and rank in the services.

The integration efforts for both race and gender have resulted in an American armed force whose ethnic/racial/gender diversity is quite different today from the force of World War II. For example, at the end of the war, women comprised 2.3% of the total active military strength (280,000 out of 12 million; Holm, 1992); by

1971, they were only 1% (about 40,000; Holm, 1992); but by March of 1994, they were over 12% (over 198,000; DEOMI, 1994). Black members' representation has grown from 5.9% in 1949 (Young, 1982) to 19.3% (more than 325,000; DEOMI, 1994) in March 1994. Total minority representation in the active services in March 1994 was over 28% (471,000; DEOMI, 1994).

Although the desegregation of the services after World War II set the services on course for these dramatic changes, the pathway to the future would prove to be full of potholes.

The Civil Rights Era

Desegregation of the services did not lead to an end of racial discrimination and strife, nor did it result in full integration (from an attitudinal perspective) of minority members (Lovejoy, 1977). By the early 1960s, with the civil rights movement in full swing, pressure to improve conditions for minority servicemembers continued to swell. Proponents of civil rights in the public sector and the Kennedy administration urged DoD to take action to end segregation in reserve units and in the housing and schools serving military members in communities near military bases (MacGregor, 1981).

Secretary of Defense Robert McNamara formed a committee (designated a presidential committee because DoD requested presidential appointment of its members) to address the issue (MacGregor, 1981). President Kennedy announced the establishment of the President's Committee on Equality of Opportunity in the Armed Forces on June 24, 1962 (MacGregor, 1981). It is often known as the Gesell committee, after its chairman, Gerhard Gesell.[2] The work of this committee had greater support within DoD than did the Fahy committee, perhaps because it had it roots within the DoD, rather than directly from the executive branch (MacGregor, 1981). The work of this committee established EO for minority soldiers, both on and off the installation, as a direct command responsibility and linked EO to military efficiency (MacGregor, 1981). It resulted in DoD Directive 5120.36 (July 1963), supporting EO for all servicemembers and giving commanders authority to declare off-limits those establishments in the civilian community that discriminated on the basis of race, creed, or na-

tional origin (Hope, 1979; MacGregor, 1981). The directive also established a focal point for EO management within DoD and required the services to develop their own manuals and regulations to implement the policy. Between 1964 and 1966, such regulations were published (Hope, 1979).

The Vietnam Era

Shortly after the implementation of these policies, the Vietnam War began. With it came increased numbers of black and other minority servicemembers. But many of these servicemembers, inspired by the civil rights era and with enhanced awareness of inequities, were more vocal concerning EO issues. As they became more militant, racial unrest in the form of riots and incidents occurred across the services (Binkin et al., 1982; Hope, 1979). Official investigations into the causes of these disturbances resulted in a document (called the Rearden report, after the chairman of the investigating team, Frank Rearden III) supporting charges of discrimination. In response, among other things, the services were required to establish EO/human relations officers and human relations councils in all major units, to improve use of minority members across the occupational spectrum, and to remove leaders who failed to take action against discrimination (Hope, 1979). Subsequently, other investigations and incidents led to congressional involvement and culminated in a 1969 directive from the House Armed Services Committee for the DoD to establish mandatory race relations seminars for all servicemembers (Hope, 1979).

In January 1970, Defense Secretary Melvin Laird created the Interservice Task Force on Education in Race Relations to develop a plan to implement the program. Colonel Lucius Theus (a black Air Force officer eventually promoted to major general) chaired the committee, which later came to bear his name. The Theus committee delivered its report to the secretary of defense on July 31, 1970 (Lovejoy, 1977). In September, an implementation committee (the Krise committee) was directed to test the educational approach outlined in the Theus report. Late that year, Colonel Edward Krise (who became the Defense Race Relations Institute's [DRRI] first director), chairman of the committee, delivered a report on the pilot program to

DoD. The report gave specific suggestions on how to carry out the Theus committee's recommendation to establish DRRI (Lovejoy, 1977). A draft DoD directive was developed, and the process of "coordination" began within DoD. Finally, spurred by one more racial incident (a particularly destructive riot at Travis Air Force Base in May 1971), the Theus committee's plan for race relations education was codified into DoD Directive 1322.11 in June 1971 (Hope, 1979; Nalty, 1986). In the words of one observer, "This directive outlined the most comprehensive race relations education program ever attempted by any major institution in this country" (Hope, 1979, p. 41).

Founding of DEOMI

DoD Directive 1322.11 chartered the Defense Race Relations Institute (DRRI; later renamed Defense Equal Opportunity Management Institute [DEOMI]) and the Race Relations Education Board (RREB), a high-level committee that was to oversee DRRI and to provide policy guidance for race relations education (Day, 1983). Others (Day, 1983; Hope, 1979; Lovejoy, 1977) have chronicled the early history of the RREB and DRRI; we shall not repeat it here. Suffice it to say that the establishment of DRRI (DEOMI) marks the beginning of the modern approach to intercultural training in the military. The following discussion updates the descriptions of DEOMI provided by Day (1983) and others (e.g., Hope, 1979; Lovejoy, 1977).

Current Policy, Training Philosophy, Staffing, and Programs

Day (1983), Lovejoy (1977), and Hope (1979) chronicle the evolution from DEOMI's initial course (lasting 6 weeks and primarily focusing on black/white issues and individual racism) to the present 16-week course (with broad inclusion of material relating to other racial-ethnic groups, gender issues, institutional discrimination, and organizational development). Between 1971 and the present, DEOMI has gone through a number of organizational changes, but the basic approach to intercultural training in the military has remained the same. DEOMI still trains the trainers by using small

group interaction, lectures, and exercises as the primary training methods. DEOMI graduates still serve as advisors and trainers in their respective services. Over the years, however, the size of DEOMI and the scope of its mission have expanded to meet the changing needs of the military. In the next section, we describe current (1994) policy and training practices at DEOMI.

Current Policy

As mentioned previously, the DoD Human Goals outlines the broad philosophy for intercultural relations within the military. A number of DoD and service directives provide the regulatory framework for this broad philosophy. The two key documents at the DoD level are DoD Directive 1350.2 (Department of Defense Equal Opportunity Program, December 1988) and DoD Instruction 1350.3 (Affirmative Action Planning and Assessment Process, February 1988).

DoD Directive 1350.2 amends, cancels, or consolidates a number of previous directives (e.g., DoD Directive 1100.15, Department of Defense Equal Opportunity Program, and DoD Directive 1322.11, Education and Training in Human/Race Relations for Military Personnel) into a unified policy statement. DoD Directive 1350.2 calls for compliance with standards of fair treatment ("Discrimination . . . shall not be condoned or tolerated"), establishment of affirmative action programs (with an annual reporting requirement), and "education and training in EO and human relations at installation and fleet unit commands, Military Service accession points, and throughout the professional military education (PME) system."

Training Philosophy

From its early days, DEOMI's training philosophy has mirrored the military's approach to EO and cultural diversity. Five main principles provide the foundation: (a) a focus on *behavioral change* and *compliance* with stated policy; (b) an emphasis on EO and intercultural understanding as *military readiness issues;* (c) an understanding that *equal opportunity is a commander's responsibility* and that a *DEOMI graduate's function is to advise and assist the commander* in carrying out this responsibility; (d) a belief that *education and training* can bring about the desired behavioral changes; and (e) reliance on *affirmative action plans* as a method for ensuring equity and diversity.

Especially important in the military's approach to intercultural training is the emphasis on education as a means to achieve *behavioral change* and *compliance* with directives (Hope, 1979; Lovejoy, 1977; Thomas, 1988). Although the Race [later *Human*] Relations Education Board has been abolished, DoD Directive 1350.2 reemphasizes DEOMI's educational function and charters the Defense Equal Opportunity Council (DEOC) to provide policy advice and guidance on EO matters. The DEOC, in its present form, includes the under secretary of defense for personnel and readiness as its chair and the service secretaries as members. Among DEOC's four objectives is the charge to "assist in developing policy guidance for *education and training* in EO and human relations for DoD personnel" (DoD Directive 1350.2, December 23, 1988, p. 4-1).

The belief that EO and cultural understanding are *military readiness issues* is clearly iterated in DEOMI's current mission briefing (given to distinguished visitors to the institute); but this idea was evident in the 1971 issue of DoD Directive 1322.11 (which established DEOMI). That directive says the educational program is designed to prevent racial problems from impairing "combat readiness and efficiency" (Hope, 1979). A negative EO climate is thought to detract from readiness by leading to racial incidents or other disruptive events, whereas a positive EO climate may be an enhancer of readiness by improving cohesion and other organizational factors (Knouse, 1994).[3]

DoD Directive 1350.2 also reinforces the concept that *equal opportunity is a commander's responsibility.* The directive identifies the chain of command as the "primary and preferred channel for correcting discriminatory practices and for ensuring that human relations and EO matters are enacted" (p. 2). Commanders are also given broad powers in dealing with discrimination (affecting military members, their families, and DoD employees) arising from nonmilitary sources (e.g., housing or service providers, various organizations associated with the military). The desire to help commanders with this responsibility led the first DEOMI staff to develop a handbook for com-

manders, designed to be "supportive of the commander's responsibility to develop a program in race relations" (Lovejoy, 1977, p. 106). This Commander's Notebook contained a statement that the EO program "must be . . . consistent with the philosophy and behavior of the local commander" (Day, 1983, p. 246). The DRRI program of instruction identified one major objective as giving the students the "capability and judgment to work with commanding officers in determining the specific needs of a race relations . . . program" (Hope, 1979, p. 42).

As we discussed previously, the belief that education and training can bring about behavioral changes leading to enhanced intercultural relations permeates DEOMI's history. The primary purpose of the Theus committee was to develop a plan for an educational program to improve race relations (Lovejoy, 1977), and DRRI and HREB were subsequently founded to implement this plan. The Krise committee, charged with planning the implementation, "was responsible for a significant innovation . . . that of concentrating on behavioral rather than attitude change" (Lovejoy, 1977, p. 24). According to Judge L. Howard Bennett, deputy assistant secretary of defense for civil rights at the founding of DRRI and perhaps the driving force behind the philosophy of behavioral change through education, the educational program could work by providing greater understanding, appreciation, and respect among the groups that make up the military (Hope, 1979).

Use of *affirmative action plans* to manage EO and diversity has also been a standard practice in the military services. DoD Directive 1350.2 establishes 10 reporting categories for which the services must provide plans and assessments on an annual basis:

Recruiting/accessions
Composition
Promotions
Professional military education (PME)
Separations
Augmentation/Retention
Assignments
Discrimination/Sexual harassment
   complaints
Use of skills
Discipline

Details of the reporting process are spelled out in the supplement to the directive, DoD Instruction 1350.3. DEOMI's curriculum includes training for EO advisors on these requirements and how to implement affirmative action programs.

Staffing

Current DEOMI staff include military and civilians, divided into directorates (e.g., curriculum, training, support, research). In addition, at any given time, as many as 300 students may be enrolled in the courses described below.

Training Programs

Over the years, DEOMI has adapted to the times, providing expanded or specialized training programs and adding research and consulting capabilities to meet the needs of the services. The current course offerings are described below.

The Equal Opportunity Advisor Course

This is the linchpin of DEOMI's training programs. A resident course of 16 weeks' duration, it is designed to train EO staff advisors for commanders throughout all services. It evolved from DEOMI's original course (discussed previously) and is thought to epitomize the "DEOMI experience." Although a variety of training techniques are used, the focus is on small group exercises, practicums, and lecture presentations. Students are led through a carefully designed curriculum designed to develop intrapersonal awareness, interpersonal understanding, and organizational skills. It covers cultural factors and unit cohesion (139 hours), communication skills (62 hours), staff advisor skills (50 hours), leadership (31 hours), and service-specific skills (20 hours). In addition, an extensive guest lecture series (94 hours) covers diverse topics related to EO in the military.

In DEOMI's early years, students were generally volunteers. Currently, students may volunteer, but many, especially from the Army, are simply assigned EO duties as part of their normal career rotation. Assignment to EO duties varies by service (e.g., Army graduates serve for only 2 or 3 years as EO advisors and then return to their original military specialty; Air Force graduates serve for a career). Most students are mid- to senior-grade noncommissioned officers, with the largest numbers coming from the Army. As with all DEOMI courses, civilians employed by the services may also attend. Few officers (other than DEOMI staff and some reserve components officers) have attended the course during recent years. The Army, however, sent 16 officers to the course in 1994, reversing a trend away from officer involvement in EO programs. These officers are to serve at the major command level throughout the Army. Another watershed event in 1994 was the training of Marine Corps EO advisors in this course for the first time (although marines had participated in other DEOMI courses and a few marine officers had graduated from the 16-week course because they were to join the DEOMI staff). The American Council on Education recommends 23 semester hours of undergraduate credit for graduates of this course.

Although the 16-week resident course is the crown jewel in DEOMI's course offerings, several other courses supplement it.

The Reserve Components Course

This course is designed to parallel the Equal Opportunity Staff Advisor Course, yet it is offered on a schedule compatible with reserve components training. It consists of two resident phases at DEOMI, each 2 weeks long, plus a nonresident, correspondence phase. The graduates are qualified to serve as EO advisors in the various reserve components (e.g., National Guard, reserves). Its curriculum and training methods are similar to those for the 16-week course. Students may be officers or mid- to senior-grade noncommissioned officers.

The Equal Opportunity Program Orientation for Managers

This is a 2-week course designed to acquaint program managers at the higher levels of command with EO issues. It includes an orientation to such topics as prejudice and discrimination, program management, and service policies. Students are typically senior noncommissioned officers or officers in the grades of O-3 (lieutenants from the Navy and Coast Guard; captains from the other services) to O-6 (captains in the Navy or Coast Guard; colonels in the other services).

Equal Employment Opportunity Courses

Beginning in 1994, DEOMI assumed responsibility for training civilian employees of the services who are responsible for equal employment opportunity (EEO) programs. The three courses are designed to serve the needs of EEO advisors at different strata (from counselor to managerial levels) in the EEO system. The courses are each 2 weeks long and cover cultural awareness, EEO complaint processing, EEO law, communication skills, counseling skills, and dispute resolution techniques.

Senior Noncommissioned Officer Equal Opportunity Workshop

This is a 1-week course that orients senior noncommissioned officers toward EO issues. The students are typically first sergeants, master chiefs, sergeant majors, or chief master sergeants. They have considerable influence over the day-to-day management of personnel within their commands and can contribute much toward the human relations climate. The course uses many guided discussions, exercises, and case studies to involve the students in their own learning process.

Senior Executive Leaders Equal Opportunity Training

In March 1994, Secretary of Defense Perry issued a memorandum calling for DEOMI to train newly selected admirals and general officers, as well as senior executive service personnel, in EO topics. The 2-day workshops are designed to give these senior leaders personal insight into broad EO and diversity issues and to help them become more effective as senior managers within the services.

Mobile Training Teams

Since 1990, DEOMI has conducted a number of mobile training seminars at the request of

military and civilian agencies. The mobile training interventions are focused on the specific needs of the organization. For example, perhaps a unit has a need for sexual harassment training and sex discrimination training. A team from DEOMI will develop an appropriate program and deliver it on site. The requesting unit pays the travel costs for the team, but there is no charge for the training. Members of DEOMI's staff are also available for consultation to help identify training needs and other EO/diversity concerns within the units.

Other Services

Besides its extensive training programs, DEOMI offers a number of other services to help military commanders improve the EO and diversity climate within their commands. These services include the following:

Research

When DEOMI was founded, research (in the sense of student and program evaluation) was an integral part of the institution. It was used to validate and develop curriculum, to assess the impact of training on students and on those in the field, and to supplement curriculum materials. After the institute programs were well established, however, the interest in research waned. In 1986, the research program was reinstituted, and a research directorate was established. Research services include conducting original research on areas of interest in military EO, monitoring and disseminating findings, and providing resource materials to policymakers, commanders, EO advisors, and other interested individuals. Adjunct researchers from the services and civilian institutions of higher learning augment the DEOMI research staff through internships, summer faculty research programs, and the DEOMI visiting professor (sabbatical) program.

The summer research program, currently conducted through the Office of Naval Research, has been the vehicle through which the Research Directorate is able to magnify its efforts to provide a solid research base to the military's EO programs. Since the initiation of the summer program in 1987, close to 30 university faculty members have participated, several of them more than once. Approximately 20% were from historically black colleges (HBCs), and a number of the remainder were members of minority groups on the faculties of predominantly white institutions. The research topics have been quite broad and thus reflect the interests of both DEOMI and the individual faculty members. At least one effort, the measurement of EO climate (discussed below and in Chapter 14) has had significant impacts on the various services. Thirteen of the summer projects have dealt with aspects of EO climate; 13 have also focused on women's issues, including sexual harassment; 5 researched accessions policy; and the same number dealt with racial disparities in the system of military justice. The remainder looked at such diverse topics as evaluating the DEOMI curriculum (2 projects), Hispanic issues (2 projects), and EO policy (3 efforts).

Climate Analysis

The Directorate of Research also conducts the Military Equal Opportunity Climate Analysis Survey (MEOCS) program (Dansby & Landis, 1991; Landis, 1990; Landis, Dansby, & Faley, 1993). The MEOCS is an organizational development survey covering EO and organizational effectiveness issues. It is offered free to commanders of military organizations. DEOMI provides a confidential feedback report to the commanders and maintains a database of survey results by service. The feedback report provides comparisons between unit and database results, as well as internal comparisons (e.g., minority-majority, men-women) to help commanders better plan actions to improve the climate. This voluntary program has been quite popular with commanders (more than 2,000 requested the survey between June 1990 and October 1995); the result is a database of more than 400,000 records. The MEOCS is discussed further in Chapter 14 of this book.

Electronic Bulletin Board

The electronic bulletin board allows EO advisors, service leadership, researchers, and interested others to access and share information. Many research publications, statistics, case studies, and other resources are available for download. Also, the system serves as a vehicle for networking and E-mail among EO advisors and DEOMI staff.

Equal Opportunity Conference and Research Symposium

The Worldwide Equal Opportunity Conference (hosted by DEOMI December 5-9, 1994) was meant to be the first of many such conferences. In addition to training programs, seminars, and workshops, a research symposium was also conducted. Paper presentations and panel discussions contributed toward increased awareness of EO/EEO research and sharing of ideas for future projects and practical application.

Library

Over the years, the DEOMI library has developed an extensive collection of materials relating to EO and diversity issues. It contains more than 12,000 books and 250 periodicals, as well as CD-ROMs for 1,500 periodicals and 100 ethnic newspapers. Its selected journals, books, reports, and CD-ROM resources are perhaps the best source for military EO information in the world. The library is a resource for staff, students, and adjunct researchers.

National/International Initiatives

Since 1993, DEOMI has provided consultation and assistance for national and international efforts to improve intercultural training and understanding. In 1994, a separate directorate was established to further the national/international goals of the institute. DEOMI teams have worked with universities, police departments, fire departments, the Department of Justice, Chambers of Commerce, schools, youth groups, and other agencies to help improve the diversity climate. In the international arena, DEOMI has consulted with agencies from Russia and other former Eastern Bloc nations, South Africa, Canada, Great Britain, and Germany. These efforts support national democratization initiatives.

SUMMARY AND DISCUSSION

In this chapter, we described the history and philosophy of intercultural relations in the armed forces, the current policies, and the training programs and methods used to implement the programs. Central to the military training effort is the Defense Equal Opportunity Management Institute (DEOMI), a unique institute dedicated to training and research in EO and diversity issues within the military. Since 1971, DEOMI has served as a focal point for intercultural training.

In keeping with the military culture, intercultural training in the services is a pragmatic business. Using a system of centralized training (based at DEOMI) for the trainers and decentralized delivery at various levels throughout the services, military leaders hope to influence the behavior of servicemembers to maintain compliance with stated policy. And that policy endorses principles of equity, opportunity, and fair treatment, not limited by a person's color, race, ethnicity, or gender.

Many would argue that this approach has made the military the most successful major institution in the United States in implementing the goal of EO for people of all racial/ethnic backgrounds. Indeed, in March 1994, 54 minority generals and admirals were serving on active duty (DEOMI, 1994; also 11 women were in the general/flag officer ranks). This representation at the most senior levels of the services is even more impressive, given that the military must "grow its own" generals and admirals. There is no opportunity for lateral recruitment from other societal institutions; all general/flag officers must come through the ranks, a process that takes about 26 years. Therefore, the current generals and admirals started in the system about 1968. On the basis of the numbers of minority officers within the personnel "pipeline," we predict the number of minority general/flag officers will double by 2005 (if force levels are maintained at predicted levels). General Colin Powell, an African American who rose to the highest military position in the nation, serves as an important and symbolic reminder that minority members with the right abilities have the opportunity to reach the top in today's military services.

Clearly, the integration of women and minorities into the military has been a success. In elucidating the reasons for this situation, we point out five possibilities that, taken together, suggest patterns to be followed by other organizations:

1. Speedy change is better than slow, incremental policies. The integration of blacks was achieved in a fairly fast fashion because of wartime needs. Women, however, had to endure a much slower process to no clear benefit.

2. Providing opportunities for contact (Allport, 1954; Amir, 1976) acts to weaken prejudice and to lay the foundation for later integration policies. Hence, the experience of whites who served with blacks in World War II made acceptance of integration possible in 1948.

3. Making salient the contrast between segregationist policies and the fundamental precepts of the society can act to increase dissonance around the past practices. Having fought a world war to eliminate racism, the country was less willing to accept segregation at home. Myrdal (1944) called this an "American dilemma."

4. The role of top leadership cannot be overemphasized. President Truman provided strong leadership that, when combined with the tradition of military compliance with civilian authority, led to efforts to produce change.

5. Efforts to institutionalize nondiscriminatory behavior (the subject of this chapter) are important. In the military, this was accomplished by

   a. Development of a cadre of people whose raison d'etre was to eliminate discrimination. Although this approach eventually caused problems with the chain of command, the foundation was established for EO to be an important aim of the service. Paradoxically, because this cadre was composed of a disproportionate number of minorities and women, they were often not taken seriously by commanders.

   b. Development of a body of knowledge, about minority groups and women, that could be used to counter stereotypes when they arose in the field.

c. Development of a technology directed toward changing behavior and attitudes. This technology consists of curricula, lesson plans, group exercises, films, and videotapes. (modified from Kauth & Landis, 1994)

Despite these successes, the senior leadership in the military understands the need to press its efforts in this area. In a pivotal memorandum to all services on March 3, 1994, Secretary of Defense Perry stated it this way: "Equal opportunity is not just the right thing to do, it is also a military and economic necessity.... The Military Services have led our nation in expanding opportunities for minority groups.... However, I believe we can and should do better" (March 3, 1994, memorandum from Secretary of Defense William J. Perry to all service chiefs and department heads). In the memorandum, one of five initiatives designed to accomplish this objective states the secretary's desire that all personnel receive EO training and specifically mentions training for senior leaders (generals, admirals, and senior executive service civilians). DEOMI's programs serve as the fulcrum for leveraging the training across the services.

The editors of this volume present a model (Figure 1.2) describing the relationships among numerous variables in intercultural behavior. The military approach to intercultural training, though recognizing the importance of effective predispositions and responses, is clearly focused on the behavioral side of the model. Through education designed to enhance intercultural sensitivity and awareness and through sanctions designed to ensure compliance, military leaders hope to intervene in the intercultural behavior process to support principles of equity and diversity. The model predicts that such behaviors, with reinforcement from the recipient, or host, will strengthen, especially if the social system supports such interactions.

Balance theories of attitude change (e.g., Brehm & Cohen, 1962; Festinger, 1957; Heider, 1958; Osgood & Tannenbaum, 1955), especially cognitive dissonance theory (Brehm & Cohen, 1962; Festinger, 1957), predict some positive attitude change as a result of behavioral compliance if the compliance is not per-

ceived to be the result of extreme coercion or large incentives and if the new behavior is seen as central to the individual's self-perception. The perceptions of coercion and incentive are individual matters. Some military members who come into the services with negative attitudes toward EO policies may justify their counterattitudinal intercultural behaviors on the basis of level of coercion or incentives; others may change their attitudes if coercion and incentives are perceived as weak. In any case, from the military perspective, if behavioral interventions lead to increased positive affect toward others from diverse backgrounds, it would be a bonus. But attitude change per se is not the stated goal.

No program, particularly one as complex and far-reaching as the military's, is free of problems that may limit overall effectiveness. We mention just two. The first problem is that the theoretical orientation of the DEOMI curriculum was fundamentally set in the early 1970s. Hence, the discussion of the conceptual underpinnings of intercultural or EO training include a focus on dissonance and institutional discrimination. The group exercises tend to reinforce a view of racism that is traditional, to use McConohay's term (McConohay, 1986). Contact theory is briefly, if at all, mentioned, and there is virtually no recognition of the newer conceptualizations derived from Tajfel, Brewer, Gaertner, Larewood, and others (Brewer & Miller, 1984; Gaertner & Dovidio, 1986; Larwood & Gattiker, 1985; Larwood, Gutek, & Galliker, 1984; Tajfel & Turner, 1979). These approaches have been shown (e.g., by Amir and his colleagues; see Chapter 22, this volume) to be quite useful in changing both attitudes and behaviors.

A second problem is the organization and use of research on EO issues. The permanent research staff across DoD that focused entirely on EO issues is quite modest, given the size and importance of the issue. At DEOMI, the current staff consists of two Ph.D.-level research psychologists (one of whom is the division director), three MA-level researcher/administrators (one of whom is a military officer), and several noncommissioned officer-level persons who perform the various administrative duties necessary to keep the operation on track. Several of the staff spend most of their time ministering to the MEOCS database (see Chapter 14, this volume). Until recently (1993), the director was an Air Force lieutenant colonel and thus subject to rotation every 3 or 4 years. These staff are supplemented by summer researchers (see above) in residence for 10 weeks and a full-time sabbatical leave faculty member (who spends an academic year in the directorate). The upshot has been that it is very difficult to maintain a coherent and consistent research program. As a counter, the directorate has placed most of its effort into developing and enhancing the MEOCS and leaving other issues to be handled on an "as time is available basis." What the group does, it does extremely well with limited resources; but, it has hardly reached its potential as the military's center for EO research, a role that was envisioned for it by the DEOC in 1987 and that was assigned, though, without the necessary funding.

If research is poorly funded at DEOMI,[4] the situation elsewhere in DoD is hardly better. The Army Research Institute has not done any significant research in the EO arena since the late 1970s (Thomas, 1988). To our knowledge, the only Navy program is centered at the Navy Personnel Research and Development Center (NPRDC) in San Diego (Rosenfeld, Edwards, & Thomas, 1991), an effort being scaled back at this time. Except for an occasional graduate thesis, the situation is even grimmer in the Air Force. All of these considerations must make us cautious in anticipating high impacts from the EO programs described in this chapter.

The long-term result of the military's program remains to be seen. What will happen to intercultural relations as the force reductions continue? How will societal demographic and attitudinal changes affect the military of the future? Will there even be a need for such training as the 21st century unfolds? How will increases in the number of women in the military affect intercultural relations in the military? Will backlash from majority men (the "reverse discrimination" concerns) have a significant affect on the services? Will policies regarding homosexual participation be revised, and how might this affect the services? (Kauth & Landis, 1994). These and other questions remain to be answered. Truly, at least for intercultural relations and training in the military, these are interesting times.

Notes

1. For example, Senator Richard Russell (D-GA) had this to say:

> The mandatory intermingling of the races throughout the services will be a terrific blow to the efficiency and fighting power of the armed services. . . . It is sure to increase the number of men who will be disabled through communicable diseases. It will increase the rate of crime committed by servicemen. (Power of the Pentagon, 1972)

Also typical of the early attitude toward women in the military is a 1945 statement by Brigadier General C. Thomas, Director of the Division of the Plans and Policies at Marine Corps Headquarters, who commented, "The opinion generally held by the Marine Corps is that women have no proper place or function in the regular service in peacetime. . . . The American tradition is that a woman's place is in the home" (Stremlow, 1979, p. 1).

2. Gesell, at the time of his appointment, was a Washington lawyer and acquaintance of Secretary McNamara's special assistant, Adam Yarmolinsky, and a close friend of Burke Marshall, then head of the Civil Rights Division in the Department of Justice.

3. Although this is a quite reasonable rationale, it is important to note that it has never been subjected to an empirical test, even though cohesion does seem to be related to unit effectiveness (Siebold & Lindsay, 1991). One problem has been the lack of agreement on what constitutes cohesion. In addition, it has been difficult to carry out a field test under realistic conditions.

4. The total DEOMI (operating) budget is less than $2.5 million. Even with the addition of the assigned military personnel on staff, the total is considerably less than $7.0 million. Considering the size of the active duty and reserve force, this amounts to less than $3 annually per service person being expended on EO issues. At the same time, this amount is far greater than that being spent by any other governmental agency at any level.

References

Allport, G. W. (1954). *The nature of prejudice*. Reading, MA: Addison-Wesley.

Amir, Y. (1976). The role of intergroup contact in change of prejudice and ethnic relations. In P. A. Katz (Ed.), *Toward the elimination of racism* (pp. 245-308). Elmsford, NY: Pergamon.

Binkin, M., Eitelberg, M. J., Schexnider, A. J., & Smith, M. M. (1982). *Blacks and the military*. Washington, DC: Brookings Institution.

Brehm, J. W., & Cohen, A. R. (1962). *Explorations in cognitive dissonance*. New York: John Wiley.

Brewer, M., & Miller, N. (1984). Beyond the contact hypothesis: Theoretical perspectives on desegregation. In N. Millerand & M. Brewer, *Groups in contact: The psychology of desegregation* (pp. 281-302). San Diego: Academic Press.

Dansby, M. R., & Landis, D. (1991). Measuring equal opportunity in the military environment. *International Journal of Intercultural Relations, 15*, 389-405.

Day, H. R. (1983). Race relations training in the U.S. military. In D. Landis & R. W. Brislin (Eds.), *Handbook of intercultural training: Vol. 2. Issues in training methodology* (pp. 241-289). Elmsford, NY: Pergamon.

Defense Equal Opportunity Management Institute (DEOMI). (1994). *Semi-annual race/ethnic/gender profile of the Department of Defense active forces, reserve forces, and the United States Coast Guard* (Statistical series pamphlet No. 94-4). Patrick Air Force Base, FL: Author.

Festinger, L. (1957). *A theory of cognitive dissonance*. Stanford, CA: Stanford University Press.

Gaertner, S. L., & Dovidio, J. (1986). The aversive form of racism. In. J. Dovidio & S. Gaertner (Eds.), *Prejudice, discrimination, and racism* (pp. 61-90). San Diego: Academic Press.

Heider, F. (1958). *The psychology of interpersonal relations*. New York: John Wiley.

Holm, J. (1992). *Women in the military: An unfinished revolution*. Novato, CA: Presidio.

Hope, R. O. (1979). *Racial strife in the U.S. military: Toward the elimination of discrimination*. New York: Praeger.

Kauth, M., & Landis, D. (1994, August). *Applying lessons learned from ethnic and gender integration to the United States military*. Paper presented at the Annual Convention of the American Psychological Association, Los Angeles.

Knouse, S. B. (1994). *Equal opportunity climate and total quality management: A preliminary study* (DEOMI technical report). Patrick Air Force Base, FL: Defense Equal Opportunity Management Institute.

Landis, D. (1990, January). *Military Equal Opportunity Climate Survey: Reliability, construct validity, and preliminary field test*. Oxford: University of Mississippi, Center for Applied Research and Evaluation.

Landis, D., Dansby, M. R., & Faley, R. H. (1993). The Military Equal Opportunity Climate Survey: An example of surveying in organizations. In P. Rosenfeld, J. E. Edwards, & M. D. Thomas (Eds.), *Improving organizational surveys: New directions, methods, and applications* (pp. 210-239). Newbury Park, CA: Sage.

Larwood, L., & Gattiker, U. E. (1985). Rational bias and interorganizational power in the employment of management consultants. *Group and Organization Studies, 10*, 3-17.

Larwood, L., Gutek, B., & Gattiker, U. E. (1984). Perspectives on institutional discrimination and resistance to change. *Group and Organization Studies, 9*, 333-352.

Lovejoy, J. E. (1977). *A history of the Defense Race Relations Institute (DRRI)*. Patrick Air Force Base, FL: Defense Equal Opportunity Management Institute.

MacGregor, M. J. (1981). *Integration of the armed forces, 1940-1965*. Washington, DC: United States Army, Center of Military History.

McConohay, J. (1986). Modern racism, ambivalence, and the modern racism scale. In J. Dovidio & S. Gaertner (Eds.), *Prejudice, discrimination, and racism* (pp. 91-126). San Diego: Academic Press.

Myrdal, G. (1944). *An American dilemma*. New York: Harper & Row.

Nalty, B. C. (1986). *Strength for the fight: A history of black Americans in the military*. New York: Free Press.

Osgood, C. E., & Tannenbaum, P. H. (1955). The principle of congruity in the prediction of attitude change. *Psychological Review, 62*, 42-55.

Power of the Pentagon. (1972). *Congressional Quarterly Weekly Report*, pp. 34-35.

Rosenfeld. P., Thomas, M. D., Edwards, J. E., Thomas, P. J., & Thomas, E. D. (1991). Navy research into race, ethnicity, and gender issues:

A historical review. *International Journal of Intercultural Relations, 15,* 407-426.

Siebold, G. L., & Lindsay, T. J. (1991, October). Correlations among ratings of platoon performance. *Proceedings of the 33rd Annual Conference of the Military Testing Association* (pp. 67-72). San Antonio, TX: U.S. Air Force Armstrong Laboratory Human Resources Directorate and the U.S. Air Force Occupational Measurement Squadron.

Stremlow, M. V. (1979). *A history of women marines 1946-1977.* Washington, DC; U.S. Marine Corps, History and Museums Division.

Tajfel, H., & Turner, J. (1979). An integrative theory of intergroup conflict. In W. Austin & S. Worshel (Eds.), *The social psychology of intergroup relations* (pp. 33-47). Monterey, CA: Brooks/Cole.

Thomas, J. A. (1988). *Race relations research in the U.S. Army in the 1970s: A collection of selected readings.* Alexandria, VA: U.S. Army Research Institute for the Behavioral and Social Sciences.

Young, W. L. (1982). *Minorities and the military: A cross-national study in world perspective.* Westport, CT: Greenwood.

12

Cross-Cultural Training
in Organizational Contexts

RABI S. BHAGAT

KRISTIN O. PRIEN

AS international companies begin to compete with each other in the global marketplace, the role of cross-cultural training becomes increasingly important. Issues such as how to educate host country employees and how to train the international manager for his or her international role are receiving increased attention from researchers and practitioners in the field of intercultural training. Practitioners charged with the responsibility for human resource activities must incorporate cross-cultural issues into training activities. Researchers should also examine the difficult issues of training across cultures as they develop better models of training in organizational contexts.

The globalization of markets, increased diversity of the workforce, and use of Third World nationals by transnational organizations have made issues of training important in the remainder of this decade. Advances in both transportation and communication technology have made it possible for individuals from dissimilar cultures to interact as fellow employees of these transnational corporations. Employees of global corporations are required to interact not only with employees of subsidiaries located in different cultures but also with customers, foreign governments, and social institutions of dissimilar cultures. Globalization requires that organizations adopt a cross-cultural perspective to be successful in accomplishing their goals in the context of a global economy. Miriam Erez, in her chapter from *Handbook of Industrial and Organizational Psychology* (1994), discusses cross-cultural issues in industrial and organizational psychology and notes that a series of political and economic changes occurring in different parts of the world make it necessary for multinational organizations to adopt a strong intercultural perspective in the socialization and training of managers. It is abundantly clear that interpersonal patterns, norms, and values that make an employee effective in one culture will not necessarily result in effectiveness in a dissimilar culture (e.g., Adler & Kiggundu, 1983; Arvey, Bhagat, & Salas, 1991; Drenth & Groenendijik, 1984; Ronen, 1989).

In writing this chapter, we note that management education in the United States is taking on an international perspective. For example, in a 1990 symposium at the University of Michigan, practicing managers and management educators emphasized that management education should prepare individuals to manage in a global economy by including foreign languages, cross-cultural issues, and international internships in the curriculum (Barnett, 1990).

Although interactions between individuals from dissimilar cultures can take many forms in the organizational setting, the interactions and the outcomes of interactions between expatriate managers and host country nationals are of crucial importance to organizations. Expatriate assignments, which can be for a short duration or an extended period, require the expatriate manager to live in the foreign country (the host country) and to manage the operations of a subsidiary. Unfortunately, these assignments are not always successful because the adaptation to a foreign culture is not easy for the assignee or his or her family. The employee's failing to complete the overseas assignment or performing at less than an optimal level can be attributed to difficulties associated with adaptation to novel situations encountered in the host county environment (Bird & Dunbar, 1991; Caudron, 1992). Managers' lack of success in expatriate assignments has negative consequences for multiple parties, including host country nationals, the expatriate manager, and the employing organization (Triandis, 1994). It has been estimated that the financial consequences to U.S. organizations may be as much as $2.5 billion in a year. Estimates show that the typical cost associated with a failed expatriate assignment can be as high as the manager's annual salary (Dowling & Schuler, 1990; Lissy, 1993). Therefore, the financial impact alone of nonexistent, insufficient, or poorly designed training for expatriate managers is sufficient to warrant a careful consideration of organizational training in the cross-cultural context.

A first step in the assessment of cross-cultural training, however, is model develop-ment in the context of previous research. Without a grounded framework for understanding the processes and content involved in this type of training, researchers and practitioners are often working in a vacuum. Without appropriate theory-driven guidance, even the best-intended efforts are likely to fail.

Current Trends in Expatriate Employment

The experience of Asian and Western European multinational corporations (MNCs), as well as some U.S. firms, has been that the success of expatriate assignments is enhanced when employees and their families are prepared for their cross-cultural experience (Tung, 1987). A growing number of expatriate employees are being sent abroad from the United States. In 1991, U.S. private industry had an estimated 80,000 employees on overseas assignment (Gowing & Armitage, 1993). Although these employees do include technicians and professionals, as well as managers ("U.S. Engineers Will Work in Japan," 1993), scant information is available as to the proportion of these who fall into the managerial category. Most of the available academic research (Black, 1992; Ronen, 1989) and practitioner advice (Dowling & Schuler, 1990; Mendenhall & Oddou, 1991), however, assumes that the expatriate U.S. employee will be a manager. It may be assumed, however, that the problems that would apply to expatriate managers would apply to expatriate technicians and professionals as well.

Unfortunately, many overseas assignments are not successful (for a further review, see Hesketh & Bochner, 1994). Some expatriate employees may simply perform at less than their full potential; other employees may pack up and return home (voluntarily or involuntarily). The number of expatriate failures has been variously estimated at between 16% to 40% of those assigned (Dowling & Schuler, 1990); 25% to 50% of those assigned (Bird & Dunbar, 1991); and approximately 30% (Tung, 1987). The cost to organizations of these failures has been variously estimated as well. The total cost to the organization for an expatriate employee may be as high as three to five times that employee's annual salary (Van Pelt & Wolniansky, 1990), with the cost of a failure estimated to range between $250,000 and $1,000,000 per employee (Caudron, 1991). Another comparable estimate (Leonard, 1994) is that the cost of a 3-year expatriate assignment may be as much as $1,000,000. The total may be as much as $2 billion in a year (Dowling & Schuler, 1990) or up to $2.5 billion (Lissy, 1993).

In addition, salaries, benefits, and travel expenses may not be the only financial costs the firm incurs from an expatriate failure. Anecdotal evidence of the costs of expatriate failures is abundant. For example, Dowling and Schuler (1990) cite the example of an expatriate employee caught attempting to smuggle a small quantity of brandy into a fundamentalist Muslim country. Not only was the employee expelled from the country, but the employing firm was also prohibited from conducting business in that country. Good intentions, though, are not sufficient. Other serious misunderstandings of dissimilar cultures often involve lack of knowledge, a function of inadequate training. For example, numerous anecdotes tell of well-intentioned U.S. sales and marketing personnel who translate an innocuous English-language product name or advertising slogan with less than positive consequences. Ricks documents many of these instances, which range from unintentional humor to outright offenses in the host country, in his 1993 book *Blunders in International Business.*

Faced with such difficulties, multinational firms often attempt to circumvent the expatriate problem by recruiting home country nationals to manage the operations of their subsidiaries. A survey of the *Forbes* 500 companies found that most firms select expatriate managers from the host country (Hayden, 1990). Many European MNCs follow a similar strategy (Kopp, 1994). A variation on this approach is adopted by many Japanese multinationals. These companies hire American employees, train these employees in Japan, and then send them back to the United States to manage the operation of the U.S. subsidiaries (Bird & Mukuda, 1984; Patterson, 1990). This approach, however, which seems to avoid the issue of cross-cultural training, may be laden with other difficulties. First, host country nationals may not have the necessary job-related skills and knowledge for senior-level positions. This problem becomes acute in the context of a less developed or developing nation. A second and perhaps a more difficult problem associated with such an avoidance of cross-cultural training pertains to

the development and implementation of global strategies. Host country nationals may not fully appreciate the need for coordination in a global context unless they are trained to understand the nature and evolution of markets that go beyond the border of their own environments (Dowling & Schuler, 1990; Scullion, 1991). Although these difficulties can be surmounted, the effort and expense required to build and implement a global strategy responsive to local conditions may be beyond the reach of all but the largest firms (Anfuso, 1994; Bartlett & Ghoshal, 1992).

A more realistic solution is to prepare managers for their foreign assignments with some form of cross-cultural training. That training programs do work is shown by the example of many East Asian firms that do extensively train managers for overseas assignments. A recent survey shows that 86% of Japanese multinationals report less than a 10% failure rate for their expatriates (Hogan & Goodson, 1990). This impressive rate of success is because of the extensive training that Japanese expatriates receive. Employees may be sent to one of the firm's overseas facilities for a year of training. Other possibilities include company-sponsored graduate training in a foreign university and intensive and sophisticated language and cultural training programs lasting from 3 months to 1 year (Tung, 1987). An example of this is found in the 1991 article "Taking the Cultural Blinkers Off," which describes the "globalization" programs of large Korean firms such as Samsung. Employees participating in this program are sent abroad at full salary (plus expenses) to become acculturated to a new language and culture. Such a cross-cultural emphasis is not necessarily found only in Asian firms. Western European firms have a higher success rate with expatriates and engage in more formal training activities than do U.S. firms (Hamill, 1989; Tung, 1987).

U.S.-based organizations, however, are not totally lacking in examples of successful expatriate training. The U.S. Department of State, related federal agencies and departments, and the U.S. military have a long history of success with programs designed to prepare the employee, spouse, and family for extensive overseas assignments. These programs include general training in cultural adaptation, education on specific aspects of the host country culture, and language training (Gowing & Armitage, 1993).

Few private-sector firms in the United States, however, engage in such training. As recently as 1984, 68% of U.S. firms surveyed did not have any training programs in place (Goldstein, 1989). It has been estimated that only 30% of expatriate employees receive any form of training at all (Dowling & Schuler, 1990). For those few firms that do have training programs, training is often only of brief duration. As Arvey et al. (1991) found, over half (57%) of the programs offered by U.S. firms last 1 week or less, with very few (14%) lasting as long as 1 month. Over 80% of the firms surveyed focused on training the employee only, with no provision for training the spouse or family. This is a crucial gap because training for the spouse is critical to the success of expatriate assignments. Many premature returns, even for the most technically sophisticated manager, are because of the spouse's failure to adjust to a dissimilar culture (Briody & Chrisman, 1991; Solomon, 1994; Tung, 1987).

A related difficulty with training programs is that they rarely include female managers for overseas assignments. Research evidence (as cited by Triandis, 1994) has shown that, for whatever reason, women find it more difficult to adjust to a different culture than do men. In addition, hardly any encouragement is given to female managers for assignments in overseas locations (Dowling & Schuler, 1990; Harris, 1993). In fact, it has been estimated that 90% of managers on overseas assignments are male (Solomon, 1994). Given that, in recent times, a substantial majority of managers in the high technology and financial services industries are women and that these companies often have subsidiaries in different countries, the need to adequately train female managers for overseas roles becomes even more important as these industries pursue joint venture agreements. Stereotypical assumptions governing the success of female managers in overseas assignments have not been found to have much merit (Adler, 1987; Barnum, 1994).

Many employers cite limited resources and lack of suitable expertise as barriers to effective cross-cultural training. Many organizations have explored alternative routes to training, by bringing in management consultants (Carson, 1989; Kitsuse, 1992). Another possibility is government-sponsored training programs specifically designed to help multinationals launch business ventures overseas. For example, the Mexican government offers a program entitled Mastering Mexico to assist expatriates and their families in adjusting to Mexico (de Lopez, 1992). In addition, organizations can foster employees' and their family members' initiatives in self-training, in which prospective expatriates take a proactive role in gathering information for the overseas assignment from published sources and from those who have already completed one or more expatriate assignments.

Some U.S. organizations have found that a commitment to training for expatriates is an effective use of organizational resources. The problem, however, is the limited research evidence supporting the anecdotal evidence of training effectiveness. Black and Mendenhall (1990) reviewed the previous studies of cross-cultural training and found little research in this area—surprising, in light of the financial impact of failed expatriate assignments. At this point, we summarize current research in this area, using the framework suggested by Triandis (1977) to categorize training program content (see Tables 12.1 and 12.2).

As has been noted earlier, cross-cultural training is best conducted in a theoretically rigorous and contextually embedded vein. At this point, we review some theoretical frameworks that are useful for conceptualizing the many facets of cross-cultural training in organizations.

Previous Theoretical Frameworks

Several theoretical frameworks are available for understanding the content and processes involved in cross-cultural training. Each model focuses on a different portion of the individual's learning and application of knowledge, skills, and attitudes related to work and organizational behavior in the cross-cultural setting. In discussing these various models, we make use of several concepts suggested by Triandis (1994).

Culture Assimilator

In the culture assimilator approach, as developed by Triandis and others (Fiedler, Mitchell, & Triandis, 1971), the focus is on cognitive

(text continued on p. 223)

TABLE 12.1 Cross-Cultural Training Applied Studies

Study	Source of Employees	Type of Training		Program Evaluation
		Affective vs. Cognitive vs. Behavioral	*General vs. Specific*	
Hogan & Goodson, 1990	Various MNCs in Japan	Cognitive; possibly behavioral	Specific	Expatriate failure vs. success
Van Pelt & Wolniansky, 1990	N/A	N/A	N/A	Employee perceptions of overseas assignments more positive and lower costs to organizations if training provided
Caudron, 1992	N/A	Cognitive and behavioral	Specific	Costs of training vs. costs of expatriate failures
Ettorre, 1993	N/A	Cognitive, affective, and behavioral	General and specific	Organizational success in the future will depend on management's awareness of cross-cultural factors; both predeparture and repatriation training essential to make optimal use of employees' knowledge
Gowing & Armitage, 1993	U.S. citizens	Affective, cognitive, and behavioral	General and specific	N/A
Laabs, 1993	U.S. and foreign countries	Primarily cognitive	General	High levels of trainee retention
McGarvey & Smith, 1994	U.S. firms	Cognitive (language training)	Specific	N/A

NOTE: N/A denotes area not included in article.

TABLE 12.2 Cross-Cultural Training Research Studies

Study	Theoretical Model	Type of Organization	Type of Training			Research Design	Results
			Affective vs. Cognitive vs. Behavioral	General vs. Specific			
Black & Gregersen, 1991	Social learning	N/A	N/A	N/A		Survey; cross-sectional; no control group	Spouse adjustment greater with self-initiated predeparture training; spouse adjustment less with company-initiated training
Domsch & Lichtenberger, 1991	N/A	German MNCs with employees in China or Brazil	Cognitive and behavioral	Specific		Survey; cross-sectional; no control group	Expatriate managers perceive that behavioral training should be added to cognitive training
Gregersen, 1992	Antecedents of organizational commitment	Various organizations in Europe and Asia	N/A	N/A		Survey; cross-sectional; no control group	Training prior to repatriation not significantly associated with ease of reintegration after assignment
Gregersen & Black, 1992	Antecedents of organizational and job commitment	Various organizations in Europe and Asia	N/A	N/A		Survey; cross-sectional, no control group	Predeparture training has a significant, positive impact on organizational commitment
Harrison, 1992	Cultural assimilator and social learning	Civilian employees of U.S. military in Japan	Cognitive and behavioral	Specific		Laboratory study; cross-sectional; control groups	Combined cognitive and behavioral training is more effective than either method alone

(continued)

TABLE 12.2 (Continued)

Study	Theoretical Model	Type of Organization	Type of Training			Research Design	Results
			Affective vs. Cognitive vs. Behavioral	General vs. Specific			
Thomas & Ravlin 1995	N/A	U.S. employees of Japanese-owned firms	N/A	N/A		Laboratory study; cross-sectional; no control groups	Perceived cultural adaptation increases perceived managerial effectiveness
Guzzo, Noonan, & Elron, 1994	Psychological contract	Various organizations in 63 countries	N/A	N/A		Survey; cross-sectional; no control group	Perceived organizational support for expatriates positively associated with organizational commitments, which, in turn, is negatively associated with intent to quit
Earley, 1987	Training model	U.S. electronics firm in Korea	Cognitive and affective	Both		Quasi experimental; cross-sectional; control group received no training	Both cognitive and affective training positively associated with self-perceived adjustment; self-perceived adjustment positively associated with performance; combined cognitive and affective training more effective than either type of training alone.
Naumann, 1993	Job satisfaction	Employees of U.S. MNCs in Hong Kong, Korea, Taiwan, and China	N/A	N/A		Survey; cross-sectional; no control group	Individuals reporting more adequate training also reported higher levels of job satisfaction

NOTE: N/A denotes area not included in the article.

222

learning. The *culture assimilator* is a programmed training exercise in which individuals are presented with descriptions of various situations and possible responses to those situations. What is learned is that cultures differ and that different behaviors will have different effects in different settings.

Social Learning Theory

Black and Mendenhall (1990) view the process of cross-cultural training as social learning, wherein the individual is acquiring the social skills necessary to function in another culture. They classify these skills into three categories. Skills in the first category are those necessary for the individual to preserve his or her self-image in an alien culture. Skills in the second are those necessary to interact with individuals from another culture. Skills in the third are the cognitive skills necessary for the individual to learn about the foreign culture.

Traditional Industrial-Organizational
Psychology Model of Training

In the traditional model, as discussed by Ronen (1989), the focus is on the training process. The traditional training model (Goldstein, 1974, 1989; Goldstein & Gessner, 1988; Wexley & Latham, 1981) contains three basic steps, each with substeps or components (adapted from Goldstein, 1974):

1. Training needs assessment
   • perform organizational analysis
   • perform job analysis
   • perform person analysis
   • determine instructional objectives

2. Training and development activities
   • select and design instructional
     programs
   • conduct training activities

3. Evaluation of training goals
   • develop evaluation criteria
   • develop evaluation model
   • determine if training goals are met

In the *training needs assessment* phase of this general model, the needs of the organization and

of the particular jobs within the organization are first determined in terms of the job skills necessary for individuals to perform jobs within the organization. Next, individuals' possession of those job skills is measured and instructional objectives are formulated to close any gaps between organizational needs and individuals' skills. In the cross-cultural setting, training needs assessment usually focuses on the knowledge, skills, abilities, and attitudes necessary for individuals from one culture to interact effectively with individuals from another culture. The assumption is that employees possess the general management or technical skills necessary for performing jobs in the multinational organizations; the cross-cultural knowledge and skills may be deficient.

Training and development activities involve those activities in which individuals acquire job-related knowledge and skills. Usually, multiple training methods can be used to accomplish any instructional objective. This use is of critical importance when individuals from one culture conduct training activities for individuals from another culture. For example, classroom participation and discussion, in which the instructor is a leader rather than an authority, may be effective in Western cultures but not in Asian cultures. In this example, the Western trainer would be well advised to choose a different training method, such as a lecture, when training individuals from these cultures.

The last step, *evaluation of training goals,* is the step most often omitted. It is as important in cross-cultural training setting, however, as in any other setting. For MNCs, failures in training can be quite expensive. The failure of one expatriate manager to adapt to the host country can cost the organization as much as $1,000,000. In addition, the expatriate manager's performance deficiencies can also be costly to the organization. Assessing training program effectiveness involves several considerations. First, did the participants learn the course content? Second and more important, can and will the participants apply the training program content on the job (will the training *transfer* to the work setting)?

The training model has one limitation as it relates to training in the cross-cultural setting. This model assumes that learning is based on the acquisition of knowledge, rather than on change in attitudes. Training in the cross-cultural setting, however, requires more than *knowledge* of differences; it also requires *acceptance* of differences. This attitudinal change may be the most difficult portion of training in the cross-cultural setting.

Hesketh and Bochner (1994) address these shortcomings in their review of cross-cultural training. They suggest that this traditional training model, especially as applied in cross-cultural settings, should be modified. They do not suggest that the traditional model be scrapped, but that it be expanded. Individuals should be taught how to learn, as well as specific skills, and the skills that are taught should be adaptable or transferrable to the demands of changing jobs in a dynamic environment. Furthermore, the focus of training should be placed on the trainee, rather than on the trainer or the training method.

Job Characteristics

Bird and Dunbar (1991) view the success or failure of expatriate work assignments as depending on the characteristics of the expatriate job. Using the Hackman and Oldham job characteristics model (1980), they describe typical overseas assignments in terms of this model and how typical expatriates will view their new job. The authors point out that expatriates must often adjust to a different job, as well to as a different culture.

Individual Characteristics

Individual characteristics may have an effect on the success or failure of an expatriate assignment. Mendenhall and Oddou (1985) suggest that individual differences, such as self-efficacy and human relations skills, are key factors in expatriate success. As discussed by Ronen (1989), such personal traits or attributes as courtesy, sensitivity, and tolerance for ambiguity will contribute to training success, as well as to ultimate job performance. Although some of the individual differences described by Ronen (e.g., dependability, imagination) may be relatively stable and not amenable to adult learning or training, others may be more amenable to training, such as general sensitivity to different cultures.

We believe it is important that the training literature in the cross-cultural context be understood with some strong theoretical underpinnings. With this goal in mind, we provide a theoretical framework that incorporates previous research and theory in training in general and in intercultural training in particular. One main point we would like to convey is that training effectiveness is a function of many factors. These include individual-level variables, such as predispositions, cognitive style, motivational state, and family status; job-level variables, such as job characteristics; and organizational-level variables, such as culture and strategy.

A New Theoretical Approach

A model for intercultural training effectiveness is presented below. In developing this model, we made the assumption that a rigorous assessment of the various needs associated with intercultural training has already been conducted. Our criterion for success of the assignees in the overseas role is conceptualized at three levels (see Figure 12.1). First, we are concerned with the effectiveness in the work role of the assignee. Second, we consider the impact of training for organization-specific criteria for success in the overseas role. Third, following the suggestions made by Triandis (1994), we also view effectiveness from the point of view of the host country setting.

In developing rigorous training programs, the viewpoints of the following parties could be useful (Triandis, 1994):

Immediate supervisors in the host country subsidiary
Immediate supervisors in the home country headquarters
Family of the expatriate
Governmental representatives in the host country
Local nationals in the host country

The point is that, unlike training conducted in the domestic setting, cross-cultural training for transnational corporations has important implications for a number of groups whose well-

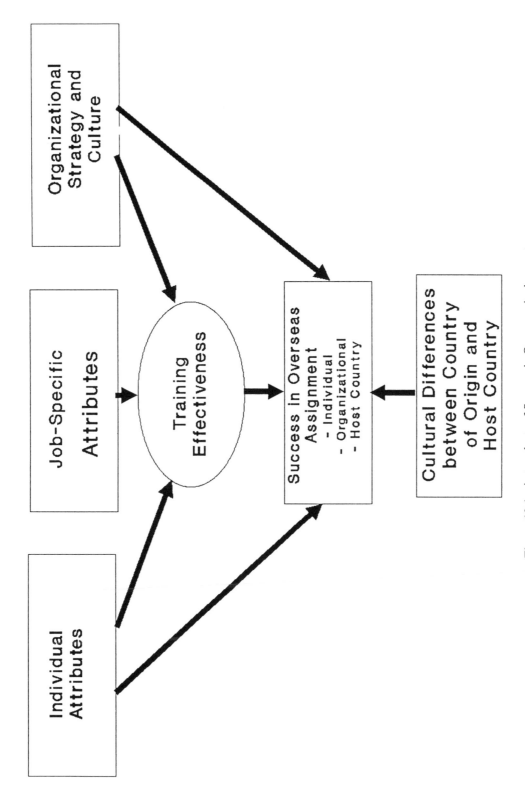

Figure 12.1. Antecedents of Success in Overseas Assignments

being is affected by the outcomes of cross-cultural training.

Individual and Family Attributes

It should not be surprising that certain individual-level attributes contribute to success in the overseas role (Arvey et al., 1991; Black, Mendenhall, & Oddou, 1991). Ronen (1989) made a strong case for the importance of cross-cultural sensitivity and intercultural competence (referred to as *multiculturalism*) in enhancing success in overseas assignments. Attributes such as cognitive flexibility, adaptability, tolerance for ambiguity, non-ethnocentricism, positive self-image, outgoingness, and extroversion have been associated with success in the overseas role.

Attributes of the family are also important. The extent to which the spouse of the international assignee is willing to relocate to a foreign country, the extent of social support network, and opportunities for children's schooling or spouse's work are quite important but have not been explicitly considered in previous training efforts. The importance of these factors is usually discovered after the international assignee has experienced failure in his or her role and has returned to company headquarters with considerable disappointment.

Job-Level Attributes

Even though little is known in this area, job-level attributes, in our opinion, are likely to have profound complicating effects. Although Arvey et al. (1991), Ronen (1989), and Feldman and Tompson (1993) suggest the importance of these factors, the existing literature does not provide a great deal of empirical grounding pertaining to the role of these job-level attributes. In one study (Naumann, 1993), expatriate job satisfaction was linked to job-level attributes or characteristics. The findings, however, showed that the relationship between desirable job characteristics and job satisfaction was similar for both domestic and expatriate managers. Job-level attributes include such variables as the complexity of the technical skills involved, the need for knowledge of host country and headquarters operations, and the complexity of interpersonal and administrative activities.

Organizational-Level Attributes

Even in situations in which training design is effective, it is important to keep in mind the importance of contextual factors in evaluating the criteria for success. Many multinationals may have a long-term orientation in overseas assignments, but the training may be designed with a short-term orientation. In our review of the literature, we get the distinct impression that the trainers are often not apprised of the strategy involved in the overseas operations. One cannot separate the strategy involved in the multinational mission from the human resource strategy involved in placing the international assignee. Most trainers are well-intentioned individuals and provide training with a plethora of individual-level interventions designed to help the individual adjust to his or her role in the overseas context. More often than not, these individual-level interventions are at odds with the overall organizational strategy involved in the multinational mission. In fact, we are of the opinion that, unless such strategies are explicitly articulated and then incorporated into the design of the training, the effectiveness of the intercultural training will be limited.

Cultural Differences

Our model shows that success in the overseas assignment is strongly affected by cultural differences between the host country and the country of origin. We suggest that cultural differences should be viewed in terms of both objective and subjective cultures (Bhagat & McQuaid, 1982; Triandis, 1972). The greater the cultural differences between the host country and the country of origin in terms of various facets of objective culture, the less the reported level of success in the overseas assignment. Differences in objective culture deal with differing food habits, roads and infrastructure in general, dress habits, and so on. The more experience an assignee has had with exotic sights, sounds, foods, smells, and people, the less the adjustment for the assignee. Culture shock is often a function of both objective and subjective culture-based differences. People react to specific cues and behave according to norms of the subjective culture of the country of origin. When people are in unfamiliar environments and when they behave in unpredictable ways, they are likely to lose *control*. Loss of control is associated with experience of stress, helplessness, and depression. Subjective, culture-based differences, which are reflected in differing belief systems, attitude structures, stereotype formations, norms, roles, ideologies, values, and task definitions, cause significant problems for the international assignee. These difficulties will be reflected in the success or failure of the assignment. Even individuals without previous knowledge of the host country culture, however, can be sensitized to the various aspects of the culture and to cultural differences in general (Triandis, Brislin, & Hui, 1988). Such training will lessen the adverse effects of cultural differences as conceptualized in our model.

Directions for Future Research

The field is open for researchers interested in the design and evaluation of cross-cultural training for expatriates. As pointed out by Triandis (1994) and as discussed in our model, some evidence suggests that training for expatriates will have beneficial consequences for the organization, the individual, and the members of the host country who will come in contact with the expatriate and his or her family members. More research is needed, however, to firmly establish this linkage between training and organizational outcomes, especially in light of the reluctance of U.S. firms to commit the necessary resources to ensure meaningful training for expatriates. Moreover, as organizations, both in the United States and in Europe and Asia, are forced to define their competition and be competitive on a global rather than a national or even regional basis, organizations' need for globally aware and cross-culturally competent managers, professionals, and even technicians can only increase. The practitioner literature in this area is primarily anecdotal, perhaps not a surprising finding in view of the lack of a generally accepted theoretical framework for research in this area. The research agenda must be based on theoretically rigorous models. As pointed out by Black and Mendenhall (1990), rigorous research on cross-cultural

training has been scarce. Moreover, research designs have been cross-sectional, rather than longitudinal, and control groups have not often been employed. It would be necessary for transnational organizations to invest in designing rigorous training programs for their expatriates. Resources dedicated to research on expatriate training would be productively invested.

Future research can follow several paths. Some of the more interesting are as follows. First, as pointed out in the previous paragraph, research designs in this area have been lacking in rigor. Despite the difficulties associated with organizational research in cross-cultural training, however, it is possible to design a study with at least some features of experimental control. An example of innovative research design is the 1992 study by Harrison, in which civilian employees of the U.S. military were the subjects. In this study, individuals were separated into groups and exposed to various types of training or, for the control group, no training at all. Longitudinal designs, though requiring a greater commitment of time by the researcher and the organization, would also be valuable.

A second area of research design to be refined is in problem definition and outcome measurement. Practitioner studies and, to some extent, research studies seem to rely on the same sources for the number of U.S. expatriate employees, rates of expatriate failure, and the associated costs. These estimates vary wildly across sources. As Gowing and Armitage (1993) point out, neither researchers nor practitioners really knows the exact number of expatriate employees that U.S. multinationals currently employ. The costs associated with such employment are also presumed to be quite high, but precise figures are not currently available. For future research in this area to have an appreciable effect on important outcomes, we recommend that more effort be directed at quantifying the nature of these outcomes.

A third promising direction for future research is to examine and develop a taxonomy of types of expatriate employees. Much research in this area has assumed that the expatriate employee is a manager, male, and with a family. Although male managers are the most common expatriates, women and professional and technical employees are also sent on overseas assignments. Women have not been traditionally considered for overseas assignments (Dowling & Schuler, 1990; Harris, 1993) because of both women's social roles in the United States and gender roles (real or perceived) in host countries. With the changing role of women in Western cultures, as well as in other parts of the world, however, the need is for a better understanding of the factors responsible for the success of female managers in expatriate roles. Technical employees, whose expatriate job assignment often involves the transfer of a new technology to the host country (Kedia & Bhagat, 1988), may well be in considerable need of appropriate cross-cultural training.

Finally, future research should be oriented to the needs of practitioners. As has been pointed out by an eminent researcher in industrial-organizational psychology (Campbell, 1990), much research in industrial-organizational psychology fails to meet the needs of the practitioners it purports to serve. Thus, future research in the area of expatriate selection and training should have a strong practitioner focus, with the goal of solving problems of interest to those firms faced with the need to staff multinational facilities.

References

Adler, N. J. (1987). Pacific Basin managers: A *gaijin*, not a woman. *Human Resource Management, 26*(2), 169-192.

Adler, N. J., & Kiggundu, M. N. (1983). Awareness at the crossroad: Designing translator-based training programs. In D. Landis & R. W. Brislin (Eds.), *Handbook of intercultural training: Vol 2. Issues in training methodology* (pp. 124-150). Elmsford, NY: Pergamon.

Anfuso, D. (1994, November). HR unites the world of Coca-Cola. *Personnel Journal,* pp. 112-121.

Arvey, R. D., Bhagat, R. S., & Salas, E. (1991). Cross-cultural and cross-national issues in personnel and human resources management: Where do we go from here? *Personnel and Human Resources Management, 9,* 367-407.

Barnett, C. K. (1990, Spring). The Michigan global agenda: Research and teaching in the 1990s. *Human Resource Management,* pp. 5-26.

Barnum, C. (1994, April). U.S. training manager becomes expatriate. *HRMagazine,* pp. 82-84.

Bartlett, C. A., & Ghoshal, S. (1992, September-October). What is a global manager? *Harvard Business Review,* pp. 124-132.

Bhagat, R. S., & McQuaid, S. J. (1982). The role of subjective culture in organizations: A review and directions for future research. *Journal of Applied Psychology Monographs, 5,* 355-389.

Bird, A., & Dunbar, R. (1991, Spring). Getting the job done over there: Improving expatriate productivity. *National Productivity Review, 10*(2), 145-156.

Bird, A., & Mukuda, M. (1984, Winter). Expatriates in their own home: A new twist in the human resource management strategies of Japanese MNCs. *Human Resource Management,* pp. 437-453.

Black, J. S. (1992). Socializing American expatriate managers overseas: Tactics, tenure, and role innovation. *Group and Organization Management, 17*(2), 171-192.

Black, J. S., & Gregersen, H. B. (1991). The other half of the picture: Antecedents of spouse cross-cultural adjustment. *Journal of International Business Studies, 22*(3), 461-477.

Black, J. S., & Mendenhall, M. (1990). Cross-cultural training effectiveness: A review and theoretical framework for future research. *Academy of Management Review, 15*(1), 113-136.

Black, J. S., Mendenhall, M., & Oddou, G. (1991). Toward a comprehensive model of international adjustment: An integration of multiple theoretical perspectives. *Academy of Management Review, 16*(2), 291-317.

Briody, E. K., & Chrisman, J. B. (1991). Cultural adaptation on overseas assignments. *Human Organization, 50*(3), 264-282.

Campbell, J. P. (1990). The role of theory in industrial and organizational psychology. In M. D. Dunnette & L. M. Hough (Eds.), *Handbook of industrial and organizational psychology* (Vol. 1, pp. 39-73). Palo Alto, CA: Consulting Psychologists Press.

Carson, W. M. (1989). Prepare them to thrive in foreign countries. *Journal of Management Consulting, 5*(4), 30-32.

Caudron, S. (1991, December). Training ensures success overseas. *Personnel Journal, 70*(12), 27-30.

Caudron, S. (1992, July 6). Surviving cross-cultural shock. *Industry Week, 241*(13), 35-38.

Domsch, M., & Lichtenberger, B. (1991). Managing the global manager: Predeparture training and development for German expatriates in China and Brazil. *Journal of Management Development, 10*(7), 41-52.

Dowling, P. J., & Schuler, R. S. (1990). *International dimensions of human resource management.* Boston: PWS-Kent.

Drenth, P. J. D., & Groenendijik, B. (1984). Work and organizational psychology in cross-cultural perspective. In P. J. D. Drenth, H. Thierry, P. J. Willems, & C. J. De Wolff (Eds.), *Handbook of work and organizational psychology* (pp. 1197-1229). New York: John Wiley.

Earley, P. C. (1987). Intercultural training for managers: A comparison of documentary and interpersonal methods. *Academy of Management Journal, 30*(4), 685-698.

Erez, M. (1994). Toward a model of cross-cultural industrial and organizational psychology. In H. C. Triandis, M. D. Dunnette, & L. M. Hough (Eds.), *Handbook of industrial and organizational psychology* (Vol. 4, pp. 559-608). Palo Alto, CA: Consulting Psychologists Press.

Ettorre, B. (1993, April). A brave new world: Managing international careers. *Management Review,* pp. 10-15.

Feldman, D. C., & Tompson, H. B. (1993). Expatriation, repatriation, and domestic geographical relocation: An empirical investigation of adjustment to new job assignments. *Journal of International Business Studies, 24*(3), 507-529.

Fiedler, F. E., Mitchell, T., & Triandis, H. C. (1971). The culture assimilator: An approach to cross-cultural training. *Journal of Applied Psychology, 55,* 95-102.

Goldstein, I. L. (1974). *Training in organizations: Needs assessment, development, and evaluation* (2nd ed.). Monterey, CA: Brooks/Cole.

Goldstein, I. L. (1989). Critical training issues: Past, present, and future. In I. L. Goldstein & Associates (Eds.), *Training and development in organizations* (pp. 1-22). San Francisco: Jossey-Bass.

Goldstein, I. L., & Gessner, M. J. (1988). Training and development in work organizations. *International Review of Industrial and Organizational Psychology,* pp. 43-72.

Gowing, M. K., & Armitage, M. A. (1993, October). *Federal government initiatives for managing cultural diversity.* Speech presented at Diversity: Managing for Strategic Advantage, Skills for a Global Market Workshop presented at Fogelman Executive Center, Fogelman College of Business and Economics, Memphis State University, Memphis, TN.

Gregersen, H. B. (1992). Commitments to a parent company and a local work unit during repatriation. *Personnel Psychology, 45,* 29-54.

Gregersen, H. B., & Black, J. S. (1992). Antecedents to commitment to a parent company and a foreign operation. *Academy of Management Journal, 35*(1), 65-90.

Guzzo, R. A., Noonan, K. A., & Elron, E. (1994). Expatriate managers and the psychological contract. *Journal of Applied Psychology, 79*(4), 617-626.

Hackman, J. R., & Oldham, G. R. (1980). *Work redesign.* Reading, MA: Addison-Wesley.

Hamill, J. (1989). Expatriate policies in British multinationals. *Journal of General Management, 14*(4), 18-33.

Harris, H. (1993). Women in international management: Opportunity or threat? *Women in Management Review, 8*(5), 9-14.

Harrison, J. K. (1992). Individual and combined effects of behavior modeling and the cultural assimilator in cross-cultural management training. *Journal of Applied Psychology, 77*(6), 952-962.

Hayden, S. (1990, August). Our foreign legions are faltering. *Personnel,* pp. 40-44.

Hesketh, B., & Bochner, S. (1994), Technological change in a multicultural context: Implications for training and career planning. In H. C. Triandis, M. D. Dunnette, & L. M. Hough (Eds.), *Handbook of industrial and organizational psychology* (Vol. 4, pp. 191-240). Palo Alto, CA: Consulting Psychologists Press.

Hogan, G. W., & Goodson, J. R. (1990, January). The key to expatriate success. *Training and Development Journal, 44*(1), 50-52.

Kedia, B. L., & Bhagat, R. S. (1988). Cultural constraints on transfer of technology across nations: Implications for research in international and comparative management. *Academy of Management Review, 13*(4), 559-571.

Kitsuse, A. (1992, September). At home abroad. *Across the Board,* pp. 34-38.

Kopp, R. (1994). International human resource policies and practices in Japanese, European, and United States multinationals. *Human Resource Management, 33*(4), 581-599.

Laabs, J. J. (1993, August). How Gillette grooms global talent. *Personnel Journal,* pp. 65-76.

Leonard, B. (1994, April). "Guardian angels" help overseas employees. *HRMagazine,* pp. 59-60.

Lissy, W. E. (1993, January/February). International issues. *Compensation & Benefits Review,* p. 17.

de Lopez, R. S. (1992, May). Moving to Mexico: New job location also means a new home. *Business Mexico,* pp. 46-47.

McGarvey, R., & Smith, S. (1994, January). Speaking in tongues. *Training,* pp. 113-116.

Mendenhall, M., & Oddou, G. R. (1985). The dimensions of expatriate acculturation: A review. *Academy of Management Review, 10*(1), 39-48.

Mendenhall, M., & Oddou, G. R. (1991). *Readings and cases in international human resource management.* Boston: PWS-Kent.

Naumann, E. (1993). Organizational predictors of expatriate job satisfaction. *Journal of International Business Studies, 24*(1), 61-80.

Patterson, T. D. (1990). The global manager. *World, 24*(2), 10-17.

Ricks, D. A. (1993). *Blunders in international business.* Cambridge, MA: Blackwell.

Ronen, S. (1989). Training the international assignee. In I. L. Goldstein & Associates (Eds.), *Training and development in organizations* (pp. 417-454). San Francisco: Jossey-Bass.

Scullion, H. (1991, November). Why companies prefer to use expatriates. *Personnel Management,* pp. 32-35.

Solomon, C. M. (1994, April). Success abroad depends on more than job skills. *Personnel Journal,* pp. 51-60.

Taking the cultural blinkers off. (1991, December). *Business Korea,* pp. 44-45.

Thomas, D. C., & Ravlin, E. C. (1995). Responses of employees to cultural adaptation by a foreign manager. *Journal of Applied Psychology, 80*(1), 133-146.

Triandis, H. C. (1972). *The analysis of subjective culture.* New York: John Wiley.

Triandis, H. C. (1977). Theoretical framework for evaluation of cross-cultural training effectiveness. *International Journal of Intercultural Relations, 1,* 19-46.

Triandis, H. C. (1994). *Culture and social behavior.* New York: McGraw-Hill.

Triandis, H. C., Brislin, R., & Hui, C. H. (1988). Cross-cultural training across the individualism-collectivism divide. *International Journal of Intercultural Relations, 12,* 269-289.

Tung, R. L. (1987). Expatriate assignments: Enhancing success and minimizing failure. *Academy of Management Executive, 1*(2), 117-126.

U.S. engineers will work in Japan. (1993, June). *Quality,* pp. 11-13.

Van Pelt, P., & Wolniansky, N. (1990, July). The high cost of expatriation. *Management Review, 79*(7), 40-41.

Wexley, K. N., & Latham, G. P. (1981). *Developing and training human resources in organizations.* Glenview, IL: Scott, Foresman.

13

The Foreign
Teaching Assistant as Expatriate Manager

MARK E. MENDENHALL

THE number of foreign graduate students in American graduate programs is rapidly increasing (Heller, 1986); for example, fewer American students are entering the fields of science, mathematics, and engineering, and foreign student enrollments are making up for that deficit (Lee, 1991). The field of engineering provides a cogent example of this trend. Khafagi (1990) observed that, in 1980, 40,772 foreign students were enrolled in accredited engineering programs at U.S. universities; by 1989, the number of foreign students in these programs had increased to 50,292; and in 1987, 55% of the doctoral degrees awarded in engineering schools went to foreign students.

This trend does not seem to be abating. The governmental policy of the People's Republic of China, India, Japan, Singapore, South Korea, and Taiwan is to rely on the United States and other countries for the training of their citizens at the graduate levels in the fields of science and engineering (Wolff, 1993). These nations simply cannot handle the internal student market for high-quality graduate programs in these fields.

By all accounts, this trend is on the increase, not only in engineering but also in other disciplines, such as business administration (Roth & Hester, 1990). The University of Minnesota is a good example of this trend. There, 25% of the TAs consist of international graduate students, and in engineering and the sciences at Minnesota, over half of the TAs are international graduate students (Gokcora, 1989). It is logical to assume that foreign teaching assistants (TAs) might encounter some difficulty in teaching American students because of differences in socialization surrounding teaching norms across cultures. The research literature bears out this assumption.

Rao has noted, "There is a slow but increasing body of research indicating the hardened lack of receptivity to foreign TAs by U.S. students" (1993, p. 4). This lack of receptivity has been termed the *Oh No! syndrome (ONS)*, referring to "a first impression by homogeneous students to a perception that their teacher is very unlike themselves" (Rao, 1993, p. 4). Numerous studies have investigated the problems foreign students encounter in American classrooms as they try to teach effectively in those classrooms; unfortunately, it is beyond the scope of this chapter to review the extant literature in detail (e.g., see Bailey, 1982; Bresnahan & Kim, 1991; Brown, 1988; Gokcora, 1989; Hinofitis & Bailey, 1980; Keye, 1980; Orth, 1982; Rao, 1993; Rojas-Gomez & Pearson, 1990; Rubin & Smith, 1990; Shahenayati, 1987; Wol-Young, 1989).

The conflicts that can pour out of the interaction of American students with foreign TAs can spill over the classroom and ripple beyond the university to state legislatures. Both the Ohio and Michigan Legislatures have attempted to take up legislation to hold universities accountable in ensuring that college instructors be verbally understandable to their students.

Whether contention is limited to the classroom, the department chair or dean's office, university grievance committees, or the state legislature, the issue of assisting foreign TAs in their teaching skills must be addressed by university administrations throughout the United States.

Seeing Foreign Teaching Assistants Through New Lenses

Traditionally, foreign graduate TAs have often been viewed as "students who 'help out' faculty." Their roles are often viewed as subordinate to those of the faculty, as somehow "less critical" to the health of the department and the university. I would like to shift that perspective for a moment and, by doing so, see whether new insights can be gained into how best to deal with the "foreign TA problem."

My aim in this chapter is to view foreign graduate TAs as "expatriate managers" and, by so doing, to create perhaps some new ways of understanding their role more comprehensively. Viewing foreign graduate TAs as managers might provide added insights into how better to manage, train, and motivate them.

I do not suggest or propose specific training methodologies or programs for foreign TAs; this has already been done by a number of

scholars (e.g., see Constantinides, 1988; Dege, 1981; Mestenhauser, 1981; Sadow & Maxwell, 1982; Sarkisian, 1986; Zukowski-Faust, 1984). Rather, I seek to extrapolate principles, issues, and themes from the theoretical literature on expatriate managerial adjustment/training to the challenge of preparing foreign graduate students to be effective TAs.

I hope a discussion of these issues will serve primarily two purposes: (a) to enhance the existing design of training programs for foreign graduate TAs and (b) to serve as a reference or guide against which existing TA training programs for foreign students can be measured in terms of their validity and efficacy potential. This latter purpose is especially important if administrators are interested in selecting existing programs for implementation, rather than in custom designing their own training programs.

The Foreign Teaching Assistant as an Expatriate Manager

During the past 15 years, a significant amount of research has investigated the skills and conditions necessary for expatriate managers to adjust to and perform well in the host cultures in which they have been assigned to work. There are significant parallels between foreign TAs and expatriate managers. Both have tasks to accomplish. To accomplish those tasks, both must communicate well enough—despite language deficiencies—to work with host nationals to complete those tasks. Both have their performance evaluated. Both are remunerated for their efforts. Both hold positions of authority over host nationals. Both must hold host nationals accountable for their performance at work. Both find themselves in situations in which they must advise and counsel host nationals. Both work in organizations in cultures that are different from their native cultures. Both must learn the ropes of their new organizations. Both must simultaneously adjust to the cultural norms outside their work organizations, as well as to those within their organizations. I find the similarities between foreign TAs and expatriate managers to be quite extensive; within each of those similarities mentioned above lay a host of specific issues, skills, and processes that must be mastered. Expecting expatriate managers and foreign TAs to "hit the ground running" in their new roles is naive and perhaps even unethical.

Dimensions of Expatriate Productivity and Adjustment

Black, Mendenhall, and Oddou (1991) summarized the foundational assumption on which most of the research in the field of expatriate adjustment is based:

> When an individual leaves a familiar setting and enters an unfamiliar one, old routines are upset thus creating psychological uncertainty. . . . [This triggers] a desire to reduce the uncertainty inherent in the new setting, especially regarding new behaviors that might be required or expected. . . . To the extent that various factors either increase or decrease uncertainty, they either inhibit or facilitate expatriate adjustment. (pp. 301-302).

An extension of this assumption is that expatriates who are able to decrease uncertainty in their lives overseas are better able to perform their tasks and are thus more effective employees than those who cannot reduce uncertainty in their lives while abroad.

Black et al. (1991) reviewed the dimensions that influence the triggering and reduction of uncertainty and linked them conceptually into a theoretical model of expatriate adjustment. The core dimensions of that model are reviewed, and a discussion of how each dimension likely influences foreign graduate TAs is conducted.

An illustration of the model is provided in Figure 13.1.

The model has two main stages. The first stage, anticipatory adjustment, involves the making of preliminary cognitive and emotional adjustments regarding the overseas experience before actually going overseas. "The basic premise is that if appropriate anticipatory adjustments are made, the actual adjustment in the new international setting will be easier and quicker" (Black et al., 1991, p. 305). People tend to do this naturally; unfortunately, they often make these adjustments on the basis of their own cultural experience, biases, and stereotypes and on misinformation about the host culture. Thus, anticipatory adjustment, when based on correct information, is highly useful; when it is founded on false information,

however, it actually impedes overseas adjustment.

I once took a group of American business students to Switzerland, where part of their overseas experience was to take courses from Swiss professors. My students assumed that norms of appropriate classroom and laboratory behavior did not differ around the world and that, if they did differ, they would not be that different between the United States and Switzerland. Their assumption turned out to be wrong.

They complained that the Swiss professors did not allow any discussion in the classroom and that they seemed annoyed whenever the American students asked them questions. The more egalitarian norms of the American classroom were replaced for them, almost overnight, with the more authoritarian norms of the Swiss classroom. Their anticipatory adjustments in this aspect of overseas life were inaccurate and thus counterproductive to their performance as students.

Dimensions that influence anticipatory adjustment, either positively or negatively, are the degree to which expectations concerning the job itself are accurate and the efficacy of the selection process. Pre-job training and previous experience working overseas create more accurate expectations of the foreign job experience; this, in turn, heightens efficacious anticipatory adjustment. Organizational factors also influence the expatriate's anticipatory adjustment. Black et al. (1991) stated,

> The closer the selected individual matches the needs of the firm, the easier the individual's adjustment. . . . [E]xpatriates who have been selected on the basis of a wide array of relevant criteria and from a pool of candidates will experience the easiest and quickest cross-cultural adjustment. (p. 307)

Without training or previous experience, foreign TAs will likely rely on their own experience regarding what constitutes normative behavior in the classroom (both for teachers and students) when they step into the classroom. Can a work situation that is more prone to failure exist than this one?

There is no doubt that training needs to occur long before the foreign TA steps into the classroom or the laboratory. The situational subtleties of communication, authority patterns,

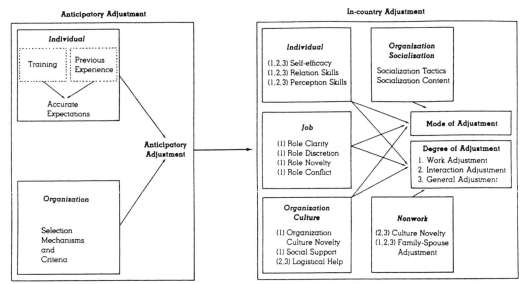

ᵃ Numbers in parentheses indicate the numbered facet(s) of adjustment to which the specific variable is expected to relate.

Figure 13.1. Framework of International Adjustment
SOURCE: Toward a comprehensive model of international adjustment: An integration of multiple theoretical perspectives. *Academy of Management Review, 16*(2), Black, Mendenhall, & Oddou, 1991, p. 303. Copyright © 1991, The Academy of Management, Briarcliff Manor, NY. Used with permission.

influence tactics, and impression management all need to be taught to the foreign TA. This training is necessary to modify inaccurate expectations about the nature of their job.

In-Country Adjustment Dimensions

Unfortunately, U.S. universities are not able to train foreign TAs before they come to the United States, and thus they come with a bundle of anticipatory adjustments about almost everything in the U.S. culture—including what they should do if they are asked to be a TA. What must they know to overcome their inaccurate anticipatory adjustments regarding the U.S. classroom?

In the in-country adjustment box in Figure 13.1, a variety of dimensions are illustrated, all of which have significant influences on degree of adjustment. Research on expatriate managers has discovered that the adjustment phenomenon is a multidimensional one; that is, the expatriate adjusts to work, interaction with host nationals, and the general conditions of the society (these are listed in Figure 13.1 as "work

adjustment," "interaction adjustment," and "general adjustment"). Notice that the subdimensions within the individual, job, organization culture, and nonwork boxes have numbers in parentheses next to them. These numbers correspond to the numbers given to the three dimensions of adjustment (1 = work adjustment, 2 = interaction adjustment, 3 = general adjustment). The numbers next to the subdimensions indicate the dimension of adjustment that the subdimension influences. For example, the subdimension of self-efficacy influences all three dimensions of adjustment. The subdimension of role clarity influences only the work adjustment dimension of adjustment.

The areas necessary to consider in designing training programs for foreign TAs are those that directly influence work adjustment. Only those areas are discussed in this chapter. Of course, it could be argued that work adjustment is not independent of the other two dimensions of adjustment. The extant literature is not developed enough to either refute this argument or confirm it. The research literature, however, does confirm that the antecedent variables in the model do influence the dimensions of adjustment; thus, the remaining focus of this chapter is to delineate more clearly these antecedent variables and to discuss their coverage in cross-cultural training program design.

The Individual Dimension

Many researchers have focused on finding the individual skills that are necessary to successfully adjust to a new culture. To discuss this literature is beyond the scope of this chapter (for reviews of this literature, see Black, Gregersen, & Mendenhall, 1992; Black et al. 1991; Mendenhall & Oddou, 1985). Black et al. (1991) collapsed these skills into three subdimensions: self-efficacy, relation, and perception.

Self-Efficacy. The ability to remain self-confident and trusting in one's ability to handle diverse situations in a foreign environment is an idea close to that of Bandura's notion of self-efficacy (Bandura, 1977). *Self-efficacy* has been defined as "the expectation that one can, by one's personal efforts, master situations and bring about desired outcomes" (Hall & Lindzey, 1978, p. 624). It has been observed that,

> Individuals with higher levels of self-efficacy tend to persist in exhibiting new behaviors that are being learned, even when those efforts are not successful, longer than do individuals with less self-efficacy. The more individuals attempt to exhibit new behaviors in the foreign situation, the more chances they have of receiving feedback, both positive and negative. These individuals can then use this feedback to reduce the uncertainty of what is expected of them and how they are doing, and they can correct their behavior to better correspond to expectations. (Black et al., 1991, pp. 307-308)

Enhancing the self-efficacy of TAs regarding their ability to successfully meet the challenges of their jobs and to continually grow in their abilities to do so should be an important part of any TA training program. Research shows that levels of self-efficacy can be increased via training (see Hall & Lindzey, 1978, pp. 612-625.).

Relation Skills. Research shows that expatriates who possess high levels of interpersonal skills before going abroad are more likely

to adjust successfully than expatriates who possess lower levels of interpersonal skills (Mendenhall & Oddou, 1985). Mendenhall and Wiley (1994) observed,

> Expatriates high in relational skills seem to be able to apply principles of human interaction to cross-cultural situations, adapting these principles to the unique norm structure of the host cultures they find themselves in. Some of these skills have to do with the strategic use of certain kinds of behaviors to create friendship bonds with host nationals. (p. 613)

American faculty struggle at times to communicate well with their students, both formally and informally; thus, it should surprise no one that foreign graduate students will need extensive training in this skill. Content will need to include norms of communication in the areas of kinesics, proxemics, the relationship of authority to communication patterns, slang, nonverbal communication, and numerous other issues that link to communication, such as sexual harassment.

Training content in programs for TAs should focus not only on teaching the communication norms of the United States but also on building up TAs' confidence in practicing those norms and feeling good about learning via experimentation.

Perception Skills. It is clear from the research literature that people from different cultures often misunderstand each other because of learned perceptual differences (for reviews, see Oddou & Mendenhall, 1984; Stening, 1979). One key to adjustment overseas is the ability to enlarge one's perceptual framework to incorporate cognitive schemata that are common to most host nationals' perceptual frameworks (for a review, see Mendenhall & Oddou, 1985). Thus, any training program designed for foreign TAs must also include instruction on how to develop a flexible, internal perceptual system; a delineation of "perceptual norms" common to American university students; strategies of how to learn about these perceptual norms throughout their assignment; and a review of how human cognitive systems function. Without this background knowledge, foreign TAs might tend to process the behaviors of their students through their own perceptual filters (which might not fit their current situation at all) and to choose counterproductive behaviors.

The Job Dimension

Subdimensions associated with the nature of a foreign TA's actual job also influences the degree to which he or she may be successful in carrying out the tasks associated with that job. These influences pertain to the job's role clarity, role discretion, role conflict, and role novelty.

Role Clarity. This concept refers to,

the extent to which what is expected of the individual is clear and unambiguous. Obviously, it is hard to adjust to something that is unclear or ambiguous, and research has found this to be true for both American and Japanese [expatriate] managers. (Black et al., 1992, p. 127)

Foreign TAs must have a fairly clear sense about their role—what is expected of them from faculty and students in terms of appropriate role behavior as a TA. Without this clarity, it will be virtually impossible for the foreign TA to accomplish the task.

Role Discretion. This concept is,

the amount of freedom individuals have in their jobs. . . . [It] involves flexibility in determining what work to do, when and how to do it, and whom to involve. Having greater role discretion enables people to configure their work so that they can use past successful behaviors and approaches more easily. Researchers have found positive impacts of role discretion on work adjustment for both American and Japanese [expatriate] managers." (Black et al., 1992, p. 126)

Once trained in the requisite skills regarding their job, foreign TAs have to be given enough flexibility to experiment with their newfound skills. Forcing foreign TAs to teach within a confined set of expectations and within a rigid class structure will not enhance their success.

Role Novelty. This refers to the degree to which the TA role is a new and unfamiliar one

to the foreign TA. If the person has never taught or assisted students before, then role novelty will be high. If he or she has had previous experience in working with American students, especially if that experience was successful, then role novelty will be low.

It is important to discuss this issue in the training program because it allows foreign TAs to build realistic expectations for themselves in their upcoming job experience. If they know they are walking into a situation that is high in role novelty, they will understand that they will likely make some mistakes and that they will have a lot to learn. This is a very healthy attitude for them to have, one that will allow them to progress positively once in their actual assignment.

Role Conflict. This subdimension involves "the extent to which conflicting demands or expectations are placed on individuals at work" (Mendenhall & Wiley, 1994, p. 615) and can potentially be the cause of many problems for foreign TAs. If foreign TAs are told to run a class within very specific guidelines and are then reproofed for not being engaging enough in the classroom, role conflict exists and only exacerbates an already troubled situation.

Having a clear congruence between tasks associated with their job, faculty expectations, and reward systems will go a long way in creating a successful experience in the classroom for the foreign TA. Providing this information to them in a training program also has the healthy side effect of forcing faculty and administrators to evaluate the existing degree of congruence in these three areas to ensure that congruence indeed does exist.

The Organization Culture Dimension

In the organization culture dimension, the two subdimensions that relate to overseas work adjustment are organization culture novelty and social support. *Organization culture novelty* refers to the degree to which the culture of the university department is similar to work cultures the foreign TA has experienced in the past. Norms regarding how to deal with students who complain to department chairs, how exams should be conducted and what types of exams are acceptable, the acceptability of using films and other audiovisual materials in the classroom, how much reading should be assigned to students, and so on differ across departments and across universities. The degree to which the culture is novel to the foreign TA will influence his or her success as a TA. Thus, special care should be taken in delineating the norms of the department to the foreign TA in the training program.

It has been theorized that social support from organizational members and other significant others enhances job adjustment overseas (Black et al., 1991). Living and working overseas is an experience of transformation, and although change can be exhilarating, it often comes with some growing pains. After a lecture goes somewhat badly, whom can the foreign TA turn to? It is critical that someone who can unconditionally accept the foreign TA's efforts and work from that stance to build the TA's skills be available. This is difficult to formalize via faculty assignments. Thus, in training, the TA must be told about this vital support need and that he or she will need to seek out such a person. Ideally, it would be a faculty member, but it could just as well be another graduate student, friend at a local church, and so on. The key is that the person must be able to empathize with the foreign TA's work experience, unconditionally accept his or her efforts, and be a positive influence in helping the TA learn from his or her errors.

The Nonwork Dimension

In the nonwork dimension, the subdimension related to work adjustment overseas is that of family-spouse adjustment. Research in the area of expatriate adjustment has shown that the degree to which the spouse and other family members adjust to their overseas situations influences the degree to which the expatriate manager can focus his or her energies on the job (Black, 1988; Black & Stephens, 1989; Tung, 1981).

Many foreign TAs are married and thus should be informed that if they desire to be successful as a TA, they will need to budget time to spend with their families and to pay attention to their spouses' adjustment to the American culture. It would not be a bad idea for the spouse to be included in the training program so that he or she can learn what his or her spouse is facing in their role as TAs. This in itself would bring a degree of unity to the couple and would allow

for more meaningful conversations between them as the TA discusses and shares the ups and downs of the semester with his or her spouse. Of course, TAs from some cultures might feel quite uncomfortable having their spouses with them during their training; thus, it is mandatory that, before the spouse is invited, the TA is first asked whether this would be acceptable.

Assessing Training Needs: A Decision Framework

Obviously, foreign TAs may be taught in a variety of ways about the content that relates to the above adjustment dimensions. How should one go about designing a new training program for foreign TAs? How can one select from the various "packaged" training programs that exist for foreign TAs? It is not a good idea to recreate the wheel, but how does one know which wheel of the many different sizes that exist out there is best for one's situation?

Black and Mendenhall (1989) established a theory-based framework for assessing the training needs of expatriate managers. Using social learning theory as their undergirding rationale, they reasoned that training needs to be differentiated by the level of "training rigor" required to successfully train the expatriate. *Rigor* is the degree of cognitive involvement necessary for trainees to expend in order to grasp the knowledge and skills they need to successfully perform their task. The authors note that,

> In general, the social learning theory literature and the cross-cultural training literature provide evidence to strongly suggest that the more rigorous the training the more effectively the trainee will be able to actually and appropriately execute the learned behaviors. The basic explanation for this relationship is that rigor . . . increases the level of attention and retention, thereby improving [skill] reproduction proficiency. (p. 523)

Contextual factors influence the level of rigor necessary for training success: culture novelty, degree of interaction with host nationals, and job novelty.

Culture Novelty. This is the degree to which the norms and values of the host culture significantly differ from those of the TA's host culture.

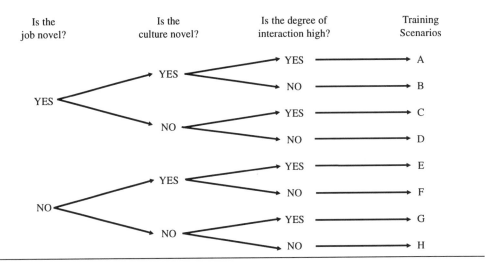

Figure 13.2 A Decision Framework for Assessing Training Needs

The larger the novelty, the more difficult the learning challenge because "the more difficult it will be for the individual to attend to and retain the various models of appropriate behavior" (p. 523).

Degree of Interaction With Host Nationals. This is "the degree of expected interaction between the individual and members of the host culture" (p. 534). This variable can be assessed by considering the frequency of interaction between TAs and students, the importance of the quality of that interaction, and the nature of that interaction; for example, is the common interaction one way versus two way in nature? Is it routine versus unique? Is it face-to-face versus written? Should it be formal versus informal? Will the interaction pattern be sustained versus infrequent?

Job Novelty. This refers to the fact that "the more novel the tasks of the new job in the new culture, the more assistance the individual will need through rigorous training to produce the desired and necessary behaviors to be effective in the new job" (Black & Mendenhall, 1989, p. 525). One way that administrators can evaluate the degree of novelty for training purposes is to consider the following questions in relation to the foreign TA's past job or general work experience:

Are performance standards the same?
Is the degree of personal involvement required in the work the same?
Are the types of tasks to be done similar?
Are the bureaucratic procedures that must be followed similar?
Are the resource limitations, legal restrictions, and technological limitations familiar?
Is the freedom to decide how work gets done the same?
Is the discretion about what work gets done similar?
Are the choices about what work gets delegated similar?

These questions (Black & Mendenhall, 1989, p. 526) can be used to create a job analysis of the TA's job tasks by the administrator who oversees TAs.

What Type of Training
Program Do You Need?

Figure 13.2 illustrates a simplified version of Black and Mendenhall's (1989) decision framework for selecting/designing cross-cultural training programs. As an administrator considers the issues inherent in each question in the decision tree, he or she progresses to an end-

A

    Level of Rigor   : High
        Duration   : 60–180 hours
        Approach   : lectures, factual briefings, books, culture assimilators, role plays, cases, simulations, field experiences.
        Training Content : Equal emphasis on job and culture. Stress job demands, constraints, and choices. Include topics like economic, political, historical, and religious elements of the culture.

B

    Level of Rigor   : Moderate
        Duration   : 2–60 hours
        Approach   : Lectures, films, books, cases, role plays, and simulations.
        Training Content : Equal emphasis on job and culture.

C

    Level of Rigor   : Moderate
        Duration   : 2–60 hours
        Approach   : Lectures, films, books, cases, role plays, and simulations.
        Training Content : Strong emphasis on job demands, constraints, and choices, less on culture.

D

    Level of Rigor   : Low to moderate
        Duration   : 20–40 hours
        Approach   : Lectures, factual briefings, cases
        Training Content : Strong emphasis on job but little emphasis on culture.

E

    Level of Rigor   : Moderate
        Duration   : 40–80 hours
        Approach   : Lectures, films, books, culture assimilators, cases, role plays, simulations
        Training Content : Little emphasis on job and most emphasis on culture, including economic, political, historical, and relikgious aspects.

F

    Level of Rigor   : Low to moderate
        Duration   : 20–60 hours
        Approach   : Lectures, films, books, cases
        Training Content : Little emphasis on job but more emphasis on culture.

G

    Level of Rigor   : Low to moderate
        Duration   : 30–60 hours
        Approach   : Lectures, films, books, cases, role plays
        Training Content : Little emphasis on job but more emphasis on culture.

H

    Level of Rigor   : Low
        Duration   : 4–8 hours
        Approach   : Lectures, films, books
        Training Content : Little emphasis on either job or culture.

Figure 13.3. Training Scenarios From Figure 13.2

point labeled with a letter. Each letter represents a "training scenario." The training scenarios are delineated in Figure 13.3.

The requisite features for each training scenario are discussed in terms of the level of rigor required, amount of time the program likely will require, training approaches that should be used, and type of content that should be covered.

Depending on the context of the situation the administrator faces, the training program design may need to differ; thus, the "one package takes care of all" approach to developing training does not apply in cross-cultural training. For example, foreign TAs from England, Australia, or New Zealand may require a training program different from that of foreign TAs from Bangladesh, Taiwan, or Nigeria. To suppose differently is to naively believe in something that is not true—namely, that all foreign TAs come to the United States with the same cultural socialization regarding education, teaching, and communication and with the same levels of experience in teaching, lecturing, and counseling.

Training Content

Once the level of rigor for the TA training program has been decided, the next question becomes, What issues need to be addressed, in terms of content, when designing cross-cultural training programs? The previous section, presented a review of a model that subsumes the skills and environmental influences necessary for expatriate productivity. This is the content that should be taught in what the framework refers to as "job content." In some training scenarios, the program should contain extensive training in the cultural system of U.S. society. For some foreign TAs, this may be a critical context they need in order to make sense of their students' behavior.

As administrators and faculty consider the issue of what content their programs should contain to meet the requisite level of rigor dictated by the above decision-tree model, they should consider with great care all of the dimensions discussed above. This chapter does not provide an easy solution to the acculturating and training of foreign TAs, but I do believe it reflects accurately the degree of analysis needed to facilitate teaching effectiveness among foreign TAs.

SUMMARY

It is beyond the scope of this chapter to suggest a specific, content-fleshed-out, comprehensive training program to the reader. I am wary of such attempts because each department will have unique training needs; I do not believe that "one size fits all" when it comes to cross-cultural training. I do think, however, it should be clear that to provide the kind of training that foreign TAs truly need should not be taken on in a cavalier fashion and should not be done quickly and without much forethought. In this sense, universities are really not much different, it seems to me, from corporations. Most corporations do not invest time and money in training their expatriate managers; indeed, it is more common for expatriate managers to receive virtually no training at all. Yet, is this not irrational? Consider the following:

The military trains its soldiers before sending them into battle, churches educate and train their missionaries before sending them out to proselytize, and governments train secret agents before they go under "deep" cover, but U.S. firms send employees overseas cold. Such a "sink-or-swim" approach would seem irresponsible and unreasonable to the military, clergy, or government; why then does it seem logical to the industrial [academic] sector? . . . Living and working overseas involves adjustments and stress of a high magnitude. Placing individuals in such conditions without giving them the tools to manage these conditions seems not only economically costly to the firm, and personally costly to the individuals, but simply wrong. (Black & Mendenhall, 1991, p. 201).

I believe that viewing foreign TAs as if they were expatriate managers is a useful way to enlarge one's sense of what training needs they require in order to perform their jobs more productively. One should not fall into the same ethical trap as companies and assume that the "best and the brightest" will be able to figure out on their own how to best do their job; working in a new culture is difficult and requires specific skills, many of which are not required in the same richness domestically. The sooner people realize this, the better it will be for foreign TAs.

Postscript

I am tempted to stop here and not bring up the following issue. It would be difficult enough for many administrators to embrace what I have written about so far, let alone deal with the issue of reentry training, but I think it is an issue that needs to be considered by university administrators.

What happens when a foreign graduate student successfully adapts to U.S. university and cultural life, graduates, and then returns to his or her home culture? The research literature is clear: Another adjustment, usually quite a traumatic one, will occur.

Most companies do not offer their expatriate managers any prereturn training because they assume that one should not need any training to return to one's home culture—after all, individuals should already understand it because they were socialized in it. Unfortunately, empirical research provides a counterintuitive reality. The process, simplified, goes something like this:

> While the [foreign TA] is away, the home culture has not remained frozen . . . [V]alues, fads, laws, norms, music, sports, cuisine, and other basic aspects of life undergo change. . . . In the meantime the [foreign TA] has been busy learning a new culture, and if the [foreign TA] adjusted well, has learned to value certain aspects of this new culture. When it comes time to return home, the [foreign TA] develops expectations about what it

will be like living and working back home, relating with old friends and family, and enjoying aspects of the home culture enjoyed before the overseas assignment. Upon return the [foreign TA] realizes the following: the home country is not the same country as when the expatriate left. The country has changed. . . . Old friends and relatives are not the same. They have undergone a variety of life changes and they no longer are the same people that the expatriate has frozen in his/her memory. . . . Coming home to a place that is supposed to be familiar, but is not, is stressful. (Mendenhall, Punnett, & Ricks, 1995, p. 491)

Issues that "repatriates" often face on return include declines in quality of life, standard of living, social status, and housing; life changes in family members; intolerance for aspects of the home culture that seem inferior to those of the host culture; disorientation of identity; and being seen by fellow citizens as somehow different because of their overseas experience (Black et al., 1992).

It can be argued that it is not the university's responsibility to offer reentry preparation training to foreign graduate students on their graduation. It is highly unlikely, however, that they will receive it anywhere else, and research shows that they do need it. My suggestion is that offering such training is perhaps not the most expedient thing to do but that it is the right thing to do for foreign graduates of U.S. institutions. When an institution goes beyond its raison d'etre and creates programs that uplift and edify its members, it carves a reputation that, in turn, feeds the institution in the future in many ways and means. Expending the extra effort for both entry and reentry training for foreign graduate students benefits all of the university's stakeholders and the university itself.

References

Bailey, J. M. (1982). Teaching a second language: The communicative competence of non-native speaking teaching assistants. *Dissertation Abstracts International, 43,* 10A. (University Microfilms No. 83-06009)

Bandura, A. (1977). *Social learning theory.* Englewood Cliffs, NJ: Prentice-Hall.

Black, J. S. (1988). Work role transitions: A study of American expatriate managers in Japan. *Journal of International Business Studies, 19,* 277-294.

Black, J. S., Gregersen, H. B., & Mendenhall, M. (1992). Global assignments: Successfully expatriating and repatriating international managers. San Francisco: Jossey-Bass.

Black, J. S., & Mendenhall, M. (1989). A practical but theory-based framework for selecting cross-cultural training methods. *Human Resource Management, 28*(4), 511-539.

Black, J. S., Mendenhall, M., & Oddou, G. (1991). Toward a comprehensive model of international adjustment: An integration of multiple theoretical perspectives. *Academy of Management Review, 16*(2), 291-317.

Black, J. S., & Stephens, G. K. (1989). The influence of the spouse on American expatriate adjustment in overseas assignments. *Journal of Management, 15*, 529-544.

Bresnahan, M., & Kim, M. (1991, August). *American undergraduate receptivity to foreign teaching assistants: An issue of English proficiency?* Paper presented at the Fourth International Conference on Social Psychology and Language, Santa Barbara, CA.

Brown, K. (1988). Effects of perceived country of origin, education status, and native speakerness on American college students' attitudes. *Dissertation Abstracts International, 49*, 1710A-1711A. (University Microfilms No. 88-15268)

Constantinides, J. C. (Ed.). (1988). *Wyoming/NAFSA Institute on Foreign TA Training: Working papers* (Vol. 2). Washington, DC: National Association for Foreign Student Affairs.

Dege, D. B. (1981, May). *Format and evaluation of the cross-cultural component of a foreign teaching assistant training program.* Paper presented at the Annual Meeting of the International Communication Association, Minneapolis, MN.

Gokcora, D. (1989, November). *A descriptive study of communication and teaching strategies used by two types of international teaching assistants at the University of Minnesota and their cultural perceptions of teaching and teachers.* Paper presented at the National Conference on the Training and Employment of Teaching Assistants. Seattle, WA.

Hall, C. S., & Lindzey, G. (1978). *Theories of personality* (3rd ed.). New York: John Wiley.

Heller, S. (1986). Teaching assistants get increased training: Problems arise in foreign student programs. *Chronicle of Higher Education, 33*(9), 9, 12-13.

Hinofitis, F. B., & Bailey, K. M. (1980). American undergraduates' reactions to the communication skills of foreign teaching assistants. In J. C. Fisher, M. A. Clarke, & J. Schacter (Eds.), *On TESOL 80. Building bridges: Research and practice in teaching English as a second language* (pp. 120-136). Washington, DC: TESOL.

Keye, Z. A. (1980). An exploratory study of students' written responses to foreign teaching assistant presentations. *Dissertation Abstracts International, 41*, 11A. (University Microfilms No. 76-08642)

Khafagi, B. (1990). Influence of international students on the U.S. educational system and professional practice. *Civil Engineering, 60*(11), 67-69.

Lee, S. (1991, May 27). Train 'em here, Keep 'em here. *Forbes*, pp. 110-116.

Mendenhall, M., & Oddou, G. (1985). The dimensions of expatriate acculturation: A review. *Academy of Management Review, 10*(1), 39-47.

Mendenhall, M., Punnett, B. J., & Ricks, D. (1995). *Global management.* Cambridge, MA: Blackwell.

Mendenhall, M., & Wiley, C. (1994). Strangers in a strange land: The relationship between expatriate adjustment and impression management. *American Behavioral Scientist, 37*(5), 605-620.

Mestenhauser, J. (1981). Foreign students as teachers: Lessons from the Program in Learning with Foreign Students. In G. Althen et al. (Eds.), *Learning across cultures: Intercultural communication and international educational exchange* (pp. 143-149). Washington, DC: National Association for Foreign Student Affairs.

Oddou, G., & Mendenhall, M. (1984). Person perception in cross-cultural settings: A review of cross-cultural and related literature. *International Journal of Intercultural Relations, 8*, 77-96.

Orth, J. L. (1982). University undergraduate evaluational reactions to the speech of foreign teaching assistants. *Dissertation Abstracts International, 43*, 12A. (University Microfilms No. 83-09183)

Rao, N. (1993, November). *The Oh No! syndrome: Understanding the negative reactions of undergraduates toward foreign teaching assistants.* Paper presented at the 79th Annual Meeting of the Speech Communication Association, Miami Beach, FL.

Rojas-Gomez, C. F., & Pearson, J. (1990). Students' perceptions of the credibility and homophily of native and non-native English speaking teaching assistants. *Communication Research Reports, 7*(1), 58-62.

Roth, E. F., & Hester, T. (1990). Globalization 101. *World, 24*(2), 24-25.

Rubin, D. L., & Smith, K. A. (1990). Effects of accent, ethnicity, and lecture topic on undergraduates' perceptions of nonnative English-speaking teaching assistants. *International Journal of Intercultural Relations, 14,* 337-353.

Sadow, S. A., & Maxwell, M. A. (1982, May). *The foreign teaching assistant and the culture of the American university.* Paper presented at the 16th Annual Convention of Teachers of English to Speakers of Other Languages, Honolulu, HI.

Sarkisian, E. (1986). Learning to teach in an American classroom: Narrowing the culture and communication gap for foreign teaching assistants. In M. Svinicki (Ed.), *To improve the academy: Resources for student, faculty, and institutional development* (pp. 120-131). Greenvale, CT: New Forums.

Shahenayati, S. (1987). A comparison of native and non-native English-speaking teaching assistants. *Dissertation Abstracts International,* 48, 1436A. (University Microfilms No. 87-13979)

Stening, B. W. (1979). Problems of cross-cultural contact: A literature review. *International Journal of Intercultural Relations, 3,* 269-313.

Tung, R. (1981). Selecting and training of personnel for overseas assignments. *Columbia Journal of World Business, 16*(2), 68-78.

Wolff, M. F. (1993). Asian graduate students still flocking to U.S. *Research-Technology Management, 36*(6), 5-6.

Wol-Young, S. (1989). *A profile of communication skills of foreign teaching assistants in a major Midwestern university.* Unpublished doctoral dissertation, University of Cincinnati.

Zukowski-Faust, J. (1984). Problems and strategies: An extended training program for foreign teaching assistants. In K. M. Bailey, F. Pialorsi, & J. Zukowski-Faust (Eds.), *Teaching assistants in U.S. universities* (pp. 76-86). Washington, DC: National Association for Foreign Student Affairs.

14

The Use of Equal Opportunity
Climate in Intercultural Training

DAN LANDIS

MICKEY R. DANSBY

RICK S. TALLARIGO

THIS chapter covers three domains relating to the general topic of equal opportunity (or diversity) climate (EOC) in organizations. The model is the large organization with a well-defined and understood bureaucratic structure. This model reflects the facts that the study of EOC grew out of concerns within the United States military and that reliable and valid measurement requires a certain minimum of respondents in each unit; hence, a large organization.

In the sections that follow, we first give an overview of the climate construct (or metaphor) as a perceptual measure and place the study of EOC within that context. Second, we describe

a particular approach to the assessment of EOC, the Equal Opportunity Climate Survey (EOCS) and its various incarnations. Finally, we describe how the EOCS is used in changing an organization to one that values and supports differences that contribute to the unit's objectives.

Background

Organizational science is moving at a quickening pace to address the imperatives of workforce diversity. The combined effects of public events (e.g., Tailhook incident, Thomas-Hill hearings [e.g., Mayer & Abramson, 1994],

AUTHORS' NOTE: This chapter was prepared when the first author was on sabbatical at the Directorate of Research, Defense Equal Opportunity Management Institute, Patrick Air Force Base, FL. The opinions in this chapter are those of the authors and do not necessarily represent those of the U.S. government, the Department of Defense, or their agencies.

charges of sexual harassment against public figures) and public law (e.g., Civil Rights Act of 1991, Americans with Disabilities Act of 1990) have spurred increased recognition of the importance of understanding and managing organizational climates. As with total quality programs, diversity programs affect multiple areas of the organization: recruiting and selection, promotions, compensation, and strategic planning. What tools are available for studying organizational climates in organizations? What relevance is there for understanding workforce diversity from the standpoint of perceptual assessments of the organizational social climate? In this section, we describe generally the role of perceptual measures in organizational development. We argue specifically that perceptual climate measures have an important role in managing workforce diversity. For the purposes of this discussion, we assumed that perceptions of organizational climate include social perceptions (inferences drawn about others on the basis of expressive characteristics; Bruner & Tagiuri, 1954), as well as perceptions of organizational characteristics.

Origins of Perceptual Measures of the Work Environment

The force-field theory of Kurt Lewin (1948) is often cited as the origin of the measurement of organizational climate. Lewin considered organizational climate to be instrumental among the forces shaping individual values, motivation, and behavior. Before Lewin, however, were the Western Electric "Hawthorne" studies. Originally designed as industrial engineering studies of the effects of illumination and other manipulations of the work environment, the series of studies, begun in 1924, resulted in no less than a paradigmatic shift in how organizational behavior is viewed. No longer was a direct relationship presumed between environment and individual behavior. Rather, individual workers were postulated to react differently to identical environments as a result of attitudes, motives, and perceptions regarding coworkers, job, or organization (Sonnenfeld, 1982). Unable initially to make sense of the experimental data, the Hawthorne experimenters induced the importance of perceptions. As reported by Locke (1976), the Hawthorne researchers "discovered . . . that workers have

minds and that the appraisals they make of the work situation affect their reaction to it" (p. 1299).

In the 1930s, Lewin incorporated individual appraisals, or perceptions, into the formal study of social climates and dynamics in the small group. As a refugee from Nazism and as an experienced Gestaltist, he posited in the group environment those forces he experienced personally. He pioneered the study of leadership climate. More important for our purposes in this chapter, Lewin's ideas of social justice and equity were very much part of his formulations of the organizational climate (Lewin, 1948). Since then, the use of perceptual measures in organizational studies has been commonplace.

Use of Perceptual Measures in Organizational Studies

Aside from their use in assessing organizational climate, workers' perceptions serve as raw data for several important organizational processes. For example, job redesign is typically predicated on workers' perceptions of such job characteristics as skill variety, job autonomy, task identity, intrinsic feedback, and task significance (Hackman & Oldham, 1976). An assumption of the job characteristics model is that a worker responds to the job as he or she perceives it. The motivational value of a job is predictable from the job characteristics perceived by its incumbents—this, despite the arguments proposed by social information theorists that perceived job characteristics represent the results of a social influence process rather than the objective characteristics of a job (e.g., Salancik & Pfeffer, 1978). Another example of perceptual data in common use is ratings of leadership and supervisory skills. Feedback to supervisors from subordinates, peers, and superiors (so-called 360-degree feedback systems; Bracken, 1994) has been found to be highly effective for developmental purposes. Other uses of perceptual data include job evaluation (Schwab & Wichern, 1983), job analysis (McCormick, Jeanneret, & Mecham, 1969), employee selection using assessment centers (Finkle, 1976), performance appraisal (Mohrman, Resnick-West, & Lawler, 1989), and assessments of organizational culture (discussed below). Perceptual measures have played and continue to play crucial roles in understanding and managing human processes endemic to organizations.

Evolution of the Climate Construct

In this section, we discuss the dynamic nature of climate: how it has been conceptualized and its relation to other relevant perceptual measures.

Subjective Versus Objective Measurement

Researchers have long sought to define organizational climate, and definitions have varied over the years. For many researchers, *organizational climate* was defined as directly observable measures of organizational structural, technological, and systemic characteristics. Others held to the perceptual, subjectivist view. The varying definitions of climate reflect this dual nature. Forehand and Gilmer (1964) defined climate as consisting of characteristics that (a) distinguish the organization from other organizations, (b) are relatively enduring over time, and (c) influence the behavior of people in the organization. Litwin and Stringer (1968) defined climate as objective characteristics of organizations describing the "personality" of the organization. Rentsch (1990) described the evolution of the climate construct from the 1960s to the 1990s. In the 1960s, the definition emphasized enduring, objective organizational characteristics. In the 1970s, the focus shifted to perceptions, rather than directly observable organizational characteristics. The 1980s saw an interest in the meaning and sense making that individuals perceive in their environments, implicating the cultural aspects of organizations. Finally, the 1990s returned to an appreciation of the objective value of group perceptions while acknowledging the potential for variability of perceptions within organizations.

Climate Content

Taxonomies of organizational climate have reflected both the subjective/objective distinc-

tion and a consistent theme of equity in the social environment. For example, dimensions identified by Litwin and Stringer (1968) included structure, individual responsibility, rewards, risks and risk taking, warmth and support, and tolerance and conflict. Campbell, Dunnette, Lawler, and Weick (1970) described four major factors in their review of the literature: (a) individual autonomy, (b) degree of structure, (c) reward orientation, and (d) consideration, warmth, and support. More extensive listings of climate dimensions have also been used by researchers. Joyce and Slocum (1984), using factor analysis, reduced a 10-factor climate model to six factors: Rewards, Autonomy, Motivation to Achieve, Management Insensitivity, Closeness of Supervision, and Peer Relations (Warmth). The elements of climate range from objective to subjective in nature. Dimensions such as degree of structure may be more objectively scored; dimensions such as reward equity have a more subjective connotation. The latter, it should be noted, can also be measured objectively as the ratio of highest to lowest earnings (Evan, 1963).

Constructs Related to Climate

In each of the above models, warmth/tolerance and reward equity play consistent roles, and the construct of EOC evolved from this conceptual basis (Landis, Dansby, & Faley, 1993). As mentioned above, equity was a theme in the early formulations of climate by Lewin; equity has been an important dimension of workers' perceptions of their organizations; equity has been the focus of a theory in its own right (viz., Adams, 1963); and, more recently, equity has been the subject of renewed interest in the study of procedural and distributive forms of organizational justice (Greenberg, 1990). Along with the resurgence of organizational justice theory in the form of procedural concerns has been an adoption of the anthropological construct of culture into organizational studies. Organizational culture, as distinct from climate (though some do not recognize the distinction), is idiographic; organizational climate is nomothetic. Culture looks for values specific to an organization; climate looks for behaviors.[1] Culture is interpreted and induced through symbols and traditions; climate is taxonomic and is reflected in consensual perception. For whatever reason, recent trends appear to indicate that culture is receiving more research attention than climate. A likely cause is the natural maturation of the climate construct. It has been around for a relatively long time, and the major issues associated with its use have been fleshed out. Culture is relatively new in the organizational science literature, and standard measures have not been as clearly delineated.

The confluence, if there will be one, of organizational justice, climate, culture, and diversity would appear to present organizational scientists a rich vein of study for some time to come. To pursue these research objectives, however, a number of methodological issues should be addressed.

Methodological Issues

Two issues are discussed: (a) the appropriateness of aggregating perceptual scores within organizations and (b) the potential import of attitudinal responses for understanding perceptual issues.

Arguments over the "objectivity" of perceptual measures of organizational climate resulted in warnings concerning making inferences about organizational climate from aggregated perceptions. Merely averaging the perceptual responses of a group or an organization does not legitimate those perceptions as homogeneous descriptions of the organizational climate. As Jones and James (1979) pointed out, such measures may be more appropriately designated as "psychological climates." Only when statistical evidence exists for the homogeneity of group responses can the averaged data be taken as representing organizational climate. In preliminary studies of this problem at the Defense Equal Opportunity Management Institute (DEOMI) and using responses to the Military Equal Opportunity Climate Survey (MEOCS), the authors found significant race- and gender-related covariation with perceptions of EOC in addition to significant cross-organizational clustering. Such evidence suggests that organizations may have multiple climates while at the same time be differentiated within a global taxonomy of climate types.

Recognizing that organizations may subsume multiple perceived climates, many authors, in reporting results of organizational surveys, have used a summarized index of the disparity between demographic groups on perceptions of the organizational climate. The index is similar to the effect size associated with the mean difference between any two comparison groups (e.g., majority/minority, men/women). Dividing the mean difference by the standard deviation of the overall group yields the d statistic (Schmidt & Hunter, 1990). We provide a context for judging the intensity of the disparity by supplying, for comparison, the mean disparity based on all organizations surveyed. The disparity index then becomes a useful tool for assessing the potential for conflict among groups within the organization.

Another issue concerns the attitude-perception distinction. What is the relationship between them? Relatively sparse recent research is available on the functional relationships between these two types of responses using a single respondent population. In an exploration of this issue, Tallarigo (1994) found an inverse relationship between attitudes and perceptions regarding equal employment opportunity (EEO). Using a shortened Modern Racism Scale (McConohay, 1986) and perceived likelihood scales of the MEOCS, respondents endorsing more tolerant racial integration views tended to perceive greater likelihood of adverse racial incidents in the organizational environment; those whose views on racial integration were less tolerant perceived less likelihood of racist behaviors in the environment. How should attitudes and perceptions be used in organizational training? Do attitudes have diagnostic import? Are ethical or privacy issues at stake in assessing and changing attitudes regarding diversity in the workplace? These questions are in need of answers as trainers and other human resource practitioners address diversity management in organizations.

Asking organizational members what they see happening in their environment has been, and probably will continue to be, a primary source of information for organizational development. Moreover, the authors would argue that perceptions ought to play such a role. It is a truism that people respond to the world, not necessarily as it is, but as they perceive it to be. Stated simply: Perceptions exist, influence

		Other Sources of Data	
		Observed	Not Observed
	Observed	Agreement	Disagreement
Perceptual Data			
	Not Observed	Disagreement	Agreement

Figure 14.1. Matrix for Assessing Agreement Between Types of Organizational Data

work behaviors, and can (and should) be measured. The "more objective" sources of data, however, must also be considered. Both are part of the perceived environment. What are the more objective measures? Commonly used data include records, incidence reports, and "expert" ratings provided by specially trained judges. Ultimately, of course, a subjective/objective dichotomy is largely a false dichotomy, and the goal becomes one of convergence between data sources of varying degrees of subjectivity and objectivity. The grid in Figure 14.1 may depict the problem more clearly.

When there is disagreement between perceptual and other sources of data, it becomes a matter of judgment as to which data source is more accurate.

Measuring organizational climates in organizations has historically and consistently included reward equity, and it is proposed that social/organizational climate is clearly relevant for the understanding of workforce diversity. Related studies of procedural justice, culture, attitude measurement, and alternative sources of information may also be part of the necessary patchwork in the study of workforce diversity.

Measurement of EOC:
Recent Findings

Working from a general desire to extend the climate construct to the diversity domain and in response to a proposal for organizational intervention and development by Dansby, Landis and his colleagues (Dansby & Landis, 1991; Landis, 1990; Landis et al., 1993; Landis & Fisher, 1987) developed the MEOCS. The

MEOCS was based on the following definition of equal opportunity climate: "The expectation by an employee that work-related behaviors directed by others toward the person will reflect merit and not one's racial/ethnic group, gender, national origin or membership in any other minority group" (Landis, 1990, p. 29).

The current version of the survey consists of 50 behaviors that require an estimate of occurrence over a fixed period of time; 27 attitude statements in Likert-scale format; measures of organizational commitment, job satisfaction, and perceived work-group effectiveness; and several demographic questions. The total time required of a respondent is approximately 40 minutes, although many complete it in significantly less time.[2]

Succeeding confirmatory factor analyses have consistently shown five reliable factors from the first 50 items: Sexual Harassment/Sex Discrimination Behaviors (SHB), Differential Command Behaviors (DCB), Positive Command Behaviors (PCB), Racist/Sexist Behaviors (RSB), and Reverse Discrimination Behaviors (RDB). The reliability indexes seem impervious to experience in that data from senior noncommissioned officers do not produce different levels from those computed from junior noncommissioned officers (Landis et al., 1993).

Construct validity of the MEOCS has also been analyzed and found to be satisfactory. Minorities and women consistently rate the EOC less favorable than do white men. Officers rate the EOC more favorable than do enlisted personnel. These results hold up across services. EOC was found to be less favorable in combat units than in service or service-support units (Tallarigo, 1992). A recent analysis found that

TABLE 14.1 Mean Scale Values for Perceived Frequency Subclass of the Military Equal Opportunity Climate Survey (MEOCS) by Minority/Majority Status, Gender, and Branch of Service

Population	Gender	Service	*SHB*	*DCB*	*PCB*	*RSB*	*RDB*	*N*
					Scales			
Minority								
	Female							
		USAF	3.60	3.85	3.59	3.88	4.01	1,002
		USA	3.56	3.72	3.37	3.70	3.89	9,266
		USN	3.51	3.81	3.48	3.55	4.04	4,138
		USMC	3.38	3.72	3.50	3.39	3.86	1,414
	Male							
		USAF	3.78	3.99	3.67	3.82	3.92	3,633
		USA	3.81	3.84	3.39	3.67	3.83	34,544
		USN	3.73	3.92	3.46	3.53	3.96	17,678
		USMC	3.70	3.90	3.56	3.49	3.91	11,129
Majority								
	Female							
		USAF	3.68	4.44	4.06	4.06	4.11	2,307
		USA	3.70	4.37	3.92	3.95	4.04	8,850
		USN	3.67	4.45	4.00	3.85	4.15	7,298
		USMC	3.47	4.39	3.98	3.60	4.10	1,640
	Male							
		USAF	4.04	4.53	4.06	4.10	3.94	12,050
		USA	4.05	4.41	3.83	3.92	3.91	58,827
		USN	4.00	4.48	3.93	3.83	4.03	35,242
		USMC	3.90	4.43	3.96	3.70	3.94	20,028

NOTE: SHB = Sexual Harassment/Discrimination Behaviors; DCB = Differential Command Behaviors; PCB = Positive Command Behaviors; RSB = Racist/Sexist Behaviors; RDB = Reverse Discrimination Behaviors.

the severity of nonjudicial punishments was also greater in combat units, as compared with support units. Hence, it would seem that the level of EOC is inversely related to discipline problems in a unit.

In June 1990, the MEOCS was released to the services for general use. The method of its use is described in a later section of this chapter. In the 5 years since its general availability, however, the MEOCS, which is administered only by request of an organizational head, has proved an extremely popular tool with commanders and every level in the services and even, in a modified form, for civilian employees in the Department of Defense (DoD). As of this writing (late 1995), close to 300,000 people in approximately 2,000 units have taken the MEOCS. The factor structure has been extremely stable, and the factor means have shown little deviation across time. Tables 14.1

and 14.2 present the factor means based on the latest database.

Additional Measures of EOC Using the MEOCS Model

University Equal Opportunity Climate Survey (UEOCS)

A version focused on the university setting was constructed by Landis and his colleagues.[3] The UEOCS-1 is a 141-item preliminary version. This version includes 69 perceptual estimation items, 10 organizational commitment statements, 6 perceived academic effectiveness items, 35 attitude items, and 21 demographic items. The perceptual estimate and attitude items were designed to parallel, to whatever

TABLE 14.2 Means on Racial Attitude Scales by Minority/Majority Status, Gender, and Branch of Service

| Population | Gender | Service | Scales | | | |
			DM	SA	RD	N
Minority						
	Female					
		USAF	3.13	4.36	3.76	1,009
		USA	3.01	4.11	3.66	9,291
		USN	3.04	4.24	3.72	4,160
		USMC	2.98	3.96	3.47	1,415
	Male					
		USAF	3.38	4.36	3.69	3,651
		USA	3.27	4.05	3.55	34,810
		USN	3.27	4.13	3.59	17,781
		USMC	3.26	4.13	3.54	11,188
Majority						
	Female					
		USAF	3.83	4.58	3.61	2,313
		USA	3.76	4.47	3.51	8,881
		USN	3.80	4.54	3.50	7,323
		USMC	3.63	3.40	3.38	1,639
	Male					
		USAF	4.24	4.41	3.30	12,073
		USA	4.11	4.24	3.25	59,462
		USN	4.18	4.33	3.17	35,432
		USMC	4.10	4.20	3.08	20,118

NOTE: DM = Discrimination Against Minorities; SA = Separatism; RD = Reverse Discrimination

extent possible, the comparable items in the MEOCS. This version was administered to a convenience sample of 611 undergraduates at the University of Mississippi, Oxford campus: 462 students were white, 63 were black, 26 were Asian, and the remainder were from smaller ethnic groups; 376 students were female, the remainder were male. The number of black students is proportionately slightly more than their fraction in the total student body (11.09% vs. 8.96%). The same was true of the female part of the sample.

Structure of the UEOCS

Exploratory factor analyses of the perceptual and attitude items reveal that each is fairly well accounted for by three factors in each set. For the perceptual estimations, the eigenvalues for the first six factors were (percentage of variance is in parenthesis): 11.95 (37.81%), 5.76 (18.22%), 3.53 (11.17%), 1.72 (5.43%), 1.43

(4.53%), and 1.21 (3.82%). The break between the third and fourth root is quite clear. After varimax rotation, the first factor was found to be marked by 18 items that appeared to denote *offensive racist behaviors directed at minorities and women.* The second factor (14 items) involved *discriminatory behaviors directed at minorities by people in authority* (e.g., administrators, faculty, fraternity/sorority officers). Thirteen items marked the last factors, and all reflected *positive interracial behaviors.*

The attitude part of the UEOCS produced two factors with the following eigenvalues: 6.51 (52.77%) and 2.79 (22.70%). The first factor ($\alpha = .87$) after varimax rotation was marked by 17 items, all of which tapped *negative attitudes toward minorities, women, foreign students, and gays, together with school pride.* The second factor (7 items, $\alpha = .72$) dealt with a feeling that *discrimination against minorities and women exists on campus* and that *not enough effort is being expended by the administration in amelioration.*

Race/Sex Differences

The first perceptual factor (Racist/Sexist Behaviors Between Students) produced a significant effect for gender ($F = 5.17, p < .02$) but not for race. The overall mean (2.39), however, indicated that all groups agreed these acts were quite likely to occur. Strong race/sex differences occurred for the second perceptual factor (Discriminatory Acts by Those in Authority). All three terms (Race, Sex, and the Race × Sex Interaction) were significant ($F = 6.68, p < .01$; $F = 11.49, p < .0008$; $F = 5.93, p < 01$, respectively). Inspection of the means indicates that the major contributor to the interaction was a difference between black males (mean = 3.21) and black females (mean = 3.65). The white males and females were not significantly different from each other, nor were they different from the black females. In other words, black males saw these behaviors as significantly more likely than did the other groups. The third factor (Positive Behaviors) was seen as slightly (though significantly) more likely by females than by males.

Strong race differences occurred with regard to the attitude items. On the first factor (Negative Attitudes Toward Minorities), the effect of race was significant ($F = 154.13, p < .0001$), with whites agreeing with these items far more than blacks (means = 2.79, 3.85, respectively). A similar pattern occurred for the second factor (Lack of Progress on Integration), with blacks agreeing more than whites (means = 2.45, 3.14, respectively).

The picture that emerges is a campus with considerable racial tension. Both blacks and whites perceived many offensive racist events occurring, but whites did not associate much negative affect with those behaviors. Blacks blamed the campus leaders for the situation, both in terms of commission and omission. The gulf between the groups was as wide, if not wider, than for any other group we have assessed.

In general, the patterns described above for the university version fit rather well with those derived from the MEOCS. Some differences, if upheld by replication both at this particular college campus as well at other institutions, should give pause to university and college administrators. The mean scores on the first factor (the equivalent to the RSB factor from the MEOCS) are among the lowest we have seen so far.[4] The lack of racial differences on this factor may indicate that, in contrast with the military findings, white students agree that these behaviors occur but may not care or realize the implications of such events. The racial differences on the attitude items give some support to this interpretation.

Equal Employment Opportunity Climate (EEOC)

Tallarigo (1994) expanded the MEOCS scales to include items tapping sexist behavior, age discrimination, sexual harassment, religious discrimination, and discrimination against the disabled. He also added scales tapping organizational trust, belief in total quality management (TQM), cohesion, traditional and modern racism, and attitudes toward women. This new instrument of 132 items was field-tested on military and civilian respondents at four DoD sites.

Structure of the EEOC

Factor analysis of the total questionnaire produced four factors accounting for 52% of the total variance. Factor 1 consisted of the Perceived Incident items (we can call them an Incident Methodology factor). Factor 2 captured the Organizational Effectiveness Measures and captured 11% of the variance. Factor 3 was a Mixed Methodology factor and will need further research to determine the underlying traits. Factor 4 was clearly the EO/EEO Attitude Scales, consisting of Traditional and Modern Racism and Attitudes Toward Women.

Population Differences

A multivariate analysis of variance with the 28 EEOC scales as dependent variables and the military/civilian designation as the independent variables produced a number of highly significant differences. In all but two cases, the military respondents scored higher than civilians, the notable exceptions being Attitudes Toward Women and one measure of Discrimination Against the Disabled. These differences are in rough accord with other comparisons between the military and civilians (see the UEOC discussion, above).

Non-American Versions

Several colleagues located in non-American universities have expressed interest in developing indigenous versions of the UEOCS. The first such version, called UEOCS-I, was prepared for students in India(n) universities.[5] Although this version was prepared in English, the lingua franca of Indian higher education, several modifications were made to make the items relevant to the Indian situation. For racial groups, three caste classifications (forward/backward, scheduled castes/tribes, and other caste minorities) were used. Items then were transformed to deal with interactions among these three groups. Items dealing with sexual and romantic relationships were often rewritten to conform with behavioral norms as perceived by our informants. The final version of the UEOCS-I consisted of 54 perceptual estimate items, 10 organizational commitment, 6 perceived academic effectiveness, 22 caste attitude, and 18 demographic items.

The UEOCS-I was administered to 175 undergraduate students in two small colleges affiliated with the same larger university in the southern part of India during the summer of 1994. Approximately 35% of the sample were female, and 65% were male (a somewhat oversampling of males and undersampling of women). In terms of caste identification, 16% were forward caste, 65% were backward caste, and 21 were scheduled caste/tribe or otherwise unidentified. This compares with the college populations of about 50% to 60% backward caste, 18% to 20% forward caste, and the rest scheduled caste/tribe.

Structure of the UEOCS-I

Three significant perceptual estimation factors were extracted with the following eigenvalues (percentage of variance is in parentheses): 6.64 (33%), 2.88 (15%), and 2.47 (13%). A sharp drop occurred after the third factor. After varimax rotation, the first factor (15 items; $\alpha = .82$) was clearly marked by items involving *discrimination and harassment of scheduled caste/tribes and women*. The second factor (8 items; $\alpha = .58$) was marked by *positive integration actions*. The last factor (4 items) seemed to reflect reverse discrimination in which members of *scheduled castes/tribes receive prefer-*

ential treatment but had the lowest reliability of all dimensions ($\alpha = .35$).

Two significant factors were obtained from the racial attitude items with eigenvalues of 2.59 (41%) and 1.11 (18%). The first factor (5 items; $\alpha = .64$) seemed to reflect *discrimination against minorities* (comparable to the DM factor in the MEOCS); the second (5 items; $\alpha = .58$) was marked by items *approving of separating the castes* (roughly comparable to the SA factor in the MEOCS).

Caste Differences

Because of the smallness of the sample, it was necessary to combine cells into a forward/backward caste and an other classification. The overall means (combining across both groups) were as follows: Discriminatory Behaviors Against Minorities and Women (DB), 3.85; Positive Behaviors (PB), 2.63; Reverse Discrimination (RD), 3.03; Discrimination Attitudes (DA), 3.52; and Caste Separation (CS), 3.21. Only the DB factor produced a significant effect ($p < .02$), and that was for Caste (mean-forward/backward = 3.90; mean-other = 3.45). These results are in accord with the other surveys that find majority groups see fewer problematical behaviors than do minority group members.

We emphasize that the UEOCS-I is a preliminary instrument. Some refinement is necessary by working with Indian colleagues, and a larger and more representative sample would increase confidence in the results and enhance precision. The results we do have, however, suggest that the MEOCS model has some generality across settings and perhaps even cultures.[6]

Other Studies Using the MEOCS Database

Relationship of EOC to Organizational Commitment

Landis, Dansby, and Faley (1994) analyzed the data from approximately 80,000 servicepeople in the MEOCS database to explore the link between climate and the individual's commitment to a service career. Grouping the perceptual estimation factors into two second-order factors (Positive Behaviors and Negative

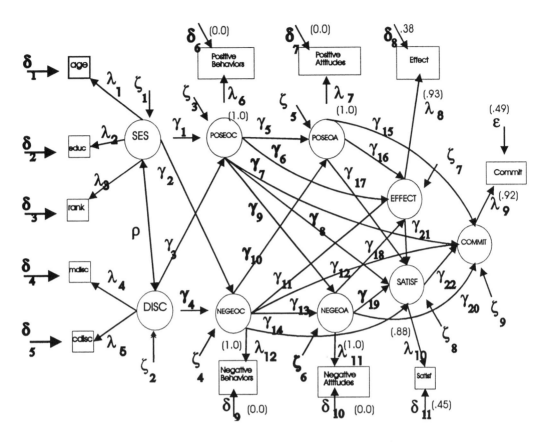

Figure 14.2. General Model
NOTE: Paths from SES and DISC to endogenous variables not shown.

Behaviors) and a similar collation for the attitude dimensions, the authors used latent variable analyses to address three hypotheses: (a) EOC (as defined by the Perceptual Estimation factors) is a significant part of the causal structure, (b) the positive second-order factors are more important than the negative factors, and (c) the structure for white males will be significantly different from similar constructions for other race/gender groups. The first and third hypotheses were strongly supported; little support was found for the second. The general model is shown in Figure 14.2; the components of that structure are given (in standard LISREL format) in Table 14.3.

Importance of EOC Variables

When the EOC variables were removed from the causal structure, the fit of the model signifi-

cantly deteriorated. The χ^2 difference was 22,770.16 (df = 12) and is significant (p < .00001). Other indices of fit showed similar differences (e.g., the root mean square residual [RMSR] went from .0348, which is acceptable [Bagozzi & Yi, 1988], to .0822, which is unacceptable; Hoelter's critical N [Hoelter, 1983] dropped from 386, which is considered good, to 144, which indicates a poor fit).

Similarity of Minority Race/ Gender Groups to White Males

The model produced an excellent fit for the white male subgroup. The fit index was .9797 (adjusted index = .9438, RMSR = .0393, and Hoelter's critical N = 320). These are all quite acceptable values. Of the race/gender subgroups, the only one that approached the white males in fit using the white male weights was

TABLE 14.3 Model Components

Name Component	From	To	Name Component	From	To
Error Terms (Manifest):			λ_{11}	NEGEOA	Negative Attitudes*
δ_1		Age	λ_{12}	NEGEOC	Negative Behaviors*
δ_2		Education	Structural Equations:		
δ_3		Rank	γ_1	SES	POSEOC
δ_4		Mdisc	γ_2	SES	NEGEOC
δ_5		Cdisc	γ_3	DISC	POSEOC
δ_6		Positive Behaviors*	γ_4	DISC	NEGEOC
δ_7		Positive Attitudes*	γ_5	POSEOC	POSEOA
δ_8		Effectiveness*	γ_6	POSEOC	EFFECTIVENESS
δ_9		Negative Behaviors*	γ_7	POSEOC	COMMITMENT
δ_{10}		Negative Attitudes*	γ_8	POSEOC	SATISFACTION
δ_{11}		Satisfaction*	γ_9	POSEOC	NEGEOA
ε		Commitment*	γ_{10}	POSEOC	POSEOA
			γ_{11}	NEGEOC	EFFECTIVENESS
Error Terms (Latent):			γ_{12}	NEGEOC	COMMITMENT
ξ_1		SES	γ_{13}	NEGEOC	NEGEOA
ξ_2		DISC	γ_{14}	NEGEOC	SATISFACTION
ξ_3		POSEOC	γ_{15}	POSEOA	COMMITMENT
ξ_4		NEGEOC	γ_{16}	POSEOA	EFFECTIVENESS
ξ_5		POSEOA	γ_{17}	POSEOA	SATISFACTION
ξ_6		NEGEOA	γ_{18}	NEGEOA	EFFECTIVENESS
ξ_7		EFFECTIVENESS	γ_{19}	NEGEOA	SATISFACTION
ξ_8		SATISFACTION	γ_{20}	NEGEOA	COMMITMENT
ξ_9		COMMITMENT	γ_{21}	EFFECTIVENESS	SATISFACTION
			γ_{22}	SATISFACTION	COMMITMENT
Measurement Model:			γ_{23}	SES	POSEOA**
λ_1	SES	Age	γ_{24}	SES	EFFECTIVENESS**
λ_2	SES	Education	γ_{25}	SES	SATISFACTION**
λ_3	SES	Rank	γ_{26}	SES	COMMITMENT**
λ_4	DISC	Mdisc	γ_{27}	SES	NEGEOA**
λ_5	DISC	Cdisc	γ_{28}	DISC	POSEOA**
λ_6	POSEOC	Positive Behaviors*	γ_{29}	DISC	EFFECTIVENESS**
λ_7	POSEOA	Positive Attitudes*	γ_{30}	DISC	SATISFACTION**
λ_8	EFFECTIVENESS	Effectiveness*	γ_{31}	DISC	COMMITMENT**
λ_9	COMMITMENT	Commitment*	γ_{32}	DISC	NEGEOA**
λ_{10}	SATISFACTION	Satisfaction*			

*Indicates fixed terms; **Not shown on Figure 14.2.

the white females. That group produced a fit index of .9642, adjusted index of .9576, RMSR = .0539, and a critical N of 362. All of these values are acceptable, with the possible exception of the RMSR, which is only slightly larger than the rule of thumb of .05 (Bagozzi & Yi, 1988). The poorest fit was produced by the two Asian groups (for Asian males, the fit index was .8215; for Asian females, it was .7623; all of the other statistics were similar to these results). The next most discrepant subgroup was the African American males. Clearly, the relation-

ships that characterize the white subgroups were not replicated in the other groups.

Indigenous Analyses of Subgroups

The model provided an adequate fit for all subgroups, with the possible exception of Asian American females. The RMSR was below .05 for all groups except the Asian American females, for whom it was .0503. Hoelter's critical N was above 200 again for all groups except the

TABLE 14.4 Indigenous Standardized Coefficients for All Race/Gender Groups

Group	WM	WF	BM	BF	HM	HF	AM	AF
Error Terms: (Manifest)								
δ_1	.75	.77	.56	.73	.82	.75	.41	.50
δ_2	.33	.16	.85	.48	.47	.43	.88	.74
δ_3	.36	.47	.92	.75	.73	.60	.99	.99
δ_4	.35	.53	.39	.49	.46	.66	.55	.61
δ_5	.79	.76	.69	.77	.67	.65	.50	.76
δ_6 [a]	.00	.00	.00	.00	.00	.00	.00	.00
δ_7 [a]	.00	.00	.00	.00	.00	.00	.00	.00
δ_8 [a]	.38	.38	.38	.38	.38	.38	.38	.38
δ_9 [a]	.00	.00	.00	.00	.00	.00	.00	.00
δ_{10} [a]	.00	.00	.00	.00	.00	.00	.00	.00
δ_{11}	.45	.45	.45	.45	.45	.45	.45	.45
ε [a]	.49	.49	.49	.49	.49	.49	.49	.49
Disturbance Terms: (Latent)								
ζ_1 [a]	1.00	1.00	1.00	1.00	1.00	1.00	1.00	1.00
ζ_2 [a]	1.00	1.00	1.00	1.00	1.00	1.00	1.00	1.00
ζ_3	.96	.98	.98	.98	.99	.99	.99	.99
ζ_4	.98	.91	.83	.86	.88	.88	.90	.83
ζ_5	.84	.91	.86	.92	.92	.92	.91	.89
ζ_6	.90	.92	.83	.88	.87	.90	.86	.94
ζ_7	.54	.57	.55	.61	.45	.62	.43	.36
ζ_8	.28	.32	.15	.26	.08	.18	.11	.14
ζ_9	.04	.11	.10	.17	.15	.17	.08	.22
Measurement Model:								
λ_1	.50	.48	.66	.51	.42	.50	.77	.70
λ_2	.82	.91	.39	.72	.73	.75	.35	.51
λ_3	.80	.73	.28	.50	.52	.63	.06	-.05
λ_4	.81	.69	.78	.72	.74	.58	.68	.62
λ_5	.46	.49	.55	.49	.57	.59	.68	.62
λ_6 [a]	1.00	1.00	1.00	1.00	1.00	1.00	1.00	1.00
λ_7 [a]	1.00	1.00	1.00	1.00	1.00	1.00	1.00	1.00
λ_8 [a]	.93	.93	.93	.93	.93	.93	.93	.93
λ_9 [a]	.87	.87	.87	.87	.87	.87	.87	.87
λ_{10} [a]	.89	.89	.89	.89	.89	.89	.89	.89
λ_{11} [a]	1.00	1.00	1.00	1.00	1.00	1.00	1.00	1.00
λ_{12} [a]	1.00	1.00	1.00	1.00	1.00	1.00	1.00	1.00
Structural Equations:								
γ_1	-.18	-.11	-.08	-.06	-.01	-.02	.03	.05
γ_2	.11	.06	.15	.06	.12	.11	.20	-.01
γ_3	.06	.02	.10	.12	.03	.03	.08	-.01
γ_4	-.03	-.29	-.38	-.37	-.32	-.32	-.25	-.25
γ_5	.27	.24	.27	.24	.27	.21	.25	.25
γ_6	.15	.16	.11	.10	.13	.10	.16	.15
γ_7	.00	-.02	.05	.01	-.01	-.02	.07	-.04
γ_8	-.05	-.07	-.02	-.04	-.01	-.07	-.01	-.02
γ_9	-.21	-.21	-.23	-.24	-.25	-.19	-.25	-.18
γ_{10}	-.02	-.05	-.05	-.06	-.02	-.06	-.03	-.04
γ_{11}	-.11	-.10	-.01	.02	-.07	-.07	-.08	-.07
γ_{12}	-.07	-.09	-.11	-.12	-.11	-.14	-.09	-.10
γ_{13}	.22	.21	.24	.22	.27	.24	.25	.16
γ_{14}	-.01	.02	.01	.03	.00	.04	.03	-.09
γ_{15}	.10	.17	.12	.20	.10	.13	.04	.09
γ_{16}	.27	.21	.28	.22	.40	.19	.32	.43
γ_{17}	-.20	-.19	-.16	-.18	-.14	-.23	-.20	-.12
γ_{18}	-.12	-.09	-.15	-.11	-.18	-.08	-.16	-.30
γ_{19}	-.02	.03	.05	.08	-.01	.03	-.04	-.05
γ_{20}	.04	.02	-.07	-.12	-.04	-.02	-.05	-.15
γ_{21}	-.63	-.56	-.74	-.65	-.85	-.68	-.77	-.74
γ_{22}	-.81	-.76	-.56	-.55	-.71	-.68	-.73	-.72
γ_{23}	-.20	-.13	-.23	-.12	.01	-.16	-.18	-.10
γ_{24}	.07	.12	-.11	-.11	.02	-.11	-.19	-.12
γ_{25}	-.03	.00	.04	-.01	-.05	-.07	.08	.18
γ_{26}	-.12	-.06	-.26	-.18	-.17	-.13	-.10	.18
γ_{27}	.01	.03	.12	-.05	.03	.09	.12	.08
γ_{28}	.11	.05	-.04	.01	-.07	-.04	-.07	-.21
γ_{29}	.06	.03	-.10	.04	-.05	-.04	-.03	-.05
γ_{30}	-.07	-.12	-.04	-.06	-.03	-.15	-.05	-.09
γ_{31}	.02	.00	.09	-.06	.09	-.06	.03	.13
γ_{32}	.15	.13	-.07	-.04	.05	.12	.06	.04
Covariance								
ρ	-.15	.02	.02	.08	-.05	-.02	.02	-.22

NOTE: a. Figures in these rows are fixed.

TABLE 14.5 Total Effects of Latent Variable Predictors on Commitment by Group

	Group							
Predictor	WM	WF	BM	BF	HM	HF	AM	AF
Satisfaction	−0.8127	−0.7603	−0.5606	−0.5486	−0.7097	−0.6805	−0.7343	−0.7226
Effectiveness	0.5119	0.4216	0.4173	0.3537	0.6038	0.4599	0.5621	0.5356
EOAP	0.3969	0.4009	0.3301	0.3707	0.4359	0.3767	0.3692	0.4057
EOAN	−0.0097	−0.0401	−0.1408	−0.1996	−0.1378	−0.0773	−0.1076	−0.2717
EOCP	0.2257	0.2028	0.2288	0.202	0.2258	0.1666	0.2704	0.2049
EOCN	−0.1295	−0.1785	−0.1696	−0.197	−0.1995	−0.2458	−0.1935	−0.1375
SES	−0.2588	−0.191	−0.4682	−0.286	−0.1439	−0.2284	−0.3817	−0.0753
DISC	0.1708	0.1747	0.1615	0.1684	0.1101	−0.0882	0.0824	0.0968

group mentioned above. By using Hoelter's critical N as an index, the best fits were obtained from the African American females (index = 549) and Asian American males (index = 414). The standardized coefficients that resulted in the above fit statistics are given in Table 14.4.

The race/gender differences noted above can be further examined by inspecting the total (direct and indirect) effects on commitment from each of the other variables (Table 14.5). It is particularly instructive to compare the effects for the African American males and Asian American females with those from white males. As noted above, the two nonwhite groups were the most different from the white male subgroup. The major differences between the white male and African American male subgroups were a much larger impact of SES for the latter group over the former (−.26 vs. −.47, respectively), a much larger impact of negative attitudes for the African American group over the white group (−.14 vs. −.01, respectively), and a much lower effect of job satisfaction for the African American group (−.56 for the African American group vs. −.81 for the white group).

For the Asian American female and white male comparison, the results show a slightly lower impact of satisfaction (−.72 vs. −.81), a much higher impact of negative attitudes (−.27 vs. −.01), and a lower impact of SES (−.06 vs. −.26). These results clearly indicate that the reasons why people feel committed to the service vary by subgroup. It should be mentioned that the dimensions being tapped by the Negative Attitudes factor involve a perception of discrimination in the work environment. In all cases, those attitudes are closely related to per-

ceived negative behaviors for the minority groups, but much less so for the white males. Figure 14.3 shows the disparity between the groups when the data in Table 14.4 are used to predict commitment and job satisfaction.

Relationship of EOC
to Unit Characteristics

Tallarigo and Landis (1995) studied the relationship of perceptual estimation dimensions to unit attributes by using multidimensional analysis. Mean unit scores on the five perceptual estimation factors were used to define distances in a five-dimensional Euclidean space. These distances were subjected to a multidimensional scaling algorithm that resulted in three dimensions. The rotated dimensions (on which each of 955 units was located) were related to a number of unit characteristics: (a) mission type (combat vs. combat support), (b) size of the unit, (c) proportion of people in the unit reported having been a victim of discrimination, (d) percentage of minorities in the unit, and (e) level of organizational commitment, job satisfaction, and perceived work group effectiveness. The first dimension, on the basis of canonical discriminant function analysis, reflected units that consist of a high percentage of alienated victims who see themselves as being ineffective. The second dimension was labeled *nonintegrated and dispirited,* and the third seemed to reflect majority individuals who feel discriminated against, as well as minorities who feel isolated. On the basis of this study, we can assert, with some degree of confidence, that

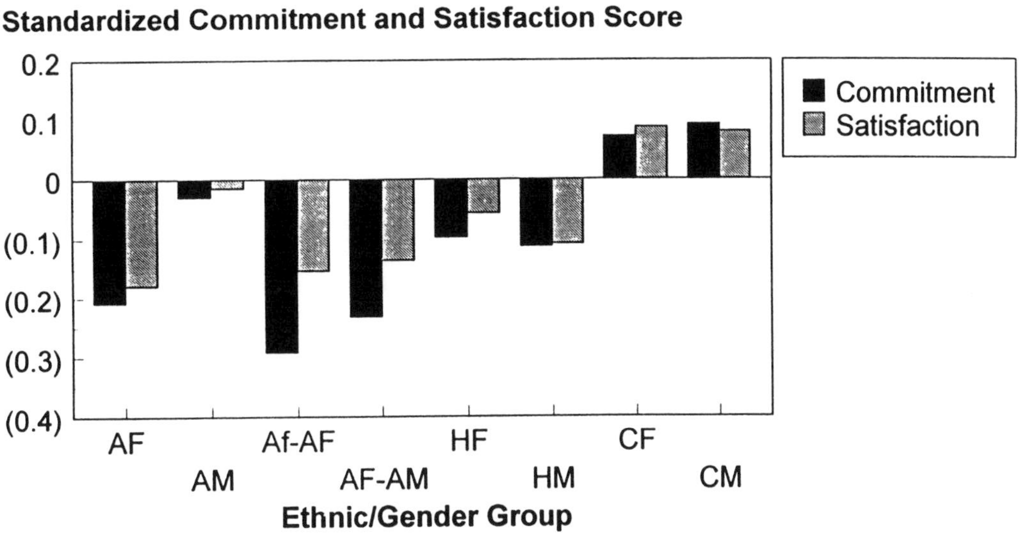

Standardized Commitment and Satisfaction Score

Figure 14.3. Predicted Commitment and Satisfaction by Group

EOC is related to objective characteristics of the organization.

Relationship of EOC to TQM

Knouse (1994) explored the potential relationship of TQM to EOC in a study of three units. Each unit had received recognition for having a TQM program and had also recently completed a MEOCS. Using the "quality" item from one of the MEOCS subscales, Knouse found significant relationships with the other climate variables. By using a regression approach, it was found that EOC is not a significant predictor of judged quality of work for majority individuals but that it is for minorities and women. This study, although provocative in its conclusions, must be considered exploratory and tentative. The sample was quite small, and no independent measures (external to the MEOCS) existed for the level of achievement of TQM.

Relationship of EOC to Group Cohesion

Neibuhr, Knouse, and Dansby (1994) correlated the EOC factors with measures of group cohesion in both a military and civilian sample. Racism and Sexism scales of six items each were constructed from the critical incident items. The MEOCS items were translated into a civilian setting for the nonmilitary version (Neibuhr, 1994). Cohesion measures were appropriate for each situation. Results indicated that sexism and racism were negatively correlated with cohesion (−.23, −.27 in the military; −.29, −.25 in the civilian) and performance (−.16, −.21 in the military; −.20, −.16 in the civilian).

The preceding discussion of results from the MEOCS database offers a macroview of the use of such surveys and how those data can be used to answer theoretically interesting questions. The basic design of the MEOCS, however, is aimed at serving individual organizations in developing more favorable organizational EOC. In the next section, we describe how this is accomplished and give the underlying philosophy for the MEOCS approach.

Use of EOC in Organizational Change

Surveys are classic tools used by organizational development (OD) consultants as a basis for organizational assessment and change (e.g.,

Bowers & Franklin, 1975; French, 1985; Hausser, Pecorella, & Wissler, 1977; E. Schein, 1969). Landis et al. (1993) describe the philosophy and program supporting the MEOCS as an aid to organizational improvement. As an OD tool, the MEOCS is well accepted by military commanders and organizational leaders in the U.S. military services (having been requested by more than 3,000 organizational heads and administered to more than 395,000 respondents). Because of the efficiencies attained by centralized administration and analysis of the survey, the MEOCS has become the most used OD survey reported in the literature. In some respects, therefore, it might serve as a contemporary model for OD survey-guided intervention in large organizations. In this section, we discuss general principles of survey-guided intervention in the context of a broader OD model developed in the U.S. Army organizational effectiveness (OE) community. These principles could readily be extended to an international and intercultural context, as discussed elsewhere in this chapter.

Background: Organizational
Surveys as an OD Tool

Bowers and Franklin (1975) describe the basic process of survey-guided development, and Hausser et al. (1977) summarize its main goal:

To facilitate interventions or changes in organizational functioning that will lead to increased organizational effectiveness by providing accurate and useful information about how an organization actually functions, how it might ideally function, and how to make the actual functioning more like the ideal functioning. (p. 5)

For a comprehensive review of the development of the survey feedback approach, see French (1985). French identifies the work of Rensis Likert at the Survey Research Center (founded in 1946) at the University of Michigan as the intellectual roots of the OD survey. Perhaps the classic intervention model is that described by E. Schein (1969). The model involves seven steps:

1. Initial contact with the client organization

2. Defining the relationship, formal contract, and psychological contract
3. Selecting a setting and a method of work
4. Data gathering and diagnosis
5. Intervention
6. Reducing involvement
7. Termination (p. 78)

Other researchers and practitioners have described similar models (e.g., Landis et al., 1993; Lippitt & Lippitt, 1978; Nadler, 1977; Umstot, 1980). Elsewhere, we have described the model used with the MEOCS (Landis et al., 1993), along with its unique features when compared with more traditional OD surveys. The MEOCS approach is based on a six-step model:

1. *Contact.* Bringing together the military commander and the survey managers at DEOMI
2. *Contract.* Setting the mutual expectations, or psychological contract, between the organization and DEOMI
3. *Data gathering.* Administration of the survey in accordance with standard guidelines
4. *Data analysis.* Processing the raw responses into meaningful information
5. *Feedback of information.* Conveying understandable and useful results to the organization's leaders
6. *Follow-up.* Using the results to effect organizational change and improvement

As discussed previously (also see Landis et al., 1993), the MEOCS measures a number of EO and organizational factors of interest to military leaders. It is a voluntary, confidential survey, with feedback returned exclusively to the requesting commander. Consequently, the MEOCS is an ideal tool for a commander who desires a self-assessment of his or her unit prior to proactive intervention to improve the productivity of the unit and the quality of life for its members. The commander controls how the survey is used; confidentiality lessens fear of the misuse of information (e.g., for political manipulation; see Zawacki & Warrick, 1976). Such control and "ownership" are critical to the success of the MEOCS as a tool for constructive change (Bowers & Franklin, 1975; Landis et al., 1993).

On receiving a letter of request from a commander, staff from DEOMI's Directorate of

Research determine which version of the survey (on the basis of gender composition and other unit demographics) is appropriate and send the requesting commander a camera-ready copy, along with answer sheets and instructions for proper administration. A unit project officer reproduces the survey booklets, administers the survey according to DEOMI's guidelines, and returns the completed response forms. Response forms are scanned into a raw data file, which is subsequently analyzed by using a commercial statistical analysis program. The data are also added to a cumulative database maintained at DEOMI. A series of computer programs developed by the second author collect and format output from the statistical program and automatically generate a feedback package, which is returned to the commander. The package includes comparisons between the unit's results and the overall database averages for the appropriate service and the military overall, as well as a number of within-unit demographic comparisons (e.g., minority/majority, women/men). These within-unit comparisons are particularly important. They often indicate gaps in perceptions among the various groups. This information can be enlightening for organizational leaders and can lead to constructive conversation to identify why the perceptions differ and what can be done to improve the organizational climate.

After the results are returned to the unit, it is up to the commander to conduct (or not) follow-up actions. Most commands have EO program advisors, who may be directed to establish an action plan. DEOMI also provides consultation and mobile training teams at the commander's request (the unit must pay for travel and per diem expenses; no charge for the consultation or training).

Organizational Effectiveness (OE) Model

As mentioned previously, the MEOCS is conducted in the context of a broader organizational intervention and is part of a systems approach to OD. In the late 1970s and early 1980s, the U.S. Army conducted an extensive OE program to help commanders and organizations become more effective. (The air force and navy had similar programs, all of which were eliminated because of budget cuts and other exigen-

cies.) A simple four-step model underscored the philosophy of the army's program, which was taught in the Organizational Effectiveness Center and School, Fort Ord, California, and the Center for Leadership and Ethics Leader Development Program at the United States Army Command and General Staff College, Fort Leavenworth, Kansas (U.S. Army Center for Leadership and Ethics, n.d.). The OE view is a systems approach, and the model (commonly known as APIE, based on the initial letters for the first word in each step) includes the following steps for rational intervention and organizational change:

1. **A**ssess current operation
2. **P**lan for change
3. **I**mplement change
4. **E**valuate change

The APIE process is viewed as continuous and is similar to other models of organizational change, such as the planned-change process discussed by Harvey and Brown (1988), Schermerhorn, Hunt, and Osborn (1991), and Hellriegel and Slocum (1992). Figure 14.4 (an abbreviated version) illustrates the iterative nature of the model.

Using OD Surveys in the APIE Model

The systems approach (e.g., Harvey & Brown, 1988; Hellriegel & Slocum, 1992; Schermerhorn et al., 1991) views organizations as open systems with inputs, processes, and outputs. The APIE model focuses on the process stage, and within the APIE context, surveys such as the MEOCS can fulfill several functions in helping organizations change and grow. They provide systems information about organizational processes; when used properly, this information can lead to quality improvement in the organization.

In general, OD philosophy emphasizes helping the client help him- or herself (E. Schein, 1969) by using a collaborative approach (Harvey & Brown, 1988). Commitment ("ownership"; Bowers & Franklin, 1975) by the top organizational leadership is essential to the success of the OD intervention. Without it, much energy may be wasted in attempts to discount the validity of the process or the results (Harvey

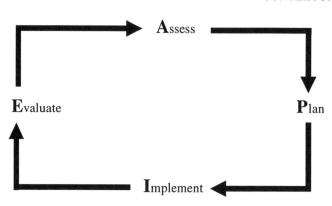

Figure 14.4. The APIE Model Provides an Apt Framework for Discussing the Use of Surveys in OD

& Brown, 1988), and few positive outcomes would be expected. The leadership also has the power to influence others (Harvey & Brown, 1988; E. Schein, 1969; V. Schein, 1985; Schermerhorn et al., 1991) and thus facilitate meaningful intervention.

Once leadership commitment to the process is attained, surveys can aid in what is commonly called a *gap analysis* (Harvey & Brown, 1988), in which a current state is compared to a desired state. The difference, or gap, between these two states is used as a basis for action planning to close the gap. Within the APIE model, the *assess* step is where the current state is determined. The survey provides a comprehensive, often less biased, view of the current state. In the case of the MEOCS, the gaps considered are in the areas of EO and OE, or more generally, human relations and organizational process. It is important to recognize that surveys are only one among many tools that may be used in gap analysis. Interviews, examination of organizational records and reports, and systematic observations are other tools that may (and should) be used as well. Information from all sources should be considered to validate and clarify survey results.

Once the current state is determined, the planning begins. In the *plan* step, potential ways of bridging the gap between the current and desired states are explored. The survey results are used as a basis for planning interventions more rationally. In providing information regarding specific concerns, the results help bring focus and direction to the planning. Broad organizational involvement is needed to foster

support for planned interventions and to help overcome the normal resistance to change (Harvey & Brown, 1988; Schermerhorn et al., 1991). Sharing the survey results with the entire organization can help in generating a sense of involvement and, by highlighting the concerns (based on information provided by unit members), motivate members to participate in the change process.

The next step in APIE is to *implement* the planned actions. Usually, the interventions will occur over some time, and it will take additional time for the actions to gain acceptance and to have an effect in the organization. The purpose of the interventions is to help close the gap between the current and desired states. Consequently, some method of assessing the effects of the interventions is needed to determine how much progress (if any) has been made in closing the gap.

This is where the survey is again useful. When the organization is ready to *evaluate* the impact of its actions, the original survey results may be used as a baseline for comparison with a second survey administered after the intervention process is completed. It is essential that the survey versions be comparable in order to use this pre-post-intervention evaluation methodology effectively. On the one hand, the results of the evaluation may reveal that the actions taken were effective; on the other hand, the results may imply that old action plans need adjustment or that new actions must be formulated. The commander and organizational staff evaluate the need for adjustment and proceed from there.

Because the APIE process is iterative, it should be repeated periodically to keep commanders aware of organizational issues and to facilitate constructive change. Because the MEOCS provides an inexpensive, informative, and useful tool for commanders who want to pursue rational change, it encourages commanders to use the APIE process. The desired result is a more effective organization with more motivated members.

SUMMARY

The use of the MEOCS as an OD/OE tool within the framework of a systems model (APIE) provides many advantages to users. Among these are gaining insight into human relations and effectiveness by using a more objective approach than is typical in many organizations, while at the same time costing the organization relatively little. The value of this information, when properly validated, is great; it can facilitate gains in effectiveness of the organization and satisfaction of its members.

In a broader intercultural context, the survey methodology also has much to offer. If properly designed, conducted, and analyzed and if the results are properly used, it can increase communication across demographic barriers. This can lead to increased sensitivity and intercultural understanding, better human relations, and increased individual satisfaction. Although the MEOCS models the process in a military context, it could easily be applied in other settings, such as communities, schools, universities, police and fire departments, other governmental agencies, businesses (especially international), and religious organizations. This potential should not be overlooked when seeking ways to improve understanding and human relations.

Notes

1. The distinction here is similar to that between emic and etic. See Chapter 2 (by Bhawuk and Triandis), this volume.

2. Strictly speaking, the first 50 items constitute the MEOCS; however, common usage has accorded the total survey with that appellation. Rather than fight a losing battle, we accede to the common will.

3. The colleagues for this version are Billy Barrios, Amy Wilson, Michael Raines, Katrina Williams, Joy Armstrong, Teresa Detterman, Ahmad Karriem, Jonathon Durm, Pyeong-Soo Jung, Cynthia Ruiz, and Marina Koval.

4. For example, a sample of 18- to 20-year-old respondents was extracted from the MEOCS database. This group's mean score on the comparable factor was 3.55.

5. The colleagues on this version are Chittibabu Govindarajulu and Manimekalai Chittibabu.

6. At this writing, colleagues are developing indigenous EOCS versions for Australia, Netherlands, Canada, and Israel.

References

Adams, J. (1963). Toward an understanding of inequity. *Journal of Abnormal and Social Psychology, 67,* 422-436.

Bagozzi, R., & Yi, Y. (1988). On the evaluation of structural equation models. *Journal of the Academy of Marketing Science, 16*(1), 74-94.

Bowers, D. G., & Franklin, J. L. (1975). *Survey-guided development: Data-based organizational change.* Ann Arbor, MI: Institute for Social Research.

Bracken, D. (1994, September). Straight talk about multi-rater feedback. *Training and Development Journal, 9,* 44-51..

Bruner, J., & Tagiuri, R. (1954). The perception of people. In G. Lindzey (Ed.), *Handbook of social psychology* (Vol. 2, pp. 634-654). Reading, MA: Addison-Wesley.

Campbell, J., Dunnette, M., Lawler, E., & Weick, K. (1970). *Managerial behavior, performance, and effectiveness.* New York: McGraw-Hill.

Dansby, M., & Landis, D. (1991). Measuring equal opportunity in the military environment. *International Journal of Intercultural Relations, 15,* 399-406.

Evan, W. (1963). Indices of hierarchical structure of organizations. *Management Science, 9,* 468-477.

Finkle, R. B. (1976). Managerial assessment centers. In M. D. Dunnette (Ed.), *Handbook of industrial and organizational psychology* (pp. 861-888). Chicago: Rand McNally.

Forehand, G., & Gilmer, B. (1964). Environmental variation in studies of organizational behavior. *Psychological Bulletin, 62,* 361-382.

French, W. L. (1985). The emergence and early history of organization development with references to influences upon and interactions among some of the key actors. In D. D. Warrick (Ed.), *Contemporary organization development* (pp. 12-27). Glenview, IL: Scott, Foresman.

Greenberg, J. (1990). Organizational justice: Yesterday, today, tomorrow. *Journal of Management, 16,* 399-432.

Hackman, R., & Oldham, G. (1976). Development of the Job Diagnostic Survey. *Journal of Applied Psychology, 60,* 159170.

Harvey, D. F., & Brown, D. R. (1988). *An experiential approach to organization development.* Englewood Cliffs, NJ: Prentice-Hall.

Hausser, D. L., Pecorella, P. A., & Wissler, A. L. (1977). *Survey-guided development II: A manual for consultants.* La Jolla, CA: University Associates.

Hellriegel, D., & Slocum, J. W. (1992). *Management.* Reading, MA: Addison-Wesley.

Hoelter, J. (1983). The analysis of covariance structures: Goodness of fit indicies. *Sociological Methods and Research, 11*(3), 325-344.

Jones, A., & James, L. (1979). Psychological climate: Dimensions and relationships of individuals and aggregated work environment perceptions. *Organizational Behavior and Human Performance, 23,* 201-250.

Joyce, W., & Slocum, J. (1984). Collective climate: Agreement as a basis for defining aggregate climates in organizations. *Academy of Management Journal, 27,* 721-742.

Knouse, S. (1994). *Equal opportunity climate and total quality management: A preliminary study (DEOMI Research Pamphlet 94-3).* Patrick Air Force Base, FL: Defense Equal Opportunity Management Institute.

Landis, D. (1990, January). *Military Equal Opportunity Climate Survey: Reliability, construct validity, and preliminary field test.* Oxford: University of Mississippi, Center for Applied Research and Evaluation.

Landis, D., Dansby, M., & Faley, R. (1993). The Military Equal Opportunity Climate Survey: An example of surveying in organizations. In P. Rosenfeld, J. E. Edwards, & M. D. Thomas (Eds.), *Improving organizational surveys: New directions, methods, and applications* (pp. 122-142). Newbury Park, CA: Sage.

Landis, D., Dansby, M., & Faley, R. (1994, April). *The relationship of equal opportunity climate to military career commitment: An analysis of individual differences using latent variables.* Paper presented at the 1994 meetings of the Psychology in DoD Symposium, Colorado Springs, CO.

Landis, D., & Fisher, G. (1987). *Construction and preliminary validation of an equal opportunity climate assessment instrument.* Patrick Air Force Base, FL: Defense Equal Opportunity Management Institute.

Lewin, E. (1948). *Resolving social conflict: Selected papers on group dynamics.* New York: Harper & Row.

Lindzey, G., & Aronson, E. (1985). *Handbook of social psychology* (Vol. 1). New York: Random House.

Lippitt, G., & Lippitt, R. (1978). *The consulting process in action.* San Diego: University Associates.

Litwin, G., & Stringer, R. (1968). *Motivation and organizational climate.* Cambridge, MA: Harvard University Press.

Locke, E. (1976). The nature and causes of job satisfaction. In M. D. Dunnette (Ed.), *Handbook of industrial and organizational psychology* (pp. 1297-1349). Chicago: Rand McNally.

Mayer, J., & Abramson, J. (1994) *Strange justice: The selling of Clarence Thomas.* Boston: Houghton Mifflin.

McConohay, J. (1986). Modern racism, ambivalence, and the Modern Racism Scale. In J. F. Dovidio & S. L. Gaertner (Eds.), *Prejudice, discrimination, and racism* (pp. 91-125). San Diego: Academic Press.

McCormick, E., Jeanneret, P., & Mecham, R. (1969). *Position Analysis Questionnaire.* West Lafayette, IN: Purdue Research Foundation.

Mohrman, A. M., Jr., Resnick-West, S. M., & Lawler, E. E., III. (1989). *Designing performance appraisal systems: Aligning appraisals and organizational realities.* San Francisco: Jossey-Bass.

Nadler, D. A. (1977). *Feedback and organization development: Using data-based methods.* Reading, MA: Addison-Wesley.

Neibuhr, R. (1994). *Measuring equal opportunity climate in organizations: Development of scales to evaluate the acceptance of diversity* (Pamphlet 94-5). Patrick Air Force Base, FL: Defense Equal Opportunity Management Institute, Directorate of Research.

Neibuhr, R., Knouse, S., & Dansby, M. (1994). *Workgroup climates for acceptance of diversity: Relationship to group cohesiveness and performance* (Pamphlet 94-4). Patrick Air Force Base, FL: Defense Equal Opportunity Management Institute, Directorate of Research.

Rentsch, J. (1990). Climate and culture: Interaction and qualitative differences in organizational meanings. *Journal of Applied Psychology, 75,* 668-681.

Salancik, G., & Pfeffer, J. (1978). A social information processing approach to job attitudes and task design. *Administrative Science Quarterly, 23,* 224-253.

Schein, E. H. (1969). *Process consultation: Its role in organization development.* Reading, MA: Addison-Wesley.

Schein, V. E. (1985). Organizational realities: The politics of change. In D. D. Warrick (Ed.), *Contemporary organization development* (pp. 86-97). Glenview, IL: Scott, Foresman.

Schermerhorn, J. R., Hunt, J. G., & Osborn, R. N. (1991). *Managing organizational behavior.* New York: John Wiley.

Schmidt, F., & Hunter, J. (1990). *Methods of meta-analysis.* Newbury Park, CA: Sage.

Schwab, D. P., & Wichern, D. W. (1983). Systematic bias in job evaluation and market wages: Implications for the comparable worth debate. *Journal of Applied Psychology, 68,* 60-69.

Sonnenfeld, J. (1982). Clarifying critical confusion in the Hawthorne hysteria. *American Psychologist, 37,* 1397-1399.

Tallarigo, R. S. (1992). [Differences between combat, combat support, and combat service support units on the Military Equal Opportunity Climate Survey]. Unpublished raw data.

Tallarigo, R. S. (1994, December). *MEOCS-EEO: Broadening the view.* Paper presented at the DoD Worldwide Equal Opportunity Conference, Cocoa Beach, FL.

Tallarigo, R. S., & Landis, D. (1995, May). *Organizational distance scaling: Exploring climates across organizations.* Paper presented at the 1995 Annual Conference of the Society for Industrial and Organizational Psychology, Orlando, FL.

Umstot, D. D. (1980). Organization development technology in the military: A surprising merger? *Academy of Management Review, 5* (2), 189-201.

U.S. Army Center for Leadership and Ethics. (n.d.). *Leader Development Program trainers course handbook.* Fort Leavenworth, KS: U.S. Army Command and General Staff College.

Zawacki, R. A., & Warrick, D. D. (1976). *Organization development: Managing change in the public sector.* Chicago: International Personnel Management Association.

Social Support and the
Challenges of International Assignments

Implications for Training

GARY FONTAINE

International Assignments

International assignments in business, diplomacy, foreign study, scientific exchange, or whatever involve journeys to "strange lands" or new *ecologies* (new sociocultural, physical, and biological environments). That is both their bane and their lure.

Several characteristics are common to the ecologies of most international assignments (Desatnick & Bennett, 1977; Fontaine, 1989). For instance, assignees confront differences associated with *people* (e.g., culture, language, physical appearance, crowdedness); *place* (seasons, climate, topography, built facilities, sights, sounds, smells, simply being far from the home to which their identity is attached); *travel* (getting there takes longer, is more complex, and requires more preparation); *time* (it usually takes longer to get things done interna-

tionally); *communication* (language can make communication with others abroad difficult, and time zones can do the same for communicating back to the "home office"); *structure* (assignees are often more responsible for structuring activities themselves); and *support* (separation from the social and organizational support groups left at home, disruption of those accompanying them, and difficulty in developing new ones). These characteristics essentially define what international assignments are and set them apart from their domestic counterparts.

Other ecological characteristics differentiate one international assignment from another (Fontaine, 1989). For instance, the specific *character* of each of the above will differentiate between assignments (e.g., assignment to an Asian or American culture with a temperate or tropical climate). In addition, assignments may differ in organizational *context* (e.g., business, diplomacy, foreign study); degrees of *power* assignees have relative to their hosts; the *standard of living* they find; and the type and novelty of the communication, transportation, manufacturing, educational, or other *technologies* needed to get tasks done. Of particular importance in this chapter are differences between assignments in *duration* (e.g., 3 days, 3 months, 3 years), whether the destination is a *cosmopolitan* urban area with a plethora of resources for support, entertainment, recreation, and so forth or a *provincial* one with very few; the availability of a supportive *expatriate community;* and a culture/language that eases or hinders entry into *host country support groups.*

The new ecologies encountered on international assignments confront assignees with significant challenges to success in terms of their adjustment, performance, and satisfaction (Black, Mendenhall, & Oddou, 1991; Dunbar, 1992; Parker & McEvoy, 1993). I have earlier (Fontaine, 1989, 1993c) identified three key challenges: (a) *coping with ecoshock* (assignees' physiological and psychological reaction to the new ecology); (b) *getting the job done* by dealing effectively with diversity; and (c) *maintaining the motivation* to continue despite almost inevitable frustration, fatigue, ecoshock, and failure. To the degree that assignees deal effectively with these challenges, their assignments will be successful. To the degree that assignees are unable to meet one or more of them, their success will be less than optimal—perhaps they will fail altogether. Improving the skills required to deal effectively with each challenge should be a central objective of training for all international assignments. Meeting that objective significantly requires understanding the roles social support plays both in producing the challenges and in providing options for dealing with them.

Social Support
and International Assignments

There has been increasing recognition among researchers, consultants, and managers of the important impact social support has on the success of international assignments (Adelman, 1988; Briody & Chrisman, 1991; Fontaine, 1986, 1989; Furnham & Bochner, 1986). Social support is typically provided by a combination of individuals or groups, including an assignee's family, friends, work group or organization, recreational, religious, hobby, or other "special interest" groups, or sometimes self-help or mutual help networks. I have previously (Fontaine, 1986; see also Furnham & Bochner, 1986) distinguished among (a) *home-country* support groups (e.g., the assignee's family, friends, and home office), (b) *home-culture* support groups (the family or workmates accompanying the assignee, those from the overseas office of their organization, or those in a larger "expat" community), and (c) *host culture* support groups (those from the host culture). The relative importance of each on any given assignment is contingent on the ecological characteristics of that assignment (e.g., its duration, the types of home-culture groups available, ease of entry into the host culture).

The social support groups identified above can serve a variety of functions (Adelman, 1988; Albrecht & Adelman, 1984, 1987; House, 1985), including the following:

Resources. Assignees need to live and work effectively abroad—money when a check hasn't arrived, food when they're sick of restaurants, transportation when their car breaks down, the clothes that protocol or custom demand when the shops are closed.

Information and *guidance* about all aspects of living and working abroad, as well as what's happening back home.

A *different perspective* from the assignee's that can assist in interpreting events that occur on assignments. This is particularly true, of course, for those from the host culture, whose perspective is especially useful for interpreting intercultural problems.

A *similar perspective* to the assignee's that can validate his or her identity, maintain confidence, and provide a feeling of being understood—"We're OK, even if those people stare at us and laugh at us because we're brown people in a white place, or white people in a brown place, or blue-eyed people in a brown-eyed place, or brown-eyed people in a blue-eyed place."

People with whom to *compare* adjustment, performance, and satisfaction on the assignment. Particularly valuable are those in the destination from the assignee's home culture; particularly dangerous are those niving and working in the very different ecology back home.

People with whom to *share responsibility* and *effort* for the tasks of working and living abroad. Success abroad requires teamwork; when assignees are too tired or stressed, others can "pick up the slack."

An island of *familiarity* in a sea of novelty. When the world seems so different and unpredictable, a social support group can be almost like home. This is particularly true of those from back home—thus, the clubs, associations, and bars in which expatriates congregate.

Love and sex and *intimacy* are generally essential to social completeness internationally, as well as at home. One need only note the prevalence of international marriages—or the plethora of "girlie bars" and "escort services"—in major international destinations.

Companionship. Both the good and bad times are better when shared with others. Companionship does not necessarily mean "liking." On an international assignment, less emphasis must be on liking than back home, where there are more choices.

This list is illustrative, not exhaustive. Supplementing it are a range of functions commonly provided, in part (though rarely entirely), by an assignees' organization. These latter are often referred to as *organizational support* (Copeland & Griggs, 1985; Fontaine, 1989; Harris & Moran, 1991) and include the following:

Preparation for the assignment through *screening,* opportunities for *self-selection, orientation* to the destination, and professional/technical, language, and intercultural *training*

Assistance with *health, passport, visa, banking, tax, communication,* and *moving* arrangements

Arrangements for the *travel* itself

Provisions for *accommodation, security, transportation,* and continued *orientation* and *training* while on the assignment

Description of *assignment objectives*

Status, recognition, and *career relevance* appropriate for the assignment

Compensation and *incentives* that are adequate, including a base salary at home-country levels, a cost-of-living allowance, an education allowance for dependents,

tax equalization, recreation, vacations, and home leaves

Staff support and the time, budget, facility, materials, communication, and other *resources* needed to do the job

Performance appraisal based on realistic objectives for the assignment

Understanding of the *special problems* of international assignments

Assistance in *managing stress* and *fatigue*

Assistance in the *reentry* process

And all of the above need to be distributed fairly among home and host culture recipients to minimize conflict.

Although the above lists illustrate the functions that social support groups can serve on international assignments, they do not provide clear implications for training in skills to develop, maintain, and make best use of support groups to fulfill these functions. To do that requires an explicit model of the challenges that must be dealt with effectively to produce assignment success, the roles of social support in those challenges, and the skills required to maintain or develop that support. Only then can the social support-related objectives of training be identified and programs be designed to fulfill those objectives (McCaffery, 1986). Although less than desirable theoretical development has occurred in the intercultural field, models of varying degrees of comprehensiveness are available from which to choose (e.g., Barna, 1983; Black et al., 1991; Brislin & Yoshida, 1994; Furnham & Bochner, 1986; Gudykunst, 1991). One such model (Fontaine, 1989, 1993c) was introduced earlier. Its implications for social support skills and examples of training techniques used to help develop those skills structure the remainder of this chapter.

Social Support and the Three Challenges

The First Challenge:
Coping With Ecoshock

I have presented a model of ecoshock (Fontaine, 1993c; see also Taft, 1977) in which international assignments are seen as confronting assignees with new *arrays of activities and experiences* that typically involve increased nov-

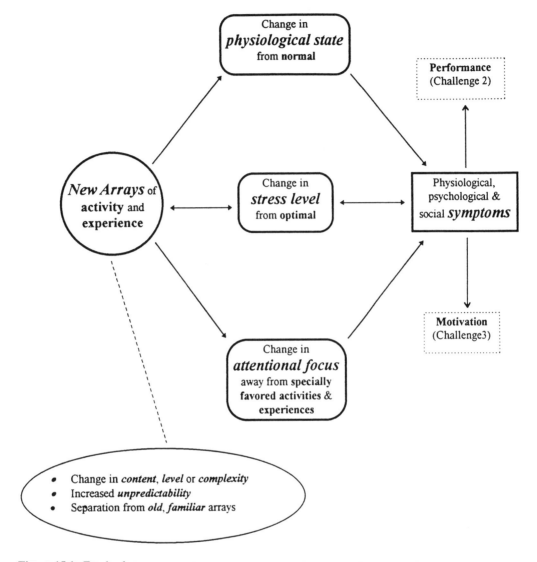

Figure 15.1. Ecoshock

elty, decreased familiarity, changes in stimulus levels or complexity, and—perhaps most significantly—unpredictability (see Figure 15.1). Any of the ecological characteristics of international assignments presented earlier (e.g., those associated with people, travel, communication) may contribute to these arrays, but certainly those associated with the *disruption of social support* are among the most important (Briody & Chrisman, 1991; Fontaine, 1986; Furnham, 1988; Furnham & Bochner, 1986). When assignees leave behind family, friends, and work-mates, they leave behind much of what is familiar in their world—for many people, the most important part of their familiar world. Although intercultural specialists have tended to emphasize the impact of what is encountered abroad as the source of culture shock (or ecoshock), it is at least as much because of what—or who—is left behind. Further, because those accompanying assignees abroad are struggling in the face of the same three challenges, they often act and react in quite different ways than they did back home. These differences can contribute much to what is novel abroad—perhaps with added impact because it is often unexpected and thus unprepared for. Assignees expect new, unpredictable behavior from those in the new cultures they encounter; they typically do not from their wife or husband or workmate accompanying them.

Initially, at least, these new arrays of activities and experiences—particularly those associated with the physical environment—can produce *changes in physiological state* away from normal. Travel dysrhythmia, or jet lag, is one such example that occurs when one is confronted with light or darkness at a biologically irregular time, which desynchronizes important circadian rhythms (Ehret & Scanlon, 1986). Other, less studied, physiological changes are produced by changes in temperature, humidity, altitude, air quality, opportunities for physical activity, and perhaps even food and drink (see Desatnick & Bennett, 1977). Although these changes can have significant impacts on health, adjustment, performance, and satisfaction, the disruption of social support is unlikely to play a large role. Further, although techniques are available to hasten adjustment to some of these changes (e.g., jet lag), by and large assignees' bodies will adapt on their own in days, weeks, or months. Thus, the key skill in coping with this source of ecoshock is usually *patience*.

The new activities and experiences encountered abroad also produce *changes in stress levels,* away from those optimal for performance—usually increases because of unpredictability. Many assignees are faced for the first time with threats to their competence in even the most mundane tasks. Further, they are stressed if the structure of their activities is modified. The role of stress in culture shock is so central that many theorists have equated the two—that is, culture shock is seen simply as stress produced by encountering a new culture (Barna, 1983; Brislin, 1993; Furnham & Bochner, 1986). *Social support* plays an important role in stress levels both because the disruption of social support is itself a stressor and because disrupted support groups are unable to play valuable stress-buffering or -reducing roles to help assignees in coping with other assignment stressors (Fontaine, 1986).

As is the case with changes in physiological state, coping with the stress produced abroad involves time and patience for the ecology to become more familiar and predictable and for at least ambient stress levels to diminish. *Intervention* by the assignee or others may play a more important role here, though, in the form of *stress management* (Walton, 1990). This management can include efforts to strengthen existing social support groups and to develop replacement support where necessary. Both are addressed shortly.

Finally, the new ecology encountered abroad can hinder assignee *participation in specially favored activities and experiences*—that is, preclude them from *focusing their attention* on the activities and experiences that have previously been associated with optimal cognitive and affective states and optimal moods (David, 1972; Hamilton, 1981). It may, additionally, force them to focus attention on activities and experiences they do not like. Assignees may be deprived of specially favored activities and experiences because (a) they simply are not available in the destination, (b) they are available but culturally inappropriate, (c) assignees may be distracted from them by other experiences or activities, or (d) assignees may simply find that the day-to-day-burdens of surviving appear to have a higher priority.

Back home, most assignees do not live "James Bond" lives. They may not participate in specially favored activities daily, weekly, or even monthly, but they do so frequently enough for their lives to be satisfying, "to keep going." Consequently, abroad, the absence of the activities may not be felt for many months or even a year or more. Thus, long after assignees' bodies have adjusted to physiological changes and long after familiarization with the ecology has diminished the stress, assignees still just "don't like the place" or the people. Ample evidence indicates that symptoms of ecoshock related to mental health are more likely after 1 to 3 years than 1 month (Fong & Peskin, 1969; Lefley, 1989; Lin, Tazuma, & Masuda, 1979; Rumbaut, 1985; Westermeyer, 1986). Mismatches between specially favored activities and experiences and those encountered abroad may be responsible for much of that delayed effect.

The types of activities and experiences associated with optimal moods is likely to vary considerably from person to person (e.g., jogging, meditating, reading a good novel, skin diving, shopping, listening to favorite music). But for many, if not most, assignees, activities involving other people are especially valued—time spent with family, friends, and workmates. For example, people from cultures that heavily value time shared with long-time, intimate friends may be frustrated by the rapid turnover in friends encountered on assignments to mobile societies like the United States. They may put great effort into establishing close friends, only to find one after another moving away. After months or years of that, they may just give up—with, however, some serious ecoshock symptoms as side effects. Thus, disruption of social groups may well contribute in an even more significant way to ecoshock than its impact on stress—particularly for those on long-term assignments, those leaving behind key persons, or those in places where replacements are difficult to find. And, unlike changes in physiology or increases in stress, ecoshock produced by these disruptions is not ameliorated by time and patience. Without active intervention—by the assignee, professionals, or support groups—it is likely to become worse.

The Second Challenge:
Getting the Job Done

Whoever we are, our perceptions of the world—including strategies for completing the tasks of living and working in it—are developed at home within familiar, relatively stable task ecologies. To the degree these strategies are *accommodated* to the characteristics of those ecologies, the tasks are completed successfully and we are productive, satisfied people (Klemp & McClelland, 1986; Scribner, 1986; Wagner & Sternberg, 1986). If the ecology remains familiar and stable, the strategies continue to be effective and become "habits" or "rules of thumb" or "our way" of doing things (e.g., what is taught in MBA programs!). Because "our way" continues to work and because those around us share in it, "our way" becomes "*the* way." But often forgotten is that it works—not because it is the way, but because it remains appropriate to the ecology in which it was developed, because of the *strategy-ecology link* (Fontaine, 1989; see also Berry, 1975; Pandey, 1990).

International assignees are confronted with unfamiliar and changing ecologies, and the appropriateness of "our way" becomes problematic. They are faced with the second challenge: Given that we expect and are skilled in doing things one way and our hosts expect and are skilled in doing them another, how are we going to do them well together? Should assignees continue to do things "our way" or try to adopt "their way" (their "our way"!) or "compromise" (defined here as doing some things "our way" and some things "their way") or what? I (and others) have suggested (Fontaine, 1989, 1993c; Kimmel, 1989; McCaffery, 1986) that, rather than select specific "our way," "their way," or "compromise" strategies, this second challenge requires a more generic strategy in which these—or frequently, other—specific strategies are selected on the basis of which is best accommodated to the new task ecologies encountered abroad. These latter often include ways beyond those typically preferred by the participants within their cultures. They have been called *third cultures* (Casmir & Asuncion-Lande, 1989). I have called them *international microcultures (IMCs)* (Fontaine, 1989, 1993c) to emphasize that the accommodation required is most often at the task or microlevel. An IMC consists of the shared perceptions by the participants in a specific task about the most effective way to complete that task. It has been suggested that, within these third cultures or IMCs, most successful international activity occurs.

The majority of social support mechanisms have traditionally been directed at helping assignees cope with the culture shock encountered abroad (Briody & Chrisman, 1991; Fontaine, 1986). In that sense, they have facilitated dealing with the second challenge only in that the more adjusted the assignee, the better he or she is likely to perform. It is important to note that although the first and second challenges are related in this way, there is an important difference between them: Although coping with ecoshock is essentially an *individual* challenge (although supportive others can help), developing effective strategies to complete tasks is most commonly a *mutual* challenge; the assignee and the host must work them out together. Therein lies a key support role in terms of the second challenge—assisting assignees in networking with hosts likely to be able to help them and with whom they are likely to work effectively together (Brislin & Yoshida, 1994).

As suggested above, the optimal strategy for dealing with the second challenge is the use of IMCs. Anecdotal evidence suggests that IMCs occur less commonly through conscious, planned development than through the often fortuitous coming together of participants who have learned to do things internationally as situations demand—not as past habits dictate. I have suggested that such people often exist in loose networks in active areas of international activity around the world; I have labeled these *IMC networks* (Fontaine, 1989; see also Kimmel, 1989; Saunders, 1987). They are networks because they work with—or at least know about—each other. In most major places of international activity, IMC networks develop. In places where they have not gelled, effective activity tends to be an irregular, transient phenomenon: Sometimes it happens, often it doesn't. IMC networks are brought together by the participants' reputations, "old hands," cultural "informants," embassy advisors, management institutes, professional societies, or chambers of commerce. These groups, and IMC networks themselves, thus provide a significant support function directly related to the second challenge.

The Third Challenge:
Maintaining the Motivation

The third challenge involves the *will* to continue. It is particularly critical on international assignments because coping with ecoshock takes time and patience and because developing IMCs or third cultures takes more time than doing things at home; these cultures typically are new and may require negotiation, preparation, and skill development.

A broad range of motives brings people to assignments, keeps them there, and lures them back internationally again. Some are *extrinsic* (e.g., seeking a salary increase or career advancement). Some are more *intrinsic* to the international character of the assignment (e.g., the desire to live in another country or to learn new skills; Dunbar, 1992). I have identified seven major factors that comprise the motivational profiles of several types of assignees (Fontaine, 1993b): job-oriented travelers, getaway-from-home travelers, recreational travelers, explorers, presence seekers, travel consumers, and followers. In reality, of course, any given assignee is motivated to varying degrees by combinations of the above factors representing his or her "motivational profile." These profiles are likely to change over time. Also, some profiles are more supported by the des-

tination ecology than others, and the *profile-ecology match* is likely to have a significant impact on both ecoshock and assignee satisfaction.

The initial motive that brought an assignee abroad (e.g., getting a promotion, escaping from home) may be insufficient to keep him or her there long enough to deal successfully with the first two challenges. In such a case, it is important to assist the assignee in modifying the motivational profile. Relevant to the focus of this chapter, such intervention can include *supporting existing social groups* (e.g., the family) so that an assignee is not motivated to return home early because of dissatisfactions and *expanding their motivational profile* to include motives more supported by the destination ecology. The latter can include *enmeshing the assignee in new social groups* (Briody & Chrisman, 1991) from which new motives to remain can evolve that stem from the rewarding group activities, relationships with its members, or other benefits of participation. Both supporting existing social groups and enmeshing assignees in new ones thus become key focal points in the support of international assignees.

**Training in the Skills to Develop
and Maintain Social Support Abroad**

I earlier stressed that any training program designed to improve success on international assignments must focus on skill objectives derived from a sound model of the determinants of that success. I summarized one such model conceptualized in terms of three challenges and suggested that assignment success is based on the degree to which each is dealt with effectively. I tried to make the case that social support plays a key role in all three challenges. As such, training for international assignments needs to focus significantly on the skills to develop and maintain support abroad (see also Adelman, 1988; Albert, 1986; Black & Mendenhall, 1990). I turn now to an examination of these skills and some training issues and techniques associated with them. In doing so, I follow a sequencing based on their inclusion in my own international assignment training seminars. Most of the skills in this sequence reflect a generic approach to training in which the emphasis is on teaching trainees the skills to learn how to learn what will work best for themselves in their own specific international assignment ecology (Hughes-Wiener, 1986; McCaffery, 1986; Steele, 1980).

Identifying the Social Support Provided at Home

This skill involves identifying the range of social support needs being provided for at home. The need to identify personal support requirements by examining the functions of support groups at home may seem obvious, but in my experience, few assignees have ever thought much about it. As is true of much else in people's lives, they often do not give much thought to or recognize the importance of social support until it is disrupted or gone. Many people do not fully appreciate the importance of social support in their lives until they find themselves on an international assignment.

Training can assist assignees in identifying their support needs at home and which individuals or groups are filling these needs. I typically give trainees an exercise (see Figure 15.2) in which they are asked to list their needs and the people providing for them. Initially, the lists tend to be rather brief and obvious (e.g., food, money, affection). I then have trainees exchange lists, facilitate a discussion of items on the lists, and ask them to add to their lists as appropriate. The second-iteration lists are usually much more complete (e.g., including the needs for identity, social comparison, and so forth discussed earlier). I then have trainees examine the *pattern* of individuals or groups filling their needs. This task is to help them in determining whether their needs are being filled by a variety of support groups or whether they are concentrated in a few. These differing patterns of support have important implications for support needs on their assignment, as is described shortly.

Identifying Social Support Needs on the Assignment

This skill involves predicting social support needs on the assignment on the basis of the previous examination of needs at home and expectations about the assignment ecology. Rarely are all assignees' support groups relocated with them; they may or may not be accompanied by their families, perhaps by some of their workmates, probably not by their friends or other support groups (e.g., recreational, hobby, or self-help groups to which they may belong). On the basis of an assessment of which groups are accompanying them, they can identify what needs will go unfilled on their assignment and, consequently, what their support requirements will be.

Training can assist assignees in developing the above skill. Again, I typically ask trainees to list which of their needs will be unfilled abroad on the basis of their previous identification of needs at home, who is filling them, and who is accompanying them (see Figure 15.2). At this point, assignees can see the importance of the pattern of support earlier identified. If their needs were being provided for by a few individuals that are accompanying them, then their support situation abroad is likely to be relatively favorable. If those few individuals are not accompanying them, then they may be "in big trouble." Generally, those whose needs are being provided for by a broader variety of support groups are more flexible (though they will almost always have to replace some—but probably not all—support).

At this point, as well, training can include discussion of the degree to which home-country support groups (those left behind) will continue to provide some level of support. On very short-term assignments (up to a month), they may not be missed at all. On other short-term assignments (up to 2 years), they may continue to provide some level of support based, in part, on the communication media available, their skills and those of the assignee in using the media, and the opportunities for home leave. On longer term assignments, the chance of home-country support groups continuing to play important support needs is considerably diminished. Assignees must recognize that the effectiveness of mediated support over time and distance is usually overestimated. Most needs occur locally, and support is most effective if local as well.

Assignees must also recognize that they probably played important support roles themselves in those home-country groups and that the latter, over time, will be forced to replace the assignee and become committed to that replacement—whether at work or at home. It is

My support needs at home?	Who fills them at home?	Filled abroad?	Who is available abroad?
_____	_____	Y N	_____
_____	_____	Y N	_____
_____	_____	Y N	_____
_____	_____	Y N	_____
_____	_____	Y N	_____
_____	_____	Y N	_____
_____	_____	Y N	_____
_____	_____	Y N	_____
_____	_____	Y N	_____
_____	_____	Y N	_____

What gives me my identify at home?	Available abroad?
_____	Y N
_____	Y N
_____	Y N
_____	Y N
_____	Y N

Figure 15.2. Social Support Exercise

useful at this point also to alert assignees that even those support groups accompanying them may not function as "supportively" as they did before. They, too, are likely to experience ecoshock, and it is not uncommon for family and workmate relationships to become more mutually destructive than supportive. This possibility needs to be taken into account in soberly predicting support needs on the assignment (as too, then, does the advisability of going at all!).

Assignees must recognize, as well, that the stress and fatigue of an international assignment and the difficulties of dealing effectively with the challenges encountered on it may increase the _level_ of current social support needs (e.g., the need for relaxing times with their familiar, predictable family) and increase the _types_ of social support needs (e.g., IMC networks may be required abroad but not at home). Again, this possibility needs to be taken into account in predicting support needs.

The skill in identifying support needs on the assignment should involve an examination of the kinds of activities and experiences associated with _optimal moods_ and the degree to which all or some of them require social support. Recall that failure to participate in such

Supported

List below activities you most *enjoy*	at *home?*	abroad?
_____	+ −	+ −
_____	+ −	+ −
_____	+ −	+ −
_____	+ −	+ −
_____	+ −	+ −
_____	+ −	+ −
_____	+ −	+ −
_____	+ −	+ −
_____	+ −	+ −
_____	+ −	+ −
Net Score	[ ]	[ ]

Supported

List below activities you most **dislike**	at *home?*	abroad?
_____	+ −	+ −
_____	+ −	+ −
_____	+ −	+ −
_____	+ −	+ −
Net Score	[ ]	[ ]

Figure 15.3. What I Like to Do

activities for whatever reason can be an important cause of ecoshock—particularly on longer term assignments. As with social support needs, most people do not give much attention to the role of these activities and experiences until they are gone.

Training can assist assignees in this process. I typically ask trainees to list their favorite activities, the degree to which each is supported (e.g., available, accessible, affordable, culturally appropriate) at home, and the degree to which they expect each to be supported abroad (see Figure 15.3). They then compute a net score based on the number of activities supported at home minus those supported abroad. Typically, this score is positive, an indication that their optimal moods are likely to be more supported at home than abroad, and they can see the need to intervene in some way if they are to maintain positive moods. This intervention can involve making sure they continue to engage in specially favored activities—whatever the cost. I refer to this as *attentional regulation* (Fontaine, 1993c; see also Hamilton, 1981). It can also involve finding new replacement activities that provide the same positive moods but that are more supported by the destination ecology. I refer to this as *attentional flexibility.* Both have implications for social support and training in social support skills to the extent that old activity preferences involve people or that replacement preferences can involve people.

Identifying Social Support Opportunities Available on the Assignment

This is essentially an *exploring* or *scouting* skill (Steele, 1980). It involves identifying the support groups accompanying assignees (e.g., family members, workmates), what the organization provides in terms of home culture and host culture personnel and their dependents, and what is available in the wider host culture. Of particular concern is (a) identifying the support provided by the organization's overseas office and (b) assessing whether the destination ecology contains a large and functioning expat community with structured means for integrating newcomers or if assignees must find home-culture groups on their own or depend largely on opportunities in the host culture. It is necessary to assess (c) whether the assignment is to a cosmopolitan, urban destination with a variety of activities and experiences available and familiar with the needs of foreigners or a more provincial destination with limited opportunities. And it is also necessary to (d) determine the degree to which language, culture, security, and attitudes toward the assignee's country facilitate or hinder entry into host culture support groups.

Training can assist exploration skills by identifying relevant sources of information and what to look for in those sources. It can guide assignees in gathering and interpreting orientation information in book or video libraries, finding informants knowledgeable about the destination, or making best use of a site visit. It

can assist in making contact with assistance centers, finding sponsors or informal social contacts, monitoring newspapers or club notices, visiting recreational or educational facilities, and so forth. Generally, training can help people learn how and what to look for, ask for, and interpret.

Training can also help assignees in identifying a broad range of support options available, going beyond the types of groups they typically turn to at home. This range is often necessary because assignees may have to expand the number and types of support groups required, they may find their success rate in getting into groups lower, or the groups encountered abroad may function quite differently in terms of support than similar groups back home (see below). Again, I typically have trainees develop lists of support opportunities available. I encourage them to be as creative, flexible, inclusive, and uncritical as possible at this stage. I then have them exchange lists, facilitate a brainstorming-like session, and have them add to their lists as appropriate.

Matching Unfilled Needs With Available Support

This is probably the key social support skill on international assignments. It requires assignees to know themselves in terms of their support needs and to know what opportunities are available. But most important, it requires *making the match*. On the one hand, making the match should be based on an understanding of the *resource requirements of the needs* (e.g., physiological, psychological, social) and the *resources provided by available support groups*. Then, needs and groups are matched on *resources* the group provides, rather than on the type of group. It is important for assignees to understand that the same type of group abroad may not provide the same resources provided at home. At home, a university may provide just the kinds of recreational opportunities required for optimal moods; abroad, the university may provide for no recreation at all. At home, a church may provide baby-sitting services; abroad, it may provide only religion. At home, bars might be a good place to meet members of the opposite sex; abroad, that may only be the case if you are willing to pay for meeting them. Making the match may well involve matching different groups to the same need (assignees may meet the opposite sex in church or at a tennis club instead). A frequent complaint from dissatisfied assignees abroad is "there is nothing to do and no one to do anything with." What they often really mean is "there is nothing *familiar* to do and no one *familiar* to do it with." One reason why successful assignees often appear to live very different lifestyles overseas is that they find they require very different support groups to fill their needs.

On the other hand, although making the match should involve the kind of understanding described above, in my experience it is at least as often based on intuition or luck. For that reason, training needs, in part, to simply provide encouragement for assignees to get out into the world and experiment—and to motivate them to stay long enough for luck to have a chance!

Maintaining Existing Relationships

Often, of course, making the match produces the recognition that at least some social support needs require the maintenance of ongoing social relationships. Typically, these are with home country groups (e.g., maintaining close relationships with those in the home office so that the assignee is not forgotten in the organization while abroad) and home culture groups (e.g., the assignee's accompanying spouse and children). As described earlier, maintenance of the former is made more problematic over time by distance and communication barriers; maintenance of the latter is made difficult because they, too, are usually experiencing ecoshock. Further, for a variety of reasons, assignees involved in international lives often find themselves in intercultural relationships—marriages or work groups. These relationships often have special challenges of their own to successful maintenance (Fontaine, 1990).

Finally, in training I make the case that *every time a family or work group is relocated together, members are faced with a new relationship.* For example, a husband and wife generally meet each other at home and in that ecology develop procedures for making decisions, handling money, entertaining themselves, allocating time, resolving conflict, and so forth, tasks on which the maintenance of relationships is based. Overseas, however, the couple are often surprised and upset to find one

partner thinking and acting in new ways in response to the new ecology—ways that may come as a surprise to the other partner too. And the procedures for making decisions, handling money, allocating time, and so forth that worked so well at home may no longer be as effective. In a very real sense, every move to a new destination produces a new marriage (or work group)—one the participants may or may not be happy with.

A key to maintaining any relationship during times of change—or intercultural relationships anytime—is (a) recognizing differences in perception (e.g., attitudes, values) that may cause relationship problems and (b) developing consensual solutions to those problems. The quality and stability of a relationship is not based solely on the number of its problems, but significantly on the partners' ability to solve them (e.g., see Ting-Toomey, 1994): One relationship may have a plethora of problems but will survive if the partners have developed effective conflict resolution strategies; another may have only one problem but will collapse if the partners cannot resolve it.

Kelley and his colleagues describe several attribution-related difficulties with important implications for the maintenance of relationships abroad (Berley & Jacobson, 1984; Fincham & Bradbury, 1990; Fletcher & Fincham, 1991; Harvey, Wells, & Alvarez, 1976; Orvis, Kelley, & Butler, 1976). *Attribution conflict* involves differences in the perceived cause of a given event in a relationship. Frequently, it is not the event itself that produces problems, but to what that event is causally attributed. For instance, a husband's arriving home intoxicated in the early morning hours might be attributed by his wife to his stress on the job, his lack of consideration for her, social pressure by his workmates, or another woman. Which particular attribution she makes and how appropriate she thinks it is will largely determine her reaction and any subsequent conflict. If she attributes it to lack of consideration and if he attributes it to social pressure and if they are aware of their differences, then they are experiencing attribution conflict. The common *symptoms* of such conflict are *arguments and fights often expressing direct or indirect hostility.*

Ignorance of attribution conflict occurs when one or both of the partners are unaware of their differences (e.g., the husband assumes the wife also attributes it to social pressure). In such cases, the *symptoms* are more likely to be *feelings of loss of responsiveness, synchrony, or enthusiasm* in the relationship. *Attributional ambiguity,* however, occurs when a relationship has so many potential problems that participants cannot arrive at a stable, consensual definition of what the real problems are (e.g., is it money, or value differences, or job pressures, or the children, or what?): One day, the cause seems like one thing and another day another. Such ambiguity can make the development of active, intervening solutions (so popular in at least Western cultures) difficult. The *symptoms,* then, are *problem-solving difficulties and threats to relationship stability.*

Research on intercultural interaction in work groups (Davidson & Feldman, 1971) and marriages (Fontaine & Dorch, 1980) suggests that intercultural relationships experience more of these attributional difficulties than intracultural ones. There is plenty of reason to expect that families or work groups experiencing new attitudes and behaviors in response to the ecological changes associated with international assignments would have difficulties with them too. Thus, a valuable international assignment training focus is on helping participants improve their skills in dealing with these attribution-related difficulties. In my own training, as much as possible, I try to have families or work groups participate in training together. In most cases, simply alerting them to the potential for attribution conflict and ambiguity, the symptoms, and the solutions is useful—particularly for those in intracultural relationships, who often never anticipate that problems might arise overseas (in my experience, those in intercultural relationships are more likely to anticipate them). But in training, they can also be asked to explore their attitudes about a variety of events occurring in their lives and work abroad in an attempt to identify areas of change or difference and potential conflict. The ability to do this on a continuing basis beyond training is likely to have significant positive impact on relationship maintenance.

Developing, Maintaining, and Dissolving New Relationships

Although making the match often involves maintaining existing support groups, it also commonly requires developing, maintaining, and—when necessary—dissolving relationships with new support groups. Usually, these are home culture groups at work or in an expat or ethnic community and/or host culture groups at work or in the wider host culture. The selection of home culture versus host culture groups is heavily dependent on ecological characteristics of the assignment (e.g., is an expat community available, or are mechanisms in place for easing entry into host culture groups?). Important concerns can also arise about the impact of each on adjustment. Although emphasis on building relationships with home culture groups might be most advisable in the short term, in the longer term, reliance on them may hinder adjustment (Kim, 1987).

Developing and maintaining support with home culture groups largely involve the same kinds of behaviors as they would at home but with a few qualifications. For instance, the selection of relationships abroad is much more constrained by *availability;* the range of choices to fill support needs is simply not as broad as at home. Consequently, assignees often find themselves in relationships with people very different from those they would choose at home and whose primary value is that they're there! If assignees do not recognize this necessity, they are apt to find themselves very lonely. Further, the *time frame* available to form, maintain, and dissolve relationships abroad is often artificially dependent on the assignment-related coming and going of people. If assignees do not recognize this dependence, they will likely find their social feelings and behaviors out of sync with those of others.

Developing, maintaining, and dissolving relationships with host culture groups can be particularly challenging—especially outside of formal host or welcoming groups that may have structured introduction procedures. The *complexity* of strategies for relationship development, maintenance, and dissolution should not be underestimated (e.g., Derlega, 1984; Duck, 1993; Furnham & Bochner, 1986). They are among the most difficult things people do in life. They require the most synchronized of behavioral initiatives and responses. The rules governing them are very culturally specific (e.g., Duck, 1993; Ting-Toomey, 1991, 1994). They differ from Sydney to Brisbane; from academic to professional; from 40-year-olds to 30-year-olds. They are so complex that even in one's own culture one commonly fails with them. Only a small percentage of the relationships (business or personal) that people wish for or need in their lives ever come to fruition—probably a very small percentage. And many of one's attempts to amicably dissolve those that one does establish end in a mess. And that's at home!

So, how can assignees be expected to do it abroad? How do international relationships ever get initiated, much less maintained? One answer may be that, in many cases, the culturally specific rules—that at home serve as a "test" for the appropriateness of the other person as a business or personal partner—are thrown away. If others do not meet the test at home, one doesn't do business with them. If others do not meet the test abroad, one may excuse them: They, after all, shouldn't be expected to know the rules. But without rules, people are swimming in rough seas.

Rules have a function. They are, as just mentioned, a screening device, a way to tell whether the other person has the same values, is predictable, and is to be trusted. Rules keep participant behaviors in synchrony and help business move along efficiently. Without rules, there is no such screening and perhaps no such synchrony.

Those skilled at developing, maintaining, and dissolving relationships at home may or may not be equally skilled abroad in different and changing ecologies. A socially skilled person is generally seen as someone who knows the rules or at least exhibits the appropriate behaviors (Cronen & Shuter, 1983). But in *international situations,* where rules differ and where conformity to them may not be so rigidly required, *a very different kind of social skill is necessary.* On an international assignment, a socially skilled person is not the one who knows rules well, but rather is the one who can survive in rough seas by grasping whatever the wind, waves, and tide present him or her. This skill is so different that quite different kinds of people may have it. The socially skilled person at home, the person who has learned so well strategies specific to the rules of his or her culture and who has practiced them to a routine may be socially inept in international situations. And vice versa: The successful international professional who appears so suave at the embassy reception may be a social klutz chatting over beers at a barbecue with neighbors back home.

Assignees may be forgiven abroad for not knowing all the relationship rules, but they first have to be met. Thus, an important skill in establishing relationships abroad is being able to put oneself in the right place at the right time. Assignees need to know *where* the behavior settings are that provide opportunities to meet relevant others and to develop relationships (e.g., meetings of professional societies, cocktail parties, sports' clubs, dinners). These settings vary considerably from culture to culture, and the skill to find them is usually based more on clever planning than on spontaneity. Further, assignees need to know how to *access* the settings (e.g., get invitations or tickets). An important social support objective of training can be to provide information about both location and access.

A prerequisite to initiating interactions once in the appropriate behavioral settings is having sufficiently high *self-confidence* (Coopersmith, 1967)—at a time when ecoshock often erodes confidence. Some assignees seem to be skilled at quickly *personalizing* a place and having a sense of *belonging*. This skill is particularly important for those who must relocate frequently to very different ecologies.

Often, an assignee's identity is based on ties to a city or organization or family. Apart from them, the person feels adrift. To be effective in establishing supportive relationships on international assignments, the basis of assignees' identity must be more portable. But what is portable? Clothes that feel part of them—especially if their business or gender requires them to wear something different most the time (suits, saris, sarongs, jeans, muu muus, or shorts). Posters, tapes, photos, hobbies, sports, hiking, jogging, knitting, reading, pets, or their own car can also work. Or being sure to take time for themselves. But they must not go too far into this identity maintenance: Too much emphasis on who they *were* may inhibit seeing who they *must be* to adapt to the overseas destination. They need a balance.

Training can help assignees with *quick personalization* (Steele, 1980). I often have assignees begin the process by listing objects, behaviors, or experiences that make them feel like "themselves" or "at home" or that are central to their "identity" (see Figure 15.2). Again, prior to an assignment, assignees often have not given these much thought. I then have assignees examine their lists to look for what may be either *portable* or *available* in the destination and have them plan to make use of them as quickly as possible after arrival.

Once contact has been made with appropriate support groups and interaction has been initiated, other skills are needed to *maintain* the relationships. Internationally, home culture support groups may tolerate a lot of deviance because they need all the people they can get (it takes lots of expats to put on a golf tournament). They will forgive assignees for anything—probably even cheating—as long as they participate! Host culture groups can be less forgiving. They may not need assignees at all and, with an assignee's first mistake, may dissolve back into the city.

The behaviors associated with maintaining relationships are just as complex and culturally specific as those for forming relationships. Certainly, recognition of the roles of *attribution conflict, ignorance of attribution conflict,* and *attribution ambiguity,* mentioned earlier in the context of maintaining home culture relationships, apply here as well. Because some level of conflict based at least on cultural differences seems inevitable, awareness of—and skills for dealing with—the *conflict resolution strategies* of the other culture is important (Fontaine, 1990; Romano, 1988). The maintenance of intercultural relationships typically requires a great deal of *mutual trust* and *giving the benefit of the doubt*—the latter, often, at times of stress when assignees and hosts are least inclined. All of these skills should be a focus for social support on international assignments.

Finally, assignees need to remember that their assignments will end (one hopes, successfully). They will have to say good-bye and go home. Thus, they need to have relationship *dissolution* skills as well. How they say good-bye can be important. It will affect how those in the expat community and in the host culture remember the assignee. International communities are small and mobile; assignees may run into the people elsewhere and need them. And how assignees say good-bye can also affect how those left behind—particularly host cul-

ture groups—treat the next person who comes along on assignment to that destination.

It is important for assignees to recognize that the meaning of "dissolving" relationships and the behaviors associated with it are again very culturally specific. In U.S. culture, for instance, relationships and the obligations they entail may be totally dissolved with no future obligations. In many other cultures, that is not so; the obligations may be diminished or changed, but the relationship in some sense remains and the obligations are never eliminated. One day, the assignees may find a previous host on their own front door needing some major "favors"!

Then there is the need to *reestablish* support back home. If the assignment has been a long one, the steps may be quite similar to those on the assignment itself (Austin, 1986; Martin, 1984). Not infrequently, it is easier to establish new support groups back home—make new friends—than it is to rekindle old ones. Training can at least alert soon-to-be returnees to this possibility prior to their reentry. Better yet, it can help them prepare for it prior to their assignment abroad in the first place.

What Organizations Can Do

As noted, the organization for which an assignee works can provide for many of an assignee's needs associated with both working and living abroad. It can provide services as diverse as cost of living allowances, staff support, satellite communications, and access to schools, swimming pools, and golf courses. And because the organization is most commonly more established in the destination than the individual assignees are, it can be particularly useful in helping assignees establish relationships with home culture and host culture support groups. But the organization rarely provides everything; in all cases, assignees will need the skills to develop a substantial amount of their support on their own. The organization can help them toward that end by providing training in at least the skills identified in this chapter.

References

Adelman, M. B. (1988). Cross-cultural adjustment: A theoretical perspective on social support. *International Journal of Intercultural Relations, 12*(3), 183-204.

Albert, R. (1986). Conceptual framework for the development and evaluation of cross-cultural orientation programs. *International Journal of Intercultural Relations, 10,* 197-213.

Albrecht, T. L., & Adelman, M. B. (1984). Social support and life stress: New directions for communication research. *Human Communication Research, 11*(1), 3-32.

Albrecht, T. L., & Adelman, M. B. (Eds.). (1987). *Communicating social support.* Newbury Park, CA: Sage.

Austin, C. N. (1986). *Cross-cultural reentry: A book of readings.* Abilene, TX: Abilene Christian University Press.

Barna, L. M. (1983). The stress factor in intercultural relations. In D. Landis & R. W. Brislin (Eds.), *Handbook of intercultural training* (Vol. 2, pp. 19-49). Elmsford, NY: Pergamon.

Berley, R. A., & Jacobson, N. S. (1984). Causal attributions in intimate relationships: Toward a model of cognitive-behavioral marital therapy. In P. C. Kendall (Ed.), *Advances in cognitive-behavioral research and therapy* (Vol. 3). San Diego: Academic Press.

Berry, J. W. (1975). Ecology, cultural adaptation, and psychological differentiation: Traditional patterning and acculturative stress. In R. W. Brislin, S. Bochner, & W. J. Lonner (Eds.), *Cross-cultural perspectives on learning* (pp. 207-228). New York: John Wiley.

Black, J. S., & Mendenhall, M. (1990). Cross-cultural training effectiveness: A review and theoretical framework for future research. *Academy of Management Review, 15,* 113-136.

Black, J. S., Mendenhall, M., & Oddou, G. (1991). Toward a comprehensive model of international adjustment: An integration of multiple theoretical perspectives. *Academy of Management Review, 16,* 291-317.

Briody, E. K., & Chrisman, J. B. (1991). Cultural adaptation on overseas assignments. *Human Organization, 50*(3), 264-282.

Brislin, R. (1993). *Understanding culture's influence on behavior.* Orlando, FL: Harcourt Brace Jovanovich.

Brislin, R., & Yoshida, T. (1994). *Intercultural communication training: An introduction.* Thousand Oaks, CA: Sage.

Casmir, F. L., & Asuncion-Lande, N. (1989). Intercultural communication revisited: Conceptualization, paradigm building, and methodological approaches. In J. A. Anderson (Ed.), *Communication yearbook* (pp. 278-309). Newbury Park, CA: Sage.

Coopersmith, S. (1967). *Antecedents of self-esteem.* New York: Freeman.

Copeland, L., & Griggs, L. (1985). *Going international: How to make friends and deal effectively in the global marketplace.* New York: Random House.

Cronen, V. E., & Shuter, R. (1983). Forming intercultural bonds. In W. B. Gudykunst (Ed.), *Intercultural communications theory: Current perspectives.* Beverly Hills, CA: Sage.

David, K. H. (1972). Intercultural adjustment and applications of reinforcement theory to problems of "culture shock." *Trends, 4*(3), 1-64.

Davidson, A. R., & Feldman, J. H. (1971). *An attribution theory analysis of interracial conflict in job settings* (Technology Report No. 11). Urbana: University of Illinois, Department of Psychology.

Derlega, V. J. (1984). *Communication, intimacy, and close relationships.* San Diego: Academic Press.

Desatnick, R. L., & Bennett, M. L. (1977). *Human resource management in the multinational company.* New York: Nichols.

Duck, S. (1993). *Individuals in relationships.* Newbury, Park, CA: Sage.

Dunbar, E. (1992). Adjustment and satisfaction of expatriate U.S. personnel. *International Journal of Intercultural Relations, 16*(1), 1-16.

Ehret, C. F., & Scanlon, L. W. (1986). *Overcoming jet lag.* New York: Berkley.

Fincham, F. D., & Bradbury, T. N. (1990). Cognition in marriage: A program of research on attribution. In W. Jones & D. Perlman (Eds.), *Advances in personal relationships* (Vol. 2). Greenwich, CT: JAI.

Fletcher, G. J. O., & Fincham, F. D. (1991). *Cognition in close relationships.* Hillsdale, NJ: Lawrence Erlbaum.

Fong, S. L. M., & Peskin, H. (1969). Sex-role strain and personality adjustment of China-born students in America. *Journal of Abnormal Psychology, 74,* 563-567.

Fontaine, G. (1986). Roles of social support systems in overseas relocation. *International Journal of Intercultural Relations, 10,* 361-378.

Fontaine, G. (1989). *Managing international assignments: The strategy for success.* Englewood Cliffs, NJ: Prentice-Hall.

Fontaine, G. (1990). Cultural diversity in intimate relationships. In D. Cahn (Ed.), *Intimates in conflict* (pp. 209-224). Hillsdale, NJ: Lawrence Erlbaum.

Fontaine, G. (1993a). The experience of a sense of presence in intercultural and international encounters. *Presence: Teleoperators and Virtual Environments, 1,* 1-9.

Fontaine, G. (1993b). Motivational factors of international travelers. *Psychological Reports, 72,* 1106.

Fontaine, G. (1993c). Training for the three key challenges encountered on all international assignments. *Leadership and Organization Journal, 14*(3), 8-14.

Fontaine, G., & Dorch, E. (1980). Problems and benefits of close intercultural relationships. *International Journal of Intercultural Relations, 4,* 329-337.

Furnham, A. (1988). The adjustment of sojourners. In Y. Y. Kim & W. B. Gudykunst (Eds.), *Cross-cultural adaptation.* Newbury Park, CA: Sage.

Furnham, A., & Bochner, S. (1986). *Culture shock: Psychological reactions to unfamiliar environments.* New York: Methuen.

Gudykunst, W. B. (1991). *Bridging differences.* Newbury Park, CA: Sage.

Hamilton, J. A. (1981). Attention, personality, and self-regulation of mood: Absorbing interest and boredom. In B. A. Maher (Ed.), *Progress in experimental personality research, 10,* 282-315.

Harris, P. R., & Moran, R. T. (1991). *Managing cultural differences.* Houston: Gulf.

Harvey, J. H., Wells, G. L., & Alvarez, M. D. (1976). Attribution in the context of conflict and separation in close relationships. In J. H. Harvey, W. J. Ickes, & R. F. Kidd (Eds.), *New directions in attribution research* (pp. 235-260). New York: John Wiley.

House, J. S. (1985). Barriers to work stress: I. Social support. In W. D. Gentry, H. Benson, & C. J. deWolff (Eds.), *Behavioral medicine: Work, stress, and health.* The Hague, The Netherlands: Martinus Nijhoff.

Hughes-Wiener, G. (1986). The "learning how to learn" approach to cross-cultural orientation. *International Journal of Intercultural Relations, 10*(4), 485-505.

Kim, Y. Y. (1987). Facilitating immigrant adaptation: The role of communication. In T. L. Albrecht & M. B. Adelman (Eds.), *Communicating social support* (pp. 192-211). Newbury Park, CA: Sage.

Kimmel, P. R. (1989). *International negotiation and intercultural exploration: Toward cultural understanding.* Washington, DC: U.S. Institute of Peace.

Klemp, G. O., & McClelland, D. C. (1986). What characterizes intelligent functioning among senior managers. In R. J. Sternberg & R. K. Wagner (Eds.), *Practical intelligence: Nature and origins of competence in the everyday world* (pp. 31-50). New York: Cambridge University Press.

Lefley, H. P. (1989). Counseling refugees: The North American experience. In P. B. Pedersen, J. G. Draguns, W. J. Lonner, & J. E. Trimble (Eds.), *Counseling across cultures.* Honolulu: University of Hawaii Press.

Lin, K. M., Tazuma, L., & Masuda, M. (1979). Adaptational problems of Vietnamese refugees: Part 1. Health and mental health status. *Archives of General Psychiatry, 36,* 955-961.

Martin, J. (1984). The intercultural reentry: Conceptualization and directions for future research. *International Journal of Intercultural Relations, 8,* 115-134.

McCaffery, J. A. (1986). Independent effectiveness: Reconsideration of cross-cultural orientation and training. *International Journal of Intercultural Relations, 10,* 159-178.

Orvis, R. R., Kelley, H. H., & Butler, D. (1976). Attributional conflict in young couples. In J. H. Harvey, W. J. Ickes, & R. F. Kidd (Eds.), *New directions in attribution research* (pp. 353-386). New York: John Wiley.

Pandey, J. (1990). The environment, culture, and behavior. In R. W. Brislin (Ed.), *Applied cross-cultural psychology* (pp. 254-277). Newbury Park, CA: Sage.

Parker, B., & McEvoy, G. M. (1993). An initial examination of a model of intercultural adjustment. *International Journal of Intercultural Relations, 17,* 355-379.

Romano, D. (1988). *Intercultural marriage: Promises and pitfalls.* Yarmouth, ME: Intercultural Press.

Rumbaut, R. G. (1985). Mental health and the refugee experience: A comparative study of Southeast Asian refugees. In T. C. Owan (Ed.), *Southeast Asian mental health: Treatment, prevention, services, training, and research* (pp. 433-486). Washington, DC: National Institute of Mental Health.

Saunders, H. H. (1987). *Beyond "us and them"— Building mature international relationships: The role of official and supplemental diplomacy.* Washington, DC: Brookings Institution.

Scribner, S. (1986). Thinking in action: Some characteristics of practical thought. In R. J. Sternberg & R. K. Wagner (Eds.), *Practical intelligence:*

Nature and origins of competence in the everyday world (pp. 13-30). New York: Cambridge University Press.

Singleton, W. T., Spurgeon, P., & Stammers, R. B. (Eds.). (1980). *The analysis of social skill.* New York: Plenum.

Steele, F. (1980). Defining and developing environmental competence. In C. P. Alderfer & C. L. Cooper (Eds.), *Advances in experimental social processes* (pp. 225-244). New York: John Wiley.

Taft, R. (1977). Coping with unfamiliar cultures. In N. Warren (Ed.), *Studies in cross-cultural psychology* (Vol. 1, pp. 121-153). San Diego: Academic Press.

Ting-Toomey, S. (1991). Intimacy expressions in three cultures: France, Japan, and the United States. *International Journal of Intercultural Relations, 15,* 29-46.

Ting-Toomey, S. (1994). Managing conflict in intimate relationships. In D. D. Cahn (Ed.), *Conflict in personal relationships.* Hillsdale, NJ: Lawrence Erlbaum.

Wagner, R. K., & Sternberg, R. J. (1986). Tacit knowledge and intelligence in the everyday world. In R. J. Sternberg & R. K. Wagner (Eds.), *Practical intelligence: Nature and origins of competence in the everyday world* (pp. 51-83). New York: Cambridge University Press.

Walton, S. (1990). Stress management training for overseas effectiveness. *International Journal of Intercultural Relations, 14*(4), 507-528.

Westermeyer, J. (1986). Migration and psychopathology. In C. L. Williams & J. Westermeyer (Eds.), *Refugee mental health in resettlement countries* (pp. 39-59). Washington, DC: Hemisphere.

16

Models of Diversity Training

BERNARDO M. FERDMAN

SARI EINY BRODY

DURING the past decade, attention to diversity has grown exponentially in U.S. organizations. The exigencies of an increasingly multiethnic, multicultural, and bigender labor force have led more and more corporations, governmental and nonprofit agencies, and educational institutions to implement a variety of training programs and related initiatives focused on reaping the benefits and avoiding the pitfalls associated with diversity. The results of one recent survey (Wheeler, 1994), for example, showed that 79% of 406 companies were using or planning to use some type of diversity training. In another set of surveys (as reported by Caudron, 1993), the proportion of organizations indicating they had or were planning diversity-training programs increased from 47% to 75% between 1990 and 1991. Finally, in a 1994 poll of 2,313 organizations with more than 100 employees, 56% re-

ported providing diversity training, compared with 40% in 1992 (Silverstein, 1995).

Despite the growth of diversity training, the term does not refer to any one specific activity. It can be used to describe many workplace interventions, ranging from 1-hour briefings to organizationwide change initiatives. Although diversity training efforts typically have some features in common—for example, a focus on domestic diversity and its implications for the workplace—such efforts can vary broadly in how they are conceptualized and implemented. The driving forces, the assumptions and goals, and the strategies and techniques employed can differ significantly between one diversity training initiative and another. In this chapter, we explore the assumptions, goals, strategies, and conceptual frameworks that guide diversity training efforts—in short, the "why, what, and

AUTHORS' NOTE: We are very grateful to Judith H. Katz for her extensive, thoughtful, and helpful comments on previous drafts of this chapter.

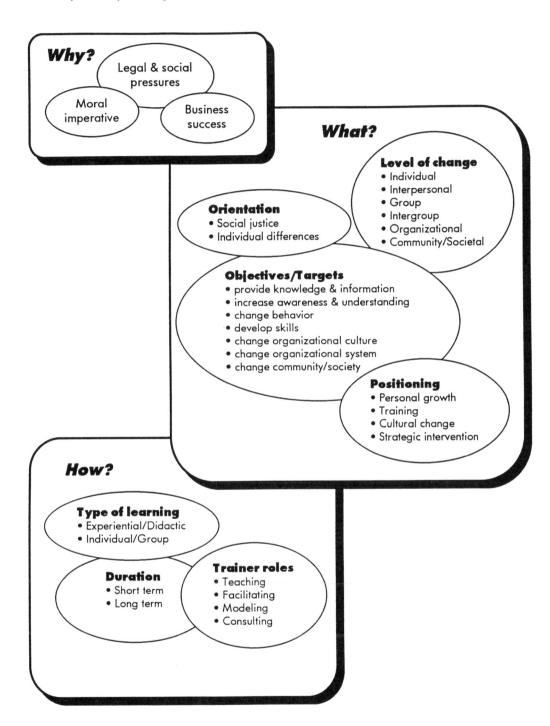

Figure 16.1. Diversity Training: The Why, What, and How

how" of diversity training. Our intent is not to provide a comprehensive review of training techniques or designs or to address the broader dynamics of cultural diversity in organizations (see e.g., Chemers, Oskamp, & Constanzo, 1995; Cox, 1993; Ferdman, 1992; Triandis, Kurowski, & Gelfand, 1994), but rather to consider the range of issues underlying the planning and use of diversity training. Figure 16.1 presents the framework for the chapter and a summary of the topics discussed.

It is important to highlight at the outset that diversity training is one component of a larger set of diversity initiatives and interventions. Many organizations in the United States actively employ a variety of strategies and techniques to deal with the increasing heterogeneity of the workplace and the community. In large part, the definition, goals, and focus of diversity training depend on whether or not organizations use it as part of a broader strategy for integrating and working with diversity.

Understanding that diversity training can be only one component of diversity initiatives becomes especially important when distinguishing between diversity training and intercultural training. Pruegger and Rogers (1994), following Triandis (1986), describe intercultural training as being "concerned with increasing our ability to communicate with culturally diverse people and monitoring and adjusting our behavior to deal effectively with those of different cultures" (p. 370). Brislin and Yoshida (1994b), focusing on intercultural communication training, define this as "formal efforts designed to prepare people for more effective interpersonal relations when they interact with individuals from cultures other than their own" (pp. 2-3). Diversity training can overlap greatly with intercultural communication training in that it often incorporates the same goal. Moreover, many methods and tools included as components of diversity training are derived or adapted from intercultural training approaches. Indeed, these are often discussed interchangeably (e.g., see Chapter 4, this volume; Triandis et al., 1994). Thus, telling diversity and intercultural training apart can be difficult sometimes if the focus is solely on techniques and training modules. A hallmark of much diversity training is its connection to organizational needs and objectives. Also, in contrast with intercultural training, working effectively across cultural differences comprises only one focal issue for most diversity training initiatives.

At a minimum, diversity training implies a concern for the impact of differences among people on their interactions and on the organization, including issues related to working in and with a heterogeneous workforce. More broadly, it can address issues related to the implications of diversity for organizational change as it is affected by competition, customers, products, and the marketplace. The definitions of diversity in specific organizations, however, can range from those focused on race, gender, ethnicity, and other group-based categorizations, to those that encompass individual differences, lifestyles, and job functions (Wheeler, 1994). Many, but not all, of these differences are reflected in cultural diversity. Thus, definitions of diversity can also vary in the degree to which they employ culture and cultural differences as central concepts. In part, these choices may depend on an organization's motivation and goals for undertaking diversity training. We discuss these in more detail in the following section.

The "Why" of Diversity Training

Organizations conduct diversity training for a multiplicity of reasons. Some of these reasons are more explicit than others. In this section, we discuss some underlying motivations that prompt organizations to introduce diversity training. These factors are important not only in affecting whether or not training is adopted but also in determining the role of the training in the organization and the form it takes.

We discuss three general categories of motivators: (a) the moral imperative, (b) legal and social pressures, and (c) business success and competitiveness (Cox, 1993). Although we treat them separately in this discussion, these arguments typically cut across diversity initiatives. In most cases, they operate jointly in various combinations to prompt and frame organizational approaches to diversity. Because the stimulus that leads organizations to embark on diversity initiatives and diversity training efforts may not always be clear, explicit, or stable over time, it can be useful to consider how different rationales can relate to the road taken.

Many, if not most, diversity initiatives embrace inclusion as a desirable goal. This concept cuts across all three types of motivations but is framed differently and takes on different connotations within each. Similarly, the various motivations can be reflected in alternative visions of the "ideal" organization and different goals for diversity efforts. Thus, we give *inclusion* and *vision and goals* special attention as we discuss each of the three driving forces behind diversity training.

The Moral Imperative

The history of the United States is often cast in terms of the struggle for justice and equality and against oppression. This legacy has had a strong impact on the motivation for diversity initiatives and on how they are framed. Debates over how best and most fairly to deal with differences in society have long been a feature of civic discourse in the United States (e.g., see Ferdman, 1990, in press; Frederickson & Knobel, 1982; Glazer, 1988; Kitano, 1991; Taylor, 1992). This pattern continues during the 1990s, and diversity training is very much in the middle of the debate (e.g., see Macdonald, 1993; Mobley & Payne, 1992; Silverstein, 1995; Swisher, 1995).

Fundamental disagreements persist in the United States whether it is best to strive for assimilation, amalgamation (the melting pot), or pluralism. The notion of multiculturalism is a relatively recent entrant into this debate and is also the source of much contention. Diversity training and other diversity initiatives grounded in the moral imperative typically adopt the orientation that pluralism and multiculturalism are the best options for all individuals, groups, and society in that these choices are likely to lead to the most positive outcomes. *Multiculturalism* means recognizing and valuing the range of cultural and other group-based differences among people (see, e.g., Katz, 1989). It also entails seeing these differences as providing essential contributions to society and therefore striving to eliminate invidious and ethnocentric comparisons, as well as finding ways to foster positive expression of the differences. Berry (1993) and Cox and Finley-Nickelson (1991) describe pluralism or integration as involving the coexistence in one society or organization of groups that differ

along cultural dimensions while maintaining distinct ethnic and cultural identities and practices.

A related perspective stemming from the moral imperative emphasizes the importance of acknowledging and working to address the long history of racism, sexism, and conflictual intergroup relations in the United States. Because certain groups have been and continue to be the targets of widespread, pervasive, and institutionalized discrimination, its impact is still very much a part of the American fabric. Proponents of the moral imperative argue that it is incumbent on the beneficiaries of this historical pattern of oppression, discrimination, and bias to begin to truly "level the playing field" in a way more consistent with the values of liberty, equality, and justice. Leveling the playing field involves, in part, heightening awareness of the inequities and recognizing, for example, how the experiences of people of color and White women have differed from those of White men.

Thus, the desire to contribute to the development of a better society by "doing the right thing" can be an important motivation for diversity training. As many businesses recognize the important role they occupy in society, they acknowledge responsibilities toward their members and toward the larger communities in which they operate, including the obligation to increase opportunities for all people and to help their stakeholders—whether employees, potential employees, customers, or residents of the community—live a better life.

Addressing diversity constructively can be one aspect of this. Cox (1993), for example, points out that "it is certainly prudent to include, among many goals of organizations, social responsibility objectives such as promoting fairness and improving economic opportunities for underachieving members of society" (p. 12). Most organizations that engage in diversity initiatives, however, do not explicitly frame these in the context of the moral argument. This is not usually a primary or overt reason for U.S. organizations implementing diversity training programs (e.g., see Morrison, Ruderman, & Hughes-James, 1993; Wheeler, 1994). Nevertheless, the moral perspective (with the associated struggle against oppression) is very much a part of the language and background of diversity in organizations (e.g., see Cross, Katz, Miller, & Seashore, 1994) and thus offers a useful lens for understanding diversity training and other diversity initiatives.

Inclusion. When President Clinton first took office in 1993, he pledged that his government would "look like America." What he meant is that every citizen should believe that she or he was adequately represented in the government; this can happen to the extent that the demographic diversity of the country is reflected among public officials at all levels. Justice and fairness, the reasoning goes, demand that artificial obstacles based on the legacy of prejudice and discrimination be removed, such that all individuals have equitable chances to succeed. Group identities and cultural differences should not be the basis for invidious distinctions or hurdles. Instead, people should be proud of them and find ways to use them for the benefit of all. These values are reflected in Maya Angelou's (1993) poem "On the Pulse of Morning," written for and recited at President Clinton's inauguration.

Viewed from the perspective of the moral imperative, inclusion implies not only eliminating barriers to opportunity based on group differences but also supporting every individual to reach her or his full potential (e.g., see Jamison, 1984; Taylor, 1992) without requiring cultural assimilation.[1] Not only does every person have the right to become her or his best possible self, but to the extent that society encourages this, all will benefit. Thus, in this approach, inclusion is seen as providing benefits to individuals, groups, organizations, and society as a whole. The dilemma here, then, becomes how best to accomplish inclusion of both individuals and groups (e.g., Ferdman, 1995). Terry (1994) describes the challenge this way:

> The problem of the "one and the many" . . . now frames the problems of everyday life. How much unity, how much diversity is the right mix to build a creative and long-term viable future in neighborhoods, communities, the nation, and the globe? The temptations and pressures to err in either direction are enormous. Yet the challenge confronts us: Build a unified society without uniformity. (p. 113)

Even among those who agree that inclusion "without uniformity" is a worthy goal, there is disagreement on the best way to get there. Be-

cause of this disparity, the moral imperative can take on a variety of forms when applied through organizational diversity initiatives, depending on the orientation—social justice or individual differences—that is adopted (see the discussion below regarding alternative orientations to diversity training).

Vision and Goals. The moral imperative and its variations are associated with particular visions of the "ideal" organization that are, in turn, related to the goals set for diversity initiatives and the criteria used to assess their effectiveness. Although proponents of the moral arguments for diversity initiatives often disagree as to whether or not the focus should be on reducing systemic oppression or on accepting and valuing the full range of human variation, they agree that the ultimate emphasis must be on both individual and social change. Organizational efforts are seen as but one piece of this broader agenda. Cobbs (1994) frames it this way: "In our organizations, we must fight to make valuing diversity a bedrock value and not something that is optional or somehow outside the parameters of how business is conducted" (p. 27).

At the individual level, successful diversity initiatives should result in greater personal fulfillment and growth and in more interpersonal effectiveness. At the societal level, successful diversity initiatives should promote more social integration and participation and result in more open communities and workplaces where prejudice, discrimination, and systemic oppression are eliminated as barriers to individual and group advancement. Cobbs (1994) connects these as follows: "Diversity will help us get in touch with our humanity. When I can celebrate differences with others, I don't have to oppress or be oppressed" (p. 28). From the moral perspective, the ultimate goal is essentially "better human beings" (J. H. Katz, personal communication, May 1995).

Legal and Social Pressures

In part because of the moral imperative, but also because of the civil rights struggles of the 1950s and 1960s and the ensuing civil rights legislation, federal regulations, and court rulings, organizations in the United States have faced legal and social demands to become more inclusive (Cox, 1993), at least in numbers, if not otherwise. These pressures include equal employment opportunity (EEO) laws, affirmative action (AA), and the Americans with Disabilities Act (ADA). Businesses that enter into contracts with the federal government become subject to EEO/AA laws and regulations. The ADA requires employers to make "reasonable" accommodations for employees and potential employees with disabilities; it also requires that public accommodations, buildings, transportation, and telecommunications be accessible to people with disabilities (Pati & Bailey, 1995; Prince, 1995). Addressing sexual harassment has also become a prominent issue. More and more organizations realize they must take active steps to prevent lawsuits charging discrimination or harassment.

Whether or not organizations view addressing diversity as the right thing to do or as good for business, they are finding themselves under legal pressure to do so. When motivated primarily by legal pressures, the focus of interventions tends to be on specific, targeted groups. Groups not covered by legal mandates—for example, gays and lesbians—would not be addressed. Also, such interventions may be very limited in nature—for example, simply posting information about what constitutes sexual harassment, what to do if one is a victim, and what behaviors should be avoided.

Beyond legal requirements, the demographic shifts in the U.S. population (e.g., larger proportion of people of color and immigrants, more women in the workforce) and the recognition that these changes are occurring has brought wider consciousness of intergroup relations and of the range of group-specific needs. Groups that previously felt pressured simply to blend in now resist this and demand acceptance and inclusion without assimilation as a precondition. In many companies, groups such as women, African Americans, Latinos and Latinas, gays and lesbians, working parents, and persons with disabilities have formed caucus or affinity groups to share experiences, to support each other, and to challenge discrimination. External organizations have also raised consciousness regarding the unique perspectives and needs of diverse groups.[2] Organizations face the need to find constructive ways to help a variety of internal and external constituencies work together more effectively. When motivated in this way, diversity initiatives tend to be focused more broadly and are less constrained by legalistic definitions of "protected groups." Nevertheless, if the impetus is primarily external and framed solely in terms of special interests, it can be difficult for the organization to articulate clear and forceful arguments for starting and continuing the intervention such that it speaks to all of its members and is perceived as intrinsically linked to the organization's best interests.

Thus, diversity training can be used to respond to pressures from both internal and external groups and to reduce the chances of lawsuits. In some organizations, diversity training has been implemented as part of consent agreements stemming from successful legal challenges to current practices. In such organizations, the initial motivation for diversity training is based chiefly on legal and social pressures and is thus chiefly reactive, rather than proactive.

Inclusion. Inclusion as seen from the perspective of legal and social pressures primarily involves removing illegal barriers—whether racial discrimination, sexual harassment, or facilities inaccessible to persons with disabilities—or obstacles perceived to be unfair. Thus, the approach tends to be primarily reactive: Inclusion is considered attained when no one complains; action is taken only when challenges or grievances are brought.

A primary focus of this type of approach has been on the number of representatives of various types of groups in the organization, in part reflecting the emphasis of affirmative action. Typically, less attention has been paid to the experience of people who have already entered the organization. More recently, however, the Department of Labor has called attention to movement into higher-level jobs with its "glass ceiling" initiative (Federal Glass Ceiling Commission, 1995).

When diversity training is driven primarily by legal and social pressures, the concept of inclusion can become quite controversial because what is viewed from one group's perspective as an appropriate and fair measure taken to remedy intergroup inequities can be viewed by another group as unfair, wrong, or divisive. Recently, for example, the political establishment in the United States has become embroiled in heated debate regarding the wisdom and efficacy of affirmative action programs. Many diversity consultants (e.g., Gardenswartz & Rowe, 1993; Katz & Miller, 1995; Solomon, 1993) argue that initiatives framed solely from this perspective are much less likely to be successful because they encounter more resistance from members of groups that do not feel included or believe they have something to lose—in particular, White men.

Vision and Goals. Diversity initiatives motivated primarily by legal and social pressures tend to be reactive. This is especially so when training has been ordered by a judge or by a legal settlement. Often, however, organizations that start for these reasons eventually move toward other motivations, especially the business-based argument. If they do not, there is little incentive to maintain active efforts and to make the necessary long-term investments.

The vision to be strived for from this perspective involves complying with the law and avoiding legal jeopardy, as well as averting conflict and maintaining smooth relations among relevant constituencies while steering clear of politics as much as possible. When aimed in this way, the goal of the training becomes making sure employees know which behaviors are permissible and which are impermissible—for example, with regard to hiring—rather than changing the organizational culture. To the extent a diversity initiative is motivated solely by legal and social pressures, it is less likely to address such issues as systemic oppression, cultural diversity and its implications for the workplace, and the potential benefits for the organization. Although these may be touched on, this will tend to be in relatively superficial ways. For example, in addressing inclusion of persons with disabilities, an organization may make the minimally necessary physical accommodations without embarking on any training directed at modifying the organizational climate within which such persons will work.

In this approach, success is defined in terms of avoiding problems and representing target groups across the organization to a degree acceptable to internal and external constituencies, but no more. The effectiveness of a diversity training initiative will be gauged on the basis of prevention of lawsuits and complaints. Illustrating the pervasiveness of this perspective, Noble (1994) reports on a survey of more than 300 companies that was conducted in New York

by the Center for the New American Workforce and that found the following:

> Most of the companies indicate they are doing what is necessary to comply with government employment law and little more. For the most part they have not taken the step beyond what would move diversity out of a pigeon hole in the personnel department and into the strategic center of the corporate environment. . . . What companies think of . . . is compliance with affirmative action guidelines and disability law. (p. 27)

Efforts prompted by this motivation are those most likely to be limited to briefings and short courses with little if any experiential content.

Business Success and Competitiveness

Perhaps the most pervasive and widely discussed motivation for diversity initiatives in general and diversity training in particular is the expected impact on business success and the bottom line. As viewed from this perspective, increasing globalization and a more diverse domestic workforce are push factors (organizations that do nothing will lose ground), whereas the benefits to be had from working effectively across differences are pull factors (organizations that take advantage, it is argued, will do better and be more competitive; e.g., see Buntaine, 1994a; Cox & Blake, 1991; Jackson & Alvarez, 1992; Thomas, 1990, 1992).

Wheeler (1994) reported that 85% of the organizations responding to his survey cited business need or competitiveness as the primary motivator for using diversity training. In contrast with initiatives framed in terms of affirmative action and equal opportunity, which are based more on the legal and moral arguments, those focused on organizational effectiveness are more likely to be viewed as essential to the organization, to involve more human and financial resources, and to be strategically focused.[3]

Buntaine (1994a) argues for the need not only to frame the business case for diversity but also to go beyond using it as a sales tool and to be as clear as possible about the benefits that organizations can gain from becoming more inclusive (see also Cox & Blake, 1991). These benefits, in Buntaine's view, include improvements among employees in retention, skills, performance, and development; in the market-place in terms of being better prepared to work with customers, partners, and suppliers and expanding the range of business opportunities; in the community in terms of a better business climate and quality of life for stakeholders; and in the organization's performance, including productivity and the capacity to deal with change effectively and creatively.

McEnrue (1993) conducted interviews with senior managers at a number of Los Angeles firms who told her of the advantages they had gained from "diversity management": "According to them, the efforts had not only improved their understanding of customer needs but also led to new product development, joint ventures, improved employee relations, an enhanced public image, and lower labor costs" (p. 22). From this perspective, diversity training is only one example of a range of organizational actions that can be taken to capitalize on diversity.

Inclusion. From the vantage point of business success, inclusion is about making sure the organization uses all productive capacity and potential to the full extent. If employees can be more effective and if the belief is that diversity training will help them do so, then the organization can be more productive and successful. Miller (1994a) describes the concept this way:

> Inclusive groups encourage disagreement because they realize it leads to more-effective solutions and more-successful adaptations to a changing environment. Instead of pressuring members to leave their individual and cultural differences outside, inclusive groups ask everyone to contribute to the full extent of their being. (p. 39)

By valuing and encouraging and ultimately including the full contributions of all members, organizations will have a broader range of talent available and will be much more likely to succeed. In this vein, Miller (1994a) goes on to affirm:

> The times require speed, adaptability, and the ability to see as much of the landscape as possible. Diversity gives organizations a greater probability of achieving those capabilities than does monoculturalism. An organizational culture biased toward maximum diversity and inclusion offers the greatest po-

tential for 360-degree vision and the broadest resource base for adaptability, growth, creativity, productivity, and high performance. (p. 44)

Thus, inclusion from the vantage point of business success is not limited to particular groups or categories of people. All individuals must be included in their full uniqueness and complexity. Doing this, however, typically includes recognizing the group-based differences among people (Ferdman, 1995). Moreover, once organizations learn to adopt an inclusive orientation in dealing with their members, this will also have a positive impact on how they look at their customer base, how they develop products and assess business opportunities, and how they relate to their communities.

Vision and Goals. From the perspective of business success, diversity and inclusion become a key strategic lever for organizational viability and effectiveness. In the same way that teams can be used as a workplace design to bring about higher performance, diversity is used as a means to an end. The goal is to make the organization the best it can be. If this takes including more views, including a variety of people, empowering workers, and effecting social change, so be it, as long as the organization is more successful.

The vision of where the organization is headed becomes quite broad from this angle:

> Inclusive and equitable employment practices are only a beginning to the business case. It takes an integrated and sustained effort comprised of *a range* of internal and external strategies and human resource initiatives—*all connected to strengthening business performance*—to demonstrate the full value of thinking and behaving inclusively. (Buntaine, 1994a, p. 221)

Because of this systems view, the business success motivation is the most likely to lead to a strategic approach to diversity training, in which the training is only one component of a long-term organizational change intervention. Whether the focus of the training component is on individual behavior and attitudes or on individual improvement, the ultimate goal is a more effective organization. In this view, the success of the initiative is measured in terms of movement toward both the full use of people and the accomplishment of organizational aims, including strategic objectives that go beyond the workforce.[4]

Combining Motivations

In actuality, the motivations for instituting diversity training rarely operate alone and are more often than not combined in complex ways. For example, a diversity effort can be seen to work to reduce oppression and thereby help people work together more effectively and so result in more profits for the organization. Also, often organizations start out for one reason—for example, they perceive legal risks—but then as a result of an initial intervention, other motivations emerge; they realize that a better workplace can result from the process of change.

Even when the primary motivation is business success, the implementation of the diversity initiative and the content of diversity training are often framed by the moral imperative. Certainly, the motivation for many consultants remains social change (e.g., see Chesler, 1994), but they have learned to make this more palatable to organizations by demonstrating how this can be quite consistent with and actually contribute to achieving business-related goals.

The "What" of Diversity Training

Diversity training programs can vary widely in both their explicit and implicit goals and in the philosophies that underlie their design. The orientation of the training, the levels of changes it seeks to make, its objectives, and its positioning as an intervention within the organization are key aspects distinguishing alternative approaches to diversity training.

Orientation

As suggested by the preceding discussion of the various motivations for diversity training and the corresponding perspectives on inclusion, organizations can adopt a variety of orientations to frame their diversity initiatives. These orientations can have important implica-

tions for the range of issues addressed in training and for the training processes used. Two such orientations are discussed here.

Miller (1994b) juxtaposes descriptions of the orientations taken by those favoring a focus on individual differences and those favoring a social justice approach. Jackson and Hardiman (1994) term these the *social diversity* and *social justice* approaches. The major difference between these is the first focuses on culture and on the ways people vary as individuals, assuming it is necessary to move forward and stop holding on to the past, whereas the second focuses on the continuing need to work against discrimination and to reduce systemic oppression (see also Morrison et al., 1993). Miller describes the perspectives as follows:

> There is a belief that diversity should be about individual differences. . . . But there is also a belief that diversity should be about correcting the injustices visited upon people and groups. . . . The Individual Differences perspective assumes the fundamental issue of diversity is to create understanding between different individuals. But it too often includes an underlying assumption that addressing discrimination and oppression will result in "pointing fingers of blame" rather than providing a basis for common ground. . . . [In contrast,] the Social Justice perspective calls for addressing discrimination and oppression head-on: identifying what they are, where they are, how they work, what mechanisms perpetuate them, and how to eliminate them. (pp. xxvi-xxvii)

This distinction parallels that made by Judith Palmer (1994), who describes three paradigms that frame work on diversity in organizations: I, the Golden Rule; II, right the wrongs; and III, value all differences. The focus of Paradigm I, the Golden Rule, is on viewing "everyone as an individual and . . . [as] more similar than . . . different" (p. 253). In this view, the goal is to avoid conflict, to eliminate prejudice and other barriers to equal opportunity, and to see everyone as an individual, rather than as a member of groups. Paradigm II, right the wrongs, focuses on remedying the injustices visited on those groups that have been the victims of systematic disadvantage. In this approach, the goal is to ensure that target groups are no longer hampered by discrimination; to do so, systemic barriers and disadvantages must be removed. Finally, Paradigm III, value all differences, focuses on "appreciat[ing] the heritage and culture of many different groups and . . . respond[ing] to the self-image and uniqueness of each individual" (p. 256). Here, the goal is to expand the range of understanding and acceptance of all members of the organization and therefore to permit each person to contribute fully and uniquely. This view incorporates a broad definition of diversity: "In Paradigm III, *diversity* means consciously and sensitively deploying the talents of all the groups in the organization without emphasizing or putting priority on any specific difference or group" (p. 257). Paradigm II is similar to the social justice perspective; Paradigm III most closely resembles the individual differences view.

Miller, Palmer, and Jackson and Hardiman all argue that the most effective diversity initiatives address both systemic issues and individual differences and thus find a way to maintain both orientations simultaneously.[5] This view contrasts with the approach often taken in intercultural training programs, which, though they acknowledge and deal with group-based cultural differences, do not typically address power differences or historically rooted patterns of discrimination.

Levels of Change

An important dimension along which diversity training programs vary is the levels of change—individual, interpersonal, group, intergroup, organizational, community/societal—that are targeted. This choice will have a direct impact on the training approach. The diversity training and the larger initiative of which it is a part may seek changes at any one of these levels, or more typically, in some combination.

At the *individual level,* training programs focus on changing people's attitudes and/or behavior or, at the very least, on imparting knowledge and information. At the *interpersonal level,* the goal can be to help employees develop more effective communication patterns or to deal with problematic relationships. At the *group level,* the focus may be on team building and on developing efficacy. At the *intergroup level,* changes may be sought in the patterns of relations between men and women, among racial or ethnic groups, or among the range of

identity groups present in the organization. At the *organizational level,* the changes desired are focused on making the organization as a whole more inclusive and more effective—for example, by removing discriminatory practices and other barriers. The diversity initiative in the case of a focus at the organizational level is designed to create major changes in the culture, structure, processes, and/or systems of the organization. Finally, some diversity initiatives may seek to affect the *community/societal level* in a way that diminishes oppression and increases pluralism and multiculturalism across a wide range of settings and people.

When focused primarily at the level of individual or interpersonal change, diversity training programs are more likely to be specific, temporary initiatives that do not require top management involvement and that are housed in Human Resources or Training Departments. This approach typically minimizes the amount of commitment and the resources allocated to attaining the program's goals. When the desired level of change is restricted to the individual or the interpersonal, organizations are more likely to experience resistance to the training and to find it difficult to develop convincing rationales for taking on the work.

In contrast, to the degree the training is designed as part of a broader organizational-level change effort, it is more likely to be infused throughout all levels of the organization and to require more resources and a longer commitment. In this approach, diversity training is one of a larger set of ingredients designed to move the whole organization in the desired direction. In describing one such initiative, O'Mara, Garrow, and Johnston (1994) write:

> The strategy from the beginning was to positively impact the organization culture through planned organizational change. . . . The project began with the assumption that training was only one of several potential interventions and that organizational systems, practices, and policies would likely need changes. (pp. 2-3)

Training geared toward organizational-level change is also linked to desired changes at the interpersonal or group level (e.g., teamwork aimed at modifying affiliation and communication patterns; see Cobbs, 1994) and the intergroup level (e.g., interdepartmental interventions). The difference is that these changes are viewed as important components facilitating and supporting the strategically based process. From a strategic or systems-change perspective, diversity training is not an end point that can be simply checked off once it is done; rather, it is a means to a much broader end.

The targets for change are important in determining not only the objectives of the training, discussed in the next section, but also the criteria for assessing whether or not the intervention has been effective. Issues related to training effectiveness are discussed later in the chapter.

Objectives/Targets

The various levels of change are closely associated with the range of objectives targeted by the diversity training. These can include providing knowledge and information, increasing awareness and understanding, developing skills, changing the organizational culture and systems, and changing the surrounding community and society. Each of these is discussed below.

Wheeler (1994) separates these objectives into two broad groups, macro and micro:

The micro objectives are those addressing specific skills, knowledge or behavior . . . while macro objectives encompass issues such as culture change, greater retention, improved productivity, or increased sales to diverse markets. . . . There are generally multiple objectives within a program or a training strategy. (pp. 18-19)

An integral part of setting the objectives for diversity training programs is setting priorities regarding the primary goals the organization would like to accomplish via the program. The methods and techniques used to accomplish the goals of diversity training will be affected by the motivation for the initiative, as well as by its orientation and desired level(s) of change. Although the objectives of many diversity training efforts are related to those of intercultural training, the connection is not always straightforward. Indeed, much of what falls under the scope of diversity training can more properly be seen as one component of broader organizational development and change initiatives. Intercultural training typically focuses on chang-

ing individual behavior and attitudes and on preparing individuals to cross cultural boundaries (e.g., Brislin & Yoshida, 1994, 1994b). In contrast, the focus of organizational development is on "planned change of human systems" (Porras & Robertson, 1992, p. 720), such as changing an organization's culture. In organizational development interventions, attitudinal and behavioral change are sought to support the broader strategic and cultural change.

Provide Knowledge and Information. Most, if not all, diversity training programs incorporate as a basic objective imparting information to participants. Such information can range from equal opportunity laws and organizational policies against sexual harassment to the nature of the demographic and social changes making it necessary to address inclusion and diversity in the workplace. When this objective is the only one, it can be addressed with relatively short informational briefings or lectures or with audiovisual and written materials. In many cases, training for employees (in contrast with that for managers) focuses on this objective. In Wheeler's (1994) survey, only 36% of respondents rated communication of policies an important objective for diversity training. However, 60% rated education an important objective. This included imparting information about diversity issues, concepts, and terminology.

Increase Awareness and Understanding. According to Cobbs (1994), the first step on the path to celebrating people's differences and accepting diversity as an advantage, rather than as a drawback, is to understand the grounds for prejudice and to get familiar with the "thoughts, attitudes, feelings, and assumptions that block our understanding and embracing of diversity" (p. 26). Hence, the objective of increasing awareness and understanding involves addressing the topic of diversity and differences, including race, ethnicity, gender, religion, and other group-based memberships and the ways they affect the workplace and the trainee.

Carnevale and Stone (1994) describe this type of training as aimed "at heightening awareness of diversity issues and revealing workers' unexamined assumptions and tendencies to stereotype" (p. 30). Awareness-based training programs seek to help participants understand cultural differences and become conscious of the dynamics that affect their interactions with people from different cultural backgrounds (e.g., Gudykunst & Hammer, 1983). Lindsay (1994) describes this type of learning as a stage in which participants "explore differences as well as understand the societal phenomena of oppression and dominance" (p. 3). To this end, Sue (1991) suggests using exercises that work to uncover stereotypes and images of different racial and cultural groups. Participants can thereby explore differences based on demographics (e.g., gender, race, age), learn how such differences affect their own and their peers' work behavior, and eventually be introduced to the value added by diversity and differences and so gain appreciation for their own and others' values, beliefs, and attitudes. In many ways, this process is analogous to the type of learning addressed in management courses on diversity (see Ferdman, 1994; *Journal of Management Education,* 1994). It is also the area most similar to traditional intercultural training.

Increasing awareness is a primary target for most diversity training. Wheeler (1994), for example, reports that 93% of the companies he surveyed rated this an important objective for diversity training. Despite the overwhelming consensus that awareness must be incorporated into diversity training as a key objective, there is less agreement regarding the issues about which participants need to become aware. In making this choice, the issues raised earlier—including the motivations for the diversity training, the orientation adopted, and the level(s) of change desired—will have a great impact. Awareness-based training can focus on a range of topics, including cultural style differences, the dynamics of prejudice, and the nature of oppression. Training motivated by the moral imperative, grounded in the social justice orientation and/or targeted at systemic organizational or societal change, will be more likely to target awareness of oppression and its manifestations in the workplace as a key objective.

Develop Skills. One criticism of training focused primarily on building awareness is that participants do not know what to do with their new learning and how to apply it in the workplace (Carnevale & Stone, 1994). Skill-based training attempts to address this deficiency by targeting behavioral as well as attitudinal changes. Sue (1991) mentions such techniques

as "role-playing, communication training, watching cross-cultural interactions, behavioral rehearsal, and analyzing organizational development and goals" (p. 103) as being potentially useful to this end. The goal is to develop skills that will help employees work effectively in the context of diversity, including the ability to communicate cross-culturally, to deal effectively with conflict, and to be more flexible and adaptable (Carnevale & Stone, 1994). Additional competencies can include mentoring and partnering effectively across gender, ethnic, and other types of differences (e.g., Buntaine, 1994b). Katz and Miller (1993) list 14 skills that they believe are critical for people who work in culturally diverse organizations. To those already mentioned, they add skills related to supporting the change process and flourishing as it happens, including:

> Having the courage to speak out, raise issues and act on opportunities for change. . . . Working actively to remove the barriers and blocks that may limit the inclusion of all people's talents. . . . Setting challenging but realistic expectations for change and of each other—realizing it is not a pass/fail test. . . . Tracking progress, and recognizing change doesn't occur in a straight line. (p. 32)

Skill-based training approaches are based on the argument that, to manage their diverse workforces effectively, managers need to develop their communication skills, learn how to exchange feedback, improve their interaction with their coworkers and customers, and enhance their listening skills. Managers should learn how to be attentive to the content of their employees' performance, rather than to the style of their delivery. Thus, if their employees have the desired capabilities and talents to perform efficiently but their techniques are different, it should not stand as a barrier to success (Cobbs, 1994). According to Wheeler (1994), skill-based training "is offered primarily to managers and supervisors" (p. 20). Carnevale and Stone (1994) expand the target trainees and include employees, as well as employers: "Skill-based training provides tools to promote effective interaction in a heterogeneous work setting. It has three important objectives: building new diversity-interaction skills, reinforcing existing skills, inventorying skill-building methodologies" (p. 31).

Change Organizational Culture and Systems. Wheeler (1994) reports that 73% of respondents to his survey thought cultural change should be a key objective of diversity training. Also, 73% rated "linkages with other programs and initiatives" as important. As Wheeler points out, however, "making the linkages is easier said than done" (p. 20).

When the diversity training is designed as one component of a larger strategic intervention, it often incorporates some of the elements described above. However, these are integrated in a way that maintains in focus the broader goal of organizational cultural and systems change. Individual-level learning is viewed as a stepping stone or ingredient of the larger changes. When the objective is creating an inclusive workplace (Miller & Katz, 1995), diversity training must provide opportunities for participants to experience what this might be like and to gain the necessary practice that will enable implementing changes in organizational norms and values, policies, and systems. "The education helps to build the new culture, in conjunction with the systems change work that is simultaneously occurring" (J. H. Katz, personal communication, May 1995).

When changing the organizational culture and systems is the target for diversity training, careful attention must be given to the mix of attendees in terms of level in the organization, roles in the change effort, and support and responsibilities once the training is over. The participants should have work- or business-related connections with each other to increase the likelihood that learning will be transferred outside the training context and result in new systems and cultural patterns in the organization. The training events must be integrated with the overall process of change in such a way that they build on each other. Also, the way the training is implemented, who attends when, and how it affects and integrates with other parts of the diversity initiative and the organization's activities are important considerations.

Change the Community. Although community or societal change is not typically a core objective for corporate diversity initiatives, once major organizational changes are underway this can become integrated into broader efforts and aligned with the work done by other related organizations. Such efforts are currently underway in the City of San Diego, with its Livable Communities initiative, and in Columbus, Indiana, where a number of community and business organizations are engaged in strategic cultural change efforts simultaneously. In San Diego, the City's Centre for Organizational Effectiveness and its external consultant, The Kaleel Jamison Consulting Group (headquartered in Cincinnati, Ohio), sponsored a Diversity Institute in 1994 that brought together groups of change agents from a variety of businesses, community groups, and governmental agencies to learn more about strategic approaches for developing inclusive organizations.

Positioning

Although many diversity training programs share components and objectives, they can often be differentiated by how the training is positioned in the organization and within the broader diversity initiative. How the diversity training program is presented to and perceived by members of the organization—whether as a means to individual development and growth, as training to improve productivity, as a vehicle toward organizational cultural change, or as an essential part of a strategic intervention—will greatly affect both its content and process and thereby its effectiveness.

To increase the success rate of diversity training programs, top management support and involvement are essential (Morrison et al., 1993; Wheeler, 1994). Commitment on the part of management is linked to allocating more resources to accomplish training goals, to considering diversity training as part of the business strategy, to assessing the organization's needs before the training as well as following the training, and to serving as a model for employees, thus in turn increasing their commitment and involvement. When these factors are present, the training is more likely to be presented and to be seen as pivotal for the organization in meeting its objectives.

The issue of when to include training in the context of an organizational initiative is controversial. Elsie Cross, Frederick Miller, and Price Cobbs (see Morrison et al., 1993) advocate education and training as an important first stage in the diversity effort, after doing a comprehensive organizational assessment. Other practitioners, in contrast, such as Ann

Morrison, encourage training later on in the process.

The rationale provided by the first group to support their argument is that a training program will create a paradigm shift, will increase awareness, understanding, and skills of those at the top level of the organization who must lead the change effort, and will serve as the "unfreezing" stage of the change process toward a well-managed, diverse workforce and toward a more inclusive workplace. Those who support positioning diversity training midway or later in the change process explain that a change in attitudes and beliefs is a long-term process, one the organization cannot afford to be waiting for if it is to meet its objectives. Also, they argue, "diversity has to exist before training on how to manage it is offered" (Morrison et al., 1993, p. 44), so energy and resources must be committed to ensuring that members of diverse groups are represented. Finally, they point out, behavioral changes will foster corresponding changes in attitudes, rather than the other way around. Thus, they suggest starting with significant systems changes before emphasizing training.

The first group counters that moving toward inclusion must begin with learning how to work effectively with the range of differences that currently exist in the organization before addressing new ones (Miller & Katz, 1995). Moreover, diversity training positioned as part of a cultural change effort or as part of a strategic intervention will go beyond attitude change to include behavioral changes as a target. Judith Katz (personal communication, May 1995) describes the preferred sequence as follows: (a) Identify and remove barriers, (b) increase awareness and skills, (c) develop new competencies, (d) change systems and rules, and (e) hold members of the organization accountable.

The "How" of Diversity Training

The way diversity training is oriented and focused, as discussed in the preceding section, will have implications for how it is implemented. Here, we discuss three process aspects of diversity training—type of learning, duration, and trainer roles and competencies—that can vary widely across organizational diversity initiatives.

Type of Learning

Type of learning will differ according to the strategy and techniques adopted by trainers and the level of change addressed. Two basic learning approaches used in diversity training are didactic and experiential learning. Also varying will be whether the focus is on individual or group learning.

Experiential/Didactic Learning

Lindsay (1994) suggests that learning objectives can be defined along a continuum describing their level of required experiential involvement, such that providing information and increasing awareness will be on the low end of the continuum and organizational culture change will be on the high end. Gudykunst and Hammer (1983) distinguish between the didactic and experiential approaches to learning. The basic premise of the *didactic approach* is that interaction among people from different cultures will be more effective when there is a reciprocal understanding of the other's culture. The didactic approach is most suited to diversity training that targets primarily knowledge objectives and some awareness because it is based on the cognitive domain and typically involves frontal presentation or group discussion. Pruegger and Rogers (1994) point out that cognitive learning (didactic) is most effective in providing information; however, it is not sufficient to cultivate cross-cultural sensitivity. Didactic methods can also be useful to provide training participants with models that will frame conversations and other more experiential activities, so as to infuse these with new perspectives and ideas and increase the chances for valuable insights.

The *experiential approach* presumes that the best learning occurs through active engagement and participation. This type of learning can involve simulations and role playing, as well as group discussions of individual and collective experiences. According to Pruegger and Rogers (1994), such methods affect attitudes and promote communication skills because participants can transfer the learning to real-life situations outside the training context.

When the objective of the training is to change the organizational culture and systems and so it is positioned as part of a strategic intervention, a high degree of experiential learning is typically used. However, role plays and simulations are less useful unless they are explicitly connected to the organizational issues at hand. In strategically designed diversity education, the experiential techniques most likely to be used involve participants in sharing their own data and perspectives in the context of the training session, as well as in the workplace and in their lives. A key aspect of the training experience for participants pertains to learning how to engage effectively with each other on the issues of diversity and inclusion as they apply to their work lives and to the organization, so as to enhance skills for dealing with and working across differences. Thus, the orientation in this approach is more toward the here and now and toward learning about how differences can be bridged effectively in the training group.

One application of this perspective is a technique called *Perception Exchange,* first developed in the 1970s by the Kaleel Jamison Consulting Group, in which participants grouped along ethnic and gender lines draw pictures describing their views of their organization and the experiences of different groups in it. Later, these pictures are presented to the whole group and discussed. For many trainees, it is the first time they realize that not everyone experiences the work environment in the same way they do and that the variations are often connected to racial, ethnic, and gender identities.[6] This can be a powerful, profound, jarring, and ultimately enriching experience, in particular for those unaccustomed or unwilling to think about how group memberships differentially affect people at work. At the same time, participants are able to develop a shared organizational diagnosis based on the perspectives of everyone in the group, not just a limited subset of people or on a majority view. This process, paradoxically, leads the group to a more coherent, complete, and ultimately inclusive view of their organizational system and can serve as a powerful motivator for developing the knowledge and skills that will undergird broader changes in the organizational culture.

Individual/Group Learning

The positioning of the training and the desired changes also are related to whether the focus is on individual or group learning.[7] In many diversity training programs, participants are brought together without regard to their function in the organization or their relationships to other participants. In these organizations, individuals might volunteer for particular sessions on the basis of availability, for example. Some organizations do not go beyond ensuring that all participants are in roughly the same hierarchical level. These approaches are most likely to be adopted when the objective of the training is to change behavior or to develop individual skills and the level of change desired is primarily the individual or the interpersonal. This type of pattern may also be seen when diversity training is one component of a broad menu of courses offered by Training or Human Resources Departments. In this approach, although participants may learn from each other during the course of the training, each takes away the learning individually and therefore has little support or shared experience back in the day-to-day workplace.

When the diversity training is part of a more systemic intervention, more attention must be given to the configuration of the participant group and to the learning that takes place at the group and the organizational levels so that it is more likely to affect what happens when everyone goes back to his or her work site. By ensuring that participants in sessions come from the same work location or function and/or are otherwise connected operationally, the training can affect more directly the culture of interaction of that group. A key issue from this perspective, then, is not only what each person learns but also what all people in the room, as a collective, learn. In the more systemic approach, work teams are often asked to attend training sessions together so that the learning will be collective. When participants form small groups for discussion or other activities, much attention is given to the composition of those groups such that they make sense, given organizational needs and realities, and the tasks typically deal with real organizational issues affecting the business. Similarly, when the focus is on group-level learning, much time and energy are allocated to developing collective norms for the training setting that ideally will be carried back to the organizational setting. These norms (and the process of deriving them) help provide the group with a safe place in which to experiment with the potential of inclusion for more effective work interactions. It becomes for many participants the first time that they experience a work-related environment where they can both be fully themselves and get work done.

Duration

The duration of the diversity training, both in terms of specific sessions and in the organization as a whole, will also vary greatly across organizations. Again, as with type of learning, the degree to which the training is seen as part of a system change process versus an opportunity for personal growth or training of employees will have a great bearing on the intensity and length of the diversity training. Those organizations that have embarked on a process of cultural change will see diversity training as part of a long-term process and will have more intensive sessions over more days. For example, in the approach used by The Kaleel Jamison Consulting Group, educational sessions lasting a minimum of 2 and ideally 3 days are held off-site and residentially. Top leaders of the organization are asked to commit to a total of from 12 to 15 days of training as a way to become clear not only about their own personal interactions and skills but also about how the issues of diversity and inclusion connect to all aspects of the business. In this approach, training and education are seen as ongoing processes, rather than as something to check off. Returning to the learning group over a period of time provides an opportunity to deepen the learning and to apply it in the workplace without thinking that the process has to be instantaneous. The payoff from this type of investment is the development of skills and competencies for effectiveness and of meaningful plans for oneself, the group, and the organization (J. H. Katz, personal communication, May 1995).

Trainer Roles and Competencies

The roles adopted by trainers are an important aspect of the process of diversity training. This aspect relates to the stance taken by those doing the work and affects, for example, who is seen as qualified to do it and what the required competencies are. The functions that trainers may be called on to do include teaching, facilitating, modeling, and consulting.

Teaching is a function and competency required of all cultural diversity trainers. Almost all diversity training involves helping participants learn new information and develop new skills. Doing this effectively requires being flexible, having the knowledge base, and being able to deal with conflict constructively. Skills related to facilitation, modeling, and consulting, however, are more likely to be called on to the extent that the training is positioned as a strategic intervention or as part of organizational cultural change. For example, when the group learning mode is preferred, the trainer's ability at *facilitating* and processing group interactions becomes critical. In this mode, every participant in the session must be attended to and considered. Much of the facilitator's task revolves around helping create a group context in which every participant is included. Thus, the trainer working from this role must be proficient in helping create a learning community that allows participants to take risks and to feel safe, as well as to share their new knowledge and insights with each other.

Modeling is important because, for many participants, the notion that it is possible to work effectively across differences is somewhat new and even disconcerting. When the trainers (who typically differ from each other along important identity group dimensions) can model how this is done by the way they conduct themselves and work together, this can be a very important source of learning for participants. To model effectively, it is critical to work in diverse teams. Those who work from this perspective believe that diversity training is difficult, if not impossible, to do alone.

Finally, *consulting* is critical when working with leaders and managers. The consultants for diversity training sessions based on a strategic model must be ready at a moment's notice to shift gears and to redesign sessions to meet the needs of the specific group and the specific organization as they relate to the overall objectives for the change effort. Trainers in a consulting mode need to keep the whole organization and the change effort in focus as they lead a specific training event. This means they are familiar with the results of the organizational assessment and the broader organizational issues affecting the participants. Some consulting firms conduct interviews with all participants prior to training sessions, in large part as a way to accomplish this.

Given the variety of approaches to diversity training, the issue of assessing competency of trainers is made quite complex, yet is quite important. In a survey conducted by the GilDeane Group (1993) of 45 diversity specialists or "consumers of diversity training services" (p. 1), over half of the respondents said that sometimes trainers are not adequately prepared or qualified. Although a number of requisite skills probably cut across models of training—Wheeler (1994), for example, lists "sensitivity, knowledge of self, self-disclosure, candor, ability to respect all cultures, ability to 'design on the fly,' [and] maturity" (p. 33)—ultimately the particular roles the trainer will be called on to perform in the context of the overall diversity intervention will be the critical determining factor. Thus, the mix of skills that are appropriate for delivering training geared at individual and interpersonal change and targeted at changing behavior will not be the same as that needed to work effectively toward changing an organization's culture and systems as part of a strategic intervention.

What Works (and What Doesn't): Issues in Assessing Effectiveness of Diversity Training

We have presented a structure to frame the range of activities comprising diversity training but have said little about effectiveness. Although this is a critical issue for organizations, it is a question that has few answers based on systematic empirical research. In part, research-based answers are scarce because the field lacks investigations that directly assess the impact of the types of factors addressed in this chapter, such as orientation, level of change, positioning, and trainer roles. Also, as the GilDeane Group (1993) points out, there are few, if any, reliable measurement tools and many sought-after changes take a long time to become apparent. Assessments of effectiveness that do exist tend to compare activities that vary on a whole range of dimensions at once and often do not make explicit the researchers' values with regard to diversity (e.g., Ellis & Sonnenfeld, 1994).

Most important, it is difficult, if not impossible, to take an objectivist stance regarding the assessment of effectiveness in that no definitive consensus has emerged regarding what the goals of training should be and how one would know that they have been accomplished. Because the definition of effectiveness will be linked to the reasons for undertaking training and to its objectives, what works and what does not can only be evaluated in the context of specified objectives and criteria. Moreover, if a focus is placed on traditional training evaluation models (e.g., Goldstein, 1991), this is likely to ignore the ways diversity training is more like organizational development and should be evaluated from that perspective.[8]

Despite these concerns, on the basis of extensive experience with diversity efforts, consultants and managers have developed useful perspectives regarding the parameters of diversity training that make it more or less effective. Sims and Sims (1993), for example, point out that diversity training is most effective in organizations that are committed to inclusion and that make it part of the organization's culture:

> [By developing such a culture] committed to diversity and difference training [organizations] (1) empower their employees to feel good about themselves in relation to their individual uniqueness . . . and work; (2) have employees who are more likely to work hard and produce more; and (3) have clear values and expectations for performance and behavior. (p. 78)

Similarly, Wheeler (1994) argues that, for diversity training to be effective, it should be closely linked with the business strategy. He also points out that, often, the problem is that organizations do not clearly specify what they hope to accomplish with the diversity training. In such cases, it would be quite difficult, if not impossible, to assess effectiveness.

A survey conducted by the GilDeane Group (1993) resulted in a list of reasons underlying the failure of diversity training programs. Some major factors cited were insufficient leadership support and lack of commitment on the part of members of the organization, who perceived diversity training as the end result, rather than as the means to a much broader end. In addition, failure to integrate diversity into management systems, policies, and practices was cited as another common pattern in organizations that fail to accomplish the goals of the training.

In another survey sponsored by the Society for Human Resource Management (SHRM)

Foundation and Commerce Clearing House (Rynes & Benson, cited in "Quick-Fix," 1995), 713 members of SHRM were asked about their organization's diversity initiative; 50% of respondents whose companies had done long-term evaluation said the program had mixed or negligible effects, whereas 18% said the program had been ineffective. On the basis of the survey results, Rynes and Benson concluded that effective diversity training programs have the following features: (a) They have top management support, (b) they are integrated with the organization's strategic plans, (c) they are mandatory and comprehensive, (d) all participants are respected by the trainers, (e) they are carefully evaluated, and (f) they hold managers accountable once the training is over ("Quick-Fix," 1995).

Clearly, the general consensus is that broad-based, long-term, strategically focused initiatives are more likely to be effective than narrowly focused, poorly resourced, short-term efforts. This view is generally derived from and consistent with the business success motivation for engaging in diversity training. Many more specific issues, however, are less clear. For example, the impact of alternative learning types or the appropriate mix of trainer roles and competencies are issues for which more investigation could be useful. To adequately assess effectiveness in the future, however, researchers and practitioners will need to be much more specific about how this concept is defined and then measure appropriately. It will not be possible to make blanket assertions about effective or ineffective diversity training. We will only be able to answer such questions as, How many days of training are best? or, What skills should trainers have? only when we consider them in the context of particular and clearly articulated models of diversity training and of inclusive organizations (e.g., Miller & Katz, 1995).

Concluding Comment

We started the chapter by pointing out that diversity training is a broad term that encompasses a whole range of activities. The framework presented here is designed to enable making sense of these variations along a selected set of dimensions that are not always immediately apparent but that are nevertheless crucial in distinguishing one diversity training initiative from another. One of our goals has been to show how the various dimensions link with and flow into each other such that, for example, effective training motivated by the desire for business success is more likely to seek organizational change and to be positioned as a strategic intervention. It is our hope that, in articulating these dimensions, we will contribute to more specific and informed discussions of, decisions about, and assessment of diversity training. More critically, we hope this will add yet more energy to the work of developing organizations that are at once truly inclusive and effective.

Notes

1. Many organizations continue to frame inclusion primarily in terms of fitting in. In these organizations, diversity efforts tend to focus on getting people in the door and then on assimilating them to existing styles and structures (e.g., see Cox & Finley-Nickelson, 1991). Although it is possible to construct morally based arguments that limit inclusion simply to such conditional participation, we believe that organizational initiatives conceived in this way cannot be properly labeled *diversity initiatives* (see also Katz, 1989; Thomas, 1990).

2. Recently, for example, the Denny's restaurant chain faced a series of lawsuits based on claims that it had discriminated in its service of African American customers. Also, the NAACP and other national and local organizations have often worked with businesses to help them find constructive ways to better serve their communities in a more equitable and broad-based manner.

3. Judith H. Katz (personal communication, May 1995) distinguishes between two versions of the competitiveness perspective. One, which she terms *the HR*, or *organizational effectiveness approach*, focuses on the ways diversity can contribute to organizational performance primarily by helping people work together better (e.g., through greater intercultural understanding and appreciation). This approach highlights the "soft side" of business. A second approach focuses on the "hard" aspects of business through development of the "Business Case,"

a solid, clear cut link to the achievement of strategic business objectives. The business case must explain how becoming a culturally diverse organization will be a crucial lever for future organizational success. . . . The business case must directly link to customers, products, performance, and a way of doing business. (Katz & Miller, 1991, p. 3)

This approach is harder to implement and is also more rarely seen in place. (For a review and additional discussion of the competitive advantages of diversity, see Cox & Blake, 1991.)

4. Judith H. Katz ties the full use vision to the HR or organizational effectiveness approach (see Note 3), in which the goal is to help people develop greater understanding of diversity and corresponding skills for functioning well in a multicultural workplace. She connects the strategic vision to the business case approach, in which the goal is not only to increase employee competencies but also to deal more effectively with a range of organizational issues, including external customers and stakeholders, as well as product development, marketing, and continuous improvement.

5. The concept of individual differences as it is described here explicitly encompasses the ways people vary on the basis of their cultural backgrounds (see Ferdman, 1995).

6. See also in this regard the work of Clayton Alderfer (e.g., Alderfer, 1992), which focuses on changing race relations in organizations and is based on intergroup theory (e.g., Alderfer, 1986). In the Race Relations Competence Workshops (Alderfer, Alderfer, Bell, & Jones, 1992) that he and his colleagues developed for the pseudonymous XYZ Corporation, race-alike and cross-race groups formed an important part of the training, which built on a prior organizational diagnosis that highlighted both differences and similarities in how Black and White men and women experienced and perceived race relations in the organization.

7. See Senge (1990) for a discussion of the differences and relationships between personal mastery and team learning.

8. Although, see Chesler (1994) and Jackson and Hardiman (1994) for discussions of how multicultural organizational development diverges in important ways from traditional approaches to organizational development (OD).

References

Alderfer, C. P. (1986). An intergroup perspective on group dynamics. In J. Lorsch (Ed.), *Handbook of organizational behavior* (pp. 190-222). Englewood Cliffs, NJ: Prentice-Hall.

Alderfer, C. P. (1992). Changing race relations embedded in organizations: Report on a long-term project with the XYZ Corporation. In S. E. Jackson & Associates, *Diversity in the workplace: Human resources initiatives* (pp. 138-166). New York: Guilford.

Alderfer, C. P., Alderfer, C. J., Bell, E. L., & Jones, J. (1992). The Race Relations Competence Workshop: Theory and results. *Human Relations, 45,* 1259-1291.

Angelou, M. (1993). *On the pulse of morning.* New York: Random House.

Berry, J. W. (1993). Ethnic identity in plural societies. In M. E. Bernal & G. P. Knight (Eds.), *Ethnic identity: Formation and transmission among Hispanics and other minorities* (pp. 271-296). Albany: State University of New York Press.

Brislin, R. W., & Yoshida, T. (1994a). The content of cross-cultural training: An introduction. In R. W. Brislin & T. Yoshida (Eds.), *Improving intercultural interactions: Modules for cross-cultural training programs* (pp. 1-14). Thousand Oaks, CA: Sage.

Brislin, R. W., & Yoshida, T. (1994b). *Intercultural communication training: An introduction.* Thousand Oaks, CA: Sage.

Buntaine, C. S. (1994a). Beyond smiling faces. In E. Y. Cross, J. H. Katz, F. A. Miller, & E. W. Seashore (Eds.), *The promise of diversity: Over 40 voices discuss strategies for eliminating discrimination in organizations* (pp. 219-221). Burr Ridge, IL: Irwin.

Buntaine, C. S. (1994b). Developing cross-gender partnership competencies: Exploring the seven C's. In E. Y. Cross, J. H. Katz, F. A. Miller, & E. W. Seashore (Eds.), *The promise of diversity: Over 40 voices discuss strategies for eliminating discrimination in organizations* (pp. 259-266). Burr Ridge, IL: Irwin.

Carnevale, A. P., & Stone, S. C. (1994, October). Diversity beyond the Golden Rule. *Training & Development,* pp. 22-38.

Caudron, S. (1993, April). Training can damage diversity efforts. *Personnel Journal,* pp. 51-62.

Chemers, M., Oskamp, S., & Constanzo, M. (Eds.). (1995). *Diversity in organizations: New perspectives for a changing workplace.* Thousand Oaks, CA: Sage.

Chesler, M. (1994). Organizational development is not the same as multicultural organizational development. In E. Y. Cross, J. H. Katz, F. A. Miller, & E. W. Seashore (Eds.), *The promise of diversity: Over 40 voices discuss strategies for eliminating discrimination in organizations* (pp. 240-251). Burr Ridge, IL: Irwin.

Cobbs, P. M. (1994). The challenge and opportunities of diversity. In E. Y. Cross, J. H. Katz, F. A. Miller, & E. W. Seashore (Eds.), *The promise of diversity: Over 40 voices discuss strategies for eliminating discrimination in organizations* (pp. 25-31). Burr Ridge, IL: Irwin.

Cox, T., Jr. (1993). *Cultural diversity in organizations: Theory, research, and practice.* San Francisco: Berrett-Koehler.

Cox, T., Jr., & Blake, S. (1991). Managing cultural diversity: Implications for organizational competitiveness. *Academy of Management Executive, 5*(3), 45-56.

Cox, T., Jr., & Finley-Nickelson, J. (1991). Models of acculturation for intra-organizational cultural diversity. *Canadian Journal of Administrative Sciences, 8,* 90-100.

Cross, E. Y., Katz J. H., Miller, F. A., & Seashore, E. W. (Eds.). (1994). *The promise of diversity: Over 40 voices discuss strategies for eliminating discrimination in organizations.* Burr Ridge, IL: Irwin.

Ellis, C., & Sonnenfeld, J. A. (1994). Diverse approaches to managing diversity. *Human Resource Management, 33,* 79-109.

Federal Glass Ceiling Commission. (1995). *Good for business: Making full use of the nation's human capital—The environmental scan: A fact-finding report of the Federal Glass Ceiling Commission.* Washington, DC: Author.

Ferdman, B. M. (1990). Literacy and cultural identity. *Harvard Educational Review, 60,* 181-204.

Ferdman, B. M. (1992). The dynamics of ethnic diversity in organizations: Toward integrative models. In K. Kelley (Ed.), *Issues, theory, and research in industrial/organizational psychology* (pp. 339-384). Amsterdam: North Holland.

Ferdman, B. M. (Ed.). (1994). *A resource guide for teaching and research on diversity.* St. Louis, MO: American Assembly of Collegiate Schools of Business.

Ferdman, B. M. (1995). Cultural identity and diversity in organizations: Bridging the gap between group differences and individual uniqueness. In M. Chemers, S. Oskamp, & M. Constanzo (Eds.), *Diversity in organizations: New perspectives for a changing workplace* (pp. 37-61). Thousand Oaks, CA: Sage.

Ferdman, B. M. (in press). Values about fairness in the ethnically diverse workplace. *Transnational Journal of Diversity Studies.*

Frederickson, G. M., & Knobel, D. T. (1982). A history of discrimination. In T. F. Pettigrew, G. M. Frederickson, D. T. Knobel, N. Glazer, & R. Ueda, *Prejudice* (pp. 30-87). Cambridge, MA: Harvard University Press.

Gardenswartz, L., & Rowe, A. (1993). *Managing diversity: A complete desk reference and planning guide.* Burr Ridge, IL: Irwin.

GilDeane Group. (1993). *Cross-cultural and diversity trainers: Do they know what they're doing? The complete report on the May, 1993 survey conducted by Cultural Diversity at Work.* Seattle, WA: Author.

Glazer, N. (1988). The future of preferential affirmative action. In P. A. Katz & D. A. Taylor (Eds.), *Eliminating racism: Profiles in controversy* (pp. 329-340). New York: Plenum.

Goldstein, I. L. (1991). Training in work organizations. In M. D. Dunnette & L. M. Hough (Eds.), *Handbook of industrial and organizational psychology* (2nd ed., Vol. 2, pp. 507-620). Palo Alto, CA: Consulting Psychologists Press.

Gudykunst, W. B., & Hammer, M. R. (1983). Basic training design: Approaches to intercultural training. In D. Landis & R. Brislin (Eds.), *Handbook of intercultural training: Vol. 1. Issues in theory and design* (pp. 118-154). Elmsford, NY: Pergamon.

Jackson, B., & Hardiman, R. (1994). Multicultural organizational development. In E. Y. Cross, J. H. Katz, F. A. Miller, & E. W. Seashore (Eds.), *The promise of diversity: Over 40 voices discuss strategies for eliminating discrimination in organizations* (pp. 231-239). Burr Ridge, IL: Irwin.

Jackson S. E., & Alvarez, E. B. (1992). Working through diversity as a strategic imperative. In S. E. Jackson & Associates, *Diversity in the workplace: Human resources initiatives* (pp. 13-29). New York: Guilford.

Jamison, K. (1984). *The Nibble Theory and the kernel of power: A book about leadership, self-empowerment, and personal growth.* New York: Paulist.

Journal of Management Education. (1994). [Whole issue]*18*(4).

Katz, J. H. (1989). The challenge of diversity. In C. Woolbright (Ed.), *Valuing diversity on campus: A multicultural approach* (pp. 1-21). Bloomington, IN: Association of College Unions International.

Katz, J. H., & Miller, F. A. (1991). *Creating a culturally diverse organization: Ten keys for success.* Unpublished manuscript, The Kaleel Jamison Consulting Group, Inc., Cincinnati, OH.

Katz, J. H., & Miller, F. A. (1993). Skills for working in culturally diverse organizations. *OD Practitioner, 25*(4), 32-33.

Katz, J. H., & Miller, F. A. (1995). On the path to a multicultural organization. *Cultural Diversity at Work, 7*(3), 6ff.

Kitano, H. H. L. (1991). Goals. In *Race relations* (4th ed., pp. 10-27). Englewood Cliffs, NJ: Prentice-Hall.

Lindsay, C. P. (1994). Experiential approaches to teaching diversity: Type of training and levels of involvement. In B. M. Ferdman (Ed.), *A resource guide for teaching and research on diversity.* St. Louis, MO: American Assembly of Collegiate Schools of Business.

Macdonald, H. (1993, July 5). The diversity industry. *New Republic,* pp. 22-25.

McEnrue, M. P. (1993). Managing diversity: Los Angeles before and after the riots. *Organizational Dynamics, 22,* 18-29.

Miller, F. A. (1994a). Forks in the road: Critical issues on the path to diversity. In E. Y. Cross, J. H. Katz, F. A. Miller, & E. W. Seashore (Eds.), *The promise of diversity: Over 40 voices discuss strategies for eliminating discrimination in organization* (pp. 33-45). Burr Ridge, IL: Irwin.

Miller, F. A. (1994b). Preface: Why we chose to address oppression. In E. Y. Cross, J. H. Katz, F. A. Miller, & E. W. Seashore (Eds.), *The promise of diversity: Over 40 voices discuss strategies for eliminating discrimination in organizations* (pp. xxv-xxix). Burr Ridge, IL: Irwin.

Miller, F. A., & Katz, J. H. (1995). Cultural diversity as a developmental process: The path from monocultural club to inclusive organization. In J. W. Pfeiffer (Ed.), *The 1995 annual: Vol. 2. Consulting* (pp. 267-281). San Diego: Pfeiffer.

Mobley, M., & Payne, T. (1992, December). Backlash! The challenge to diversity training. *Training & Development,* pp. 45-52.

Morrison, A. M., Ruderman, M. N., & Hughes-James, M. (1993). *Making diversity happen: Controversies and solutions.* Greensboro, NC: Center for Creative Leadership.

Noble, B. P. (1994, November 6). Still in the dark on diversity. *New York Times,* p. F27.

O'Mara, J., Garrow, G., & Johnston, S. (1994, May). *A story of valuing diversity as a systems change initiative.* Paper presented at the American Society for Training and Development International Conference and Exposition, Anaheim, CA.

Palmer, J. (1994). Diversity: Three paradigms. In E. Y. Cross, J. H. Katz, F. A. Miller, & E. W. Seashore (Eds.), *The promise of diversity: Over 40 voices discuss strategies for eliminating discrimination in organizations* (pp. 252-258). Burr Ridge, IL: Irwin.

Pati, G. C., & Bailey, E. K. (1995). Empowering people with disabilities: Strategy and human resource issues in implementing the ADA. *Organizational Dynamics, 23*(3), 52-69.

Porras, J. I., & Robertson, P. J. (1992). Organizational development: Theory, practice, and research. In M. D. Dunnette & L. M. Hough (Eds.), *Handbook of industrial and organizational psychology* (2nd ed., Vol. 3, pp. 719-822). Palo Alto, CA: Consulting Psychologists Press.

Prince, B. (1995). Aspirations and apprehensions: Employees with disabilities. In C. Harvey & M. J. Allard (Eds.), *Understanding diversity* (pp. 140-148). New York: HarperCollins.

Pruegger, V. J., & Rogers, T. B. (1994). Cross-cultural sensitivity training: Methods and assessment. *International Journal of Intercultural Relations, 18,* 369-387.

Quick-fix diversity efforts are doomed. (1995, January). *Training,* pp. 18, 20.

Senge, P. M. (1990). *The fifth discipline: The art and practice of the learning organization.* Garden City, NY: Doubleday.

Silverstein, S. (1995, May 2). Workplace diversity efforts thrive despite backlash. *Los Angeles Times,* pp. 1, 14.

Sims, S. J., & Sims, R. R. (1993). Diversity and difference training in the United States. In R. R. Sims & R. F. Dennehy (Eds.), *Diversity and differences in organizations: An agenda for answers and questions* (pp. 73-92). Westport, CT: Quorum.

Solomon, E. J. (1993). Recognizing resistance: Creating readiness for organization change. *Diversity Factor, 1*(2), 16-20.

Sue, D. W. (1991). A model for cultural diversity training. *Journal of Counseling and Development, 70,* 99-105.

Swisher, K. (1995, February 13-19). Diversity training: Learning from past mistakes. *Washington Post National Weekly Edition,* p. 20.

Taylor, C. (1992). *Multiculturalism and "the politics of recognition."* Princeton, NJ: Princeton University Press.

Terry, R. W. (1994). Authenticity: Unity without uniformity. In E. Y. Cross, J. H. Katz, F. A. Miller, & E. W. Seashore (Eds.), *The promise of diversity: Over 40 voices discuss strategies for eliminating discrimination in organizations* (pp. 113-114). Burr Ridge, IL: Irwin.

Thomas, R. R. (1990). From affirmative action to affirming diversity. *Harvard Business Review, 68*(2), 107-117.

Thomas, R. R. (1992). Managing diversity: A conceptual framework. In S. E. Jackson & Associates, *Diversity in the workplace: Human resources initiatives* (pp. 306-317). New York: Guilford.

Triandis, H. C. (1986). Toward pluralism in education. In S. Modgil, G. K. Verma, K. Mallick, & C. Modgil (Eds.), *Multicultural education: The interminable debate.* London: Falmer.

Triandis, H. C., Kurowski, L. L., & Gelfand, M. J. (1994). Workplace diversity. In H. C. Triandis, M. D. Dunnette, & L. M. Hough (Eds.), *Handbook of industrial and organizational psychology* (Vol. 4, pp. 769-827). Palo Alto, CA: Consulting Psychologists Press.

Wheeler, M. (1994). *Diversity training: A research report* (Report No. 1083-94-RR). New York: Conference Board.

PART III

Area Studies: Intercultural Training for Critical Parts of the World

17

Reentry Training for Intercultural Sojourners

JUDITH N. MARTIN

TERESA HARRELL

I have been a stranger in a strange land.

—Moses, Exodus 2:22

Alas! and now where on earth am I? What do I here myself?
—Odysseus (on returning home to Ithaca)

"Why was I going home?" he asked himself. But he knew why. It was time. In order not to lose all that he had gained, he had to move forward and risk it all.
—James Baldwin, *Another Country*

WRITERS throughout history have described the sometimes bittersweet experience of sojourning, from Moses' description of travel abroad in biblical times, to Odysseus' return to Ithaca after 20 years of hardship and struggle, to James Baldwin's (1962) description of return to the United States, a country of racism and prejudice. However, the notion of systematic professional training to assist sojourners in these transitions is a relatively recent phenomenon (see Brislin & Van Buren, 1974; Marsh, 1976).

In this chapter, we first present definitions and theoretical assumptions. Second, we provide an overview of current theoretical conceptualizations of reentry and the implications for training. Third, we outline a general training model and describe training issues and content for particular sojourner groups.

Definitions

Intercultural reentry is the process of reintegration into primary home contexts after an intercultural sojourn (N. Adler, 1981; Martin, 1984). *Intercultural sojourn* refers to an intensive and extended visit into cultural contexts different from those in which one was socialized. In addition, a sojourn differs from migration in that the immigrant plans an indefinite stay, and some form of assimilation is often the goal. Also, the sojourn differs from everyday intercultural interactions for individuals who have been socialized into pluralistic societies. The difference is that sojourning involves cultural immersion on a daily basis, 24 hours a day (see Gudykunst's [1983] typology of strangers).

In this chapter, we focus on the reentry experience of individuals returning from an overseas sojourn, although much of the extant reentry literature could apply to readaptation after an intensive intercultural experience within national borders. The reentry experience may vary, depending on the *purpose* of the intercultural sojourn, whether one travels abroad as a student, a corporate employee, as military personnel, technical assistance worker, government employee, or missionary (Austin, 1983, 1986). The majority of research has investigated student and corporate returnees, and therefore this chapter focuses on these two groups:

> *Student sojourner returnees:* Those who travel abroad to study and return to their home country as students to continue their academic program
> *Professional sojourner returnees:* Those whose motivation for travel is for professional reasons (e.g., international students, corporate employees) and who return home to a professional environment

More discussion in the literature is needed about the distinction between professional returnees and student returnees. Granted, at some point when students become professionals, the lives of both groups converge into the professional arena. Until that occurs, though, the concerns and stakes are different. For instance, students go abroad for many reasons: They want to pursue a foreign degree or expertise because it is considered more prestigious in the job market back home or because is not available in the home country. Student sojourners leave home for language acquisition, to pursue their interest in area studies, to accompany their parents on an overseas assignment, to be exchange students, or just because they want to see more of the world (Koester, 1985, 1987).

Professional sojourners' motivations for going overseas are directly connected to their professional responsibilities. There are two categories of professional sojourners: One is the professional who has been sent by her government or employer to acquire certain expertise in the form of training from an academic institution, foreign company, or government; the second is the professional who goes abroad on a work assignment.

The professional who goes abroad for training may be an international student who will integrate into the workforce immediately on return, or a midcareer professional who can enhance her career by overseas training. Either the employer finances the training or works with the sojourner to secure funding from other sources. Professional sojourners who are not sent abroad by their employers usually receive some type of professional leave, with or without pay. Funding is available from special honorary fellowships (e.g., Fulbright, Rockefeller Foundation). Once these professional sojourners become students, their status at their host institutions may be viewed differently. They may or may not be recognized for their previous work experience or their professional position.

What distinguishes these sojourners from student sojourners is the expectation that the professionals will return to (former) employment immediately after the overseas sojourn (Glaser, 1978; Hu & Pedersen, 1986a, 1986b) and stay on the job for a certain period of time after receiving the overseas training (Harrell, 1994).

The second type of professional sojourners goes abroad on a work assignment; this group includes technical assistance workers, corporate employees, and missionaries. Their assignment may last for several months or years. It is ideal if the professional sojourners are able to stay abreast of events that take place in the home office and can return home at regular intervals. Sometimes, the professional and social lives overseas become intertwined because the social context is so closely connected to the status in the work environment. For example, it is not uncommon for professional sojourners to get to know their colleagues much better overseas. This is especially true for the military, missionaries, and the foreign service personnel because they often live in the same communities or in enclaves. Then there are certain societies, such as Japan, where socializing with colleagues is encouraged (Harris & Moran, 1991).

In addition to our focus on student and professional sojourners, our review of literature is primarily, though not exclusively, U.S. centered. Reentry training may vary dramatically from country to country because cultural attitudes toward sojourning vary, from suspicion of anyone who leaves the homeland and thus makes readaptation difficult—for example, Japan (Goodman, 1990; Kobayashi, 1981; LaBrack, 1981; White, 1988)—to the other extreme of viewing international sojourning as normal, with no need for training on return—for example, Western Europe. The need is for more scholarship investigating how reentry experiences vary from country to country.

Assumptions

Several fundamental notions of intercultural sojourning underlie all theoretical and practical notions of reentry. First, the sojourner's readaptation to the home culture must be considered within the context of the entire sojourn; the reentry phase is only one aspect of the intercultural sojourn. Second, the reentry transition is similar to other adult transitions, in that all transitions involve loss and change for the individual and present opportunities for personal and intellectual growth (J. Bennett, 1977; Bridges, 1980). The amount of time it takes to make the transition is highly individualistic. Third, sojourner adaptation and reentry are complex phenomena comprising cognitive, affective, and behavioral processes, and scholars have yet to formulate comprehensive theories of adaptation (Furnham, 1988; Kim, 1988; Searle & Ward, 1990). Each theoretical approach, however, contributes to conceptual understanding and has implications for designing and implementing reentry training. Familiarity with these various approaches can facilitate the development of comprehensive, grounded theory for training.

Research, Theory, and Training

Scholars, practitioners, and sojourners have noted the importance of theory-based training refined by dialogue between researchers and trainers. We believe that theoretical and research endeavors should be grounded in intercultural realities and that training should be grounded in appropriate theories. We hope this chapter will promote this dialogue.

Researchers, practitioners, and trainers can enhance each other's work in several ways. For example, (reentry) trainers can help researchers ground their research in intercultural experience by

1. Identifying general training issues that need to be studied—for example, Why are reentry training programs often not attended by returnees? Which sojourners are most likely to benefit from training? At what point in the intercultural sojourn should reentry training take place? Which reentry issues are most salient for which sojourner groups (personal adaptation issues vs. professional [re]integration issues)? How does the overseas experience change the values and attitudes of the sojourner, and how do these changes affect the reentry experience?

2. Identifying specific hypotheses derived from training that can be tested empirically—for example, sojourners who are aware of the process of reentry are more likely to benefit from training programs than those who deny the existence of a reentry phenomenon; sojourners are most receptive to training several months after their return home.

3. In providing assistance in the interpretation of specific research results—for example, do the results of reentry studies make sense, given the trainers' experiences? What questions should be investigated in subsequent research?

Conversely, being familiar with research and theory can assist trainers

1. In providing information that will help in conceptualizing and designing the training—for example, from theoretical models, what are the most critical reentry issues that need to be addressed in training? psychological processes? professional reintegration issues? personal issues—for example, what are sojourner characteristics and skills that facilitate reentry adaptation?

2. In evaluating the reentry training—for example, what types of training are most effective for particular sojourner groups (e.g., Is the particular training effective)? What are appropriate measures by which to evaluate training?

In the next section, we review the traditional and current theoretical approaches to reentry. There are many approaches to cultural adaptation overseas, and no one theory has been developed to explain the sojourn experience (for literature reviews, see Furnham & Bochner, 1986; Kim & Gudykunst, 1988). We selected three theoretical approaches that have been adapted to the reentry phase of cultural adaptation, and although none explain the totality of the reentry experience, each contributes something to our understanding of the process and to our expertise in reentry training.

Theoretical Approaches to Reentry

W-Curve Theory

The early literature on reentry was based on social-psychological notions and conceptualized adaptation (and readaptation) as the sojourner's feelings of comfort or satisfaction reflecting the degree of congruence between the sojourner and environment. The most important social-psychological theory is the W-curve theory, in which the feeling of satisfaction and well-being is posited to change over time. According to this theory, the sojourn overseas occurs in a predictable U-curve fashion: The sojourner has a feeling of euphoria immediately on entry into the foreign culture, but that changes to culture shock and discomfort and then to a gradual feeling of fit and comfort (Lysgaard, 1955; Oberg, 1960; Thomas & Harrell, 1994; Torbiorn, 1982).

This U-curve process is repeated again on reentry, and the entire process is referred to as the *W-curve of adaptation and readaptation* (Gullahorn & Gullahorn, 1963). This repatriation is as important and intense as, and sometimes more challenging than, the overseas adjustment (N. Adler, 1981; Sussman, 1986). It is often unexpected, and sojourners are often not prepared for the extent to which they experience confusion and disorientation on return to their home environment.

Early studies were based on U.S.-educated international students who were returning to their home countries in professional capacities. Several studies identified both personal and professional aspects of reentry (Gama & Pedersen, 1977; Gullahorn & Gullahorn, 1963),

stressing that, for the professional sojourner, personal and professional issues go hand in hand and that professional integration is as important as, if not more so, personal readaptation. Later research, however, concentrated more on social psychological (re)adaptation, and the professional integration issue was ignored (Harrell, 1994).

Psychological Adjustment

As noted, these early studies conceptualized (re)adaptation in terms of psychological health, and more recent studies in the same tradition measure reentry with mental health questionnaires—for example, psychological depression scales (Rogers & Ward, 1993; Ward & Kennedy, 1992; Weissman & Furnham, 1987). Recent empirical research has focused on testing the viability of the U- and W-curve process (see Church, 1982, for a review of literature; see Nafziger, 1995, for an example of an empirical test of the W-curve) and on identifying variables that influence their entry and reentry adjustment and problems experienced by returnees (Church, 1982; Furnham, 1988; Lonner, 1986; Martin, 1984; Uehara, 1986).

Professional Integration

Professional integration is often viewed as the missing link in the transition from overseas to reentry for professional sojourners. Professional integration "expands on the cultural reentry concept to include the professional dimensions of reentry" (Hood & Schieffer, 1983, p. 2). The value of the overseas experience and how it affects the eventual career of the student sojourner or the professional sojourner has been overlooked in the reentry literature.

Many issues cause professional integration shock when a sojourner returns to the home country workplace. The most profound are the role/status reversal issues. Professional sojourners often return to their previous work environments to become persona non grata. After an assignment of several years abroad, they return to work environments that sometimes seem more unfamiliar than the overseas environment. A returned employee may experience a decrease in the level of professional responsibilities and decision-making powers, fewer subordinates to supervise, feelings of not being valued, undefined job description and assignments, and an office space usually designated to someone of lower status. For example, Torbiorn (1982) found that the most troublesome reentry aspect for Swedish corporate employees was their unwillingness to accept a decrease in economic and professional status.

Financial concerns are also part of professional integration. It is not uncommon for the professional sojourner to receive additional financial incentives while assuming overseas duty. In retrospect, these seem rather generous, compared with the home country salary schedule and benefits—for example, housing allowances or free housing, cars and drivers, free airplane tickets to return home, tuition paid for dependents' education (Harris & Moran, 1991). Giving up these benefits leads to financial concerns on return (N. Adler, 1981; Copeland & Griggs, 1985; Harrell, 1994).

Often, professionals go overseas because they have been told that this will give them a competitive edge for promotions within the company or that every manager within the organization is expected to go overseas at least once in her career. Consequently, when they return, they expect to be promoted or at least rewarded for their tour of duty. For these reasons, the professionals are often unprepared for the changes they encounter within the organization on their return. They may have a new and unfamiliar supervisor who is not aware of their previous work history and performance, and often their overseas accomplishments and responsibilities go unrecognized. They may be dismayed by the inability to use newly acquired competencies (N. Adler, 1981) and the lack of opportunity to share experiences from the overseas assignments (Copeland & Griggs, 1985; Harrell, 1994). Often, the predeparture promises that were made to give them some incentive and motivation for accepting the overseas assignments are not kept. Their work teams are no longer the same because their former colleagues, as well as their former subordinates, may have been promoted. In fact, some of their former subordinates may have acquired positions of equal or higher status than the professional sojourners' status.

Another aspect of professional integration is the jealousy or lack of support and loyalty from their new supervisors, colleagues, and subordinates (Gama & Pedersen, 1977; Harrell, 1994).

Initially, they may find themselves out of the informal information loop. The corporate culture may have changed with the introduction of new technology, or support for learning new technologies that are essential for completing their tasks may be lacking.

In addition to describing personal and professional aspects of reentry, this social-psychological research has also contributed to the reentry training literature by identifying factors that facilitate or inhibit the reentry process for both student and professional sojourners. Being familiar with these factors may help trainers to assist returnees in successful psychological adaptation. Three sets of variables that influence reentry are sojourner background variables, host environment variables, and reentry environment variables.

Influences on Reentry

Sojourner Background Variables

Sojourner background variables include characteristics that the sojourner brings to the sojourn and reentry experience: nationality, age, gender, religion, ethnicity, socioeconomic background, previous intercultural experience, and personality. It seems clear that nationality affects the personal and professional reentry. As noted above, societies vary in their attitude toward reentry, and much has been written about the difficulties of Japanese returnees (Kobayashi, 1981; Labrack, 1981). Brabant, Palmer, and Gramling (1990), in their study of 96 returned international students, found that the sojourners' nationality was sometimes associated with reentry problems. Specifically, Nigerians experienced greater problems than students of other nationalities; as one Nigerian student wrote:

> U.S.A. education and social life tends to draw so many into a world of fantasy. This induces a lot of students to believe that their home country is completely underdeveloped. The reality of an underdeveloped system tends to disappear after a few years of stay in the U.S.A. Emphasis should be laid on actual reality by constantly reminding students of their original background. (p. 398)

The research seems to suggest that younger sojourners (adolescence) have a more difficult time readapting, perhaps because they are more changed by the overseas experience than adults, who have already been fully socialized into their primary cultural environment (Gullahorn & Gullahorn, 1963). An exception is Brabant et al.'s (1990) study in which no relationship was found between age and adaptation. Returnee issues may vary with age. Younger returnees are more concerned with the personal relationships that are often affected by their absence (Martin, 1986a, 1986b), whereas postuniversity and professionally established returnees may be more concerned about professional reintegration (Gama & Pedersen, 1977; Harrell, 1994).

Female returnees seem to have more difficulty with social-psychological reentry than male returnees, particularly those who sojourn in countries where they experience more liberal gender roles than in their own country (Brabant et al., 1990; Gama & Pedersen, 1977; Harrell, 1994). They may also experience more professional problems on reentry, in that they may find themselves a small minority in the workforce, and that position may lead to isolation and loneliness (N. Adler, 1984, 1986; Boakari, 1982). Kim (1988) emphasizes that gender findings in the adaptation literature should be treated with caution because gender is often confounded with other variables (e.g., spousal roles).

Religion is also posited to influence reentry adaptation, but few studies have investigated this variable. Brabant et al. (1990) found that religious affiliation was related to family/ personal problems; that is, Near Eastern and Islamic students proportionately experienced greater problems with family than students of other religions. This difficulty probably occurs because of the more liberalizing changes students experience overseas that may cause family conflict on their return.

Previous intercultural experience would seem to facilitate readaptation. N. Adler (1981), in her study of corporate returnees, found that overseas adaptation (but not satisfaction) was related to general reentry effectiveness, but there is little empirical evidence to corroborate this finding. Personality characteristics of the sojourner (e.g., openness, flexibility) seem to facilitate transitions in general (Bennett, 1977;

Kim, 1988). Personality variables as predictors of cultural adaptation fell out of favor for a while with researchers (Church, 1982), but there seems to be a return to valuing the role of personality in the adaptation process (Chapter 5, this volume; Harris & Moran, 1991; Kealey, 1989; Kim, 1988).

Two factors that have been almost completely neglected in reentry research are ethnicity and socioeconomic status. We know these variables influence a sojourn abroad (e.g., international students from Africa and Asia experience more hostility in the United States and England than Western European students; Aldegan & Parks, 1985; Church, 1982; Zwingmann & Gunn, 1983), but scant literature explains how sojourner ethnicity affects reentry.

An exception is Harrell's (1994) investigation of U.S.-educated Indonesian professional returnees. In her interviews, Harrell discovered differences between the reentry experiences of Chinese and indigenous Indonesians. Of those interviewed, all of the Chinese students returned to the lucrative private sector, whereas all but two indigenous Indonesians returned to public-sector jobs. She emphasizes the need for future studies of ethnicity and reentry.

An example of how ethnicity may influence reentry is an African American student who travels to Jamaica and enjoys the status of a majority culture member and, while there, perhaps serves as a cultural broker to white students on the same program. On returning to the United States, this same student resumes minority status and experiences a decrease of the support and status present in Jamaica.

It also seems possible that minority group sojourners are more experienced and facile in negotiating cultural transitions and may experience less difficulty in reentry transitions. At any rate, the relationship between ethnicity and reentry is not easy to understand, particularly because of the limited information on how various countries treat ethnic groups in their sending sojourners overseas. For example, from anecdotal information we know that, in many countries, certain ethnic groups are not included in the selection pool when students are sent abroad to study.

Discovering the relationship between social class and reentry has also been difficult. Brabant et al. (1990) found no relationship between social class and reentry problems but did note little variation in this variable. This lack of variation occurs because of few lower-class participants, just as few U.S. students or professional sojourners represent nonmajority cultures. Brislin (1981) identified similar gaps in the U.S. literature because most sojourners who travel abroad are self-selected and fairly homogeneous (white, middle-class, educated).

Host Environment Variables

The sojourners' experiences in the host country affect both personal and professional reentry. It is difficult to identify specific variables that affect reentry, however, because they are so interrelated. Although the length of the overseas stay may be important, it is probably the degree to which the sojourner is integrated into the host society that influences the reentry experience. Several studies have indicated that, for professional and student sojourners, those who are more integrated into the host country have more difficult personal reentry on return (Harris & Moran, 1991; Sussman, 1986). N. Adler (1981) found the converse was true for corporate employees; those who resisted contact with the host culture overseas were rated most effective by their colleagues on their return.

Another influence on reentry is the degree of difference between the host and home environments; that is, the more different the host culture from the home culture, the more difficult reentry will be. Again, it is probably the greater the difference, the more adaptation and value change are required on the part of the sojourner. This greater change in the sojourner's outlook contributes to a more difficult reentry (Harrell, 1994; Uehara, 1986), although N. Adler (1981) found no relationship between cultural distance and reentry difficulty among corporate employees.

Another variable affecting reentry is the amount of contact the sojourner maintains with friends and family at home. For example, research findings suggest that sojourners who maintain communication with friends and family at home while abroad or who return home from time to time if on an extended sojourn seem to have an easier time of readapting (Brabant et al., 1990; Harrell, 1994; Martin, 1986b). This sustained contact allows sojourn-ers to keep abreast of changes and events at home and causes fewer surprises on return.

Reentry Environment Variables

Several variables in the reentry environment influence returnees' experiences. One is the support system available to the sojourner. A great deal of research identifies the importance of social support in the *overseas* experience (Adelman, 1988; Chapter 15, this volume; Furnham & Bochner, 1986; Kim, 1988), and a few studies have systematically investigated this aspect of reentry.

Returning U.S. students report that their relationships with family and sometimes with friends often provide them with emotional support during reentry (Martin, 1985, 1986a, 1986b; Wilson, 1985); however, colleges and universities often do not provide them with a supportive environment. Rather, they report that their institutions penalize student returnees by not showing flexibility in transfer of credit, financial aid, and registration deadlines (Kauffmann, Martin, & Weaver, 1992).

The same may be said for returning professionals. They often report that they feel out of touch with the home office, that the skills they learned overseas are not appreciated, and that the environment is not supportive (N. Adler, 1981; Torbiorn, 1982). Harrell (1994) found that the greatest support for professional sojourners during reentry came from supervisors and colleagues who had also studied abroad.

Although the traditional focus on the social-psychological aspects of the reentry experience is important and has contributed to our knowledge about the experience, unanswered questions remain. For example, it is still not clear what the relationship is between time and psychological (re)adaptation—that is, that readjustment follows a predictable timeline. Certainly, empirical research has not confirmed the utility of the U-curve in overseas sojourning (Brislin, 1993; Kealey, 1989; Klineburg & Hull, 1979).

Also, it is not yet known which factors are most salient for particular sojourner groups (e.g., student returnees vs. professional returnees). Not all of the variables that affect psychological adaptation or professional integration have been identified. Further, it is not clear how these variables interact to determine the degree of difficulty that any one sojourner may experience on reentry.

This gap in the literature may also be a result of this particular research tradition—the variable analytical approach that tries to identify all of the variables that affect a particular phenomenon and then measure the relationships among these variables by statistical tests. Although earlier studies have lamented the lack of rigorous quantitative studies, perhaps it is time for more qualitative, in-depth studies that describe specific problems encountered by a variety of returnee groups.

A final contribution of the early research on reentry is the identification of difficulties, both personal and professional, experienced by returning student sojourners. The Inventory of Reentry Problems, published 20 years ago, encompasses six general areas and is still applicable to most sojourners (Asuncion-Lande, 1976):

1. Cultural adjustments (e.g., identity problems, adjustment to daily personal and work routines)
2. Social adjustments (e.g., feelings of social alienation, superiority, frustration as a result of conflicting attitudes)
3. Linguistic adjustments (adoption of speech mannerisms that may be misinterpreted by people at home)
4. National/Political adjustments (e.g., changes in political conditions, adoption of new political views)
5. Educational adjustments (e.g., absence of professional education programs and support groups, relevance of American education)
6. Professional adjustments (e.g., inability to communicate what was learned, resistance to change by colleagues, high expectations)

Harrell (1994), from her research on returned Indonesian students, identifies a seventh problem—financial concerns. This list provides a guideline for trainers in developing the content of training.

To summarize, this social-psychological literature contributes to reentry training by emphasizing the processual nature of the intercultural experience, emphasizing the importance of both personal and professional reintegration, and identifying variables that affect reentry and problems experienced by returnees.

Expectations Model

A second theoretical perspective is also grounded in social-psychological literature. Researchers have noted the importance of sojourner expectations in adaptation to the foreign environment (Black & Gregersen, 1990; Chiu, 1995; Furnham, 1988; Gullahorn & Gullahorn, 1963; Hawes & Kealey, 1981; Kealey, 1989; Searle & Ward, 1990; Weaver, 1993) and especially in their return to the home culture. In fact, many scholars have emphasized that a distinguishing characteristic of the reentry experience is that it is *unexpected* (N. Adler, 1976; Brislin & Van Buren, 1974; Gama & Pedersen, 1977; Martin, 1984; Torbiorn, 1994; Westwood, 1984; Westwood & Lawrance, 1988; Westwood, Lawrence, & Paul, 1986).

Applying the *expectancy value model,* a social-psychological theory (Feather, 1982), to sojourner adaptation, Furnham (1988) suggests that the sojourner has expectations about the impending experience that are then fulfilled or unfulfilled; fulfilled expectations lead to positive evaluations of the experience and ultimately to good adjustment, whereas unfulfilled expectations lead to negative evaluations and poorer adjustment. This model has empirical support (Weissman & Furnham, 1987).

Expectancy violation theory, used originally in investigations of nonverbal behavior (Burgoon, 1983, 1992), further refines the role of expectations in sojourning. Unlike expectancy value theory, not all unfilled expectations lead to negative evaluations and outcomes. Rather, unfulfilled expectations may be violated either positively or negatively. Expectations perceived as negatively violated (things turn out worse than expected) do lead to negative evaluations (Burgoon & Walther, 1990). Those violated positively (things turn out better than expected), however, lead to positive evaluations and outcomes.

Recent research findings confirm these hypotheses. Several studies report that overmet expectations lead to positive well-being in international students in New Zealand (Rogers & Ward, 1993), in corporate employees in Japan (Black & Gregersen, 1990), and in returned

U.S. students (Lobdell, 1990; Martin, Bradford, & Rohrlich, 1995). Conversely, when adaptation is much more difficult than anticipated, sojourners tend to experience psychological problems, as reported in studies of international students (Rogers & Ward, 1993), West Indian and Asian immigrants in Britain (Cochrane, 1983), and Vietnamese immigrants in Australia (Krupinski, 1975).

Implications for Training

The contributions of this research to training is the emphasis on setting expectations about reentry early in the sojourn experience. Given the findings that overmet expectations lead to greater satisfaction, it may be good to overprepare sojourners. For example, Westwood and his colleagues have outlined reentry training based on expectations theory for returning international students (Westwood, 1984; Westwood & Lawrance, 1988; Westwood et al., 1986). The training begins prior to the return, and students are encouraged to explore indepth what their personal and professional expectations are for their return. They are also presented with firsthand information about reentry from those who have experienced reentry.[1]

A second example of long-term reentry training is the overseas study program at the University of the Pacific. LaBrack (1993) provides an excellent description of how predeparture and reentry training are combined and linked in this program.

The same topics (stereotyping, cultural patterns of values and communication, identity, and culture shock) are explored both prior to and on return from the overseas experience in training sessions. In the postreturn sessions, sojourners are encouraged to examine ways in which they and others in their social network have changed. In this way, not only are students assisted in developing realistic expectations in each phase of the sojourner experience, but the sojourn is also seen as a process and thus crosscultural learning is facilitated and made relevant to personal and academic experience. This emphasis on holistic, processual learning tries to avoid what LaBrack terms *the shoebox effect,* wherein the experience of the year abroad are "put away" on return and are not integrated into subsequent learning.

Reentry Systems Theory

Another theoretical approach, based on general systems theory, conceptualizes adaptation as a stress-adaptation-growth cycle (Kim, 1988). Martin (1993) proposed extending this theory to include the reentry phase of adaptation (Martin, 1993; Rohrlich & Martin, 1991)[2]; that is, reentry adaptation is conceptualized as a cycle of stress-adaptation-growth. The sojourner is under stress in the reentry environment and learns to adapt through communication with others in the reentry environment. This adaptation leads to personal and intellectual growth. The model incorporates much of previous social-psychological research (reviewed above) in identifying important variables but is unique in its emphasis on *the role of communication* and growth in the adaptation process and on the comprehensive nature of reentry.

The model includes the following components:

1. Sojourner characteristics
   - Cultural background
   - Personality attributes
   - Preparedness for change
2. Home environment characteristics
   - Receptivity
   - Conformity pressure (e.g., social segregation)
3. Communication of the returning sojourner
   - Communication competence
   - Interpersonal communication with members of home culture
   - Mass communication consumption in home culture
   - Interpersonal communication with other returnees
   - Mass communication consumption of media from former host culture (e.g., exposure)[3]
4. Readaptation outcomes
   - Psychological health (e.g., absence of severe stress, feeling comfortable at home)
   - Functional fitness (e.g., professional reintegration, also congruent with the social skills approach; Furnham & Bochner, 1986)
   - Intercultural identity (e.g., changes in identity)

Perhaps the most important contribution of the model is the expanded notion of reentry adaptation; that is, the fourth component (outcomes) extends the social psychological model (emphasis on the affective feeling aspect) to include cognitive and behavioral aspects, which can include professional integration.

Psychological Health. This dimension of reentry adaptation has been discussed—the feeling of well-being, a fit between returnee and environment.

Functional Fitness. This facet of adaptation is the behavioral aspects of reentry and encompasses at least two dimensions of reentry. The first dimension is the social skills needed to negotiate social life in the home environment; this is congruent with Furnham and Bochner's (1986) social skills approach to adaptation (can the returnee function in daily social life?). The second dimension relates to the behavioral skills needed for professional (re)integration (can the returnee function effectively in professional contexts?).

Reentry into the professional milieu is part of the readjustment of many sojourner groups because of how their overseas experiences influence job searches, initial employment decisions, or reintegration into the workplace. This means that, eventually, the adjustment and readjustment strategies that each sojourner develops to deal with life's transitions are transformed into valuable life lessons. Thus, the sojourner continues to discover ways to make sense out of a personal transformation that is often rarely understood or valued by nonsojourners. However, the sojourner must develop strategies for coping and fitting into routines that include the personal worldviews of others.

Unlike other arenas of one's life, the workplace requires a certain capacity of readiness, fitness, and efficiency so that professional responsibilities can be immediately assumed. This expectation of workplace fitness does not usually accommodate reentry shock.

Intercultural Identity. Many scholars have discussed the idea that sojourners often undergo significant personal and cognitive changes that may alter the very core of their sense of personal and cultural identities (P. Adler, 1975, 1982; J. Bennett, 1993). This is particularly true of individuals who belong to an ethnic majority

group (e.g., whites in the United States) for whom an overseas sojourn is the first extensive experience of being in the minority. Individuals who live on the cultural margins because of multiple cultural transitions abroad or domestic pluralism have been labeled *marginal* (Stonequist, 1937), *third-culture persons* (Useem, Donoghue, & Useem, 1963), *multicultural* (P. Adler, 1982), *cultural mediators* (Bochner, 1982), and more recently, *borderland dwellers* (Anzaldua, 1987). Scholars usually either tout the strength of the marginal position or note the inherent stress and tensions. The point is that this is a very important aspect of sojourning and one that is often salient in reentry training. Although not all sojourners develop a multicultural attitude, almost all deal with a heightened sense of cultural identity to some degree.

Implications for Training

The systems approach to reentry contributes several notions to reentry training. First, reentry training should assist sojourners to deal with stress. The notion that intercultural adaptation is stressful has been suggested by a number of researchers and trainers (Barna, 1983; Dyal & Dyal, 1981; Selye, 1974; Walton, 1990). Specific suggestions for incorporating stress-reduction in reentry is described by Martin (1993), including Brammer and Abrego's (1981) interventions and Holmes and Rahe's (1967) stressful life events.

A second contribution of this model is the emphasis on effective sojourner communication with friends, family, and coworkers on reentry and the importance of gaining social support during reentry transitions (Adelman, 1988; Albrecht & Adelman, 1987; Kim, 1978, 1988). It has been suggested that, through communication, one makes a successful reentry (Martin, 1986b).

Dealing With Intercultural Identity Issues

M. Bennett (1993) developed a model of intercultural sensitivity, based on attitudes toward cultural differences, that extends Kim's notion of the intercultural identity aspect of adaptation. This model has six stages—three stages of ethnocentric thinking (e.g., cultural differences do not really exist or, at best, are not important) and three stages of ethnorelative thinking (e.g., differences are appreciated, multiple frames of reference are experienced). The final stage of ethnorelativistic thinking is characterized as integrative—constructive marginality, wherein individuals are truly multicultural; they live on the margins between cultures, outside all cultural frames of reference, and struggle with the total integration of ethnorelativism.

LaBrack (1993) suggests that, before U.S. students go abroad, their thinking is often characterized as one of the three ethnocentric stages (denying, defensive, minimizing). After their return, they are more enthnorelative in their attitude and understanding of cultural differences (accepting, adapting, integration). M. Bennett (1993) gives suggestions for assisting individuals to progress toward increased ethnorelativism. As such, this model is an excellent tool to assist sojourners, both students and professionals, in understanding and developing their sense of cultural identity.

J. Bennett (1993) elaborates on the final phase of this model (constructive marginality) and relates the concept of ethnocentrism/ethnorelativism to cultural identity development. Although many returnees do not reach this stage of cultural identity, it is useful for those sojourners who experience multiple cultural transitions and reentries. Bennett states that, at this last stage of complete cultural relativism, there are two potential responses for the marginal person: encapsulated or constructive marginality. The *encapsulated marginal person* responds to cultural marginality with a compromised ability to establish boundaries and to make judgments and becomes trapped by marginality. In contrast, the *constructive marginal person* maintains control of choice and is able to construct contexts intentionally and consciously for the purpose of creating his or her own identity.

Bennett goes on to discuss the particular training challenges of working with both types of marginal individuals. She suggests that the challenges for the trainer of encapsulated marginals is to model a consistent appreciation for diversity of perspectives because they often see only the negative side of multiple perspectives. For example, student returnees need to learn to make connections between their intercultural experience and their academic learning. Overall, returnees need to learn to appreciate, synthesize, and take individual control of their lives. Constructive marginals, however, need to learn how to think in a context defined and assessed by their construction of reality—because they already appreciate the diversity of experience of intercultural transitions. They also need to explore the ethical and boundary issues in accepting multiple frames of reference.

To summarize the contributions of the three theoretical approaches to reentry, the W-curve/early theories emphasized reentry as a complex process, incorporating both psychological and professional aspects and identification of factors that influence personal and professional reentry. Expectations theory emphasizes not only that the events that occur during reentry cause difficulty but also that the mind-set/perceptions of the returnee play an important role. This perspective also emphasizes that reentry training must start early in the sojourn and that it is better to overprepare than underprepare sojourners. Reentry systems theory emphasizes the importance of communication in reentry and conceptualizes reentry as a complex experience. This perspective incorporates the psychological adjustment notions but is particularly valuable in stressing the role of behavioral fitness and intercultural identity development in the reentry experience.

Designing Reentry Training for Specific Sojourner Groups

As with any training, the trainer should conduct a needs assessment of the training context, answering the Who, Why, What, How, Where, and What For questions (see Chapter 4, this volume). In this section, we first describe salient characteristics for the two sojourner groups and outline and discuss a general, long-term model for reentry training based on the theoretical notions outlined above. In this discussion, we identify the various training concerns specific to professional and student sojourner groups. The emphasis is not on specific training strategies, but on a comprehensive understanding how reentry issues should be incorporated at every phase of the sojourn.[4] As noted, professional and student sojourners have different reentry concerns.

Student Returnees

The typical U.S. student sojourner is usually an undergraduate whose study abroad is part of liberal education, not necessarily tied to a major. The emphasis for this sojourn is on personal and intellectual growth, rather than on professional development (see Carlson, Burn, Useem, & Yachimowicz, 1990; Kauffmann et al., 1993). For most student sojourners, cognitive and moral developments are not yet matured and cultural identity not yet completely formulated, particularly for members of dominant ethnic cultures (Perry, 1970; Smith, 1991).

The goal of reentry training for student sojourners is usually to assist them in understanding their personal and intellectual growth and changes in their cultural identity, to feel more comfortable in their home environment, and to be able to function effectively in that environment.

Professional Returnees

For professional returnees, the sojourn and related reentry training are usually professionally, rather than personally, focused. Although an overseas sojourn is always personally challenging, the professional sojourner's personal and cultural identity is usually already formed, and so the challenge for them during the sojourn is to adapt enough to complete a task, usually with a preestablished structure to assist them.

On return, family issues—the readaptation of spouses and children—are important but secondary. The training goals are usually to assist the sojourner in being functionally fit for the job.

Reentry Training Model

The professional integration model developed by Harrell (1994) and presented here (see Figure 17.1) has been modified to include the training demands and activities of both student and professional returnees. The training needs of both groups converge at different phases during their overseas experiences. This is especially true when the professional sojourner has embarked on a study-abroad experience or the student sojourner is preparing to enter the professional arena. Components in the model are therefore designed with both returnee groups in mind.[5]

The model offers a comprehensive conceptualization of the overseas experience, as well as those training activities designed to prepare sojourners to go overseas and repatriate, and is congruent with the theoretical notions discussed earlier in the chapter. The model comprises four training phases:

1. The predeparture phase
2. The overseas experience phase
3. The pre-reentry phase
4. The reentry phase

These phases have been developed as a way to operationalize the training and orientation experiences of the overseas sojourner. Even though the model is presented in a linear mode, it should be understood that the phases are not considered discrete, but as a continuum, a continuous flow of activity, sometimes overlapping, and the parts cannot be separated.

The model also assumes that the overseas experience—whether the sojourner embarks on the experience as a student or a professional—influences professional reentry or eventual entrée into professional life. For this reason, this model also considers issues related to career development, from the very beginning, when the sojourner is selected or decides to go abroad, to continuous reentry preparation during the sojourner's time overseas. A strategy is developed and implemented that ensures a smoother transition, repatriation, into the eventual work environment (Boakari, 1982; Denney & Eckert, 1987; LaBrack, 1981).

Predeparture/Pre-Reentry Phase

As designated in the model, predeparture/pre-reentry training begins in the home country 3 to 6 months prior to departure, initiates preparation for the overseas experience, and creates a framework for the sojourner to understand the orientation while also considering those issues paramount to repatriation—as a student or a professional. Components of this training include seminars, activities, and individual sojourner projects that could be implemented in both home and host country, depending on where the training resources exist. Much has

Predeparture/Pre-reentry (Home/Host Country)	Overseas Experiences (Host Country)	Pre-reentry (Host/Home Country)	Professional Reentry (Home/Host Country)
–Professional integration Orientation (PS, SS) Professional reentry (PS) –Implications for reentry on career decisions (PS) Character of the work environment –Identify the establish (PS) support system and protocol for professional overseas acculturation, adjustment, and reentry –Career development for student sojourners entering the job market for the first time (SS) –Identify skills and competencies (PS, SS) Inventory before departure Inventory on return –Language training (PS, SS) –Country specific cultural Orientation (PS, SS) Host culture (PS, SS) Overseas employer (PS) Foreign higher educational system (SS) Home culture comparison/contrast (PS, SS) –Host country professional affiliations Mentor identification (PS, SS) Host families (PS, SS) Home country citizens (PS, SS) Host country nationals (PS, SS) –Contact corporate supervisor (PS) –Contact academic advisor (SS)	–Adjustment issues (PS, SS) Family presence or absence in host country Cultural, gender, status, and age issues Financial considerations –Professional orientation (PS, SS) Professional relationships Professional responsibilities –Professional organizations (PS, SS) Conference participation Training opportunities –Professional networking (PS, SS) –Academic experiences (SS) Internships Academic rigor Research and publishing Professorial relationships –Nonformal educational experiences Living/lifestyle experiences Student organizations Community organizations social activities (PS, SS) Host families Cultural activities Travel –Host country employment (PS, SS) –Maintain home connections (PS, SS) Employer contact/briefings Travel home E-mail –Employer and faculty training (PS, SS) Specific country orientation Cross-cultural orientation	–Professional briefings and debriefings (PS) –Critical evaluations (PS) –Exit interviews (PS, SS) –Career development (PS, SS) Interviews with home country supervisors Update resume Networking with home staff –Repatriation orientation (PS, SS) Political and economic Social and cultural Readjustment Cultural contrast orientation Language assessment Foreign and national language –Consult with mentors (PS, SS) –Periodic visits to home country if possible (PS, SS) –Academic concerns (SS) Financial aid applications Registration Housing application Campus employment Status of the degree program Transfer of credits to home institution from the study abroad experiences –Internships (SS) –Alumni Association (PS, SS)	–Readjustment issues (PS, SS) Family adjustment Cultural, gender, status, and age issues Financial adjustment Social readjustment –Resumption of employment (PS) –Job search (PS, SS) –Employment (PS, SS) Evaluation of experiences Organizational orientation Management structure Formal and informal Organizational policies Formal and informal Organizational culture Job satisfaction Compensation, benefits, promotions Quality of work relationships Awareness of employer expectations Awareness of employee expectations concerning readjustment –Professional development (PS, SS) –Consult with mentors (PS, SS) –Consult other returnees (PS, SS) –Foreign language retention (PS, SS)

Figure 17.1. Professional Integration Training Model for Professional and Student Sojourners

SOURCE: From *Professional Integration of Indonesian Graduate Degree Holders From U.S. Colleges and Universities in the Fields of Business Administration, Education, and Engineering,* a dissertation by T. Harrell, 1994, University of Minnesota. Copyright 1994 by T. Harrell. Adapted with permission.

been written describing content and methods for overseas predeparture training.

Professional integration orientation is a viable component of predeparture training, particularly for professional sojourners. Sending employees abroad is an investment in the company's resources and therefore its future dividends. If reentry is not considered, according to Copeland and Griggs (1985), there is

a costly "brain drain" of the corporation's international expertise. An outstanding number of repatriated personnel leave their companies shortly after return from abroad. And seeing that international assignments may be risky for one's long-term career, others in the company become unwilling to go. (p. 204)

Even before departure, professional sojourners should be encouraged to consider the *implications for reentry on career decisions* and the *character of the work environment* when they return, to begin a process of setting realistic expectations.

Training should also help the professional sojourner *identify the established support system* and protocol for acculturation throughout the entire sojourn experience. Similarly, student sojouners should be presented with ideas of how the overseas experience may be integrated into their career decisions and to begin to think of career strategies they may explore on return.

Foreign language training is an ongoing enterprise that starts in the home country and continues in the host country. Ideally, language proficiency will remain a part of the sojourners' repertoire of competencies. Professional sojourners, unlike student sojourners, may not need to use the host country language in the work environment because many multinational organizations use the home country language as the *lingua franca* in the workplace. They should be encouraged, however, to acquire minimum linguistic competence to enable them to be more independent and comfortable while living in the host country. Language proficiency not only makes life easier but also facilitates cultural understanding. Language provides the foundation for understanding the subtle nuances of a culture. The formal language that may be required in the academic or business arena may be different from the language used in everyday life.

Trainers should provide at least introductory, *country-specific information* and a cultural immersion activity before departure from the home country. Cultural immersion activities give sojourners the opportunity to experience a culture or subculture group activity that is unfamiliar or different from their own (e.g., Barnga, Ecotonos[6]). The goal of this activity is to provide the sojourner with an experience of feeling marginal or outside a familiar cultural milieu. The opportunity to debrief this experience serves as an "inoculation," helps the sojourners in understanding some of the reactions they may have during their overseas sojourn, especially when they are introduced to new environments (Chiu, 1995).

Student sojourners need information about the culture of their overseas institution, the academic requirements and academic conduct expected of them in the overseas institution. In addition, it is important for sojourners to meet with student and professional sojourners who have recently returned. All training sessions and activities should include a component that introduces the student or professional to what might be expected on return to the home country. This sets up the expectation that the sojourn is a complex experience that engages the total individual and has far-reaching effects and that it does not begin with the arrival in the host country and end when leaving the host country.

Sojourners need some training regarding adjustment issues they may encounter during their overseas experiences. Some intercultural trainers encourage sojourners to keep journals as a way to chronicle their experiences and their reactions to their experiences. Professional sojourners should receive an orientation to their overseas workplace, including the work environment, protocol for professional relationships, and the work ethic that is practiced. Student and professional sojourners who are sponsored need to contact their sponsors and participate in additional training programs implemented by their sponsors. This is important because most sponsoring agencies have requirements/stipulations that sojourners must adhere to in order to receive funding.

Orientation sessions are most helpful when they include presentations by host country nationals who are still in contact with the status and events of their country and who have an understanding of their own cultural origins, as well as an understanding of the sojourners' home country culture. The more astute the host country nationals are about the cultural differences between sojourners' home and host culture, the more effective they will be in the predeparture training in helping sojourners develop realistic expectations.

It is also important that *host country professional affiliations* be identified—that is, that the sojourners be introduced to potential mentors from their host and home country who understand both cultures. Whenever possible, professional sojourners should be encouraged to contact their supervisor and colleagues in their overseas work environments and institutions. Professional sojourners should expect to receive some information about the nature of the work they will be expected to perform in the host country and how this experience will affect their career in their home corporation when they repatriate.

Overseas Experience

Training during the overseas experience takes place in the host country. It is anticipated that orientation will continue to include assistance with cultural *adjustment,* particularly if family issues are involved. In addition, training should include current affairs of the country—for example, the status of the economy, social-political climate, level of literacy, public health and safety, status of men and women, and arts and culture. Language training in the host country focuses even more on increasing the level of the sojourners' proficiency.

Sojourners are immersed in the host country culture while continuing to consult with mentors who will serve as cultural interpreters. Sojourners should be encouraged to write journals so that they can continue to record their first impressions to their experiences and their reactions to those impressions.

Professional orientation provides information about the work of the sojourners' *host professional organizations* (corporations or academic institutions). Training sessions in the host country give sojourners the opportunities to discuss their experiences, check out the appropriate cultural behavior, discuss the day-to-day challenges, relate how they are adjusting, and solicit support and resources for increasing their psychological comfort and their behavioral competence in the new cultural contexts.

Professional opportunities are important for both student and professional returnees. The professional sojourner should be encouraged to strengthen work-related relationships and networks, attend conferences, and develop mentoring relationships.

Although student returnees may be less focused on these types of relationships, they should be encouraged to develop professional relationships and *academic activities* related to their academic major. They also should be encouraged to become involved in *nonformal educational experiences* and *social activities,* to be active in the student and community life—which will assist them in their cultural adaptation and competence.

As sojourners reach the end of their overseas experiences, they need to consider specific issues related to repatriation. As noted earlier, it is important that they have established and *maintain contact* with their home country support system. Professional sojourners often have the ability to return to the home country at various intervals, either for vacation or work-related travel. This gives them the opportunity to visit the home office and to find out what changes have occurred.

Pre-Reentry Phase

As professional sojourners prepare for their return to the home office, they need to think about their own career development and the strategies they will use for reacculturating themselves in their organizations. For example, *in professional briefings,* they may have interviews with home country supervisors to find out as much as possible about their new work assignment and the supervisors and colleagues with whom they will be working. Student sojourners should also continue to consider how this overseas experience fits into their *career development.*

Because student sojourners often do not have the same financial resources available for occasional travel home as many professional sojourners, they need to prepare, while still overseas, for their return to their home country institution and to deal with *academic concerns.* For this reason, they need to maintain contact with their academic and financial aid advisors and to take care of academic concerns. Friends may need to preregister sojourners for classes and to find living accommodations for them before they return to the home country and institution. Arrangements need to be made in advance for the transfer of academic credit or other documentation from their host institutions. The policies related to acquiring documents may be very different from the policies practiced in the home institution.

Repatriation training during the pre-reentry phase for both student and professional sojourners should include specific information about the political and economic status of the home country. In addition, sojourners should be provided with information that will help in setting their expectations about social and cultural readjustment challenges during reentry. If training cannot take place in the host country because of financial constraints, this information can be provided by way of mail. For example, newspaper headlines and clippings can be sent that will communicate with the sojourner the major national events. Short essays about reentry can be sent. Newsletters or other information from university or corporation can help keep sojourners in touch with events.

Reentry Phase

Repatriation or reentry is an ongoing process that can last for several months or a lifetime. Sojourners experience many changes in perceptions about their cultures, their home countries, home workplaces, and academic institutions. As indicated in the model, many training issues can be addressed in the reentry phase. Psychological *readjustment issues* need to be addressed. The sojourners need to feel comfortable, once again, in home contexts. Family readjustment issues may also need to be addressed. Training strategies to assist psychological readjustment has been discussed extensively (Martin, 1993, Westwood, 1984). In addition, social readjustment needs to occur, and social and behavioral competencies sometimes need to be relearned (Austin, 1987).

Financial issues are of concern to both student and professional sojourners. Repatriation can be a costly process. Getting resettled in the home country economy can be very expensive. This aspect of reentry has often been overlooked in the many lists of reentry concerns.

Employment issues and job searches are usually a concern for both student and professional returnees. Professional sojourners need to evaluate their overseas work/study experience and to (re)adjust to the home organization. They need to become familiar with the management structure, organizational policies, and organizational culture.

They also need to know what employer expectations are for their professional work and their readjustment. This can be done through formal briefings, as well as through more informal relationships with their mentors and other employee returnees. Professional sojourners need to continue their professional development through networking, retaining their relationships with their host country colleagues and forging new collegial relationships. They should also maintain their language competence.

Student returnees need to consider ways in which their overseas experience can help them in reaching their professional goals, as well as their academic goals. This may be done by retaining their personal and *professional affiliations* from abroad, by retaining their *language competence,* and by joining professional organizations and participating in conferences and organizational activities. Formal reentry training in the academic setting should include a session on assessing the impact of an overseas study experience on academic and professional goals and incorporating these impacts into future plans (Mestenhauser, 1988).

SUMMARY

We reviewed research and theoretical conceptualizations of reentry for both student and professional returnees. We identified a number of research issues that should be addressed, outlined a training model, and provided suggestions for implementing comprehensive reentry training that begins when the initial decision is made to travel abroad, through the return and reintegration of the professional and student sojourner.

Notes

1. Additional anecdotal descriptions of individuals' personal reentry experience may be found in contemporary literature—for example, Paul Theroux's (1986) "Yard Sale"; Bill Holm's (1990) *Coming Home Crazy.* Also see F. M. Boakari's (1982) account of returning home to Africa after years of study in the United States and Marcia Miller's (1988) paper *Reflections on Reentry After Teaching in China.*

2. For a more comprehensive discussion of how this model can be applied to reentry, see Martin (1993).

3. A number of testable hypotheses emerge from the relationships among these four components. For example, on the one hand, the greater the participation in (other returned sojourner) communication, the greater the initial short-term development of (home) communication competence; on the other hand, the greater the participation in (other returned sojourner) communication, the less the subsequent long-term development of (home) communication competence.

4. For a list of resources (organizations and bibliographic material), see Martin (1993).

5. In the model, if a training activity is considered more appropriate for a professional sojourner, this is indicated by (PS). If the activity is more appropriate for a student sojourner, (SS) is designated. If an activity relates to both groups, this is indicated by (PS, SS).

6. These are cultural simulations available from Intercultural Press, Box 700, Yarmouth, ME 04096.

References

Adelman, M. (1988). Cross-cultural adjustment: A theoretical perspective on social support. *International Journal of Intercultural Relations, 12,* 183-204.

Adler, N. (1976). *Growthful reentry theory.* Unpublished mimeo, University of California, Graduate School of Management, Los Angeles.

Adler, N. (1981). Reentry: Managing cross-cultural transitions. *Group and Organization Studies, 6*(3), 341-356.

Adler, N. J. (1984). Women in international management: Where are they? *California Management Review, 26,* 78-89.

Adler, N. J. (1986). Do MBA's want international careers? *International Journal of Intercultural Relations, 10,* 277-300.

Adler, P. (1975). The transition experience: An alternative view of culture shock. *Journal of Humanistic Psychology, 15*(4), 13-23.

Adler, P. (1982). Reflections on cultural and multicultural man. In L. A. Samovar & R. E. Porter (Eds.), *Intercultural communication: A reader* (pp. 389-406). Belmont, CA: Wadsworth.

Albrecht, T. L., & Adelman, M. B. (1987). *Communicating social support.* Newbury Park, CA: Sage.

Aldegan, F., & Parks, D. (1985). Problems of transition for African students in an American university. *Journal of College Student Personnel,* pp. 504-508.

Anzaldua, G. (1987). *Borderlands/La frontera.* San Francisco: Spinster/Aunt Lute.

Asuncion-Lande, N. (1976). Inventory of reentry problems. In H. Marsh (Ed.), *Reentry/transition seminars: Report on the Wingspread colloquium* (pp. 4-5). Washington, DC: National Association for Foreign Student Affairs.

Austin, C. N. (1983). *Cross-cultural reentry: An annotated bibliography.* Abilene, TX: Abilene Christian University Press.

Austin, C. N. (1986). *Cross-cultural reentry: A book of readings.* Abilene, TX: Abilene Christian University Press.

Austin, C. N. (1987). Cross-cultural reentry. In C. Dodd & F. F. Montalvo (Eds.), *Intercultural skills for multicultural societies* (pp. 70-82). Washington, DC: SIETAR International.

Baldwin, J. (1962). *Another country.* New York: Dial.

Barna, L. M. (1983). The stress factor in intercultural relations. In D. Landis & R. W. Brislin (Eds.), *Handbook of intercultural training* (Vol. 2, pp. 19-49). Elmsford, NY: Pergamon.

Bennett, J. M. (1977). Transition shock: Putting culture shock in perspective. *International and Intercultural Communication Annual, 4,* 45-52.

Bennett, J. M. (1993). Cultural marginality: Identity issues in intercultural training. In R. M. Paige (Ed.), *Education for the intercultural experience* (pp. 109-136). Yarmouth, ME: Intercultural Press.

Bennett, M. J. (1993). Toward ethnorelativism: A developmental model of intercultural training. In R. M. Paige (Ed.), *Education for the inter-*

cultural experience (pp. 21-72). Yarmouth, ME: Intercultural Press.

Black, J. S., & Gregersen, H. B. (1990). Expectations, satisfaction, and intention to leave of American expatriate managers in Japan. *International Journal of Intercultural Relations, 14,* 485-506.

Boakari, F. M. (1982). Foreign student reentry: The case of the hurrying man. *NAFSA Newsletter, 34,* 33-49.

Bochner, S. (Ed.). (1982). *Cultures in contact.* Elmsford, NY: Pergamon.

Brabant, S., Palmer, C. E., & Gramling, R. (1990). Returning home: An empirical investigation of cross-cultural reentry. *International Journal of Intercultural Relations, 14,* 387-404.

Brammer, L., & Abrego, P. (1981). Intervention strategies for coping with life transitions. *Counseling Psychologist, 9,* 19-36.

Bridges, W. (1980). *Transitions.* Reading, MA: Addison-Wesley.

Brislin, R. W. (1981). *Cross-cultural encounters: Face-to-face interaction.* Elmsford, NY: Pergamon.

Brislin, R. W. (1993). *Understanding culture's influence on behavior.* Ft. Worth, TX: Harcourt Brace Jovanovich.

Brislin, R. W., & Van Buren, H. (1974). Can they go home again? *International Education and Cultural Exchange, 9,* 19-24.

Burgoon, J. K. (1983). Nonverbal violations of expectations: Explication and initial test. *Human Communication Research, 4,* 129-142.

Burgoon, J. K. (1992). Applying a comparative approach to expectancy violations theory. In J. G. Blumler, J. M. McLeod, & K. E. Rosengren (Eds.), *Comparatively speaking: Communication and culture across space and time* (pp. 53-69). Newbury Park, CA: Sage.

Burgoon, J. K., & Walther, J. B. (1990). Nonverbal expectancies and the evaluative consequences of violations. *Human Communication Research, 17,* 232-265.

Carlson, J. S., Burn, B. B., Useem, J., & Yachimowicz, D. (1990). *Study abroad: The experience of American undergraduates.* Westport, CT: Greenwood.

Chiu, M. L. (1995). The influence of anticipatory fear on foreign student adjustment: An exploratory study. *International Journal of Intercultural Relations, 19,* 1-44.

Church, A. (1982). Sojourner adjustment. *Psychological Bulletin, 91,* 540-572.

Cochrane, R. (1983). *The social creation of mental illness.* White Plains, NY: Longman.

Copeland, L., & Griggs, L. (1985). *Going international: How to make friends and deal effectively in the global marketplace.* New York: Random House.

Denney, M., & Eckert, E. (1987, May). Re-entry shock: Torn between two cultures. *Worldspeak,* pp. 10-11.

Dyal, J. A., & Dyal, R. Y. (1981). Acculturation, stress, and coping: Some implications for research and education. *International Journal of Intercultural Relations, 5,* 301-328.

Feather, N. T. (1982). *Expectations and actions: Expectancy value models in psychology.* Hillsdale, NJ: Lawrence Erlbaum.

Furnham, A. (1988). The adjustment of sojourners. In Y. Y. Kim & W. B. Gudykunst (Eds.), *Cross-cultural adaptation: Current approaches* (pp. 42-62). Newbury Park, CA: Sage.

Furnham, A., & Bochner, S. (1986). *Culture shock: Psychological reactions to unfamiliar environments.* New York: Metheun.

Gama, E. M. P., & Pedersen, P. (1977). Readjustment problems of Brazilian returnees from graduate studies in the United States. *International Journal of Intercultural Relations, 1,* 46-58.

Glaser, W. A. (1978). *The brain drain: Emigration and return.* Elmsford, NY: Pergamon.

Goodman, R. (1990). *Japan's international youth: An emerging new class of school children.* New York: Oxford University Press.

Gudykunst, W. B. (1983). Toward a typology of stranger-host relationships. *International Journal of Intercultural Relations, 7,* 401-415.

Gullahorn, J. T., & Gullahorn, J. E. (1963). An extension of the U-curve hypothesis. *Journal of Social Issues, 14,* 33-47.

Harrell, T. (1994). Professional integration of Indonesian graduate degree holders from United States colleges and universities in the fields of business administration, education, and engineering. (Doctoral dissertation, University of Minnesota, 1994). *Dissertation Abstracts International,* 9428921.

Harris, P. R., & Moran, R. T. (1991). *Managing cultural differences* (3rd ed.). Houston, TX: Gulf.

Hawes, F., & Kealey, D. J. (1981). An empirical study of Canadian technical assistance: Adaptation and effectiveness on overseas assignment. *International Journal of Intercultural Relations, 5,* 239-258.

Holm, B. (1990). *Coming home crazy.* Minneapolis, MN: Milkweed.

Holmes, T. H., & Rahe, R. H. (1967). The Social Readjustment Rating Scale. *Journal of Psychosomatic Research, 11,* 213-218.

Hood, M. A. G., & Schieffer, K. J. (Eds.). (1983). *Professional integration: A guide for students from the developing world.* Washington, DC: National Association for Foreign Student Affairs.

Hu, L. T., & Pedersen, P. (1986a). *Reentry adjustment of returned Taiwanese students from abroad in engineering and related fields.* Syracuse, NY: Syracuse University.

Hu, L. T., & Pedersen, P. (1986b). *Research on the reentry of international students in engineering and related fields.* Syracuse, NY: Syracuse University.

Kauffmann, N., Martin, J. N., & Weaver, H. (with Weaver, J.). (1992). *Students abroad, strangers at home.* Yarmouth, ME: Intercultural Press.

Kealey, D. J. (1989). A study of cross-cultural effectiveness: Theoretical issues, practical applications. *International Journal of Intercultural Relations, 13,* 387-428.

Kim, Y. Y. (1978). Toward a communication approach to the acculturation process. *International Journal of Intercultural Relations, 2,* 197-224.

Kim, Y. Y. (1988). *Communication and cross-cultural adaptation.* Philadelphia: Multilingual Matters.

Kim, Y. Y., & Gudykunst, W. B. (Eds.). (1988). *Cross-cultural adaptation: Current approaches. International and Intercultural Communication Annual, 11.*

Klineberg, O., & Hull, W. F. (1979). *At a foreign university: An international study of adaptation and coping.* New York: Praeger.

Kobayashi, T. (1981). *Kaigai Shijo Kyooiku, Kikoku Shijo Kyooiku* [Overseas children's education, returning children's education]. Tokyo: Yuhikaku.

Koester, J. (1985). *A profile of the U.S. student abroad.* New York: Council on International Educational Exchange.

Koester, J. (1987). *A profile of the U.S. student abroad: 1984 and 1985.* New York: Council on International Educational Exchange.

Krupinski, J. (1975). Psychological maladaption in ethnic concentrations in Victoria, Australia. In I. Pilowsky (Ed.), *Cultures in collision.* Adelaide: Australian National Association for Mental Health.

LaBrack, B. (1981). Can you go home? *Kyoto English Center Journal, 80-81* (two-part series).

LaBrack, B. (1993). The missing linkage: The process of integrating orientation and reentry. In R. M. Paige (Ed.), *Education for the intercultural experience* (pp. 241-280). Yarmouth, ME: Intercultural Press.

Lobdell, C. L. (1990). *Differential effects of expectations in the context of intercultural reentry adjustment.* Unpublished master's thesis, Arizona State University, Tempe.

Lonner, W. J. (1986). Foreword. In A. Furnham & S. Bochner (Eds.), *Culture shock: Psychological reactions to unfamiliar environments* (pp. xv-xx). New York: Metheun.

Lysgaard, S. (1955). Adjustment in a foreign society: Norwegian Fulbright grantees visiting the United States. *International Social Science Bulletin, 7,* 45-51.

Marsh, H. (Ed.). (1976). *Reentry transition seminars: Report on the Wingspread colloquium.* Washington, DC: National Association for Foreign Student Affairs.

Martin, J. N. (1984). The intercultural reentry: Conceptualization and directions for future research. *International Journal of Intercultural Relations, 8,* 115-134.

Martin, J. N. (1985). The impact of a homestay abroad on relationships at home. *Occasional Papers in Cultural Learning* (No. 6). New York: AFS International/Intercultural Programs.

Martin, J. N. (1986a). Communication in the intercultural reentry: Student sojourners' perceptions of change in reentry relationships. *International Journal of Intercultural Relations, 10,* 1-22.

Martin, J. N. (1986b). Patterns of communication in three types of reentry relationships: An exploratory study. *Western Journal of Speech Communication, 50,* 183-199.

Martin, J. N. (1993). The intercultural reentry of student sojourners: Recent contributions to theory, research, and training. In R. M. Paige (Ed.), *Education for the intercultural experience* (pp. 301-328). Yarmouth, ME: Intercultural Press.

Martin, J. N., Bradford, L., & Rohrlich, B. (1995). Comparing predeparture expectations and post-sojourn reports: A longitudinal study of U.S. students abroad. *International Journal of Intercultural Relations, 19,* 87-110.

Mestenhauser, J. A. (1988). Adding the disciplines: From theory to relevant practice. In J. A. Mestenhauser, G. Marty, & I. Steglitz (Eds.), *Culture, learning, and the disciplines* (pp. 133-

167). Washington, DC: National Association for Foreign Student Affairs.

Miller, M. (1988). *Reflections on reentry after teaching in China* (Occasional Papers in Intercultural Learning, #14). New York: AFS Center for the Study of Intercultural Learning.

Nafziger, K. L. (1995). *The reentry adjustment of short-term student sojourners: A growth curve analysis of the U-curve hypothesis.* Unpublished doctoral dissertation, University of Illinois, Urbana-Champaign.

Oberg, K. (1960). Culture shock: Adjustment to new cultural environments. *Practical Anthropology, 7,* 177-182.

Perry, W. (1970). *Forms of intellectual and ethical development in the college years: A scheme.* New York: Holt, Rinehart & Winston.

Rogers, J., & Ward, C. (1993). Expectations-experience discrepancies and psychological adjustment during cross-cultural reentry. *International Journal of Intercultural Relations, 17,* 185-196.

Rohrlich, B., & Martin, J. N. (1991). Host country and reentry adjustment of student sojourners. *International Journal of Intercultural Relations, 15,* 163-182.

Searle, W., & Ward, C. (1990). The prediction of psychological and sociocultural adjustment during cross-cultural transitions. *International Journal of Intercultural Relations, 14,* 449-464.

Selye, H. (1974). *Stress without distress.* Philadelphia: J. B. Lippincott.

Smith, E. (1991). Ethnic identity development: Toward the development of a theory within the context of majority/minority status. *Journal of Counseling and Development, 70,* 181-188.

Stonequist, E. (1937). *The marginal man.* New York: Scribner.

Sussman, N. M. (1986). Reentry research and training: Methods and implications. *International Journal of Intercultural Relations, 10,* 235-254.

Theroux, P. (1986). Yard sale. In T. J. Lewis & R. J. Jungman (Eds.), *On being foreign: Culture shock in short fiction* (pp. 273-280). Yarmouth, ME: Intercultural Press.

Thomas, K., & Harrell, T. (1994). Counseling student sojourners: Revisiting the U-curve of adjustment. In G. Althen (Ed.), *Learning across cultures* (pp. 89-108). Washington, DC: National Association for Foreign Student Affairs.

Torbiorn, I. (1982). *Living abroad: Personal adjustment and personnel policy in the overseas setting.* New York: John Wiley.

Torbiorn, I. (1994). Dynamics of cross-cultural adaptation. In G. Althen (Ed.), *Learning across cultures* (pp. 31-56). Washington, DC: National Association for Foreign Student Affairs.

Uehara, J. (1986). The nature of American student reentry adjustment and perceptions of the sojourn experience. *International Journal of Intercultural Relations, 10,* 415-438.

Useem, J., Donoghue, J. D., & Useem, R. (1963). Men in the middle of the third culture. *Human Organization, 22,* 169-179.

Walton, S. J. (1990). Stress management training for overseas effectiveness. *International Journal of Intercultural Relations, 14,* 507-527.

Ward, C., & Kennedy, A. (1992). Locus of control, mood disturbance, and social difficulty during cross-cultural transitions. *International Journal of Intercultural Relations, 16,* 175-194.

Weaver, G. (1993). Understanding and coping with cross-cultural adjustment stress. In R. M. Paige (Ed.), *Education for the intercultural experience* (pp. 137-167). Yarmouth, ME: Intercultural Press.

Weissman, D., & Furnham, A. (1987). The expectations and experiences of a sojourning temporary resident abroad: A preliminary study. *Human Relations, 40,* 313-326.

Westwood, M. (1984). *Returning home: A program for persons assisting international students with the reentry process.* Ottawa: Canadian Bureau of International Education.

Westwood, M. J., & Lawrance, S. (1988). Reentry for international students. In G. MacDonald (Ed.), *International student advisors' handbook.* Ottawa: Canadian Bureau of International Education.

Westwood, M. J., Lawrance, W. S., & Paul, D. (1986). Preparing for reentry: A program for the sojourning student. *International Journal for the Advancement of Counseling, 9,* 221-230.

White, M. (1988). *The Japanese overseas: Can they go home again?* New York: Free Press.

Wilson, A. H. (1985). Returned exchange students becoming mediating persons. *International Journal of Intercultural Relations, 9,* 285-304.

Zwingmann, C. A. A., & Gunn, A. D. G. (1983). *Uprooting and health: Psycho-social problems of students from abroad.* Geneva: World Health Organization, Division of Mental Health.

18

A Framework and Model for
Understanding Latin American and
Latino/Hispanic Cultural Patterns

ROSITA DASKAL ALBERT

THIS chapter focuses on a framework for understanding Latin American cultural patterns. It emphasizes some important emic or culture-specific (Berry, 1980; Pike, 1966) features of Latin American cultures and how middle-class Latin American patterns differ from North American and Northern European patterns. It also presents a general model for understanding cultures.

The chapter focuses on Latin American and Latino/Hispanic themes. Although for comparative purposes I present data from cultures that are not Latin American, I do so with the aim of contributing to a better appreciation for the complexity, beauty, and richness of Latin American cultural patterns. This is a preliminary, limited, and, no doubt, flawed attempt to characterize with fidelity patterns that can only be understood by deep and profound experience.

Economic and environmental interdependence between North and Latin America is growing. More than 50% of the oxygen in the world is produced in the Amazon rain forest. Latin America is the fastest growing market in the world for U.S. exports, and because of NAFTA and other trade blocks, the United States and other countries will be trading with Latin American countries on a scale far larger than ever before.

Economic vitality in the region is increasing (it is the second fastest growing economic region in the world), and as was made clear in the Summit of the Americas in Miami (Brooke,

AUTHOR'S NOTE: The author wishes to thank Harry Triandis for his mentoring and his interest and for making available a variety of articles, including some yet unpublished. She also wishes to thank Dan Landis, Rabi S. Bhagat, Frank Montalvo, José Gomez, Lisa Miller, Stuart Albert, and Ena Cuevas for their very helpful comments and suggestions.

1994), by the end of the 1990s, the United States expects to export more to Mexico than to Japan, and more to Latin America than to Western Europe (Brooke, 1994). Some Latin American countries expect a high rate of GNP growth for the next decade. Consequently, the current orientation of Latin American countries is toward accelerating growth and development. This is an exciting time for the Latin American region, a region that has tremendous potential.

With a population of 448,076 million in 1990 (Collier, Skidmore, & Blakemore, 1992) and rapid modernization, Latin American countries are increasingly significant players in world trade. At the same time, Latinos or Hispanics constitute the second largest minority in the United States (at least 22 million); thus, the United States is the fifth-largest Spanish-speaking country in the world (Reddy, 1990). The rapidly accelerating rate of intercultural contact with Latin Americans makes it crucial for North Americans and persons from other regions to learn more about Latin American cultures.

In a broad overview such as this, I can neither cover all significant patterns of differences that exist nor adequately cover cultural patterns specific to any given country. My caveat is especially true for Brazil, a "continent-country" with unique cultural patterns stemming from its Portuguese/African/Indian heritage. (Perhaps I am more acutely aware of this because I am a Brazilian.)

Terminology

Terminology is a sensitive area; almost every term can be problematic. In this chapter, I use the term *Latin American* to refer to individuals who were born and reside in Latin American countries. It is important to realize that people in Latin American countries do not generally view themselves as "Latin American," but rather as Colombians, Brazilians, and so forth. *Latino* or *Hispanic* is used for persons of Latin American origin or ancestry in the United States. Although the term *Latino* is not without problems (it has been used pejoratively in some places, and specific designators such as Chicano, Mexican American, Puerto Rican, Cuban, and so on are often preferred), it seems to be currently preferred to *Hispanic* by members of the culture, in part because it reflects their Latin American origins. Some Latinos reject the term

Hispanic, seeing it as a designator imposed on them from the outside, one that incorrectly denotes Spanish, rather than Latin American, origins. Given the greater acceptability of *Latino* but the fact that most of the studies reported here use *Hispanic,* both terms are used.

Following the convention of many Latin Americans, I use the term *North American* to denote U.S. citizens. (Although *American* is sometimes used, Latin Americans point out that they are also "American." Although citizens of Mexico and Canada are geographically North Americans, they are usually referred to as *Mexicans* and *Canadians.*) *Anglo American* is used to refer to mainstream persons in the United States. (Even though many Americans are not descendants of Anglo Saxons and would find this designator strange, mainstream culture is considered to be predominantly white, Anglo Saxon, and Protestant.) This is the term most frequently used by Latinos to refer to members of the mainstream U.S. culture.

General Considerations

A surprising 75% of the population is now urban (Portes & Schauffler, 1993) and predominantly young. The mixture of races has been extensive, with mestizos and mulattos representing majorities of the population in several countries. This mixture has affected cultural patterns, which reflect varying combinations of European, African, and Native American elements.

Because of different colonial histories and extensive intermixing, the dynamics of race relations tend to be different in Latin American cultures than they are in the North American culture. In reviewing the literature, Lisansky (1981) indicates that some authors discuss the commingling of race and class in various countries, whereas others argue that, in some places, social differentiation by class is far more important than differentiation by racial characteristics. Still others suggest that differetiations based on color and physical characteristics are made but that class and achievement make it possible for people to transcend race. Montalvo (1987; personal communication, May 14, 1995) relates he discovered that the history of race relations in the Americas is not as idyllic as he had been led to believe as a child; he has proposed that color is a critical variable overlooked by researchers and has called for greater attention to it in studies of acculturation and assimilation of Latinos into American society.

An example of how Latin American experiences and views may differ from North American perceptions is provided by Tumin and Feldman's (1969) study of Puerto Ricans in the island. The authors found that 75% denied skin color had an effect on educational and economic opportunities and that 85% thought they were accorded the same respect irrespective of skin color. Many indicated, however, that color did matter in personal relations and the population is split between the judgments that "it is better to be white" and that "color doesn't matter."

The North American sojourner may well encounter people in a number of areas—such as in Brazil and Puerto Rico, for example—who believe there is little or no racial discrimination in their country and who are proud of their record of race relations. The wise sojourner will guard against the tendency to apply a North American lens to race and class relations in Latin America and will try to learn how the people in a particular location view these relations.

History, Geography, Language, and Religion

Each country has a unique history and geography and other unique elements that contribute to the culture of its people. Obviously, it is wise to learn as much as possible about each country before going there or interacting with its citizens. Few things annoy Brazilians more than the assumption that they speak Spanish (we speak Portuguese) or that the capital of Brazil is Buenos Aires (our capital is Brasília)! History is very important to Latin Americans and to those seeking to understand them: Some countries, such as Mexico, trace their history for 3,000 years.

Latin American countries are overwhelmingly Catholic, and the Church has historically played a major role in the societies of most countries. Liberation theology has emerged from Latin America. Mixtures of Catholicism with African and Native American religions have also emerged, creating unique practices and beliefs.

Of course, learning the language of a given country is always very useful for communica-

tion and facilitates the enactment of cultural behaviors. But although these factors are important and the reader is strongly encouraged to learn as much as possible about them, they are insufficient. It is necessary to look specifically at intercultural relations and at cultural patterns.

International and Intercultural Relations

All of the countries are former colonies of European countries and have had relations with the United States. These relations have, at times, been difficult and been characterized by a love-hate relationship. At various points, citizens of some Latin American countries have felt treated as inferiors and have been offended by the way the American government treated their country or people. This has also been true of Latinos in the United States.

Currently, feelings toward the United States seem to be generally positive, and there is a great desire to increase trade with the United States. Any North American dealing with a Latin American or Latino should be aware of the history of relations and should realize that any hint of North American superiority is liable to evoke negative feelings.

The sojourner to Latin America should also keep in mind that Latin American countries are changing and modernizing at a very rapid rate, that democratically elected governments are in place, and that growth, the opening of markets, and trade are big priorities now. Finally, those interacting with Latin Americans would do well to keep in mind that the professional persons they are likely to encounter are sophisticated and often broadly educated.

Training Issues

The Need for Training

Perhaps because of the greater degree of contact and proximity between Latin American, North American, and European cultures and because people in the three regions use the same alphabet, Latin American cultures are not perceived to be as "foreign" as Asian or even African cultures. Although this perception may contribute to the feeling that one can learn to interact with Latin Americans more easily, and this is positive, it may also lead sojourners to expect greater similarity than probably exists between North American or Northern European cultures and Latin American cultures. This expectation, in turn, may result in some unexpected problems.

Unfortunately, until recently, Latin America has been either largely ignored or exploited as a region by North American or Northern European educators, businesspersons, and others. Along with the general lack of research on cultural differences (Albert, 1988) and of training, even in multinational organizations (Albert, 1994), training for interaction with Latin Americans has not received enough attention. Fortunately, the situation seems to be changing. The danger now is that ill-qualified persons will provide training. Below, I suggest some qualifications that competent trainers must have.

Characteristics of Training Providers

First and foremost, providers need to have had extensive experience living in a Latin American country because they need to know how cultural patterns are enacted in many different settings and situations and to understand their subtle variability. Second, simply being a Latin American or Latino(a) is insufficient. It takes a truly bicultural, bilingual person to comprehend the similarities and differences between the target culture and the culture of origin of the trainees in all their subtleties and to know how to convey these differences optimally. Third, it is necessary that the training provider be an intelligent reader and critic of social science research. Some studies in the literature are poorly done; others have approached Latin American cultures from an ethnocentric, North American or European perspective. Fourth, a provider should have sound knowledge of theories, concepts, and issues in intercultural communication and education, crosscultural psychology, and the patterns of cultural differences that have been found to matter. Having developed, researched, and used a variety of methods in workshops for close to 20 years, I have become convinced that a trainer must be knowledgeable about various methods and should be able to select the most appropriate ones to use for a particular audience and in a particular setting.

Focus on Latin American Subjective Cultures

The model presented here focuses on dimensions of the subjective cultures—that is the norms, values, and interpretations of behaviors, feelings, and attitudes (Triandis, 1972)—of Latin Americans. For training purposes, the major focus is on emic or culture-specific patterns and on differences between Latin American patterns and patterns from other cultures. Although I cite a few studies that show some differences among specific Latin American countries, we do not yet have enough systematic data from all or even most of the countries to make any definitive statements. A lot more research needs to be done before the commonalities and differences among Latin American cultures can be specified.

Given the relative paucity of research on the culture of any one country, I have culled information from studies in different countries and with different populations, including Latino/Hispanic groups in the United States, to provide a more complete picture. Whenever possible, I refer to the specific cultural groups or countries that a research project was based on. I refer to Latin American *cultures* to emphasize the multiplicity of Latin American cultural groups.

Caveats

In any cross-cultural interaction, it is crucial that the participant not judge another culture on the basis of his or her culture of origin. One important goal of intercultural training, therefore, should be to alert people to this and to teach them to make attributions or interpretations that are similar to those made by persons from the target culture. Intercultural sensitizers (ICSs) are designed to do this (Albert, 1983b, 1986a, 1995). For information on an ICS designed to sensitize Anglo Americans to Latino/Hispanic patterns (Albert, 1992a), please contact the author.

There are both similarities and differences among groups and among individuals. Thus, Latin Americans are both similar to and different from North Americans and Northern Europeans. There is also variability within any group. Thus, Latin Americans from one country may differ from those from another country; subcultural groups may differ from each other.

Other kinds of variability, based on gender, age, class, degree of urbanization, and region of country, also exist. Among Latinos in the United States, there is great diversity in terms of country of origin, degree of acculturation, and other factors. Some Latino patterns of behavior and perception may be additionally influenced by minority status and structural conditions in the United States.

I want to alert the reader to the dangers of stereotyping. Unfortunately, Latin Americans and Latinos have often been, and continue to be, negatively stereotyped or characterized by persons who do not understand their cultural patterns (see Kolland, 1990, for stereotypes of Mexicans; see A. Ramirez, 1988, on racism toward Hispanics). Latin Americans and Latinos are naturally very sensitive to this (e.g., see Collier, 1988; Hecht, Ribeau, & Sedano, 1990; Hernandez, 1970; Rivera, 1970; Wagner & Haug, 1971).

As Allport (1954) suggests, what is needed is evidence of true group differences. Also needed are characterizations that emphasize the Latin American and Latino worldviews and perspectives. This is what I attempt to present, focusing on what the social science literature tells us, on what I have learned from 20 years of researching and training in this area, and on a lifetime of living in both Brazil and the United States.

This chapter is more illustrative than comprehensive. I hope I correct some misperceptions. Inevitably, I make generalizations and oversimplify what is in reality very complex. I make statements about Latin Americans or Hispanics and about North or Anglo Americans that obviously do not apply to some persons or groups because they differ from the prevalent pattern. I want the reader to think of Latin Americans as generally *more likely* and North Americans as *less likely* to exhibit the patterns described, rather than to assume one group has them and the other does not. The research available on some elements or dimensions is often very sparse; a lot more work needs to be done before these patterns are adequately demonstrated. New conceptualizations and refinements in current conceptualizations are needed. Also needed is a lot more work on the variations that may exist among Latin Americans and Latino groups. Cultures are dynamic and they change. Some of the patterns I describe may already be changing. Still, I believe it is helpful to know how a pattern has traditionally operated in a culture, because this may provide a deeper understanding of the underlying premises of that culture.

For the above reasons, *I encourage the reader to consider each characterization presented below as provisional and to constantly look for additional evidence regarding a pattern—particularly unbiased evidence, preferably based on empirical research, that looks at both generalizability and variability across persons, across groups, and across countries.* My hope is that a consideration of these patterns will allow the subjective culture of Latin Americans to become clearer and more accurately perceived.

A Model for Understanding
Latin American Patterns

In intercultural interactions, persons bring with them cultural patterns of behavior, perceptions, and cognitions that are deeply ingrained and that often seem natural and universal to them. They are often unaware that these patterns are, for the most part, culturally based and that other cultures may differ in how they characteristically act, perceive, and interpret behaviors in any given situation. The role of intercultural training is (a) to create a greater awareness and understanding on the part of the trainee of cultural patterns and how they operate in the target culture, as well as how they differ from the trainee's own culture of origin; and (b) to teach the trainee how to interact effectively with persons from the other culture once he or she understands these patterns. Lack of knowledge may lead to serious misunderstandings and even conflicts (Albert, 1983a, 1983b; Albert & Triandis, 1985).

Intercultural misunderstandings occur for at least two reasons: (a) People expect the same behavior in the target culture that they find in their own culture and (b) the same behavior can be interpreted differently in two cultures (Albert, 1983a; Albert & Triandis, 1979). Thus, *understanding the behavior of Latin Americans from the point of view of insiders to the culture becomes the key.* Although many factors, such as a trainee's personality, education, demographic characteristics, roles, and situational factors, play a role in the success of intercultural interactions, the deeply ingrained cultural patterns that participants bring with them are crucial and need to be made explicit.

My model of intercultural training, therefore, emphasizes making the trainee aware of culture-specific elements and of cultural differences and making him or her understand these differences from the perspective of members of the target culture. A major goal of training is to have the trainee learn to make attributions to situations that are isomorphic with those made by the persons in the target culture (Albert, 1983a, 1986b; Albert & Triandis, 1985; Triandis, 1975). ICSs are designed to do this.

My model posits that both *emic patterns* (culture-specific patterns of perceptions, cognitions, and behaviors) and *etically derived* patterns (those that locate a culture's patterns within more general, cross-cultural dimensions or categories of perceptions, cognitions, and behaviors) are important for understanding a given culture. In addition, knowledge of *communication patterns* that are typical of the target culture is necessary for understanding and interacting with its members. Together, emic, etic, and communication patterns permit one to know what to expect, what the meanings of particular behaviors are, and how to interact appropriately with members of a given target culture.

The emic, etic, and communication patterns of any culture involve differentiations that can be classified, following Triandis and Albert (1987), as primarily *perceptual*, primarily *cognitive*, or primarily *behavioral*. Briefly stated, *perceptual differentiations* include differentiations made in a culture on the basis of attributes of persons—for example, a person's gender or status. *Cognitive differentiations* involve patterns of meanings, interpretations of actions, and values that are emphasized. *Behavioral differentiations* refer to patterns of action and activity that are preferred.

Even though I present the dimensions of culture as focusing on either perceptual, cognitive, or behavioral differentiations to provide a clearer picture of them, this categorization is, to some extent, arbitrary, and some dimensions might be placed into a different category by other researchers or trainers. (Similarly, some dimensions that I place into the emic category might be arguably considered etic by other researchers or trainers.) It is clear that perceptions, cognitions, and behaviors interact with each other in complex ways in any intercultural interaction. Furthermore, it is wise to remember that a cognitive dimension such as *collectivism*

(explained below) has clear behavioral and perceptual implications. Similarly, a behavioral dimension such as *high contact* (explained later in the chapter) has clear implications for perceptions and interpretations of the behavior.

The various emic, etic, and communication patterns characteristic of Latin American cultures are presented below in terms of elements, categories, or dimensions of culture. Although they are presented separately, they fit together into patterns that have coherence and meaning and that form a "cultural whole." This selective overview of conceptual and empirical social scientific work on emic, etic, and communication patterns focuses only on those categories and dimensions that seem most useful for understanding Latin American cultures.

The emic patterns I examine are subsumed under the meta-dimension I call the *interpersonal orientation,* which is paramount for Latin Americans. The components of this orientation include cognitive patterns that emphasize valuing *respect, dignity, loyalty,* and *simpatía* (explained below); and behavioral or action patterns that tend to emphasize *cooperation,* rather than competition, *the avoidance of criticism and of negative behaviors,* reliance on *interpersonal connections* (*palanca*), and *personalistic attention.*

The etically derived patterns I describe include Latin American perceptual patterns of *high power distance* and of both a *feminine* and a *masculine* orientation; cognitive patterns that place higher emphasis on *collectivism, familism, high Confucian work dynamism,* a *shame* orientation, and changing *orientations toward the past, the present, and the future;* and the following patterns of action: a *polychronic pattern of time use,* both *subjugation* and *mastery* over nature, a *being* orientation, a *Dionysian or emotionally expressive* pattern, and a pattern of *high uncertainty avoidance* in some instances and flexibility in others.

The communication patterns I examine include certain cognitive orientations, such as toward *language use, politeness, and associativeness and expressiveness in language use,* and behavioral emphases on *high context communication* and on *high contact.*

Emic Patterns: The Interpersonal Orientation

The social scientific literature on Latin Americans and Hispanics, as well as my own observations and data, suggest strongly that Latin Americans have an overarching cultural orientation I would call the *interpersonal orientation.* This appears to be the preeminent, meta-orientation of Latin Americans. It permeates many facets of life, from the focus on the family to the patterns of communication, the values of respect and harmonious relationships, and behavior in the workplace. This cultural orientation differs in significant ways from the fundamental orientation of North Americans and Northern Europeans. For example, Díaz-Guerrero (1975) proposes that Mexicans focus on *interpersonal reality,* or the state of affairs between two or more persons, and that North Americans focus on external *physical reality.*

The strong interpersonal orientation has been documented in numerous studies. Below, I review some components of this orientation that have been substantiated by data.

Cognitive Patterns

Respect and Dignity

Respeto (respect) and *dignidad* (worthiness, dignity) are important notions for Latin Americans and Latinos. Díaz-Guerrero and Szalay (1991) describe the socialization of Mexican children as based on traditional values of respect and obedience. Hispanics perceive criticism or insults as denoting a great lack of respect, as assaults on the other person's dignity (Díaz-Royo, 1974; Tumin & Feldman, 1971).

Triandis, Marín, Lisansky, and Betancourt (1984) have shown that, in judgments involving "trying to show dignity" to another person, Hispanics to a greater degree than non-Hispanics give higher estimates to "treats others as equal" and "respects the other." Given the power distance findings among Latin Americans described below (Hofstede, 1980), the reader should be cautioned that "treats others as equal" is only likely in horizontal relationships, and not among superiors and subordinates. In judgments about "respect," all scales showed significant differences between Hispanic and non-Hispanic subjects (Triandis, Marín, et al., 1984).

Loyalty

On the basis of their findings, Triandis et al. proposed that "showing loyalty" for another did not have a definitive meaning for non-Hispanics but that it clearly did have a meaning for Hispanics. They found that, in trying "to show loyalty" toward another person, Hispanics were more likely than non-Hispanics to believe that a person would be "honest," "friendly," and "would do what the person wanted done." They would also "defend," "respect the person," "respect the culture of," and "value the language of" the other person.

Sympatía

Latin Americans and Latinos show a strong cultural preference for *simpatía* (Triandis, Marín, et al., 1984). *Simpatía* refers to a permanent quality of a person. My definition is that a person is seen as *simpático/a* to the extent that he or she is perceived to be open, warm, interested in others, exhibits positive behaviors toward others, is in tune with the wishes and feelings of others, and is enthusiastic.

Simpatía has been found to be important for Cubans (Alum & Manteiga, 1977), Mexican Americans (Burma, 1970), and Puerto Ricans (Landy, 1959). In discussing the value that Latinos place on being *simpático,* having positive interactions with others and avoiding negative behaviors, Triandis, Marín, et al. (1984) concluded, "The ignorance of these expectancies by other cultural groups brings about discomfort and stress in intergroup relations, as shown in our data by the differences in results when the interacting dyads (actor and target) were homogenous or heterogeneous in ethnicity" (p. 1373). Triandis et al. point out that simpatía is one component of "a more general pattern of cultural differences between Hispanics and non-Hispanics in which interpersonal behaviors are more important than task achievements" (p. 1374).

Patterns of Action

Cooperation Versus Competition

Many studies provide empirical support for the notion that Latin Americans and Latinos tend to be cooperative in interpersonal and work situations, whereas Americans tend to be competitive. Triandis, Marín, et al. (1984) found that, in equal status roles, there is more competition in the North American mainstream culture than among Hispanics, a finding in agreement with the general preference of Latinos for cooperation over competition. Marín and Triandis (1985) argue that Hispanics tend to be allocentric, rather than idiocentric; that is, they pay more attention to the needs, values, goals, and viewpoints of others than to their own individual needs, goals, and values. In my experience, it is often hard for individualistic North Americans to fully comprehend this orientation. The trainee needs to learn that this orientation is deeply rooted: Whereas North or Anglo Americans are socialized for competitiveness, self-reliance, and self-assertion, Latin American and Latino children are trained for cooperation, harmony in interpersonal relations, and sensitivity to the needs and feelings of others (Díaz-Guerrero & Szalay, 1991, based on Mead, 1953; Landy, 1959; M. Ramírez, 1983; and Triandis, 1981). There is empirical support (Holtzman, Díaz-Guerrero, & Swartz, 1975) for the notion that Americans are field independent, whereas Latinos are "field sensitive," to use the words suggested by M. Ramírez (1983); thus, they are more influenced by their surroundings.

Mexican children tended to be highly cooperative in experimental games, whereas their American counterparts tended to be highly competitive (Kagan & Madsen, 1971). Moreover, in another study, Mexican children indicated they would avoid confrontation with an aggressor, whereas Anglo American and Mexican American children said they would confront the aggressor (Kagan, Knight, & Martinez-Romero, 1982). The picture may be more complicated for Mexican Americans. Some studies found more cooperation and less competition among Mexican American than among Anglo American children and adults (Kagan & Knight, 1981; Kagan & Madsen, 1971; Knight & Kagan, 1977; Triandis, Marín, et al., 1984); a few studies found either no differences between the responses of Mexican Americans and Anglo Americans (Kagan et al., 1982; Lucas & Stone, 1994) or differences only when cooperation is adaptive (Espinoza & Garza, 1985).

*Avoidance of Criticism
and of Negative Behaviors*

Mexican Americans have been described as guarding against offending others, avoiding di-

rectly questioning another's beliefs or actions or direct criticism, placing a great emphasis on manners and courtesy in interpersonal relations, and making social relations appear harmonious or positive (Madsen, 1972; Murillo, 1976).

Latinos and Latin Americans have been described as valuing avoidance of negative behaviors, such as criticizing, insulting, and fighting (Díaz-Royo, 1974; Fitzpatrick, 1971; Heller, 1966; Madsen, 1972; Rubel, 1970; Triandis, Hui, et al., 1984). In my own research, I have noticed that Latinos express a concern with "not offending" the other person more frequently than Anglo Americans.

On the basis of navy recruits' estimates of behaviors and data from monolingual Puerto Ricans, Triandis, Marín, et al. (1984) concluded, "It is clear from the data that Hispanics expect much more positive behaviors in positive social situations than non-Hispanic respondents. . . . [T]he expected deemphasis of negative behavior in negative situations was found for all samples except for our bilingual respondents" (p. 1373).

In apparent contrast with other researchers, Ferdman and Cortes (1992) found that many Hispanics in their sample tended to deal with conflict at work "openly, directly and immediately." Yet, they point out, this did not mean a display of strong negative emotions; they found, as did other researchers (e.g., Collier, 1988), that Hispanics report working to maintain control over their anger. Ferdman and Cortes's findings accord with what I have observed. These diverse examples illustrate the difficulty of coming to a characterization of Latin American and Latino behaviors. Perhaps an emphasis on positive behaviors may not mean avoidance of dealing with conflicts or that different samples in different situations behave differently. At this point in time, our knowledge base is insufficient to specify precisely what behaviors occur in what situations for what group of participants and how these behaviors are enacted.

Interpersonal Connections

On the basis of an ethnographic study in Colombia in schools, governmental, and corporate settings, Archer and Fitch (1994) describe *palanca* (literally, "a lever"; interpersonally, "a connection"; p. 83) as a common pattern and a powerful cultural myth. They explain *palanca* as the instrumental form of an interpersonal relationship.

Palanca provides a means by which individuals can transcend general rules, procedures, and the effects of scarcity by interacting with powerful others to gain what they need. The idea of *palanca* is rooted in a more fundamental notion that a person's identity is largely constituted by relationships with others. It is also tied to the notion of hierarchy and power distance because it is the more powerful persons who can help others. Archer and Fitch state: "Acting as a *palanca* to transcend scarcity and/or rules is viewed as a favor, and sometimes as an obligation, of interpersonal relationships" (p. 84).

It is interesting to note that the Latin American notion of being embedded in a rich interpersonal network may be at variance with some assumptions of human resource training as it is typically carried out in North America, such as the idea that one should develop and empower the individual. (For a discussion of the need to incorporate intercultural research and practice into organizational settings, both domestically and internationally, see Albert, 1992b, 1994, and Triandis & Albert, 1987).

Personalistic Attention

My own research on Latino or Hispanic/ Anglo American differences (Albert, 1986a, 1992a), as well as personal observations, suggests that Latin Americans and Latinos expect, and at times prefer, personalized, individualized attention, rather than being treated in a standardized way like everyone else. In Latin American cultures, individuality is valued and greater distinctions are made on the basis of status, class, being a member of the in-group, and other attributes of the persons interacting. So, giving special attention to members of the in-group or to a high-status person is not viewed in the same it might be in the United States.

In summary, then, emic components of an overarching interpersonal orientation are found among Latin Americans and Latinos. This orientation includes cognitive patterns that emphasize respect, dignity, loyalty, and *simpatía,* as well as patterns of action such as coopera-tion, avoidance of criticism and of negative behaviors, use of interpersonal connections, and personalistic attention.

Etic or Cross-Cultural Dimensions

In this section, I review dimensions of culture that have emerged from cross-cultural conceptualizations and research focusing on a variety of cultures. Often, but not always, Latin American cultures tend to be toward one end of the continuum, whereas North American and Northern European cultures tend to be toward the other end of the continuum. Measurement of these dimensions is still evolving (Singelis, Triandis, Bhawuk, & Gelfand, 1995).

It is important to keep in mind that the variations found are for cultural groups, and not for specific individuals; thus, within a given culture there may be individuals who differ from the pattern described here. So, the reader should see these as differences of degree, rather than of kind, and keep in mind, as Kluckhohn and Strodbeck (1961) indicate in their seminal work, that all cultures have all of the orientations; it is more a matter of a greater prevalence or preference for one pattern over the other patterns.

Perceptual Patterns

Two important perceptual patterns distinguish Latin American cultures from other Western cultures: high power distance and more differentiated gender roles.

High Versus Low Power Distance

Hofstede (1980, 1991) defines *power distance* as "the extent to which the less powerful members of institutions and organizations within a country expect and accept that power is distributed unequally" (1991, p. 28). His research with managers indicates that Latin American countries have high power distance scores and that the United States and non-Latin European countries have low scores. Hofstede (1991) sees differences in power distance between cultures persisting for long periods of time. Triandis (1995) and Singelis et al. (1995)

propose that "verticality" be seen as "the acceptance of inequalities among people, and power distance as norms establishing and rewarding some forms of inequality" (Singelis et al., 1995, p. 269).

The components of high power distance that Hofstede measured were as follows: (a) Employees were frequently afraid to express disagreement with their managers, (b) employees perceived that their boss had autocratic or paternalistic styles, and (c) employees expressed a *preference* for these management styles, rather than for more participatory styles.

I find the power distance dimension extremely important in interactions between North Americans and Latin Americans because it can be very different in the two cultural patterns. In my research, Latino students were most likely to blame students, rather than teachers, in the episodes presented to them (Albert, 1983b) and to select attributions indicating a greater power distance between teachers and students than did Anglo Americans (Albert, 1992a). This finding reflected the fact that the teacher in many Latin American cultures is considered to be much higher in status than students and is treated with respect. (This does not mean, however, that the teacher is viewed as distant. Often, it is quite the opposite; he or she is frequently viewed as close to students and is treated with affection. Variations, of course, occur from place to place in how teachers and students behave toward one another.)

Triandis, Marín, et al. (1984) also found evidence of high power distance among Hispanics. Even though Díaz-Guerrero and Szalay (1991) did not find more references to authority and respect in Mexico and Colombia than in the United States, in their word-association task with college students, they too indicated that, in the literature, Hispanic cultures are frequently characterized as authority oriented. In an apparent contrast to this, Ferdman and Cortes (1992) found that Hispanic managers in the United States preferred a participatory, open-door leadership style, did not like close supervision, and were willing to challenge their superiors.

This diversity of findings illustrates the difficulty of providing generalizations regarding any of the dimensions. Ferdman and Cortes explain the discrepancy between their study and Hofstede's as perhaps due to the fact that their data came from a company in the United States, with managers who had minority status. They

also cite situational and organizational factors and perceptions of ethnicity. Differences in the social class of the managers in their managerial level and in the time frame at which the different studies were conducted may also account for the differences in their results.

The above discussion suggests that knowledge of *how* power distance is enacted in various Latin American cultures in different settings and in different roles is most important. This is one reason for my earlier suggestion that only persons with deep experience with Latin American cultures provide this kind of training.

An important feature of power distance in Latin American countries is class. Class differences are salient and very important to Latin Americans. Most countries have a large lower class, a small middle class, and a very powerful upper class. Interestingly, the greater power distance of Latin Americans probably stems not only from their European roots, as is commonly supposed, but also from some of the indigenous cultures. Condon (1985) notes, "In most tribes, certainly in the dominant tribes such as the earlier Mayans and the late-flourishing Aztecs, class lines were rigid as though etched in stone, justified and maintained in a theocratic state" (p. 3). The many ramifications of high power distance include how the roles of parents, teachers, and bosses are enacted (Albert, 1992a; Díaz-Guerrero & Szalay, 1991; Hofstede, 1991), the use of status symbols, and language use (Spanish has two forms of address, *tu* and *usted,* the later denoting respect).

The reader is cautioned that although this orientation is highly general, variations and changes occur in specific situations and at different times. How and when to show respect in each cultural milieu is highly specific, depending on the context, the participants, and the norms that have developed. Thus, training in the proper forms of interaction with persons from different statuses is necessary. It is also very important to avoid making judgments based on one's own culture and to understand the views and perspectives of the members of the target culture.

Gender Roles

Gender roles have generally been more differentiated for Latin Americans and Latinos than for North Americans and Northern Europeans. (This is why Latin American students in the United States reportedly have had a hard time with differences in gender roles [Pollard, 1989].) As Lisansky (1981) notes,

> *Machismo* or manliness as an ideal is discussed by authors on all Hispanic groups. Defined in various ways, it is a constellation of values, ideals and behaviors appropriate to the realization of manhood. An important element of machismo is the maintenance of the male's dignity and respect, or honor. (p. 206)

In a recent review, Casas, Wagenheim, Banchero, and Mendoza-Romero (1994) contend that some authors think the construct of machismo is pervasive among Hispanics and plays a pivotal role in defining the traditional culture; others think it is less ingrained. Still others acknowledge that machismo played a defining role vis-à-vis the traditional culture but that it is on the decline as a result of acculturation in the United States, modernity, and economic advancement.

An important thing for the sojourner to realize is that this term tends to have different meanings for Latin Americans and Hispanics than it does for North or Anglo Americans (Díaz-Guerrero & Szalay, 1991; Guilbault, 1992; Mirandé, 1988). As Hutchison and Poznanski (1987) put it,

> For many North Americans and Europeans *machismo* conjures up the image of aggressive males showing off, competing with each other, and dominating women. A more accurate interpretation, based on our discussion of "image" earlier, is that Latin men behave in accordance with their image of what a man should be: strong, respected, and capable of protecting and providing for women and his family. (p. 88)

Female behaviors and ideals have received less attention in the social science literature. The ideal woman was traditionally viewed as one who remained totally above reproach and was submissive (Lisansky, 1981). Fitzpatrick (1971) and others note that despite the cultural ideal of female subordination and the preservation of appearances, women have had a great deal of influence in the home, where middle-class women have often played a managerial role supervising maids and other household staff. They have also had much influence over their sons and have tended to be active in public affairs (Fitzpatrick, 1971; several Latin American countries have even had female presidents). Lisansky notes that although some authors argue that sex role differentiation continues, a number of authors describe a liberalization or changes in Hispanic sex roles in the United States. As an example, a recent study by Herrera and DelCampo (1995) found that working-class Mexican American women want their husbands' role to include household and child-care responsibilities.

Gender roles seem to be changing in Latin America, especially in the cities; upper-middle and middle-class women are entering the workforce in large numbers. Since 1960, women's labor force participation in Latin America has grown twice as fast as women's worldwide participation (Acevedo, 1995). Women have also gained many rights. Several countries (Brazil and Argentina) have passed legislation facilitating or legalizing divorce, extending maternity leave, and giving women more equality in the family (Safa, 1995). Still, gender differentiations tend to be much greater than those found in the United States and Northern European countries.

Cognitive Patterns

Among the important cognitive dimensions of Latin American cultures are collectivism and familism, Confucian work dynamism, a shame orientation, and a changing orientation toward the past, the present, and the future.

Collectivism Versus Individualism

Collectivism versus individualism is a fundamental dimension of cultural differences (Hofstede, 1980; Hui & Triandis, 1986; Kluckhohn & Strodbeck, 1961; Triandis, 1995).

Triandis (1995) identifies four "defining" attributes that distinguish collectivistic from individualistic cultures:

1. In collectivistic societies, like Latin American societies, individuals define themselves as part of a group; in individualistic societies, like American society,

individuals focus on a self-concept that is autonomous from groups.

2. In collectivistic societies, personal goals overlap with the goals of members of the person's in-group (e.g., family, clan); even when they do not, people believe it is "obvious" that in-group goals take precedence (Schwartz, 1990).

3. The behavior of collectivists can best be predicted from norms, perceived duties, and obligations (Bontempo & Rivero, 1992; Miller, 1994). Among individualists, behavior can best be predicted on the basis of attitudes and internal processes, as well as contracts made by the individual.

4. For collectivists, relationships are of the greatest importance and are maintained, even if the costs to the individual exceed any benefits. Individualists, in turn, tend to terminate relationships when the costs exceed the benefits (Kim, Triandis, Kagitçibasi, Choi, & Yoon, 1994).

Hofstede (1980) found that the most individualistic countries were the United States, Australia, and Great Britain; they ranked 1, 2, and 3 out of 53 countries. In contrast, the Latin American countries have generally been found to be collectivistic. They ranked from 22/23 to 53 among 53 countries or regions for individualism. The 5 countries with the lowest individualism scores—that is, the most collectivistic— were Latin American countries. (As my students astutely have pointed out, the scale was one of individualism; they wondered whether it would have been so labeled had the researcher come from a collectivistic culture!)

This dimension is very important for those preparing to interact with Latin Americans, because the usual North American pattern is to think first and foremost of one's own wishes, needs, and views, whereas the Latin American pattern is to express what is good for the other. So, trainees need to understand that a fundamental cognitive shift is required. In my training experience, this is a hard shift to bring about. It takes an experienced and knowledgeable trainer to prepare people to deal with a culture that presents a challenge to their most basic assumptions and values. Trainees need to be prepared not only to encounter different patterns but also to learn how their customary patterns is viewed; for example, they need to learn that Latin Americans may interpret individualistic behaviors as selfish and egotistical.

It is important to point out the distinction between individuality and individualism (Kluckhohn & Strodbeck, 1961). Although Latin American cultures can be generally characterized as collectivistic, *individuality,* or the recognition of individual uniqueness, is highly important in these cultures (Gillin, 1965; Grebler, Moore, & Guzman, 1970; Kluckhohn & Strodbeck, 1961; Lisansky, 1981; Madsen, 1973; Magaffey & Barnett, 1962; Mintz, 1966; Saunders, 1954; Szalay, Ruiz, Strohl, Lopez, & Turbyville, 1978; Wagenheim, 1972).

Familism. Among collectivists, greater differentiation is made between members of the in-group and outsiders than is generally the case in individualistic cultures. The in-group in Latin American societies is defined by one's extended family—not only the nuclear family, but also grandparents, aunts and uncles, and cousins, often second- and third-degree cousins. No institution in Latin America is more important than the family. Consequently, familism is extremely strong in Latin American cultures (Fitzpatrick, 1971; Triandis, 1981). It is so important that it has traditionally been common for Latin Americans to extend the family status to good friends by making them godparents (*compadres,* or godfathers; *comadres,* or godmothers) of their children.

Díaz-Guerrero and Szalay (1991) conducted a study with comparable samples of Mexican, Colombian, and U.S. university students of the same age and educational level, half of whom were male and half female. The students responded to different stimulus words by providing word associations. On the basis of a thoughtful interpretation of the results, they characterized Mexican family relations as "exceptionally affect laden, with a great emphasis on love, reflecting strong emotional interdependence" (p. 2). In fact, they concluded that, in the Mexican conception of self, social roles and qualities such as "understanding and helpfulness" predominate. "The dominant role characteristics reflect the idea of interdependence, the ideals of the unity and cohesion of the family above the individual" (p. 2). This contrasts with the American view of the self as "an independent, self-reliant individual who has positive personal and social qualities and who makes his own decisions along his own interests" (p. 2). The responses of the Colombians were similar to those of the Mexicans.

In the training I provide, I give examples of various family roles and how they are seen differently in Latin American cultures and in North American culture. There are some interesting and important differences; space limitations prevent me from detailing them here.

Confucian Work Dynamism

To investigate whether an "Eastern" instrument would yield different dimensions of cultural differences, a survey of values based on Confucian notions was administered to university students in 22 countries. Researcher Michael Bond and others (Chinese Culture Connection, 1987) found support for dimensions similar to Hofstede's, plus a new dimension, which they labeled *Confucian work dynamism.* This factor includes such things as the value of thrift, persistence, having a sense of shame, and ordering relationships by status. It has a negative correlation with reciprocation, personal steadiness, protecting your "face," and respect for tradition. Results indicate that Brazil, the only Latin American country in the sample, was high in this dimension, as were the five economic "dragons" of Taiwan, Hong Kong, Japan, South Korea, and Singapore. The United States, by contrast, was low on this dimension. This finding contradicts the stereotypical assumption of Latin Americans as people who do not work hard. The authors speculate that certain values tapped by this dimension may lie at the root of the "stunning economic development" of the societies that rank high.

Shame Versus Guilt. One important element of the Confucian work dynamism is having a sense of shame. The sense of shame seems to be rather pronounced in Latin American cultures. Benedict (1946) first proposed that some cultures socialize people by making them feel ashamed of behaviors that do not fit the mores and that other societies socialize them by making people feel guilty. Shame is a social means of control; guilt is an internalized means of control. The former is used more often in collectivistic cultures; the latter is used in individu-

alistic cultures. Albert (1986a, 1992a) found empirical evidence for the view that Latin Americans are more likely than North Americans to select attributions or interpretations of behavior involving shame when choosing interpretations to situations involving interactions between North American teachers and Latin American students.

Time Orientation

Kluckhohn and Strodbeck (1961) proposed a classification of various value orientations. Three general time orientations were proposed: past, present, and future. The authors state,

> Obviously, every society must deal with all three *time* problems. . . . Where they differ is in the preferential ordering of the alternatives (rank order emphases), and a very great deal can be told about the particular society or part of a society being studied and much can be predicted about the direction of change within it if one knows what the rank-order emphasis is. (p. 14)

Although North Americans have been commonly considered to be future oriented, Latin Americans have been historically considered to be present oriented (Kluckhohn & Strodbeck, 1961). This means that Latin Americans as a rule are less likely to plan activities ahead of time in their personal or organizational life and are much more likely than North Americans to do things on the spur of the moment. This behavior is something sojourners must adjust to.

The unpredictability of the economic and, in some places and times, the political environment have probably contributed to this behavior and have made flexibility desirable. To be sure, many observers would say that North American organizations have been shifting to a present-time orientation (these days, one often hears the lament that companies focus only on the short-term performance, rather than plan for the long term).

At the societal level, some observers have lamented the ahistorical orientation of North Americans. In contrast, Latin American countries have traditionally tended to emphasize history in their curriculum. These countries now emphasize development and the future, and people in the middle class are becoming more future oriented. In fact, Hofstede (1980) argues that the Confucian work dynamism value should be relabeled *long-term orientation* and, as the reader will recall, in that dimension the U.S. sample was low (short-term oriented), whereas the Brazilian sample was high (long-term oriented.)

The reader is cautioned that time orientation of a cultural group depends on the social class one is focusing on and on the particular aspect of the culture one is describing. I currently characterize the general personal orientation of middle-class Latin Americans as present-to-future oriented.

Patterns of Action

Polychronic Versus Monochronic
Time Orientation

Hall (1984) characterizes two orientations toward time and activity: (a) polychronic, P-time, in which people do many things at once and (b) monochronic, M-time, in which individuals do one thing at a time. The former is characteristic of Latin Americans, the latter of North Americans and Northern Europeans. Hall discusses how different what he calls *American European (AE) time* is from what he calls *Colonial Iberian-Indian (CII) time*. According to Hall, when CII persons meet someone in the street and find out that a mutual friend is in the hospital, they change everything and go to see that friend. Although this may happen in some places, one must be careful in generalizing from this example; obviously, such behavior would vary according to the obligations of the person, the importance of the friend, and a number of other factors. In urban areas, people tend to be more monochronic than in rural areas. Yet, the general observation that Latin Americans tend to give higher priority to people than to schedules is basically correct.

The old stereotype of the Latin American always being late comes from judging a polychronic culture by using monochronic standards and by misunderstanding the different meanings and duration of time in Latin American cultures. The reader should also understand that it is possible to err by assuming that everybody and everything runs late: A colleague of mine once missed a boat that only came to a remote area of Brazil once a week because she was sure it would be late; it wasn't!

The monochronic North Americans tend to stress following a schedule. Hall (1984) explains that, for CII people, the schedule is not internalized as it is for North Americans or Europeans; it is external and carries less weight than networks of family and friends. Thus, according to Hall, being late does not convey a negative message and is not seen as an insult. Of course, what is considered late is also different in Latin American cultures.

Hall explains the many implications of the two systems. Thus, taking one's turn, seeing people in private, making appointments, and many other customs are examples of M-time. For Latin Americans, time is not as fixed and compartmentalized; it is more fluid and more flexible. Some Latin Americans might see North Americans as slaves to the clock, and they will sometimes be annoyed by what they would consider the North American disregard for human values (Hutchison & Poznanski, 1987). An interesting implication drawn by Hall is that employers do not schedule a subordinate's work for him or her, because this would be an invasion of the employees individuality!

Much more could be said about the polychronic features of Latin American societies. North Americans and Northern Europeans interacting with Latin Americans will do well to understand this crucial difference; otherwise, they might be frustrated or might misinterpret the Latin American pattern.

Orientation Toward Nature

Kluckhohn and Strodbeck (1961) propose three orientations toward nature: subjugation to nature, harmony with nature, and mastery over nature. They indicate that, on the one hand, the "Spanish American" culture in the Southwest exhibited a preference for the view that humans are subject to nature, both in attitudes toward events like the damage done by storms and in attitudes toward illness and death. The "Texan" (Anglo American community), on the other hand, clearly had an orientation favoring mastery over nature.

As Latin America has urbanized and modernized, impressive and massive projects, such as hydroelectric plants, have been built, and many in the elite would probably be characterized as feeling mastery over nature. Yet, it is possible that the majority of the population still feels subjugated to nature (see West, 1990), largely for lack of resources. It is my impression that this is changing as a result of industrialization, yet the emphasis may be different from the mastery emphasis found for the United States. Díaz-Guerrero and Szalay found that, in associations to the word *future*, "development" and "progress" were emphasized by Mexicans and Colombians, whereas U.S. Americans emphasized technology and science. I speculate that many Latin Americans may be moving toward a mastery orientation and, among some segments of the population, such as those concerned with the environment, toward an attitude of harmony with nature.

Activity Orientation. This dimension centers on the nature of people's mode of self-expression in activity. Some cultures prefer a *Being* orientation, others a *Being-in-Becoming* orientation, and still others a *Doing* orientation (Kluckhohn & Strodbeck, 1961). The Being orientation is found where the preference is for "the kind of *activity* which is a spontaneous expression of what is conceived to the 'given' in the human personality" (p. 16). Mexican society illustrates the Being pattern preference "in its widely ramified patterning of *fiesta* activities" (p. 16). The North American culture exhibits a preference for the Doing orientation: North Americans usually plan "activities" to do with friends: They must play tennis or jog or "do something."

The negative stereotype of the Latin American as lazy derives from misconceptions based on applying the standards of a Doing culture to judge behavior in a Being culture, because people in the two types of cultures tend to do things somewhat differently. Latin Americans, in turn, may see the North American as having a somewhat mechanical orientation to both activities and people and as someone who is always rushing to do more and more things without stopping long enough to reflect on the ultimate meaning and purpose of all this activity. Díaz-Guerrero and Szalay (1991) found "an interesting cluster of Mexican reactions dealing with being, existence and development, totally unparalleled by the U.S. group" (p. 99). They note that the distinction between the Doing and Being orientations is subtle but important and dif-

ficult to measure. They found that the Colombian view is close to the Mexican view.

It is mistake to draw from this distinction the implication that Latin Americans do not work hard. Many work extremely hard and under very difficult conditions (many people travel 2 hours to work each way every day), especially the vast numbers of people who are poor and work at very low wages. There may be differences in the way work is viewed in the North and Latin American cultures. Díaz-Guerrero and Szalay (1991) found that although in North American culture work seems to be viewed as a main source of satisfaction, identity, or respect, responses from Mexicans and Colombians indicated that work seems to have more instrumental value for them, with necessity and providing for their family as primary considerations.

Although Latin Americans may be changing toward a greater Doing orientation as their societies become serious international competitors, North Americans are being urged to seek more balance, more community, and to focus more on spiritual development, and these are Being and Being-in-Becoming patterns! In yet another example of the value of the Being orientation, when people in North American society have serious or terminal illnesses, they are told to "take one day at a time" and "smell the flowers"—that is, to adopt a present-oriented, Being pattern.

Dionysian Versus Apollonian Cultures

A related dimension is that of Apollonian versus Dionysian cultures. This dimension, originally proposed for different personality types (Morris, 1942), reflects stoicism and control of desires in the face of events and difficulties (Apollonian) at one end of the continuum, and expressiveness at the other end of the continuum (Dionysian). Latin Americans tend to express their emotions openly, be these emotions of grief, pain, or joy; the more measured, at times stoic response to pain and pleasure of some North Americans and Northern Europeans may seem odd to them. (Of course, any individual may or may not fit this or any other predominant cultural pattern.) This expressiveness is seen in many arenas.

In a study of communication satisfaction, Hecht et al. (1990) found that Mexican American students were dissatisfied "if the Mexican

American respondent does not feel free to express emotions and/or the Anglo conversational partner is unwilling or unable to express emotions" (p. 40). The authors point out that this seems consistent with the literature on Mexican American culture and language.

Uncertainly Avoidance/Flexibility

Hofstede (1991) defines *uncertainty avoidance* as "*the extent to which the members of a culture feel threatened by uncertain or unknown situations.* This feeling is, among other things, expressed through nervous stress and in a need for predictability: a need for written and unwritten rules" (p. 113). The greater the job stress, the attitude that company rules should not be broken, and the intention to stay with the company for a long time, the higher the uncertainty avoidance score. He found that Latin American countries tend to be high or moderate in this dimension and that the United States tends to be low.

Although it is true that many Latin Americans generally intend to stay with a company a long time and that, historically, political or economic instability may have led to feelings of uncertainty in many regions, at the interpersonal level I find it difficult to reconcile many of the characteristics that Hofstede discusses under uncertainty avoidance with the behavior of the majority of Latin Americans I know. His findings may due to the fact that the aspects of uncertainty avoidance he actually measured were rather limited.

I find that Latin Americans tend to be very flexible in terms of interpersonal relations, especially when dealing with those of equal or higher status, rules in organizations and bureaucracies, and plans. Often, they seem much more flexible than North Americans. Corroboration for this view comes from Ferdman and Cortes (1992), who note that Hispanics value flexibility, and from Lisansky (1981), who indicates that Latin Americans are more flexible than Hofstede's description seems to imply.

In conclusion, Latin American cultures stress cognitive patterns and patterns of action which differ in many respects from those of North American and Northern European cultures. Among other characteristics, Latin American cultures tend to emphasize high power distance, differentiated gender roles, collectivism and familism, Confucian work dynamism, a changing orientation toward the past, present, and future, a polychronic pattern of time use, traditional subjugation toward nature that is changing to mastery over nature, a Being orientation, emotional expressiveness, and uncertainly avoidance coupled with flexibility in many domains.

Communication Patterns

As was done for other sections of the chapter, I consider first some cognitive patterns and then some patterns of action.

Cognitive Patterns

Politeness and Relational Themes

Latin Americans and Latinos tend to be socialized into politeness, with an emphasis on warm interpersonal relations (Díaz-Guerrero & Szalay, 1991; Szalay & Brent, 1967). In a study of conversational rules, Collier (1988) found that Mexican Americans mentioned politeness most frequently and also cited role prescriptions, especially cultural prescriptions, and relational climate as important. In intercultural conversations with Anglo Americans, they also saw their cultural identity sometimes threatened by negative stereotypes.

In general, the speech patterns of North Americans may strike Latin Americans as too blunt, too direct, and too plain. Hecht et al. (1990) provide the following quote to illustrate the dissatisfaction felt by a Mexican American male in conversation with an Anglo American: "The other person was blunt and seemed to find it easy to say that there was no solution but to dissipate the relationship" (p. 40). The authors give this as an example of the importance of *relational solidarity,* one of seven categories of relational themes regarding communication satisfaction for Mexican Americans.

Orientation Toward Language Use

Latin American cultures tend to value music, art, and linguistic prowess highly. A number of Latin American writers have received Nobel Prizes in literature, pioneering new forms of prose. World-class writers include Octavio Paz, Carlos Fuentes, and Gabriel García Márquez. Facility with language and the ability to be eloquent is admired, and many presidents, governors, and ambassadors have been writers. Language is often used expressively and associatively, rather than strictly pragmatically.

Written communication is much less common in routine affairs than in the United States, despite vast improvements in mail systems in recent years, although faxes are now commonly used in major cities. Latin Americans tend to strongly prefer personal, preferably face-to-face, communication over more impersonal means of communication.

Patterns of Action

High and Low Context Communication

Hall (1976) distinguished high context from low context communication:

> A high context (HC) communication or message is one in which most of the information is either in the physical context or internalized in the person, while very little is in the coded, explicit, transmitted part of the message. A low context (LC) communication is just the opposite; i.e., the mass of the information is vested in the explicit code. (p. 79)

High-context communication tends to occur in collectivistic cultures, and in these societies people expect more from others than do persons in low-context cultures.

Latin American cultures would be classified as high context; that means Latin Americans will not be as explicit as Northern Europeans or North Americans, especially if they need to ask a favor or if they have to say no. The meanings of messages they send and receive are often conveyed by gestures and other nonverbal signals, by the rank and position of those speaking, and by reading between the lines. This is difficult for those who come from a low-context culture, like the German or U.S. cultures, because individuals from these cultures are not used to having to pay this much attention to context factors and to "decipher" what is being conveyed.

Murillo (1976) indicates that Mexican Americans are likely to use elaborate and indi-

rect expressions in an effort to make social relations harmonious. North Americans or European who do not understand this pattern may misinterpret it, believing that Latin Americans are not forthcoming or that they are trying to hide something.

High-Contact Versus Low-Contact Cultures

Paralinguistic Behaviors. In my research, Latinos were perceived as speaking louder and more than Anglo Americans (Albert & Nelson, 1993). This is part of the more expressive pattern described above. Yet, yelling in the street or being rowdy in restaurants or parties, which I have seen North American college students do, especially in a crowd, is considered rather offensive by Latin Americans.

Eye Contact. In my research, I found that when a student would lower her eyes while being addressed by a teacher, Anglo Americans interpreted this as disrespectful because the student was not looking directly at the teacher. In actually, according to Latino cultural patterns, the student was showing respect to the teacher by averting her eyes (Albert, 1992a).

Gestures. As a rule, Latin Americans use gestures much more frequently than North Americans, and gestures are used to express feelings, to answer questions, to call people or send them away, to greet them, and so on. Training should include specific gestures and their meanings and cautions about those that are offensive to members of the target culture.

Proxemic Patterns. In terms of interpersonal distances, Latin American usually stand and sit much closer to each other than do North Americans. They do so at distances that may be uncomfortable to many North Americans, Northern Europeans, and Asians.

Hall (1959) explains that the distances people keep are very specific and culture bound. Although he delineates rather precisely the distances that feel comfortable to North Americans, he does not offer concrete distances for Latin Americans, except to say that the close distances Latin Americans use may evoke either sexual or hostile feelings in North Americans. He also points out that Latin Americans may perceive North Americans as distant, cold, and unfriendly and that North Americans may perceive Latin Americans as "breathing down our necks, crowding us, and spraying our faces" (p. 185). Notice how negative these perceptions are! Training should help people from each culture interpret the other cultural pattern in a less negative way.

Tactility. The amount of touch is also much greater among Latin Americans than among North Americans. Ferdman and Cortes (1992) found that many Hispanic managers mentioned the importance of touching other people, both literally and figuratively. Latin Americans touch people frequently and do so for many reasons, as a way to establish personal rapport with them. The kinds of touching that are appropriate, however, are highly specific and dependent on the relationship and the particular context. A sojourner needs to be a good observer, because the rules that govern touching are subtle and complex, and the wrong kind of touch can be interpreted negatively.

In my research, when I asked teachers and students to respond to scenarios depicting commonly occurring situations, Anglo Americans more than Latinos selected the interpretation that the North American teacher was uncomfortable with the fact that Latin American students would touch him or her (Albert & Triandis, 1979).

Shuter (1976) investigated the distances and axis or angle measurements at which persons in the street interacted with another person in three Latin American countries. The Costa Ricans interacted at a more direct axis and at smaller distances than either Panamanians or Colombians (female dyads had smaller distances than male dyads). Colombians had a significantly lower contact score for both touching and holding (with females having higher contact scores for both) than either Costa Ricans or Panamanians.

This example demonstrates two important things:

1. Some variations occur in the behavioral patterns of persons from different Latin American countries. More research is needed to document both the differences and the similarities between countries and regions.
2. It is important for a trainer to have first-hand knowledge of the patterns in a particular country and setting. Otherwise, he or she might unwittingly and unintentionally mislead people.

In summary, Latin Americans tend to be expressive and associative, prefer face-to-face communication, emphasize politeness and relational themes, and use high-context and high-contact communication.

SUMMARY

There appear to be substantial differences in the basic cultural frames of reference of Latin Americans, on the one hand, and persons from other cultures, particularly North Americans and Northern Europeans, on the other. In this brief chapter, it is not possible to convey them all. I selectively highlighted some of the more characteristic, emic Latin American cultural patterns and some of the most important and salient dimensions of difference between Latin American cultures and other Western cultures. I also discussed the communication patterns that tend to be preferred by Latin Americans.

Values, expectations, norms, and behaviors, the strands that form the fabric of a culture, are extremely complex and multifaceted. They in-

teract with each other in complementary and intricate ways, and countervailing tendencies are at times present. The task of conveying them adequately in training is crucial and very challenging. If this chapter has helped the reader to better understand and appreciate Latin American cultural patterns and related training issues, it will have fulfilled its mission. For as Inman, quoted in Hanke (1959) and in Hutchison and Poznanski (1987), states,

Latin America has something to contribute to an industrialized and mechanistic world concerning the value of the individual, the place of friendship, the use of leisure, the art of conversation, the attractions of the intellectual, the equality of races, the juridical basis of international life, the place of suffering and contemplation, the value of the impracti-cal, the importance of people over things and rules. (Hanke, 1959, p. 10)

References

Acevedo, L. de A. (1995). Feminist inroads in the study of women's work and development. In C. E. Bose & E. Acosta-Belén (Eds.), *Women in the Latin American development process* (pp. 65-98). Philadelphia: Temple University Press.

Albert, R. D. (1983a). The intercultural sensitizer or culture assimilator: A cognitive approach. In D. Landis & R. Brislin (Eds.), *Handbook of intercultural training: Vol 2. Issues in training methodology* (pp. 186-217). Elmsford, NY: Pergamon.

Albert, R. D. (1983b). Mexican-American children in educational settings: Research on children's and teacher's perceptions of behavior. In E. Garcia (Ed.), *The Mexican American child: Language, cognition, and social development* (pp. 183-194). Tempe: Arizona State University.

Albert, R. D. (1986a). Communication and attributional differences between Hispanics and Anglo Americans. *International and Intercultural Communication Annual, X,* 41-59.

Albert, R. D. (1986b). Conceptual framework for the development and evaluation of cross-cultural orientation programs. *International Journal of Intercultural Relations, 2,* 197-213.

Albert, R. D. (1988). The place of culture in modern psychology. In P. Bronstein & K. Quina (Eds.), *Teaching a psychology of people: Resources for gender and sociocultural awareness* (pp. 12-18). Washington, DC: American Psychological Association.

Albert, R. D. (1992a). *Communicating across cultures.* Unpublished manuscript.

Albert, R. D. (1992b). Polycultural perspectives on organizational communication. *Management Communication Quarterly, 6*(1), 74-84.

Albert, R. D. (1994). Cultural diversity and intercultural training in multinational organizations. In R. Wiseman & R. Shuter (Eds.), *Communicating in multinational organizations* (pp. 153-165). Thousand Oaks, CA: Sage.

Albert, R. D. (1995). The intercultural sensitizer or culture assimilator as a cross-cultural training method. In S. Fowler & M. Mumford (Eds.), *The intercultural sourcebook* (pp. 157-167). Yarmouth, ME: Intercultural Press.

Albert, R. D., & Nelson, G. (1993). Hispanic-Anglo differences in attributions to paralinguistic behavior. *International Journal of Intercultural Relations, 17*(1), 19-40.

Albert, R. D., & Triandis, H. C. (1979). Cross-cultural training: A theoretical framework and some observations. In H. Trueba & C. Barnett-Mizrahi (Eds.), *Bilingual multicultural education and the professional: From theory to practice* (pp. 181-194). Rowley, MA: Newbury House.

Albert, R. D., & Triandis, H. C. (1985). Intercultural education for multicultural societies: Critical issues. *International Journal of Intercultural Relations, 9,* 319-337.

Allport, G. (1954). *The nature of prejudice.* Reading, MA: Addison-Wesley.

Alum, R. A., & Manteiga, F. P. (1977). Cuban and American values: A synoptic comparison. In *Hispanic subcultural values: Similarities and differences* (pp. 184-202). [Mosaic.] (ERIC ED 144466)

Archer, L., & Fitch, K. (1994). Communication in Latin American multinational organizations. In R. Wiseman & S. Wiseman (Eds.), *Communicating in multinational organizations* (pp. 75-93). Thousand Oaks, CA: Sage.

Benedict, R. (1946). *The chrysanthemum and the sword: Patterns of Japanese culture.* Boston: Houghton Mifflin.

Berry, J. (1980). Introduction to methodology. In H. C. Triandis & J. Berry (Eds.), *Handbook of cross-cultural psychology* (pp. 1-28). Boston: Allyn & Bacon.

Bontempo, R., & Rivero, J. C. (1992). *Cultural variation in cognition: The role of self-concept in the attitude behavior link.* Paper presented at the meeting of the American Academy of Management, Las Vegas, NV.

Brooke, J. (1994, December 9). On eve of Miami Summit Talks, U.S. comes under fire. *New York Times,* p. A4.

Burma, J. H. (1970). A comparison of the Mexican-American subculture with the Oscar Lewis culture of poverty model. In J. H. Burma (Ed.), *Mexican-Americans in the United States: A reader* (pp. 17-38). Cambridge, MA: Schenkman.

Casas, J. M., Wagenheim, B. R., Banchero, R., & Mendoza-Romero, J. (1994). Hispanic masculinity: Myth or psychological schema meriting clinical consideration? *Hispanic Journal of Behavioral Sciences, 16*(3), 315-331.

Chinese Cultural Connection. (1987). Chinese values and the search for culture-free dimensions of culture. *Journal of Cross-Cultural Psychology, 18,* 143-164.

Collier, M. J. (1988). A comparison of conversations among and between domestic culture groups: How intra- and intercultural competencies vary. *Communication Quarterly, 36*(2), 122-144.

Collier, S., Skidmore, T. E., & Blakemore, H. (Eds.). (1992). *Cambridge encyclopedia of Latin America and the Caribbean* (2nd ed.). Cambridge, UK: Cambridge University Press.

Condon, J. (1985). *Good neighbors.* Yarmouth, ME: Intercultural Press.

Díaz-Guerrero, R. (1975). *Psychology of the Mexican.* Austin: University of Texas Press.

Díaz-Guerrero, R., & Szalay, L. B. (1991). *Understanding Mexicans and Americans: Cultural perspectives in conflict.* New York: Plenum.

Díaz-Royo, A. T. (1974). *The enculturation process of Puerto Rican highland children.* Unpublished doctoral dissertation, University of Michigan.

Espinoza, J., & Garza, R. T. (1985). Social group salience and interethnic cooperation. *Journal of Experimental and Social Psychology, 21,* 380-392.

Ferdman, B. M., & Cortes, A. C. (1992). Culture and identity among Hispanic managers in an Anglo business. In S. Knouse, P. Rosenfeld, & A. Culbertson (Eds.), *Hispanics in the workplace* (pp. 246-276). Newbury Park: CA: Sage.

Fitzpatrick, J. P. (1971). *Puerto Rican Americans: The meaning of migration to the mainland.* Englewood Cliffs, NJ: Prentice-Hall.

Gillin, J. (1965). Ethos components in modern Latin American culture. In D. Heath & R. Adams (Eds.), *Contemporary cultures and societies of Latin America* (pp. 503-517). New York: Random House.

Grebler, L., Moore, J. W., & Guzman, R. C. (1970). *The Mexican American people: The nation's second largest minority.* New York: Free Press.

Guilbault, R. del C. (1992). Americanization is tough on "macho." In R. Holeton (Ed.), *Encountering cultures* (pp. 34-36). Englewood Cliffs, NJ: Prentice-Hall.

Hall, E. T. (1959). *The silent language.* Garden City, NY: Doubleday.

Hall, E. T. (1976). *Beyond culture.* New York: Anchor.

Hall, E. T. (1984). *The dance of life.* New York: Anchor.

Hanke, L. (1959). *South America.* New York: Van Nostrand.

Hecht, M. L., Ribeau, S., & Sedano, M. V. (1990). A Mexican American perspective on interethnic communication. *International Journal of Intercultural Relations, 14*(1), 31-55.

Heller, C. S. (1966). *Mexican American youth: Forgotten youth at the crossroads.* New York: Random House.

Hernandez, C. A. (1970). *Mexican Americans' challenge to a sacred cow* (Monograph No. 1). Los Angeles: University of California, Mexican American Culture Center.

Herrera, R. S., & DelCampo, R. L. (1995). Beyond the superwomen syndrome: Work satisfaction and family functioning among working-class, Mexican American women. *Hispanic Journal of Behavioral Sciences, 17*(1), 49-60.

Hofstede, G. (1980). *Culture's consequences.* Beverly Hills, CA: Sage.

Hofstede, G. (1991). *Cultures and organizations: Software of the mind.* New York: McGraw-Hill.

Holtzman, W. H., Díaz-Guerrero, R., & Swartz, J. D. (1975). *Personality development in two cultures.* Austin: University of Texas Press.

Hui, C. H., & Triandis, H. C. (1986). Individualism-collectivism: A study of cross-cultural researchers. *Journal of Cross-Cultural Psychology, 17,* 225-248.

Hutchison, W. R., & Poznanski, C. A. (with Todt-Stockman, L.) (1987). *Living in Colombia.* Yarmouth, ME: Intercultural Press.

Kagan, S., & Knight, G. P. (1981). Cooperation-competition and self-esteem: A case of cultural relativism. *Journal of Cross-Cultural Psychology, 10,* 457-467.

Kagan, S., Knight, G. P., & Martinez-Romero, S. (1982). Culture and the development of conflict resolution style. *Journal of Cross-Cultural Psychology, 13,* 43-58.

Kagan, S., & Madsen, M. C. (1971). Cooperation and competition of Mexican, Mexican-American, and Anglo-American children of two ages under four instructional sets. *Developmental Psychology, 5,* 32-39.

Kim, U., Triandis, H. C., Kagitçibasi, C., Choi, S-C, & Yoon, G. (1994). *Individualism and collec-*

tivism: Theory, method, and applications. Thousand Oaks, CA: Sage.

Kluckhohn, F., & Strodbeck, F. (1961). *Variations in value orientations.* New York: Harper & Row.

Knight, G. P., & Kagan, S. (1977). Acculturation of prosocial and competitive behaviors among second- and third-generation Mexican American children. *Journal of Cross-Cultural Psychology, 8,* 273-284.

Kolland, F. (1990). National cultures and technology transfer. *International Journal of Intercultural Relations, 14*(3), 319-336.

Landy, D. (1959). *Tropical childhood: Cultural transmission and learning in a rural Puerto Rican village.* Chapel Hill: University of North Carolina Press.

Lisansky, J. (1981). *Interpersonal relations among Hispanics in the United States: A content analysis of the social science literature* (Technical Report No. 3). Urbana: University of Illinois, Department of Psychology.

Lucas, J. R., & Stone, G. L. (1994). Acculturation and competition among Mexican Americans: A reconceptualization. *Hispanic Journal of Behavioral Sciences, 16*(2), 129-142.

Madsen, W. (1973). *Mexican Americans of South Texas* (2nd ed.). New York: Holt, Rinehart & Winston.

Magaffey, W., & Barnett, C. R. (1962). *Cuba: Its people, its society, its culture.* New Haven: HRAF.

Marín, G., & Triandis, H. C. (1985). Allocentrism as an important characteristic of the behavior of Latin Americans and Hispanics. In R. Díaz-Guerrero (Ed.), *Cross-cultural and national studies of social psychology* (pp. 85-114). New York: Elsevier North-Holland.

Mead, M. (1953). *Cultural patterns and technical change.* Paris: United Nations Educational, Scientific, and Cultural Organization.

Miller, J. G. (1994). Cultural diversity in the morality of caring: Individual-oriented versus duty-based interpersonal moral codes. *Cross-Cultural Research, 28,* 3-39.

Mintz, S. W. (1966). Puerto Rico: An essay in the definition of a national culture. In *Status of Puerto Rico: Selected background studies for the U.S.-P.R. Commission on the Status of P.R.* Washington, DC: Government Printing Office.

Mirandé, A. (1988). Que gacho es ser macho: It's a drag to be a macho man. *Aztlan, 17,* 63-69.

Montalvo, F. F. (1987). *Skin color and Latinos: The origins and contemporary patterns of ethnora-*

cial ambiguity among Mexican Americans and Puerto Ricans. San Antonio, TX: Our Lady of the Lake University, Worden School of Social Service.

Morris, C. (1942). *Paths of life.* New York: Harper & Row.

Murillo, N. (1976). The Mexican American family. In C. A. Hernandez, M. J. Haug, & N. N. Wagner (Eds.), *Chicanos: Social and psychological perspectives* (pp. 15-25). St. Louis, MO: C. V. Mosby.

Pike, K. (1966). Etic and emic standpoints for the description of behavior. In A. Smith (Ed.), *Communication and culture* (pp. 152-163). New York: Holt, Rinehart & Winston.

Pollard, W. R. (1989). Gender stereotypes and gender roles in cross-cultural education: The culture assimilator. *International Journal of Intercultural Relations, 13,* 57-72.

Portes, A., & Schauffler, R. (1993). Competing perspectives on the Latin America informal sector. *Population and Development Review, 19*(1), 33-60.

Ramirez, A. (1988). Racism toward Hispanics: The culturally monolithic society. In P. A. Katz & D. A. Taylor (Eds.), *Eliminating racism: Profiles in controversy* (pp. 137-158). New York: Plenum.

Ramírez, M., III. (1983). *Psychology of the Americas: Mestizo perspectives on personality and mental health.* New York: Pergamon.

Reddy, M. (Ed.). (1990). *Statistical record of Hispanic Americans.* Detroit: Gale Research.

Rivera, J. S. (1970). Chicanos—Culture, community, role: Problems of evidence and a proposition of norms toward establishing evidence. *Aztlan, 1*(1), 37-51.

Rubel, A. J. (1970). Perceptions of social relations: A comparative analysis. In J. H. Burma (Ed.), *Mexican Americans in the United States: A reader* (pp. 211-224). Cambridge, MA: Schenkman.

Safa, H. I. (1995). Women's social movements in Latin America. In C. E. Bose & E. Acosta-Belén (Eds.), *Women in the Latin American development process* (pp. 227-241). Philadelphia: Temple University Press.

Saunders, L. (1954). *Cultural differences and medical care of the Spanish-speaking people of the Southwest.* New York: Russell Sage.

Schwartz, S. H. (1990). Individualism-collectivism: Critique and proposed refinements. *Journal of Cross-Cultural Psychology, 21,* 139-157.

Shuter, R. (1976). Proxemics and tactility in Latin America. *Journal of Communication, 26,* 46-52.

Singelis, T. M., Triandis, H. C., Bhawuk, D. S., & Gelfand, M. (1995). Horizontal and vertical dimensions of individualism and collectivism: A theoretical and measurement refinement. *Cross-Cultural Research, 29*(3), 240-275.

Szalay, L. B., & Brent, J. (1967). The analysis of cultural meanings through free verbal associations. *Journal of Social Psychology, 72,* 161-187.

Szalay, L. B., Ruiz, P., Strohl, J., Lopez, R., & Turbyville, L. (1978). *The Hispanic-American cultural frame of reference.* Washington, DC: Institute of Comparative Social and Cultural Studies.

Triandis, H. C. (Ed.). (1972). *The analysis of subjective culture.* New York: John Wiley.

Triandis, H. C. (1975). Culture training, cognitive complexity, and interpersonal attitudes. In R. Brislin, S. Bochner, & W. Lonner (Eds.), *Cross-cultural perspectives on learning* (pp. 39-77). Beverly Hills, CA: Sage.

Triandis, H. C. (1981). *Some dimensions of intercultural variation and their implications for interpersonal behavior.* Unpublished manuscript.

Triandis, H. C. (1995). *Individualism and collectivism.* Boulder, CO: Westview.

Triandis, H. C., & Albert, R. D. (1987). Cross-cultural perspectives on organizational communication. In F. M. Jablin, L. L. Putnam, K. Robert, & L. Porter (Eds.), *Handbook of organizational communication* (pp. 264-295). Newbury Park, CA: Sage.

Triandis, H. C., Hui, C. H., Albert, R. D., Leung, S., Lisansky, J., Díaz-Loving, R., Plascencia, L., Marín, G. B. H., & Loyola-Citron, L. (1984). Individual models of social behavior. *Journal of Personality and Social Psychology, 46,* 1389-1404.

Triandis, H. C., Marín, G., Lisansky, J., & Betancourt, H. (1984). *Simpatía* as a cultural script of Hispanics. *Journal of Personality and Social Psychology, 47*(6), 1363-1375.

Tumin, M. M., & Feldman, A. (1969). Social class and skin color in Puerto Rico. In M. M. Tumin (Ed.), *Comparative perspectives on race relations* (pp. 197-214). Boston: Little, Brown.

Tumin, M. M., & Feldman, A. (1971). *Social class and social change in Puerto Rico.* Indianapolis, IN: Bobbs-Merrill.

Wagenheim, K. (1972). *Puerto Rico: A profile* (2nd ed.). New York: Praeger.

Wagner, N. N., & Haug, M. J. (1971). *Chicanos: Social and psychological perspectives.* St. Louis, MO: C. V. Mosby.

West, D. (1990). *Between two worlds: The human side of development.* Yarmouth, ME: Intercultural Press.

19

Sociocultural and Contextual Challenges
of Organizational Life in Eastern Europe

Implications for
Cross-Cultural Training and Development

EDWARD DUNBAR

THE creation of favorable intercultural and business partnerships with the Eastern European Community (EEC) has lately received a great deal of attention in the United States. This, of course, is a consequence of the demise of the Soviet-dominated state market system, which had predominated throughout the EEC since the end of World War II. Concurrent with the political transformation of the EEC, there has been a growing recognition of the need for U.S. organizations to internationalize their operations (Kanter, 1991; Schweiger, Csiszar, & Napier, 1993). Accordingly, there are compel-

ling reasons for the creation of a cultural and economic partnership between the EEC and the United States. The implications of this partnership are considered in this chapter concerning two broad areas: (a) the operational barriers and psychological constructs that mediate U.S.-EEC relations and (b) the relationship of these factors to the perceived need for intercultural skills by U.S. staff to live and work in the EEC.

The partnership between the United States and the EEC can be considered in the context of interpersonal, intergroup, and organizational domains. Areas of particular emphasis include

AUTHOR'S NOTE: The author would like to express his thanks to Annette Haraldsted with the U.S.-Baltic Chamber of Commerce and Ralph Seifer with the World Affairs Council for their assistance regarding the current research.

The term *Eastern European Community (EEC)* as used in this chapter refers to those countries formerly dominated by the Soviet Union. As is suggested later, the referencing of this varied geopolitical region as a community is itself open to question. In the context of this discussion, the term is applied largely with respect to U.S. perceptions of the region as being a unified sociocultural environment and of intergroup attitudes that shape intercultural relationships.

international trade policy, regulatory affairs, diplomatic protocol, and economic policy. A less tangible but equally crucial factor concerns the interpersonal and intergroup attitudes that shape intercultural relationships. I argue that, without the development of intercultural skills in U.S. businesspersons who live and work in the EEC, the current opportunity for partnership may be missed entirely. Areas in need of immediate attention include the selection, preparation, and development of U.S. staff to work in the EEC. It is also essential to foster leadership and team-based approaches of EEC managers to transform organizations that must now participate in a market-driven economy.

Contextual Factors in Operations in the EEC

Three dimensions that mediate international business performance are (a) the sociocultural challenge (the "cultural toughness") of interpersonal processes encountered in a given country or region (Mendenhall & Oddou, 1985), (b) the unique operational challenges (e.g., barriers to production, personnel management, and market development) encountered, and (c) the competency of expatriate staff to implement corporate strategy in the context of a specific cultural milieu (Stephens & Black, 1991). Each of these dimensions influences the introduction of new products or services abroad, as well as the creation of international joint ventures and multinational business partnerships. Regarding international business operations, prior research has identified a variety of salient cultural and contextual variables, including ergonomic/human factors variability (Chapanis, 1974; Meskati, 1989), economic risk analysis (Dela Torre & Neckar, 1988), and sociotechnical system integration (Doktor & Lie, 1991). Prior study has also served to identify the operational challenges frequently encountered by corporate personnel abroad. In a survey of repatriated U.S. managers, Korn-Ferry (1981) identified 14 barriers to international business operations. A subsequent study of expatriate U.S. managers and technical personnel that included the dimensions of the Korn-Ferry survey yielded three factors that characterized the problems of working internationally (Dunbar, 1988): (a) work-related cultural differences, (b) production and manufac-

turing practices, and (c) business support (personnel-related) resources. For senior expatriate German and U.S. executives, these three factors reflected significant differences in the perceived operational challenges encountered in doing business in North America and Japan (Dunbar, 1994b). Further examination of the factor structure of international operations challenges was examined in a survey with Fortune 500 human resources executives (Dunbar & Ehrlich, 1985). This study identified three factors of international business challenge: (a) intercultural differences, (b) manufacturing and production practices, and (c) marketing and accounting practices.

A related issue in the challenge of expatriate performance abroad concerns the maturity of the organization's international operations. The performance of international operations has been related to the complexity and maturity of the products and services that are provided abroad (Dela Torre, 1975; Egelhoff, 1982). In their study of the performance of international strategic business units, Gronhaug and Kvitastein (1992) proposed that international operations varied in the complexity of the product and services provided. As suggested by Anderson and Coughlan (1985), as products become more complex, the challenge to international effectiveness increases. Gronhaug and Kvitastein proposed four categories that characterize the operations found in international markets: (a) provision and acquisition of raw materials, (b) manufactured products, (c) services, and (d) high-technology intensive products. Their findings indicate that product complexity is related to organizations asserting more control and influence on their international operations.

Psychological Principles of Organizational Life in the EEC

Independent of the myriad of economic and organizational challenges found in the EEC, the interpersonal and intergroup relationship between U.S. and EEC persons is mediated by attitudinal, cultural, and cognitive factors. Some EEC area experts believe the current emphasis on the development of manufacturing, finance, and technology in the EEC may indeed be overlooking the more fundamental concerns of the social and cultural integration of the former Eastern Bloc with Western market-driven organizations (Enyedi, 1994). In the Landis and Bhagat framework of intercultural behavior (see Chapter 1, this volume), both cultural variation (e.g. cultural values and worldviews) and social psychological variables mediate individual and organizational performance. Individuals responsible for shaping and implementing international business relationships in the EEC would do well to consider two psychological constructs that characterize the unique challenges of group relations in the EEC: healthy paranoia and learned helplessness.

The psychological construct of healthy paranoia has traditionally been applied to the relationship of majority-minority relations in North America (Ridley, 1984). In terms of the EEC, healthy paranoia is salient to the understanding of both political and organizational life during the period of Soviet control after World War II (Weiner, 1994). As suggested by Rigby (1972), the state-run societies of the EEC were typified by totalitarianism, monoparty rule, a command economy, and terror. Against this backdrop, healthy paranoia characterizes the organizational suspiciousness and interpersonal guardedness that has existed in state-controlled companies. This natural suspiciousness (healthy paranoia) is reflected in the proscribed leadership behavior of managers from the advent of Soviet domination of the region until the recent demise of the state-run systems. Indeed, the impact of self-proclaimed U.S. business consultants in the EEC during the past few years has only exacerbated the problems of out-group suspicion and guardedness fostered under the Soviet state-dominated system.

A second psychological construct characteristic of organizational life in the EEC concerns the learned helplessness of leadership under the state-controlled system. The research of the past two decades concerning learned helplessness is vast (Seligman, 1975). Based on social learning principles, *learned helplessness* has been experimentally defined as the belief than an individual has no control over the rewards and punishments received from interacting with his or her environment (Garber & Seligman, 1980). In terms of the EEC, the learned helplessness model is reflective of the nature of organizational behavior in a state-run and -regulated marketplace. As Nagy (1993) observed concerning managerial behavior in the Soviet-dominated state system, "The success of managers depended little or not [at all]

on company profitability or competitiveness, since they operated as monopolies in a shortage economy at home, or in the completely distorted Comecon market" (p. 82). Indeed, one of the most profound consequences of the learned helplessness of the state-run system on organizational life in the EEC can be observed in managerial behavior.

It has been noted frequently that most managers in the EEC are not adequately prepared to perform in a market-driven organization. Some of the most notable managerial problems have been related to ineffective presentation skills, a reluctance to communicate and interact across functional areas within the organization, and poor time-management skills (Karvalics, 1993). Recent evidence of the impact of the state-run system on organizational leadership was illustrated by a study of achievement motivation in Bulgaria (VanderHorst, 1994). In studying employee and managerial achievement styles, it was found that achievement via collaboration ("vicarious achievement") predominated, whereas personal ("direct power") and social ("instrumental power") achievement needs were significantly lower. The emphasis on achievement through participation was attributed to the oppressive organizational structure of Bulgarian companies under the state-run system, as well as the emphasis on technical skills at the expense of leadership and teamwork practices. In the context of the EEC, the constructs of healthy paranoia and learned helplessness are salient to the understanding of how a state-run system can compromise individual leadership, particularly with respect to personal achievement and decision making.

Psychological Principles of U.S. Perceptions of the EEC

Of equal concern to U.S.-EEC relations is the social psychology of U.S. organizations and their employees in viewing the EEC. With respect to U.S. organizations, the psychological constructs of social identity theory, the mythology of expatriation, and cultural worldviews all serve as determinants in the development of organizational relationships. Traditionally, U.S. business theorists have paid an inordinate amount of attention to the deficits of the host countries in which American organizations have established operations without consideration of how Western or U.S. beliefs compromise performance. Individuals and groups on both sides of the cultural divide of East and West have been socialized to view one another with a mix of suspicion, competitiveness, and bewilderment.

The first of the three psychological constructs is social identity theory (SIT). As has been demonstrated by experimental social psychologists, SIT is characterized by in-group identification and more negative out-group attributions (Tajfel, 1982; Tajfel & Turner, 1979). One of the more interesting and consistent observations of SIT concerns the observation that out-group members are typically perceived to be more homogeneous than in-group members. In the context of the U.S.-EEC relationship, this observation suggests that persons of the U.S. parent organization will be seen as being more diverse in their behaviors, perceptions, beliefs, and actions than their EEC counterparts. An unexplored question is whether this attributional tendency toward homogeneity would extend to the perception of the EEC as a region; that is, U.S. businesspersons may view the EEC as being more uniform and monolithic than it actually is. In terms of the EEC, possible attributions about the former Eastern Bloc might include viewing the EEC as a monolithic socioeconomic system that is undifferentiated with respect to readiness to compete in a global market economy. Additional regionwide assumptions might include viewing all EEC managers as inept or dishonest or mistrusting of their Western counterparts. Indeed, viewing the EEC as an economic backwater may fail to recognize the contribution of the Soviet scientific establishment on such high-technology industries as computer software, biotechnology, and agribusiness (Jones & Wiseman, 1994).

There is also substantial debate and confusion concerning the experience of U.S. staff who work and live abroad. Such misrepresentations may obscure an organization's accurate appraisal of the challenges faced by its international employees. This dilemma has been referred to by Dunbar and Katcher (1990) as the *four myths of expatriation,* which are the second of the three psychological constructs. The authors have characterized organizational assumptions concerning expatriation as (a) "our person in Havana" (suggesting that the international reassignment is rarely problematic for staff who had been deemed competent when

viewed in terms of performance in the United States), (b) "the lost employee" (Heenan, 1970; characteristic of the isolated expatriate who has limited contact with domestic management and operations), (c) "the ugly American" (the expatriate employee who is reified for having failed to meet the goals and objectives of the international assignment; this person is typically recalled prior to completion of the posting), and (d) "the cultural relativist" (the idealized multicultural expatriate, capable of dealing with all cultural issues at all times in all settings). As suggested by these expatriate myths, many U.S. parent organizations formulate a basic global assumption concerning the experience of their expatriate personnel. This formulation reflects the need for organizations to characterize the international assignment in a manner that simplifies the process of working internationally, obscures differences in the experiences of the individual, and typically views life outside the United States as being inferior and undesirable.

An additional determinant of international performance of U.S. organizations abroad concerns the failure to adequately comprehend the sociocultural worldviews of the host culture. Research on cultural worldviews (the third psychological construct) is based on an anthropological field study conducted during the past 30 years, concerning proscribed group behaviors and belief systems (Hofstede, 1980; Kluckhohn, 1962). The traditional dimensions of the Kluckhohn model (human nature, person-environment relations, temporal emphasis, personal development, and individual-group relations) have also been considered in the context of organizational behavior. These cultural worldview dimensions have been employed as markers of organizational cultural assumptions. These include perception of the employee (the human nature dimension in the Kluckhohn model), competitive philosophy of the organization (person-environment relations), organizational goals (temporal emphasis), employee performance (personal development), and leader-group relations (individual-group relations). Of concern to the development of organizational relationships in the EEC is how accurately U.S. organizations assess the differences of cultural worldviews in terms of the workplace. Recognition of the role of cultural belief systems in understanding managerial behavior of international operations has been increasing (Doktor, Tung, & Von Glinow, 1991).

It has been suggested that the U.S. practice of exporting leadership and organizational development programs internationally has failed to consider the differing assumptions of group decision making, authority, problem solving, and achievement styles. This may lead to unanticipated consequences for both the expatriate and the host country employee. Put simply, not knowing the belief systems of the host country can in and of itself be a cause of organizational failure internationally.

Concerning the cultural worldviews of the EEC, Bieliauskas (1994) has suggested that many of the recently autonomous Eastern European states are experiencing a crisis of national identity and are redefining their basic assumptions regarding personal rights and responsibilities of the citizenry and leadership. Certain observations can be made about the cultural worldviews of organizations under the Soviet-style state economy, including the distrust and need for control of employees, the submersion of managerial decision making under collectivization, and the establishment of organizational goals that were at once viewed as fatalistic (with quotas and 5-year plans dictated by state agencies) and unrelated to the needs of the employees of the organization. The market-driven organizational worldview of many Western firms is in contrast, if not at odds, with the external, fatalistic, and monolithic structure of Soviet-style organizations. These worldview differences are embedded in the operational and workplace barriers encountered by Western managers who are heading operations in the EEC today.

Characteristics of Intercultural Effectiveness

As reported by Kealey and Ruben (1983), evidence suggests that expatriate attributes of personality, cultural knowledge, and reported intercultural behaviors are predictive of adjustment and performance abroad. As suggested by Hawes and Kealey (1981), self-reported cultural skills and cognitions were found to predict more favorable ratings of intercultural effectiveness by host country cohorts. Their research has underscored the salience of awareness of culture as a factor in working internationally. In addition, their research has supported the notion that intercultural adjustment is mediated by a variety of intrapsychic and behavioral factors.

The implications of prior research indicate that adequate criteria exist by which organizations can select, brief, and train personnel for international relocation. As such, irrespective of the myth of expatriation adopted by the sponsoring organization, training and development efforts can improve the adjustment and effectiveness of staff working abroad. The dimensions of expatriate adjustment need to be considered in terms of the perspective of both expatriate (U.S.) and host (EEC) persons. It has also been determined fairly clearly that personality traits play a role (if not the singularly determinant role) in intercultural adaptation. As proposed by the Landis and Bhagat model of intercultural effectiveness (see Chapter 1, this volume), personality characteristics are an antecedent factor in formation of intercultural behavior. This is certainly the contention of many scholars of cultural immersion and intercultural adjustment. Personality traits such as sociability, complex social cognition, and intrapsychic hardiness have all been discussed as desirable attributes of the culturally skilled individual.

Researching Expatriate Challenge and Performance in the EEC

The original research reported in this chapter examines the perceived operational challenges found in the operations of U.S.-owned companies. In addition, factors of expatriate effectiveness were examined concerning cultural cognitions, behaviors, and personality traits that were perceived as desirable for living and working in the EEC. The respondent survey group consisted of 112 U.S. business leaders responsible for the development and direction of their organization's operations in the EEC. The management group consisted of individuals who had product or project management responsibilities for the region. Participants were identified through Eastern European trade and business councils based in North America. The participants' parent organizations were all for-profit, U.S.-owned companies. Industry representation included multinational telecommunications (4% of the respondent sample), financial services (14% of the sample), business consulting (38%), import-export firms (24%), and manufacturing/consumer products

TABLE 19.1 Country-Specific "Cultural Toughness" Ratings as Reported by U.S. Business Leaders

		Cultural Differences		Governmental Regulatory		Political Stability		Toughness Index	
	N	M	SD	M	SD	M	SD	M	SD
Bulgaria	37	3.25	1.11	3.75	.84	3.50	1.52	10.50	2.92
Czech Republic	52	2.38	.92	2.00	.56	2.54	.56	6.92	1.08
Estonia	57	2.83	.70	2.52	.51	2.02	.82	7.36	1.39
Finland	33	1.71	.46	1.70	.46	1.18	.39	4.61	1.10
Hungary	42	2.22	.43	2.00	.67	1.92	.60	6.14	1.21
Latvia	57	2.98	.76	3.11	.98	2.55	.90	8.64	2.28
Lithuania	42	2.71	.66	2.65	.73	2.43	.88	7.79	2.11
Poland	31	2.77	.84	2.97	.71	2.45	1.12	8.19	1.82
Romania	31	3.32	1.47	3.30	1.28	3.55	1.44	9.97	3.89
Slovakia	39	2.75	.84	3.25	.44	2.50	.51	8.50	1.52
Mean Rating		2.61	.67	2.72	.76	2.90	1.90	7.43	2.14

NOTE: 5 = very challenging, 3 = somewhat challenging, 1 = not very challenging.

companies (21%). Information was also recorded for the countries that U.S. organizations were doing business with, the length of time doing business in the EEC, and the number of countries where regional offices and facilities had been established. The civil war in the former Yugoslav republics resulted in information about this region of the EEC being omitted from the survey.

The vast majority of U.S. organizations had been involved in the EEC for a very brief period; the mean length of time conducting business in the EEC was 4.5 years (SD 2.63). Respondent organizations were found to be active in multiple countries in the EEC; the mean number of countries with which U.S. organizations were active was 4.59 (SD 2.71). The total number of organizations active in each EEC country is reported in Table 19.1. It should be noted that two organizations reported being active in Albania; this information was not reported separately. Nearly half (49.1%) of the sample had not established a regional office in the EEC; the mean number of EEC countries in which regional offices were operating was 2.97 (SD 2.47).

In addition, individual telephone interviews were conducted with 11 area experts and government trade representatives for the EEC countries. These individuals were all on staff with their respective countries' diplomatic consulate or trade association. These structured interviews were based on the same items and scaling used in the questionnaires with the U.S. respondents; as such, the same dimensions were examined and measured equivalently with both sample groups to allow for comparison between the two groups. The interview subjects had spent an average of 10 years living in the United States (mean of 10.54, SD 8.24).

I. Measures

Cultural Toughness Index

Individual country ratings addressing cultural toughness were developed, incorporating three dimensions salient to the EEC (Weiner, 1994). These dimensions were identified as (a) Sociocultural Value Differences, (b) Governmental/Regulatory Controls, and (c) Political Instability/Risk. Ratings were based on a 5-point Likert-type scale, with higher scores reflecting greater cultural toughness/challenge. These ratings were aggregated for each country to provide an overall estimate of the perceived cultural toughness. The means and standard deviations for each country, as well as for the region as a whole, are reported in Table 19.1.

Operational Challenges Index

The Operational Challenges Index (Dunbar, 1988) examined the business-related chal-

TABLE 19.2 Business-Related Problems in the EEC by Country as Reported by U.S. Business Leaders

	Work-Related Cultural Differences		Production Manufacturing Practices		Business Support Practices		Operational Challenge Index	
	Mean	*SD*	*Mean*	*SD*	*Mean*	*SD*	*Mean*	*SD*
Bulgaria	3.85	.42	4.19	.11	4.08	.73	4.01	.41
Czech Republic	3.96	.49	4.23	.21	4.19	.61	4.10	.37
Estonia	3.62	.57	3.93	.52	3.71	.85	3.74	.56
Finland	3.72	.45	4.25	.28	3.95	.60	3.94	.38
Hungary	3.84	.47	4.23	.22	3.94	.73	3.99	.43
Latvia	3.86	.66	4.00	.47	4.02	.81	3.98	.56
Lithuania	3.92	.85	4.15	.39	3.72	.88	3.77	.47
Poland	3.92	.33	4.19	.11	4.49	.38	4.15	.20
Romania	4.22	.33	4.17	.45	4.55	.48	4.40	.36
Slovakia	3.89	.27	3.93	.57	3.39	.57	3.97	.38
Mean Rating	3.92	.64	4.07	.54	4.08	.77	4.00	.57

NOTE: 5 = very challenging, 3 = somewhat challenging, 1 = not very challenging.

lenges to operations in each EEC country. The measure consists of 12 items scored on a 3-point Likert scale, with higher scores indicating greater difficulty in running operations in the given country. The factor scales defined in prior research were employed and yielded three subdimensions of challenge in doing business abroad; (a) Work-Related Cultural Challenges, (b) Production and Manufacturing Challenges, and (c) Business Support Challenges. The summary scores for the Operational Challenges scores are presented in Table 19.2. In addition, comparison group data for the Operational Challenges scores are reported for U.S. staff in Western Europe, Japan, and developing countries; this information is compared to the aggregated EEC ratings from the current study and is presented in Table 19.3.

*Cultural Skill, Awareness,
and Experience*

Intercultural cognitions, experiences, and behaviors thought to be desirable in working in the EEC were examined. Measuring dimensions of cultural skill suggested in the work of Hawes and Kealey (1979) and Tucker (1978), eight items reflecting specific cultural skill and experiences were administered in the questionnaire, as well as in the individual interviews.

*Personality Dimensions
of Expatriate Effectiveness*

The measurement of personality traits attributed to international expatriate success were examined for what has been called the *Big Five dimensions of personality* (Goldberg, 1992). A 5-point semantic differential employing word pairs from the NEO Five Factor Questionnaire was administered in the survey and structured interviews (Costa & McCrae, 1991). The personality dimensions examined included neuroticism (hereafter referred to as *stress tolerance*), social introversion (referred to as *social extroversion*), openness to experience, agreeableness, and conscientiousness. The neuroticism score was reversed so that higher values reflect lower neuroticism ratings and hence higher stress tolerance. The descriptive statistics for the five personality dimensions are reported in Table 19.4.

II. Qualitative Analyses

In addition to the questionnaire data, two open-ended questions were content analyzed: (a) ratings for complexity of products and services provided by U.S. organizations in the EEC and (b) the perceived personal challenges encountered by expatriates in the EEC.

TABLE 19.3 Comparison of Operational Challenges for U.S. Staff by Differences in International
Assignment[a]

	Mean	SD
I. Work-Related Intercultural Challenges:		
Eastern Europe[b]	3.92	.64
Western Europe[c]	3.23	.76
Japan[d]	3.31	.64
Developing states[e]	3.96	1.02
II. Manufacturing/Production Challenges:		
Eastern Europe	4.07	.54
Western Europe	2.72	.78
Japan	3.07	.49
Developing states	4.01	.88
III. Business Support Challenges:		
Eastern Europe	4.08	.77
Western Europe	2.96	.89
Japan	3.40	.90
Developing states	3.71	.56

a. Ratings for each dimension are 5 = more of a problem than in the U.S., 3 = no more of a problem than in the U.S., 1 = Less of a
problem than in the U.S.
b. N = 112 U.S.-based business leaders involved with EEC operations
c. N = 48 U.S. managers based in Western Europe
d. N = 21 U.S. executives based in Japan
e. N = 80 U.S. managers based in developing countries

Complexity of Products and Services

The categories proposed by Gronhaug and
Kvitastein (1992) to characterize international
operations abroad were examined. These four
categories were used as coding dimensions in
content analysis of responses to the open-ended
question "What are the primary areas of opportunity for business development in Eastern
Europe?" The categories and reported frequencies of endorsement were (a) provision and
acquisition of raw materials (20%), (b) manufactured products (36%), (c) business devel-
opment/consultation services (65%), and (d)
high-technology intensive products (42%).
Responses were scored for each of the four
product/service categories by the author and a
university research assistant. The interrater correlation of agreement for the four dimensions
was .78.

Expatriate Personal Challenge

Five categories of expatriate personal challenge were scored for the open-ended question
"What do you think are the primary challenges
that U.S. expatriates experience in living in
Eastern Europe?" The rating dimensions were
based on the categories of expatriate challenges
as defined in structured interviews by Hawes
and Kealey (1979) in their study of the international transfer of Canadian personnel. The categories and response frequencies were as follows: (a) modification of work/professional
roles (47%), (b) managing intercultural relationships (78.6%), (c) personal behavioral and
stress management (65%), (d) managing interpersonal relationships with other expatriates (8.9%), and (e) adjusting to social/environ-
mental challenges (91%). The mean interrater
coefficient of reliability for these five dimensions was .86.

Method

The current study employed survey research
data relying on psychometric ratings, as well as
qualitative data derived from open-ended survey items and the individual interviews. Tabu-
lation of the qualitative data was analyzed by

TABLE 19.4 U.S. Business Leaders and EEC Country Representatives: Scale Means and Standard Deviations for Operational Challenges, Desired Expatriate Cultural Competencies, and Big Five Personality Traits

	Mean	SD	Mean	SD
I. Operational Challenges[a]				
Work-related intercultural differences	3.92	.64	3.27	.41
Production practices	4.07	.54	3.02	.69
Business support practices	4.08	.77	3.57	1.06
Summary score	4.02	.65	3.27	.66
II. Cultural Competencies				
Speaks and understands the primary language of the country	3.33	1.01	3.00	1.00
Lives in host country communities	2.37	1.03	2.60	2.19
Committed to the transfer of technical/business skills to host country persons	3.88	.81	3.63	.92
Knowledgeable about the country (history, religion, geography, politics, economics)	3.37	1.25	3.00	1.09
Demonstrates solid business/technical skills	4.61	.49	4.36	.51
Sensitive to the political climate of the country	4.05	.53	2.09	.94
Has a high tolerance for stress and uncertainty	4.37	1.21	3.09	1.84
Sensitive to the image of Americans in this country	3.54	.97	2.72	2.05
III. Personality Traits				
Stress tolerance (neuroticism)	10.11	1.84	9.50	.53
Social extroversion	9.60	2.44	11.80	1.93
Openness to experience	9.77	1.76	8.20	1.55
Agreeableness	7.34	1.64	9.00	2.58
Conscientiousness	7.90	1.62	8.40	1.43

NOTE: Ratings for each dimension are 5 = more of a problem than in the U.S., 3 = no more of a problem than in the U.S., 1 = Less of a problem than in the U.S.

using content analytic methods. Pearson and Spearman correlations were computed for the cultural toughness ratings and operational challenges dimensions in relationship to the level of activity in the EEC ratings of U.S. organizations. A principal components factor analysis was computed with the scale items measuring intercultural skill. Multivariate analysis of variance (MANOVA) of the data (employing univariate *F*-tests with Scheffe contrasts with each of the independent variables) was computed to examine the relationship of the Big Five dimensions of personality with the intercultural skill dimensions identified in the factor analysis. Results of data analysis based on the survey data individual country scores were computed for the Cultural Toughness dimensions and the three Operational Challenge scales. This information is summarized in Tables 19.1 and 19.3, respectively.

The Operational Challenges dimensions were compared for the U.S. business leaders with the EEC country representatives. In addition, comparison group data are presented with U.S. corporate staff assigned to other international sites (e.g. Western Europe, Japan, and developing states); this is summarized in Table 19.4. The Operational Challenges dimension for the U.S. business leader group was comparable to the U.S. expatriate comparison group data for the Work-Related Intercultural Challenge score. The Operational Challenge scales for Production/Manufacturing and Business Support were substantially higher than those for Western Europe and Japan and equivalent to the factor ratings reported with U.S. staff working in developing countries. Differences in the Operational Challenges scores on the Production/Manufacturing and Business Support dimensions were noted for the U.S. business leaders and the EEC country representatives.

Cultural Toughness and Operational Challenges in the EEC

The dimensions of Cultural Toughness and Operational Challenges were examined in relationship with organizational characteristics of industry type, product complexity, and level of activity in the EEC (the number of countries doing business in and the number of offices opened in the EEC). Results indicated that differences of industry type and product complexity were related to the perceived difficulties in doing business in the EEC. Univariate analysis of variance results were significant for the Operational Challenges score ($F = 10.23$, $p < .001$); financial service operations were reported to be significantly more operationally challenged when compared with the other industry groups. Differences in the Product Complexity scores were significantly related to the Operational Challenges score for provision and acquisition of raw materials ($r =. 21$, $p < .01$) and high-technology businesses ($r = -.24$, $p < .004$). Organizations that were characterized as more involved in the EEC (total number of countries doing business in and number of regional offices operating in) had significantly higher Cultural Toughness scores ($r = .67$, $p < .001$) but did not report greater operational challenges than less active U.S. companies.

Expatriate Challenges in the EEC

The five dimensions of expatriate challenge in living and working in the EEC were examined in relationship to workplace challenges and cultural toughness. Spearman (nonparametric) correlations were computed between the Expatriate Challenges dimensions and the Operationals Challenge and Cultural Toughness indices. Results indicated that expatriate challenge to modify professional/work roles was significantly related to both the Cultural Toughness ($r = .31$, $p < .001$) and Operational Challenges ($r = .22$, $p < .01$) indices; this was also true for reported social/environmental expatriate challenge (Cultural Toughness $r = .32$,

$p < .001$; Operational Challenges $r = .22$, $p < .009$).

Dimensions of Expatriate Skill in the EEC

An orthogonally rotated varimax factor analysis of the eight cultural skill items identified three factors that accounted for 76% of the total variance. The identified factors were assessed according to the scree criteria as set forth by Cattell (1967). Items with a loading of greater than .35 were retained in the analysis, as suggested by Stevens (1992) for analysis of factors with samples of 100 or more subjects. The factors were described as (a) International Business Skill, (b) Intercultural Sensitivity, and (c) Sensitivity to the International Business Partnerships (see Table 19.5).

The relationship of the Cultural Toughness dimension and the Operational Challenges Index with the three factors of cultural skill was examined in a 6×3 factorial MANOVA. A significant multivariate effect was found ($F = 59.33$, $p < .001$). Univariate F-test results were computed for each cultural skill factor. The unique predictors for the Operational Challenge score were the dimensions of International Business Skill ($T = 4.97$, $p < .001$, $\beta = .82$) and International Partnership Sensitivity ($T = 5.50$, $p < .001$, $\beta = .38$). The Cultural Toughness-Political Challenge score was uniquely predicted by the Partnership Sensitivity factor ($T = 2.49$, $p < .02$, $\beta = .39$). The Cultural Toughness-Governmental/Regulatory Challenge score was inversely related to the factor for Partnership Sensitivity ($T = -3.95$, $p < .001$, $\beta = -.55$). The Cultural Toughness-Intercultural Differences score was predicted by all three cultural skill factors: Intercultural Skill ($T = 3.09$, $p < .003$, $\beta = .79$), International Business Skill ($T = -2.98$, $p < .004$, $\beta = .71$), and Partnership Sensitivity ($T = 2.41$, $p < .001$, $\beta = .39$).

The Big Five dimensions of personality were examined in relationship to the three factors of intercultural skill and experience. A 3×5 factorial MANOVA was computed with the intercultural skill factors employed as the dependent variables. A significant multivariate effect was found ($F = 18.52$, $p < .001$). All three of the intercultural skill factors were significantly

TABLE 19.5 Factor Analysis of Desired Expatriate Cultural Competencies and Experiences

	Factor One *International Business Skill*	Factor Two *Intercultural Sensitivity*	Factor Three *Intercultural Partnership Sensitivity*
Speaks and understands the primary language of the country	−.75	.45	
Lives in host country communities	−.41	.72	
Is committed to the transfer of technical/business skills to host country persons			.82
Is knowledgeable about the country (history, religion, geography, politics, economics)		.89	
Demonstrates solid business/technical skills	.79		
Is sensitive to the political climate of the country	.82		
Has a high tolerance for stress and uncertainty	.85		
Is sensitive to the image of Americans in the country	.35		.69
Eigenvalue:	3.16	1.67	1.21
Pct. Variance:	39.5	20.9	15.6

NOTE: Factor loadings ≥ .35 are reported.

related to the Big Five dimensions of personality. Univariate F-tests and adjusted R^2 results are reported in Table 19.6.

Implications for Research and Training

The original research presented above examined the contextual and operational challenges reported by U.S. executives and area experts involved with operations in the EEC. Ratings of the skills, awareness, and personality traits attributed to effectiveness in working in the EEC are reported for U.S. business leaders and EEC country and trade representatives. In response to research on SIT, this study examined the degree of differentiation that U.S. business leaders evidenced in their attitudes about the EEC. The survey results illustrate a consistent if modest variation between countries in the reported cultural toughness and operational challenge encountered. As such, it appears that, through involvement with the EEC, there is some recognition of the diversity of the region, at least regarding issues related to establishing business operations there. Those Eastern European countries characterized as most adherent to the practices of a state-run system, Romania and Bulgaria, were seen as being the most difficult environments in which to successfully do business. By contrast, Finland, a country historically more autonomous than the rest of Soviet-dominated Eastern Europe, was viewed as being the least operationally challenging country on the three Cultural Toughness dimensions and the Operational Challenges Index. Differences by product type and service were noted regarding difficulty of doing business in the EEC. Financial service operations and the acquisition and transfer of raw materials were found to be particularly problematic areas for doing business in the EEC.

By comparison, businesses engaged in high-technology areas reported fewer operational challenges; in effect, more technically complex

TABLE 19.6 MANOVA Results for Intercultural Skill and Big Five Personality Clusters

	F Ratio	Sig.	Adjusted R^2	β	T-Value	Sig.
	18.52	.001				
International Business Skill	30.40	.001	.57			
Stress tolerance (low neuroticism)				.67	8.53	.001
Social extroversion				.68	9.36	.001
Conscientiousness				.49	5.53	.001
Openness to experience				.01	.01	.99
Agreeableness				−.30	−4.31	.19
Intercultural Sensitivity	14.36	.001	.38			
Stress tolerance (low neuroticism)				.49	5.29	.001
Social extroversion				−.05	−.56	.57
Conscientiousness				.53	5.01	.001
Openness to experience				.33	5.52	.001
Agreeableness				−.09	−1.09	.28
International Partnership Sensitivity	7.23	.001	.22			
Stress tolerance (low neuroticism)				−.05	−.49	.62
Social extroversion				.13	1.31	.19
Conscientiousness				.25	2.05	.04
Openness to experience				.58	5.83	.001
Agreeableness				−.04	−.41	.68

businesses and services were less problematic areas in which to do business than other areas, such as business consultation. This finding may reflect the relatively more adept technical human resources available in the EEC vis-à-vis the governmental controls, regulations, and management practices in some of the countries.

Culturally Skilled Behavior as Related to Personality Type

As has been noted, expatriate effectiveness in the EEC was comprised of a combination of cognitive, behavioral, and personality dimensions. Consistent with other research efforts, a multidimensional model of intercultural effectiveness was proposed. Factor results identified three dimensions of effectiveness, the first being related to doing business in the EEC. Intercultural experience and knowledge about the host country was isolated as a second desirable attribute. Finally, U.S. businesspersons indicated that awareness of issues related to U.S.-EEC technology transfer and the political climate of the host culture were a distinct and important factor in effectively working in the EEC. These factors of intercultural effective-

ness appear to be viewed as more desirable because challenges to living and working in the EEC are greater. Also, there was generally satisfactory agreement of the importance of these dimensions of intercultural effectiveness for both U.S. and senior EEC country representatives.

An area in need of further examination concerns the relationship between intercultural skills and the Big Five dimensions of personality. In the research reported here, intercultural skills (e.g. knowing about the history, culture, and language of the country) were related to the traits of Stress Tolerance, Openness to Experience, and Conscientiousness. Effective International Business Skills (e.g., possessing solid technical and work-related skills, being sensitive to the image of Americans abroad) was predicted by higher stress tolerance (lower neuroticism), greater conscientiousness, and social extroversion (the latter being the most highly desired trait as reported for the EEC country representatives). As viewed by U.S. managers and area specialists, it appears that being more effective in the international workplace is not equivalent with being interculturally effective in living abroad, at least with respect to the personality traits related to these two dimensions of effectiveness in living and working abroad. Sensitivity to the development of intercultural business partnerships shares the traits predictive of intercultural sensitivity—namely, an openness to differences and greater conscientiousness. It is also worth note that the items concerning host country language skill and residence in host country communities (vs. expatriate enclaves) loaded on the factor for Intercultural Sensitivity and significantly negatively loaded on the factor for International Business Skill. This finding suggests that living in a host country community and being adept at the host country language were not viewed by American executives as being related to effectiveness in the international workplace. Rather, international business effectiveness was attributed to business competencies, greater stress tolerance, and awareness of international protocol. This, in turn, was predicted by a more socially outgoing and mindful (conscientious) interpersonal style.

These findings hold implication for assessment of the readiness to work and live in the EEC. As evidenced by the work of Kealey and others, however, self-report or opinions of other persons from the parent company may not accurately reflect intercultural effectiveness as viewed by the host country person (as well as that of third-country national staff). The study presented here illustrates how U.S. personnel view effective international and intercultural behavior. It is quite another thing to believe that the noted attributes of international business effectiveness would be appraised the same by cohorts from the EEC.

Implications for Personnel Selection and Orientation

Individuals who evidence personality characteristics of stress tolerance, social extroversion, and openness to experience will be more successful in the international assignment. Equally, the dimensions of cultural knowledge and skill as suggested by Kealey and others were thought to positively contribute to intercultural effectiveness in working in the EEC. As has been discussed by Kealey (Chapter 5, this volume), evidence suggests that personality traits and sociocultural knowledge contribute to both the adjustment and effectiveness of North American personnel in working interna-

tionally. In terms of the findings presented in this chapter, there is reasonable agreement as to the desirability of a social style that is open to new experiences, socially amiable and outgoing, and that demonstrates a tolerance for stress and ambiguity. U.S. staff living and working in the EEC certainly face a variety of cultural, operational, and governmental barriers. As such, there is a good match of the selection criteria set forth by Kealey and his colleagues; there is also general agreement on this point between U.S. businesspersons and the EEC country representatives.

Many human resources professionals acknowledge a surprisingly limited number of qualified candidates for many international assignments (Russell, 1978), even when the selection criteria noted above are not considered. The reality faced by many cross-cultural training programs is that, often, less than ideal candidates are selected for the expatriate assignment (Black & Porter, 1991). When considered in the context of the Landis and Bhagat model, it is likely that U.S. organizations will need to devote as much, if not more, time to the behavioral rehearsal (expatriate orientation and training) as to the selection of staff (based on personality and skill dimensions) to work in the EEC.

Results of the study described here underline the need for organizations to effectively orient, train, and monitor the performance of expatriates in the EEC. The EEC community poses a variety of challenges related to operational practices and leadership behavior that are distinct from those of Western Europe. Even experienced international managers may be unaccustomed to working with a workforce as technically competent on the one hand and as unaccustomed on the other to a quality-driven and team-oriented approach to organizational performance as that found in many regions of the EEC. These challenges will likely be documented in the international training and organizational development literature in the future.

One issue of critical importance to work life in the EEC, however, cannot be as easily deferred to later times—namely, the need to resolve conflict within and between current geopolitical communities. Like it or not, if Western organizations intend to develop meaningful and profitable relationships with the EEC, they must be prepared to respond to the quickly changing social differences of the EEC as related to political, national, and ethnic tension and animosity.

Conflict Mediation in the EEC

An issue of the utmost importance to cross-cultural consultation in the EEC concerns the need to address ethnic and national conflict throughout the EEC. As is grimly demonstrated by the tragedy of Bosnia-Herzegovina, no single issue is of greater importance in the EEC. The social, economic, and historical sources of intergroup conflict in the EEC are numerous. These include the historical ethnic animosities found throughout the region, the already mentioned themes of institutional paranoia, and the experience of conflict for power that is occurring between the former leadership of the Soviet-dominated regimes and the various reform groups (including both pro-Western and nationalist groups). Independent of these factors is the shroud of anti-Semitism, which is an issue of current concern to many in the EEC. As the writer Laszlo Vegel (1993) states, "The Jewish question—I experience it from day to day— is the crystallization point of the anti-minority movement" (p. 13). As is all too evident to even the casual student of European history, the transition from a nationalist to a fascist social ideology is very much part of the collective consciousness of the region. As suggested by Vegel, anti-Semitism in the region may well serve as a bellwether of the xenophobia and opposition to ethnic and national minority populations broadly. When put into the context of applied psychological practice, the "minority problem" poses a challenge with respect to framing any intervention to group conflict. Although SIT may well contribute substantially to the understanding of the formation of natural out-group biases, any serious understanding of the dilemma of group relations in the contemporary EEC must also hearken back to the notion of group-endorsed social pathology as suggested by the work of Adorno, Frenkel-Brunswik, Levinson, and Sanford (1950) in their study of fascism and the authoritarian personality.

The implications for cross-cultural interventions in this regard are numerous. As suggested by Tzeng and Jackson (1994) social group conflict can be characterized by three theoretical models of group relations: (a) social contact theory (SCT), (b) social identity theory (SIT), and (c) realistic group conflict theory (RGC). In terms of the U.S.-EEC partnership, the historical relationship since World War II has been one driven by realistic group conflict (the geopolitical conflict of East and West ideologies), whereas the more recent and desirable experience is predicated on a gradual increase in social contact (particularly in the area of international business), as well as the development of mutual goals and objectives (the alleviation of realistic conflict needs through shared mutual needs).

In this new relationship, the redefining of ingroup versus out-group is inherent to the fostering of an interdependent relationship. Conversely, the relationship between the EEC states is significantly mediated by SIT, as is evidenced by the separation of the Czech and Slovak states and the carnage of the former Yugoslav region. Out-group bias is additionally mediated by attitudes reflecting psychological well-being (Dunbar, 1994a). Increasing evidence suggests that out-group bias is a product of social attributions and experience (e.g., SCT, SIT) and personality characteristics (e.g., openness to experience, authoritarianism, personality traits of prejudiced beliefs and cognitions). To appreciate the psychological dynamics of intercultural conflict in the EEC, one could simply turn the identified criteria of expatriate effectiveness on its head; that is, social avoidance, restricted social cognition, and a lack of emotional engagement are some of the belief systems at work in the ethnic conflict being played out in regions of the EEC.

Conflict management consultation is directly applicable to organizations throughout the EEC, as well. Areas of attention include training in diplomatic protocol, team building with multinational groups, and intergroup relations training for multiethnic organizations. A unique population in the EEC that will require provision of psychological consultation is the refugee groups from the former Yugoslav states in other regions of the EEC. The unique stressors associated with this population most notably concern the remediation of trauma secondary to the civil conflict of the Bosnia debacle (Marsella, Bornemann, Ekbad, & Orley, 1994). To consider conflict management in terms of the Landis and Bhagat model, training and development programs in the EEC need to address affective and cognitive dimensions of negative out-group attribution on the one hand, and to establish a mechanism of social support and reinforcement on the other hand to endorse the development of new behaviors that are inclusive rather than exclusive, collaborative rather than combative.

It has often been said that, to sound authoritative in organizational climate research, it should always be reported that employees are dissatisfied with their compensation and that communication should improve. One cannot go wrong by suggesting that training in the EEC needs to address conflict resolution. In my opinion, corporate training efforts to mediate the ethnic, national, and culture-based animosities between historically intact groups runs the risk of exacerbating the problem it serves to alleviate. As has been demonstrated by other organizational development specialists, team-building efforts with non-Western work groups can easily increase conflict and illwill, rather than resolve it (Bourgeois & Boltvinik, 1981).

Indeed, at this writing, Eastern Europe is the site of one of the bloodiest interethnic conflicts of the century: the warfare in the former Yugoslav republics. The tragedy of Bosnia-Herzegovina clearly underscores the power of ethnic and cultural issues in the region. With respect to the topic of training and development activities, however, little of substance can be gained directly in responding to armed civil conflict. I propose that attainable training and development goals be pursued, irrespective of how appealing it may be to attempt to provide large-scale, systematic change through organizational intervention programs. A great deal needs to be done with respect to developing organizational structures, creating team-oriented leadership behaviors, and establishing working intercultural relationships. Intercultural trainers must choose wisely where to focus their efforts and resources if they are to contribute meaningfully to the forging of a healthy relationship between the United States and the EEC.

References

Adorno, T., Frenkel-Brunswik, E., Levinson, D. J., & Sanford, R. N. (1950). *The authoritarian personality.* New York: Wiley Science.

Anderson, E., & Coughlan, A. (1985). International market entry and expansion via independent integrated channels of distribution. *Journal of Marketing, 51,* 51-77.

Bieliauskas, V. J. (1994, August). *International consultation: The quest for freedom and identity in Eastern Europe.* Invited address, 102nd Annual Convention of the American Psychological Association, Los Angeles.

Black, J. S., & Porter, L. W. (1991). Managerial behaviors and job performance: A successful manager in Los Angeles may not succeed in Hong Kong. *Journal of International Business Studies, 22*(1), 99-113.

Bourgeois, L. J., & Boltvinik, M. (1981). OD in cross-cultural settings: Latin America. *California Management Review, 23*(3), 75-81.

Cattell, R. B. (1967). The scree test for the number of factors. *Multivariate Behavioral Research, 1,* 245-276.

Champanis, A. (1974). National and cultural variables in ergonomics. *Ergonomics, 17*(2), 153-175.

Costa, P. T., & McCrae, R. P. (1991). *Revised NEO Personality Inventory and NEO Five-Factor Inventory: Professional manual.* Odessa: Psychological Assessment Resources.

Dela Torre, J. (1975). Product life-cycle as a determinant of global marketing strategies. *Atlanta Economic Review, 25*(5), 9-14.

Dela Torre, J., & Neckar, D. H. (1988). Forecasting political risks for international operations. *International Journal of Forecasting, 4*(2), 221-241.

Doktor, R. H., & Lie, J. (1991). A systems theoretic perspective upon international organizational behavior: Some preliminary observations and hypotheses. *Management International Review, 31,* 125-133.

Doktor, R. H., Tung, R., & Von Glinow, M. A. (1991). Future directions for management theory development. *Academy of Management Review, 16*(2), 362-365.

Dunbar, E. (1988). *Adjustment of U.S. expatriate staff: A survey report.* Unpublished doctoral dissertation, Columbia University.

Dunbar, E. (1994a, August). *Experiencing and coping with social group based conflict.* Paper presented at the 102nd Annual Convention of the

American Psychological Association, Los Angeles.

Dunbar, E. (1994b). The German executive in the U.S. work and social environment: Exploring role demands. *International Journal of Intercultural Relations, 18*(3), 277-291.

Dunbar, E., & Ehrlich, M. (1985). *Career pathing practices of U.S. multinational organizations* (Technical report, Columbia University Project on International Human Resources). New York: Columbia University.

Dunbar, E., & Katcher, A. (1990). International relocation training: Exploring the myths of expatriation. *Training and Development Journal, 44*(9), 45-48.

Egelhoff, W. (1982). Strategy and structure in multinational corporations: An information processing approach. *Administrative Sciences Quarterly, 27,* 435-458.

Enyedi, G. (1994). Metropolitan integration in Europe. *Hungarian Quarterly, 35,* 100-105.

Garber, J., & Seligman, M. (Eds.). (1980). *Human helplessness: Theory and application.* San Diego: Academic Press.

Goldberg, L. R. (1992). The development of markers of the big-five factor structure. *Psychological Assessment, 4,* 26-42.

Gronhaug, K., & Kvitastein, O. (1992). Distribution involvement in international strategic business units. *International Business Review, 2*(1), 1-15.

Hawes, F., & Kealey, D. (1979). *Canadians in development: An empirical study of adaptation and effectiveness in the overseas assignment.* Ottawa: Canadian International Development Agency.

Hawes, F., & Kealey, D. (1981). An empirical study of Canadian technical assistance. *International Journal of Intercultural Relations, 5,* 239-258.

Heenan, D. (1970, May-June). The corporate expatriate: Assignment to ambiguity. *Columbia Journal of World Business,* pp. 49-54.

Hofstede, G. (1980). Motivation, leadership, and organization: Do American theories apply? *Organizational Dynamics, 3,* 27-33.

Jones, A., & Wiesman, R. (1994). U.S. trade figures with the Baltic. *U.S.-Baltic Chamber of Commerce Quarterly, 1*(1), 2-3.

Kanter, R. M. (1991, May-June). Transcending business boundaries: 12,000 world managers view change. *Harvard Business Review,* pp. 151-164.

Karvalics, A. (1993). How much is a Hungarian manager worth? *Business and Economy in Hungary, 5,* 25, 34-38.

Kealey, D., & Ruben, B. (1983). Cross-cultural personnel selection criteria, issues, and methods. In D. Landis & R. Brislin (Eds.), *Handbook of intercultural training: Vol. 1. Issues in theory and design* (pp. 155-175). Elmsford, NY: Pergamon.

Kluckhohn, C. (1962). Universal categories of culture. In S. Tax (Ed.), *Anthropology today.* Chicago: University of Chicago Press.

Korn-Ferry International. (1981). *The repatriation of the American international executive.* New York: Author.

Marsella, A., Bornemann, T., Ekbad, S., & Orley, J. (1994). *Amidst peril and pain: The mental health and well-being of the world refugees.* Washington, DC: American Psychological Association.

Mendenhall, M., & Oddou, G. (1985). The dimensions of expatriate acculturation: A review. *Academy of Management Review, 10,* 39-47.

Meshkati, N. (1989). *Technology transfer of large-scale technological systems to the Third World: An analysis and agenda for research.* Invited paper for the World Bank Program in Risk Management, the World Bank and Swedish Rescue Services Board, Karlstad, Sweden.

Nagy, A. (1993). Plus ca change: Changes in establishment attitudes under socialism. *Hungarian Quarterly, 34,* 77-92.

Ridley, C. (1984). Clinical treatment of the nondisclosing black client. *American Psychologist, 39,* 1234-1244.

Rigby, T. H. (1972). Totalitarianism and change in communist systems. *Comparative Politics, 4*(3), 433-453.

Russell, P. (1978). *Dimensions of overseas success in industry.* Unpublished doctoral dissertation, Colorado State University, Ft. Collins.

Schweiger, D. M., Csiszar, E. N., & Napier, N. K. (1993). Implementing international mergers and acquisitions. *Human Resource Planning, 16*(1), 53-70.

Seligman, M. (1975). *Helplessness: On depression, development, and death.* New York: Freeman.

Stephens, G. K., & Black, J. S. (1991). The impact of spouse's career orientation on managers during international transfers. *Journal of International Business Studies, 28*(4), 417-428.

Stevens, J. (1992). *Applied multivariate statistics for the social sciences* (2nd ed.). Hillsdale, NJ: Lawrence Erlbaum.

Tajfel, H. (1982). Social psychology of intergroup relations. *Annual Review of Psychology, 33,* 1-39.

Tajfel, H., & Turner, J. C. (1979). An integrative theory of intergroup conflict. In W. G. Austin & S. Worchel (Eds.), *The social psychology of intergroup relations* (pp. 33-48). Pacific Grove, CA.: Brooks/Cole.

Tucker, M. (1978). *The measurement and prediction of overseas adjustment in the Navy* (U.S. Navy contract number N00600-73-D-0780). Denver, CO: Center for Research and Education.

Tzeng, O. C. S., & Jackson, J. W. (1994). Effects of contact, conflict, and social identity on inter-ethnic group hostilities. *International Journal of Intercultural Relations, 18*(2), 259-276.

VanderHorst, N. (1994, May). *Achieving styles in Eastern Europe: A case study of Bulgaria.* Paper presented at the Annual Convention of the Western Psychological Association, Kona, HI.

Vegel, L. (1993). Balkan testament. *Hungarian Quarterly, 34,* 3-21.

Weiner, R. (1994). *Change in Eastern Europe.* New York: Praeger.

20

Russia and the West
Intercultural Relations

WALTER G. STEPHAN

MARINA ABALAKINA-PAAP

TRYING to paint a portrait of Russia for Western readers is a daunting task. All societies are constantly evolving and, of necessity, researchers in intercultural relations can only capture an instant in this process of change. But when this process has been accelerated by the cyclotron of revolution, as is the case with Russia, then one is left presenting a single frame from a movie on fast forward.

Our reaction to this dilemma is not to attempt the impossible task of presenting an up-to-the-second portrait of Russia, but rather to try to dig deeper for the essential nature of Russian national character. We seek to offer readers a glimpse of those enduring aspects of Russian character that lie behind and shape the changes that are taking place and that are most likely to remain after these changes run their course.

Despite our attempt to present the enduring characteristics of Russians, we cannot ignore the current realities of the Russian social system. All systems of government rely on a social contract between the rulers and the ruled. In the 1980s, the Soviet government failed to live up to its end of the contract; it could no longer fulfil the needs of the governed for security and the basic requisites of life in modern societies. The fall of the Soviet system left many people in Russia disillusioned and alienated—stripped of the system of beliefs and norms that had guided their public, and to some extent their private, lives for decades. Insecure about their future and their place in the world, Russians approach contacts with the West with a deep ambivalence. They have a great pride in Russian history and culture, coupled with a deep concern over the implications of their economic and political instability. This ambivalent aspect of current relations with the West may have its roots in a more pervasive ambivalence noted by Western observers of Russian character.

In attempting to present a portrait of Russian character, we have been greatly hampered by the limited number of studies on this subject. Until the 1990s, few Westerners were allowed into the Soviet Union to conduct comparative empirical investigations. The Soviet Union itself did not promote the study of national character, so Soviet investigators conducted few studies. Soviet researchers were particularly discouraged from studying anything that might reflect negatively on the Soviet Union, such as alcoholism, divorce, prostitution, and crime (Brief & Collins, 1994). Thus, the available evidence was both meager and biased.

Another reason for the lack of empirical studies of Russian character is that many Russians believe their national character is too complex, too spiritual, too sensitive, and too instinctive for any empirical investigation to capture or for any non-Russian to understand. They are skeptical of any attempt to describe and explain with logic and reason all the twists and turns of their nature. As the famous Russian poet of the 19th century, Tyutchev, said:

> *With the mind alone Russia cannot be*
> *understood,*
> *No ordinary yardstick spans her greatness;*
> *She stands alone, unique—*
> *In Russia one can only believe.*

In this chapter, we present the accumulated wisdom of astute observers of Russia through the years, along with the limited information that can be gleaned from empirical studies of Russia. Specifically, we first present a portrait of Russian national character as seen by foreigners whose observations are not empirically based. Then, we sketch a parallel portrait as it emerges from the limited empirical studies of foreigners' perceptions of Russia. Next, we introduce information from studies done in Russia, as a corrective to the previous two portraits. We also speculate about differences between Russia and the West on a variety of dimensions frequently used to compare cultures. Along the way, we discuss the implications for intercultural relations of the discrepancies between foreigners' views of Russians and Russians' views of themselves.

Intergroup Perceptions

From the perspective of intercultural relations, there are two basic reasons for trying to understand intergroup perceptions and the realities behind them. First, the way one cultural group views another determines the expectations concerning the group, the initial behavioral reactions to the group, and the attributions most likely to be used to explain the behavior of members of the other culture. Second, to the degree that the in-group's view of the out-group does not match the out-group's views of itself, misunderstandings and conflicts are likely to arise.

Perceptions of Russians

Russia as Seen by Western Observers

"It is a task of extraordinary importance to let go of ideological and psychological prejudices and stereotypes. We must work out realistic perceptions of one another. This is especially important for the world's two greatest nuclear superpowers" (Frank & Melville, 1989, p. 199).

Writing of the Russian peasantry before the Communist revolution, Dicks (1952, 1990a, 1990b) argued they were characterized by a deep ambivalence seen in mood swings that oscillated from a zest for life, vitality, and spontaneity to deep melancholy, suspicion, and hostility. Their ambivalence also appeared in their outward civility and inward disobedience. They vacillated between feeling they were worthless and feeling they were superior to the rest of humankind. The ambivalence also appeared in attitudes toward authority, which were a volatile mixture of submissive love and deep resentment. Russian peasants apparently did not practice the Socratic dictum of moderation in all things.

Relying on a variety of sources, Mead (1951) portrayed Russians as an uncontrolled, even impulsive, group of people. She concluded that the distinctions between the individual and the group are less finely drawn in Russia than in the West. She also argued that Russians place a great emphasis on equality. Here is her succinct portrait of the traditional Russian character.

Traditional Russian character structure . . . developed individuals prone to extreme swings in mood from exhilaration to depression, hating confinement and authority, and yet feeling that strong external authority was necessary to keep their own violent impulses in check. In this traditional character, thought and action were so interchangeable that there was a tendency for all effort to dissipate itself in talk or in symbolic behavior. While there was a strong emphasis on the need for certain kinds of control—by government, by parents and teachers—this control was seen as imposed from without; lacking it, the individual would revert to an original impulsive and uncontrolled state. Those forms of behavior which involve self-control rather than endurance, measurement rather than unstinted giving or taking, or calculation rather than immediate response to a situation were extremely undeveloped. The distinctions between the individual and the group and between the self and others were less emphasized than in the West, while the organization of the *mir,* the large extended families, and religious and social rituals stressed confession and complete revelation of self to others and the merging of the individual in the group. (p. 26)

Clyde Kluckhohn (1961), another well-known American anthropologist, wrote that Russians

[show] a great need for intensive face-to-face relationships with others. . . . They value people in terms of what they are rather than in terms of what they have done. . . . Russians are expressive and emotionally alive. . . . They accept the need for impulse control but are nevertheless rather prone to excessive indulgence. . . . They are less [persistent] than Americans and more acceptant of the passive sides of their nature. . . . Russians demand and expect . . . loyalty, respect, and sincerity from their group. . . . In spite of the passion of Russians for close social interaction, they exhibit considerable mistrust of others. . . . The Russians value identification with and participation in the collectivity more than Americans. (pp. 614-615)

Several decades later, Peabody (1985), in summarizing the work of a variety of investiga-

tors, concluded that Russians depend strongly on the group to provide emotional support and moral guidance. They also have a tendency to express their impulses, rather than control them. To Peabody, the Russians represent the antithesis of the Protestant ethic: They display little concern with achievement, are low on impulse control, are intensely personal in relationships, and are more oriented toward the group than the individual.

As difficult as it is to form a coherent image of the traits comprising Russian national character, it is even more difficult to form an impression of their interpersonal style. Russians have a reputation in the West for hardiness and stoicism; they present themselves in public as indifferent, pushy, and discourteous; and they betray little emotion (Gannon, 1994). Russians may bump into or push people without apology, and they speak directly, often bluntly (Miller, 1960). Yet, they value establishing close interpersonal relationships to a much greater degree than in most parts of the Western world. And, in established interpersonal relationships, they are warm, generous, spontaneous, and emotional.

Many Western observers have emphasized the enormous importance that friends and friendship have for Russians (Bialer, 1985; Richmond, 1992; Smith, 1976, 1990). Russians use more gradations of closeness when they refer to their personal relationships than most Westerners do. For example, a person whom Americans would without hesitation refer to as a friend might be referred to by a Russian as a *priyatel*—someone closer than a simple acquaintance, but still not as close as a friend. Friends are people one can confide in and from whom one can expect complete understanding and support. According to Smith (1976),

Within the trusted circle, there is an intensity in Russian relationships that Westerners find both exhilarating and exhausting. When they finally open up, Russians are looking for a soul-brother not a mere conversational partner. They want someone to whom they can pour out their hearts, share their miseries, tell about family problems or difficulties with a lover or a mistress, to ease the pain of life or to indulge in endless philosophical windmill tilting. (p. 147)

Russians prefer to have a small number of friends with whom they can be completely open and sincere. From a conversation *po dusham* ("soul to soul"), Russians derive the greatest joys and relief in their lives.

How can the paradox of being cold and impolite on the one hand and extremely warm and emotional on the other hand be explained? It appears that a much greater distinction exists between the public and private spheres of life in Russia than in the West. Hence, Russians seem far colder in public than most Westerners but seem much warmer in private than most Westerners. The distinction between the public and private spheres is important for interpersonal relations, but also for other behaviors, as will become clear as our discussion proceeds. To students of intercultural relations, the sharp distinction between how people are treated in the private versus the public spheres is reminiscent of the idea that collectivistic cultures make greater distinctions between the in-group (usually the family) and the out-group than individualistic cultures (Triandis, 1990).

It is important to underscore the impressionistic nature of these observations by Westerners. Even the most astute observers have had only a limited exposure to Russian culture and necessarily generalize from a narrow base of experience. In addition, their observations are subject to all of the implicit and explicit biases created by their own national backgrounds and personal experiences. Another problem is the complexity of the culture they are attempting to portray. Russia covers a vast geographical area and is home to more than 100 nationality groups, in addition to the dominant Slavic culture (the group to which much of the following analysis probably applies best). There are rural-urban differences, and despite all attempts by the Communists, stratification by social classes (social stratification related to power, privilege, and access to resources) existed during the Communist era and has become even more significant in the present. The richness and complexity of Russian culture is rarely adequately portrayed by foreign observers.

The View of Russia That Emerges From Empirical Research

A Gallup poll conducted in the United States during World War II (known as the Great Patriotic War in Russia) found that the adjectives most frequently chosen by Americans to describe Russians were hardworking, brave, radical, ordinary, and progressive (see Table 20.1; Gallup, 1982, cited in Yatani & Bramel, 1989). After the war, Buchanan and Cantril (1953) found that Americans saw Russians as cruel, hardworking, domineering, and backward. This survey found a remarkably high degree of consensus among the other seven sampled Western countries that Russians possessed these characteristics. Three decades later, Peabody (1985) examined the stereotypes of Russians held by students from seven European countries. He found that Russians were perceived to be serious, hardworking, firm, intelligent, thrifty, persistent, cautious, inflexible, passive, and self-confident. In Peabody's study, the strong consensus among these European respondents was that the Russians were high on impulse control and moderately assertive. Interestingly, these two traits contrast strongly with the traditional, more impressionistically derived views of Russians presented earlier. Peabody believes that the perceptions of Russians as controlling their impulses and as being assertive are inaccurate. He argues that these perceptions are a product of low levels of contact with Russians. He also suggests that his respondents may have been unduly influenced by official views of the Russian people made available to the Western media. More recently, Stephan et al. (1993) asked U.S. students to rate Russians on 38 traits. The authors found that Russians were perceived as disciplined, hardworking, obedient, serious, strong, proud, orderly, conservative, competitive, emotional, and patriotic.

Although it is difficult to summarize across these studies, it is clear that Westerners' views of Russians have fluctuated over time and reflect Russia's stance toward the West at the time of the surveys. Hardworking is the only trait that occurs in all four studies; the *serious* trait appears twice; and the idea of conservativeness (cautious) also appears twice. Contradictory traits occur in several surveys (conservative/progressive, emotional/emotionally controlled). The variability of the results probably reflects the lack of information concerning Russians possessed by the respondents to these surveys.

These empirical studies are subject to all of the limitations that characterize most cross-cultural research. The samples used in most of these studies were not representative or comparable, the instruments employed suffer from

TABLE 20.1 Americans' Stereotypes of Russians

Gallup (1941)	Buchanan & Cantril (1953)	Peabody (1985)	Stephan et al. (1993)
hardworking	cruel	serious	disciplined
brave	hardworking	hardworking	hardworking
radical	domineering	firm	obedient
ordinary	progressive	intelligent	serious
progressive	backward	thrifty	strong
		persistent	proud
		cautious	orderly
		inflexible	conservative
		passive	competitive
		self-confident	emotional

equivalence problems, the testing conditions were not the same, and the data were gathered at different points in time. Our confidence in the results increases in those instances where they are replicated across studies, but so few comparable studies have been done that we have reason to question even the replicated findings that do occur (e.g., hardworking). With these reservations in mind, it does appear that views of Russians were the most negative during the Cold War period and became less negative as the Cold War began to thaw. This conclusion is substantiated by surveys of attitudes toward Russia.

Americans' Attitudes Toward Russia

During the first half of the 20th century, attitudes toward Russia were largely negative in Europe and the United States (with the exception of World War II). The Europeans looked down on the Russians, and most Americans were virulently anti-Communist.

Opinion polls taken before World War II indicate that, in the United States, Russia was one of the world's least preferred countries (Walsh, 1944). For instance, in a 1937 Gallup poll of Americans, Russia ranked last when they were asked which European country they liked best. Only 1% of Americans said they liked Russia best. In 1939, a comparable survey revealed that only 12% of British respondents said they liked Russia best (Gallup, 1941, cited in Yatani & Bramel, 1989). The vast majority of Americans in the early surveys considered communism to be the single greatest threat to their way

of life. Until 1939, they even preferred fascism to communism (Yatani & Bramel, 1989).

Although views toward Russia during World War II clearly softened, anti-Communist and anti-Russian sentiment increased markedly after the war. In 1954, a National Opinion Research Center poll indicated that over 90% of Americans held negative attitudes toward the Soviet Union. Opinions in this survey, which was conducted yearly thereafter, gradually became more positive until 1974, then declined until 1980, but rose again in the mid-1980s (Yatani & Bramel, 1989; see also Nincic, 1985; Smith, 1983). One study done in the early 1980s indicated that Americans viewed the Soviet Union as a Nazi-style totalitarian regime, perceived the Soviet leaders as fanatics or cynics, and because of the long history of conflicts between the two countries, dehumanized the Soviet people and devalued their experiences, aspirations, thoughts, and fears (Bialer, 1985).

Public opinion toward Russia became increasingly positive during the Gorbachev era (1985-1990) because Russia was no longer perceived by Westerners as a major threat to world peace. In 1989, a national survey revealed that two thirds of Americans believed that, by the year 2000, the United States and Russia would be living together peacefully (Holsti, 1991).

At least until well into the 21st century, Westerners are likely to bring to their relationships with Russians the burden of the hostile relations between Russia and the West that prevailed during nearly all of the 20th century. The extremely negative attitudes and feelings of suspicion and distrust that existed during much of the 20th century are likely to carry over to future relations with Russians as a set of largely unacknowledged negative feelings and assumptions. It may have been only a Cold War that was fought with the Russians, but it is likely to continue to create a chilly climate for years to come.

Empirical Studies of Russian Character

Cross-national studies of personality traits are few in number and limited in scope, but those that exist offer some interesting glimpses into Russian character. Inkeles (1968) compared a sample of Russian immigrants with an American sample. The researcher found that the Russians have a higher need for affiliation and are more dependent on others and the group for emotional support but are lower on needs for approval and autonomy than Americans. The Russians are more emotionally expressive, more passive, and more pessimistic than the Americans. In addition, they are less concerned with individual achievement than the Americans.

Mikheyev (1987) proposed that there is a high level of suspiciousness in the Russian character that is directed toward one another, as well as foreigners. He cites as support a survey he conducted indicating that, in a sample of former Soviet citizens, 62% believed people are basically evil, whereas only 6% of Americans believed this. He argued that life in Russia is seen as a constant struggle for survival where strength, endurance, and a capacity to tolerate suffering are valued traits. Because other people are seen as greedy, selfish, and cruel, one has to be constantly on guard in relations with others, except for one's family and friends.

The results of these studies and others using immigrant samples may have been influenced by the types of respondents used. Immigrants are a select group, and their experiences after they leave the Soviet Union may affect their perceptions. Nevertheless, the difference in general outlook between Americans and Russians in these studies is noteworthy.

A study comparing citizens of Russia and England on Eysenck's measures of personality found that Russian women were lower on extraversion than British women, whereas Russian men were higher on neuroticism than British men (Hanin, Eysenck, Eysenck, & Barrett, 1991). In another study, Russians and Americans were compared by using the Comrey Personality Scales (Brief & Comrey, 1993). This study found that Russians were less trusting, less energetic (some items here concern motivation to work), less empathic (generous and helpful), and less emotionally stable (more depressed and pessimistic) than Americans. Consistent with Bronfenbrenner's (1970) research on obedience, Russian males were found to be more conforming and orderly than American males, although no cross-national differences were found for females. American males scored higher on masculinity than Russian males, but no differences were found for females.

An extensive set of cross-national studies has been conducted comparing Russians and Americans on authoritarianism (McFarland, Ageyev, & Abalakina-Paap, 1992; McFarland, Ageyev, Abalakina-Paap, & Djintcharadze, 1993). These studies have found a consistent and, to many Westerners, surprising result: Russians are less authoritarian than Americans. The authors' interpretation of this finding is that the Western belief that Russians are authoritarian is based on the totalitarianism of the Communist system of government in the former Soviet Union. The authors believe that Westerners make the mistake of equating Russian character with the Soviet political system and assume the Russian people are as authoritarian as their political system. In a more recent study, these investigators found that Russian students thought their parents and friends expected lower levels of authoritarianism from them than did American students' parents and friends (McFarland, Ageyev, Abalakina-Paap, & Djintcharadze, 1993). Thus, low levels of Russian authoritarianism may be partially a result of greater conformity to the wishes of parents and friends who prefer low authoritarianism.

One of these investigators (Ageyev, 1993) also argues that Russian culture is actually more tolerant of deviance and more forgiving than American culture. During the Soviet era, Russians conformed to conventional norms when in public, but they did so less in private, where they were known for their irony, sarcasm, and wit aimed at those in authority. Ageyev argues that these private anti-authoritarian attitudes are a type of self-protective reaction to totalitarianism and that they are consistent with the findings from the personality measures of authoritarianism.

These investigations have also presented evidence indicating that Russians have less experience with the types of child-rearing practices thought to lead to authoritarianism than do Americans (McFarland, Ageyev, & Djintcharadze, 1993). Soviet child-rearing practices did not reflect the authoritarianism of the state. Although Bronfenbrenner (1970) presented evidence that official policy in the former Soviet Union was to instill obedience and self-discipline in children, the techniques used to do this were generally not punitive ones. He found that child-rearing manuals advocated the use of reasoned persuasion and positive encouragement, rather than physical punishment. Reprimands and deprivation of privileges or withdrawal of love were considered to be permissible, however. Bronfenbrenner (1970) also reported the results of several studies indicating that Russian children at the time were more obedient than American children. Consistent with Bronfenbrenner's thesis, McFarland, Ageyev, and Abalakina-Paap (1993) found that Russian child-rearing practices were less punitive than those of Americans.

Additional evidence of Russian anti-authoritarian attitudes comes from a study by Hamilton, Sanders, and McKearney (1995). In this study, a lower percentage of Russians than Americans said they would obey a superior officers' command to shoot civilians suspected of aiding the enemy during wartime. The percentage of Russians who said they would obey this order was 21%; the comparable percentage from a 1976 study done in the United States was 31%.

Another set of intriguing findings from McFarland, Ageyev, and Abalakina-Paap indicated that, with regard to the distribution of resources, Russians preferred equity (distribution based on merit) more than Americans did and that they preferred equality (equal distribution regardless of merit) less than Americans did (McFarland et al., 1992). The authors attribute these differences to growing disenchantment with the official norms for the distribution of resources prevailing during the Communist era that were based on need ("From each according to his ability to each according to his need").

Data from these empirical studies of Russian national character are limited in breadth and depth, but to the extent that they are valid, they suggest some problems are likely to arise during intercultural relations. First, Westerners appear to assume that Russians are highly authoritarian and this is not the case. Second,

Americans and other Westerners are unlikely to appreciate the degree to which Russians are collectivistic and retain communal feelings for the group. On the one hand, the impersonality with which Westerners are likely to be treated in public and the mistrust they may be subjected to may surprise and dismay them. On the other hand, the warmth and trust they will receive if they can penetrate the reserves of this public impersonality may be equally surprising to Westerners.

Russian Views of Russians

Official Views of Russian Character During the Communist Period

During the Communist period in Russia, party ideologues created an image of the ideal Soviet citizen. As described in official documents, Soviet citizens were supposed to put the interests of the state above their own. They were expected to be patriotic, be proud, struggle against imperialism, support their families, respect work, be honest and friendly, observe the laws, and take an active role in the life of the country and the collective (Dicks, 1952; Heller, 1988; Mikheyev, 1987; Shlapentokh, 1989). This *Homo sovieticus* was expected not to be impulsive or spontaneous, but rather to overcome these tendencies through planned, purposeful activity. Private feelings and desires were supposed to be suppressed.

Mead (1951) painted a similar picture of the type of person the Communists attempted to create:

> The Bolshevik is expected to develop a strong internal conscience, an ability to produce the highest level of activity without external prodding or stimulation. . . . There must be no diffuseness in his behavior, it must be continually focused and purposeful, measured, calculated, planned, and appropriate. Within his behavior there must be a rigid subordination of personal and private feeling to the demands of the final goals of the Party. (p. 28)

The official political ideology in Soviet Russia claimed that the average citizen was close to this ideal and stated that the majority of people followed the model established for them

TABLE 20.2 Russians' Stereotypes of Americans

Melnikova (1990)	*Stefanenko (1990)*	*Stephan et al. (1993)*
aggressive	hungry for success	ambitious
strong	enterprising	spontaneous
power hungry	relaxed in behavior	dignified
quick	professionally competent	competent
brave	self-confident	energetic
dangerous	individualistic	enterprising
energetic	pragmatic in relations	competitive
noisy	materialistic	patriotic
	communicative	independent
	ethnocentric	sociable
	thrifty	
	diligent	

(Shlapentokh, 1989). The reality was far from this ideal, and attempts to solve practical problems often required Soviet leaders to come to terms with this reality. Soviet leaders well into the 1980s chided their people for failing to live up to these high standards and criticized them for poor work habits, lying, stealing, egotism, and cynicism. Thus, there was a clash in the Soviet system between the idealized public code of conduct and the reality of life in Soviet Russia. The result was the emergence of private codes of conduct at variance with the official ones (Smith, 1976, 1990). The difference between official and private codes of conduct is nicely illustrated in an example provided by Mikheyev (1987). In the official code, stealing from the state was a more serious crime than stealing from an individual; in the private code, however, stealing from the state was not even recognized as an offense, whereas stealing from other individuals was a serious offense.

Nevertheless, the Soviet state did manage to control much of the behavior, and even the thinking, of its people. It did this through a monopoly on power, the distribution of wealth and prestige, its control over education and the media, and the use of repression (Gannon, 1994). In totalitarian countries, such as Russia, social control is maintained through external sanctions (Alt & Alt, 1964; Inkeles & Bauer, 1961). The government assumes that all of its people are to be distrusted and that therefore sanctions must be used to control their behavior. One consequence of the termination of totalitarianism is that greater reliance must be placed on internal control mechanisms to replace the absent external controls. Currently, in Russia, there is a

lack of clear guidelines for conduct. This is one among many factors contributing to the chaos of contemporary Russian life.

Empirical Studies of Russians'
Views of Russians and Americans

Unfortunately, few empirical studies of Russians' views of themselves or others were conducted during the Communist era. Therefore, the studies that do exist are all quite recent. In a study of Russians' views of Americans, Melnikova (1990) found that a sample of Russian workers perceived Americans as aggressive, strong, power hungry, quick, brave, dangerous, energetic, and noisy (Table 20.2). The Russian workers also believed that there was little social justice in the United States and that there was political persecution and terrorism.

In a sample of Russian students, Stefanenko (1990) found that Americans were perceived as hungry for success, enterprising, relaxed in behavior, professionally competent, self-confident, individualistic, pragmatic in relations, materialistic, communicative, ethnocentric, thrifty, and diligent. Stephan et al. (1993), in their study of Russian students, found that they perceived Americans as ambitious, spontaneous, dignified, competent, energetic, enterprising, competitive, patriotic, independent, and sociable. Thus, there was considerable agreement between these last two studies.

Stefanenko (1990) also examined Russian students' views of Russians and found they perceived Russians as hospitable, friendly, patriotic, humane, socially dependent, and

TABLE 20.3 Russians' Stereotypes of Russians

Stefanenko (1990)	Stephan et al. (1993)
hospitable	tough
friendly	patient
patriotic	hospitable
humane	adaptable
socially dependent	wasteful
responsive	materialistic
	obedient
	friendly
	emotional
	passive

responsive (see Table 20.3). She concluded that Russians view themselves as quite different from Americans. Stephan et al. (1993) found that Russian students perceived Russians as tough, patient, hospitable, adaptable, wasteful, materialistic, obedient, friendly, emotional, and passive.

The Stephan et al. (1993) study found that the correlation between the Russian and American students' views of Americans was quite high (.77). Thus, there was a very high level of agreement between Russian college students' perceptions of Americans and Americans' perceptions of themselves. Although the Russian students perceived that Americans are quite different from them, they appear to know what these differences are.

The American students, too, saw Russians as different from Americans, but there was a relatively low level of agreement between Americans' perceptions of Russians and Russians' perceptions of themselves (.13). Thus, the American students appear not to understand Russian culture well enough to perceive Russians as the Russians perceive themselves. Taken together, these results indicate that the Russian students' views of Americans are largely positive and that they appear to be more accurate than Americans' views of Russians (assuming the autostereotypes of each group are accurate).

The contrasts between the recent empirical studies of Westerners' views of Russians (Peabody, 1985; Stephan et al. 1993) and Russians' views of themselves are interesting (Stefanenko, 1990; Stephan et al., 1993). There is some agreement that Russians are obedient, passive, emotional, strong, proud, and patient.

The Russians, however, also see themselves as adaptable but wasteful, whereas they are seen by Westerners as inflexible but thrifty. The Russians also see themselves as friendly and hospitable, but Westerners do not mention these traits. And Westerners see Russians as hard-working and conservative, but the Russians do not mention these traits in their self-descriptions. These results suggest that if Westerners interacting with Russians rely on the perceptions of Russians prevalent in their cultures, they will be led astray about as often as they will make accurate assumptions.

These empirical results point to another important difference between Russians and Americans. On the one hand, Russians view Americans as a highly pragmatic and materialistic people. This view is consistent with Americans' views of themselves. On the other hand, Russians appear in these studies to be exactly the opposite—nonpragmatic and nonmaterialistic—with only one exception: In the Stephan et al. (1993) study, Russian students described Russians as materialistic, which is probably a reflection of recent changes in the Russian economy.

In Russian culture, the words *pragmatic* and *materialistic* have always had a negative connotation because they are the opposite of spirituality, which many Russians believe to be at the core of their national character. As one contemporary Russian writer put it when discussing the Russian soul,

Logical categories are inapplicable to the soul. But Russian sensitivity, permeating the whole culture, doesn't want to use logic—logic is seen as dry and evil, logic comes from the devil—the most important thing is sensation, smell, emotion, tears, mist, dreams, and enigma. (Tolstaya, 1990, p. 4)

Russians believe that emotions, rather than material considerations, should guide an individual's behavior. "Emotionality is considered a positive attribute, and some of the most convincing arguments between Russians appeal to the irrational element of human existence" (Gannon, 1994, p. 135). This perceived antagonism between logic and spirituality (nonpragmatism) is at least partially responsible for Russia's difficulties in making the transition to a free-market economy. It also means that, on many occasions, Russians and Americans are speaking different languages; the voice of reason and the voice of emotion do not always harmonize.

Russians' Attitudes Toward Americans

Just as Russia was perceived to be an enemy by Americans during the Cold War, so the United States was presented as an enemy in official Russian propaganda. One study of the content of speeches by Politburo members in the period from 1971 to 1978 indicated, "The enemy image is the preponderant image of the United States offered by all the members in all eight years" (Herrman, 1985, p. 682).

The Russians' attitudes toward Americans were, in a number of respects, the mirror image of Americans' views of Russians. For instance, Bronfenbrenner (1961) argued that each country viewed the other as aggressive, believed the government of the other country exploited and deluded its people, said leaders of the other country were untrustworthy, and thought the policies of the other country verged on madness. Another study content-analyzed the speeches of President Kennedy and Premier Khrushchev and found that each leader presented the other nation as imperialistic and militaristic but that each presented his own country as the champion of peace and freedom (Eckhardt & White, 1986). Thus, each country viewed the other in similarly negative terms.

The average Russian's attitudes toward Americans were more complex and ambivalent than simply viewing them as the enemy. In compliance with the official propaganda, Russians during the Communist era publicly displayed a certain amount of hostility toward Westerners, but privately they often expressed highly positive attitudes toward the West. An indirect indication of this positivity was an intense interest in information about the West. This interest was common for people in all strata of Russian society (Shlapentokh, 1989), but particularly for intellectuals. During the Communist era, the intellectuals had more opportunities to obtain firsthand information about the West than other segments of Russian society because they could read and speak foreign languages, English being the most popular (Pozner, 1991; Shlapentokh, 1989). Interestingly, in the late 1980s, there were more teachers of English in Russia than there were students of Russian in the United States (Axtell, 1990).

Although censored, the official media also provided substantial information about the West. As a result, Russians were quite knowledgeable about Western culture, movies, music, and literature. A study in the southern Russian city of Taganrog found that Russians were well informed in foreign history and culture, particularly that of the United States. In a representative sample of the population, only 6% did not know the major American political figures of the 20th century and only 9% could not answer questions about the main events in U.S. postwar history (Grushin & Onikov, 1980, cited in Shlapentokh, 1989). Russians have always been fascinated with Western lifestyles, and many have tried to imitate them in their own lives.

By contrast, the virtual blackout in the Western media concerning Russian culture meant that, for most of the 20th century, Americans and Western Europeans received little or no information about Russia. As a result of this blackout, most Westerners are largely ignorant of Russian history and culture. Many Americans are ignorant of even the most important events in Russian-American relations. For example, one national survey in the United States found that 28% of respondents thought Russia fought against the United States in World War II (*New York Times* poll, cited by Silverstein & Flamenbaum, 1989).

It is important to stress the role mass media played in creating the images of Russia that were presented in the West. Although journalists may claim to be objective, their reporting is inevitably flawed by their own biases and those of their editors. Pozner (1991) noted that, in his encounters with many Moscow-based U.S. journalists during the Cold War, he found that most of them, like Americans in general, had very negative views of the Soviet Union. And although they did report the facts, the choice of those facts was such that it supported their views. The other reason for negative reporting was the sensationalism of the American media. As one American journalist confessed in private conversation with Pozner, the stories about Russia that were most likely to appear on television or on the first page of a newspaper were those of corruption, drugs, alcoholism, and dissidents. Thus, the biased image presented in the American mass media was central to the creation of the misconceptions of Russian culture prevalent in the West.

A parallel phenomenon occurred in Russia, where the official Soviet media were pressured to present only negative information about the West, such as information on unemployment, the homeless, crime, and drug abuse. It appears, however, that in Russia there was also a great deal of skepticism concerning the official media. Thus, the image of America and Americans appears not to have been affected as much by the media as was the case in the West.

Differences Between Russians and the West on Dimensions Used for Cultural Comparisons

Although we lack the systematic data to be precise on these issues, it is possible to categorize Russian culture on many of the dimensions commonly used to conceptualize cultural differences, such as those discussed by Hofstede (1980) and Triandis (1990). Although it is largely speculative, at the very least the following discussion may serve as a basis of hypotheses that can be tested in future research.

A strong argument can be made that Russians are more collectivistic than Americans or other Western individualistic cultures (Kerberly, 1983). They stress family ties more, place a greater emphasis on interpersonal relations, and value the in-group over the individual. The Russian language has no word equivalent to the English word for privacy, a concept near and dear to individualistic cultures.

The Russians appear to be even less concerned with uncertainty avoidance than Ameri-cans and people from a number of other Western cultures because they have had to live with uncertainty for so long. In some situations, Russians appear to be very tolerant of ambiguity. For instance, one study found that "87% of the decisions approved at meetings are abstract and do not specify the time when recommendations are to be fulfilled" (Voinova & Chernakova, 1979, cited in Shlapentokh, 1989, p. 113). Also, the Russian people appear to be quite tolerant of deviance. Even during the most repressive periods of recent Russian history, many Russians displayed deviant behaviors in private although they would never have done so publicly.

Power distance is probably more important in Western Europe than in either Russia or the United States. A legacy of communism and a hallmark of individualism is an emphasis on equality. Social class distinctions are de-emphasized in both Russia and the United States but appear to retain considerable importance in European countries.

Russians appear to make greater distinctions between the sexes and may be characterized as emphasizing more traditional conceptions of masculinity and femininity than most cultures in the West. Russians follow different norms for relations between the sexes in their public and private lives. In the Stalinist constitution of 1936, men and women were declared to be equal "in all spheres of economic, state, cultural, public, and political life." Russian women receive equal pay for equal work, and they are better educated than Russian men, although a great many work in jobs that have less prestige than the jobs held by men. In their private lives, the position of Russian women is characterized by inequality: They do most, if not all, household work, and they take care of the children. Because the overwhelming majority of them work full time, they carry a double burden. Very appropriately, Smith (1976) refers to Russian women as "liberated but not emancipated" (p. 166).

The Russian norms for male-female interactions differ substantially from Western norms both in public and in private. For example, it is common in Russia for a man to open doors for a woman, to help her into her coat, and to help her get out of the bus by supporting her with his hand. Fewer and fewer men in the West display these kinds of behaviors, and as a result, Russian women often regard them as rude, boorish, and uncivil. Therefore, some Western women may perceive Russian men as patronizing when they are only trying to be polite.

Unlike many other collectivistic cultures, Russia does not appear to be a high-context culture (in high-context cultures, words convey only a portion of a message, and to a great extent, the message is communicated implicitly). Similar to the United States and other individualistic cultures, Russia is a low-context culture that emphasizes direct, spontaneous communication (Dicks, 1990a, 1990b). With respect to emotional expressiveness, Russians make a distinction that Westerners do not: They are less likely to express emotions in public settings (unless they are drinking) and more likely to express them in private settings. Russia is a relatively high-contact culture where people often physically touch each other, but again there is a distinction between public and private life. The high-contact nature of Russian culture is most likely to surface in close interpersonal relationships.

Intercultural Relations
Between Russia and the West

Many Westerners were taught to hate and fear Russians during their formative years (Cohen, 1985). As late as 1983, an American President, Ronald Reagan, was characterizing the Soviet Union as the "evil empire." According to Reagan,

> They are the focus of evil in the modern world. It is a mistake to ignore the facts of history and the aggressive impulses of the evil empire, to simply call the arms race a giant misunderstanding and thereby remove yourself from the struggle between right and wrong, good and evil. (quoted in Bar-Tal, 1990, p. 69)

One likely outcome of being socialized during a time when Russia was viewed as an enemy in the West and vice versa is that Westerners and Russians may experience anxiety when interacting with each other, at least initially. Stephan and Stephan (1985) suggest that anxiety is particularly high when groups have a history of antagonism, have little prior personal contact, possess negative stereotypes of one another, are ethnocentric, perceive the out-group to be different from the in-group, and know little about the other group. These conditions apply remarkably well to the interactions of many Westerners with Russians. Clearly, historical relations between Russia and the West have frequently been antagonistic, personal contact has been scant, the mutual stereotypes contain many negative components, many Westerners are ethnocentric, they perceive Russians to be different from people in the West, and they know little about Russian culture, customs, norms, values, and beliefs. Hence, it is likely that intergroup anxiety pervades the initial phases of social interactions between Russians and Westerners.

The arousal created by intergroup anxiety can lead to the amplification of the dominant behavioral responses in the situation (Stephan, Stephan, Wenzel, & Cornelius, 1991). For instance, if the interaction situation calls for politeness, anxious people on both sides will respond with extreme politeness, perhaps to the point of being excessively solicitous. Intergroup anxiety can also lead to extreme evaluations of members of the other group, as well as strong emotional reactions (Stephan & Stephan, 1989). For example, if the outcomes of the contact between Russians and Westerners are favorable, positive evaluations of the out-group and positive emotions would be expected, whereas if the outcomes are unfavorable, extreme negative evaluations and emotions would be expected. Anxiety can also affect cognitive processing, typically in ways that sustain previous expectancies, stereotypes, and attitudes. Westerners may rely more on stereotypes when they are anxious. Thus, in many instances, intergroup anxiety may distort social relations between Russians and Westerners in ways that promote negative outcomes and perceptions.

The negative views of Russians held by Westerners can also bias their processing of new information about the two countries. One study found that altruistic actions (economic aid to an African country) were attributed by Americans to self-serving motives if the actions were engaged in by the Soviet Union but that the same actions were attributed to more positive motives if they were engaged in by the United States. A similar bias occurred for the interpretation of negative actions (sending arms to an African nation). In this case, the motives were seen as more negative if the Soviets engaged in these actions than if the Americans did so (Sande, Goethals, Ferrari, & Worth, 1989;

also see Burn & Oskamp, 1989). The investigators argue that these attributions occur in the service of maintaining the view that Americans are more moral than Russians.

The ignorance of Russian history and culture that we mentioned earlier can also create problems in intercultural interactions. Westerners often carry into these interactions an incorrect picture of Russians and their culture that may lead them to commit a variety of errors in the course of interacting with Russians. Westerners' expectations and the behaviors based on them will often be inappropriate. For their part, the Russians may believe that the Westerners' ignorance of Russia indicates a lack of respect for Russians and their culture. All of these factors are likely to create barriers to effective communication by causing misunderstandings and, in some cases, conflict (see Table 20.4).

In Russia, the difference between public and private spheres of life was reinforced during the Communist era by a state bureaucracy that took a negative view of individualism and that discouraged people from being warm, natural, or spontaneous in public. Because their public lives were subject to scrutiny and because they could not openly speak their minds, Russians' private relations became more intense. The intensity of Russians' close relationships may create problems when Westerners interact with them. Dissatisfaction is very likely to be mutual. Westerners often see such intense relationships as too demanding and emotion-laden. In turn, when Russians fail to establish the "soul-to-soul" connection they are seeking, they may conclude that Westerners are cold and may find their relations with them superficial and unsatisfactory.

Some confusion and misunderstanding may also be generated in social interactions between Russians and Westerners because of different norms for nonverbal behavior. One of the most noticeable of these norms concerns smiling. Every American visitor to Russia is surprised by the fact that people there do not smile. It is often interpreted as unfriendliness, coldness, or even as a sign of oppression (Pozner, 1991). The truth is that, in Russia, smiling or greeting and talking to strangers, which is so common in the United States, is non-normative and may even be interpreted as an attempt to make an unwanted sexual advance, particularly if it occurs in a large city (Pozner, 1991; Richmond, 1992). To Russians, smiling at a stranger "appears naive or even suspect" (Richmond, 1992, p. 41).

SUMMARY

For centuries, travelers, diplomats, military analysts, scientists, and academics have tried to document and describe the differences between Russia and the West. Psychology arrived late on the scene. Only recently has psychology broadened its horizons to include attempts to understand the origins of cultural differences. In addition to its purely academic value, understanding cultural influences in behavior has tremendous practical importance—for diplomacy, business, science, and tourism. In this chapter, we noted the apparent differences between Russians and Westerners on a wide variety of dimensions commonly used to conceptualize culture. Unfortunately, at this critical juncture, psychology lacks the empirical data necessary to draw definitive conclusions about the nature and origin of these differences between Russia and the West and their effects on intercultural relations.

Trying to understand other cultures is never easy, but in the case of Russia, the usual problems are compounded by the fact that, for most of this century, Russia was a closed society. Those few foreigners who visited Russia during the 70 years of Communist rule were prevented from establishing the kinds of personal relationships that would have provided insights into Russian culture. Thus, Westerners were exposed to Russians' public lives but not to their private lives. We attempted to show that this distinction—between public and private life— is important in all spheres of life in Russia. Now that the iron curtain has been raised, foreigners are rediscovering Russia. They have started the difficult task of learning, but much remains to be done.

No culture can avoid being stereotyped because stereotypes are such useful cognitive shortcuts to deal with the enormous amounts of

TABLE 20.4 Some Do's and Don'ts

Do's

- When visiting somebody's home, bring flowers. Flowers are always appreciated, and they are a must for special occasions. The number of flowers should be odd, except at funerals, when it should be even.
- Try to establish personal contacts with the people you are doing business with. Not only will it speed all your business transactions, but it will also help you get to know and understand the Russian culture better.
- When asked, be open about your income, cost of housing, cars, and entertainment. Russians are genuinely interested in the American way of life, and it is customary in Russia to openly discuss these issues.
- If you are a woman, accept the courteous behavior of Russian men, and if you are man, engage in this kind of behavior to avoid being perceived as uncivil.
- Russians are very much concerned with their own and other people's appearance, so dress appropriately; theater, concert, or other formal occasions require dressing up.
- Be careful. Crime is on the rise, and foreigners in Russia do not enjoy any special protection.
- Keep the telephone numbers of people you want to get in touch with in Russia in a safe place; the telephone directories in Russia are scarce, and directory assistance is hard to get.
- Be patient. In conversations or in business affairs, Russians do not like to get directly to the matter, so everything takes longer there.
- Do try to see Russians at home, and when invited, expect to have a several-course meal and drinks.
- Russians like to receive and will appreciate presents, even small ones. Presents can also facilitate business relationships.
- Be a little skeptical about people of the opposite sex who show a romantic interest in you. Some Russians are desperate to leave their country.
- Try to learn the alphabet; being able to read Cyrillic will at least help you find your way around.

Don'ts

- Do not be offended if seated at a restaurant table with someone else. Try to use the occasion to get to know the Russians.
- Do not expect thank-you notes from Russians. They believe that oral expressions of gratitude for a present or a favor are enough. Russians will not expect these notes from you, either.
- Do not talk too loud in public places. It is viewed as rude and inconsiderate, and if this conversation is not in Russian, Russians may take it personally.
- It is not customary in Russia (particularly in big cities) to talk to or smile at strangers, so do not interpret this behavior as coldness and unfriendliness.
- Do not be dismayed by the large crowds you will frequently encounter in Russia. Also, try not to take pushing, touching, and other behavior in crowds personally.
- Do not be shocked when strangers, particularly older people, make comments and even recommendations about your appearance or behavior.
- Do not be surprised by a late night call or even a visit from a Russian friend. Close relationships with Russians come at a cost, and they will be willing to repay you tenfold.
- Do not assume that everybody speaking Russian is a Russian. There are more than 100 ethnic groups in Russia. Do not hesitate to ask about a person's nationality because, with the recent political developments, people are increasingly aware of these issues.
- In response to a Russian's openness, do not hesitate to open your soul. It is expected from people Russians consider their friends, and it is a sign of true acceptance.
- Do not try to keep up with Russians when drinking, particularly if they are drinking vodka. Russians expect people to drink "bottoms up" but will readily accept a religious or health excuse.
- Do not shake hands or hand something over a threshold. It is considered bad luck.
- Do not walk on grass; use the pathways.
- Do not put your feet on tables. It is considered rude, uncivil, and unsanitary.
- Some public places in Russia may not be as clean as similar places in the West. Try not to be disconcerted if they are untidy, littered, and unkempt.
- Do not expect much business to be done by telephone or by mail; Russians prefer face-to-face transactions. And do not put much trust in agreements that are not written on paper.
- Russians prefer to keep doors closed. So, do not assume that a closed office door means that nobody is there. Also, do not assume that a closed bathroom door means it is occupied. Knock on the door to make sure.

social information we encounter every day. Stereotypes help people categorize one another and social events, but if these stereotypes are inaccurate because they are overgeneralized, unduly negative, or just plain wrong, they create problems in intercultural relations. In this chapter, we demonstrated that the stereotypes of Russians held by Westerners are distorted by the historical antagonisms that existed between the former Soviet Union and Western countries. These inaccuracies will create problems with which both Russians and Westerners will have to contend for years to come.

We emphasized differences between Russian culture and the cultures of the West because the differences create problems when cultural groups interact with one another. We would also like to point out that the cultures of Russia and the West share much in common. In fact, the similarities may be greater than the differences. These similarities help make visiting and working in Russia a pleasure, although the differences mean it is also a challenge.

We end where we began by reiterating that Russia is going through a period of social upheaval and that, without doubt, this transition and the major economic and political changes that occur during it will leave their mark on Russian national character. These changes may be years or even generations in the making. What aspects of Russian character will endure and what aspects will disappear remain to be seen. If we have done our job well, we have at least provided a point of reference against which such changes can be compared.

References

Ageyev, V. (1993, July). *Why are Russians less authoritarian than Americans? A social ecological explanation.* Paper presented at the International Society of Political Psychology, Boston.

Alt, H., & Alt, E. (1964). *The new Soviet man.* New York: Bookman.

Axtell, R. (1990). *Do's and taboos around the world* (2nd ed.). New York: John Wiley.

Bialer, S. (1985). The psychology of U.S.-Soviet relations. *Political Psychology, 6,* 263-273.

Bar-Tal, D. (1990). Causes and consequences of delegitimation: Models of conflict and ethnocentrism. *Journal of Social Issues, 46,* 65-82.

Brief, D. E., & Collins, B. E. (1994). *A cross-national study of American and Russian national character: An example of research protocol.* Unpublished manuscript, University of California, Los Angeles.

Brief, D. E., & Comrey, A. L. (1993). A profile of personality for a Russian sample: As indicated by the Comrey Personality Scales. *Journal of Personality Assessment, 60,* 267-284.

Bronfenbrenner, U. (1961). The mirror-image in Soviet-American relations: A social psychologist's report. *Journal of Social Issues, 17,* 45-56.

Bronfenbrenner, U. (1970). *Two worlds of childhood: U.S. and U.S.S.R.* New York: Russell Sage.

Buchanan, W., & Cantril, H. (1953). *How nations see each other.* Westport, CT: Greenwood.

Burn, S. M., & Oskamp, S. (1989). Ingroup biases and the U.S.-Soviet conflict. *Journal of Social Issues, 45,* 73-90.

Cohen, S. F. (1985). *Sovieticus.* New York: Norton.

Dicks, H. (1952). Observations on contemporary Russian behavior. *Human Relations, 5,* 111-176.

Dicks, H. (1990a). Notes on the Russian national character. In E. Trist & H. Murray (Eds.), *The social engagement of social science* (pp. 559-573). Philadelphia: University of Pennsylvania Press.

Dicks, H. (1990b). Some notes on the Russian national character. In C. E. Black (Ed.), *The transformation of Russian society* (pp. 636-651). Cambridge: Harvard University Press.

Eckhardt, W., & White, R. K. (1986). A test of the mirror-image hypothesis: Kennedy and Khrushchev. *Journal of Conflict Resolution, 11,* 325-332.

Frank, J. D., & Melville, A. Y. (1989). The image of the enemy and the process of change. In A. Gromyko & M. Hellman (Eds.), *Breakthrough* (pp. 199-208). New York: Walker.

Gallup, G. H. (1941). *The Gallup poll.* New York: Random House.

Gannon, M. J. (1994). *Understanding global cultures.* Thousand Oaks, CA: Sage.

Grushin, B., & Onikov, L. (Eds.). (1980). *Massovaia informatsiia v sovetskom promyshlennon gorode.* Moscow: Politizdat.

Hamilton, V. L., Sanders, J., & McKearney, S. J. (1995). Orientations toward authority in an authoritarian state: Moscow in 1990. *Personality and Social Psychology Bulletin, 21,* 356-365.

Hanin, Y., Eysenck, S. G., Eysenck, H. J., & Barrett, P. (1991). A cross-cultural study of personality: Russia and England. *Personality and Individual Differences, 12,* 265-271.

Heller, M. (1988). *Cogs in the wheel: The formation of Soviet man.* New York: Knopf.

Herrman, R. K. (1985). Analyzing Soviet images of the United States: A psychological theory and empirical study. *Journal of Conflict Resolution, 29,* 665-697.

Hofstede, G. (1980). *Culture's consequences.* Beverly Hills, CA: Sage.

Holsti, O. R. (1991). American reactions to the USSR: Public opinion. In R. Jervis & S. Bialer (Eds.), *Soviet-American relations after the Cold War* (pp. 23-47). Durham, NC: Duke University Press.

Inkeles, A. (1968). *Social change in Soviet Russia.* Cambridge, MA: Harvard University Press.

Inkeles, A., & Bauer, R. A. (1961). *The Soviet citizen.* Cambridge, MA: Harvard University Press.

Kerberly, B. (1983). *Modern Soviet society.* New York: Pantheon.

Kluckhohn, C. (1961). Studies of Russian national character. In A. Inkeles & K. Geiger (Eds.), *Soviet society: A book of readings* (pp. 607-618). Boston: Houghton Mifflin.

McFarland, S. G., Ageyev, V., & Abalakina-Paap, M. (1992). The authoritarian personality in the United States and the former Soviet Union: Comparative studies. In W. F. Stone, G. Lederer, & R. Christie (Eds.), *Strength and weakness: The authoritarian personality today* (pp. 199-228). New York/Berlin: Springer-Verlag.

McFarland, S. G., Ageyev, V., & Abalakina-Paap, M. (1994). Authoritarianism in the former Soviet Union. *Journal of Personality and Social Psychology, 63,* 1004-1010.

McFarland, S. G., Ageyev, V., Abalakina-Paap, M., & Djintcharadze, N. (1993, July). *Why are Russians less authoritarian than Americans?* Paper presented at the International Society for Political Psychology, Boston.

McFarland, S. G., Ageyev, V., & Djintcharadze, N. (1993). *Russian authoritarianism two years after communism.* Unpublished paper, Western Kentucky University, Bowling Green.

Mead, M. (1951). *Soviet attitudes toward authority.* New York: McGraw-Hill.

Melnikova, O. T. (1990). The USSR and the USA: Stereotypes and mutual perceptions. In V. A. Vinogradov (Ed.), *Toward understanding: Communication and present day realities* (pp. 65-74). Moscow: Vneshtorgizdat.

Mikheyev, D. (1987). The Soviet mentality. *Political Psychology, 8,* 491-523.

Miller, W. (1960). *Russians as people.* New York: E. P. Dutton.

Nincic, M. (1985). The American public and the Soviet Union: The domestic context of discontent. *Behavioral Science, 22,* 345-357.

Peabody, D. (1985). *National characteristics.* Cambridge, UK: Cambridge University Press.

Pozner, V. (1991). *Parting with illusions.* New York: Avon.

Richmond, Y. (1992). *From nyet to da: Understanding the Russians.* Yarmouth, ME: Intercultural Press.

Sande, G. N., Goethals, G. R., Ferrari, L., & Worth, L. T. (1989). Value-guided attributions: Maintaining the moral self-image and the diabolical enemy image. *Journal of Social Issues, 45,* 91-118.

Shlapentokh, V. (1989). *Public and private life of the Soviet people.* New York: Oxford University Press.

Silverstein, B., & Flamenbaum, C. (1989). Biases in the perception and cognition of the actions of enemies. *Journal of Social Issues, 45,* 51-72.

Smith, H. (1976). *The Russians.* New York: Ballantine.

Smith, H. (1990). *The new Russians.* New York: Random House.

Smith, T. W. (1983). American attitudes toward the Soviet Union and communism. *Public Opinion Quarterly, 47,* 277-292.

Stefanenko, T. G. (1990). Moscow students' images of Americans and Soviets. In V. A. Vinogradov (Ed.), *Toward understanding: Communication and present-day realities* (pp. 74-83). Moscow: Vneshtorgizdat.

Stephan, W. G., Ageyev, V. S., Stephan, C. W., Abalakina, M., Stefanenko, T., & Coates-Shrider, L. (1993). Soviet and American stereotypes: A comparison of methods. *Social Psychology Quarterly, 56,* 54-64.

Stephan, W. G., & Stephan, C. (1985). Intergroup anxiety. *Journal of Social Issues, 41,* 157-176.

Stephan, W. G., & Stephan, C. W. (1989). Emotional reactions to interracial achievement outcomes. *Journal of Applied Social Psychology, 19,* 608-621.

Stephan, W. G., Stephan, C. W., Wenzel, B., & Cornelius, J. (1991). Intergroup interaction and self-disclosure. *Journal of Applied Social Psychology, 21,* 1370-1378.

Tolstaya, T. (1990). Notes from underground. *New York Review of Books, 37,* 3-5.

Triandis, H. C. (1990). Theoretical concepts that are applicable to the analysis of ethnocentrism. In R. W. Brislin (Ed.), *Applied cross-cultural psychology* (pp. 34-55). Newbury Park, CA: Sage.

Walsh, W. B. (1944). What the American people think of Russia. *Public Opinion Quarterly, 8,* 513-522.

Yatani, C., & Bramel, D. (1989). Trends and patterns in Americans' attitudes toward the Soviet Union. *Journal of Social Issues, 45,* 13-32.

21

Developing Expatriate Managers for Southeast Asia

GRAHAM WILLIAMS

RITCHIE BENT

Hong Kong

At the mouth of the busy Pearl River, just south of Canton, lies the British Colony of Hong Kong—a territory of 6 million people, with a geographical area of less than 1,100 km^2 and an economy that for the last decade has been the envy of the Western world. Currently rated as the eighth largest trading nation on earth and widely recognized as a major financial center, Hong Kong's future seems promising as China continues to look toward this small enclave as a major source of foreign investment and expertise.

In 1984, the historic Sino-British Joint Declaration was signed, signifying the return of sovereignty to China in 1997 and the start of a unique transition that, for the next decade, was to reposition the territory as an important strategic player in China's economic growth. But the strategic value of Hong Kong is not limited to China alone. Many Western companies now

view the territory as an important bridgehead for penetration into one of the largest untapped consumer markets in the world: greater China. Hong Kong's sound legal system, political stability, advanced infrastructure, talented workforce, and long-standing relationship with China positions the territory as one of the most attractive operational bases in the region. The specter of 1997 and rapidly rising costs have so far done little to dampen the enthusiasm of foreign companies keen to locate their people in Hong Kong. Evidence of this is seen in the recent growth of the territory's expatriate population, with an additional 17,202 professional/ managerial staff arriving in Hong Kong during 1993, representing a 21% growth over the previous year (Hong Kong Census and Statistics Department, 1994)—a trend likely to continue as China opens its doors further to the outside. But herein lies the major dilemma facing foreign firms: On average, a company can expect the cost of an expatriate manager to be twice that of his or her local counterpart (Wyatt, 1994); this expectation gives rise to two compelling questions that form the basis for this chapter: Why do companies continue to send expensive expatriates overseas, and what measures can be taken to ensure that these managers are both operationally and culturally effective?

To provide perspective, the study begins with a general overview by defining the role of the "international" manager, looking at some reasons why organizations choose expatriates (defined for the purposes of this study as native English speakers) to run their overseas operations and what are the steps taken to help with the cultural integration of these managers. Consideration is then given to some longer-established and more recent studies that have attempted to explain the nature of national culture and its impact within the work context. In this respect, particular emphasis is given to overseas Chinese, who are broadly defined as those who have settled outside mainland China.

We then introduce four key components considered vital for successful expatriate acculturation. These are supported and supplemented by the findings of our own research, from which emerges two models: one that proposes an enhanced learning cycle for the effective expatriate manager, and another that serves to bring together the various competencies in the form of a composite whole.

In presenting these findings, it is our intention to provide a useful balance of theory and practice that should be of interest to researchers in the field, individuals and organizations planning to base themselves in Hong Kong, and professionals already in place. The findings are also broadly applicable to the other Chinese-dominated, high-growth areas of the region, such as Singapore, Taiwan, and more recently, the southern Chinese Special Economic Zones. In concluding, we offer some practical advice to the expatriate manager, based on the authors' combined 25 years of experience in the region. We begin with an insight into the broader meaning and role of the "international manager."

The International Manager

Different cultural preferences, national tastes and standards, and business institutions are vestiges of the past. . . . The world's needs and desires have been irrevocably homogenized. This makes the multinational corporation obsolete and the global corporation absolute. . . . Instead of adapting to superficial and even entrenched differences within and between nations, the global corporation will seek sensibly to force suitably standardized products and practices on the entire globe. (Levitt, 1983).

First-time visitors to the major Asian cities of Hong Kong, Singapore, and Taipei are often heard to remark that, generally, there is little difference between these and other large cities: Businesspeople with mobile phones pressed to their ears rush from one meeting to the next, seemingly oblivious of anything going on around them. Sign boards advertise brand names common to all major cities in the Western world, and sophisticated shop fronts display designer goods that carry price tags similar to those in Manhattan or Bond Street. One may detect a ring of truth in Levitt's words and be forgiven for thinking that, culturally, there is little difference between what is now observed in the commercial East and West.

If we are to assume at this point that certain differences that may not be immediately apparent do exist among managers of different cultures, a question inevitably arises as to what impact this may have within the business context. Drucker (1988) helps shed some light on this dilemma in declaring that *what* managers do is the same the world over but that *how* they do it is embedded in their tradition and cultures. An interesting parallel is that this "how" appears to differentiate the international manager from his or her domestic counterpart and, to some extent, offers the key to operating successfully in a culturally foreign environment.

No true consensus appears to have been reached as yet about what constitutes an international manager. Barham and Wills (1992) talk in terms of someone who can manage across a number of countries and cultures simultaneously, perhaps on a regional or global basis. Adler (1986) refers to them as chameleons who are capable of acting in many ways, not experts rigidly adhering to one approach. The French organization Rhone-Poulenc describes them as "managers who think world, not France" (Reid, 1991, p. 15). Although lacking an agreed definition, the concept of the international manager now appears to be widely accepted as someone capable of operating beyond the domestic boundaries of his or her home country, working effectively with people of a differing culture, and in many cases, actually living in the host country as an expatriate.

The competencies required of an international manager appear to be broad and wide ranging. Recent research in this area has been conducted by Barham and Wills (1992) of the Ashridge Management College in Britain, in which several leading businesses in Europe, Asia, and North America were surveyed. The key managerial characteristics to emerge from this research include the following:

Strategic awareness
Adaptability to new situations
Sensitivity to different cultures
Relationship skills
Ability to work in multicultural teams
Language skills
Understanding international marketing
International negotiating skills

Interestingly, their findings appear to emphasize the softer "people skills," rather than the hard technical skills, an observation that tends to reinforce the views of other authorities in the field. Adler (1986), in prescribing the skills required for managing multicultural teams, identifies

Recognizing differences from the beginning
Creating clear and broad goals to which everyone can relate
Giving mutual power and respect
Encouraging feedback to help bring cohesion to a team

Marsick, Turner, and Cederholm (1989) identified the need for international managers to

Read cross-cultural cues
Develop active listening skills
Tolerate and manage ambiguity
Negotiate when the rules of the game are unclear

Although many of the competencies described are equally applicable to domestic managers, the weighting that one assigns to each serves to differentiate the requirements for an international manager.

Why Choose Western Managers to Work in Southeast Asia?

In March 1994, the Employers Federation of Hong Kong staged a conference that attracted more than 300 representatives from the major companies in Hong Kong. The theme of the conference centered around the equalization of terms for local and expatriate employees. Its purpose was to establish what could be done to curb the rapidly escalating costs of expatriates in Hong Kong. A major issue to arise was why companies continued to employ expensive expatriates even though talented local staff were readily available.

Each international company has its own reasons for choosing expatriates, but it is possible to generalize: Many foreign companies view Southeast Asia, and in particular China, as a strategically significant market for long-term business growth. During the start-up stage, many prefer to rely on loyal, tried and tested employees, rather than on locally appointed hires, to initiate their operations until suitable local replacements have been identified and trained. Among other things, this choice allows the organization a certain level of control and also the opportunity to develop valuable experience that cannot be provided by business schools or flying visits to international operations. In certain areas of business, it is also still difficult to find the appropriate level of experience and expertise locally. In Hong Kong, these areas currently include management development professionals, attorneys in international commercial law and risk management, certain telecommunication specialists, and regionally mobile general managers who are able to move at a moment's notice. Many companies also view the presence of expatriates as a powerful means of imparting their corporate culture onto the foreign subsidiary and thus ensuring a desired level of predictability and control over the affairs of the unit.

The expatriate debate is likely to continue for many years, but it is likely that expatriates will remain a common feature of foreign enterprise for the foreseeable future. With this thought in mind, we now turn toward the steps taken by several major organizations to develop their international managers.

Preparing Managers to Work Internationally

There appears to be little consistency in the approach adopted by international corporations to prepare their managers for international assignments. Most, however, perhaps not surprisingly, recognize the need to physically integrate their managers into the local culture while still retaining the bonding influence inherent in the corporate culture. Barham and Oates (1991) provide an illustrative summary of the practices of some large European and North American companies.

For example, the Italian car manufacturer Fiat places strong emphasis on its English-language programs for graduates. This involves a 100-hour course integrated into the introductory, 5-month training scheme. In addition to providing a useful skill, Fiat management see this approach as giving the graduates a strong signal that they are working in an international environment. The company's vice president for management development, Vittorio Tesio, explains that language teaching goes farther than simply providing proficiency in a foreign tongue and that it also helps people understand other cultures. Building on this, part of the education process for their more senior managers involves "traveling seminars" in which a week is spent looking at other industries in various countries. This endeavor has a powerful impact on the attitude of the participants in that it enables them to see that the world is different and, in doing so, helps develop respect for the foreign competitors.

Kanter (1989), in commenting on General Electric's (GE) Management Development Institute at Crotonville, describes it as more than a corporate college; but in effect a synergy center enables people to identify and tackle common problems together. In keeping with many international corporations, GE management see a major objective of formal core programs to be the creation of networks and a common understanding that ensures that all of their international managers are playing by the same standards and employing the same rules. What perhaps distinguishes GE from many other

companies is its use of foreign business schools. Despite having its own residential center and access to many other major schools in the United States, a large group of company executives are sent to the French business school INSEAD each year. Company management insist on their participants living locally in an environment of total cultural immersion, which they believe nurtures a greater global outlook for their managers.

The British trading giant Jardine Matheson has globally more than 220,000 employees and a trading base that, for the past 160 years, has been in Hong Kong. The company places high priority on the integration of its international managers into the local culture. At present, more than a quarter of its employees are located in Hong Kong, including nearly 200 Western managers. The company uses a number of mechanisms to achieve the cultural integration of these managers—some explicit, others more implicit. In most cases, the company's management development initiative is seen as a major vehicle in this respect.

An advantage this company has over others is that its annual intake of international graduates, drawn primarily from the United States, Australia, and Britain, start their working careers in Asia with relatively few preconceptions about Asians. On arrival, they commence a 2-year management training program undertaken jointly with the locally recruited Chinese graduates. The format of the training is project based, with the participants spending much of their time in their business units. At regular intervals and under the guiding hand of an external and internal facilitator, they are brought together to discuss their experiences.

Although the cultural issue is not overtly addressed, through the course of mixed group meetings the subject tends to arise as a natural matter of course. A choice of Mandarin or Cantonese language training forms an integral part of the 2-year training syllabus. Although some international graduates arrive already fluent in an Asian language, the training module itself is designed to achieve only a general working knowledge of the chosen language, with a view to creating empathy and understanding among the cultures, rather than a high level of fluency.

The company also has in place a series of integrated core management development programs that are attended by most executives during the course of their careers. Again, although not addressing the cultural issue directly, the heavy emphasis placed on team development activities encourages the issues to emerge naturally. When addressed, it is done within the context of working together effectively as a multicultural business team, rather than of trying to hypothesize and identify why Asians may operate differently from Westerners.

One major midcareer program run annually at a UK business school and in Hong Kong for the past 7 years does attempt to address the cultural issue directly. The 1-day module has drawn a number of different responses from the participants. In general, although both Western and Asian participants found that it had heightened their level of awareness, most thought they already had sufficient experience of other cultures to cope with difficulties encountered at work. In an interesting response, witnessed by one author on two occasions, both Asian and Western participants responded adversely to the process. They expressed concern that by trying to highlight the differences, the facilitator was effectively destroying a harmony that already existed within the group. This observation perhaps serves to highlight some of the potential dangers of cross-cultural training and development.

Up to this point, we have considered the broader issues of international management and the implications involved in firms helping their executives integrate into foreign working environments. Many companies, however, are beginning to realize that different parts of the world may require different skills and that the competencies required in an international manager are perhaps more geographically specialized than at first expected. With this thought in mind, attention now turns toward the East and the emergence of the "Asia manager."

The East Asia Manager

In 1992, one of the more enduring debates to arise from the formation of a single European market was whether the process would give birth to a Euromanager. This debate has taken on a new dimension as the Asia Pacific Rim assumes growing economic importance and as commentators, academics, and consultants have started to contemplate the emergence of a new breed of international executive: the *Asia manager* (Syrett, 1993). For the purpose of this chapter, this term will be defined as an executive of Western origin, probably a native English speaker, who is required to work with the overseas Chinese in Asia.

The cultural complexity of Asia, particularly from a business perspective, almost defies description. Naisbitt and Aburdene (1990) note that the countries of this region have more than 1,000 languages and possess the most varied religious and cultural traditions in the world. Redding and Armitage (1993) reinforce this view in identifying the region as being divided between organizations that have radically different structures from each other and commercial values that differ from those of their Western counterparts.

Redding and Armitage illustrate this by highlighting four major organizational types operating in the region that are largely foreign to the West: (a) the large Japanese corporation, which relies on company loyalty, networks of suppliers, and large internal labor markets; (b) the Korean *chaebol,* which is based on family ownership but continues to retain much of the competitiveness and work intensity of the Japanese companies; (c) the Chinese family businesses, which are controlled by owner managers and are highly flexible, adaptive, and efficient; and (d) the large Hong Kong trading *hongs,* which are usually family owned but are run along Western managerial lines. The other organizational types, more of Western origin but nevertheless prevalent in the region, are the multinational corporations and their hybrid offshoots. The free-market economies of Hong Kong, Singapore, and increasingly Taiwan and Southern China have resulted in the emergence of all these forms except the Korean *chaebol* and, in turn, have created a high level of complexity and challenge for those involved in business.

Based on the observations presented so far, a broad competency template has begun to emerge for the international manager. The cultural and business diversity of the region, however, suggests that a more complex competency set may be required for the Western manager operating in Southeast Asia. In addition to the generic managerial skills, one can surmise that the competencies may also include the following:

Tolerance for high levels of ambiguity

Sensitivity and responsiveness to different cultures

An open mind

Being prepared to move to and work in different countries

Informed knowledge of Asia

Perhaps above all, ability to span the gray divide between East and West

It is this much-debated and largely intangible "gray divide" between the overseas Chinese and Western races that we now explore. In drawing comparisons, we are mindful that wide individual differences can occur both within and among cultures, and for these reasons, only broad generalizations can be made. By applying our own findings and those of others to the multicultural work context, however, we hope to provide a meaningful comparison and ultimately produce a more practical and usable set of conclusions. We begin with a summary of the better-known cross-cultural research findings.

Understanding the Overseas Chinese

Our own work has been largely based in Hong Kong, but studies of the overseas Chinese also include the Chinese working in other Asian countries and even those just across the border from Hong Kong in southern China. It seems a reasonable assumption that, for an expatriate manager to be effective in Hong Kong and other countries that are predominantly Chinese, he or she should have a good understanding of the overseas Chinese and their culture. This is only a starting point, of course, and requires appropriate actions to follow from that understanding.

Hofstede (1981) defines culture as the collective programming of the human mind that distinguishes one group from another. Perhaps we should remember that this is a Western interpretation of culture. But what is the collective programming of the Hong Kong Chinese mind? This programming has been considered and researched from many perspectives. We start by looking briefly at some independent aspects of Chinese culture before considering cross-cultural studies that sought to identify the general dimensions of culture.

1. *Confucian principles.* Many researchers and academics (Bond, 1986; Kirkbride, Tang, & Shae, 1989; Redding, 1990) believe that the roots of Chinese culture (particularly for the overseas Chinese) spring from the Chinese philosophy of Confucianism and, to a lesser extent, from Taoism and Buddhism. Hofstede (1991) makes an interesting contrast between Western and Chinese religions. Western religions (Christianity, Judaism, Islam) are based on the existence of a "Truth" accessible through the Bible or the Koran. The Chinese religions are not based on the assumption of a truth; rather, it is what one does or how one lives, not what one believes, that is important. For example, Confucian teaching advocates patience, perseverance, hard work, education, and moderation in all things. A further Confucian teaching stresses respect for authority and that stability and harmony are based on an unequal relationship between people (Hofstede, 1991). Redding and Casey (1976) see this manifested in a reluctance by employees to share information and aversion of participative systems of management.

2. *Harmony.* Harmony is also perceived as linked to Confucian teaching. Tang and Kirkbride (1986) explain their research finding about the Hong Kong Chinese manager's preference for avoiding conflict in terms of maintaining harmony even at the expense of productivity and efficiency.

3. *Importance of the group.* Hsu (1949) highlights the need for the individual to control emotions, to avoid conflict, and generally to adapt to the collectivity. Individuals are expected to put their own interests second to the interests of the group.

4. *Face.* Concern for face is seen as more salient for the Chinese than for other cultures. It is linked to the previous section in that it follows from a high sensitivity to group belonging and peer opinion. Goffman (1955) defines *face* as the positive social value a person effectively claims for himself by the line others assume he has taken during a particular contact. Concern for face probably occurs in all cultures; however, Redding and Ng (1982) investigating the role of face for overseas Chinese (including Hong Kong), argue that the degree of impact of face issues is much higher for overseas Chinese. They further argue that any explanation of behavior in organizations is incomplete without

taking into account the face concepts that are specific to the Chinese.

5. *Trust.* Bond (1991) defines *trust* as "committing something of oneself, such as material resources or information, to the care of another, when one has no effective control over how the other may use it" (p. 37). Bond found that the Hong Kong Chinese are comparatively more trusting of their immediate family than Americans but that there is no difference in terms of trusting strangers.

6. *Fate.* Bond (1986) studied the extent to which managers believed rewards were gained as a result of external factors—luck or fate—as compared with internal factors—skill and effort. He found that Hong Kong Chinese managers show a much stronger bias toward luck or fate as compared with Western managers.

7. *Preference for the tangible and concrete.* Bond (1991), following Nakamura's (1964) work on Asian thinking, argues that the preference among Chinese for the tangible and concrete may be linked to early schooling and the need to memorize not less than 3,500 characters to be considered literate. He suggests that the early and repeated memorizing of these characters results in a holistic outlook and a preference for the tangible, rather than the abstract. This preference then may lead to an evaluation of ideas in terms of their immediate application.

8. *Importance of context.* Peterson (1993) describes the Chinese as a high-context society in that they tend to perceive events and relationships within the context in which they occur, rather than as in the West, where in the business context, rules and procedures are generally perceived as more important.

We have looked at some broad dimensions of culture that have been suggested as differentiating Chinese and Westerners. Often, it is a matter of degree, rather than absolutes; for example, Westerners, too, are concerned about face, and there may be considerable variations among the Chinese themselves on these dimensions. The picture is further complicated, for example, by the influence of Western culture in Hong Kong, which does not affect everyone equally. Lau and Kuan (1988) suggest that the Hong Kong ethos represents a mixture of traditional Chinese culture and modern cultural traits fostered by the particular nature of Hong Kong society itself.

Dimensions of Culture

Probably the most comprehensive analysis of cultural differences was carried out by Hofstede (1980), in which he surveyed 116,000 employees of IBM working in 40 countries, including Hong Kong. Hofstede's study found four dimensions of national culture.

1. Collectivism versus individualism
2. Power distance
3. Uncertainty avoidance
4. Masculinity versus femininity

1. *Collectivism versus individualism.* This dimension relates to the degree of cohesiveness, integration, and loyalty to the group, as opposed to individuals looking after their own interests. Hong Kong came out high on the collectivism dimension. Although Hofstede's sample was drawn from a multinational company, Redding (1990) found similar results among Chinese family businesses. Collectivism implies the importance of relationships between group members; additionally, Tu (1984) describes Chinese society as being constructed of morally binding relationships connecting all; and Redding (1990) describes the extensive use of *Guanxi,* or contacts, in doing business in China.

2. *Power distance.* This dimension refers to the extent to which people accept that power in organizations should be distributed unequally. Thus, a high power distance culture like Hong Kong accepts wide differences in power in organizations. This acceptance suggests that a high level of autocratic behavior from managers is acceptable by subordinates. This situation links with the Confucian ethic of respect for those in authority.

3. *Masculinity versus femininity.* Masculinity refers to societies high in so-called masculine characteristics, such as strong needs for achievement, assertiveness, status, and recognition. *Femininity* refers to the presence of female qualities, such as sensitivity and concern for others' welfare. Hong Kong, for example, was in the middle on this dimension.

4. *Uncertainty avoidance.* This is a measure of the society's ability to tolerate uncertainty. Hong Kong came out low on uncertainty avoidance, a finding that indicates a relatively high tolerance for opinions and behaviors dif-

ferent from one's own and that the people are low in anxiety.

One criticism of Hofstede's work is that he studied employees of a large multinational company, so his findings might not be generalizable to the whole populations of the countries studied. But in Hofstede's (1991) view, the only thing that could explain the differences between national groups within the organization was the culture itself. This view is supported by Laurent (1983), who found that multinational companies do not reduce national value differences among their employees.

A major criticism that can be leveled against Hofstede is he used an instrument developed by Westerners and therefore biased toward Western values and language. To counter this criticism, Bond (1991) asked a group of Chinese social scientists from Taiwan and Hong Kong to design a questionnaire that was then administered in 23 countries. The results overlapped with Hofstede's results. The dimensions of individualism versus collectivism, power distance, and masculinity versus femininity emerged, but not uncertainty avoidance. Instead, Bond found a fourth dimension, which he termed *Confucian dynamism*. This dimension seems to be more related to "virtue," whereas uncertainty avoidance is more related to "truth."

A further obfuscation of the cultural dimensions comes from Trompenaars's (1993) study, which identified within one company extreme differences in individualism and power distance related to the department in which employees were working.

Hofstede's work, although published in 1980, was started many years earlier and so may now be rather dated; for example, the Hong Kong data were collected in the early 1970s. More recently, Trompenaars (1993) published the results of his 10-year study covering 15,000 managers from 28 countries, including Hong Kong. Trompenaars found five dimensions of culture.

1. Universalism versus particularism (rules vs. relationships)
2. Collectivism versus individualism (the group vs. the individual)
3. Neutral versus emotional (the range of feelings expressed)

4. Diffuse versus specific (the range of involvement)
5. Achievement versus ascription (how status is accorded)

Two of these suggest significant differences between Western and Hong Kong Chinese managers. *Universalism versus particularism* indicates the degree of importance placed on relationships. The Hong Kong managers' inclination toward particularism indicates a stronger emphasis on relationships, rather than on rules: A trustworthy person is one who honors changing circumstances, rather than his or her word, and several perspectives in reality exist relative to each person.

Diffuse versus specific deals with the degree of openness between people. Hong Kong Chinese managers are inclined toward the diffuse end of the continuum, and this is characterized by a more closed, formal, and reserved approach to relationships and a reluctance toward self-disclosure, particularly to those not in close relationships.

The literature on the culture of Hong Kong Chinese managers is interesting and gives some indicators for understanding and dealing with managers in Hong Kong. The picture is complicated but may be even more so if one remembers that most investigations into culture start from a Western perspective. As Maruyama (1984) says in his exploration of alternative concepts of management,

A move from European and North American (ENA) theories to Asian, African and Arabic theories is to cross a theoretical difference at a very different level compared to a move from one theory to another within ENA. The difference is at the epistemological level i.e. in the structure of perceiving, thinking and reasoning. (p. 101)

Previously, Cole and Scribner (1974) noted, "As yet there is no general theory or conceptual framework in psychology that would generate specific hypotheses about how culturally patterned experiences influence the development of cognitive processes in the individual" (p. 6). Nakamura (1964), however, in his study of thinking of Eastern peoples, gives the following characteristics as typical of Chinese thinking.

Emphasis on the perception of the concrete

Nondevelopment of abstract thought

Emphasis on the particular, rather than the universal

Practicality as a central focus

Concern for reconciliation, harmony, and balance

Interestingly, all of these seem to have been discovered in the cultural investigations of Hong Kong managers. Perhaps, though, it needs to be emphasized that Nakamura's list does not do justice to the richness of Chinese thinking. Needham's (1978) discussion of the Chinese approach to causal explanation and Northrop's (1944) discussion of intuitive concepts and ideas illustrate some of the complexity of Chinese thinking. Redding (1990) summarizes the difference between Western and Chinese cognition as follows:

Western cognition. Logical, sequential connections. Use of abstract notions of reality that represent universals. Emphasis on cause.

Chinese cognition. Intuitive perception and more reliance on sense data. Non-abstract. Non-logical (in the Cartesian sense). Emphasis on the particular, rather than the universal. High sensitivity to context and relationships.

Maruyama's (1984) article highlights the complexity of the different theoretical conceptions across cultures, and he discusses a variety of endogenous theories that Westerners previously had been totally unaware of and, in some of his Japanese examples, had misinterpreted by using Western ways of thinking. It seems possible that Westerners are not even aware of some Chinese theoretical and meta-theoretical differences. Certainly, Chinese philosophy does seem replete with theories (e.g., see Chan, 1963; Fung, 1947), though it is difficult to say which are influencing managers today.

The examples given above illustrate some of the complexity involved in understanding the behavior and thinking of the Hong Kong Chinese. We have carried out some qualitative research with Hong Kong Chinese who had worked with both Hong Kong and Western managers. Part of this research asked respondents to identify the differences they perceived

between Hong Kong Chinese managers and Western managers. The differences they identified tie in well with earlier findings but are perhaps expressed in a more straightforward way.

According to our Chinese respondents, Hong Kong Chinese managers, compared with Western managers, are

More hardworking

More serious

More analytical

More long-term thinking

More subjective in judgments

More formal

More conscious of differences in levels

More autocratic

More demanding

More secretive of plans

More concerned to get group decisions

Less likely to delegate

Less friendly, but more considerate of people

Less receptive to new ideas

Less open

Less creative

Less flexible

The flavor of the culture comes through in these findings, although some contradictions are apparent. For example, perhaps in the Hong Kong Chinese culture it is possible to be both more autocratic and more concerned to get group decisions. An alternative explanation is that the people being compared varied from case to case. One must also remember that the comparisons were drawn with Western managers who may not be typical. For instance, does the typical Western manager choose to work in Hong Kong?

So far, we have highlighted the growing trend of companies in sending expatriate managers to Asia. We have also identified and discussed some of the research findings concerning cultural differences between Chinese and Westerners, including our own findings from Hong Kong. Now we come to the intriguing question, What are the competencies required of an expatriate manager in Asia, and how can these be developed?

The Effective Expatriate Manager

Research on work related to cross-cultural interactions shows that between 16% and 40%

of all expatriate managers given foreign postings end their assignments early because of their poor performance or inability to adjust to the foreign environment and that up to 50% of those who do not return early function at a low level of effectiveness (Black & Mendenhall, 1990). Solutions usually proposed for this problem are appropriate selection and training (Mendenhall & Oddou, 1985; Tung 1981). However, it seems that cross-cultural training is not very widespread. According to Black and Mendenhall, only 30% of managers sent on expatriate assignments (of 1 to 5 years) receive cross-cultural training before their departure. Usually, discussion of cross-cultural training focuses on predeparture training, though Thiagarajan (1971) argues that cross-cultural training can be most effective if it is conducted after the trainee has lived and worked in the host culture for a short time. We agree with this position and that learning from one's own experience of the culture may be the most effective. Predeparture training may even be counterproductive because it may lead to a separation of intellectual and emotional learning and to the formation of false assumptions and stereotypes. Only when a person actually lives and works in the other culture will the cross-cultural issues become real and enable effective learning to take place. This actuality places the responsibility for cross-cultural learning firmly with the manager concerned, although the organization (or the manager) can provide useful support through a mentor, support group, and/or concurrent formal and informal training.

Mendenhall and Oddou (1985) suggest four components of successful expatriate acculturation, and most of the findings from our Hong Kong research fit into these four components. We then suggest a modified model, however, building on their work but also taking account of our own and others' research and using our experience with managers in Hong Kong.

The four components suggested by Mendenhall and Oddou (1985, 1986) are

1. Self-oriented dimension
2. Other-oriented dimension
3. Perceptual dimension
4. Cultural-toughness dimension

The *cultural toughness* dimension refers to the gap between the home culture of the expatriate and the culture in which he or she is working. After posting, the expatriate manager can do nothing about this. It can be an important consideration in selecting expatriate managers, however, and for the expatriate manager at the stage of deciding whether to accept a particular overseas posting or not.

We now consider Mendenhall and Oddou's first three dimensions, adding in some of the findings from our survey of expatriate managers and locals in Hong Kong.

Self-Oriented Dimension

The self-oriented dimension covers activities that maintain or strengthen the expatriate's self-esteem, self-confidence, and feelings of well-being. To some extent, the activities in this dimension are based on the individual's interests and personality. So, individuals will come up with their own personal answers that work for them. The subdimensions, however, do provide areas to focus on.

According to Mendenhall and Oddou (1985), this dimension is composed of three subfactors.

1. *Reinforcement substitution.* This subfactor involves replacing activities that bring pleasure in the home culture with similar, yet different, activities from the host culture. From our experience, some of these reinforcement substitution activities can also help with the other-oriented dimension—for example, enjoying Chinese food with locals and going for country walks with locals. Obviously, there are a great many possible substitutes, and expatriates who find parallel substitutes for their interests and activities tend to adjust more successfully in the host culture.

2. *Stress reduction.* Entering a new culture often produces stress for expatriates. Those who can deal with stress will adjust more successfully to the new culture. Ratiu (1983) discusses the use of stability zones by those who adjust well. *Stability zones* are activities, such as meditation, religious practices, writing, and a favorite pastime (e.g., sports), into which the manager is able to withdraw temporarily. Interestingly, Ratiu reports that the most effective expatriates have greater ease and readiness with which they can recall and discuss culture shock. They are more aware of the stress, more able to talk about and use it as a positive learning experience. This finding may indicate that perhaps new expatriate managers should try to

become aware of their culture shock and be prepared to talk about it and learn from it.

3. *Technical competence.* Possessing the necessary technical expertise seems to be an important aspect of expatriate adjustment. An expatriate who does not have the required level of expertise is likely to have problems of adjustment.

Mendenhall and Oddou (1985) are suggesting general areas within the self-oriented dimension that will help expatriates manage effectively. Our interviews with effective Asia managers in Hong Kong also added some factors specific to Hong Kong in the self-oriented dimension that worked for them:

Proactively trying to understand their culture
Playing by the rules and becoming less easy-going
Giving more explicit instructions and being more specific in communication
Leading more by example
Taking more care to present an image of fairness
Becoming more tolerant and patient
Becoming less aggressive

Other-Oriented Dimension

The other-oriented dimension is concerned with interacting effectively with locals and, according to Mendenhall and Oddou (1985), consists of two subfactors; relationship development and willingness to communicate.

1. *Relationship development.* Establishing close relationships with locals enables the newcomer to understand the intricacies of the new culture and to behave appropriately and not make the usual cross-cultural mistakes. Research indicates that long-lasting friendships with locals is an important factor in successful adjustment.

2. *Willingness to communicate.* Communication skills that seem important in successful adjustment are as follows:

Willingness to use the local language
Confidence in interacting with locals
Use of "conversational currency" (e.g., anecdotes, jokes, proverbs, local news stories related to the culture)
Desire to understand and relate with locals

These two relationship factors seem particularly important for the East Asia manager. As one of our local respondents commented, "Chinese working culture is more people-oriented. Establishing personal relationships with local staff is important."

In our survey of local Chinese staff in Hong Kong, we asked what Western managers did that seemed helpful in enabling them to fit into the local culture. Their answers included the following:

Trying to understand local customs
Being familiar with the local culture
Reading local newspapers/magazines
Integrating with locals—trying to get along with them, rather than trying to create a distinct circle of expatriates
Having plenty of discussion with local colleagues, but not just work related
Taking an active role in joining local colleagues' activities in Karaoke, mahjong, lunch
Appreciating Chinese food
Learning the local language, or at least key phrases/expressions
Learning about local staffs' attitudes toward different managerial styles and using an appropriate style
Having an open mind

This last example—having an open mind—seems particularly important and is a major factor influencing the next major dimension to be covered—the perceptual dimension.

Perceptual Dimension

People from different cultures often misinterpret each other's behavior because of learned cultural differences in the way they perceive, interpret, and evaluate social behaviors. However, it is not just a question of having some understanding of the local culture. Research shows that expatriates who adjust well are nonjudgmental and nonevaluative when interpreting the behavior of locals. They make looser or less rigid evaluations and are more willing to change their perceptions and interpretations. They tend to use stereotypes more self-consciously and tentatively and do not relate to locals in stereotypical ways (Ratiu, 1983). Their concern is with description and interpretation, as opposed to the less well

Well adjusted
expatriate cycle

less well adjusted
expatriate cycle

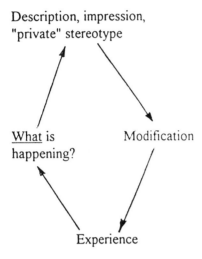

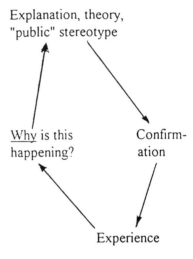

Figure 21.1. Ratiu's Proposed Learning Cycles

SOURCE: J. Raitu, Thinking internationally: A comparison of how international executives learn. *International Studies of Management and Organization, XIII* (1-2), p. 147. Copyright M. E. Sharpe, Inc. Used with permission.

adjusted expatriates who tend to seek early explanations and rapid conclusions. Ratiu sees the less well adjusted as looking backward to try to pick up from their new experience data that will confirm their previous conclusions. The better adjusted are more forward looking, trying to find out more and more to improve the tentative picture they already have.

This dimension seems to be more than just perceptual, as labeled by Mendenhall and Oddou. Our experience agrees with Ratiu's (1983) suggestion that the well-adjusted expatriate uses a particular learning cycle that is different from the learning cycle being used by the less well adjusted (see Figure 21.1).

Ratiu (1983) based his proposed learning cycles on the model of Kolb and Fry (1975). The basic difference between the two cycles is that the well-adjusted or most international expatriate managers are much more tentative in their dealings with foreign nationals and, in particular, in their perception of foreign nationals. The less well adjusted seem to be searching for more definite answers about the differences between their own culture and the foreign culture as if they are looking for ways to differentiate their own culture from the new culture. They are also quicker to attribute definite differences to the foreign nationals, in contrast with the better-adjusted expatriates, who tend to be more subjective and tentative.

Williams (1980) had developed the learning cycle further to include the role of others in the learning process and, bearing in mind that the other-oriented dimension of successful cross-cultural management includes the learning from locals to improve understanding, we suggest an enhanced learning cycle for the effective expatriate manager. Following the suggestion from some respondents in our survey concerning the importance of open-mindedness, we see this as a facilitating factor impinging on every stage of the learning cycle and have thus put it at the core of our model (see Figure 21.2).

Learning from experience really involves trying to make sense of what happens to you by a construction of what reality means for any

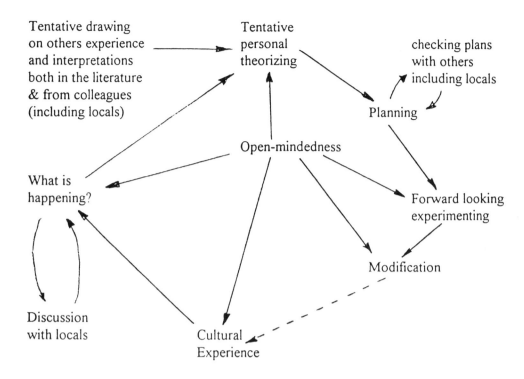

Figure 21.2. Effective Expatriate Managers' Learning Cycle

particular situation. We believe that the effective expatriate manager has a much looser, more tentative construction of this cultural reality. The less-effective expatriate manager wishes for more certainty to explain what is happening and so will jump more readily to accept theories and explanations and then try to fit any further experience into these. The more-effective expatriate is more open-minded and more ready to change his or her own tentative personal theory as he or she undergoes new experiences or as new information becomes available.

After considering this learning cycle, it is interesting to speculate on the value of predeparture training. Usually, this training involves learning about the characteristics of the new culture. Almost inevitably, this will involve a degree of stereotyping. Usually, there is a range of behavior, and "cultural facts" are really only someone's idea of average behavior in that culture. As well as the variations in behavior, the average behavior may be changing. In Hong Kong, for example, the move seems to be toward more Westernization over the last few years, in our experience. Cultural facts perhaps can become outdated.

The real key to the effectiveness of cross-cultural training is how the cultural facts and stereotypes are received. If they are taken as definite objective facts, then the training may do more harm than good: It may inhibit open-mindedness and hence cultural learning. If the cultural facts and stereotypes are perceived as only tentative, then the managers can perhaps be encouraged to continue learning in a flexible, open, ongoing attempt to increase their understanding of the host nationals and their culture. Perhaps the effective expatriate is able to continually question and challenge his or her own values and assumptions concerning the host culture. A potential indication of this quality is the extent to which the manager is judgmental and evaluative regarding the local staff both individually and as a group. Judgmental and evaluative perceptions and behavior may indicate a more rigid, less open approach to the culture, which may be less effective.

Managerial Cultural Competence

Managerial cultural competence, the ability to manage effectively in a foreign culture, is a combination of several factors. Here, we draw on Mendenhall and Oddou's (1985) analysis but modify and build on it by using our own and Ratiu's (1983) research:

Managerial Cultural Competence Factors

1. Self-oriented dimension comprising three subfactors

    a. Reinforcement substitution
    b. Stress reduction
    c. Technical competence

2. Other-oriented dimension comprising

    a. Relationship development
    b. Willingness to communicate

3. Cognitive dimension

    a. Perceptual
    b. Nonjudgmental, nonevaluative attitude
    c. Loose/Flexible interpretations of situations
    d. Open-minded, tentative, intuitive approach to learning

Mendenhall and Oddou suggest a fourth dimension, *cultural toughness,* which is basically a measure of the compatibility of the two cultures concerned, that of the expatriate manager and that of the host country. These researchers seem to imply that this dimension is solely dependent on the cultures of the two countries involved.

In our experience, this dimension also has an individual element. An individual manager's personality and background experience may help him or her feel more at ease or at home with a particular culture or, alternatively, more ill at ease with the culture. We term this situation *cultural compatibility,* and it consists of two factors: the cultural toughness referred to by Mendenhall and Oddou, and the compati-

bility of the individual with the culture. So, the fourth factor becomes

4. Cultural compatibility

    a. Individual compatibility
    b. Cultural toughness

These different factors of cultural competence interact with each other and can be represented as in Figure 21.3.

Some Practical Advice for Western Managers Working in the Chinese-Dominated Regions of Southeast Asia

In this chapter, we attempted to provide the reader an insight into the complexity and challenge facing the Western manager new to the Southeast Asian, Chinese work environment. We began with a brief introduction to some of the more well established research findings and, in doing so, identified several fairly well defined differences between Chinese and Western people. Much of this research, however, was conducted and commented on by Western observers and, as such, was influenced by the personal biases and values of that particular cultural group. A second important caveat in assessing the practical worth of these findings is that although certain differences have been identified, they tend to be general in nature and, as such, cannot be used to predict the behavior of specific individuals. For example, it would be risky to assume that a Chinese employee is less likely to question the actions of the boss than is his or her Western counterpart.

By introducing models, our intention was to provide the expatriate manager moving to Asia for the first time a series of mental tools and frameworks that will help him or her derive the most from initial experiences. Of course, managers can do a number of things prior to their posting to culturally attune themselves to the new country—language tuition, for example. It is our belief, and one shared by many seasoned expatriate managers, that managers never really become fully attuned until they have actually lived among the culture concerned. Central to successful cultural acculturation is the need to

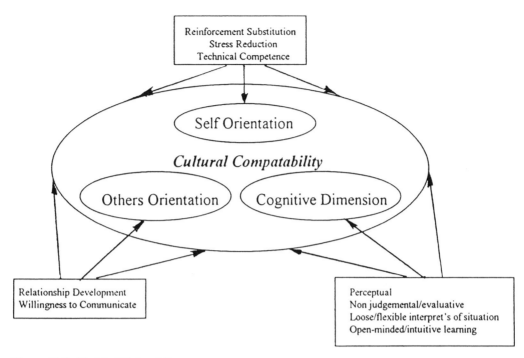

Figure 21.3. Model of Cultural Competence

remain open-minded and to recognize that, from a managerial perspective, although some approaches may be different in the host country, they are not necessarily less effective and, indeed, in many cases may be considerably more so!

We mentioned at the beginning of this chapter that the competencies required in an international manager are perhaps more geographically specialized than at first expected. We continue to support this view but add that the degree of open-mindedness needed for a Westerner to adapt to a Southeast Asian working environment in itself requires microcompetencies that may be less important for local postings, such as those within Europe. These competencies were identified as individual compatibility and cultural toughness, which may not be readily transferable to all individuals. On this basis, we argue that some expatriate managers are inherently more operationally effective within an overseas Chinese work environment than others and, in this respect, would require careful initial selection by the companies concerned.

We end with some comments from local respondents in our research who were asked what advice they would offer newly arrived Western managers who had never lived or worked in Asia before:

- Become familiar with the local culture; before the posting, try to talk to someone who's been working in that culture before.
- Read local newspapers. Keep up to date with current local issues and show your interest by discussing these with local staff.
- Learn some Cantonese, at least some greetings, but preferably more.
- Mix well with local colleagues: Attend local social activities with them, communicate and try to integrate.
- Get to know the local culture and managerial style.
- Bear in mind that many colloquial terms you bring with you are not understood, even the ones you think are common in your own country.

- Keep doing research and learn about the culture. Let this show in your interaction with locals.

Two respondents in particular gave their advice in terms of how they picture an effective Western manager:

The effective Western manager asks, considers, and rewards inputs from his subordinates; he works damn hard and mixes well with the locals but mustn't get too friendly with subordinates so that he can still maintain control over them and be able to get the work done efficiently.

An effective Western manager usually creates a more friendly image amongst local staff. He knows and is willing to learn more about local society so when he discusses with his staff about work or socializes with the local employees, he shows his interest in them. Remember, the "personal touch" is important in Chinese society. If a Western manager makes staff feel that he considers himself distinct and "higher" than Chinese staff, he is not going to be accepted. Being different is all right; showing that you think you are superior in not a good idea.

References

Adler, N. J. (1986). *International dimensions of organizational behavior* (Kent International Business Series). Boston: Kent.

Barham, K., & Oates, D. (1991). *The international manager.* London: Economist Books.

Barham, K., & Wills, S. (1992). *Management across frontiers: Identifying the competencies of successful international managers* (Ashridge Management Research Group, Report 929). Berkhamsted, UK: Ashridge Management College.

Black, J. S., & Mendenhall, M. (1990). Cross-cultural training effectiveness: A review and a theory framework for future research. *Academy of Management Review, 15*(1), 113-136.

Bond, M. H. (1986). *The psychology of the Chinese people.* Cambridge, UK: Oxford University Press.

Bond, M. H. (1991). *Beyond the Chinese face.* Cambridge, UK: Oxford University Press.

Chan, W. T. (1963). *A source book in Chinese philosophy.* Princeton, NJ: Princeton University Press.

Cole, M., & Scribners, S. (1974). *Culture and thought.* New York: John Wiley.

Drucker, P. (1988, September-October). Management and the world's work. *Harvard Business Review,5,* 65-76.

Fung, Y. L. (1947). *The spirit of Chinese philosophy* (E. R. Hughes, Trans.). London: Routledge & Kegan Paul.

Goffman, E. (1955). On face work: An analysis of ritual elements in social interaction. *Psychiatry, 18*(3), 213-231.

Hofstede, G. (1980). *Culture's consequences: International differences in work-related values.* Beverly Hills, CA: Sage.

Hofstede, G. (1981). Culture and organizations. *International Studies of Management and Organization, 10*(4), 15-41.

Hofstede, G. (1991). *Cultures and organizations: Software of the mind.* New York: McGraw-Hill.

Hong Kong Census and Statistics Department. (1994). Hong Kong: Government Information Service Publication.

Hsu, F. L. K. (1949). Suppression versus repression: A limited psychological interpretation of four cultures. *Psychiatry, 12,* 223-242.

Kanter, R. M. (1989). *When giants learn to dance.* New York: Simon & Schuster.

Kirkbride, P. S., Tang, S. F. Y., & Shae, W. C. (1989). The transferability of management training and development: The case of Hong Kong. *Asia Pacific Human Resource Management, 27*(1), 7-9.

Kolb, D., & Fry, R. (1975). Toward an applied theory of experiential learning. In C. L. Cooper (Ed.), *Theories of group processes* (pp. 33-51). Chichester, UK: Wiley.

Lau, S., & Kuan, H. (1988). *The ethos of the Hong Kong Chinese.* Hong Kong: Chinese University Press.

Laurent, A. (1983). The cultural diversity of Western conceptions of management. *International Studies of Management and Organization, 13*(1-2), 75-96.

Levitt, T. (1983, May-June). The globalization of markets. *Harvard Business Review, 21,* 92-102.

Marsick, V. J., Turner, E., & Cederholm, L. (1989). International managers as team leaders. *American Management Review.*

Maruyama, M. (1984). Alternative concepts of management: Insights from Asia and Africa. *Asia Pacific Journal of Management, 1*(1), 100-111.

Mendenhall, M., & Oddou, G. (1985). The dimensions of expatriate acculturation: A review. *Academy of Management Review, 10,* 39-47.

Mendenhall, M., & Oddou, G. (1986). Acculturation profiles of expatriate managers: Implications for cross-cultural training programs. *Columbia Journal of World Business, 21,* 73-79.

Naisbett, J., & Aburdene, P. (1990). *Megatrends 2000.* London: Sidgwick Jackson.

Nakamura, H. (1964). *Ways of thinking of Eastern peoples: India-China-Tibet-Japan.* Honolulu: University of Hawaii Press.

Needham, J. (1978). *Science and civilization in China.* Cambridge, UK: Cambridge University Press.

Northrop, F. S. C. (1944). The complementary emphases of Eastern intuitive and Western scientific philosophy. In C. A. Moore (Ed.), *Philosophy East and West.* Princeton, NJ: Princeton University Press.

Peterson, R. B. (Ed.). (1993). *Managers and national culture: A global perspective.* Westport, CT: Quorum.

Ratiu, I. (1983). Thinking internationally: A comparison of how international executives learn. *International Studies of Management and Organization, XIII*(1-2), 139-150.

Redding, S. G. (1990). *The spirit of Chinese capitalism.* New York: de Gruyter.

Redding, S. G., & Armitage, C. (1993). *Management development in Asia-Pacific: Molding managers for success* (Economist Intelligence Unit Research Report). London: EIU.

Redding, S. G., & Casey, T. W. (1976). Managerial beliefs among Asian managers. In R. L. Taylor, M. J. O'Connell, R. A. Zawacki, & D. D. Warwick (Eds.), *Proceedings of the Academy of Management 36th Annual Conference of the Academy of Management,* 351-355.

Redding, S. G., & Ng, M. (1982). The role of "face" in the organisational perception of Chinese managers. *Organisation Studies, 3,* 201-219.

Reid, P. (1991). *Global management: Culture, context, competence* (Ashridge Management Research Group Report 916). Berkhamsted, UK: Ashridge Management College.

Syrett, M. (1993, May). Directions. *Ashridge Journal,* pp. 26-30.

Tang, S. F. Y., & Kirkbride, P. S. (1986). Developing conflict management skills in Hong Kong: An analysis of some cross-cultural implications. *Management Education and Development, 17*(3), 287-301.

Thiangarajan, K. M. (1971). Cross-cultural training for overseas management. *Management International Review, II*(4-5), 69-85.

Trompenaars, A. (1993). *Riding the waves of culture.* London: Economist Books.

Tu, W. M. (1984). *Confucian ethics today: The Singapore challenge.* Singapore: Federal Publications.

Tung, R. L. (1981). Selection and training of personnel for overseas assignments. *Columbia Journal of World Business, 16*(1), 68-78.

Williams, G. (1980, January). *Improving the management effectiveness of the school principal.* Paper presented at the Fourth Commonwealth Council for Education Administration Regional Conference, Nicosia, Cyprus.

Wyatt Consulting Group. (1994). *1994 Compensation report, Hong Kong.* Hong Kong: Far East Survey Unit of the Wyatt Company.

22

Training Teachers and Students for Intercultural Cooperation in Israel
Two Models

HANNA SHACHAR

YEHUDA AMIR

THIS chapter focuses on the possibilities of schools making a positive contribution for coexistence in multicultural societies. At first, two major orientations in multiracial societies—integration and pluralism—as well as their relevance in schools are discussed. Then some background information on Israel, where both orientations exist in one country, are presented. Following, two intervention models for furthering cultural coexistence and its implementation in Israeli schools are elaborated. Finally, some prospects for the future are suggested.

A major demographic characteristic of many countries is their newly developed social structure of ethnic or racial diversity that resulted from massive population movements, easily facilitated by modern transportation technolo-

gies. Examples of this development are (a) Europe, following the immigration of workers to central and northern Europe from Third World countries; (b) typical immigrant countries, such as the United States, Canada, and Israel; (c) the collapse of European colonialism and subsequently the movement of native residents to the colonial "motherland" (e.g., Indians and Pakistanis to England); (d) results of wars; (e) results of population exchange or transfer (e.g., Turkish Bulgarians to Turkey, Cypriots of Turkish and Greek origin, Muslims in India). The tendency toward cultural diversity gained additional momentum as a result of a new trend evidenced after World War II in many countries for minorities, even ancient ones, to achieve cultural independence or equal rights, which included religious autonomy or equality and revival of old and sometimes even forgotten languages, native traditions, and laws (e.g., the Basques in Spain, the French in Canada).

In many of these cases, these new populations, immigrants, or old ethnic subgroups have acquired in the host country some kind of cultural equality. As a result, a process started in that country to change from a unicultural, uniethnic, and unilinguistic society to a multicultural one. In such a multicultural society, the question arises, what style of social and cultural life does that society or country prefer? Is it in the convergent direction, such as social and cultural intermixing, a melting pot orientation, or is the divergent ideology predominant, emphasizing cultural or even political separation, ethnic pluralism, and so forth? A society's preference in one direction will have direct consequences in many spheres of life, such as work, housing projects, social and community behavior, governmental policies, and schools and education.

The problem is that, at times, especially when social changes occur, societies are not always clear about their orientation on this issue. In such cases, discontinuity, disorientation, and a cognitive entanglement may be the result for the next generation.

In general, countries and societies have chosen an avenue of cultural ideology to direct their social life with regard to ethnic intergroup coexistence. The most prevailing choices are as van Oudenhoven and Willemsen (1989) stated: "Assimilation and pluralism form the two poles of a dimension reflecting the degree to which a minority group is supposed to adapt to the majority" (p. 247). National examples of these different solutions can easily be provided. Switzerland could serve as a relatively extreme example of ethnic pluralism. A number of ethnic groups differentiated on religious, cultural, linguistic and, to some extent, historical bases live side by side with a high degree of own-group liberty and self-expression, as well as of intergroup tranquility and mutual respect, under a very general umbrella of national institutions and unity. At the other extreme (assimilation or melting pot policy), we could categorize some of the South American countries, with their Spanish, Indian, and sometimes black racial ancestors, the United States, and some European countries—at least with regard to their official cultural proclamation, though not always in line with the practical behavior of the individual majority group members.

Canada could serve as an intermediary example where ethnic pluralism is the official national policy and, to a large extent, is also accepted as a social norm. Still, one gets the impression that the policy of pluralism is a result—and to some extent, a rational compromise initiated by the Anglo-oriented majority group—of a political necessity. Actually, many majority group members and leaders prefer the country and its society to continue to be Anglo culturally oriented and believe that, in the long (but not too long) run, it will indeed be so.

Israel is an example where, in one country, both social orientations of living separately and together take place.

Multiculturalism in the Schools

Once a society has made its choice, schools may follow this direction, trying to implement educational programs that will facilitate this orientation and aiming at preparing the future generation to accept the preferred social consensus and to live accordingly as adults. After all, social continuity is, in practice, a major mission carried out by the educational system and the schools. Still, the question of how this topic is represented and dealt with in the curriculum and other educational programs in the schools remains. The general impression is that the answer to this question is quite simple and straightforward—namely, hardly, if at all. Schools and learning contexts in many European, North American, Middle Eastern, and even Southeast Asian and Pacific Ocean countries generally exclude this topic from the curriculum and hardly deal with it in extracurricular activities. In a number of countries (e.g., United States, Israel), attempts are made to involve such contents in the schools, but they are sporadic, rare, and generally on an experimental basis.

The result is that the preparation of children through the schools for an ethnically mixed society is minimal and, in many countries, practically nonexistent. Assuming that the need exists, the question is, can something be done about it? Is enough knowledge and information available to help the schools and direct them regarding the assimilative or integrative orientation, or alternatively concerning the pluralistic preference?

The answer to this question is a positive one. Many intervention programs for students and the schools have already been developed, primarily during the last 20 years. Many of these programs have also been thoroughly studied and evaluated. Research results have extensively contributed to the improvement of some of these approaches and programs (Johnson & Johnson, 1981).

Two major intervention orientations and subsequent techniques are presently implemented in schools that have chosen to deal with the issue of multiculturalism. One orientation is labeled *school integration* and is generally practiced in schools in which students from different ethnic or racial backgrounds are in constant contact on a day-to-day basis within the school. The other orientation, sometimes referred to as *intercultural learning,* does not require actual intergroup contact in the schools; it focuses on learning about positive aspects of the "other" culture(s) and aims at de-emphasizing the superiority of one's own culture, as well as accepting differences. The second orientation may be used in ethnically homogeneous schools where intergroup contact does not exist. Still, it may also be practiced in ethnically integrated schools, in addition to their dealing with intergroup interventions based on ethnic contact.

Later, we elaborate on these two orientations, specifically as implemented in Israeli schools. To help the reader more fully understand their relevance in Israel, we provide in the next section some background information about the ethnic composition of Israel and its educational structure.

Demographic Background and Educational Structure of Israel

On the one hand, ethnic integration is a clear-cut national policy and an accepted social norm regarding the ethnic Jewish groups originating from Western (primarily European) and Middle Eastern (primarily Muslim) countries. On the other hand, for the Israeli Jews and Arabs, the policy is pluralism, which is accepted by both Jewish and Arab groups.

Israel's demographic composition can be described briefly as follows: A Jewish majority comprising about 84% of the population and an Arab (including Druze) minority of about 16%.

The Jewish population stems primarily from two geographical origins: those who originally emigrated from European, North American, and other "Western" countries (e.g., South Africa), and those who came from Asia and North Africa, most of them Middle Eastern Muslim countries. At present, these two groups have more or less equal portions in the country.

Differences in cultural background and considerable differences in educational and occupational levels have resulted in a high correspondence between ethnic background and social class. Westerners acquired solid social positions, whereas many Middle Easterners were found at the bottom of the social ladder. This situation produced intergroup tension that was and still is, to some degree, accompanied by prejudice and social distance. Despite this social-cultural cleavage, members of both groups identify themselves as members of a common Jewish nation and show a basic sense of identification with the land and people of Israel. Ethnic interaction and integration are generally accepted as a national norm. As such, there is broad acceptance and strong social consensus of the goal of ethnic mixing and social integration of the groups, and no institution or group opposes this orientation in principle. On a day-to-day basis, however, there are still clear traces of interethnic tension between the groups (Amir, Sharan, & Ben-Ari, 1984).

The intergroup situation of the Jewish majority and the Arab minority in Israel can be typified as two groups living side by side as distinct entities. Their relations are characterized by an almost total separation in most areas of life and by some pronounced negative feelings and attitudes toward each other. Jews are generally oblivious to the realities of the Arab sector and do not exhibit much interest in Arabs and their culture. Israeli Arabs have a strong feeling of minority discrimination and a heightened sensitivity to their being ignored by the Jewish majority. This state of affairs has been sustained and intensified by the continuous conflict and tension between Israel and its Arab neighbors. Lately, however, probably as a consequence of the peace treaty some 15 years ago between Israel and Egypt, and currently between Jordan and Israel, as well as between Israel and the Palestinians, some change in the attitudes of both sides in the acceptance of the principle of coexistence appears to have taken place. Both groups seem to have realized that they will have to make political compromises and live together in one way or another (Amir & Ben-Ari, 1989; Louis Guttman Institute, 1993; Peled & Bar-Gal, 1983). Still, one should also take into account that neither side is interested in attaining social and cultural integration or in promoting interpersonal relations of an intimate nature with the other group. Each group prefers to retain its cultural and national uniqueness, social and physical separation, as well as a distinct group identity. Consequently and probably as a result of the present-day political scenarios and changing tendencies toward concrete peaceful solutions in this geographical area, cultural pluralism seems to be the mode of living together preferred and accepted by both Israeli Jews and Arabs.

Israel's school structure is quite different for these two intergroup situations. Although there is no law or any other institutional requirement for separation, Arab and Jewish students generally attend separate, ethnically homogeneous schools. This trend developed for the following reasons: (a) The vast majority of Arabs and Jews live in different towns, villages, and neighborhoods; (b) both groups prefer separate educational institutions because of national, religious, linguistic, and a variety of other reasons. As a consequence, children and youths of both groups have only a minimal opportunity to meet and communicate with each other.

For the Jewish population, the schools are ethnically mixed with regard to students from Western and Middle Eastern backgrounds. In elementary schools, this ethnic mixing is less extensive. The reason for this is that neighborhoods are sometimes socioeconomically homogeneous, elementary schools are generally neighborhood schools, and there is still a correlation between ethnic background and socioeconomic status (SES). In junior high schools (which are generally attached to senior high schools), however, there is a national policy of ethnic mixing. Thus, ethnic mixing at the high school level is a national policy, as well as the general practice in the country.

In the following sections, two models of intercultural interventions in the schools are presented. The first program is implemented in a large number of ethnically mixed Jewish junior high schools and in a somewhat different version in elementary schools. The second program is being carried out in a number of Arab and Jewish schools.[1]

School Integration Model

Heterogeneity in the student population creates manifold challenges for schools and teachers, who often are ill-prepared to cope with them. The problems posed by the students' heterogeneity affect school administration and are exacerbated by the relative lack of adequate teacher preparation for dealing with this issue. As a result of this confluence of causes, schools have devised various ways of their own to limit the effects of the problem.

Two approaches can be identified for coping with the heterogeneous classroom in multicultural schools. One approach claims that students' cultural or ethnic diversity constitutes an impediment to student academic progress and is not beneficial. The more accomplished learners are prevented from progressing at their own pace, and slower learners are not taught at a pace that takes their needs into consideration. This approach, therefore, would advocate the use of initial assessment of students' learning abilities and needs, often by use of standardized tests, followed by assignment of students to ability groups on the basis of their test scores. Finally, teachers will adapt subject matter and study materials according to the particular needs of each level. Of note is the fact that the teaching method employed in the various ability groups is almost entirely of the traditional frontal type of whole-class instruction.

The second approach asserts that cultural diversity among students in the same school provides an opportunity, as well as a resource, for mutual enrichment for both the students and the teachers. That can be realized, however, only if the school plans students' learning experiences in such a way as to take advantage of the situation.

Obviously, the learning experiences designed by each approach will differ considerably. The first approach, "assessment-assignment-adaptation of materials," employs a system of ability grouping and tracking students in separate classes according to their level of achievement. The second approach seeks to change the instructional method from the traditional whole-class type to a more cooperative, interactive style of teaching and learning in which students have unmediated contact with one another. The first approach is by far the more prevalent one because it appears to simplify matters for schools and teachers who face the need to cope with culturally heterogeneous classes every day. This approach, however, also exacts a high price in terms of the potential academic progress of all students and in terms of achieving the social goals of fostering positive interaction between members of different ethnic and cultural groups.

Research and experience have shown that separation of students according to achievement level negatively affects their self-image (Eitan, Amir, & Rich, 1992) and their chance for academic advancement (Cahan, Linchevski, & Igra, in press). It was found that twice the number of students are transferred to lower levels than are promoted to higher ones (Rich, Shachar, & Shafir, 1988). Moreover, the quality of the learning materials, educational environment, and teachers is distinctly lower in the lower tracks, compared with the higher ones. In Israel, there is a 75% overlap between academic track and ethnic group, such that students of Middle Eastern background are concentrated in the lower tracks.

Put together, these data express a clear social message transmitted by the educational system, intentionally or unintentionally. The message is that there are "more and less equal" students as a function of their ethnic background. Inevitably, the school exerts a decisive effect on the students' future status in society.

The second approach, the school integration approach, maintains that diversity in the student populations constitutes an opportunity for enrichment for both the students and the teachers. Despite its sound grounding in theory and research, this approach is not widely used in schools. The primary reasons for its relatively limited adoption by schools is found in the latters' organizational features and in the professional and educational thinking of the teaching staff (Shachar & Sharan, 1995). We elaborate on this topic later in this chapter.

The theoretical basis of the second approach includes the contact theory for creating positive intergroup relations among different ethnic groups. *Contact theory* requires that the following conditions prevail in the intergroup contact situation: (a) All members of the interacting group must have equal status; (b) the situation requires cooperation, not competition, among members of the different groups; (c) the intergroup contact must be meaningful and involving for the participants, and not superficial; (d)

the situation must be sanctioned by the relevant authority; and (e) participants must derive pleasure and satisfaction from the situation (Allport, 1954; Amir, 1969, 1976; Cook, 1962).

The relevant instructional methods whose effects were assessed in a large number of empirical studies involve cooperation among students of different academic levels, cultural and ethnic groups, as well as learning experiences with a high level of complexity, initiative, and mutual interdependence among students (Aronson, Blaney, Stephan, Sikes, & Snapp, 1978; Cohen et al., 1994; Sharan, 1980, 1994; Sharan & Sharan, 1976; Slavin, 1983, 1990; Slavin & Madden, 1979).

The full range of cooperative learning methods is available in recent publications (Sharan, 1994). In general, cooperative learning is an instructional strategy that involves several variations based on a number of common features:

- Classrooms are divided into small heterogeneous groups of students (3 to 5 per group), which constitute the social units in which learning is pursued.
- Students in these groups interact directly with one another with respect to the learning materials while this interaction is unmediated by the teacher.
- Student interaction includes mutual assistance, cooperation, and exchange of ideas, feelings, and materials as they pursue a common academic goal.
- The small groups assume responsibility for selecting, planning, implementing, and presenting their learning outcomes.

Clearly, these features represent a significant change in classroom life and learning. They refer to all major dimensions of classroom learning and behavior—dimensions such as the teachers' function, the students' behavior, the nature of the learning task, the classroom organization, and the interpersonal communication among the students and between students and teachers.

When the above dimensions are changed and when the cooperative learning features are implemented, they create a living and learning environment that allows a large scope of contributions made by the students to fulfill the common goal of the group. It also allows an ongoing process of improvement in the social

TABLE 22.1 Comparison Between Two Educational Approaches Based on Contact Theory

	First Approach	*Second Approach*
Contact Conditions	*Assessment-Assignment-Adoption*	*Cooperative Learning*
Equal status	Absent: Students assigned to ability groups according to academic level	Present: All group members share same activity
Cooperation and not competition	Absent: Prevailing instructional method fosters competition	Present: Learning tasks based on cooperation
Meaningful situation and not superficial	Often absent: Learning tasks are routine and imposed by teachers	Often present: Students are empowered to make choices and decisions
Support by relevant authorities	Absent when school authorities employ a policy of tracking and ability grouping	Present when school adopts instructional methods supporting cooperation
Satisfaction	Depends on chance factors such as an unusual teacher	Present: Students manage their own behavior

relations among different groups in the classroom.

Implementation of the kind of learning environment required by the cooperative learning methods is dependent on considerable investment of time and energy in cultivating the appropriate skills needed by teachers and principals. Acquiring the skills necessary for employing cooperative learning methods in the classroom, however, is only one of several steps that must be taken to ensure effective use of these methods in the classroom. The other necessary steps deal with the school as an organizational unit.

The two approaches discussed above can be compared in terms of the extent to which each one fulfills various conditions of the contact theory and thereby contributes to improving intergroup relations. The comparison is made clear by Table 22.1.

Necessary and Sufficient Conditions for Implementing Cooperative Learning in Heterogeneous Schools

It is widely accepted that in-service or preservice training for teachers is the necessary condition for bringing about the implementation of cooperative learning in heterogeneous schools. Yet, it has been observed by many teacher trainers that a discrepancy exists between the input in teacher training efforts and the output of teachers' teaching behavior in classrooms. In many cases, apropos these observations, trainers redoubled their efforts and tried to improve the way in-service training courses were conducted. This was done on the assumption that the improvement would yield better results, or in other words: More and better training will produce better results in the classroom.

During the course of years, as greater appreciation was gained of the relevance of a systems approach to understanding schools, it became clear that in-service training is indeed a necessary condition for achieving ongoing change in classroom instruction. However, it is certainly not a sufficient one. Providing training for teachers, either as individuals or in small groups, does not yield desired results.

It became quite apparent that personnel at all levels of the school, including principals, department coordinators, and teachers, must be involved in the in-service training efforts. The unique function of each level of personnel had to be taken into consideration when constructing the training model presented here.

Time and experience have shown even that was not enough to effect real change. Having all levels of school personnel acquire relevant knowledge is only one dimension of the picture. A second dimension of the instructional change effort is for personnel at any level of the

TABLE 22.2 A 4-Stage Working Model for Implementing Cooperative Learning in Secondary
Schools

	Stage 1 *Learning what to do*	Stage 2 *Learning how to do*	Stage 3 *Getting the experience*	Stage 4 *Establishing the change*
Principals	Defining the principal's role as facilitator for changing teaching methods in the school	Setting up a schedule for collaborative planning by teachers	Expanding cooperative learning; developing new methods of eval- uation	Establishing cooperative learning as a norm in school life
Coordinators	Defining the role of coordinators; acquiring the necessary skills to lead cooperative plan- ning by teachers' teams	Leading team planning; sharing observations of classrooms and drawing conclusions	Developing teamwork and planning alternative ways of student evalua- tion	Ongoing assessment of goals and means in co- operative learning
Teachers	Introducing cooperative learning methods and their rationale, including initial imple- mentation	Collaborative planning of lessons; implemen- tation with peer obser- vation	Ongoing team planning and implementing co- operative learning and alternative ways of eval- uation	Using cooperative learn- ing and alternative eval- uation regularly
Students	—	Initial exposure to co- operative learning; analyzing differences between techniques	Developing cooperative skills and self-regulated learning	Mastering different learning techniques and skills

school to have time for well-planned experience, for building appropriate norms of professional behavior and decision making concerning the instructional change.

Several stages of professional development
intervene between the acquisition of knowledge and skills and the daily implementation of
cooperative learning. During these intervening
stages, teachers make mistakes that may provide the raw material for analyzing and understanding their work, so they can gradually reach
a high level of professional competence.

Table 22.2 presents a 4-stage training model
designed to bring about an ongoing change of
instructional methods in multicultural schools.
The model shows that each level of the school
requires specific skills needed for implementing instructional and social change—namely,
changing the instructional method as a prerequisite for positive contact among students.

Students

In the first stage, the change does not affect
the students. In the second stage, the students

begin to have initial experiences in cooperation. They are given tasks and learning materials that require them to negotiate with one another, to listen to and assist one another, and to
plan learning activities together.

Cooperation and mutual assistance are skills
that students do not ordinarily possess. This is
especially true when students have been socialized into a system of classroom learning that
emphasizes listening to teachers' verbal presentations and following teachers' instructions and
where evaluations of their behavior stress the
value of not talking and of obeying authority.
An example of this state of affairs occurred during an experiment that encompassed nine
classes of eighth-grade students. One class was
to carry out a group investigation project in
which students were organized into heterogeneous groups. The students were given learning
materials and guidelines for proceeding with
their work, and the teacher told them to begin.
Everyone remained silent: No one moved or
talked. Once again, the teacher told them to begin their work, whereupon a few hesitant movements became evident, accompanied by smiles
that reflected the students' confusion. Fifteen

minutes elapsed before students slowly began to proceed with the task at hand.

Later analysis of this situation by several teachers suggested a possible explanation for the students' "strange" behavior. This particular school has a reputation for being very conservative, demanding a high standard of achievement, and insisting on strict, even rigid, rules of discipline. Teachers are required to maintain strict discipline and silence during class sessions. When the prevailing behavioral norms were changed suddenly and even dramatically, students found it difficult to change their behavior. It was hard to believe that it was permissible for them to talk and to act freely in the classroom without the threat of punishment.

In the second and third stages of the model, students engage in an analysis of their own study processes and of a variety of learning strategies. Furthermore, they are asked to compare different styles of learning. The goal is to assist students in becoming more effective learners (Joyce & Weil, 1986). In the fourth stage, students are to have gained some mastery of different learning styles and study tasks, cooperating with one another in planning group tasks that allow each group member to make a contribution according to his or her ability.

Teachers

In the first stage, teachers participate in inservice training devoted to instructional methods and to the theory and research on which they are based. As part of the in-service course, teachers implement in their classrooms portions of the new methods they are learning. In the second and third stages, they engage in cooperative planning with colleagues of lessons and instructional units and implement these plans in their classrooms while observing each other, receiving feedback, and reaching conclusions about their work. In the third and fourth stages, teachers are to reach a reasonable degree of competence in the use of a range of instructional methods and in the ability to make the professional decisions that must accompany the use of these methods. Teachers must be able to solve social and learning problems that arise from the use of these methods in the heterogeneous classroom. Among these problems is the question of how to evaluate students in a way that reflects the change in their style of learning as a function of the newly adopted instructional methods.

Subject Coordinators

A school undergoing change in its basic work patterns is in need of a group of high-level professional people who can lead the school during the process. In a school with 500 to 1,500 students and teachers, no one person, however talented, can bear the brunt of the change all alone. Consequently, according to our model, a group of people is selected that participates in an intensive course in both the instructional and organizational roles required for implementing the change process. The subject coordinator's role, according to our model, is to help construct and maintain ongoing cooperation among teachers who comprise the subject-matter teams in the school for purposes of planning, implementation, evaluation, and improvement of instruction according to the models acquired in their in-service training course.

Principals

Principals play a determining role in the success (or failure) of the school change project. It often happens that principals do not have the knowledge necessary for fulfilling this role successfully. According to our model, in the first stage, principals learn what their role is in facilitating the implementation of the agreed-on change. A principal's role is constructed gradually during the course of the in-service training, all the while cooperating with the team of change agents who conduct the in-service courses.

During the subsequent stages of change, cooperation with the principal moves from the training site to the school, where the principal must revise the school schedule so that teachers and students have greater flexibility for experimenting with the new forms of learning and instruction. The principal's critical role is in gradually institutionalizing the change in the life of the school.

Consultation in the School

In the second stage of our model, the teaching staff continue to receive consultation with the change agents 1 day a week after the teachers have begun to engage in planning and implementing what they have learned. The change agents must now assist teachers in the process of implementing the new methods in the classroom and in planning future lessons. The consultant must be present during the planning, classroom implementation, and evaluation of the new methods during the third and fourth stages of the change process, as well as during the second stage.

The school consultant's role is to assist the school in developing local personnel for roles of instructional leadership. These people are needed to continue the process of change and of institutionalizing the change after the involvement of the external change agent is discontinued.

Pilot studies that examined two groups of about 125 teachers from six schools in which this model was implemented found that the group of teachers who had succeeded in developing skills of cooperative staff work expressed greater confidence in their ability to develop their students' social skills than did their colleagues in another group, who perceived their staff work as much less developed.

In sum, the model of in-service teacher training presented here attempts to identify the necessary and sufficient conditions for preparing educators to cope effectively with culturally and ethnically heterogeneous classes of students. The model takes into consideration the knowledge and differentiated functions that must be acquired by members of the school staff. It also takes into consideration the amount of time these processes require to unfold so that teachers can become competent in the use of appropriate instructional methods for coping with the social reality they confront in their classes.

Cognitive-Informational Model

In the previous section, we described the rationale and the program of a model for change in ethnic relations based on interpersonal contact between the relevant groups. In many inter-group conflict situations, however, interventions based on contact are not possible (because the groups live apart or have no common language), sometimes even not desirable (e.g., because the groups show resistance to meeting each other). The conflict still exists, and positive change is needed, sometimes urgently.

An example of the latter case are Jews and Arabs living in Israel. Both groups are citizens of the same country, but as already mentioned, they live apart and by their own preference. Thus, there is little chance and opportunity for intergroup contact. What can be done under such conditions to improve intergroup relations and perceptions? It seems that the cognitive-informational approach may provide appropriate tools to deal with this problem.

The cognitive approach is based on information given to one group about the other group by means of mass communication and educational programs. The main assumption behind such a program is that ignorance and lack of information comprise the first stage in the development of prejudice, stereotypes, and the consequent tension between groups (Myrdal, 1944; Williams, 1947). Studies about ignorance of ethnic out-groups and prejudice provide direct support for the idea that these two concepts are related positively (Murphy & Likert, 1938; Nettler, 1946). Indirect support for this assumption comes from the studies that demonstrate a negative correlation between the educational level attained by respondents and the extent of their prejudices and discriminatory tendencies toward out-groups (Harding, Proshansky, Kutner, & Chein, 1969; Wagner & Schoenbach, 1984).

The educational programs to improve intergroup relations can be divided into two types. The first type focuses on the history of the different groups in the society and highlights their achievements and contributions. This kind of program stresses the similarities between the different groups and is supposed to enhance attraction and understanding. Among 39 studies summarized by Stephan and Stephan (1984), 24 found that educational materials succeeded in reducing prejudice, 14 found that such programs had no effects, and 1 found an increase in prejudice. In contrast, the second type of program stresses group differences. Misperceptions and real dissimilarities are assumed to be the bases of conflict. According to this view, programs should explain and legitimate the differences among groups, rather than ignore them. The vast majority of such programs have been used in cross-cultural situations in which the participants are provided with information on cultural differences. Many of these are based on the orientation of the cultural assimilation (Albert, 1983; Brislin, Cushner, Cherrie, & Yong, 1986; Cushner, 1989; Malpass & Salancik, 1977; Triandis, 1975).

An underlying assumption common to both types of programs is that members of one group must understand the cultural system of the other group before they can understand individual members of this group. Accordingly, an abundance of training materials in the culture assimilator format have been developed (Fiedler, Mitchell, & Triandis, 1971). This technique requires that both the target audience and the target culture should be specified and that the materials should be designed specifically for each combination of audience and target culture. The evaluation of this training suggests that its main contribution is in developing greater understanding of the other culture and better adjustment to it (Brislin, Landis, & Brandt, 1983).

An Alternative Training Approach

The assumption of the culture assimilator approach that training materials must be prepared for each combination of target audiences and target cultures demands great specificity in the development of the training materials, and as a result, their usage is very costly. To overcome this problem, an alternative strategy[2] can be suggested. Rather than produce specific tools, it may be advisable to develop general training materials that focus on cognitive processes mediating the perception of another culture. The notion is to adopt a general cross-cultural sensitivity model whereby more sophisticated thinking regarding cross-cultural interaction is encouraged. Whereas the objective of the first approach is to bring an individual to awareness of his or her ignorance regarding a particular culture, the general approach seeks to make the individual aware of his or her cognitive processes and how they affect perception, attitudes, and behavior relevant to any other cultural group. Treatment of cognitive processes should improve awareness and organization of

specific information regarding the other cultural groups and should eventuate in improved intergroup perceptions and attitudes.

The theoretical basis for this approach is as follows: People everywhere are bombarded with immense amounts of information, not all of which can possibly receive their full attention. Everyone has a structural framework by means of which new information is processed and that has the characteristics of a schema (Kelley, 1972). This schema serves to sensitize the individual to elements in the environment that are consistent with it and to dismiss inconsistent elements. Understanding the ways an individual responds to and organizes this information should provide much insight into the process of intergroup perception, intergroup relations, and intergroup differences. Following are the main cognitive processes by which the individual organizes and responds to information, each of which must be taken into account. Participants must learn and be aware of them when developing a change program created to improving intergroup perceptions and relations.

1. Categorization. Because not all pieces of information can be attended to, people group bits of information into categories for more efficient organization. The process of categorization involves the narrowing of perceived differences among objects categorized together and the exaggeration of differences between categories (Taylor, Fiske, Etcoff, & Ruderman, 1978). The categorization process allows one to react to others more easily, although not necessarily more accurately (Tajfel, 1969) because the individual often relies on insufficient cues. *Stereotypes* are a part of the categorization process. These are generalizations of motives and characteristics ascribed to individuals because of their group membership, with little or no consideration of differences among the individuals making up the group.

2. Differentiation. Given that people become accustomed to one set of categories, they are likely to use those categories when faced with new information. One reason for misunderstanding and miscommunication among people from different cultures is that they differentially treat pieces of information within a category. Also, if people make many differentiations within a certain area, they are said to be cognitively complex, rather than cognitively simple. According to Davidson (1975), the relation between complexity and cross-cultural effectiveness is assumed to exist because a cognitively simple person has a single framework within which to evaluate the observed behavior of others in the target culture. People have a more complex cognitive schema when dealing with in-group members, compared with the simple cognitive schema when dealing with out-groups (Doise, Deschamps, & Meyer, 1978; Wilder, 1982).

3. In-Group—Out-Group Distinction. A major base for forming categories about other people and for differentiating information within those categories is the tendency to form in-groups and out-groups (Tajfel, 1981). According to this process, individuals have a tendency to accentuate intracategory similarity and intercategory differences. In addition, to preserve a positive social identity for one's own group, this process will stress the negative characteristics of the out-group and the positive ones of the in-group (Tajfel, 1981).

4. Attribution. The attribution process deals with the tendency of people to judge the causes and intentions of the other's behavior. The strong tendency is to use "internal" causes when analyzing the behavior of others (Weiner, 1979). This means that one uses trait labels instead of situational or social context factors. This error—making trait judgments and not taking situational factors into account—has been called the *fundamental attributional error* (Ross, 1977).

No theoretical antagonism exists between the specific and the general approaches to cross-cultural training. Rather, the one may complement the other. The general approach can serve as a preparatory stage for the specific one and can facilitate the specific training stage. Consider the two approaches as a training package wherein the former encourages more sophisticated thinking about cross-cultural interaction and the latter concentrates on understanding and accepting a specific culture. Therefore, the first stage has the potential of changing the individual schema, widening its perspective, and making it cognitively more complex, thereby making the person more receptive to the new information in the second stage.

Following the above considerations and conceptualizations, three types of training programs were developed and consequently implemented: (a) a general program that was similar for Israeli Arab and Jewish students (except for the language used—namely, Hebrew and Arabic), (b) a specific program for Arabs about various Jewish cultural aspects, and (c) a specific program for Jews about various Arab cultural aspects.

The general program was mainly based on the four cognitive processes specified above. The two specific programs were developed following pilot studies on each ethnic group that were designed to discover the main components of misinformation or prejudice of one group about the other one. For each of these three program types, a 24-hour program was developed, aiming at concentrating on up to eight topics, each one to comprise at least 3 hours of learning and training. All programs included exposure to verbal and audiovisual materials, formal lectures, exercises, analyses of incidents, discussions, and role playing.

The specific program for the Arabs included the following topics: the Jewish family, Jewish identity, relations between religious and secular Jews in Israel, ethnic groups in Israel, the Holocaust and its impact on Jews in Israel, and the Arab-Israeli conflict. The specific program for the Jews included these topics: the Arab family, the status of Arab woman, Arab settlements in Israel, minority-majority relations, and the identity of Arabs living in Israel.

Within each of the above contents, three major considerations guided the choice of materials and implementation: (a) emphasis on the similarities between the Arab and Jewish cultures, norms, and behavior, (b) emphasis on positive and acceptable phenomena, and (c) illustration of the "subjective culture" (Triandis, 1972) from each group's point of view.

Thus, for instance, regarding the Jewish target groups on the topic of the identity of Arabs living in Israel, the following goals were set up: To acquaint students with different conceptions of identity, to emphasize the complex nature of Israeli Arab identity and compare this with similar phenomena within Jewish subpopulations, to evaluate the strength of the nationalistic element and examine the reasons and rationale for its predominance, and to point out different patterns of adjustment among Israeli

Arabs and, for comparison, young Israeli Jews. Basically, this unit aims at examining rationally the components of Israeli Arab identity: the element of nationalism and the element of Israeli citizenship. The fact that Arabs are citizens of the state of Israel and at the same time part of the Palestinian Arab nation creates conflict between the two elements, particularly when tensions escalate between Israel and the Arab states. Factors responsible for the predominance of one element over the other are studied, and ways in which Israeli Arabs cope with this are dealt with. Possible comparisons of a similar nature regarding minority subgroups within the Jewish population are also included.

Research results on the pilot administration of these programs show the following general findings:

- The specific program tends to narrow the gap between the respondents' relative positive attitudes, perceptions, and attributions toward their own group as compared with the other one. This can occur as a result of some positive shift of the "others" or some less positive (not necessarily negative) outlook on one's own group.
- The general program consistently lowers the certainty of the respondents regarding his or her relatively negative attitudes, perceptions, and attributions toward "other" groups; in other words, as a result of the exposure to the specific program, participants seem to be less sure about their relatively negative outlook on "others."

Teachers were trained for these programs, which were consequently carried out on groups of late adolescent students and evaluated on a before-after experimental design. The programs were carried out while some political tension between the two ethnic groups prevailed in the country. Nevertheless, they were very favorably received by the participants. As stated, results indicated that each type of program produced positive results in certain but different areas. Consequently, a combined version (including both general and specific components) is being prepared, to be carried out on both groups in the near future. It is hoped that this improved program will produce, for both groups, more positive results than have been found for each of the programs separately.

Prospects for the Future

The trend around the world seems, for reasons specified above, to be toward multiculturalism. In other words, societies and countries will increasingly comprise ethnically, racially, and culturally different subgroups. These societies will have to learn to live together and to accept the idea of "unity within diversity," an idea that is not easy to live by.

Many among the younger generation are already learning through international traveling and the mass media, especially television programs, about cultures other than their own, as well as diverse customs and ways of life. Such exposure may serve as a first step toward multicultural understanding and possibly may facilitate intergroup acceptance and coexistence. Future development of multimedia technologies in and out of schools may enable students from one part of the globe to establish contacts and communicate with peers from other continents. This contact, however, will be more frequent among the affluent and higher SES groups and will leave behind large portions of the population deprived of the relevant and meaningful exposure to other ethnic groups. Yet, these latter groups are more vulnerable to the negative aspects of intergroup relations, such as xenophobia, prejudice, bigotism, and skinheads.

Thus, a major function of the educational systems should be to deal with these pressing and threatening social problems in one way or another. In this chapter, we presented two models of intervention in schools that differ from each other in a number of aspects: length of time invested in the training, purposes to be achieved, materials that construct the training, and the required processes. Any attempt to implement these models should take into consideration such factors as the characteristics of the involved groups, specific goals to be achieved, and available resources.

Schools have the advantage of having the future generation totally at their disposal and the possibility to prepare them adequately for life. It seems that living constructively in multicultural social settings will be a common goal in many communities around the world. Therefore, high priority should be given to schools by political decision makers to carry out this highly important and complex social task in one way or another.

Notes

1. These programs were designed and developed by the Institute for the Advancement of Social Integration in the Schools and the Winston Institute for the Study of Prejudice at Bar-Ilan University in Israel.

2. The authors would like to thank Rachel Ben-Ari for her contribution in the conceptualization of this approach.

References

Albert, R. D. (1983). The intercultural sensitizer or culture assimilator: A cognitive approach. In D. Landis & R. W. Brislin (Eds.), *Handbook of intercultural training* (Vol. 2, pp. 186-217). Elmsford, NY: Pergamon.

Allport, G. W. (1954). *The nature of prejudice.* Reading, MA: Addison-Wesley.

Amir, Y. (1969). Contact hypothesis in ethnic relations. *Psychological Bulletin, 71,* 319-342.

Amir, Y. (1976). The role of intergroup contact in change of prejudice and ethnic relations. In P. A. Katz (Ed.), *Toward the elimination of racism* (pp. 245-308). Elmsford, NY: Pergamon.

Amir, Y., & Ben-Ari, R. (1989). Enhancing intergroup relations in Israel: A differential approach. In D. Bar-Tal, C. F. Grauman, A. W. Kruglanski, & W. Stroebe (Eds.), *Stereotypes and prejudice: Changing conceptions* (pp. 243-257). New York/Berlin: Springer-Verlag.

Amir, Y., Sharan, S., & Ben-Ari, R. (Eds.). (1984). *School desegregation.* Hillsdale, NJ: Lawrence Erlbaum.

Aronson, E., Blaney, N., Stephan, C., Sikes, J., & Snapp, M. (1978). *The jigsaw classroom.* Beverly Hills, CA: Sage.

Brislin, R., Cushner, K., Cherrie, C., & Yong, M. (1986). *Intercultural interactions: A practical guide.* Beverly Hills, CA: Sage.

Brislin, R. W., Landis, D., & Brandt, M. (1983). Conceptualizations of intercultural behavior and training. In D. Landis & R. W. Brislin (Eds.), *Handbook of intercultural training* (Vol. 1, pp. 1-34). Elmsford, NY: Pergamon.

Cahan, S., Linchevski, L., & Igra, N. (in press). *Ability grouping and mathematical achievement in Israeli junior high schools.* Megamot: (Hebrew).

Cohen, E., Lotan, R., Whitcomb, J., Balderrama, M., Cossey, R., & Swanson, P. (1994). Complex instruction: Higher order thinking in heterogeneous classrooms. In S. Sharan (Ed.), *Handbook of cooperative learning methods.* Westport, CT: Greenwood.

Cook, S. W. (1962). The systematic analysis of socially significant events: A strategy for social research. *Journal of Social Issues, 18,* 66-84.

Cushner, K. (1989). Assessing the impact of a culture-general assimilator. *International Journal of Intercultural Relations, 13*(2), 125-146.

Davidson, A. (1975). Cognitive differentiation and cultural training. In R. Brislin, S. Bochner, & W. Lonner (Eds.), *Cross-cultural perspectives on learning* (pp. 79-94). Beverly Hills, CA: Sage.

Doise, W., Deschamps, J. C., & Meyer, G. (1978). The accentuation of intracategory similarities. In H. Tajfel (Ed.), *Differentiation between social groups* (pp. 79-94). San Diego: Academic Press.

Eitan, T., Amir, Y., & Rich, Y. (1992). Social and academic treatment in mixed-ethnic classes and change in student self-concept. *British Journal of Educational Psychology, 62,* 364-374.

Fiedler, R., Mitchell, T., & Triandis, H. (1971). The culture assimilator: An approach to cross-cultural training. *Journal of Applied Psychology, 55,* 95-102.

Harding, J., Proshansky, H., Kutner, B., & Chein, I. (1969). Prejudice and ethnic relations. In G. Lindzey & E. Aronson (Eds.), *Handbook of social psychology.* Reading, MA: Addison-Wesley.

Johnson, D., & Johnson, R. (1981). Effects of cooperative and individualistic learning experiences on interethnic interaction. *Journal of Educational Psychology, 73,* 454-459.

Joyce, B., & Weil, M. (1986). *Models of teaching* (3rd ed.). Englewood Cliffs, NJ: Prentice-Hall.

Kelley, H. H. (1972). Causal schemata in the attribution process. In E. E. Jones (Ed.), *Attribution: Perceiving the causes of behavior.* NJ: General Learning Press.

Louis Guttman Israel Institute for Applied Social Research. (1993). *Press releases of June and October, 1993.* Jerusalem, Israel: Author.

Malpass, R., & Salancik, G. (1977). Linear and branching formats in culture assimilator training. *International Journal of Intercultural Relations, 1,* 76-87.

Murphy, G., & Likert, R. (1938). *Public opinions and the individual.* New York: Russell & Russell.

Myrdal, G. (1944). *An American dilemma.* New York: Harper & Row.

Nettler, G. (1946). The relationship between attitude and information concerning the Japanese in America. *American Sociological Review, 11,* 177-191.

Peled, T., & Bar-Gal, D. (1983). *Intervention activities in Arab-Jewish relations: Conceptualization, classification, and evaluation.* Jerusalem, Israel: Israel Institute for Applied Social Research.

Rich, Y., Shachar, H., & Shafir, D. (1988). *Heterogeneous schools in Tel-Aviv.* Research report (unpublished paper), Institute for the Advancement of Social Integration in the Schools, Bar-Ilan University, Ramat-Gan.

Ross, L. (1977). The intuitive psychologist and his shortcomings: Distortion in the attribution process. In L. Berkowitz (Ed.), *Advances in experimental social psychology* (Vol. 10). San Diego: Academic Press.

Shachar, H., & Sharan, S. (1995). Cooperative learning and the organization of secondary schools [Special issue]. *School Effectiveness and School Improvement, 6*(1).

Sharan, S. (1980). Cooperative learning in small groups: Recent methods and effects on achievement, attitudes, and ethnic relations. *Review of Educational Research, 50,* 241-271.

Sharan, S. (Ed.). (1994). *Handbook of cooperative learning methods.* Westport, CT: Greenwood.

Sharan, S., & Sharan, Y. (1976). *Learning in small groups.* Englewood Cliffs, NJ: Educational Technology.

Slavin, R. (1983). *Cooperative learning.* New York: Longman.

Slavin, R. (1990). Comprehensive cooperative learning models: Embedding cooperative learning in the curriculum and the schools. In S. Sharan (Ed.), *Cooperative learning, theory, and research.* New York: Praeger.

Slavin, R., & Madden, N. (1979). School practices that improve race relations. *American Educational Research Journal, 16,* 169-180.

Stephan, W. G., & Stephan, C. W. (1984). The role of ignorance in intergroup relations. In N. Miller & M. B. Brewer (Eds.), *Groups in contact: The psychology of desegregation.* San Diego: Academic Press.

Tajfel, H. (1969). Social and cultural factors in perception. In G. Lindzey & E. Aronson (Eds.), *Handbook of social psychology* (Vol. 3). Reading, MA: Addison-Wesley.

Tajfel, H. (1981). *Human groups and social categories: Studies in social psychology.* Cambridge, UK: Cambridge University Press.

Taylor, S. E., Fiske, S. T., Etcoff, N. L., & Ruderman, A. J. (1978). Categorical and contextual bases of person memory and stereotyping. *Journal of Personality and Social Psychology, 36,* 778-793.

Triandis, H. C. (1972). *The analysis of subjective culture.* New York: John Wiley.

Triandis, H. C. (1975). Cultural training, cognitive complexity, and interpersonal attitudes. In R. Brislin, S. Bochner, & W. Lonner (Eds.), *Cross-cultural perspectives on learning.* New York: John Wiley.

van Oudenhoven, J. P., & Willemsen, T. M. (1989). Toward a useful psychology of ethnic minorities. In J. P. van Oudenhoven et al. (Eds.), *Ethnic minorities: Social psychological perspectives* (pp. 237-251). Amsterdam: Swets and Zeitlinger.

Wagner, U., & Schoenbach, P. (1984). Links between educational status and prejudice: Ethnic attitudes in West Germany. In N. Miller & M. B. Brewer (Eds.), *Groups in contact: The psychology of desegregation*

Weiner, B. (1979). A theory of motivation for some classroom experiences. *Journal of Educational Psychology, 71,* 3-25.

Wilder, D. A. (1982). Perceiving persons as a group: Categorization and intergroup relations. In D. Hamilton (Ed.), *Cognitive processes in stereotyping and intergroup behavior.* Hillsdale, NJ: Lawrence Erlbaum.

Williams, R. M., Jr. (1947). *The reduction of intergroup tensions: A survey of research on problems of ethnic, racial, and religious group relations.* New York: Social Science Research Council.

23

Understanding Across the Sexual Orientation Gap

Sexuality as Culture

MICHAEL W. ROSS

MARÍA EUGENIA FERNÁNDEZ-ESQUER

ANNETTE SEIBT

THE conception of sexual lifestyle as culture has been developed during the past four decades but has intensified with the focus on sexual communities arising from the HIV/AIDS pandemic. Indeed, the common use of the term *gay community* with regard to social, cultural, and public health areas has emphasized the organized nature of this group, as well as the sense of identity based on sexual orientation. The term *gay* refers to those who self-identify with this community; the term *homosexual* refers to the sexual behavior on which such an identity is based. Not all homosexual people identify themselves as gay (although the vast majority of gay people who are sexually active engage in homosexual behavior). The gay community in Western nations has developed its own argot, traditions, organizations, folklore, relational styles, and behaviors, and to the outsider, approaching gay people may result in as much culture shock as approaching any other group with a different cultural milieu. Further, and particularly important to note, the differences between gay and lesbian subcultures are significant, the more so because of their comparatively separate development since the 1970s. For this reason and because the bulk of the research is on the gay male subculture, we examine the gay male subculture in this chapter.

The definition of *culture* used here is that used by Linton (1938): the "sum total of the

AUTHORS' NOTE: The authors thank John Hart, at the University of Sydney; and Joyce Yost, at the University of Texas, for helpful comments on earlier drafts of this chapter.

knowledge, attitudes and habitual behavior patterns shared and transmitted by members of a particular society." In the case of the homosexual subculture, the homosexual milieu is embedded within a larger culture, and it is the sexual identity that forms the basis for the thoughts and beliefs, along with the knowledge of the subculture that is transmitted on entry into it. This "culture" is contrasted with "nature" in the same sense that it is used by Rosaldo and Lamphere (1974): that what was assumed to be "natural" (inherent in a homosexual genetic condition, personality, or master status) previously is now recognized as being due to common cultural or subcultural stereotypes. Because this social world is the creation of homosexual persons, any understanding of the homosexual world must understand the traditions, thoughts, and activities of its inhabitants.

What is particularly different about sexuality as culture is the degree to which it is submerged within other cultures that also tend to affect it. Because homosexual behavior is still stigmatized and often criminalized and because there is usually no way of identifying people who have sex with members of their own gender apart from self-disclosure or their identification with the gay subculture, this is essentially a hidden sector of the broader community. Thus, this is a culture in which membership may be transient or episodic and in which there is no tradition to be developed by parental or familial transmission. In fact, the identity may often precede acculturation, and acculturation will usually commence with involvement in the gay subculture. Role models and gatekeepers are thus likely to play a disproportionate significance in gay acculturation. Further, models of acculturation based in ethnic differences are not entirely appropriate as models, given the late learning of the culture and its often transient nature or invisible attributes.

However, there are important similarities. Migrants moving from one country to another may have to learn the ways and means of other ethnic cultures as adults. A person who becomes immersed in a gay or ethnic culture after adolescence and becoming an adult in a different culture gradually becomes more aware of patterns of personal interaction, customs, and rituals of a different group. The phenomenological experience of culture change is similar: First, a "migrant" walking into a new ethnic or sexual culture will usually focus primarily on people, particularly their gestures, forms of dress, speech (although for those migrating to another country with a different language, the focus will be on learning the new language, rather than on the new dialect or accent), and patterns of social interaction. Second, the migrant will begin to infer values, attitudes, and norms based on his or her own understanding of the behaviors observed. Third, the migrant will attempt to imitate and adopt what has been observed. At first, this imitation will be conducted on a trial-and-error basis in an attempt to fit it within existing habits and patterns of behavior dictated by the culture of origin. Fourth, to the extent the migrant attempts to join in the new culture, multiple patterns of adaptation will occur. Some of these changes will include discarding previous patterns or an attempt to blend old and new. Over time, the migrant will retain a pattern of behavior that has been uniquely adopted: The tapestry of cultural change for the individual will contain strands that are old, new, or a combination of both. Murray (1979) applies this model of ethnicity to the homosexual subculture and argues that gay men in North America are a "quasi-ethnic community." The model was implied much earlier, however, by the famous American novelist James Baldwin in the title of his work (which encompasses homosexual orientation), *Another Country* (1962).

What Is a Gay Culture?

A considerable amount of discussion has revolved around what constitutes a gay community or "gay subculture." Weeks (1985) talks about "a sense of wider ties, of what we can best call sexual community. It is in social relations that individual feelings become meaningful, and 'identity' possible" (p. 189). The cultural dimension, Weeks goes on to suggest, is where "group life of gay men and women came to encompass not only erotic interaction but also political, religious and cultural activity" (p. 189). This transition from nature to culture, and the construction of a culture, Weeks argues, is what Malinowski (1929) refers to as social differences creating cultural ones—where culture determines the situation, the place, and the time of the sexual act. Malinowski takes a relativist position in which the evolution of cultures is a function of culture over nature—in which the variations in society and culture are not "natural," but rather are based on societal evolution. And although Malinowski points out that culture determines the situation, the place, and the time for the physical act, it can also be argued that reciprocally, in the case of the gay subculture, the social situation also creates the subculture. In the case of the gay community, the *expression* of the sexual behaviors associated with the subculture is itself a product of the society in which the subculture is embedded. Further, the stigmatization that has determined the situation, time, and place of sexual contact, and the stereotypes that have been imposed on the subculture, have themselves produced internalized and definable aspects of subculture. Thus, the gay subculture is located within, and created by the very pressures in, the community that separated it off. Warren (1974) comments cogently that the gay community is not necessarily bounded by places and times because gay people do not necessarily have to live together geographically to feel a sense of community; secrecy and stigma give them that. The political and ideological direction of the gay movement, however, has also subsequently defined the subculture.

Culture as Civilization

Altman (1982) questions whether there is such a thing as a gay culture or a gay sensibility. He notes that although Sontag believes that Jews and homosexuals are the preeminent creative minorities in contemporary urban culture, it is problematic whether a gay culture exists in the aesthetic sense. Altman notes four ways in which the term *gay culture* is used, the most significant being that of lifestyle (considered to be as important as class and ethnicity in defining identities in the United States). The second is its use with regard to aesthetic products, such as art and literature growing out of a gay lifestyle. Third, he argues, is the assumption that art produced by gay people is automatically gay culture (an assumption he dismisses). Fourth, a homosexual sensibility is a product of being a minority. This latter point, the issue to which a lifestyle is linked to the experience of concealment, is in direct opposition to the conception of a gay "lifestyle" that involves any degree of openness about sexual orientation to the wider

culture; that is, one would expect any characteristic of a subculture based on concealment to decay in proportion to the growth of any characteristic based on identifiable lifestyle. We argue, however, that Goodwin's (1989) conception of gay folklore allows both a historical tradition (based on concealment or, as Stoller, 1976, also notes, clowning, mimicry, and caricature as resistance mechanisms), as well as an overt lifestyle that is identifiably gay.

Nevertheless, Altman also notes that items of clothing, fashions of speech and gesture, and personal accoutrements including makeup may have been ways of conveying a predilection that did not destroy the homosexual man's status in the eyes of the world but that can be communicated obliquely to other gay people at a level above a threshold for them but below that for the "straight" world. It is not uncommon for gay men and lesbians to refer to their "gay radar" as a means of picking up these subtle cues regarding the presumed sexual orientation of others. Unfortunately, Berger, Hank, Rauzi, and Simkins (1987) found that, with the exception of lesbian subjects, detection of sexual orientation by heterosexual and homosexual people was not different from chance, a finding suggesting that, empirically, the gay radar concept is questionable. From the 1970s, however, Altman notes, the gay subculture is also about self-affirmation and assertion and with a need to express a sense of community with other homosexual people and a view of the world based on the particular experience of being homosexual. And to the extent that experience is altered, so too gay culture itself changes (Altman, 1982). It is important to note the change across time of what the gay culture was and is and that gay culture, as any culture, is a dynamic process and both time- and place-specific.

This latter point is well illustrated by the change in fashions in homosexual men. Prior to the 1970s, the popular image and point of identification of overt gay men was a degree of flamboyance, even femininity, in dress and mannerisms. The so-called Castro clone look (named after the Castro Street area of San Francisco), however, which is at the time of this writing still fashionable as an identificatory style for many gay men, is the antithesis of this: jeans, checked shirt and boots, clipped hair, and sometimes a mustache. Nevertheless, as Altman argues, the *tradition* of "camp," which is perhaps the most classic form of gay male culture, still is a significant basis of Western male gay culture. *Camp* refers to a witty, feminine, flamboyant mode of social and verbal interaction with exaggerated mannerisms and expression, a so-called queeny behavior. Note the continuing use of the term *queen,* itself a traditional expression that can be traced back nearly 300 years to the first descriptions of homosexual men. This interest in ornamentation and emotion itself, however, is culture-bound in the sense that Western culture has defined this as feminine. Gagnon and Simon (1973) describe camp as an expression of community characteristics and an interpersonal communication characteristic, without an equal degree of commitment to this behavior on the part of its members and involving exaggerated feminine mannerisms or "goofing around." Leznoff and Westley (1956) sum this up as an indication that gossip about sex, the adoption and exaggeration of feminine behavior, and the affectation of speech represent a way of affirming that homosexuality is accepted and has the collective support of the group.

Civilization as Community

Altman (1982) goes on to argue a critical point: To what extent have the various developments in human rights in the past two decades created a genuine gay community (held together not just by external hostility and commercial venues but also by self-created institutions and images)? The growth of the very term *gay community,* we suggest, along with the proliferation of gay bookshops, counseling services, churches, press, academic journals, radio programs, choirs and theater groups, sports and other special interest groups, and the other institutions that go to form the external facade of a community of common interests, confirms the sense of community, although not always necessarily culture. Although Altman suggests that the absence of common territory and common language (as in nationality) to bind gay people together makes gay culture particularly important, it is difficult to be precise about what constitutes this culture. We argue, however, that, in large metropolitan areas, gay areas, gay organizations, and the traditional camp dialect constitute territory, language, and institutions. Further, there are subcultural norms with regard to

relationships (with greater acceptance of non-monogamous and non-exclusive relationships). This constitutes, in the view of some writers at least, a "gay people." The only major difference is that this culture is learned from role models and mentors, rather than from parents. Altman argues that the creation of a minority culture based on identification, rather than on birth, means a greater consciousness of the symbols of identity, although these are predominantly urban and middle-class ones. Finally, Altman notes, there is a gay *heritage* with regard to the increased interest and publication on the history of the culture and its icons. This heritage, Harry and De Vall (1978) suggest, through the rise of gay institutions and media, helped provide gays with a sense of collective identity by increasing awareness of the existence of each other. Prior to this, the authors suggest, gays could be described as a "historyless" people. It has now become possible for a recorded history of the gay collectivity, as opposed to a history of gay individuals. The advent of a collective identity among gays and the means for disseminating it (the gay media) has led to a gay subculture that is now as much a creation of its media as its lifestyle. Thus, it is possible to describe gay culture as a "culture in progress," currently developing the markers of a full culture. It must also be noted that a reciprocal process, the mainstreaming of gay culture through arts, fashion, and media, is contagious and adds to the refining and distilling of a gay culture through repeated feedback loops.

Goodwin (1989) notes a further important aspect of gay culture: argot. He notes that the gay subculture has its own language, traditions, and behavioral codes that one needs to know in order to function comfortably and effectively within it. Usually, he argues, a subculture will develop an argot, a private method of communicating even when among outsiders; use of the argot also serves as a means of mutual identification and helps foster subcultural cohesion. Although competent use of the language is not required for membership in the subculture, an understanding of it is almost inevitable because exposure guarantees acquisition of the argot's meaning. Goodwin suggests that being forced to form a secret system for interacting and for meeting people similar to themselves meant that gay people had to develop a private means of communication and that such a form of communication includes humor and folklore. This is context dependent: The less gay the context, the more likely the folklore or humor functions for identification and covert communication. As Goodwin notes, verbal agility is common in the gay subculture, where a sharp wit and a sharp tongue are prized possessions, and he speculates that this is because of the oral nature of the subculture and the pervasiveness of humor in the gay community. Puns and double entendres, often with multiple levels of meaning, inversion of terms (a pejorative word is used in a positive sense), intonation, and the development of new terms and jokes all play a part in making up the gay argot.

Rodgers (1979) identifies more than 12,000 terms in his dictionary of gay slang, although many of these are words borrowed from the specialized language of other groups, such as sex workers and actors. Linguists build on the macrosociologists' notion of group, status, role, and social function (Gumperz, 1982), noting that bilingual behavior reflects both an underlying set of general rules and lower-order nonshared language-specific rules. The gay subculture may possess these lower-order rules because language is a socially and culturally (or subculturally) constructed symbol system. It can be used in ways that reflect both macrolevel social meanings and create and reflect microlevel social meanings. Thus, a functionally distinct subculture would be expected to evolve an argot that reflects the degree to which it is differentiated from the macroculture, as Rodgers has demonstrated.

Visual cues are also important in recognition. Apart from the commonly recognized pink triangle and the lowercase Greek letter lambda (λ), such things as pinky rings (on the small finger), keys worn on the belt, black leather articles of clothing (to express an interest in sadomasochistic activities), and in the early 1980s, colored handkerchiefs to indicate interest in particular sexual activities (although the code was apparently so complicated, depending also on the pocket it was worn in, that it did not last long). Other visual cues noted by Goodwin (1989) are eye contact and proximity. Slightly sustained eye contact indicates sexual interest (often also referred to as "cruising"), and closer proximity (perhaps even including brushing past someone or slight sustained touching of arms or legs) also indicates sexual interest; and if that interest is not reciprocated, the other person will gently and imperceptibly withdraw

from contact. These cues may have a different meaning in a heterosexual context; for example, eye contact may signal recognition to a nongay person.

The folklore itself, Goodwin notes, is grounded in shared and secret knowledge, and for this reason much of the material is nonsensical to outsiders. Some of this material may flout the values nominally espoused by the dominant heterosexual culture and, by asserting normalcy, create and help maintain cohesion within the subculture. Humor, according to Goodwin, is one of the most obvious folkloric forms used to preserve a sense of group. Such jokes and anecdotes not only function as entertainment but also act as attention-getting devices, lighten the burdens of day-to-day life and oppression, emphasize the sharing of something outsiders cannot understand, and preserve a sense of group by making people feel safe and understood within the subculture.

Cross-Cultural Approaches to Homosexual Behavior

A number of models of homosexuality are culturally specific, and it must be recognzied at the outset that any homosexual subculture is itself located in a culture, which will superimpose on that subculture the relevant model of homosexual behavior. Although we discuss in this chapter the homosexual subculture in Western countries, and more particularly Anglophone Western countries, even in the United States the Latino gay subculture and the African American gay subculture may differ. An example is the so-called Latin model of homosexuality (Carrier, 1985; Parker, 1989). In societies based on Mediterranean cultures, the homosexual role is conceptualized as taking the receptive (or feminine) role in sex. The individual who takes the insertive role is not conceptualized as homosexual and is usually not stigmatized, provided he also engages in heterosexual sex. This conceptualization may also be dependent on age, with sexual behavior that involves taking a receptive role more acceptable or less labeled in younger partners or if there is an age difference between the partners. Thus, for Latino homosexuals, there is likely a much greater degree of label splitting by gender typing of behavior, with those men who are solely inserters in penetrative sexual acts not necessarily being labeled as homosexual, and those engaging in receptive sexual acts not only being labeled as homosexual but also frequently assuming feminine behaviors ranging from cross-dressing at one extreme to situation-specific camp behavior at the other. Evidence suggests greater sex-typed behavior in some Latino gay subcultures (Alonso & Koreck, 1989; Carrier, 1985; Parker, 1987).

The sex role prescriptions of the culture in which the gay subculture is embedded will have a significant impact on the behavior exhibited by those in the gay subculture. Ross (1983) compared homosexual men in Sweden and Australia on sex roles and found that, in the more sex-role-rigid and antihomosexual society (Australia), significantly more feminine sex typing of homosexual men occurred, whereas in Sweden, it did not differ significantly from the heterosexual population. These data suggest that the models of sex roles adopted in gay subcultures may reflect those in the wider cultural unit.

Other diametrically opposed models of homosexual behavior may occur in other cultures, as in the Sambia of Papua-New Guinea. Herdt (1981) notes that homosexual contact in this culture has a ritual role in which older men will have repeated homosexual contact with younger men over a number of years as part of initiation rites. The younger males act as fellators of older males to obtain the masculinizing effect of ingested semen. As they graduate to adulthood, they are, in turn, fellated (the practice apparently does not continue after marriage, when heterosexual relations commence). Thus, ingestion of semen is seen as *masculinizing,* and homosexual activity is regarded as a normal part of male development in the Sambia, whereas the same behavior in Western societies would be regarded as *feminizing.* These two examples illustrate well the profound cultural variation in the interpretation of homosexual behaviors and the gender roles attributed to them, as well as the enormous cross-cultural variation in what might be described on purely behavioral grounds as homosexual cultures (in the Sambia) or subcultures (in the case of Western homosexual behavior). Further, significant cultural variations are found in the actual homosexual sexual behavior engaged in, often depending on the degree of development of the gay subculture (Ross, 1986). One heterosexual myth that those entering the gay male subculture face is the belief that anal intercourse is universal and defining. Anal intercourse is not necessarily the most common or the most preferred sexual activity, nor was it even prior to the HIV pandemic (Ross, 1986).

Given that cultural prescriptions may be internalized but inaccurate, as Read (1980) notes, much subcultural behavior, such as camp, is essentially ritual reenactments of the heterosexual's myths about homosexuals but using deliberate distortions and exaggerations to devalue the "truth" of the myths and communicating and identifying the homosexual's existential experience of inclusion and exclusion. The imposed stereotype of the effeminate male is acted out in such ritual reenactments in such a way as to exaggerate and make fun of it. In this analysis, the form of the subculture becomes a reflection or internalization of the heterosexual mythology about homosexuals. It is interesting to speculate on whether, with the decline of the opposite-gender identification myth of the homosexual, a significant change in subculture behavior will occur or whether it has become so entrenched as tradition and heritage that it will continue.

History of Development of Gay Communities

A number of assumptions about gay subcultures are both culture-bound and temporally bound. Trumbach (1989) asserts that using "sociological models to study homosexual behavior in any society other than that of the modern Western world" is both dangerous and fallacious because the gay minority model we use in describing the gay subculture has only been established since the early 1700s in northwestern Europe and is peculiar to time and place. Both Greenberg (1988) and Trumbach argue cogently that, until 1700, the sodomite of traditional European culture from the 12th century was a man who had sex with boys and women: Both were considered to be less powerful, and the status of the active male was not compromised (in much the same way as "Latin" homosexuality, described above).

After 1700, the sodomite began to be defined around the role of the transvestite male. From this time, any sexual desire by one male for another, regardless of whether the partner was an adult male or a boy, would be characterized as effeminate sodomy. A series of arrests in the first decade of the 18th century revealed the existence of the new style of sodomite, who was labeled a "she-whore" and enacted the role in the privacy of clubs. This enactment included kissing and dancing together, sometimes dressing as women, and often being referred to by women's names. These behaviors are documented in both England and the Dutch Republic, and by around 1750, men who had sex with men often conformed to the new role of the effeminate sodomite. This was the homosexual role that was later characterized by 19th-century psychologists as the homosexual and that has become a tradition in the gay subculture, at least while a substantial number of gay men acculturated into this model when they came out are still active in the gay subculture.

It is apparent, however, that over the centuries since the homosexual was identified as a "type," several major changes have occurred in the conception of what a gay person should be like—from the mentally ill, the effeminate, to the macho man—and undoubtedly the conception of the gay man will continue to change. It is also possible that the growth of urban areas to the point where people of like interests reached a critical mass may have played some part, as London and Amsterdam were among the largest northwestern European cities in the 18th century. Interestingly, Harry and De Vall (1978) note the relationship between city size and number of gay bars in the late 20th century, with cities over 250,000 having at least one gay bar, and a correlation between city size and number of gay bars being 0.53.

Characteristics of Gay Communities and Satellite Cultures

Urbanization and the development of homosexual and gay communities generally proceed together. In a comprehensive analysis of the development of such communities, Harry and De Vall (1978) note that the emergence of a range of organizations catering to the needs and tastes of a particular minority is problematic for any stigmatized minority group that attempts to make its behavior invisible. The transformation of organizations serving invisible and secretive populations from "black market" to conventional markets may be explained by the concept of "institutional completeness," as described by

Breton (1964). Breton suggests that at one extreme is a community consisting of a network of interpersonal relations; at the other, is a more formal structure containing organizations of various sorts, including religious, educational, political, recreational, and professional ones, along with welfare and mutual aid groups, electronic and print media, and commercial and service organizations. Harry and De Vall make the point that this cycle of development is fueled by the process of migration to urban centers, with such migration providing opportunities for entrepreneurs (who also have a vested interest in these and will work to strengthen the ethnic or other identity that keeps their clientele as large as possible). The authors also indicate that, in North America, the development of gay communities, both through general population increases and the migration of gay people to larger urban centers (which may better facilitate their lifestyle), strengthens a gay identity. We believe the increased commercial and political visibility of these urban gay subcultures or satellite cultures further acts as a magnet to larger urban areas and thus accelerates this trend.

Humphreys (1979) refers to the gay subcultures in larger metropolitan areas as "satellite cultures," more visible, with their own media and services, and often also catering to more specialized needs within the gay subculture (e.g., leather bars, Western bars, hustler bars). As a result of this, Harry and De Vall suggest (1978) that

> gays have been transformed from a statistical aggregate of quasi-isolated individuals into members of a self-conscious and interacting community. If institutional completeness were carried further, there would be a full-fledged political economy for male homosexuals, with a well-developed market providing a wide range of goods and services and a variety of job opportunities for male homosexuals serving other male homosexuals. (p. 136)

In the time since they wrote this, such institutional completeness has developed in the major cities of the Western world.

Residential concentrations of gay people, according to Harry and De Vall, serve as protective devices (e.g., greater information to informal news and informational networks, provision of exchange of a variety of small interpersonal services, insulation from heterosexual neighbors). Areas most commonly chosen may be those with a predominance of apartment buildings and older houses, where smaller household units (the great majority of gay households contain one or two persons) are more suited to gay men's lifestyles. Indeed, Levine (1977) suggests that, in some major urban centers, these are ghettos in the sense that there is relative social isolation, segregation, and the development of a special subculture. It must be noted that although a minority of gay people live in such areas, their importance as a centerpiece for gay lifestyle, community, and culture is highly important. We believe that gay tourism, now a multimillion dollar industry that centers on such gay meccas, plays a large part in the maintenance and dissemination of gay culture. Gay tourism, which includes gay resorts, trips to gay cultural settings such as San Francisco, New York, Fire Island, and Amsterdam, and is catered to by gay travel companies, gay hotels, and gay sexual services, plays a large part in the development and dissemination of the Western gay culture and its maintenance. In part, this may be because of the larger discretionary income of gay men. Harry and De Vall suggest that the past few decades have seen a substantial increase in entrepreneurs (heterosexual and homosexual) who cater to the gay market. The influence of gay tourism may actually mean that the Western gay subculture may become a dominant gay subcultural model throughout the world.

In contrast, gay life in rural areas and small towns is much more informal. Harry and De Vall (1978) indicate that gay life in such communities too small to support even a mixed (gay and heterosexual) bar appears to be largely lacking in specialized institutions. In small towns, gay life consists mainly of friendships and acquaintanceships with perhaps a dozen other gay people. Entry to such a network is negotiated with some difficulty and considerable circumspection, they report, because of the stigma and the fact that, in smaller places, most people know or know of other people and the option for anonymity is significantly reduced. Newcomers may need to search for those who, on demographic grounds, might be assumed to be gay, such as older unmarried men or those who appear effeminate, or to make sexual contacts that may later develop into social ones in parks and public conveniences or local highway truck stops. In many cases, owing to the problem of recognition in small communities, some men may only make sexual contacts at regional cities or larger towns. Harry and De Vall suggest that the first institutions to arise are those associated with the sexual marketplace— informally, the cruising areas and public conveniences, followed by the bars, bathhouses, and other more formal sexual meeting places. We believe it is possible to chart the development of gay subcultures and their development into satellite cultures by the degree of complexity and development of their organizations.

Development of Gay Subcultures

Initially, the development can be distinguished as sexual. The first stage is the *sexual informal stage,* in which informal sexual contact places, such as public conveniences, parks, and other informal contact places, become recognized. In the second or *sexual formal stage,* gay bars, bathhouses, and other formal areas for sexual contact may develop. The development of formal organizations for social contact and the development of a sense of community beyond sexual contact usually follow this as the third stage. This tends to be followed by the fourth stage, in which rights and services to protect civil rights or to address problems in the gay community (e.g., a legal referral service, gay hot line, gay counseling service, STD/AIDS-related services) evolve. Fifth, local media services and news sheets to advertise both personal contacts and local events, along with other such cultural information, including entertainment reviews, advertisement of gay-positive or gay-accepting services, and gossip or social material, will arise. Sixth, professional and recreational organizations for gay people are set up, such as gay bowling clubs, other sports groups, and organizations for occupational groups, such as businesspeople, physicians, or attorneys may develop local chapters (although these tend to arise at a national level initially). Finally, the gay satellite culture becomes a recognized subculture center and acts as a magnet for gay people nationally and internationally, as indicated by the development of gay hotels and restaurants and other tourism-related industries. These stages are not necessarily linear, but they do give a general indication of the evolution and complexity of any gay subculture or satellite culture.

Political factors are also important. The differences between gay urban subculture centers and small towns and rural areas also include local climate and opinion, Harry and De Vall (1978) argue. Local government powers may stop the development of gay communities through the use of zoning, differential use of police power, and enforcement of other potentially discriminatory ordinances, such as the refusal to allow the use of public facilities for gay groups, and police entrapment. Tolerance by local authorities may be a significant precursor for the development of a gay subculture, and certainly for gay satellite cultures, but once it has reached a certain level of development, the economic and political power of the gay subculture creates its own economic and social momentum for its maintenance. Such examples can be seen in large satellite cultures—for example, the Castro in San Francisco, Darlinghurst in Sydney, and the Montrose in Houston, to name a few.

Community and Identity

Identity in the gay male world is not an all-or-nothing process. The development of gay identity follows a pattern, which Plummer (1981) refers to as *life cycles*—the recurrent life crises involved in becoming gay. The growing interest in life span development, through which predictable crises in adult life are charted, according to Plummer, involve for the gay world three major stages: (a) coming out to oneself, (b) coming out in the gay world, and (c) coming out in the straight world (*straight,* in this case, being the gay term for heterosexual). He notes that the first stage of identification is often the hardest because it usually has to be done alone and without support. This step involves confronting the insidious message that homosexuality is rare, a sickness or maladjustment, or just abnormal. Despite the fact that homosexuality was removed from the list of psychiatric disorders in 1973 because of the complete lack of evidence that it was associated with any psychopathology, antihomosexual attitudes (often referred to as *homophobia*) still exist that lead to self-rejection. Further, Plummer notes, one heterosexist assumption is that people assume everyone is heterosexual until

proved otherwise. However, self-awareness and the awareness that there are others, perhaps facilitated by a liberal peer group, articles, and programs in the media about homosexual people, knowledge of other homosexual acquaintances or peers, access to a gay counseling service or switchboard, or other educational experience, may make this realization less traumatic.

The second stage, that of meeting other homosexual people, marks the beginning of gay acculturation. This involves, Plummer notes, gaining access to homosexual role models that counterbalance the heterosexual models of the preceding years and that serve to dispel many myths and preconceptions about homosexual people and behavior. The gay bar is perhaps the most common and important element in this meeting process, with, more recently in larger metropolitan areas, gay support groups. At this stage, the gay individual will begin to build up social supports and role models, and lifestyle issues apart from the solely sexual preference one will develop, along with a knowledge of what we can term *gay anthropology* (a knowledge of the maneuvers and conventions about making sexual contacts and the etiquette of sexual interaction), as well as *gay culture* (which may include entertainment preferences, style of clothing, or style of food, drink, and drugs), *gay linguistics* (particular expressions or inflections or key phrases that may be used to signal sexual orientation in a coded fashion), and *gay history* (the traditions and history of a gay lifestyle). Further distinctions with regard to gay culture are made by Warren (1974), who includes gay ideology (legitimating statements or beliefs about gay identity, community, and way of life), and the gay symbolic universe, in which the ultimate integration and legitimation of both identity and world occurs. All of these confirm the existence and integrity of a core of attitudes, beliefs, and behaviors that constitute a gay subculture.

The third stage, Plummer (1981) notes, centers around relationships with the straight world: to whom and how to disclose and how to establish the continuity of identity between oneself and the world at large or to keep one's sexual orientation secret and live a life marginalized to some degree. It must be noted that the first stage involves establishing a subculture identity, often without direct knowledge of the subculture. The second stage involves learning about being a member of the subculture and its norms and mores. The third stage involves publicly identifying as a member of that subculture. This is different from the more usual development of subculture identity, which is most commonly transmitted from parents and in which there may be little choice (e.g., related to skin color or other physical characteristics). Where the cultural or subculture identity is not based on readily observable characteristics (e.g., in the case of religion or absence of physically identifiable racial characteristics), then the third stage, that of self-disclosure, may be similar in homosexuality and other stigmatized and nondistinguishable identities. Plummer does indicate, however, there will nevertheless be no immediate lifestyle available for many gay men who come out in areas without the necessary critical mass to sustain a gay subculture. For such men, particularly if they make sexual contacts in public conveniences or cruising areas, the subculture into which they enter will be predominantly one of gay anthropology (Humphreys, 1970). Or, a level of acculturation into part of the gay subculture may lead to degrees of gay acculturation. This latter point may also involve differing levels of commitment to gay relationships, from remaining single to entering into a committed gay relationship. Plummer also indicates that the person will have to make some decision on the pattern and type of sexual involvement he wants and whether to experiment with numbers of sexual partners and sexual activities.

The cultural world of the homosexual, Plummer suggests, includes at its most general all cultural forms that take homosexuality as their key concern: gay bars, discos, clubs, saunas and bathhouses, and other commercial establishments. Until the 1970s, such worlds were restricted in scope, substantially hidden from sight, and fairly culturally impoverished. Satellite cultures, more visible and public, develop, and this may extend to being a gay ghetto (an urban neighborhood that contains a number of gay institutions and a residential population that is largely gay). Further, Plummer indicates, a new lifestyle option for gays in such satellite cultures has evolved, that of working for gay institutions. This evolution, however, may be seen as an extension of the previous situation in which some occupations were reputed to attract a disproportionate number of homosexual people—for gay men, hairdressing, being a florist,

and other occupations associated with a feminine stereotype; for lesbians, the military or stereotypically masculine occupations, and the arts, which have traditionally been regarded as liberal and accepting of differences. Nowadays, it is difficult to find any occupational bias in the employment of gay people, particularly with the demise of the myth about homosexual men being feminine and lesbians masculine (although this was a strong element in the cultural traditions of the gay subcultures themselves prior to 1970).

One of the most significant dimensions of the gay subculture is what Lee (1978) terms the *gay ecosystem,* wherein sex is supplied conveniently, inexpensively, and apparently in almost inexhaustible supply. Such places of sexual contact include gay bathhouses and saunas, pornographic movie theaters and video arcades, back rooms behind some gay bars and bookshops, certain streets, beaches, classified advertisements in the gay press, phone services and computer bulletin boards, and of course the traditional public parks and public toilets. Lee comments that "anybody with enough learnt self-confidence and a knowledge of the rules of the game can find sex here." Although this gay ecosystem is a central part of the sexual side of being homosexual or gay, the gay subculture encompasses much more than just the sexual side of homosexuality: The gay ecosystem is equivalent to *homosexual behavior,* whereas the gay subculture is equivalent to a *gay identity.* This distinction may be blurred, however, if the difference between behavior and identity is not a clear one; Weston (1991) makes some parallel observations with regard to erotic and non-erotic friendships.

Community as Social Support

The gay community will function in the sense of a social support mechanism for those whose identity is as gay and who have access to other members of this community. Weston (1991) argues that the gay community constitutes a "family of choice"—one that people create—as opposed to a biological family—one that people are born into—and that gay people treat community as a cultural category implicated in the renegotiation of kinship relations. The emphasis on families organized by choice as opposed to procreation stems, in part, from the rejection that some gay people face from their biological families and, in part, from the strong immigration to large urban centers that results in separation from biological families. Further, to the extent to which gay people maintain secrecy about their sexual orientation and identity, there is a degree of alienation from biological families. Although it is important to note that many gay people have close and warm relationships with their biological families, lifestyle and distance may still present the need for an immediate and empathic family of choice. Given the frequency of alienation from biological family for the very reason that leads to membership in the gay community, the creation or adoption of families of choice is significantly associated with membership in the gay community. In this way, gay acculturation is radically different from acculturation with regard to ethnic groups, wherein the biological family is often the instrument of acculturation and the source of ethnic history and tradition. In fact, with the gay community, the opposite is the case: The acculturation leads to the creation of family, of an intimate environment in which traditional holidays (e.g., Christmas, New Year, Thanksgiving) may be celebrated.

Also just as important, however, is the social support provided by having an accepting family of choice. Social support will buffer or prevent stress, and in stigmatized communities, the need for such support to protect against marginalization, discrimination, or rejection is high. Ross (1990) has reported on the impact of discrimination on gay people and notes that the impact of a number of other life events, including work and finance-related ones and particularly ones related to relationships, will lead to distress and dysfunction. The need to have strong and accepting supports in a psychologically hostile environment is one role the family of choice plays for gay people. This has been demonstrated clearly in the AIDS crisis, with much of the support for people living with AIDS coming from volunteer support groups and "buddies" organized by the gay community (Altman, 1994).

Process of Gay Acculturation

Classical approaches to acculturation, which define it as acquiring (or incorporating) the customs of an alternative society (Mendoza, 1989),

tend to focus on measuring the degree of immersion into an alternative culture and conceptualize the degree of immersion or identification into a target culture compared with a culture of origin as being reciprocal entities. The great majority of acculturation research has looked at movement from one culture to another, rather than at the relationships between membership of a dominant culture and a subculture embedded within it, where movement may be frequent between dominant culture and subculture. We believe it is central to our understanding of acculturation for both homosexual/ bisexual and heterosexual people in the gay subculture that a model to measure acculturation in this context is developed.

Acculturation in the context of HIV prevention has usually been interpreted as acculturation from one ethnicity toward another's culture—for example, as in acculturation of Hispanic immigrants to the U.S. English-speaking culture. In this context, acculturation is closely associated with language, which is used as a surrogate marker. Acculturation to the gay subculture, though seldom labeled as such, has also been identified as related to HIV risk; this relationship underscores the importance of understanding acculturation with regard to the homosexual person. Various definitions have been used. In a longitudinal study of homosexually active men in Chicago, Joseph, Adib, Joseph, and Tal (1991) measured acculturation to the gay community in terms of amount of time socializing with gay men, along with the degree to which respondents' homosexuality was known and perceived community homonegative attitudes. The authors found that, in the short term, (6 months) the interaction between social participation with other gay men and a positive attitude to their own sexual identity significantly predicted lower sexual risk. Absence of peer support was also associated with relapse to unsafe sex (Adib, Joseph, Ostrow, & James, 1991). Connell et al. (1989), however, found that acculturation variables, including the proportion of friends who were gay men and membership of gay organizations, were not significantly associated with adoption of safe sex in a Sydney sample of gay men. This finding may have been because of lack of variance, in that the latter sample was drawn heavily from within the gay subculture, or of the measures used.

The measurement of gay acculturation may be sufficiently variable to explain the differ-

TABLE 23.1 Markers of Acculturation to the Gay Culture

Public Life	*Private Life*
I **Gay Media**	I **Social Gatherings**
National magazines, local newspapers, news sheets, novels, biographies Films and videotapes	Expeditions, travel Dinner parties
II **Gay Places**	II **Social Network**
Bars, restaurants, bath houses, coffee shops, dances	Proportion of gay friends Close gay friends
III **Gay Holidays**	III **Professional Relationships**
Stonewall celebrations, Coming Out Day, Mardi Gras	One's own gay doctor, lawyer, accountant, etc.
IV **Gay Tourism**	IV **Gay Identity**
Trips to gay meccas Gay cruises or tours	Self-identification Disclosure to others
V **Gay Organizations**	

Professional
    Doctors, lawyers, nurses
Recreational
    Jogging or bicycling clubs
Social support
    PFLAG (Parents and Friends of Lesbians
    and Gays)	

ence in results. Turner, Hays, and Coates (1993) note that *integration* into the gay community may be of special importance, particularly given that gay people may perceive more support coming from peers than from family. It appears that acculturation with the gay subculture is related to social networks and membership of gay-identified organizations. From research to date, it appears that the process of social integration into the gay subculture may best be measured by the proportion of friends who are gay, membership in gay organizations, reading of gay magazines and newspapers, and identification as being gay, all of which might indicate the degree to which norms and role models are available. Despite their problems, these measures may serve as rough and superficial markers to begin conceptualizing acculturation.

Markers for acculturation into the gay community cover all the measures of culture we discussed above. In terms of the development of

gay norms, a number of possible measures cover the realms of public and private life (see Table 23.1). These include reading of specifically gay literature, including national gay magazines, local gay news sheets, and at the literary level, gay novels or biographies. Going to places that predominantly cater to gay people, such as gay bars, restaurants, bathhouses, and other venues that are gay-identified and in which contact is made with other gay people, and the frequency of such patronage is an important index of *public* gay culture. Where such events exist, attendance at major gay celebrations and events (e.g., Stonewall marches in New York, Gay Mardi Gras in Sydney) and gay tourism (e.g., trips to gay meccas in San Francisco, New York, Amsterdam, and other centers with significant satellite cultures) may also be an index of acculturation for those with high disposable income. In the realm of culture, attendance at gay films and viewing of gay videotapes and other specifically gay-content cultural media should also be considered. Membership in national or local gay organizations is a possible indicator of acculturation and community involvement.

As people age or move into stable relationships, a transition may also occur to a more *private* gay culture, including expeditions with gay friends, dinner parties, and other time in more private settings but with gay companions. Proportion of gay friends is also a possible index of acculturation, including proportion of close friends who are gay; selecting one's professionals, such as dentist, physician, accountant, and other related services, on the basis of their sexual orientation is a further indicator where such choice is available (e.g., in the "Gay Yellow Pages"). These indices are biased toward those who live in large subcultures or satellite cultures, but it is also likely that greater acculturation is possible in these centers, either through the more accultured moving to them, or through those in them being exposed to greater possibilities for acculturation.

Finally, identity, as with other areas of acculturation, is perhaps the major index of the extent to which a gay person feels he belongs to a gay community or subculture, as is the extent to which that identity is known to friends and family. We believe it is possible to create a scale to measure degree of acculturation to the gay community and culture that incorporates some or all of these indices.

Intercultural Training for Work in Gay Communities

The implications of the work presented here for intercultural training are profound. From a theoretical point of view, we can conceptualize the gay subculture as much of a culture as racial and ethnic ones, although unlike some racial and ethnic groups, it is possible to hide one's identification with the gay community. Further, for some people, gay subculture involvement may be episodic. Nevertheless, it is possible to identify salient aspects of acculturation that may, in turn, make it possible to determine the degree of acculturation into the gay subculture. We present some of these in this chapter, with the caveat that they refer to Western gay subcultures and that those in other cultures will differ, depending on the perceptions about homosexu-

ality in the culture they are embedded in, their degree of exposure to the Western gay subculture, and the level of stigmatization and organization associated with homosexual behavior and gender relationships. Essentially, there are two areas of intercultural training: (a) heterosexuals needing to interact with the gay community (e.g., health workers, parents or siblings of gay people, entrepreneurs seeking to develop gay-oriented marketing options) and (b) gay individuals traveling interstate or overseas and wanting to make contacts in foreign gay communities. We deal with these issues of training from outside and for within gay subcultures in turn.

Training for Interaction With Gay Individuals From a Heterosexual Perspective

Consciously or not, heterosexual-identified individuals interact daily with homosexual or gay-identified individuals in nonspecific and "undercover" situations, such as on a train or bus or in administrative situations or in an office. For the most part, heterosexual-identified individuals assume that others are heterosexual in social situations. In the same situation, even if the topic is superficially about sexual matters, homosexually active or gay individuals are able and often eager to get by through use of mainstream language and inconspicuous conduct. This ability is due to having been raised and learned to mingle into the mainstream heterosexual environment.

Although homosexual persons are able to "enter" and "leave" mainstream society and return to the safer realm of the gay subculture, most heterosexual persons do not have this flexibility or ability. We know from members of ethnic or religious groups of the strength needed and the strain of having to travel between their respective groups and the mainstream environment. In contrast, most members of the mainstream culture are not able to undertake this travel, often even so far as to empathize with, mix into, or behave inconspicuously in such a subgroup. It seems to us that there are good reasons for enabling heterosexual persons to become more "knowledgeable" and to gain empathic insight into the gay subculture. We propose and briefly outline an intercultural training program with heterosexuals as the target group. Specifically, we suggest it is possible to train individuals who either have or want to understand and cross socially the sexual orientation gap, a gap that currently prevents them from knowing and enjoying a significant sector of the human species.

Although parents and siblings of persons who have "come out" as gay are often led to seek information and reflect on their attitudes toward homosexuality, others will be interested in such training for professional reasons. Stimulus is given by such professional groups as the American Medical Association (AMA), which has recently made known its new policy of urging physicians to seek greater understanding of their homosexual and bisexual patients to raise awareness and to place an onus of caring on the physician (Dunlap, 1994). This is an important shift in professional and social thinking reflected in the AMA statement and is indicative of the need to better understand clients, patients, or peers.

Young adults in general and lesbian and gay youth in particular are vulnerable to major problems, such as alcoholism, drug use, STDs/HIV, depression, and suicide. It has been suggested that adolescents who feel different from their heterosexual peers in some way they have not fully defined act out to "prove" to themselves and their social environment that they are not homosexual (Sanford, 1989). Thus, professionals such as teachers, social workers, officers in institutions, and similar workers should be particularly well-informed and sensitive professionals because a significant proportion of their clientele are likely not only to be homosexual or gay but also to have associated problems. Because most schools deny the presence of homosexuality among their student populations (Chng, 1980) and ignore the subject of homosexuality in their sexual education programs (Newton, 1982; Telljohann, Price, Poureslami, & Easton, 1995), institutions concerned with the health of the public in the broadest sense should be the targets of intercultural training, whose goals are to increase an understanding of the homosexual subculture by developing awareness of homophobic behavior (discrimination, jobs, housing), homophobic thinking (jokes, stereotyping), and homophobic societal structures (legal and administrative systems).

Such training curricula should be based on one or more psychosocial theories that help infer methodologies and the didactics for the training, as well as measures to evaluate it. The theories should include the construct of both the prevailing heterosexual and homosexual social norms in the corresponding culture because social norms were identified as an important component in the "making" of the gay subculture (Ross, 1983, 1986). In fact, the inclusion of social norms as probably the most important topic is appropriate because only a minority of people in the United States are aware of having had personal contact with a homosexual person and because only those few are able to base their attitudes on personal interaction. The formation of attitudes for those unaware of personal exposure to a homosexual person is, therefore, based on societal norms (Herek, 1984). In particular, younger people especially derive their attitudes about homosexually from the perception of what they think their peers expect them to think and how their peers expect them to behave. And the motivation to comply with peer norms is known to be especially strong during adolescence. Appropriate training methodologies should include role plays, in which the ability to verbally counter homophobic remarks or jokes from a friend, a stranger, and in a group is practiced. In addition to the normative component as a factor for behaving is the component of personal attitude. Personal attitudes toward homosexuality are determined by a person's beliefs about who and what homosexuals are and by his or her attributions as to what "causes" homosexuality. Myths, questions, and historical and/or scientific knowledge about homosexuality should be elicited from the group and expanded and discussed if necessary.

In addition to role playing and as an intellectual transfer, trainees should be asked to think of and present a situation that is most likely to happen in their respective workplaces involving the topic of homosexuality. Openly gay trainers will be able to not only desensitize participants to fear of homosexual persons and to act as models but also point to verbal and nonverbal cues that make an appropriate offer for a conversation about sexuality easier for students, clients, or friends.

Training Within the Gay Subculture

Conceptualizing the gay subculture as a culture has a number of advantages for intercultural training. In addition to broadening the definition of culture away from traditional racial and ethnic ones, it allows homosexual behavior to be approached, not as a value-laden moral or religious issue that may cause conflicts or tension, but as a separate culture due (despite the personal moral and religious positions of the intercultural trainer) respect as a community of knowledge, attitudes, and habitual behavioral patterns with its own argot, folklore, and heritage. Sensitivity to this subculture is critical to research on and the education of its members, and this sensitivity will need to be developed by trainers in the same way it is for other cultures. Most important is desensitization to the subculture, in which the individual is able to put aside preconceived ideas and is open to see the members of the subculture as individuals and as people beyond their subculture label. Nevertheless, a degree of culture shock will remain for some who find some aspects of the subculture, when they observe it closely, to be disturbing or fascinating.

It is useful to introduce the concept of heterosexism here because it may be a barrier to intercultural understanding. *Heterosexism* refers to seeing and interpreting things in the gay subculture by using the values and perceptions of the heterosexual community. It is equivalent to ethnocentrism in the anthropological context. Most readers will be familiar with the risks of using ethnocentric analyses in other cultures and of the problems in miscommunication and misinterpretation this leads to. The problem is subtler in the gay subculture because it appears on the surface to be part of the culture in which it is situated and because the language is apparently that of the dominant culture (although with differences in argot and meaning). Further, we have not commonly thought of heterosexuality as anything associated with bias because heterosexual persons usually do not have an identity as heterosexual unless in apposition with gay persons or contexts and thus do not perceive their approach as being imbued with a heterosexual bias. Intercultural training with regard to work in the gay community needs to make these issues explicit to avoid the development of misunderstanding or antagonism.

Where people are being trained to work with or in the gay subculture or satellite culture, it is important to be explicit about preexisting values and beliefs with regard to homosexuality. This openness is as important for those who are homosexual or bisexual as for those who are heterosexual, because fears, myths, and preconceptions occur from all points of view. Perhaps the most important variables to take into account are the affective ones, and desensitization is central to any introduction to the gay subculture. This desensitization is best achieved on a one-to-one basis, with a guide or gatekeeper from the subculture who is able to take the trainee to a number of gay venues with different degrees of exclusivity; explain the behaviors, argot, and etiquette; act as a buffer; and introduce the trainee to other guides or gatekeepers. The importance of becoming acquainted with gay people in a nonthreatening context cannot be overestimated; by getting to know gay people as individuals, much of the prejudice or preconceptions about homosexuality is desensitized (Herek, 1984). Generally, women appear to be more comfortable with gay men than heterosexual men are, perhaps because of the threat to identity or masculinity or discomfort with homosexuality that is more salient for men.

The issue of embarrassment is also an important one to consider if intercultural training is intended to lead to research or clinical practice. The gay subculture is far more explicit in its sexual language, and a wide range of terms refers specifically or obliquely to genitalia and sexual behavior. Discussing sexuality will therefore bring up issues of discomfort or unease in those unfamiliar with the gay subculture, and it is wise to have some familiarity with the work on discussing sexuality (see Ross & Channon-Little, 1991). Ross and Channon-Little detail the most common areas of discomfort, approaches to asking sexual questions, and ways of organizing an interview. Any discussion or interview is predicated on an understanding of the sexual argot used by the respondent and some comfort with this.

In conclusion, we have discussed the relevant research with regard to the gay male subculture and the concept of acculturation to the subculture and the more developed satellite cultures, particularly with regard to history and development, cultural differences in perception of homosexuality, gay heritage and folklore, linguistics, anthropology, and diversity. An extensive and specialized body of literature deals with all of these issues, which we have simplified somewhat here to make our central argument. We believe the gay subculture can be dealt with as a culture in the traditional sense of the term and that intercultural training is the preferred method to approach research or clinical practice. This approach has the advantage of both making possible a systematic investigation of the similarities and differences between the broader culture and the subculture embedded in it and using the intercultural construct of ethnocentrism to understand and reduce discomfort and conflict. Intercultural training with regard to the gay subculture is our preference for promoting understanding across the sexual orientation gap.

References

Adib, S. M., Joseph, J. G., Ostrow, D. G., & James, S. A. (1991). Predictors of relapse in sexual practices among homosexual men. *AIDS Education and Prevention, 3,* 293-304.

Alonso, A. M., & Koreck, M. T. (1989). Silences: Hispanics, AIDS, and sexual practices. *Differences, 1,* 101-124.

Altman, D. (1982). *The homosexualization of America.* Boston: Beacon.

Altman, D. (1994). *Power and community: Organizational and cultural responses to AIDS.* London: Taylor & Francis.

Baldwin, J. (1962). *Another country.* New York: Dial.

Berger G., Hank, L., Rauzi, T., & Simkins, L. (1987). Detection of sexual orientation by heterosexuals and homosexuals. *Journal of Homosexuality, 13*(4), 83-100.

Breton, R. (1964). Institutional completeness of ethnic communities and the personal relations of immigrants. *American Journal of Sociology, 70,* 192-203.

Carrier, J. M. (1985). Mexican male bisexuality. In F. Klein & J. Wolf (Eds.), *Bisexualities: Theory and research* (pp. 75-85). New York: Haworth.

Chng, C. L. (1980). Adolescent homosexual behavior and the health educator. *Journal of School Health, 50,* 517-521.

Connell, R. W., Crawford, J., Kippax, S., Dowsett, G. W., Baxter, D., & Berg, R. (1989). Facing the epidemic: Changes in the sexual lives of gay and bisexual men in Australia and their implications for AIDS prevention strategies. *Social Problems, 36,* 384-402.

Dunlap, D. W. (1994, December 25). AMA states new policy on sexuality: Adopts a standard that does not judge. *New York Times,* p. 30.

Gagnon, J. H., & Simon, W. (1973). *Sexual conduct: The social sources of human sexuality.* London: Hutchinson.

Goodwin, J. P. (1989). *More man than you'll ever be: Gay folklore and acculturation in middle America.* Bloomington: Indiana University Press.

Greenberg, D. F. (1988). *The construction of homosexuality.* Chicago: University of Chicago Press.

Gumperz, J. J. (1982). *Discourse strategies.* Cambridge, UK: Cambridge University Press.

Harry, J., & De Vall, W. B. (1978). *The social organization of gay males.* New York: Praeger.

Herdt, G. (1981). *Guardians of the flutes: Idioms of masculinity.* New York: McGraw-Hill.

Herek, G. M. (1984). Beyond "homophobia": A social-psychological perspective on attitudes toward lesbians and gay men. *Journal of Homosexuality, 10*(1 & 2), 1-21.

Humphreys, R. A. L. (1970). *Tearoom trade: A study of homosexual encounters in public places.* London: Duckworth.

Humphreys, R. A. L. (1979). Exodus and identity: The emerging gay culture. In M. Levine (Ed.), *Gay men: The sociology of male homosexuality* (pp. 134-147). New York: Harper & Row.

Joseph, K. M., Adib, S. M., Joseph, J. G., & Tal, M. (1991). Gay identity and risky sexual behavior related to the AIDS threat. *Journal of Community Health, 16,* 287-297.

Lee, J. A. (1978). *Getting sex.* Ontario: Musson Books.

Levine, M. P. (1979). Gay ghetto. *Journal of Homosexuality, 4,* 363-377.

Leznoff, M., & Westley, W. A. (1956). The homosexual community. *Social Problems, 3,* 257-263.

Linton, R. (1938). Culture, society, and the individual. *Journal of Abnormal and Social Psychology, 33,* 425-436.

Malinowski, B. (1929). *The sexual life of savages.* Orlando, FL: Harcourt Brace Jovanovich.

Mendoza, R. H. (1989). An empirical scale to measure type and degree of acculturation in Mexican-American adolescents and adults. *Journal of Cross-Cultural Psychology, 20,* 372-385.

Murray, S. O. (1979). The institutional elaboration of a quasi-ethnic community. *International Review of Modern Sociology, 9,* 165-177.

Newton, D. E. (1982). A note on the treatment of homosexuality in sex education classes in the secondary school. *Journal of Homosexuality, 18,* 97-99.

Parker, R. (1987). Acquired immunodeficiency syndrome in urban Brazil. *Medical Anthropology Quarterly, 1*(2), 155-175.

Parker, R. (1989). Youth, identity, and homosexuality: The changing shape of sexual life in Brazil. *Journal of Homosexuality, 17*(1 & 2), 267-287.

Plummer, K. (1981). Going gay: Identities, life cycles, and lifestyles in the male gay world. In J. Hart & D. Richardson (Eds.), *The theory and practice of homosexuality* (pp. 93-110). London: Routledge & Kegan Paul.

Read, K. E. (1980). *Other voices: The style of a male homosexual tavern.* Novato, CA: Chandler & Sharp.

Rodgers, B. (1979). *Gay talk: A (sometimes outrageous) dictionary of gay slang.* New York: Paragon.

Rosaldo, M. Z., & Lamphere, L. (1974). Introduction. In M. Z. Rosaldo & L. Lamphere (Eds.), *Woman, culture, and society* (pp. 1-15). Stanford, CA: Stanford University Press.

Ross, M. W. (1983). Societal relationships and gender role in homosexuals: A cross-cultural comparison. *Journal of Sex Research, 19,* 273-288.

Ross, M. W. (1986). *Psychovenereology: Personality and lifestyle factors in sexually transmitted diseases in homosexual men.* New York: Praeger.

Ross, M. W. (1990). The relationship between life events and mental health in homosexual men. *Journal of Clinical Psychology, 46,* 402-411.

Ross, M. W., & Channon-Little, L. D. (1991). *Discussing sexuality: A guide for health practitioners.* Sydney, Australia: MacLennan & Petty.

Sanford, N. D. (1989). Providing sensitive health care to gay and lesbian youth. *Nurse Practitioner, 14,* 30-43.

Stoller, R. (1976). *Perversion: The erotic form of hatred.* New York: Pantheon.

Telljohann, S. K., Price, J. H., Poureslami, M., & Easton, A. (1995). Teaching about sexual orientation by secondary teachers. *Journal of School Health, 65,* 18-22.

Trumbach, R. (1989). Gender and the homosexual role in modern Western culture: The 18th and 19th centuries compared. In D. Altman (Ed.), *Homosexuality, which homosexuality?* (pp. 149-169) London: GMP.

Turner, H. A., Hays, R. B., & Coates, T. J. (1993). Determinants of social support among gay men: The context of AIDS. *Journal of Health and Social Behavior, 34,* 37-53.

Warren, C. A. B. (1974). *Identity and community in the gay world.* New York: John Wiley.

Weeks, J. (1985). *Sexuality and its discontents: Meanings, myths, and modern sexualities.* London: Routledge & Kegan Paul.

Weston, K. (1991). *Families we choose: Lesbians, gays, kinship.* New York: Columbia University Press.

Name Index

Babiker, I. E., 127, 137, 140
Bagozzi, R., 253, 254, 261
Bailey, E. K., 287, 302
Bailey, J. M., 232, 241
Bailey, K. M., 232, 241, 243
Baker, J., 83, 102
Balderrama, M., 412
Baldwin, J., 307, 323, 429
Ball-Rokeach, S., 8, 11, 12
Banchero, R., 337, 346
Bandura, A., 135, 140, 235, 241
Banks, C. A., 50, 58
Banks, J., 151, 163
Banks, J. A., 50, 58
Barham, K., 384, 385, 386, 398
Barlow, D. E., 63, 78
Barlow, M. H., 63, 78
Barker, R. G., 28, 32
Barkow, J., 121, 122
Barna, L., 5, 9, 11
Barna, L. M., 266, 268, 279, 316, 323
Barnett, C. K., 217, 228
Barnett, C. R., 338, 347
Barnett-Mizrahi, C., 345
Barnlund, D., 36, 42, 58
Barnum, C., 219, 228
Barrett, P., 371, 381
Barry, H., 30, 32
Bar-Tal, D., 377, 380, 403, 412, 413
Bartlett, C. A., 218, 228
Basadur, M., 168, 181
Batchelder, D., 70, 78, 79
Bates, A., 10, 12
Bauer, R. A., 373, 381
Baxter, D., 429
Bebbington, P., 133, 134, 143
Bell, E. C., 300
Bell, R., 145
Bem, D. J., 4, 11
Ben-Ari, R., 402, 403, 412
Benedict, R., 339, 345
Bennett, J. M., 38, 42, 46, 48, 51, 58, 148, 151, 162, 163, 165, 166, 168, 181, 309, 312, 316, 317, 323
Bennett, M., 148
Bennett, M. J., 3, 7, 8, 11, 42, 58, 156, 157, 164, 316, 317, 323
Bennett, M. L., 264, 268, 279
Benson, H., 280
Benson, P., 106, 122
Benson, P. G., 89, 90, 93, 102
Berg, R., 429
Berger, G., 416, 429
Berger, P. L., 46, 58
Berkowitz, L., 34, 413
Berley, R. A., 275, 279
Berman, J., 34
Bernal, M. E., 300

Berry, J., 2, 11, 95, 102, 327, 345
Berry, J. W., 23, 31, 32, 33, 34, 124, 125, 126, 128, 130, 133, 134, 136, 137, 138, 139, 140, 141, 143, 144, 145,147, 172, 181,182, 196, 202, 269, 279, 285, 300
Best, D., 193, 202
Betancourt, H., 29, 33, 34, 333, 348
Bhagat, R. S., 78, 94, 95, 102, 217, 226, 228, 229, 327, 351, 353, 361
Bhakkal, R., 191, 200
Bhawuk, D. P. S., 7, 11, 19, 22, 32, 34, 58, 84, 89, 102,146, 185, 200, 355, 348
Bialer, S., 368, 370, 380
Biehiauskas, V. J., 353, 363
Binkin, M., 204, 205, 214
Bird, A., 168, 181, 217, 218, 224, 228
Bishop, L., 201
Black, C. E., 380
Black, J., 83, 84, 85, 89, 90, 95, 96, 98, 103, 104
Black, J. S., 43, 58, 61, 62, 79, 111, 118, 120, 122, 127, 132, 133, 148, 164, 166, 181, 217, 219, 221, 223, 226-229, 233, 234, 235, 236, 237, 238, 240, 241, 242, 265, 266, 270, 279, 314, 324, 350, 361, 362, 363, 392, 398
Blake, B., 171, 182
Blake, B. F., 43, 58, 165, 177, 179, 181
Blake, R. W., 85, 103
Blake, S., 288, 300, 301
Blakemore, H., 328, 346
Blanchard, K., 43, 58
Blaney, N., 404, 412
Blondell, T., 134, 140
Blumer, J. A., 324
Boakari, F. M., 312, 318, 323, 324
Bochner, S., 26, 32, 93, 94, 103, 125, 126, 127, 136, 137, 138, 140, 141, 142, 147, 166, 181, 217, 224, 229, 265, 266, 267, 268, 276, 279, 280, 310, 313, 315, 316, 324, 325, 348, 412, 413
Boehrer, A., 84, 105, 135, 146
Boltvinik, M., 363
Bond, M., 4, 11, 34
Bond, M. H., 22, 24, 25, 32, 34, 388, 389, 390, 398
Bontempo, R., 21, 34, 338, 345
Borden, G. A., 43, 58
Bornemann, T., 362, 364
Bose, 345, 347
Boski, P.

Bourgeois, L. J., 363
Bouvy, A. M., 140
Bowerman, W., 120, 122
Bowers, D. G., 258, 259, 261
Bowers, K. S., 94, 103
Boyer, E., 68, 79
Brabant, S., 311, 312, 313, 324
Bracken, D., 245, 262
Bradbury, T. N., 275, 279
Bradford, L., 315, 325
Brammer, L., 316, 324
Brandt, E., 85, 103
Brandt, M., 1, 11, 195, 200, 409, 412
Brandt, M. E., 126, 141
Brehm, J. W., 212, 214
Brein, M., 136, 137, 141, 166, 181
Brenes, A., 34
Brent, J., 342, 348
Brent, R., 383
Bresnehen, M., 232, 242
Breton, R., 420, 429
Brewer, M., 4, 11, 212, 214
Brewer, M. B., 413
Bridges, W., 309, 324
Brief, D. E., 367, 371, 380
Briody, E. K., 219, 228, 265, 267, 269, 270, 279
Brislin, R., 11, 12, 58, 60, 71, 79, 80, 84, 89, 102, 103, 104, 122, 126, 127, 141, 169, 171, 181, 188, 190, 191, 194, 195, 200, 201, 227, 230, 266, 268, 269, 279, 301, 345, 348, 364, 409, 412, 413
Brislin, R. W., 1, 3, 7, 8, 10, 11, 19, 22, 29, 30, 32, 34, 35, 37, 42, 43, 45, 47, 52, 58, 59, 60, 62, 66, 67, 68, 69, 72, 73, 75, 78, 79, 80, 126, 132, 141, 143, 147, 150, 164, 181, 182, 214, 284, 292, 300, 307, 313, 314, 323, 324, 382, 409, 412
Broaddus, D., 191, 200
Bronfenbrenner, U., 371, 372, 375, 380
Bronstein, P., 345
Brooke, J., 327, 328, 345
Brown, D. R., 259, 260, 262
Brown, E. D., 26, 32
Brown, K., 232, 242
Brown, L., 172, 181
Bruner, J., 245, 262
Bruner, S., 98, 103
Bruschke, J., 78, 80
Buchenan, W., 369, 380
Bujaki, M., 126, 140
Buntaine, C. S., 288, 289, 293, 300
Burgoon, J. K., 314, 324

Lederer, G., 381
Lee, J. A., 423, 429
Lee, S., 231, 242
Leeds-Hurwitz, W., 40, 59
Lefcourt, H. M., 141
Lefley, H., 12, 132, 143
Lefley, H. P., 26, 8280
Lekhyananda, D., 132, 141
Leonard, B., 218, 229
Leung, K., 21, 24, 25, 33, 34, 145
Leung, S., 348
Levine, M., 429
Levine, M. P., 421, 429
Levinson, D. J., 362, 363
Levitt, T., 384, 398
Lew, S., 129, 145
Lewin, E., 245, 262
Lewin, K., 47, 59, 76, 245
Lewis, T. J., 326
Leznoff, M., 417, 429
Lichtenberger, B., 221, 229
Lie, J., 350, 363
Liebermen, D. A., 108, 113, 115, 121, 122
Liese, L. H., 132, 147
Likert, R., 408, 413
Lin, A., 127, 136, 140, 141
Lin, K., 125, 127, 135, 143
Lin, K. M., 268, 280
Lin, N., 135, 143
Linchevski, L., 404, 412
Linden, W., 129, 143
Lindholm, K. J., 133, 144
Lindsay, C. P. 293, 295, 302
Lindsay, T. J., 213, 215
Lindzey, G., 235, 242, 262, 412, 413
Linton, H., 5, 12
Linton, R., 124, 145, 414, 429
Lippitt, G., 258, 262
Lippitt, R., 258, 262
Lisansky, J., 328, 333, 337, 338, 342, 347, 348
Lissy, W. E., 217, 218, 230
Litwin, G., 246, 262
Lobdell, C. L., 315, 325
Locke, E., 245, 262
Locke, S. A., 135, 143
Loehlin, J., 1, 12
Longabaugh, R., 28, 33
Lonner, W., 103, 348,, 412, 413
Lonner, W. J., 24, 33, 43, 58, 147, 279, 280, 310, 325
Lopez, R., 338, 348
Lorsch, J., 300
Lotan, R., 412
Lovejoy, J. E., 104, 105, 106, 107, 214
Lowe, G., 10, 12
Loyola, C. L., 348

Lucas, J. R., 334, 347
Luckmann, T., 46, 58
Lum, J., 37, 59
Lustig, M. W., 43, 59, 155, 164
Lysgaard, S., 131, 137, 143, 310, 325

Macdonald, H., 285, 302
MacGregor, M. J., 204, 205, 214
Macleod, B. M., 127, 136, 140, 141
Madden, N., 404, 413
Madsen, M. C., 334, 346
Madsen, W., 334, 338, 347
Magaffey, W., 338, 347
Mahmoudi, K. M., 113, 123
Maldanado, M., 134, 144
Malgady, R., 134, 145
Malinowski, B., 415, 416, 429
Malpass, R., 10, 12, 191, 201, 409, 412
Malpass, R. S., 32, 33
Malrick, K., 303
Mann, L., 145
Manteiga, F. P., 333, 345
Marayuma, G., 10, 12
Maruyama, M., 390, 391, 399
Marim, G. B. H., 348
Marin, G., 29, 33, 34, 333, 334, 336, 347
Marsellal, A., 12, 362, 364
Marsh, H., 307, 323, 325
Marsick, V. J., 385, 399
Martin, J., 10, 13, 127, 139, 143, 278, 280
Martin, J. M., 132, 142
Martin, J. N., 36, 37, 42, 43, 49, 56, 59, 60, 62, 79, 107, 109, 113, 114, 120,123, 149, 152, 153, 155, 164, 307, 310, 312, 313, 314, 315, 316, 322, 323, 325, 326
Martin, L., 165, 182
Martinez, J. L., Jr., 144
Martinez-Romero, S., 334, 346
Marty, G., 325
Masuda, M., 125, 127, 135, 142, 143, 268, 280
Maureas, V., 133, 134, 143
Mawhinney, T. A., 134, 140
Maxwell, M. A., 232, 243
May, W., 2, 12
May, W. H., 24, 33
Mayer, J., 244, 262
Mayton, D., 8, 12
McCaffery, J. A., 152, 164, 266, 269, 271, 280
McClelland, A., 194, 200
McClelland, D. C., 269, 280
McConokay, T., 212, 214, 247, 263

McCormick, E., 245, 263
McCusker, C., 21, 34
McDaniel, A. K., 170, 182
McDaniel, C. O., Jr., 170, 182
McDaniel, N. C., 170, 182
McDermott, S., 132, 144
McDonald, G., 326
McEnvie, M. P., 289, 302
McEvoy, G., 90, 92, 95, 104, 112, 118, 120, 123, 132, 144, 265, 280
McFarland, S. G., 371, 372, 381
McGarvey, R., 220, 230
McGrae, R. P., 355, 363
McGrew, P. 10, 12
McGrew, P. C., 190, 201
McGuire, M., 132, 144
McKeevney, S. J., 372, 381
Mclean, G. N., 201
Mcleod, J. M., 324
McNulty, M., 168, 181
McQuaid, S. J., 226, 228
Mead, M., 334, 347, 366, 372, 381
Mecham, R., 245, 263
Melnikova, O. T., 373, 381
Melville, A. Y., 367, 380
Mena, F. J., 134, 144
Mendenhall, M.,43, 58, 61, 62, 79, 85, 96, 103, 127, 132, 141, 144, 148, 164, 166, 181, 182, 217, 219, 223, 224, 226, 227, 228, 230, 231, 233, 234, 235, 236, 237, 238, 240, 241, 242, 265, 270, 279, 350, 364, 392, 393, 394, 396, 398, 399
Mendoza, R. H., 130, 144, 429
Mendoza-Romero, J., 337, 346
Merta, R., 8, 10, 12
Mestenheuser, J., 46, 60, 232, 242
Mestenheuser, J. A., 322, 325
Meshkali, N., 350, 364
Meyer, G., 410, 412
Michalis, D., 70
Michik, G. L., 24, 33
Migneault, P., 143
Mikheyev, D., 371, 372, 373, 381
Miller, A., 10, 12
Miller, A. B., 190
Miller, D., 95, 104
Miller, E., 96, 104
Miller, F. A., 285, 288, 289, 290, 293, 294, 295, 299, 300, 301, 302
Miller, J. G., 338, 347
Miller, L., 327
Miller, M., 323, 326
Miller, N., 140, 212, 214, 413
Miller, P. M., 127, 140
Miller, W., 368, 381
Millerand, N., 214

Subject Index

Acculturation, 9, 124-140
Acculturation Index (instrument), 134
Acculturation Rating Scale for
   Mexican Americans
   (instrument), 129
Adaptability. *See* Flexibility
Adaptation, 217-218, 226
Advanced experts, 19, 20 (figure), 31
   See also Experts; Lay person;
   Novices
Advanced Projects Research Agency
   (organization), 200 (note)
Affect, 25
Affective learning, 7, 8, 36, 42, 47-
   49, 51, 52, 54-55, 65-66,
   220-222
Affective meaning, 24
Affective variables, 5-6
Africa, 19, 27, 42, 52, 93, 312, 323
   (note), 328-377, 390, 402
   See also Liberia; Nigeria;
   Somalia; South Africa; West
   Africa
African Americans, 169, 210, 256,
   287, 299, 312, 418
Albania, 354.
   See also Eastern Europe
Allocentrism, 21, 31, 47
   See also Collectivism;
   Idiocentrism

Altruism, 21
Amazon rainforest, 327
Ambiguity, 45, 47, 155, 224, 226
American Council on Education
   (organization), 208
American Field Service
   (organization), 112, 119, 192
American Indians, 27, 187, 328
American Medical Association, 427
American Society for Training and
   Development (ASTD), 41, 55
Americans with Disabilities Act, 245,
   287
Anthropologists and anthropology,
   19, 23, 30-31, 40
Anxiety, 5, 10, 73-76
Anxiety/Uncertainty Management
   Theory, 73-76
Arabic countries, 186, 390
   See also Middle East
Arabs, 194, 402-411
Area simulations, 8
   See also Training and
   development activities
Area studies, 53, 67, 71, 168
Army Research Institute
   (organization), 213
Arousal seeking, 5, 8
Asia, 19, 28, 31, 112, 135-136, 312,
   315, 383-398

   See also China; Hong Kong;
   India; Indonesia; Japan; Korea;
   Malaysia; Nepal; Pakistan;
   Phillippines; Singapore;
   Southeast Asia; Taiwan;
   Thailand; Vietnam
Asian Americans, 129, 250, 254, 256
Assimilation, 37
ASTD. *See* American Society for
   Training and Development
Attitudes, 22, 38, 41, 48, 53, 63, 68,
   86, 93, 223, 227
Attribution, 27-28
Australia, 22, 69, 261 (note), 276,
   338, 386, 425
Austria, 197
   See also Eastern Europe
Aztecs, 336

Back-translation, 29
   See also Language; Translation
BAFA BAFA (exercise), 47, 70, 74
   See also Training methods
Bar-Ilan University, 412 (note)
Basques, 401
Behavioral Assessment Scale for
   Intercultural Communication
   (BASIC) (instrument), 108,
   109, 116

About the Editors

Dan Landis (Ph.D., Wayne State University) is Professor of Psychology and Director of the Center for Applied Research and Evaluation at the University of Mississippi. During 1994-95, he was Visiting Professor, and for 1995-96 he was appointed the first Shirley J. Bach Visiting Professor at the Defense Equal Opportunity Management Institute (DEOMI), located at Patrick AFB, Florida. He is the co-originator (with M. R. Dansby) of the Military Equal Opportunity Climate Survey, the founding and continuing Editor-in-Chief of the *International Journal of Intercultural Relations,* the coeditor (with R. W. Brislin) of the first edition of this handbook, the coeditor (with J. Boucher and K. Clark) of *Ethnic Conflict* (1985), and the author of more than 100 articles, book chapters, and technical reports.

Rabi S. Bhagat (Ph.D, University of Illinois) is Professor of Management in the Fogelman School of Business at the University of Memphis, Tennessee. He has published more than 45 articles, chapters, and monographs in the areas of organizational behavior, organizational theory, and cross-cultural issues in international management. He has coedited *Human Stress and Cognition in Organizations: An Integrated Perspective* (1985, with T. A. Beehr) and *Work Stress: Health Care Systems in the Work Place* (1987, with J. C. Quick, J. Dalton, and J. D. Quick). He has served on the editorial boards of several publications and was awarded the James McKeen Catell Award by the Society for Industrial and Organizational Psychology.

About the Contributors

Marina Abalakina-Paap (Ph.D., Moscow State University, Russia) is Assistant Professor at New Mexico State University. She has co-authored articles on authoritarianism, social cognition, and intercultural relations.

Rosita Daskal Albert (Ph.D., University of Michigan), an Associate Professor in the Department of Speech-Communication, University of Minnesota, is a researcher and consultant to business, educational, and governmental organizations on intercultural and diversity training. She has taught at the University of Illinois, Rutgers University, and New York University and was a visiting scholar at Harvard University. Her research, writing, and consulting have focused on Hispanic-Anglo interactions, on the development and evaluation of intercultural training (especially of the intercultural sensitizer), and on intercultural training in organizations. She is conducting research on French and American multinationals and on Brazilian culture. Her work has appeared in *Handbook of Intercultural Training, The Handbook of Organizational Communication,* the *International Journal of Intercultural Relations,*

the *International and Intercultural Communication Annual, Management Communication Quarterly,* and the *Intercultural Sourcebook.* She has 20 years of experience in intercultural education and training.

Yehuda Amir (Ph.D.) is Professor of Psychology at Bar-Ilan University, Israel. He has served as head of the Department of Psychology and the Israel Army Manpower Research Division. He has published more than 100 articles and books, mainly on intergroup conflict and cross-cultural psychology. He founded and until recently headed the Institute for the Advancement of Social Integration in the Schools and the Winston Institute for the Study of Prejudice. He is incumbent of the Thomas Bradley Chair for Ethnic Integration.

Kathleen D. Baldwin is a graduate student in the Psychology Department at the University of Alaska at Anchorage and is nearing completion of a master's degree in clinical psychology. She has long-standing personal and academic interests in cross-cultural issues within the realm of clinical and social psychology, as well as interests in issues related to effective intercultural interactions. She aims to pursue a doctoral degree in psychology, with the long-term aim of applying her research and clinical training to mental health issues facing cultural and ethnic populations unique to the state of Alaska.

Ritchie Bent (M.Sc., University of Leicester, UK) is the General Manager, People Development, for the large Asian-based multinational, Jardine, Matheson and Co. Ltd. Prior to this, he held the position of General Manager, Group Personnel Services in the company. He speaks Cantonese and has 18 years of management experience in Asia, including several years as an inspector with the Royal Hong Kong Police. Prior to joining the police, he worked in the Marketing Division of Kodak Ltd. (UK).

Dharm P. S. Bhawuk (Ph.D., University of Illinois) is Assistant Professor at the School of Management of the University of Hawaii, Manoa Campus, in Honolulu. His doctoral dissertation supported the hypothesis that people will learn better from a theory-based assimilator than from other kinds of culture assimilators; he used a multimethod approach to measure the effects of cross-cultural training. Prior to coming to Illinois, he received an MBA from the University of Hawaii, and a Bachelor of Technology in mechanical engineering from the Indian Institute of Technology, Karagpur, India. He has edited a book and has published five refereed articles in journals and nine book chapters.

Brian F. Blake (Ph.D., Purdue University) is Professor of Psychology and Director of the Consumer-Industrial Research Program at Cleveland State University. A psychologist by training, he has been previously an Assistant and Associate Professor at St. John's University and a tenured Professor at Purdue University. Since receiving his doctorate in 1969, he has been responsible for more than 150 publications, book chapters, convention presentations, and technical reports. His research has spanned disciplines as diverse as marketing, agricultural economics, social psychology, and advertising communications. He has been interested in the cross-cultural aspects of social perception and has studied the orientations of subcultures in Africa, the Middle East, and South America. His background in program evaluation is rather broad, including assessments of educational programs targeted to disadvantaged youths, analysis of large-scale domestic public information programs, and feasibility studies of community development programs.

Sari Einy Brody (M.A., Bar-Ilan University, Israel) is a doctoral student in the Industrial/Organizational Psychology Ph.D. program at the California School of Professional Psychology and is an Adjunct Faculty Member at the University of Redlands, where she instructs business management students in organizational behavior. Her research and practice interests focus on cultural diversity in the workplace and group dynamics.

Shannon C. Curtis is a master's student in consumer-industrial psychology at Cleveland State University. Her major area of interest lies in training and program evaluation. Her interest in cross-cultural communication and relations stems from numerous trips abroad, including Europe, England, St. Lucia, Sweden, Russia, and the Ukraine. She has participated in several panel discussions dealing with program evaluation in both public and private institutions.

Kenneth Cushner (Ph.D., University of Hawaii) is Associate Professor of Education and Director of the Center for International and Intercultural Education at Kent State University. He teaches in the areas of international and intercultural education, as well as social studies education. He is a frequent contributor to the professional literature in intercultural education, conducts professional development activities for many professional associations worldwide, and has developed and led international education programs for young people and educators on five continents. He is coauthor of - *Intercultural Interactions: A Practical Guide* (2nd ed., 1996) and *Human Diversity in Education: An Integrative Approach* (2nd ed., 1996).

Mickey R. Dansby (Ph.D., University of Florida) is the Director of Research for the Defense

Equal Opportunity Management Institute (DEOMI), Patrick AFB, Florida. Previously, he was a Professor at Florida Institute of Technology, consultant, independent researcher, and Adjunct Professor for Rollins College Brevard. He has published numerous articles, book chapters, and reports and has taught a wide range of courses at the graduate and undergraduate levels. He served 20 years as an officer in the U.S. Air Force, retiring in 1991 as a lieutenant colonel. While on active duty, he held a variety of educational and research positions, including 6 years as a faculty member of the U.S. Air Force Academy, Director of Research and Analysis for the Air Force Leadership and Management Development Center, and Director of Research of DEOMI from 1986 to 1991. He founded the Military Equal Opportunity Climate Survey (MEOCS) Program and many other research and consulting services at DEOMI.

Norman G. Dinges (Ph.D.) is a member of the Psychology Faculty at the University of Alaska at Fairbanks and a Visiting Faculty in Public Policy at the Institute for Social and Economic Research at the University of Alaska at Anchorage. He is active in applied research dealing with the intercultural factors and processes involved in mental health service delivery systems, as well as with issues of community and organizational levels of competence. His research and consulting activities include projects funded by NIAAA, NIMH, the Alaska Division of Health and Human Services, the Annie E. Casey Foundation, and the Robert Wood Johnson Foundation.

Edward Dunbar (Ed.D., Columbia University), is a partner of Pacific Psychological Associates, a psychological consulting group. He is an Associate Clinical Professor and Instructor in the Department of Psychology at the University of California at Los Angeles (UCLA) and a Research Psychologist at the National Research Center on Asian-American Mental Health. He has also taught in the psychology and counseling programs at Columbia University and California State University system and has worked in the human resources and organizational development functions for ITT, Great Western Bank, and Becton Dickinson, Inc. His organizational consultation experience has in-

cluded the telecommunications, health care, finance, and chemical manufacturing industries.

Bernardo M. Ferdman (Ph.D., Yale University) is Associate Professor in the Organizational Psychology Programs at the California School of Professional Psychology in San Diego, where he directs The Border Project and specializes in diversity and multiculturalism in organizations, ethnic and cultural identity, and organizational development. Since 1989, he has been a consultant affiliate with The Kaleel Jamison Consulting Group, Inc., a national firm specializing in strategic cultural change and management consulting, and from 1993 to 1995 he directed the Organizational Consulting Center at CSPP. He has consulted to a variety of organizations, including Warner Lambert, Inc., the World Bank, the Federal Aviation Administration, the City of San Diego, and the County of San Diego District Attorney's Office. He previously taught at the University at Albany, State University of New York. He is editor of *A Resource Guide for Teaching and Research on Diversity* (1994) and coeditor of *Literacy Across Languages and Cultures* (1994). In 1991, he was awarded the Gordon Allport Intergroup Relations Prize by the Society for the Psychological Study of Social Issues for his paper *The Dynamics of Ethnic Diversity in Organizations: Toward Integrative Models*.

María Eugenia Fernández-Esquer (Ph.D., University of Arizona) completed her postdoctoral fellowship in cancer prevention at the Center for Health Promotion Research and Development, School of Public Health, University of Texas, Health Science Center at Houston, where she is Assistant Professor of Behavioral Sciences. She has conducted psychological research and published in both cancer- and HIV-prevention areas, primarily in risk perception and the influence of acculturation on health behaviors and presently teaches courses in health promotion and the multicultural aspects of public health.

Gary Fontaine (Ph.D., University of Western Australia) is Associate Professor of Communication at the University of Hawaii and Principal Consultant for Strange Lands International

Assignment Specialists. He is a consultant, trainer, researcher, and author specializing in intercultural relations and international assignments with more than 20 years of professional experience dealing with organizations in the America/Asia/Pacific region.

William B. Gudykunst (Ph.D.) is Professor of Speech Communication at California State University at Fullerton. His work focuses on developing a theory of interpersonal and intergroup effectiveness that can be applied to improving the quality of communication. He is author of *Bridging Differences* (1994) and coauthor of *Culture and Interpersonal Communication* (1988, with S. Ting-Toomey), *Communicating With Strangers* (1992, with Y. Y. Kim), and *Bridging Japanese/North American Differences* (1994, with T. Nishida).

Ruth M. Guzley (Ph.D.) is an Assistant Professor of Communication Arts and Sciences at California State University at Chico. Her research interests include superior-subordinate communication, organizational commitment, training and development, and intercultural issues in organizations.

Mitchell R. Hammer (Ph.D.) is an Associate Professor of International Relations at American University, Washington, DC. His research interests include intercultural communication effectiveness and cross-cultural training. His work has appeared in *Human Communication Research, International Journal of Intercultural Relations, Journal of Black Studies,* and *Communication Yearbook,* among others.

Teresa Harrell (Ph.D., University of Minnesota) is Assistant Director for International Student and Scholar Services in the Institute of International Studies and Programs, University of Minnesota. Her dissertation research, *Professional Integration of Indonesian Graduate Degree Holders From United States Colleges and Universities in the Fields of Business Administration, Education and Engineering,* was conducted in Indonesia. Her doctorate is in the field of Education with an emphasis on international education/training and development. Her re-

search and training activities focus on overseas orientation, professional integration/reentry, cross-cultural counseling and global diversity. She has had various positions in higher education since 1972 and has been a trainer since 1979.

Richard Heslin (Ph.D., University of Colorado at Boulder) is Associate Professor of Psychological Sciences at Purdue University, West Lafayette, Indiana. His research interests have included small groups, attitude formation and change, attitude and personality measurement, nonverbal communication, and consumer behavior. He has authored over one hundred articles and papers in these areas. his books include *Instrumentation in Human Relations Training* (two editions), and *Nonverbal Behavior and Social Psychology.* His interest in cross-cultural - training research is based on earlier research with the Quechua-speaking peasants of the Chapare rain forest of Bolivia and with intense interest in issues surrounding the conduct of valid research. His papers on cross-cultural attitude assessment and training have been presented at conferences in Bradford, England, and Kingston, Ontario.

Daniel J. Kealey (Ph.D., Queen's University, Kingston, Ontario) is President of People in Development, a consulting firm specializing in cross-cultural research and international personnel selection. He has spent much of his career in international development. He has lived and studied abroad and has undertaken extensive research on the adaptation and effectiveness of advisors posted to developing countries. His publications include *Cross-Cultural Effectiveness: A Study of Canadian Technical Advisors Overseas* (1990), *Overseas Screening and Selection: A Survey of Current Practice and Future Trends* (1994), *Cross-Cultural Collaborations: Making North-South Cooperation More Effective* (1995, with D. R. Protheroe), and several related journal articles.

Judith N. Martin (Ph.D., Pennsylvania State University) is Associate Professor of Communication at Arizona State University. She has taught in Dra-el-Mizan, Algeria, and at the University of Minnesota, University of New Mexico, and the Summer Institute for Intercultural Communication (Portland, OR). She is the author of numerous articles and essays on intercultural communication. Her research interests include investigating the role of communication in facilitating cultural transitions (e.g., reentry), identifying dimensions of intercultural competence, and understanding the relationship between ethnic identity and communication. She has conducted training for various intercultural sojourner groups, including students, faculty, corporate, and technical assistance personnel.

Mark E. Mendenhall (Ph.D., Brigham Young University) holds the J. Burton Frierson Chair of Excellence in Business Leadership at the University of Tennessee at Chattanooga. His main research areas are international human resource management, leadership and organizational change, and Japanese organizational behavior. He is coauthor of *Readings and Cases in International Human Resource Management* (1991, with G. Oddou), *Global Assignments* (1992, with J. S. Black and H. Gregersen), and *Global Management* (1995, with D. Ricks and B. J. Punnett). He has also published numerous research articles in such journals as *Sloan Management Review, Academy of Management Review, Journal of International Business Studies, Columbia Journal of World Business,* and *Group and Organization Studies.* Active in the Academy of Management, he is Past President of the International Division of that organization.

R. Michael Paige (Ph.D., Stanford University) is Associate Professor in the Departments of Educational Policy and Administration, and Curriculum and Instruction, at the University of Minnesota. He has been involved in international education since 1965, when he began a 2-year Peace Corps assignment, and he has been a professional cross-cultural trainer, researcher, and consultant since 1968. He has lived and worked in Turkey, Indonesia, Thailand, the Philippines, and Kenya. The author of numerous articles on cross-cultural training and research, he is the editor of *Education for the Intercultural Experience* (1994) and training section coeditor (with J. Martin) of the *International Journal of Intercultural Relations.*

Kristin O. Prien is a doctoral student in the Department of Management at the University of Memphis, Tennessee. She has presented several papers at various academic conferences, and in 1994 she coauthored a paper that was presented at the International Congress of Cross-Cultural Psychologists held in Pamplona, Spain.

George W. Renwick is President of Renwick and Associated and has designed and conducted intercultural training programs for 65 corporations in 21 countries. With two colleagues, he conducts a workshop each summer on Cross-Cultural Training in International Corporations, and he facilities the Advanced Workshop for Experienced Trainer. A founder of the Intercultural Press, he is editor of the InterAct series and coauthor of *Managing in Malaysia.* Since 1982, he has served as a cross-cultural and management consultant to western corporations in China.

Michael W. Ross (Ph.D., University of Melbourne) taught psychiatry at Flinders University Medical School before heading the AIDS Program for the South Australian Health Commission and later serving as Director of the National Center in HIV Social Research at the University of New South Wales, Australia. He is a Professor of Public Health in the Center for Health Promotion Research and Development at the University of Texas, Health Science Center at Houston, and the author of more than 200 scientific papers and book chapters and 11 books on homosexuality, STDs and HIV, psychology, drug use and minorities, and HIV/AIDs-related burnout.

Annette Seibt (Ph.D., University of Texas) is a scientist and docent in the Center for Applied Health Sciences at the University of Lüneburg and the Polytechnic of North East Lower Saxony in Lüneburg, Germany, since 1994. Among other duties, she is responsible for health promotion training programs for key professionals from formerly socialist countries.

Hanna Shachar (Ph.D.) started her educational career as a teacher of art and painting in elementary and secondary schools. She teaches in the School of Education at Bar-Ilan University (Israel) and also heads the Junior High School Department in the university's Institute for the Advancement of Social Integration in the Schools. Her teaching work focuses on school reforming and restructuring, and she has published books and articles concerning teaching in heterogeneous classrooms and school organization.

Walter G. Stephan (Ph.D., University of Minnesota) is Professor at New Mexico State University and has also taught at the University of Texas at Austin. He has published articles on attribution processes, cognition and affect, intergroup relations, and intercultural relations. He has also coauthored with C. Stephan) *Two Social Psychologies* (1990), a textbook in social psychology; and *Intergroup Relations* (1996). He serves on the editorial boards of the *Journal of Personality and Social Psychology* and the *International Journal of Intercultural Relations.*

Rick S. Tallarigo (Ph.D., Bowling Green State University) is a senior consultant with the international consulting firm HRStrategies, Inc., Detroit, Michigan. After working in community mental health for several years, he joined the United States Air Force as a behavioral scientist, initially assigned as a training research applications officer. While on the faculty at the United States Air Force Academy, Colorado Springs, Colorado, he designed analytical and feedback methods for conducting large-scale periodic leadership development and organizational surveys. He has served as researcher at the Defense Equal Opportunity Management Institute, (DEOMI) and has authored or coauthored numerous papers, presentations, and publications in the areas of organizational and human resources studies.

Harry C. Triandis (Ph.D.) is Professor of Psychology and Labor and Industrial Relations at the University of Illinois. He has received many citations and awards, including an honorary degree from the University of Athens, Greece, for his work in cross-cultural psychology, a citation from the American Psychological Association "for the international advancement of psychology as a science," an award from the Inter-American Association of Psychology "for the advancement of psychology as a science and a profession," and the 1993 award for outstanding article in the *International Journal of Intercultural Relations,* and the Klineberg Award for Intercultural Research. He has authored 7 books, 2 monographs, more than 80 chapters, more than 90 journal articles, and has edited 9 books.

Colleen Ward (Ph.D., University of Durham, UK) has held teaching and research positions at the University of the West Indies, Trinidad; the Science University of Malaysia; the National University of Singapore; and the University of Canterbury, New Zealand. She has diverse interests in cross-cultural psychology: acculturation, gender issues, intergroup relations, and altered states of consciousness and mental health. She is Past Secretary General of the International Association for Cross-Cultural Psychology and serves on the editorial boards of the *International Journal of Intercultural Relations* and the *Journal of Cross-cultural Psychology.*

Graham Williams is in the Division of Commerce at City University of Hong Kong. He was the Founding Director of the City University of Hong Kong MBA Programme and has taught business and management in Hong Kong since 1985. Previously, as well as teaching many international management courses in the UK, he has taught in the West Indies, Africa, Europe, the Middle East, India, and Thailand.